# HANDBOOK OF RESEARCH
## ON LITERACY AND DIVERSITY

# HANDBOOK OF RESEARCH ON LITERACY AND DIVERSITY

Edited by
LESLEY MANDEL MORROW
ROBERT RUEDA
DIANE LAPP

*Foreword by Edmund W. Gordon*

*Afterword by Eric J. Cooper*

THE GUILFORD PRESS
New York    London

© 2009 The Guilford Press
A Division of Guilford Publications, Inc.
72 Spring Street, New York, NY 10012
www.guilford.com

Printed in the United States of America

This book is printed on acid-free paper.

Last digit is print number:   9   8   7   6   5   4   3   2   1

**Library of Congress Cataloging-in-Publication Data**

Handbook of research on literacy and diversity / edited by Lesley Mandel Morrow,
Robert Rueda, Diane Lapp.
    p. cm.
    Includes bibliographical references and index.
    ISBN 978-1-60623-246-0 (hardcover)
    1. Language arts—United States—Handbooks, manuals, etc.   2. English language—
Study and teaching—United States—Foreign speakers—Handbooks, manuals, etc.
3. Children of minorities—Education—United States—Handbooks, manuals, etc.
4. Multiculturalism—United States—Handbooks, manuals, etc.   I. Morrow, Lesley
Mandel.   II. Rueda, Robert.   III. Lapp, Diane.
    LB1576.H2337 2009
    372.6—dc22

                                         2008043430

# About the Editors

**Lesley Mandel Morrow, PhD**, is Distinguished Professor of Literacy and Chair of the Department of Learning and Teaching at the Graduate School of Education, Rutgers, The State University of New Jersey. Her research interests include early literacy development and the organization and management of language arts programs. Widely published, Dr. Morrow is a recipient of the International Reading Association's Outstanding Teacher Educator in Reading Award and the William S. Gray Citation of Merit, among many other honors, and is a member of the Reading Hall of Fame.

**Robert Rueda, PhD**, is Professor of Psychology in Education at the Rossier School of Education, University of Southern California. His research centers on sociocultural processes in classroom learning, motivation, and instruction, with a focus on reading and literacy in English language learners and students in at-risk conditions. Dr. Rueda is a fellow of the American Psychological Association and the American Educational Research Association, and served as associate editor of the *American Educational Research Journal*.

**Diane Lapp, EdD**, is Distinguished Professor of Education in the Department of Teacher Education at San Diego State University. Her major areas of research and instruction are issues related to struggling readers and their families who live in economically deprived urban settings. Widely published, Dr. Lapp has received numerous awards, including the International Reading Association's Outstanding Teacher Educator in Reading Award, and is a member of the Reading Hall of Fame.

# Contributors

**Arnetha F. Ball, PhD**, School of Education, Stanford University, Stanford, California

**Eurydice B. Bauer, PhD**, Department of Curriculum and Instruction, College of Education, University of Illinois at Urbana–Champaign, Champaign, Illinois

**Camille L. Z. Blachowicz, PhD**, National College of Education, National-Louis University, Chicago, Illinois

**Erica C. Boling, PhD**, Department of Learning and Teaching, Graduate School of Education, Rutgers, The State University of New Jersey, New Brunswick, New Jersey

**Cynthia H. Brock, PhD**, Department of Educational Specialties, College of Education, University of Nevada Reno, Reno, Nevada

**Margarita Calderón, PhD**, Center for Research and Reform in Education, School of Education, Johns Hopkins University, Baltimore, Maryland

**María S. Carlo, PhD**, Department of Teaching and Learning, School of Education, University of Miami, Coral Gables, Florida

**Heather Casey, PhD**, Teacher Education, School of Education, Rider University, Lawrenceville, New Jersey

**Jill Castek, PhD**, Graduate School of Education, University of California Berkeley, Berkeley, California

**Michael Cole, PhD**, Departments of Communication and Psychology, University of California San Diego, La Jolla, California

**Eric J. Cooper, EdD**, National Urban Alliance for Effective Education, Stamford, Connecticut

**Patricia A. Edwards, PhD**, Department of Teacher Education, College of Education, Michigan State University, East Lansing, Michigan

**Linnea C. Ehri, PhD**, PhD Program in Educational Psychology, The Graduate Center, City University of New York, New York, New York

**Douglas Fisher, PhD**, School of Teacher Education, College of Education, San Diego State University, San Diego, California

**Peter J. Fisher, PhD**, National College of Education, National-Louis University, Chicago, Illinois

**Nancy Frey, PhD**, School of Teacher Education, College of Education, San Diego State University, San Diego, California

**Linda B. Gambrell, PhD**, School of Education, Clemson University, Clemson, South Carolina

**Eugene E. García, PhD**, Department of Curriculum and Instruction, Mary Lou Fulton College of Education, Arizona State University, Tempe, Arizona

**Georgia Earnest García, PhD**, Department of Curriculum and Instruction, College of Education, University of Illinois at Urbana–Champaign, Champaign, Illinois

**Perry Gilmore, PhD**, Department of Language, Reading, and Culture, College of Education, University of Arizona, Tucson, Arizona

**Norma González, PhD**, Department of Language, Reading, and Culture, College of Education, University of Arizona, Tucson, Arizona

**Susie M. Goodin, MA**, Graduate School of Education, University of California Berkeley, Berkeley, California

**Edmund W. Gordon, PhD**, Teachers College, Columbia University, New York, New York; Department of Psychology, Yale University, New Haven, Connecticut

**John T. Guthrie, PhD**, Department of Human Development, University of Maryland, College Park, Maryland

**Kris Gutiérrez, PhD**, Graduate School of Education and Information Studies, University of California Los Angeles, Los Angeles, California

**Douglas K. Hartman, PhD**, Departments of Teacher Education and Educational Psychology, College of Education, Michigan State University, East Lansing, Michigan

**Robert T. Jiménez, PhD**, Department of Teaching and Learning, Peabody College of Education and Human Development, Vanderbilt University, Nashville, Tennessee

**Melanie R. Kuhn, PhD**, Department of Literacy and Language, Counseling and Development, School of Education, Boston University, Boston, Massachusetts

**Diane Lapp, EdD**, School of Teacher Education, College of Education, San Diego State University, San Diego, California

**Carol D. Lee, PhD**, Learning Sciences Doctoral Program, School of Education and Social Policy, Northwestern University, Evanston, Illinois

**Donald J. Leu, PhD**, Departments of Curriculum and Instruction and Educational Psychology, Neag School of Education, University of Connecticut Storrs, Storrs, Connecticut

**Cheryl A. McLean, PhD**, Department of Learning and Teaching, Graduate School of Education, Rutgers, The State University of New Jersey, New Brunswick, New Jersey

**Gwendolyn Thompson McMillon, PhD**, Department of Reading and Language Arts, School of Education and Human Services, Oakland University, Rochester, Michigan

**J. Gregory McVerry, MA**, Department of Educational Psychology, Neag School of Education, University of Connecticut Storrs, Storrs, Connecticut

**Luis C. Moll, PhD**, Department of Language, Reading, and Culture, College of Education, University of Arizona, Tucson, Arizona

**Danette A. Morrison, BS**, Department of Human Development, University of Maryland, College Park, Maryland

**Lesley Mandel Morrow, PhD**, Department of Learning and Teaching, Graduate School of Education, Rutgers, The University of New Jersey, New Brunswick, New Jersey

**Honorine Nocon, PhD**, School of Education and Human Development, University of Colorado Denver, Denver, Colorado

**W. Ian O'Byrne, MEd**, Department of Educational Psychology, Neag School of Education, University of Connecticut Storrs, Storrs, Connecticut

**Jeanne R. Paratore, EdD**, Department of Developmental Studies and Counseling Psychology, School of Education, Boston University, Boston, Massachusetts

**Django Paris, PhD**, Department of English, Arizona State University, Tempe, Arizona

**P. David Pearson, PhD**, Language and Literacy, Society and Culture Program, Graduate School of Education, University of California Berkeley, Berkeley, California

**Julie L. Pennington, PhD**, Department of Educational Specialties, College of Education, University of Nevada Reno, Reno, Nevada

**Pedro Portes, PhD**, Department of Counseling and Human Development Services, College of Education, University of Georgia, Athens, Georgia

**Taffy E. Raphael, PhD**, Department of Curriculum and Instruction, College of Education, University of Illinois at Chicago, Chicago, Illinois

**Timothy Rasinski, PhD**, Teaching, Leadership, and Curriculum Studies, College of Education, Kent State University, Kent, Ohio

**D. Ray Reutzel, PhD**, School of Teacher Education and Leadership, Emma Eccles Jones College of Education and Human Services, Utah State University, Logan, Utah

**Iliana Reyes, PhD**, Department of Language, Reading, and Culture, College of Education, University of Arizona, Tucson, Arizona

**Nancy L. Roser, PhD**, Department of Curriculum and Instruction, College of Education, University of Texas at Austin, Austin, Texas

**Jennifer Rowsell, PhD**, Department of Learning and Teaching, Graduate School of Education, Rutgers, The State University of New Jersey, New Brunswick, New Jersey

**Eliane Rubinstein-Ávila, EdD**, Department of Language, Reading, and Culture, College of Education, University of Arizona, Tucson, Arizona

**Robert Rueda, PhD**, Rossier School of Education, University of Southern California, Los Angeles, California

**Spencer Salas, PhD**, Department of Middle, Secondary, and K–12 Education, College of Education, University of North Carolina at Charlotte, Charlotte, North Carolina

**Karen Spear-Ellinwood, JD, EdS**, Department of Language, Reading, and Culture, College of Education, University of Arizona, Tucson, Arizona

**Brad L. Teague, MA**, Department of Teaching and Learning, Peabody College of Education and Human Development, Vanderbilt University, Nashville, Tennessee

**Dianna Townsend, EdD**, Department of Educational Specialties, College of Education, University of Nevada Reno, Reno, Nevada

**Susan Watts Taffe, PhD**, Division of Teacher Education, College of Education, Criminal Justice, and Human Services, University of Cincinnati, Cincinnati, Ohio

**Catherine M. Weber, MEd**, Department of Literacy, Language, and Culture, College of Education, University of Illinois at Chicago, Chicago, Illinois

**Ann-Marie Wiese, PhD**, Center for Child and Family Studies, WestEd, Sausalito, California

**Leisy Wyman, PhD**, Department of Language, Reading, and Culture, College of Education, University of Arizona, Tucson, Arizona

**Lisa Zawilinski, MS**, Department of Curriculum and Instruction, Neag School of Education, University of Connecticut Storrs, Storrs, Connecticut

# Foreword

## *Every Child Must Be Visible*
## *If We Are to Succeed as a World-Class Nation*

EDMUND W. GORDON

In 1965, when beginning my career as a research scientist, I published what was then a controversial essay review of the then-extant research literature on socially disadvantaged children (Gordon, 1965). I asserted what was at that time a "progressive" perspective by avoiding reference to such children as "culturally deprived." But because I was writing about the research findings available at that time, I could not avoid reporting the prevailing view that these children were different in many ways from children whose characteristics were considered normative. However, the burden of my review was to reflect the consensus that socially disadvantaged children were essentially deficient in most of the characteristics that mattered.

That modest suggestion of difference somehow gained traction, and within 10 years the widely held perspective had shifted from cultural deprivation and generalized deficiency to different and then to diverse. There was perhaps an element of political correctness in this change in perspective. Certainly it better reflects the fact that the characteristics of children who have been placed at risk of academic failure by some of their life conditions include many highly adaptive features and behaviors, but it also tends to hide or ignore the fact that academic cultures are specialized cultures that require and reward specialized, developed abilities. Life conditions and circumstances that do not enable and encourage the development of those specialized abilities tend to produce children who are deficient in the ability to handle academic work. We know in the 21st century that the absence of a certain developed ability because of the absence of opportunity to learn should not be interpreted as absence of ability to learn, and that the recognition of the fact of diverse human characteristics demands accommodation and differentiation in pedagogical treatment. In some circumstances, improved life circumstances are required. It is a source of shame that our society has moved slowly to achieve the necessary accommodations and differentiations in educational treatments, and has essentially avoided serious effort at providing improved circumstances of life for our most seriously socially disadvantaged children and those whose variance from colloquial norms is significant.

It is the society's good fortune that some of us have taken seriously the need for accommodation and differentiation in the teaching and learning transactions made available to diverse populations of students. The authors of the chapters in this handbook are among the growing number of educators who have engaged the need to adapt educational treatments to some of the diverse characteristics of learners who present themselves to our schools. In contrast to the article with which I began almost 50 years ago, these author-educators are not primarily concerned with documenting deficits but are thoughtfully and skillfully addressing the problems of accommodation and differentiation, without ignoring the fact that academic achievement and its derivative correlate, intellective competence, require some developed abilities that the life conditions of some of these children have not enabled them to achieve. The ideas and practices advanced in this book do not provide perfect solutions: Human learning, especially academic learning, is a complex process that pedagogical science cannot fully explain. Robert Schaeffer, for many years Dean of Faculty at Columbia University's Teachers College, once described teaching as a process of inquiry. But I think such chapter titles as "What Do We Know about the Discourse Patterns of Diverse Students in Multiple Settings?," "Engaging Diverse Students in Multiple Literacies in and Out of School," "Roles of Engagement, Valuing, and Identification in Reading Development of Students from Diverse Backgrounds," and "Teacher Knowledge in Culturally and Linguistically Complex Classrooms: Lessons from the Golden Age and Beyond" point us in the right direction so long as we remember that a discrete learner-characteristics-oriented pedagogy (English learner, socially disadvantaged, impoverished, learning disabled, etc.) may itself be insufficient. Learners bring more than the specific characteristics by which they can be identified to the teaching and learning situation. Rather, they come to school with a rich combination of both status and functional characteristics that constantly interact and sometimes change. Optimal interventions require the skillful orchestration of a comprehensive complex of interventions that go beyond the classroom practices. I am increasingly persuaded that effective academic learning is more likely to occur in the presence of exquisite orchestrations that exploit and enhance the complementarities between the learning and teaching opportunities that occur outside of schools, and the appropriate and sufficient teaching and learning transactions that occur in schools. Whether in school or out of school, complementar-

ity should be the guiding principle. What is required is that teaching and learning transactions out of school must complement those that occur in school, and
wherever the teaching and learning occur, these transactions should complement
the characteristics of the learning person. Such sophisticated pedagogy can make
every child into a visible and productive learner. The work that follows in this
book can help us achieve those ends.

## REFERENCE

Gordon, E. W. (1965). Characteristics of social disadvantaged children. *Review of Educational Research, 35*(5), 377–388.

# Contents

Foreword: Every Child Must Be Visible If We Are to Succeed as a World-Class Nation
EDMUND W. GORDON
ix

Introduction
LESLEY MANDEL MORROW, ROBERT RUEDA, *and* DIANE LAPP
1

## PART I. PERSPECTIVES ABOUT LEARNING AMONG DIVERSE STUDENTS

1. Relating Diversity and Literacy Theory
HONORINE NOCON *and* MICHAEL COLE
13

2. Policy Related to Issues of Diversity and Literacy: Implications for English Learners
EUGENE E. GARCÍA *and* ANN-MARIE WIESE
32

3. What Do We Know about the Discourse Patterns of Diverse Students in Multiple Settings?
ILIANA REYES, LEISY WYMAN, NORMA GONZÁLEZ, ELIANE RUBINSTEIN-ÁVILA, KAREN SPEAR-ELLINWOOD, PERRY GILMORE, *and* LUIS C. MOLL
55

4. Family Literacy: Recognizing Cultural Significance
PATRICIA A. EDWARDS, JEANNE R. PARATORE, *and* NANCY L. ROSER
77

5. Poverty and Its Relation to Development and Literacy
PEDRO PORTES *and* SPENCER SALAS
97

6. Language, Literacy, and Content: Adolescent English Language Learners
ROBERT T. JIMÉNEZ *and* BRAD L. TEAGUE
114

## PART II.  SPECIAL ISSUES CONCERNING LITERACY

 7. Academic English and African American Vernacular English:                     137
    Exploring Possibilities for Promoting the Literacy Learning of All Children
    CYNTHIA H. BROCK, GWENDOLYN THOMPSON MCMILLON, JULIE L. PENNINGTON,
    DIANNA TOWNSEND, and DIANE LAPP

 8. Engaging Diverse Students in Multiple Literacies in and Out of School         158
    CHERYL A. MCLEAN, ERICA C. BOLING, and JENNIFER ROWSELL

 9. The New Literacies of Online Reading Comprehension and the Irony             173
    of No Child Left Behind: Students Who Require Our Assistance the Most
    Actually Receive It the Least
    DONALD J. LEU, J. GREGORY MCVERRY, W. IAN O'BYRNE, LISA ZAWILINSKI,
    JILL CASTEK, and DOUGLAS K. HARTMAN

10. Roles of Engagement, Valuing, and Identification in Reading Development       195
    of Students from Diverse Backgrounds
    JOHN T. GUTHRIE, ROBERT RUEDA, LINDA B. GAMBRELL, and DANETTE A. MORRISON

11. Robust Informal Learning Environments for Youth                               216
    from Nondominant Groups: Implications for Literacy Learning
    in Formal Schooling
    KRIS GUTIÉRREZ and CAROL D. LEE

12. Assessing Student Progress in the Time of No Child Left Behind               233
    GEORGIA EARNEST GARCÍA and EURYDICE B. BAUER

13. Meeting the Needs of Diverse Learners: Effective Management                  254
    of Language Arts Instruction
    D. RAY REUTZEL, LESLEY MANDEL MORROW, and HEATHER CASEY


## PART III.  STRATEGIES FOR TEACHING

14. Cross-Language Transfer of Phonological, Orthographic,                        277
    and Semantic Knowledge
    MARÍA S. CARLO

15. Learning to Read in English: Teaching Phonics to Beginning Readers           292
    from Diverse Backgrounds
    LINNEA C. EHRI

16. Vocabulary Instruction for Diverse Students                                   320
    SUSAN WATTS TAFFE, CAMILLE L. Z. BLACHOWICZ, and PETER J. FISHER

17. Comprehension: The Means, Motive, and Opportunity for Meeting                 337
    the Needs of Diverse Learners
    SUSIE M. GOODIN, CATHERINE M. WEBER, P. DAVID PEARSON, and TAFFY E. RAPHAEL

18. Helping Diverse Learners to Become Fluent Readers                             366
    MELANIE R. KUHN AND TIMOTHY RASINSKI

PART IV. PREPARING TEACHERS TO TEACH LITERACY TO DIVERSE STUDENTS

19. Teacher Knowledge in Culturally and Linguistically Complex Classrooms:    379
    Lessons from the Golden Age and Beyond
    DJANGO PARIS *and* ARNETHA F. BALL

20. Protecting Our Investment: Induction and Mentoring of Novice Teachers    396
    in Diversity-Rich Schools
    NANCY FREY *and* DOUGLAS FISHER

21. Professional Development: Continuing to Understand    413
    How to Teach Children from Diverse Backgrounds
    MARGARITA CALDERÓN

Afterword: From "Just a Teacher" to Justice in Teaching—    431
Working in the Service of Education, the New Civil Right
ERIC J. COOPER

Author Index    437

Subject Index    451

# Introduction

LESLEY MANDEL MORROW, ROBERT RUEDA, *and* DIANE LAPP

This research handbook has been compiled to present a synthesis of investigations, issues, and questions that address the acquisition and development of literacy for children and their teachers. A special focus of the volume is on issues of diversity, policy, and equity as they impact research, theory, and practice in literacy. Attention to these issues must be a top priority if national and state goals for closing the reading achievement gap are to be accomplished (International Reading Association, 2002). This is a daunting task, because students today more than ever need to be literate to succeed in the workplace. At the same time, there is clear evidence that the achievement of all children has not been equal. More than half of all American students score below proficiency in reading (National Assessment of Educational Progress, 2005). Ample evidence indicates a growing achievement gap in reading and math between (1) minority and nonminority students, (2) those from economically poorer and richer families, (3) students whose native language is English and those whose first language is not English, and (4) students identified for special education services and those in regular education.

Nationally reported data point to four conclusions: (1) There are differences in the emerging literacy knowledge and performance of young children entering kindergarten from various racial/ethnic and socioeconomic backgrounds; (2) the gap is greater for children who enter school with a combination of risk factors (e.g., mothers with less education, living in a single-parent family, whether the family receives welfare benefits, and whether the primary language spoken in the home is not English); (3) by grade 4, there is a significant discrepancy between the reading comprehension proficiency of European American, non-Hispanic students and their African American and Hispanic peers, and this discrepancy continues through grade 12; and (4) these gaps have been stable for more than a decade. Research has documented stable differences over time between kindergarten and grade 7 (Tabors, Snow, & Dickinson, 2001) and between first grade and the end of high school (Cunningham & Stanovich, 1997); therefore, as time progresses, it becomes increasingly more difficult to undo the "failure to read" syndrome (Al Otaiba & Fuchs, 2002).

Concern about issues of diversity, policy, and equity has traditionally been viewed as a problem in urban and in poor rural districts. However, as the diversity in our country continues to grow daily, the preparation of all teachers must focus on developing proficiency in dealing with language diversity, cultural diversity, policy concerns, and equity (Lapp, Flood, & Chou, 2008; Leland & Harste, 2005; Weiner, 2006).

## THE POLICY OF NO CHILD LEFT BEHIND: PUTTING READING FIRST

Although it is very controversial, the No Child Left Behind Act of 2001 (NCLB) is the principal national legislative policy response to the illiteracy crisis in the United States and the problem of the failure to read proficiently. It is strongly driven by the recognition that illiteracy can no longer be tolerated as an inevitable state for too many groups of American students. NCLB also represents a departure from past national policy for low-income parents in the education of their children. Parents now have a wider array of educational choices, including public charter schools, and, depending on the academic progress of their children's school, the choice of external supplemental services. If children consistently fail in a given school, NCLB may include sanctions such as reorganization of that institution. Although there are countless problems with NCLB, it heightens awareness about our illiteracy problems; it stresses professional development of teachers and accountability; and it involves parents in decision making.

## ISSUES RELATED TO TEACHER QUALITY

Two important features of NCLB underscore the importance of instruction. First is the emphasis on having well-qualified teachers instructing all students, especially those at risk for school failure. Second is the emphasis on instructional practice based on educational research, that is, evidence-based practice. Well-qualified teachers and related educational specialists are essential both for early identification of students who have difficulty with early reading requirements and for tailoring reading instruction that results in mastery and continued achievement.

One consequence of this legislation is that states and school districts are under great pressure to guarantee a skilled teacher in every regular education classroom. The legislation requires that all teachers of core academic subjects (English, reading/language arts, math, science, foreign language, civics/government, economics, history, geography, arts, etc.) must be highly qualified. This means that regular education teachers must hold a state license or certificate in teaching, demonstrate competence in the subject(s) they teach, and also be able to demonstrate subject matter knowledge on the standardized tests that states select.

One question regarding the emphasis on quality teachers is: What is an effective teacher? The short answer is: One whose students learn. The effective teacher is an individual with deep knowledge of the subject matter taught, and sufficient pedagogical expertise and experience to be effective with all students. One definition of an "effective teacher" is one whose students achieve at the proficient, or competent, level on a given state's high-stakes assessments. As desirable as this sounds, this general description of the effective teacher is narrow and vague. Poor students and students of color do underachieve in school for a variety of complex reasons, but it is clear that they often enter school lagging behind their peers in academic preparation. Although schools may have little control over what happens before students come to school, they are able to guarantee that all students receive the single most important resource to reach their potential, specifically, highly qualified teachers. One continuing issue related to opportunity to learn, however, is that research has shown that well-prepared teachers often choose not to teach in communities with "at-risk" students (Peske & Haycock, 2006). When they do, they sometimes encounter little support; therefore, they are not as effective as they might be in higher-achieving middle-class schools.

## RESEARCH AND THEORY
## ABOUT EFFECTIVE AND EXEMPLARY TEACHING

A major concern in the study of exemplary teachers is to find a reliable and valid way to identify who is exemplary and to describe what these teachers do in their classrooms. Investigators have undertaken this task in several ways. Researchers have identified teachers as exemplary based on the following criteria:

- Selecting teachers with students who have excellent test scores in literacy achievement over a period of time.
- Selecting teachers whose students' test scores are beyond what would be expected from children considered "at risk" from schools that beat the odds.
- Selecting teachers based on administrator recommendations.
- Selecting teachers nominated by their peers.
- Selecting teachers nominated by parents.
- Selecting teachers nominated by students.

Researchers have used some or all of these characteristics when selecting samples to study (Block, 2001; Morrow & Casey, 2003; Pressley, Rankin, & Yokoi, 1996; Taylor, Pearson, Clark, & Walpole, 1999; Taylor, Peterson, Pearson, &

Rodriquez, 2002; Wharton-McDonald, Pressley, Rankin, & Mistretta, 1997). Taylor, Pearson, and Clark (2000), for example, studied the literacy practices of exemplary teachers in schools that beat the odds. Students in these teachers' classrooms were considered to be at risk due to family poverty, yet they scored well in literacy achievement. Two teachers in grades K–3 in 14 schools across the United States participated in the study. Each teacher was observed five times, from December to April, for 1 hour of reading instruction. Teachers also completed a written survey, kept a weekly log of reading and writing activities in their classrooms, and were interviewed in May of that school year. These effective teachers focused on small-group instruction, provided time for independent reading, monitored student on-task behaviors, and initiated strong home communication. The teachers also focused on explicit phonics instruction and the application of phonics in the context of reading and writing, asked high-level comprehension questions, and were more likely to ask students to write their responses to reading.

In a related study to determine exemplary practice, Wharton-McDonald and colleagues (1997) meticulously collected and described through surveys and interviews the most important literacy practices and routines among 89 K–3 regular education and 10 special education teachers identified by administrators as exemplary. These exemplary teachers were described by their peers and supervisors as "masterful" in the classroom, managing time, materials, and student behavior with finesse. These effective teachers held high expectations for their students and had a real sense of purpose, direction, and objectives. Topping the list of classroom characteristics and instructional practices reported by these effective, primary-level teachers was—not surprisingly—a literate classroom environment. In addition, these educators provided explicit instruction in literacy (reading and writing) skills, strategies, and concepts. They provided daily doses of both contextualized and isolated skills and strategy instruction, access to varied reading materials, and a variety of ways to engage students in reading and writing. They adapted instruction to the ability levels or needs of their students, worked to motivate students to engage in reading and writing, and consistently monitored student engagement and literacy progress through systematic accountability.

Morrow, Tracey, Woo, and Pressley (1999) intensively observed six exemplary teachers from three different school districts. Teachers selected to be observed for the study were nominated by school administrators, peers, parents, and students. The selection process also included checking these six teachers' student achievement scores over the preceding 5 years to confirm the effects of their exemplary status on student achievement measures. Approximately 25 hours of observation, as well as individual interviews, were completed on each of the six teachers. The major finding was that these six exemplary teachers provided "literacy-rich environments." Within these literacy-rich classrooms, teachers orchestrated a variety of learning settings, such as whole-class, small-group, one-on-one, and teacher-directed learning centers and social interactions with adults and peers. A rich variety of print and print-producing materials were available for the children's use on a daily basis. Teachers provided various instruction, such as spontaneous, authentic, explicit, direct, systematic, meaning-oriented, problem-solving, and open-ended approaches. They engaged children on a daily basis in shared, guided, oral, silent, independent, collaborative, and performance reading and writing. They provided regular writing, word analysis, and comprehension instruction. Moreover, they made consistent efforts to connect reading and writing instruction to thematic content taught at other times of the day. Many of these same effective practices and instructional routines were reported and confirmed 2 years later by Cantrell (1999a, 1999b) in her study of the effects of literacy instruction on primary students' reading and writing achievement.

In summary, the time distribution among regular literacy activities and lessons, and the focus of these lessons, exert measurable influences on young children's literacy growth and development. Effective teachers are masterful classroom managers who balance their instructional time, emphases, and content among a variety of alternative literacy learning activities. Effective literacy learning activities are integrally linked to activities in other parts of the day and curriculum; have an explicit purpose, with learning tasks clearly defined; and engage students across a wide variety of social settings. Synthesis of investigations about exemplary literacy practice in the elementary grades, such as those we have described, indicate that exemplary literacy teachers share the following characteristics: (1) They provide explicit literacy instruction; (2) engage students in constructive exchanges with the teacher (3) create a supportive, encouraging, and friendly atmosphere; (4) weave reading and writing throughout the curriculum; (5) integrate content-area themes into the teaching of reading and writing; (6) create a literacy-rich environment in their classrooms, with a variety of literacy materials to support instruction; (7) teach to individual needs in small-group settings; (8) have excellent organization and management skills; and (9) develop strong connections with students' parents. Teachers include daily organization and management routines, and organize their instruction so that the environment is filled with the necessary reading and writing materials to support that instruction, purposefully placed for accessibility when needed. There are explicit instructions and time for periods of social interaction for learning in whole-group, small-group, and one-on-one settings. The teacher provides many formats for reading and writing: reading aloud, shared reading, independent reading, collaborative reading, guided reading, performance of reading activities, partner/buddy reading, literature circles, and content-area reading. The teacher organizes the following writing activities: shared writing, journal writing, independent writing, reader response writing, collaborative writing, writing fiction and nonfiction, guided writing, performance of writing activities, content-area writing, and writing workshop (e.g., Allington, Johnston, & Day, 2002; Block, 2001; Cantrell, 1999a, 1999b; Morrow et al., 1999; Morrow & Casey, 2003; Pressley et al., 1996; Pressley et al., 1997; Taylor et al., 1999, 2002; Wharton-McDonald et al., 1997). While many of the researchers phrase their findings differently, the categories are remarkably similar.

Exemplary language arts classrooms are informed by sociocultural theory. According to this theory, student learning is dependent on social interaction that is heavily scaffolded, and on social organization of contexts that allows students to transform what they know with important academic knowledge and skills (Vygotsky, 1978). Well-organized classrooms are collaborative communities, with teachers guiding instruction and student participation. These rich learning contexts take into consideration the relationships among the teacher, the student, the community of the classroom, and the larger community of the school. The sociocultural perspective is based on the belief that a community of learning occurs among individuals in a well-organized and -managed classroom that is responsive to student learning needs and existing knowledge and skills, including those from home and community settings.

Although many studies of exemplary teaching imply a concern for diversity, and attention to policy and equity, a gap in this research results because these terms are often not explicitly used, nor are concerns for differences in language and cultural background given prominence.

## OVERVIEW OF THE BOOK

This book deals with issues of social class, dialect, first language, power, and privilege. The intended audience is college professors and their graduate and undergraduate students. It is also intended for classroom teachers of reading and reading specialists in districts with children from diverse backgrounds.

The stage is set for the book in a foreword with a most appropriate title: "Every Child Must Be Visible If We Are to Succeed as a World-Class Nation." This important piece is written by Professor Emeritus Edmund W. Gordon (from Columbia University).

The book is divided into four major parts. Part I addresses perspectives about learning and diverse students. Special issues concerning literacy, diversity, equity, and policy are discussed in Part II. Strategies for teaching children from diverse backgrounds are elaborated in Part III, and preparation of literacy teachers to teach children with diverse languages, cultures, and experiences is discussed in Part IV.

Part I begins with Chapter 1 by Honorine Nocon (from the University of Colorado at Denver) and Michael Cole (University of California at San Diego), who provide a historical context and discuss theory related to issues about diversity and literacy. In Chapter 2, policy related to diversity and literacy is discussed by Eugene E. García (from Arizona State University) and Ann-Marie Wiese (WestEd). Iliana Reyes, Leisy Wyman, Norma González, Eliane Rubinstein-Ávila, Karen Spear-Ellinwood, Perry Gilmore, and Luis C. Moll (all from the University of Arizona) share ideas about the discourse patterns of diverse students outside of school in Chapter 3. An area of utmost importance when we talk about diversity is family. In Chapter 4, Patricia A. Edwards (from Michigan State University), Jeanne R. Paratore (Boston University), and Nancy L. Roser (University of Texas at Austin) discuss family literacy and the importance of recognizing cultural significance. In Chapter 5, poverty and its effect on literacy are discussed by Pedro Portes (from the University of Georgia) and Spencer Salas (University of North Carolina). English language learners and literacy development are discussed by Robert T. Jiménez and Brad L. Teague (both from Vanderbilt University) in Chapter 6.

Part II highlights special issues concerning literacy. It begins with Chapter 7 by Cynthia H. Brock (from the University of Nevada), Gwendolyn Thompson McMillon (Oakland University), Julie L. Pennington and Dianna Townsend (University of Nevada), and Diane Lapp (San Diego State University), which discusses teacher talk and academic English development. In Chapter 8, Cheryl McLean, Erica Boling, and Jennifer Rowsell (all from Rutgers, The State University of New Jersey) look at engaging diverse students in multiple literacies in and out of school. This is followed in Chapter 9 by a discussion of the consequences of new literacies, poverty, and NCLB by Donald J. Leu, Gregory McVerry, W. Ian O'Byrne, Lisa Zawilinski (all from the University of Connecticut), Jill Castek (University of California Berkeley), and Douglas K. Hartman (Michigan State University), who find that the diverse students who often require the most assistance frequently receive the least. The next topic, in Chapter 10, focusing on guiding children from diverse backgrounds to become engaged readers, is written by John T. Guthrie (from the University of Maryland), Robert Rueda (University of Southern California), Linda B. Gambrell (Clemson University), and Danette A. Morrison (University of Maryland). Defining informal learning and describing such activities with children from diverse backgrounds is then discussed in Chapter 11 by Kris Gutiérrez (from the University of California Los Angeles) and Carol D. Lee (Northwestern University). Georgia Earnest García and Eurydice B. Bauer (both from the University of Illinois), in Chapter 12, discuss assessment of student progress as a guide to planning appropriate instruction. Finally, in Chapter 13, D. Ray Reutzel (from the Utah State University), Lesley Mandel Morrow (Rutgers, The State University of New Jersey), and Heather Casey (Rider University) discuss organizing and managing the language arts program with children from diverse backgrounds.

In Part III, the authors present strategies appropriate for teaching children from diverse backgrounds. Chapter 14 deals with language development in first and second languages by María S. Carlo (from the University of Miami). In Chapter 15, Linnea C. Ehri (from the City University of New York) presents studies on acquiring knowledge about print, specifically, phonological awareness and phonics. Issues related to vocabulary development are shared in Chapter 16 by Susan Watts Taffe (from the University of Cincinnati), and Camille L. Z. Blachowicz and Peter J. Fisher (both from National-Louis University). Comprehension through the construction of meaning with expository and narrative texts is discussed in Chapter 17 by Susie M. Goodin and P. David Pearson (both from the University of California Berkeley), and Catherine M. Weber and Taffy E. Raphael (from the University of Illinois, Chicago) The last strategy dealt with in this section addresses ways to help diverse learners become fluent readers, and is discussed in Chapter 18 by Melanie R. Kuhn (from Boston University) and Timothy Rasinski (Kent State University).

The fourth and final major part in the book is about preparing teachers to teach literacy to children who have diverse languages, cultures, and experiences. Chapter 19 by Django Paris (from Arizona State University) and Arnetha F. Ball (Stanford University) addresses teacher education that connects teachers' and children's knowledge. Next, in Chapter 20, Nancy Frey and Douglas Fisher (both from San Diego State University) discuss how to mentor teachers of children from diverse backgrounds during their induction year. Finally, Chapter 21, by Margarita Calderón (from Johns Hopkins University), discusses professional development that helps teachers continue to understand how to teach children from diverse backgrounds.

We began the book with a foreword to set the stage; we end with an afterword—entitled "From 'Just a Teacher' to Justice in Teaching," by Eric J. Cooper (from the National Urban Alliance for Effective Education)—to reflect.

## REFERENCES

Al Otaiba, S., & Fuchs, D. (2002). Characteristics of children who are unresponsive to early literacy intervention: A review of the literature. *Remedial and Special Education, 23*(5), 300–316.

Allington, R. L., Johnston, P. H., & Day, J. P. (2002). Exemplary fourth-grade teachers. *Language Arts, 79*(6), 462–466.

Block, C. C. (2001, December). *Distinctions between the expertise of literacy teachers preschool through grade 5.* Paper presented at the annual meeting of the National Reading Conference, San Antonio, TX.

Cantrell, S. C. (1999a). Effective teaching and literacy learning: A look inside primary classrooms. *Reading Teacher, 52*(4), 370–379.

Cantrell, S. C. (1999b). The effects of literacy instruction on primary students' reading and writing achievement. *Reading and Research Instruction, 39*(1), 3–26.

Cunningham, A. E., & Stanovich, K. E. (1997). Early reading acquisition and its relation to reading experience and ability 10 years later. *Developmental Psychology, 33,* 934–945.

International Reading Association. (2002). *Position statement on investment in teacher preparation in the United States.* Newark, DE: Author.

Lapp, D., Flood, J., & Chou, V. (2008). The promise of multiliteracies for the preparation of urban classroom teachers of reading. In L. C. Wilkinson, L. M. Morrow, & V. Chou (Eds.), *Improving literacy achievement in urban schools: Critical elements in teacher preparation* (pp. 40–60). Newark, DE: International Reading Association.

Leland, C. H., & Harste, J. C. (2005). Doing what we want to become: Preparing new urban teachers. *Urban Education, 40*(1), 60–77.

Morrow, L. M., Tracey, D. H., Woo, D. G., & Pressley, M. (1999). Characteristics of exemplary first-grade literacy instruction. *Reading Teacher, 52*(5), 462–476.

Morrow, L. M., & Casey, H. K. (2003). A comparison of exemplary characteristics in 1st and 4th grade teachers. *California Reader, 36*(3), 5–17.

National Assessment of Educational Progress. (2005). *The Nation's Report Card*. Washington, DC: National Center for Education Statistics. Available at *nces.ed.gov/nationsreportcard*.

Peske, H. G., & Haycock, K. (2006). *Teaching equality: How poor and minority students are shortchanged on teacher quality*. Washington, DC: Education Trust.

Pressley, M., Rankin, J., & Yokoi, L. (1996). A survey of instructional practices of primary teachers nominated as effective in promoting literacy. *Elementary School Journal, 96*(4), 363–383.

Tabors, P. O., Snow, C. E., & Dickinson, D. K. (2001). Homes and schools together: Supporting language and literacy development. In D. K. Dickinson & P. O. Tabors (Eds.), *Beginning literacy with language: Young children learning at home and school* (pp. 313–334). Baltimore: Brookes.

Taylor, B. M., Pearson, P. D., & Clark, K. (2000). Effective schools and accomplished teachers: Lessons about primary-grade reading instruction in low-income schools. *Elementary School Journal 101*(2), 121–165.

Taylor, B. M., Pearson, P. D., Clark, K. E., & Walpole, S. (1999). *Beating the odds in teaching all children to read* (CIERA Report No. 2–006). Ann Arbor, MI: Center for the Improvement of Early Reading Achievement.

Taylor, B. M., Peterson, D. S., Pearson, P. D., & Rodriguez, M. C. (2002). Looking inside classrooms: Reflecting on the "how" as well as the "what" in effective reading instruction. *Reading Teacher, 56*(3), 270–279.

Vygotsky, L. S. (1978). *Mind in society: The development of higher psychological processes* (M. Cole, V. John-Scribner, & E. Souberman, Eds. & Trans.). Cambridge, MA: Harvard University Press.

Weiner, L. (2006). *Urban teaching: The essentials* (2nd ed.). New York: Teachers College Press.

Wharton-McDonald, R., Pressley, M., Rankin, J., & Mistretta, J. (1997). Effective primary-grades literacy instruction = balanced literacy instruction. *Reading Teacher, 50*(6), 518–521.

# PART I

# PERSPECTIVES ABOUT LEARNING AMONG DIVERSE STUDENTS

# Relating Diversity and Literacy Theory

HONORINE NOCON *and* MICHAEL COLE

There is little debate among educational researchers that all people, barring severe biological impediment, can learn to become literate. Additionally, academics agree that we learn throughout our lifespans by building on what we have previously experienced (Bransford, Brown, & Cocking, 2000). As Snow (2001), Heath (1983), Cummins (2007), Lee (1995), Moll, Sáez, and Dworin (2001), and others have demonstrated, children with very different cultural heritages and quite different life experiences have developed rich linguistic backgrounds in their homes and home communities that teachers can use to build both learning and literacy.

As a matter of common practice, however, many teachers ignore these potentially important experiential backgrounds. Often this lack of interest reflects teachers' beliefs that home experiences of poor, minority group children are simply irrelevant to classroom learning. At other times, teachers actively seek to exclude from their classrooms what children have learned at home, because they devalue, stigmatize, or even pathologize the experiences of children whose cultures deviate from their own. This privileging of the norms of the teachers' culture is supported by public schooling, the values and practices of which in the United States are consistent with white, English-speaking, middle-class culture (Rogoff, 2003; Valencia, 1997).

The children involved are not insensitive to this situation. For example, teachers report discovering students who hide their ability to read and write in Spanish owing to fear of ridicule by fellow students (Moll et al., 2001). Moll and colleagues (2001) argue that negative teacher and peer responses to linguistic diversity reflect broad societal attitudes that contribute to the ideological and material context for learning and literacy development in ordinary classrooms. Frequently these broad societal attitudes deter teachers from recognizing the strengths that poor children, children of color, and linguistically diverse children (who are often the same children) bring to the classroom. As Lee (2001) argues, "Teachers who believe that these students cannot learn, that they contribute nothing of value from their home and community lives, and that their language is inferior are not likely to invest the energy, the tenacity, and the sheer will demanded to reengage students who have disengaged from school" (p. 118).

Ruíz (1984), in addressing U.S. language policy, defined such broad social attitudes concerning language as "orientations," or "complexes" about the role of language. Ruíz described two orientations to language that have dominated policy debate and schoolroom practice: language as problem and language as right. The language-as-problem orientation assumes that speaking (or writing) a language other than the dominant language in a society (English, for our purposes in this chapter) is a handicap to children on a personal level, and a threat to national unity and commerce on the societal level. The language-as-right orientation assumes that one's first language is so intertwined with identity and culture that its free use and maintenance are inalienable rights.

After laying out the shortcomings of these opposing views, Ruíz (1984) proposed that language policymakers and educators concerned with social justice consider a language-as-resource orientation—"language is a resource to be managed, developed and conserved," an orientation that frames "minority communities as important sources of expertise" (p. 28). Such a reorientation would render linguistic diversity a resource for all, including those from the dominant culture, in commerce, diplomacy, and learning, based on research on the positive effects of knowing more than one language (Bialystok, 2007; Wolf, 2007).

We believe that the resource orientation can be expanded to encompass many facets of diversity based on the documented value of honoring and building on students' home and community cultures. For example, the contributors to the volume edited by González, Moll, and Amanti (2005) describe productive changes in teachers, family members, and students when the funds of knowledge in homes and communities become resources to enrich instruction of mandated curricula. Similarly, Banks and colleagues (2007), Ladson-Billings (1995), Lee (1995), Mercado (2001), and Nieto (2002) have described the positive outcomes in student behaviors and academic achievement that ensue when teachers build their instruction on resources from community, youth, and popular cultures. The use of community cultural resources is also supported by Téllez and Waxman (2006), based on their meta-analysis of 25 studies on instructional practices for students with a first language other than English.

Whatever its merits, expanded use of the resource orientation in school learning and literacy development is unlikely to come about spontaneously. Collin and Apple (2007) argue that because nondominant literacies are subject to power relations favoring elites, a crucial step in the process of broadening opportunity for nonelite learners is "to collaborate in developing powerful literacies both for securing productive, rewarding labor in fast-moving informational economies and for reshaping socio-economic orders according to principles of justice and strong democracy" (pp. 436–437). We concur; this is the challenge that educators and activists for social justice in education face. Consequently, in this chapter we consider a broad range of long-standing social attitudes, or ideologies/theories, regarding literacy and diversity that play important, but not always recognized, roles in determining when and whether linguistic–cultural diversity is treated as a resource or a problem for children in their formal schooling. Our discussion is guided by two assumptions. First, diverse linguistic–cultural experiences and learning from the home are valuable resources for effective classroom teaching and learning. Second, proficiency in text literacy is an essential skill in broadening opportunities for participation in both informational economies and social change in the interest of justice.

In theorizing the relationship between literacy and diversity, with particular attention to formal education, we argue the following in subsequent sections:

- A *sociocultural–historical perspective on literacy* provides a useful lens through which to analyze the dynamic complexities of literacy development in and out of school.
- *Ideologies regarding diversity* shape school-based ideologies/theories of literacy in response to power relations and social conditions beyond school.
- The *diversity-in-literacy matrix*, which lays out the interrelations of theories of diversity and literacy, is a useful tool for analyzing current approaches to literacy practice and literacy instruction.
- A *resource orientation* to diversity is supported by educational, linguistic, and psychological research, and is essential to effective teaching for non-mainstream children, but widespread adoption of that orientation is difficult to achieve in educational institutions designed with a diversity-as-problem orientation.

We conclude with a discussion of implications of our review for classroom teaching and future research.

## A SOCIOCULTURAL–HISTORICAL PERSPECTIVE ON LITERACY

What we term a "sociocultural–historical perspective on literacy" encompasses a broad family of theories that assumes human learning and development involve the interconnected contributions of historically evolved sociocultural practices, dominant belief systems, social rules and conventions, and institutionalized divisions of labor. Reading and writing are two important examples of human abilities that require such an inclusive, systemic approach.

This view also includes the important fact that, as several authors have pointed out, oral language is central to the process of hominization and, consequently, is universal to all humans who have not experienced insult to the brain.

In contrast, the process of becoming literate involves developing proficiency in the use of the tools (i.e., symbol systems) that are the historical and cultural products of the practices of literacy among social groups (Luria, 1976; Wolf, 2007). In short, our brains are not wired to read; writing systems developed too recently to be encoded in our genes. Consequently, although there is a great deal of interesting new research on the role of literacy in shaping the brain's activities during ontogeny (summarized in Wolf, 2007), we focus on four sociocultural conceptions of literacy that have informed literacy instruction and have persisted across historical time. Each has important implications for how current researchers and practitioners think about cultural diversity and literacy.[1]

### Literacy as Gatekeeper

Human beings first became "literate," understood as the process of becoming expert in the manipulation of a system or systems of graphic symbols to acquire, store, and communicate information, in order to keep track of accounts in the trade of animals and food products (Schmandt-Besserat, 1996). As forms of social life and their associated technologies of production increased in complexity, and large numbers of human beings began to live in what we now refer to as "city-states," social groups developed more complex systems of literacy, either independently or through borrowing.[2] As part and parcel of increasing social complexity, the cultural legacies of literacy (i.e., the symbol sets and conventions for their manipulation), were kept under the control of social elites, who arranged for selected groups of people under their control to acquire and to use literacy in the interests of the state. The clear connections between state power and the benefits of literacy for those who aspired to better living conditions were made clear in an early letter from a father to a son living in ancient Egypt:

> I have seen how the belaboured man is belaboured—thou should set thy heart in pursuit of writing. . . .
>
> The small building contractor carries mud. . . . He is dirtier than vines or pigs from treading under his mud. His clothes are stiff with clay. . . .
>
> Behold, there is no profession free of a boss—except the scribe, he is the boss. . . .
>
> Behold, there is no scribe who lacks food from the property of the House of the King—life property, health! (quoted in Donaldson, 1978, p. 84fn)

So pronounced have been the sociopolitical power consequences of literacy that many scholars argue that the main function of literacy from ancient to modern times has been to facilitate the enslavement of other humans (Collins & Blot, 2003; Diamond, 2005). For example, Olson (2001) describes Luther's radical defiance of clerical textual authority, which had protected and restricted access to literacy for centuries. Luther stated "that the meaning of Scripture depended not upon the dogmas of the church [which had then to be interpreted by clerics and scribes], but upon a deeper reading of the text" (in Olson, p. 142). Luther's statement ultimately led to the "mass literacy campaigns of the German Protestant Reformers of the 16th century to create a critical mass of readers who could take advantage of the pictures and texts that the printing press made available to them" (Tyner, 1998, p. 19).

The Protestant Reformation opened the gates to mass literacy in Europe and the Western World, but as Gee (1988, p. 200), invoking Plato, commented, literacy has two sides: "literacy as liberator and literacy as weapon." Freire (2001) made the same point, arguing that literacy has been used for both personal freedom and social control.

Scribner (1984), in her analysis of literacy theory, described three metaphors for literacy, one of which was literacy as power. She notes that "it is an undisputed fact that illiteracy in America is concentrated among the poor and ethnic minorities whose problems of poverty and political powerlessness are deeply intertwined with problems of access to knowledge and literacy" (p. 12). Scribner points directly to the gatekeeping function of literacy with her metaphor of literacy as "a state of grace," as revealed in "the tendency in many societies to endow the literate person with special virtues" (p. 13). Scribner describes this as the association of literacy with mysticism in some societies, and with being "cultured" in Western societies (p. 13). Both metaphors resonate with Bourdieu's (1982/1991) formulation of exclusion and inclusion based on cultural and social capital, which we interpret as an alternative formulation of gatekeeping. One way in which literacy has been used by elites for social evaluation is as a marker of progress, to which we now turn.

### Literacy as Progress

According to several accounts, 19th-century authors had a propensity to interpret history as a progression from savagery to civilization (Diamond, 2005; Goody, 1977). This tendency is described by Cole (2005, p. 197) as a "master narrative" equating history and social evolution with progress. Both Diamond and Cole argue that writing has contributed to social change and to the perception of writing as a marker of social superiority. Diamond notes that "peoples who pride themselves on being civilized have always viewed writing as the sharpest distinction raising them above 'barbarians' or 'savages'" (2005, p. 215).

Cole (2005, p. 206) questions the idea that school-based literacy produces generalized development of cognitive skills:

> At a minimum, it seems certain that practice in representing language using writing symbols improves children's and adults' ability to analyze the sound structure and grammar of their language [Morais & Kolinsky, 2001], a finding which Peter Bryant and his colleagues have made good use of in the design of programs for the teaching of reading [Bryant, 1995; Bryant & Nunes, 1998].

Cole notes, in connection with his suspicions about the generality of the cognitive changes wrought by formal schooling, that Vai farmers from northwestern Liberia showed similar increased language-analyzing abilities even though they had acquired literacy apart from schooling. Citing further research on schooling and literacy outside of schooling, Cole (2005) concludes that schooling may prepare people for specific practices (e.g., bureaucratic work[3]) valued in modern, urbanized society; however, this is not equivalent to generalizable intellectual advancement for whole societies. Similarly, while literacy produces both individual cognitive and social change over generations, those changes are contextually situated in the practices of cultural groups and are neither neutral in terms of individual or societal change, nor are they unidirectional in terms of progress or success. As Diamond (2005, p. 215) points out, "civilized" peoples don't always defeat the "barbarians," and cultures that gave birth to literacy in what is now the Middle East and southern Mexico have faced both defeats and declines in power in the course of their histories. Still, the ideology of literacy as progress remains prevalent, informing both educational practice and policy (Cummins, 2007; UNESCO, 1951), and provoking a critical countertheory of literacy as discourse, which we now address.

### Literacy as Discourse

Tyner (1998, p. 26) summarizes the work of literacy scholars who have questioned assumptions about literacy as progress by arguing that "the elevation of print over oral cultures was a serious misstep in literacy research." She points to the work of Goody and Watt (1963) and Scribner and Cole (1981), who found that literate people do not necessarily think clearly. As a response to theories of literacy as progress, Tyner describes a theory of literacy that emerged at the end of the 20th century as research began to focus on qualitative and quantitative studies of the meaning of literacy in particular contexts—literacy as discourse. Consistent with Scribner and Cole's finding that the practice of literacy has different consequences in different cultural practices, Tyner argues that "the theory of literacy as discourse offers these students [children in diverse, multicultural societies] the tools to switch fluently between a wide range of discourses available to them in order to apply communication in strategic ways" (p. 28).

Delpit's (1995) work provides a clear example of literacy as discourse. She argues that while maintaining their home discourse, members of nondominant cultural groups must master the discourses of power to access the culture of power. Stressing the importance of that home/primary discourse as the foundation for developing expertise in other discourses, Tyner (1998) cites Gee's (1996) argument that discourses are mastered through a process of acquisition that is closer to apprenticeship than to formal and conscious learning. Nieto (1999, 2002) describes this process as an internally challenging negotiation that students who are not from the mainstream navigate in acquiring the discourse of school literacy. It also involves the institutionally and personally challenging negotiation that teachers of nonelite students need to undertake in acquiring the discourses of multicultural literacies.

Nieto's work, as well as that of Gee (1996, 2003), provides a link between literacy as discourse and the associated concept of multiliteracies across languages, dialects, registers, and media forms. The New London Group (1996) articulated the need for new pedagogies to address the issue of new media literacies. This concern was taken up recently by Collin and Apple (2007), who analyzed what they refer to as the biopolitics of workplace and school-based literacies. A theory of multiple literacies as multiple forms of discourse links to the multiple uses or functions that literacy may serve in specific contexts. We turn to that issue in the following section.

### Literacy as Tool and Practice[4]

Cole (2005) describes culture and education simultaneously as both processes and products. Similar to literacy, both culture and education use tools and serve as tools. "They overlap in their emphasis upon sustaining the life of the community by bringing about change in children" (p. 196). The life of the community is sustained by enculturating children in the practices of the community, including the practice of literacy. What is not so clear in today's rapidly changing and complex societies, with overlapping cultural groups and practices, is what sorts of tools are most appropriate to the enculturation processes to which diverse children are subjected in schools.

Gutiérrez and Rogoff (2003) address the complexity of culture and enculturation in modern society by describing "culture" as a process that entails participating in multiple practices that are at once culturally inherited and co-created by individuals in interaction. These practices often cross the boundaries of groups of individuals who share cultural commonalities, providing an explanation for within-group variation. Literacies as practices, and as tools situated within practices, can similarly be used within and across cultural communities.

With the concept of literacies as tools for human interaction in mind, we return to the last of Scribner's (1984) three literacy metaphors, literacy as adaptation:

> This metaphor is designed to capture concepts of literacy that emphasize its survival or pragmatic value. When the term "functional literacy" was originally introduced during World War I (Harman, 1970), it specified the literacy skills required to meet the tasks of modern soldiering. Today, functional literacy is conceived broadly as the level of proficiency necessary for effective performance in a range of settings and customary activities. (p. 9)

Scribner argues that the broader conception of functional literacy essentializes people and situations by assuming that a shared minimal level of literacy is universal. Her critique was prescient in light of the Reading First program and the No Child Left Behind Act of 2001 (NCLB) (Cummins, 2007). A sociocultural–historical conception of literacy as a tool situated in practice represents a move counter to the essentializing concept of functional literacy. Additionally, a sociocultural–historical approach that conceptualizes literacy as a practice, or practices, shared and transformed over time assumes that literacies themselves are dynamic. New literates not only acquire the tools of literacy but also contribute to the ongoing development of the practice of literacy, because the participation and identities of the participants themselves change in relation to the practice.

Rogoff (2003) describes literacy as both dynamic and specific. On the one hand, she recounts the ways the definition of English literacy has changed over time in the United States, from reading and reciting passages without comprehension to making inferences and developing ideas through written material (pp. 260–261). On the other hand, she describes Scribner and Cole's (1981) findings that the Vai people of Liberia used three literacies for three separate purposes (Vai script for personal writing, Arabic for memorization or study of the Qur'an, and English for business). These two examples suggest that as people engage with culturally specific literacy products in processes of becoming proficient users of different literacies, they at the same time contribute to changes in those literacies. These examples also resonate with Delpit's (1995) and Nieto's (2002) arguments that proficiency in, and navigation between, multiple literacies by diverse individuals in multicultural settings is a reasonable social goal.

However, it is important to keep in mind that neither the processes nor the products of literacy are unidirectionally benign. Proficiency, for example, assumes both access and evaluation. As we have illustrated in earlier sections, access to literacy can be restricted. Similarly, the right to assess proficiency can be restricted. Both conditions suggest the differential relations that diverse people have to the practices of literacy and to dominant cultures in their societies.

## IDEOLOGIES OF DIVERSITY

Banks and colleagues (2005) note that small hunting and gathering groups share a relatively narrow range of differences in comparison to people in modern and geographically accessible areas. Immigration, often of formerly colonized peoples, together with modern modes of transportation and communication, has increased contacts among peoples and created "amalgams and hybrids" as groups of varying ethnicities, cultures, languages, and religions come into contact in modern nation-states (Banks et al., 2005, p. 18). Bearing in mind Banks and colleagues' argument that those differences often correspond to differences in power, position, and access to resources as the historical legacy of colonization and empire building, we find valuable their definition of "diversity" as a descriptive term referring to "the wide range of racial, cultural, ethnic, linguistic, and religious variation that exists within and across groups that live in multicultural nation-states" (p. 17).[5]

"Diversity," then, as the term is used in contemporary discussions about American education, is the product of a historical process of diversification of populations occupying shared space. From a sociocultural–historical perspective, diversity is the product of past processes of diversification, as well as current processes of "distinction," or inclusion and exclusion, that re-create stratification in societies, ultimately related to the distribution of resources, including literacy (Bourdieu, 1984). The process of producing diversity (in particular, current practices of inclusion and exclusion based on factors such as home language/culture, ethnicity, and social class), has contributed to three ideologies of diversity that have had significant impact on both the literacy development and the schooling of nondominant populations. We address each of these next.

## Diversity as Deficit

The deficit ideology of diversity locates school failure in the endogenous deficiencies of children and families of color who live in poverty, particularly those whose heritage is Mexican or African American (Valencia, 1997, 2000). The deficit model has been used by both conservatives and liberals to explain the apparent inability of children from certain cultural groups to achieve academically and is code for their lack of motivation, cognitive abilities, and "culture." Valencia and Black (2002) argue that the deficit ideology was supported by both myth and science in the cultural deprivation literature of the 20th century and has been advanced in educational policy circles by the "at-risk" literature. They note that the deficit assumption underlying both bodies of literature and the policy and practice they inform "turns students into burdens and trades potential for risk" (p. 87).

Nieto (1999) notes that

> there is ample evidence that some educators believe that bicultural students [those whose home cultures are not the dominant culture which aligns with schooling] have few experiential or cultural strengths that can benefit their education. Teachers consider them to be "walking sets of deficiencies" … or "culturally deprived" just because they speak a language other than English as their native language, or because they have just one parent, or because of their social class, race, gender, or ethnicity. (p. 85)

Nurcombe, Lacey, and Walker (1999) refer to this deficit ideology as the hard-bitten attitude that "if they're any good they'll make it under their own steam; those that haven't don't deserve to" (p. 47). Nieto (2002) attributes the deficit thinking of some teachers to their whiteness and membership in the middle class. In their privilege, they are unaware that they have culture, and that that culture is the norm against which they judge students of color or students who speak languages other than English, and students from low socioeconomic status (SES) backgrounds. These students are the "others"; they have culture.

A deficit ideology of diversity often results in a compensatory approach to instruction, in which educators try to remediate the deficits of children who have been deprived of the cultural experiences valued in schools, or whose lack of English is construed as a lack of language and cognitive competence. Additionally, a deficit ideology in relation to SES can result in low expectations or the *pobrecito* syndrome, which refers to teachers who believe they are being compassionate in not asking poor students (who are most often students of color, and who frequently are learners of English as a second language) to perform, much less succeed, because they already suffer so much that it would be wrong to increase demands upon their already burdened lives.

Nurcombe and colleagues (1999) locate the deficit ideology (also referred to as "cultural deprivation" or "disadvantage") in research from the 1960s and 1970s that correlated low cognitive performance with poverty and malnutrition on the one hand, and limited language development with poverty and membership in nondominant groups on the other. They suggest that the deprivation–deficit ideology evolved "in an attempt to explain why improvement in elementary and high school facilities had not had a more significant effect upon the scholastic attainment of minority children. Deprivation was described as affecting physical, personality, and cognitive development" (p. 68).

This scientific investigation of diversity as a deficit was consistent with broad social attitudes associated with social Darwinism and white superiority that provided the rationale for European and U.S. colonialism and empire building. It was characterized in terms that are reminiscent of the white man's burden and embraced in the War on Poverty in the United States. However, it was also criticized by educational researchers and scholars, who questioned the culturally biased tests used by psychometricians and the assimilationist assumptions that underlay the quest to find a solution to the "deficits." This questioning, as well as qualitative studies of minority children and adults *in situ*, led to a new theory of diversity as difference.

### Diversity as Difference

Nurcombe and colleagues (1999) argue that theorists of cultural difference placed "more weight upon differences in the *expression* of competencies. Minority-group children are described as having more competence than psychometricians have detected. These children do not express their competence in formal test situations, partly because of social inhibition and partly because of their poor comprehension of both tester and test" (p. 64). Nurcombe and colleagues include Cole and Bruner (1971) and Labov (1970) among theorists of cultural difference. Others whose research has supported the diversity as difference ideology include Scribner and Cole (1978), Sharp, Cole, and Lave (1979), and particularly Heath (1983), whose seminal study of the ways that cultural difference plays out in schools contributed to the concept of mismatch between home and school cultures, which, as cultural difference theorists such as Rogoff (2003) would argue, were inherently equal. Gallego, Cole, and the Laboratory of Comparative Human Cognition (2001) argue that the ideology of diverse cultures as different but equal led advocates to "seek to ameliorate the relatively poor performance of non-mainstream children by creating some form of accommodation between the culture of school and the culture of the home" (p. 976). They add that educational researchers informed by the theory of diversity as difference fall into two groups—those who seek to organize classrooms to incorporate home cultural patterns, and those who seek to make the largely implicit culture of schooling explicit in a process of making children bicultural.

Although both diversity as deficit and diversity as difference ideologies continue to inform educational research, policy, and practice, diversity as difference has become the dominant paradigm. Among those adhering to that paradigm are many scholars of color, whose work has contributed to a growing ideology of diversity as strength.

## Diversity as Resource

Nieto (2002) argues that whereas teachers need to teach students the cultural capital they need to negotiate society, "teachers also need to make a commitment to become *students of their students*" (p. 217, original emphasis). By learning with and about their students, teachers can begin to build on the talents and strengths that students bring to schools. "Building on students' strengths means, first, acknowledging that students have significant experiences, insights, and talents to bring to their learning, and second, finding ways to use them in the classroom" (Nieto, 1999, p. 109). González and colleagues (2005) located strength in the diverse funds of knowledge of families and communities that can be tapped to enrich curriculum and make learning meaningful for all children.

Lee (1992) argues that three pedagogical models build on diverse students' strengths. Signifying and the interpretation of speakerly texts (Lee, 1991), talk story (Tharp & Gallimore 1988), and community funds of knowledge (Moll & Greenberg, 1990) are culturally relevant to specific populations and effective across broad populations. All three models view experience with cultural resources in the home, including oral tradition and dialogue, as strengths upon which to build literacy.

Similarly, Moll and colleagues (2001) argue that bilingual children use the social processes and cultural resources at hand, both in school and out, to develop both Spanish and English literacies. They note that "becoming literate is not solely an individual accomplishment. Children inherit the historical conventions of written language and learn them with the assistance of others (adults and peers) in specific cultural contexts or settings" (p. 435). Whereas this is consistent with a practice/tool theory of literacy, Moll and colleagues add that they are referring to more than general circumstances for learning—"to how the specific ideas and activities that constitute those circumstances help determine what literacy (or literacies) may come to mean for children or how it may form part of their lives" (p. 436). Moll and colleagues document meta-awareness about language in children who are becoming biliterate. This meta-level competence is consistent with meta-awareness about language reported by Cole (2005) and others, and metalinguistic skills observed in bilinguals reported by Bialystok (2007) and others. It is also suggestive of the metacultural skills hypothesized by Gee (2003), Lee, Spencer, and Harpalani (2003), and others in regard to diverse students who become bicultural. In these cases, diversity of language and experience can be viewed as a resource in developing metacognitive thinking.

Consideration of cognitive competencies takes the discussion of diversity as resource to a different level, unfortunately, beyond the scope of this chapter. Before moving on to the consideration of diversity in literacy development, however, we do want to point to what brain research has confirmed regarding diversity in literacy. According to Wolf (2007, p. 5), "Underlying the brain's ability to learn reading lies its protean capacity to make new connections among structures and circuits originally devoted to other more basic brain processes that have enjoyed a longer existence in human evolution, such as vision and spoken language." As we develop the ability to read, we build on the neural networks developed through our use of oral language and the associations we have learned to help us make meaning in our cultural milieu. As Wolf notes, "Comprehension of text is affected by everything the reader brings to the text. ... The dynamic interaction between text and life experiences is bidirectional: we bring our life experiences to the text, and the text changes our life experiences" (p. 160).

## INTERRELATION OF IDEOLOGIES OF DIVERSITY AND LITERACY THEORY

In the previous sections, we laid out four theories of literacy and three ideologies of diversity. We now organize these in a matrix that corresponds (on a diagonal from top left to lower right) to an attitudinal continuum, the extremes of which can be considered diversity as a problem in literacy development and diversity as a resource in literacy development (see Figure 1.1). These poles map onto other, related dichotomies in linguistics (prescriptive and descriptive approaches to grammar, second language as additive or subtractive) and epistemology (objective and subjective truth). These dichotomies and the two poles are associated with control by dominant groups in opposition to individual and group agency and contributions.

Examples of approaches to literacy that correspond to the top left pole (i.e., literacy as gatekeeper, diversity as deficit) include the Ford English School, characterized by the "melting pot." Some scholars locate early approaches to Head Start

| | Literacy as progress | Literacy as gatekeeper | Literacy as discourse | Literacy as practice/tool |
|---|---|---|---|---|
| **Diversity as deficit** | Literacy is a marker of cultural/ ethnic progress and superiority. | Literacy is the purview of elites, who have earned membership in the literacy club and who restrict access to members of the dominant culture. | | |
| **Diversity as difference** | | Literacy is available to all, but the pathways to academic literacy must be opened by the dominant culture (i.e., changes in schooling). | Literacies are discourses in which all participate, but access to the written discourse of the dominant culture must be negotiated by both educators and nonmainstream learners to expand opportunity. | Literacies are equal in value, and produce situated ontogenetic and cultural changes in cognition and the practice and tools of literacy, respectively. |
| **Diversity as resource** | | | Control of more than one discourse leads to meta-awareness and access, while honoring home discourses strengthens identity. | The negotiation of multiple literacies by all will provide all with access to enriched learning and literacy practices and tools. |

**FIGURE 1.1.** The diversity-in-literacy matrix.

at this pole, along with Reading First. At the other extreme, literacy as practice/ tool, diversity as resource, we locate the funds of knowledge approach (Gonzáles et al., 2005) and the Fifth Dimension (Cole & the Distributed Literacy Consortium, 2006), an afterschool program that is co-constructed with diverse children and adults, using locally valued content within a framework that develops print and media literacies valued in school, and that also welcomes community literacies. Other areas of the matrix correspond to programs like Achievement via Individual Determination (AVID; Mehan, Hubbard, & Villanueva, 1994), which makes the culture of schooling explicit and accessible to diverse students. AVID corresponds to the literacy-as-discourse diversity-as-difference area. Interpretation of speakerly texts (Lee, 1991) and talk story (Tharp & Gallimore, 1988) correspond to the literacy-as-discourse, diversity-as-resource area. Of course, these examples represent our interpretations of the work cited. Others may well disagree with these characterizations, based on nuances of the programs under consideration. We consider that to be a strength of the diversity-in-literacy matrix, which we offer as a tool for analyzing learning contexts and instructional approaches in terms of their relation of diversity to literacy development. In the quest to improve student outcomes, too often curricula and best practices are not analyzed critically in terms of the orientations and assumptions upon which they have been framed. Nor are the implications of those orientations and assumptions for instructional relationships and the development of diverse learners seriously considered.

In considering how sociocultural–historical approaches might help us think about diversity, Cole (1998) asked: Do we make diversity go away? Or do we harness it? Similarly, we may ask: Do we see diversity as a deficit in literacy development—a problem that we should make go away through assimilation or denial of access? Or do we see diversity as a resource in developing new practices and tools for literacy that will serve the needs of multiple groups, as well as the cause of social justice? These are the questions that educators and researchers need to ask themselves regularly to guide their work on behalf of all children. Of course, we and the contributors to this volume align with the resource–discourse–practice/ tool area of the matrix.

Assuming that diversity is a resource in the development of literacy does not mean, however, that literacy development in classrooms with diverse learners is easily accomplished, or that the practices and tools of literacy are benign (cf. Bialystok, 2007). Diversity and literacy are complex phenomena interacting in complex ways. That said, in the following section we conclude with a further consideration of the resource orientation to diversity in literacy development and its implications for classroom teaching and further research.

## A RESOURCE ORIENTATION

Sociocultural–historical theory tells us to begin our analysis of social phenomena with history and context. Our consideration of literacy and diversity has been framed by broad social attitudes concerning both of these phenomena over time and in the present. We have sought to integrate the different theories or ideologies in the diversity-in-literacy matrix, based loosely on the language orientations proposed by Ruíz (1984) and heavily on the additive and subtractive categories in relation to culture and language. Analysis of literacy theories in terms of the problem–resource continuum of orientations to diversity provides a lens on power relations and the relative social positioning of diverse literacy learners. Our integration of these theories/ideologies invites consideration of their relevance for today's teachers, teacher educators, and rapidly diversifying student populations.

An important question for concerned educators is: What ideologies inform my classroom practice and materials, or my teacher education program, or my research agenda? We suggest that identifying and developing tools, strategies, and approaches to instruction informed by theories of literacies as discursive tools and ideologies of diversity as difference and strength are in the interest of diverse learners, social justice in public education, and academic achievement. This position is informed by decades of research, and decades of resistance, both public and scholarly, to embracing a resource orientation to diversity.

It is clear that we have aligned ourselves with the area of the matrix that views diversity as a resource in literacy development. Yet we acknowledge that the development of literacy is, if not easier, at least less complex, when one is building literacy skills on the shared background of a common language and common experiences. We also know that apparently homogeneous groups mask significant forms of diversity. Teachers today must contend with rapidly increasing cultural and linguistic diversity, as well as differences in home culture and life experiences. Building learning and literacy on the backgounds of 20 or 30 elementary students or 170 secondary students is a daunting task, regardless of one's dedication to culturally and individually differentiated instruction. Even when groups of students share linguistic and cultural heritage, asking teachers to become the students of their students is asking them to challenge the status quo of a historically assimilationist institution and traditional teaching practice that is teacher-centered and based on a transmission, or broadcast, model of teaching/learning (in addition to asking them to work longer hours with inadequate pay). Teachers need to be supported by teacher education and professional development that encourages them to integrate community funds of knowledge into their curricula and provides them with tools and models of how to do so. Teachers and teacher educators, as well as educational policymakers, need to be supported by rigorous research that expands our knowledge base about the efficacy of building on students' backgrounds and the essential elements of students' diverse resources for optimal instruction and learning. To assume that our increasingly rich, multicultural diversity is a resource for the development of literacy or literacies is to assume responsibility for helping teachers to access the core elements of the backgrounds of large groups of students, and to coordinate instructional practice with those backgrounds in an institutional context designed for batch processing, and a political context that favors both assimilation and gatekeeping. Additionally, as we engage in efforts to enculturate the young in the written discourses of the codes of power, we must acknowledge that control of the practice and tools of literacy and English as a second language change the relations of families and communities to schools and to each other, even as we view them as resources. Providing broad opportunities for access and agency in our increasingly diverse society involves change, not only for the society at large but also for our institutions and the diverse constituencies that comprise our society. Ensuring that this change is productive for learners and teachers, and socially just is our ongoing challenge, a challenge that must be met with rigorous research that contributes to resource-oriented instructional and curricular design and teacher education.

## NOTES

1. Wolf (2007) provides a fascinating and accessible history of literacy as a frame for discussions of brain research on language and literacy, dyslexia, and digital media. For more on the history of literacy, see Cole (2005) and Serpell and Hatano (1997).
2. Diamond (2005) makes an interesting case for the separate development of Sumerian and Mayan writing systems, the probable separate emergence of the Chinese system, and the possible but, in his view, unlikely separate emergence of the Egyptian system.
3. Collin and Apple (2007) argue that public schooling is a form of literacy sponsorship that "(re)produces technical/administrative knowledge and differently-oriented workers 'necessary' for the US industrial economy of the 20th century" (p. 439).
4. McVee, Dunsmore, and Gavelek (2005) have written about this shift in theorizing literacy as researchers moving "toward exploring the tools and signs related to literacy practices situated within particular contexts and activities" (p. 540). See also Florio-Ruane and McVee (2000).
5. We would add other categories, in particular, gender and sexual orientation.

## REFERENCES

Banks, J. A., Au, K. H., Ball, A. F., Bell, P., Gordon, E. W., Gutierrez, K. D., et al. (2007). *Learning in and out of school: Life-long, life-wide, life-deep.* Seattle: LIFE Center, University of Washington.

Banks, J. A., Banks, C. A. M., Cortés, C. E., Hahn, C. I., Merryfield, M., Moodley, K., et al. (2005). *Democracy and diversity: principles and concepts for educating citizens in a global age.* Seattle: Center for Multicultural Education, University of Washington.

Bialystok, E. (2007). Cognitive effects of bilingualism: How linguistic experience leads to cognitive change [Special issue: Cutting edge research in bilingualism]. *International Journal of Bilingual Education and Bilingualism, 10*(3), 210–223.

Bourdieu, P. (1984). *Distinction: A social critique of the judgment of taste.* Cambridge, MA: Harvard University Press.

Bourdieu, P. (1991). *Language and symbolic power.* Cambridge, MA: Harvard University Press. (Original work published 1982)

Bransford, J. D., Brown, A. L., & Cocking, R. R. (Eds.). (2000). *How people learn: Brain, mind, experience and school.* Washington, DC: National Academy Press.

Bryant, P. (1995). Phonological and grammatical skills in learning to read. In B. de Gelder & J. Morais (Eds.), *Speech and reading: A comparative approach* (pp. 249–256). Hove, UK: Erlbaum.

Bryant, P., & Nunes, T. (1998). Learning about the orthography: A cross-linguistic approach. In H. M. Wellman (Ed.), *Global prospects for education: Development, culture, and schooling* (pp. 171–191). Washington, DC: American Psychological Association.

Cole, M. (1998). Can cultural psychology help us think about diversity? *Mind, Culture, and Activity, 5*(4), 291–304.

Cole, M. (2005). Cross-cultural and historical perspectives on the developmental consequences of education. *Human Development, 48*, 195–216.

Cole, M., & Bruner, J. (1971). Cultural differences and inferences about psychological process. *American Psychologist, 26*(10), 867–876.

Cole, M., & the Distributed Literacy Consortium. (2006). *The Fifth Dimension: An after-school program built on diversity.* New York: Russell Sage Foundation.

Collin, R., & Apple, M. W. (2007). Schooling, literacies, and biopolitics in the global age. *Discourse: Studies in the Cultural Politics of Education, 28*(4), 433–454.

Collins, J., & Blot, R. K. (2003). *Literacy and literacies: Texts, power, and identity.* Cambridge, UK: Cambridge University Press.

Cummins, J. (2007). Pedagogies for the poor: Realigning reading instruction for low-income students with scientifically based reading research. *Educational Researcher, 36*(9), 564–572.

Delpit, L. (1995). *Other people's children: Cultural conflict in the classroom.* New York: New Press.

Diamond, J. M. (2005). *Guns, germs, and steel: The fates of human societies.* New York: Norton.

Donaldson, M. C. (1978). *Children's minds.* London: Croom Helm.

Florio-Ruane, S., & McVee, M. (2000). Ethnographic approaches to literacy research. In M. L. Kamil, P. B. Mosenthal, P. D. Pearson, & R. Barr (Eds.), *Handbook of reading research* (Vol. 3, pp. 153–152). Mahwah, NJ: Erlbaum.

Freire, P. (2001). The adult literacy process as cultural action for freedom. In S. W. Beck & L. N. Olah (Eds.), *Perspectives on language and literacy: Beyond the here and now* (pp. 335–352). Cambridge MA: Harvard Educational Review.

Gallego, M. A., Cole, M., & the Laboratory of Comparative Human Cognition. (2001). Classroom cultures and cultures in the classroom. In V. Richardson (Ed.), *Handbook of research on teaching* (4th ed., pp. 951–997). Washington, DC: American Educational Research Association.

Gee, J. P. (1988). The legacies of literacy: From Plato to Freire through Harvey Graff. *Harvard Educational Review, 58*(2), 195–212.

Gee, J. P. (1996). *Sociolinguistics and literacies: Ideology in discourses.* London: Taylor & Francis.

Gee, J. P. (2003). *What video games have to teach us about learning and literacy.* New York: Palgrave/Macmillan.

González, N., Moll, L. C., & Amanti, C. (Eds.). (2005). *Funds of knowledge: Theorizing practices in households, communities, and classrooms.* Mahwah, NJ: Erlbaum.

Goody, J. (1977). *The domestication of the savage mind.* Cambridge, UK: Cambridge University Press.

Goody, J., & Watt, I. P. (1963) The consequences of literacy. *Comparative Studies in History and Society, 5,* 304–345.

Gutiérrez, K. D., & Rogoff, B. (2003). Cultural ways of learning: Individual traits or repertoires of practice. *Educational Researcher, 32*(5), 19–25.

Harman, D. (1970). Illiteracy: An overview. *Harvard Educational Review, 40,* 226–243.

Heath, S. B. (1983). *Ways with words: Language, life, and work in communities and classrooms.* Cambridge, UK: Cambridge University Press.

Labov, W. (1970). The logic of non-standard English. In F. Williams (Ed.), *Language and poverty* (pp. 153–189). Chicago: Markham Press.

Ladson-Billings, G. (1995). But that's just good teaching!: The case for culturally relevant pedagogy. *Theory Into Practice, 34*(3), 159–165.

Lee, C. D. (1991). Big picture-talkers/words walking without masters: The instructional implications of ethnic voices for an expanded literacy. *Journal of Negro Education, 60*(3), 291–304.

Lee, C. D. (1992). Literacy, cultural diversity, and instruction. *Education and Urban Society, 24*(2), 279–291.

Lee, C. D. (1995). Signifying as a scaffold for literary interpretation. *Journal of Black Psychology, 21*(4), 357–381.

Lee, C. D. (2001). Is October Brown Chinese?: A cultural modeling activity system for underachieving students. *American Educational Research Journal, 38*(1), 97–141.

Lee, C. D., Spencer, M. B., & Harpalani, V. (2003). "Every shut eye ain't sleep": Studying how people live culturally. *Educational Researcher, 32*(5), 6–13.

Luria, A. R. (1976). *Culture and cognitive development.* Cambridge, MA: Harvard University Press.

McVee, M. B., Dunsmore, K., & Gavelek, J. R. (2005). Schema theory revisited. *Review of Educational Research, 75*(4), 531–566.

Mehan, H., Hubbard, L., & Villanueva, I. (1994). Forming academic identities: Accommodation without assimilation among involuntary minorities. *Anthropology and Education Quarterly, 25*(2), 91–117.

Mercado, C. I. (2001). The learner: "Race," "ethnicity," and linguistic difference. In V. Richardson (Ed.), *Handbook of research on teaching* (4th ed., pp. 668–694). Washington, DC: American Educational Research Association.

Moll, L. C., & Greenberg, J. B. (1990). Creating zones of possibilities: Combining social contexts for instruction. In L. C. Moll (Ed.), *Vygotsky and education* (pp. 319–348). New York: Cambridge University Press.

Moll, L. C., Sáez, R., & Dworin, J. (2001). Exploring biliteracy: Two student case examples of writing as a social practice. *Elementary School Journal, 101*(4), 435–449.

Morais, J., & Kolinsky, R. (2001). The literate mind and the universal human mind. In E. Dupoux (Ed.), *Language, brain, and cognitive development: Essays in honor of Jacques Mehler* (pp. 463–480). Cambridge, MA: MIT Press.

New London Group. (1996). A pedagogy of multiliteracies: Designing social futures. *Harvard Educational Review, 66*(1), 60–92.

Nieto, S. (1999). *The light in their eyes: Creating multicultural learning communities.* New York: Teachers College Press.

Nieto, S. (2002). *Language, culture, and teaching: Critical perspectives for a new century.* Mahwah, NJ: Erlbaum.

Nurcombe, B., Lacey, P., & Walker, S. (1999). *Children of the dispossessed: Far-West preschoolers 30 years on* (2nd ed.). Stamford, CT: Ablex.

Olson, D. R. (2001). From utterance to text: The bias of language in speech and writing. In S. W. Beck & L. N. Olah (Eds.), *Perspectives on language and literacy: Beyond the here and now* (pp. 137–160). Cambridge, MA: Harvard Educational Review.

Rogoff, B. (2003). *The cultural nature of human development.* Oxford, UK: Cambridge University Press.

Ruíz, R. (1984). Orientations in language planning. *Journal of the National Association for Bilingual Education, 8*(2), 15–34.

Schmandt-Besserat, D. (1996). *How writing came about.* Austin: University of Texas Press.

Scribner, S. (1984). Literacy in three metaphors. *American Journal of Education, 93*(1), 6–21.

Scribner, S., & Cole, M. (1978). Literacy without schooling: Testing for intellectual effects. *Harvard Educational Review, 48*(4), 448–461.

Scribner, S., & Cole, M. (1981). *The psychology of literacy.* Cambridge, MA: Harvard University Press.

Serpell, R., & Hatano, G. (1997). Education, schooling, and literacy. In J. W. Berry, P. R. Dasen, & T. S. Sarawathi (Eds.), *Handbook of cross-cultural psychology: Vol. 2. Basic processes and human development* (pp. 339–376). Boston: Allyn & Bacon.

Sharp, D. W., Cole, M., & Lave, C. A. (1979). Education and cognitive development: The evidence from experimental research. *Monographs of the Society for Research in Child Development, 44*(1–2), 1–112.

Snow, C. E. (2001). Literacy and language: Relationships during the preschool years. In S. W. Beck & L. N. Olah (Eds.), *Perspectives on language and literacy: Beyond the here and now* (pp. 161–186). Cambridge, MA: Harvard Educational Review.

Téllez, K., & Waxman, H. C. (2006). A meta-synthesis of qualitative research on effective teaching practices for English language learners. In J. M. Norris & L. Ortega (Eds.), *Synthesizing research on language learning and teaching* (pp. 245–277). Philadelphia: Benjamins.

Tharp, R. G., & Gallimore, R. (1988). *Rousing minds to life.* New York: Cambridge University Press.

Tyner, K. (1998). *Literacy in a digital world: Teaching and learning in a world of information.* Mahwah, NJ: Erlbaum.

United Nations Educational, Scientific, and Cultural Organization (UNESCO). (1951). *Learn and live: A way out of ignorance of 1,200,000,000 people.* Paris: Author.

Valencia, R. R. (Ed.). (1997). *The evolution of deficit thinking: Educational thought and practice.* London: Falmer Press.

Valencia, R. R. (2000). Inequalities and the schooling of minority students in Texas: Historical and contemporary conditions. *Hispanic Journal of Behavioral Sciences, 22*(4), 445–459.

Valencia, R. R., & Black, M. S. (2002). "Mexican Americans don't value education!"—On the basis of the myth, mythmaking, and debunking. *Journal of Latinos and Education, 1*(2), 81–103.

Wolf, M. (2007). *Proust and the squid: The story and science of the reading brain.* New York: HarperCollins.

# CHAPTER 2

# Policy Related to Issues of Diversity and Literacy

## Implications for English Learners

EUGENE E. GARCÍA *and* ANN-MARIE WIESE

Educating English learners is a major concern of school systems throughout the United States given that between 1979 and 2006 the population of students who speak a language other than English at home has grown from 3.8 million to 10.8 million (from 9 to 20%) of children ages 5–17 (U.S. Department of Education, National Center for Education Statistics [NCES], 2008). Indeed, although there was an 18% increase in the number of school-age children between 1994 and 2004, the number of such children who spoke a language other than English at home increased by 162% (U.S. Department of Education, National Center for Education Statistics, 2006). The unfortunate reality is that education is not a successful experience for many of these students (August & Shanahan, 2006). Confronted with this reality, policymakers and the public have urged changes in teaching methods, adoption of new curricula, allocation of more funding, and holding educational institutions accountable. Such actions at the federal level, coupled with state and local school district levels, have and will continue to affect these students directly. Furthermore, these efforts have generally focused specifically on language when addressing English learners. Although the link between language and literacy may not seem evident, the National Literacy Panel on Language-Minority Children and Youth concluded that many factors influence second-language literacy development, including, but not limited to, second-language and first-language oral proficiency (August & Shanahan, 2006). As such, policies that focus on language have consequences for literacy as well.

In this chapter, we identify and describe educational policy as it relates to English learners, children whose primary language is a language other than English. Because the vast majority of these children, up to 75%, spoke Spanish as their native language (August, 2006; U.S. Department of Education, National Center for Education Statistics, 2006, 2008), our discussion focuses on the population of Latino, Spanish-speaking students in its treatment of policy and practice, but not to the exclusion of some 25% of the non-English-speaking students who do not speak Spanish.[1] In this analysis we concentrate on early schooling, which has been the focus of both policy and practice interventions for this population. In this chapter we discuss the following:

- *Demographic trends of the student population*, in particular, the significant increase in the number of the following: children who live in homes where a language other than English is spoken, Latino children, English learners, and so forth, both for the school-age population and birth-to-age-5 population.
- *The historical role of federal courts in establishing legal rights of English learners*, and recent trends that are undermining this legal right. This includes a discussion of landmark cases such as *Lau v. Nichols* (1974) and *Castañeda v. Pickard* (1981), as well as more recent cases in areas outside of education that have implications for educational policy as it relates to English learners.
- *The role of federal legislation in providing equal educational opportunity to English learners*, through a chronicle of the Bilingual Education Act of 1968 as part of the Elementary and Secondary Education Act, and its current counterpart, Title III of the No Child Left Behind Act of 2001 (NCLB). This includes a discussion of the accountability provisions of NCLB and how they relate to the academic achievement of English learners. In addition, the chapter addresses Reading First, and Early Reading First of NCLB, which focus specifically on literacy and the resulting implications for English learners.
- *Implications for future policy*. Since NCLB is currently up for reauthorization, this section summarizes key recommendations for revisions to the legislation relative to English learners.
- *Implications for classroom practice*. This section presents, in a question-and-answer format, responsibilities of educational agencies that serve English learners, as established by legislation and litigation.

Overall, this chapter identifies and describes federal education policy as it relates to English learners, and at the same time explores whether such policy has proven to disadvantage or to enhance the education of said population. The active track record of policy action has not left a clear path; it is still being negotiated (Wiese & García, 2006). Our chapter addresses this complex collage of policy and practice, with the goal of informing both policy and those who provide direct instructional services to these students.

## DEMOGRAPHIC TRENDS: A FOCUS ON ENGLISH LEARNERS

In considering demographic trends for English learners, it is important to acknowledge how the population varies along dimensions such as nationality, linguistic proficiency in the first language, linguistic proficiency in the second language, and socioeconomic status. This diversity is reflected within the Latino population, which includes both long-term U.S. native-born populations and immigrants from various countries of origin, each of which is associated with a unique combination of histories, cultural practices, perspectives, and traditions.

### Nation of Origin

The growth in the Latino[2] population has been driven to a high degree by immigration. In 2003, almost 25% of the total U.S. birth cohort (some 4 million newborns) were attributed to Latino mothers. Of this birth cohort, 68% were born into families in which one parent was born outside the United States. A large majority of young Latino children are of Mexican origin (68%), but substantial proportions have Puerto Rican (9%), Central American (7%), South American (6%), Cuban, or Dominican (3% each) origins. Especially important, the vast majority of young Latino children are themselves U.S. citizens (Capps, Fix, Ost, Reardon-Anderson, & Passel, 2004; Hernandez, 2006).

### Language Proficiency and Home Language Environment

English learners arrive at school with varied levels of proficiency in their native language and English. In addition, some may speak several languages prior to the introduction of English in United States schools (García, 2005; Hernandez, 2006). In general, English learner populations in the United States tend to acquire their first language in the home and to learn English formally as they enter public schooling. Differences in first-language development are most commonly attributable to differing linguistic practices in the home. In an analysis of data from the Early Childhood Longitudinal Study, Birth Cohort (ECLS-B), López and Barrueco (2006) describe the home language environments of Hispanic 9-month-olds in the country, using a national sample of children born between December 2001 and January 2002.

Latino infants comprised 26% of the total infant population, and approximately 75% of the infants resided in homes where Spanish was spoken to some extent. Furthermore, whereas roughly 33% of all young Latino children (ages 5–8) are bilingual (fluent in both English and Spanish), Latinos are more likely than other racial/ethnic groups to be English learners, and to have one or both parents also be English learners; that is, over 50% of all Latino children ages 0–8 have either a mother or father whose primary language is Spanish. Moreover, Latino children, including those from native and immigrant families, are more likely than any other racial/ethnic group to live in "linguistically isolated homes," households in which no one over the age of 13 speaks English exclusively or very well (Hernandez, 2006). On the other hand, only 5% of young Latino children in U.S.-born families live with two LEP parents, and 14% live with at least one such parent (Hernandez, 2005). Still, these children might be exposed to Spanish through relationships with extended family members (e.g., grandparents), who may be significantly involved in their care and upbringing (Zentella, 2005).

## Language Proficiency and Poverty

Analyses by Hernandez (2006) also offer some information regarding the relationship between language and poverty. Compared to children ages 0–8 in the general population, Latinos are more likely to live below the official poverty level: 17.4% of children in the general population live in official poverty compared to 27.7% of Latinos. The proportion of Latinos in poverty is intensified when we look at children who live in homes in which little or no English is spoken. This trend may be illustrated by examining differences in poverty level by Latino fathers' English fluency. In Latino homes where the father is fluent in English, 16.3% of children live below the official poverty line, compared to 30.2% in homes where the father is not fluent in English. Together, issues of poverty and lack of English-language proficiency are critical factors in understanding the educational challenges facing this population of students.

## THE FEDERAL COURTS AND ENGLISH LEARNERS: ESTABLISHING LEGAL RIGHTS

*Lau v. Nichols*, the 1974 U.S. Supreme Court decision, stands as the landmark case for establishing language-minority status as a claim for discrimination. The decision also called for providing support to LEP students to access the curriculum:

> There is no equality of treatment merely by providing students with English instruction. Students without the ability to understand English are effectively foreclosed from any meaningful discourse. Basic English skills are at the very core of what these public schools teach. Imposition of a requirement that, before a child can effectively participate in the education program he must already have acquired those basic skills is to make a mockery of public education. We know that those who do not understand English are certain to find their classroom experiences wholly incomprehensible and in no way meaningful. (p. 18)

The class action lawsuit was filed against the San Francisco Unified School District on March 25, 1970, and involved 12 U.S.-born and foreign-born Chinese students. Prior to the suit, the district initiated a pullout program in 1966, at the request of parents of LEP students. In a 1967 school census, the district identified 2,456 LEP Chinese students. By 1970, the district had identified 2,856 such students, of which more than half (1,790) received no special instruction. Also, the vast majority of these students (over 2,600) were taught by teachers unable to speak in Chinese. The district still argued that it had taken initial steps to serve the LEP students. In the end, the Court ruled in favor of the students and parents, and the majority opinion overruled an appeals court that had ruled in favor of the district.

The majority opinion relied on statutory, or legislative, grounds and avoided any reference to constitutional determination. A student's right to special educational services flowed from the district's obligations under the Title VI of the 1964 Civil Rights Act, which prohibits discrimination on the grounds of race, color, or national origin in programs or activities receiving federal financial assistance. A May 25, 1970, memorandum issued by the Department of Health, Education, and Welfare also justified the requirement of special educational services. After *Lau*, the domain of language-minority education lawsuits belonged almost exclusively to Latino litigants. Although some cases were litigated to ensure compliance with the *Lau* requirements of "affirmative steps," most subsequent cases involved issues not addressed by *Lau*: Who are these students? What form of additional educational services must be provided?

In *Aspira of New York, Inc. v. Board of Education* (1975), a community action group brought a suit on behalf of all Latino children in the New York City School District. The plaintiff argued that these students could not successfully participate in an English schooling context because of their lack of English proficiency, but that they could successfully participate in a Spanish-language curriculum (Roos, 1984). The U.S. district court hearing this case adopted a language dominance procedure to identify those students eligible for non-English, Spanish-language instructional programs.

The procedure called for parallel examinations to obtain language proficiency estimates on Spanish and English standardized achievement tests. All students scoring below the 20th percentile on an English-language test were given the same (or a parallel) achievement test in Spanish. Students who scored higher on the Spanish achievement test and Spanish-language proficiency test were to be placed in a Spanish-language program. These procedures assumed adequate reliability and validity for the language and achievement tests administered. Such an assumption was, and still is, highly questionable. However, the court argued that it acted in "reasonable manner," admitting that in the absence of better assessment procedures it was forced to follow previous (*Lau*) precedents. A subsequent case, *Otero v. Mesa County School District No. 51* (1975), concluded that a clear relationship between low academic achievement and a lack of English proficiency must be clearly demonstrated before a court could mandate special instructional services.

In the key Fifth Circuit decision of *Castaneda v. Pickard* (1981), the court interpreted Section 1703(f) of the Equal Education Opportunity Act of 1974 (EEOA) as substantiating the holding of *Lau* that schools cannot ignore the special language needs of students. The 1974 EEOA extended Title VI of the Civil Rights Act to all educational institutions, not just those receiving federal funding. Section 1703(f) of the EEOA provides the following:

> No state shall deny equal educational opportunities to an individual on account of his or her race, color, sex, or national origin by—the failure of an educational agency to take appropriate action to overcome language barriers that impede equal participation by its students in its instructional programs.

Furthermore, the court then contemplated whether the EEOA statutory requirement that districts take "appropriate action to overcome language barriers" should be further delineated. The plaintiffs urged on the court a construction of "appropriate action" that would necessitate bilingual programs that incorporated bilingual students' primary language. The court concluded, however, that Section 1703(f) did not embody a congressional mandate that any particular form of remedy be uniformly adopted.

However, the court did conclude that Congress required districts to adopt an appropriate program, and that by creating a cause of action in federal court to enforce Section 1703(f), it left to federal judges the task of determining whether a given program was appropriate. Although the court noted that Congress had not provided guidance in that statute or in its brief legislative history on what it intended by selecting "appropriateness" as the operative standard, it continued with reluctance and hesitancy and described a mode of analysis for a Section 1703(f) case. It became legally possible to substantiate a violation of Section 1703(f), following from *Lau*, on three grounds: (1) The program providing special language services to eligible English learners is not based on sound educational theory; (2) the program is not being implemented in an effective manner; or (3) the program, after a period of "reasonable implementation," does not produce results substantiating that language barriers are being overcome to eliminate achievement gaps between bilingual and English-only students. It is obvious that these criteria allow a local school district to continue to implement a program with some educational theoretical support for a "reasonable" time, making judgments upon its "positive" or "negative" effects.

Furthermore, in the *Castaneda* decision, the court again spoke, reluctantly but firmly, to the issue of program implementation. In particular, the court indicated that the district must provide adequate resources, including trained instructional personnel, materials, and other relevant support that would ensure effective program implementation. Implicit in these standards is the requirement that districts staff their programs with language-minority education specialists, typically defined by state-approved credentials or professional coursework (similar to devices used to judge professional expertise in other areas of professional education).

## LOOKING FORWARD: THE TENTATIVE LEGACY OF *LAU*

U.S. federal courts have played a significant role in shaping educational policy for bilingual students. Although hesitant at times, the courts have spoken to issues of student identification, program implementation, resource allocation, professional staffing, and program effectiveness. Moreover, they have obligated both local and state educational agencies to language-minority education responsibilities. However, in recent years the courts' role in establishing the rights of English learners has eroded as the power of *Lau v. Nichols* has been undermined. Through the cumulative impact of three cases—*Guardians Association v. Civil Service Commission* (1983), *Alexander v. Choate* (1985), and *Alexander v. Sandoval* (2001)—the court (1) established that the language of Title VI applies to purposeful discrimination, and does not extend to adverse effect; and (2) determined that plaintiffs could only sue for intentional discrimination, which has left enforcement almost entirely in the hands of the executive branch. Although *Lau* is not the only source of federal legal protection for English learners, the most likely alternatives are not a perfect substitute for *Lau* (for a thorough discussion of these alternatives, see Moran, 2004). Still, whereas the core elements of *Lau v. Nichols* are on increasingly shaky grounds, the central finding remains uncontested: an English-only curriculum can be exclusionary, whether or not that was the intent of school officials (Gandara, Moran, & García, 2004).

## FEDERAL LEGISLATION: LANGUAGE, LITERACY, AND ACCOUNTABILITY

### Bilingual Education Act, 1968–1988

From its inception in 1968 through its final reauthorization in 1994, Title VII of the Elementary and Secondary Education Act, the Bilingual Education Act (BEA), has served as the primary U.S. federal legislative effort to provide equal educational opportunity to English learners. The legislation was reauthorized on five occasions (1974, 1978, 1984, 1988, 1994). The BEA was eliminated as part of NCLB (2001), the most recent reauthorization of the Elementary and Secondary Education Act of 1965 (ESEA). Under NCLB provisions, federal funds will continue to support the education of LEP students through Title III: Language Instruction for Limited English Proficient and Immigrant Students. However, Title III differs markedly from the initial enactment of Title VII: The BEA and all subsequent reauthorizations. Overall, although the original intent of the BEA was never one of establishing language policy, the role of language became a prominent marker as the legislation articulated the goals and nature of education for English learners.

Similar to *Lau v. Nichols*, the BEA stemmed from the Civil Rights Act of 1964, as part of the "War on Poverty" legislation. The legislation was primarily a "crisis intervention" (García & González, 1995), a political strategy to funnel poverty funds to the second largest minority group in the Southwest, Mexican Americans (Casanova, 1991). The BEA intended to establish a demonstration program to meet the educational needs of low-income, LEP children. It was primarily a remedial effort, aimed at overcoming students' "language deficiencies," and these "compensatory efforts were considered to be a sound educational response to the call for equality of educational opportunity" (Navarro, 1990, p. 291). No particular program of instruction was recommended; rather, financial assistance was provided to local educational agencies (LEAs) "to develop and carry out new and imaginative ... programs" (BEA, 1968, § 702). Among the approved activities were the following programs: bilingual education, history and culture, early childhood education, and adult education for parents.

Although the aim of bilingual education (BEA) was never one of establishing language policy, the role of language became a prominent marker as the legislation articulated the goals and nature of education for English learners in various reauthorizations from 1974 through 1988. In its early years, all programs funded under the BEA featured native-language instruction, but reauthorization in subsequent years marked a shift toward English acquisition as a primary goal (Birman & Ginsburg, 1983). Bilingualism was viewed as a laudable goal, but not the responsibility of schools. Rather, families, churches, and other institutions outside the school could foster native-language maintenance (Casanova, 1991; Crawford, 1999).

## ESEA Reauthorizations of 1994 and 2001: From Bilingual Education to English Only

The 1994 reauthorization of the BEA marked a return to developing English-language proficiency in combination with native-language maintenance to the extent possible. However, the 2001 reauthorization of the ESEA, or NCLB, as it is commonly known, focuses on the goal of "English proficiency." Illustrative of this shift is the fact that the word *bilingual* has been completely eliminated from the law and from any government office affiliated with the law. The federal office that oversees the provisions of the law is now referred to as the Office of English Language Acquisition, Language Enhancement, and Academic Achievement for Limited English Proficient Students (OELA), instead of the Office of Bilingual Education and Minority Languages Affairs (OBEMLA). What was formerly known as the National Clearinghouse for Bilingual Education (NCBE) is now known as the National Clearinghouse for English Language Acquisition and Language Instruction Educational Programs (NCELA). Table 2.1 below provides a summary of key differences in how the 1994 and the 2001 reauthorizations of the ESEA address the education of LEP students.

As described in the summary of the legislation, significant changes are evident in the following areas: purpose, program, allocation of funds, and accountability and assessment. As a result of Title III of NCLB, federal funds are no longer administered via competitive grants designed to ensure equity and promote quality programs for English learners—programs that served as models to the larger

**TABLE 2.1. Significant Differences in the 1994 and 2001 Reauthorizations of the ESEA**

| Issue | 1994 Title VII: Bilingual Education Act | 2001 Title III: Language instruction, limited-English-proficient students, and immigrant students |
|---|---|---|
| Eligible populations | Limited-English-proficient students | Limited-English-proficient students |
| | Recent immigrants who "have not been attending one or more schools in any one or more States for more than three full years." [§ 7501(7)] | Immigrant children and youth: 3–21 years of age, not born in any state, "have not been attending one or more schools in any one or more states for more than 3 full academic years." [§ 3301(6)] |
| | Native Americans, Native Alaskans, Native Hawaiians, Native American Pacific Islanders | Native Americans, Native Alaskans, Native Hawaiians, Native American Pacific Islanders |
| Purpose | "(A) To help such children and youth develop proficiency in English, and to the extent possible, their native language; and (B) meet the same challenging State content standards and challenging State student performance standards expected of all children." [§ 7111(2)] | "To help ensure that children who are limited English proficient, including immigrant children and youth, attain English proficiency, develop high levels of academic attainment in English, and meet the same challenging State academic content and student academic achievement standards as all children are expected to meet." [§ 3102(1)] |
| | "The use of a child or youth's native language and culture in classroom instruction can—(A) promote self-esteem and contribute to academic achievement and learning English by limited English proficient children and youth." [§ 7102(14)] | Programs for Native Americans: "develop English proficiency and, to the extent possible, proficiency in their native language." [§ 3211(2)] |
| | The "unique status of Native American languages" and language enhancement. | |
| Programs | Competitive grants to local education agencies (schools, districts). State education agencies approve the grant application before submission but play no official role in the grant's implementation. | "To streamline language instruction educational programs into a program carried out through formula grants to State educational agencies and local educational agencies." [§ 3102(7)] |
| | "Quality bilingual education programs enable children and youth to learn English and meet high academic standards including proficiency in more than one language." [§ 7102(9)] | "To implement language instruction educational programs, based on scientifically-based research on teaching limited English proficient children." [§ 3102.(9)] |
| | Priority is given to programs which "provide for development of bilingual proficiency both in English and another language for all participating students." [§ 7116 (i)(1)] | |

*(cont.)*

**TABLE 2.1.** *(cont.)*

| Issue | 1994 Title VII: Bilingual Education Act | 2001 Title III: Language instruction, limited-English-proficient students, and immigrant students |
|-------|------------------------------------------|---------------------------------------------------------------------------------------------------|
| Allocation of funds | Cap of 25% of funds for skills achievement indicators programs, can be lifted if an applicant has demonstrated that developing and implementing a bilingual education program is not feasible. | 95% of funds must be used for grants at the local level to teach LEP children; each state must spend this percentage to award formula subgrants to districts. |
| Accountability and assessment | Local education agency (LEA) is the locus of control and is granted great flexibility on how to best serve students. LEA sets own goals and ways of assessing them. | To hold various educational agencies accountable for "increases in English proficiency and core academic content knowledge … by requiring—(A) demonstrated improvements in the English proficiency of limited English proficient students each fiscal year; and (B) adequate yearly progress." [§ 3102(8)] |

nation. Instead, resources are allocated primarily through a state formula program for language instruction educational programs (LIEPs) that are based on scientifically based research (U.S. Department of Education, 2002). LIEPs are defined as "an instruction course in which LEP students are placed for the purpose of developing and attaining English proficiency, while meeting challenging State and academic content and student academic achievement standards. A LIEP may make use of both English and a child's native language to enable the child to develop and attain English proficiency" (U.S. Department of Education, 2002, p. 20).

## No Child Left Behind Act

### Reading First and Early Reading First

NCLB added two new reading programs to the ESEA in an attempt to understand and to simplify the complexities of literacy teaching and learning (Antunez, 2002). According to the U.S. Department of Education, both Reading First and its preschool-level companion Early Reading First focus on putting proven methods of early reading instruction in classrooms. Reported preliminary evidence suggests that Reading First is being implemented in schools and classrooms as intended by the legislation (Center on Education Policy, 2006; U.S. Department of Education, 2006). Table 2.2 provides a comparison of key components of Reading First and Early Reading First.

The Reading First program provides formula grants to states, and funds are allocated to states based on the proportion of children ages 5–17 who reside within the state and are from families with incomes below the poverty line. Then state education agencies award subgrants to local education agencies on a competitive

**TABLE 2.2. Reading First and Early Reading First of the NCLB**

| Issue | Reading First (NCLB, Title I, Part B, Subpart 1) | Early Reading First (NCLB, Title I, Part B, Subpart 2) |
|---|---|---|
| Target population | Targets children in kindergarten through third grade, particularly those from low-income families. | Targets preschool-age children, particularly those from low-income families. |
| Purpose | To provide assistance to State educational agencies and local education agencies(1) in establishing reading programs for students in kindergarten through grade three that are based on scientifically reading research, to ensure that every student can read at grade level or above no later than grade 3.<br><br>(2) ... in preparing teachers ... through professional development and other support so the teachers can identify specific reading barriers facing their students and so the teachers have tools to effectively help their students to read.<br><br>(3) ... in selecting or developing effective instructional materials ... , programs, learning systems, and strategies that have been proven to prevent or remediate reading failure within a State. [§ 1201(1)] | (1) To support local efforts to enhance the early language, literacy, and prereading development of preschool age children through strategies and professional development that are based on scientifically based reading research.<br><br>(2) To provide preschool age children with cognitive learning opportunities in high-quality language and literature-rich environments, so that children can attain the fundamental knowledge and skills necessary for optimal reading development in kindergarten and beyond.<br><br>(3) To demonstrate language and literacy based on scientifically-based reading research that supports age-appropriate development of oral language (vocabulary, expressive language, listening comprehension); phonological awareness (rhyming, blending, segmenting), print awareness, and alphabetic knowledge.<br><br>(4) To use screening assessments to effectively identify preschool age children who may be at risk of reading failure.<br><br>(5) To integrate such scientific reading research-based instructional materials and literacy activities with existing programs. [§ 1221(a)(1-5)] |
| Allocation of funds | *Formula grants to states*, submitting an approved application, based on proportion of children ages 5–17 who reside within the state and who are from families with incomes below the poverty line. [§ 1202(b)(3)(A)]<br><br>*Subgrants to local education agencies on a competitive basis.* States give priority to local education agencies in which at least 15% of the children, or 6,500 children served, are from families with incomes below poverty line. [§ 1202(c)(2)(B)] | Grants awarded on a competitive basis to local education agencies and public or private organizations that serve children from low-income families. [§ 1221(b)(1)] |

*(cont.)*

**TABLE 2.2.** *(cont.)*

| Issue | Reading First (NCLB, Title I, Part B, Subpart 1) | Early Reading First (NCLB, Title I, Part B, Subpart 2) |
|---|---|---|
| Required use of local funds | Authorized activities include:<br><br>(1) Selecting and administering screening, diagnostic, and classroom-based instructional reading assessments.<br><br>(2) Selecting and implementing a reading instruction program based on scientifically based research instruction and provides such instruction to children in kindergarten through grade 3.<br><br>(3) Procuring and implementing instructional materials that are based on scientifically based reading research.<br><br>(4) Providing professional development for teachers of kindergarten through grade 3, and special education teachers of kindergarten through grade 12. [§ 1201(c)(7)(A)] | Authorized activities include:(1) Providing preschool-age children with high-quality oral language and literature-rich environments in which to acquire language and prereading skills.<br><br>(2) Providing professional development that is based on scientifically based research knowledge of early language and reading development.<br><br>(3) Identifying and providing activities and instructional materials that are based on scientifically based reading research.<br><br>(4) Acquiring, providing training for, and implementing screening reading assessments or other appropriate measures. |
| English learners | Called out in delineation of children who can be served by local funds in kindergarten through grade 3, and defined as "children who are identified as having limited English proficiency." [§ 1202(c)(7)(A)(ii)(II)(ff)] | Not specifically mentioned in the legislation. |
| Key definition | *Essential components of reading instruction.* Explicit and systematic instruction in phonemic awareness, phonics, vocabulary development, reading fluency (including oral reading skills), and reading comprehension strategies. [§ 1208(3)] | |

basis, for proposals that show promise in raising student achievement and successfully implementing scientifically based reading programs for K–3 children. Funds may support professional development for teachers and use of diagnostic and screening tools, as well as classroom-based instructional reading assessments to monitor progress and to measure how well children are reading (U.S. Department of Education, 2008). Early Reading First is one of only two NCLB initiatives that address preschoolers and focus on preparing them to enter kindergarten with necessary language, cognitive, and early reading skills. Unlike Reading First, awards in Early Reading First are made directly to local education agencies and public or private organizations on a competitive basis.

The Reading First legislation was in fact formulated from the findings of National Reading Panel (National Institute of Child Health and Human Development, 2000). The National Reading Panel (NRP) was approved in 1997 by Congress to initiate a national, comprehensive agenda for and to guide the development of policy related to reading instruction (Ramirez, 2001). After public hearings, discussion, and review of the findings of a National Research Council (NRC) report, *Preventing Reading Difficulties in Young Children* (Snow, Burns, & Griffin, 1998), the panel decided to focus on the following subtopics for study: alphabetics (phonemic awareness and phonics instruction), fluency, and comprehension (vocabulary instruction, text comprehension instruction, and teacher preparation and comprehension strategies instruction). In addition, studies of second-language acquisition, bilingualism, and biliteracy were not included, and as such, the NRP did not specifically address issues relevant to English learners.

Both Reading First and Early Reading First involve scientific research programs, defined in the legislation as "research that applies rigorous, systematic, and objective procedures to obtain valid knowledge relevant to reading development, reading instruction, and reading difficulties" [§ 1208(6)(A)]. The legislation goes on to provide more detailed guidance on the specific characteristics of the research methods. Of particular importance is the careful delineation of components of essential reading instruction for Reading First programs and the areas of early language and reading development detailed for Early Reading First programs. These flow directly from the NRP study areas delineated earlier. Reading First focuses on "explicit and systematic instruction in phonemic awareness; phonics; vocabulary development; reading fluency, including oral reading skills; and reading comprehension strategies" [§ 1208(3)]. Early Reading First focuses on "(A) recognition, leading to automatic recognition, of letters of the alphabet, knowledge of letters, sounds, blending of letter sounds, and increasingly complex vocabulary; (B) understanding that written language is composed of phonemes and letters each representing one or more speech sounds that in combination make up syllables, words, and sentences; (C) spoken language, including vocabulary and oral comprehension abilities; and (D) knowledge of the purposes and conventions of print" [§ 1222(d)(2)].

It is important to note that neither the NRP nor the resulting Reading First or Early Reading First legislation examines or makes recommendations specific to reading instruction for English learners (ELs). This is problematic on two accounts: the number of ELs that are served by Reading First schools, and the fact that literacy development for ELs includes all the challenges implicit for monolingual children and, in addition, is shaped by an array of linguistic, cognitive, and academic variables (Antunez, 2002). More than 33% of teachers who have ELs in their classes reported that no time was set aside to coordinate instruction with staff. In fact, only 10% of teachers reported that they had weekly meetings with staff to coordinate reading instruction for ELs, despite the fact that Reading First schools were significantly more likely to have adopted new materials for ELs (43 vs. 29%; U.S. Department of Education, 2006). Children who participated in Early Reading First programs were more likely than children nationally to be Hispanic (46 vs. 21%). In addition, 4 out of 10 Early Reading First parents (41%) reported that the primary language spoken in the home was something other than English. Although the NRC did not specifically address research related to English learners and literacy, the report did state that learning to speak English should be a priority for children prior to learning to read in English. Also, the NRC recommended the oral development of the home language and, when feasible, literacy development in the home language (National Institute of Child Health and Human Development, 2000). At the same time, a seminal review of the research on language-minority children and literacy found a significant gap in the research relative to ELs. In fact, not much is known about how emergent literacy skills might relate to later literacy skills outcomes (August & Shanahan, 2006). Given the linguistic, cognitive, and academic variables that compound the processes of reading for English learners, literacy instruction for these children, and relevant educational policy, require additional considerations and recommendations for instruction, both within and beyond the areas identified in Reading First (Antunez, 2002).

## Accountability and English Learners

Under NCLB, states are required to ensure that all students meet standards of proficiency in math and reading by 2014. As Congress considers reauthorization of NCLB, analyses of recent achievement data show that students designated as English learners are among those furthest behind. In eighth grade, 51% of EL students are behind Anglo-American students in reading and math. In fourth grade, 47% of EL students are behind in math, and 35% are behind in reading when compared to their white counterparts (Fry, 2007). Not surprisingly, states are subject to a number of accountability provisions that place emphasis on the assessment of ELs. NCLB delineates two sets of responsibilities for states and, hence, for districts and schools in regard to LEP students. Under Title III, they are responsible for ensuring that ELs make progress in learning English, and under Title I, that ELs become proficient in mathematics and reading/language arts. Both Title I and Title III of the NCLB include requirements for LEP students, with the ultimate goal of increasing English-language proficiency and academic achievement. Table 2.3 summarizes the main provisions of each.

The provisions concerning whether an EL must be assessed in English, and whether the results contribute toward a state's adequate yearly progress (AYP) determination, are particularly important. Accountability provisions mandate annual assessment in English for any student who has attended school in the United States (excluding Puerto Rico) for 3 or more consecutive years and attainment of "annual measurable achievement objectives" (U.S. Department of Education, 2002). States are required to hold subgrantees accountable for AYP.[3] Subgrantees must report every second fiscal year and must include a description of the program, as well as the progress made by children in learning English, meeting state standards, and attaining English proficiency. States report every second year to the Department of Education, which reports every second year to Congress. Subgrantees failing to meet AYP must develop an improvement plan with

**TABLE 2.3. Comparison of the Main Provisions of Title I and Title III of NCLB**

|  | Title I | Title III |
|---|---|---|
| Standards | Academic content standards, for all students, including LEP.<br><br>Student academic achievement Standards, for all students, including LEP. | Develop English language proficiency standards aligned with academic content standards. |
| Assessments | Academic content assessments in reading and mathematics, and science in 2007–2008. Must provide for participation of all students. | *See English language proficiency assessments for Title I.* |
| Academic assessment and LEP students | LEP students are to be assessed in a valid and reliable manner. Must be provided with reasonable accommodations when assessed, to the extent practicable, "in the language and form most likely to yield accurate data" on academic knowledge.<br><br>Students who have been in schools three years or more generally must be assessed in English. |  |
| State English language proficiency assessments | Must annually assess English language proficiency of LEP students, measuring oral language, reading, and writing skills in English. |  |
| Annual measurable objectives | Annual objectives that lead to achieving proficiency in reading/language arts and math by 2014. To be deemed as making adequate yearly progress (AYP) each district and school must show that requisite percentage of each designated student group, as well as the student population as a whole, met the state proficiency goal.<br><br>Must also show that at least 95% of students in each designated subgroup participated in these assessments.<br><br>Must demonstrate that they have met targets on other academic indicators—graduation rates in high school, attendance, etc.<br><br>Can also make AYP through "safe harbor" provision, if percentage of students considered not proficient decreased by at least 10% and the group made progress on one of the state's other academic indicators. | Establish objectives for improving LEP students' English language proficiency in speaking, reading, writing, and listening.<br><br>States receiving funds under Title III must establish annual goals for increasing and measuring progress of LEP students in (1) learning English, (2) attaining English proficiency, and (3) meeting adequate yearly progress goals in attaining academic proficiency outlined in Title I. [§ 3122(3)(A)] |
| Actions when annual targets/goals not achieved | Specific action must be taken if students do not meet state progress goals. If they do not make AYP for 2 consecutive years, they are identified for improvement. And parents must be given an opportunity to transfer to another school. If students continue to miss AYP for additional years, this can lead to corrective action or restructuring. | If they receive funding under Title II and do not meet goals for 2 consecutive years, must develop an improvement plan.<br><br>If students do not meet goals for 4 consecutive years, must modify curriculum and method of instruction, or State must determine whether to continue to fund the district and require the district to replace personnel related to the district's inability to meet goals. |

*Note.* Adapted from the U.S. Government Accountability Office (2006).

sanctions if they continue to fail for 4 years (U.S. Department of Education, 2002). In fact, failure to meet AYP can eventually result in loss of Title III funds, restructuring, and corrective action

From a policy perspective, as a result of NCLB, EL students are no longer invisible in the classroom, district, or state: Increased attention has been paid to this population of students (Cohen & Clewell, 2007). Unfortunately, the practice of assessing EL students appropriately within this policy is a significant challenge. Cognitive and linguistic abilities and educational performance of children are generally obtained by measuring specific skills, typically through standardized testing. Several concerns and problematic issues have arisen over the past few decades in relation to test development and assessment practices for culturally and linguistically diverse students. Present efforts to develop appropriate measures and procedures that take into account children's cultural and linguistic backgrounds continue, so as to not penalize those who fall outside the cultural mainstream in the United States. The goal of these tests and procedures in general is to create culturally and linguistically relevant means, and scores that accurately portray the abilities and concurrent performance levels for a diverse body of children.

Though important strides have been made in the development of appropriate tests and testing procedures for culturally and linguistically diverse students (Rhodes, Ochoa, & Ortiz, 2005), much research and development are still needed. Tests are still limited in terms of the overall number and the domains and skills they cover (Espinosa & López, 2006). Moreover, several tests developed for specific language-minority groups are merely translations of original English versions, which tend to be based on European American cultural values. Their view of competence, in many cases, is simply not applicable to other groups with different backgrounds. As such, the content and construct validity of an English measure may not be the same when translated into Spanish. Furthermore, tests with appropriate content and construct validity should contain enough items to assess an identified skill, and be standardized with representative samples of Latino children from diverse national origins, language backgrounds, and socioeconomic conditions.

In practice, most states have met the requirement of including at least 95% of ELs in reading and mathematics assessments. However, the United States Government Accountability Office (GAO) found little evidence that state tests yield valid and reliable results for ELs; although most states use some form of accommodations for ELs, there is a need for more research on which accommodations are most appropriate. Although the U.S. Department of Education has provided some support and training, state officials report that they need more guidance to develop valid and reliable assessments for both English-language proficiency and academic content areas. Without specific guidance, states may spend time developing assessments that do not adequately track student progress. Furthermore, additional research needs to be conducted and disseminated on appropriate accommodations for LEP students (U.S. Government Accountability Office,

2006). To this end, the U.S. Department of Education initiated an LEP partnership to provide states with technical assistance and resources to make content assessments more accessible and appropriate for LEP students. In addition, experts from around the country are being brought together to develop high-quality English and native-language assessments in reading and math.[4]

## IMPLICATIONS FOR FUTURE POLICY

With NCLB up for reauthorization, scholars, policymakers, researchers, and practitioners alike are weighing in on recommendations for revisions to the legislation. In 2007, fifteen leaders in education—representing K–12 and higher education, school and school system governance, civil rights and business—came together to form the Commission on No Child Left Behind, a bipartisan, independent effort dedicated to improving NCLB. Their final report provides a summary of the main NCLB provisions, discussion of the impact of NCLB implementation in various contexts, and recommendations for improving the legislation (Commission on No Child Left Behind, 2007). We briefly summarize here the Commission's specific recommendations regarding EL students.

First, the Commission recommends withholding a portion of a state's administrative funding if that state has not fully developed and implemented English-language proficiency standards, assessments, and annual measurable objectives. Second, the Commission recommends extending the time period, from 2 years to 3 years, that ELs can remain the LEP subgroup for AYP purposes, after attaining proficiency in English. This would help schools measure more accurately the achievement of ELs. Third, the Commission recommends that states use their allocation of funding to create and implement alternate assessments for ELs, to develop plans for establishing universally designed assessment systems, and to develop further and implement high-quality science assessments now required under law. Fourth, the Commission recommends that the U.S. Department of Education develop a common scale across states to determine English-language proficiency. Finally, the Commission recommends ensuring that teachers of ELs receive the training and support they need by requiring states to create an endorsement for teacher certification for those who spend more than 25% of their teaching time with ELs.

## IMPLICATIONS FOR THE CLASSROOM

As the United States advances educational policy for any of its students in an ever-diversified population, it is even more important to understand the dramatic shifts in technology, globalization, and democratization. These circumstances pose a particular challenge to educators and to those among us who look to educational agencies for help in realizing the moral imperatives of equity and social justice. García (2001a, 2001b) indicates that language will continue to be at the forefront of federal and state policy activity. As such, we have attempted to deepen an understanding of the education of ELs through the lens of educational policy. Through both litigation and legislation, several important conclusions regarding the responsibilities of educational agencies have been established. Using a question-and-answer format, Table 2.4 sets out some of these responsibilities and a practical guide for understanding the legal status of EL students, and the legal liability of the educational agencies that serve them (adapted from Roos [1984] and García [2001b]).

## CONCLUSION

Overall, this chapter has described federal education policy as it relates to ELs and, at the same time, has explored whether such policy has proven to disadvantage or enhance the education of said population. For now, policy is almost characterized by a "blind spot" when it comes to the new demographic reality, particularly the growth of ELs. Consequently, it is not surprising that policy has not delineated a clear path for practitioners (Wiese & García, 2006). These circumstances pose a particular challenge to educators and to those among us who look to educational agencies for help in realizing the moral imperatives of equity and social justice. García (2001a, 2001b) indicates that language, which inevitably has implications for literacy development, will continue to be at the forefront of federal and state policy activity.

To this end, the search for general principles of learning that work for all students must be redirected. This redirection considers a search for and documentation of particular implementations of "general" and "nongeneral" principles of teaching and learning that serve a diverse set of environments, in and out of school. This mission requires an understanding of how individuals with diverse sets of experiences, packaged individually into cultures, "make meaning," communicate that meaning, and extend that meaning, particularly in social contexts we call "schools." Such a mission requires in-depth treatment of the processes associated with producing diversity and issues of socialization in and out of schools, coupled with a clear examination of how such understanding is actually transformed into pedagogy and curriculum across the content areas, which can result in high academic performance for all students. Policy must align itself with this mission. If we can attend to policy that "counts," then we might predict that as more ELs enter the "right" kind of schools, barriers to their academic, social, and economic success and mobility will fall. In that policy arena, language distinctions will blend with other features of our society to create a more "equalitarian" society (García, 2001b), a society in which the negative effects of racial, ethnic, linguistic, and class differences are eliminated.

## TABLE 2.4.  Legal Rights of English Learners and Legal Liabilities of Educational Agencies

*Question*: Is there a legally acceptable procedure for identifying language minority students in need of special instructional treatment?

*Answer*: Yes. The legal obligation is to identify all students who have problems speaking, understanding, reading, or writing English because of a home language background other than English. To do this, a two-phase approach is common and acceptable. First, the parents are asked, through a home language survey or on a registration form, whether a language other than English is spoken in the child's home. If the answer is affirmative, the second phase is triggered, in which students identified through the home language survey are given an oral language proficiency test and an assessment of their reading and writing skills.

*Question*: Once the students are identified, are there any minimal standards for the educational program provided to them?

*Answer*: Yes. First, a number of courts have recognized that special training is necessary to equip a teacher to provide meaningful assistance to limited-English-proficient students. The teacher (and it is clear that it must be a teacher, not an aide) must have training in second-language-acquisition techniques to teach English as a second language.
Second, the time spent on assisting these students must be sufficient to ensure that they acquire English skills quickly enough so that their disadvantages in the English language classroom do not harden into a permanent educational disadvantage.

*Question*: Must students be provided with instruction in their native language as well as English?

*Answer*: At the present time, the federal obligation has not been construed to compel such a program. However, the federal mandate is not fully satisfied by an ESL program. The mandate requires English language help plus programs to ensure that students not be substantively handicapped by any delay in learning English. To do this may require either (1) a bilingual program that keeps the students up in their coursework while learning English or (2) a specially designed compensatory program to address the educational loss suffered by any delay in providing understandable substantive instruction. Finally, it is legally necessary to provide the material resources necessary for the instructional components. The program must be reasonably designed to succeed. Without adequate resources, this requirement cannot be met.

*Question*: What minimal standards must be met if a bilingual program is to be offered?

*Answer*: The heart of a basic bilingual program is a teacher who can speak the language of the students, as well as address students' limited English proficiency. Thus, a district offering a bilingual program must take affirmative steps to find teachers with these characteristics. This might include allocating teachers with language skills to bilingual classrooms, and affirmative recruitment of bilingual teachers. Additionally, it requires the district to establish a formal system to assess teachers to ensure that they have the prerequisite skills. Finally, where there are insufficient teachers, there must be a system to ensure that teachers with most (but not all) of the skills are in bilingual classrooms, that those teachers are on a track to obtain the necessary skills, and that bilingual aides are hired whenever the teacher lacks the necessary language skills.

*Question*: Must there be standards for removal of a student from a program? What might these be?

*Answer*: There must be definite standards. These generally mirror the standards for determining whether a student is in need of special language services in the first place. Thus, objective evidence that the student can compete with English-speaking peers without a lingering language disability is necessary.

*(cont.)*

**TABLE 2.4.** (*cont.*)

Several common practices are unlawful. First, the establishment of an arbitrary cap on the amount of time a student can remain in a program fails to meet the requirement that all language minority students be assisted. Second, it is common to have programs terminate at a certain grade level, for example, sixth grade. While programs may change to accommodate different realities, it is unlawful to deny a student access to a program merely because of grade level.

*Question*: Must a district develop a design to monitor the success of its program?

*Answer*: Yes. The district is obligated to monitor the program and to make reasonable adjustments when the evidence suggests that the program is not successful.

Monitoring is necessarily a two-part process. First, it is necessary to monitor the progress of students in the program to ensure (1) that they are making reasonable progress toward learning and (2) that the program is providing the students with substantive instruction comparable to that given to English-proficient pupils. Second, any assessment of the program must include a system to monitor the progress of students after they leave the program. The primary purpose of the program is to ensure that the LEP students ultimately are able to compete on an equal footing with their English-speaking peers. This cannot be determined in the absence of such a postreclassification monitoring system.

*Question*: May a district deny services to a student because there are few students in the district who speak his or her language?

*Answer*: No. The 1974 Equal Educational Opportunities Act and subsequent court decisions make it clear that every student is entitled to a program that is reasonably designed to overcome any handicaps occasioned by a language deficit. The number of students who speak a particular language may be considered to determine how best to address the student needs given the human and fiscal resources available. Still, some form of special educational services must be provided.

## NOTES

1. Throughout various contexts, such as research, litigation, legislation, and practice, a range of terms has been used to describe children who come to school with a primary language other than English. "Limited English proficient" (LEP) is the term most commonly found in legislation and litigation to refer to children whose primary language is a language other than English. "English language learner," "bilingual learner," and "English learner" are terms more commonly found in the research literature and at times in educational settings. Further distinctions can be made based on ethnicity (Latino, Asian, etc.), primary language (Spanish, Mandarin, Vietnamese, etc.), nation of origin, and other categories.

2. According to the U.S. Bureau of the Census, "The term 'Hispanic' or 'Latino' refers to persons who trace their origin or descent to Mexico, Puerto Rico, Cuba, Spanish-speaking Central and South America countries, and other Spanish cultures. Origin can be considered as the heritage, nationality group, lineage, or country of the person or the person's parents or ancestors before their arrival in the United States. People who identify their origin as Hispanic or Latino may be of any race" (*www.census.gov/ population/www/socdemo/hispanic/hispanic.html*).

3. As of February 2004, schools and districts may continue to include in AYP determinations former LEP students for up to 2 years after they no longer meet the state's definition for LEP. However, it was clarified in September 2006 that former LEP students

should not be included in the LEP subgroup for any other purpose on current state or local education agency report cards.

4. Additional information regarding the LEP partnership, and recent related resources and guidance, may be found at *www.ncela.gwu.edu/spotlight/lep.*

## REFERENCES

Alexander v. Choate, 469 U.S. 287 (1985).

Alexander v. Sandoval, 532 U.S. 275 (2001).

Antunez, B. (2002). Implementing Reading First with English language learners. *Directions in Language and Education, 15,* 12–13.

Aspira of New York, Inc. v. Board of Education of the City of New York, 394 F. Supp. 1161 (1975).

August, D. (2006). Demographic overview. In D. August & T. Shanahan (Eds.), *Report of the National Literacy Panel on Language Minority Youth and Children* (pp. 14–28). Mahwah, NJ: Erlbaum.

August, D., & Shanahan, T. (Eds.). (2006). *Report of the national literacy panel on language minority youth and children.* Mahwah, NJ: Erlbaum.

Bilingual Education Act, Public Law No. 90-247, 81 Stat. 816 (1968).

Bilingual Education Act, Public Law No. 93-380, 88 Stat. 503 (1974).

Bilingual Education Act, Public Law No. 95-561, 92 Stat. 2268 (1978).

Bilingual Education Act, Public Law No. 98-511, 98 Stat. 2370 (1984).

Bilingual Education Act, Public Law No. 100-297, 102 Stat. 279 (1988).

Bilingual Education Act, Public Law No. 103-382 (1994).

Birman, B. F., & Ginsburg, A. L. (1983). Introduction: Addressing the needs of language minority children. In K. A. Baker & A. de Kanter (Eds.), *Bilingual education: A reappraisal of federal policy* (pp. ix–xxi). Lexington, MA: Heath.

Capps, R., Fix, M., Ost, J., Reardon-Anderson, J., & Passel, J. (2004). *The health and well-being of young children of immigrants.* Washington, DC: Urban Institute.

Casanova, U. (1991). Bilingual education: Politics or pedagogy. In O. García (Ed.), *Bilingual education* (Vol. 1, pp. 167-182). Amsterdam: Benjamins.

Castañeda v. Pickard, 64b F.2d 989 (1981).

Center on Education Policy. (2006). *Keeping watch on Reading First.* Washington, DC: Center on Education Policy.

Civil Rights Act, Public Law No. 88-352, 78 Stat. (1964).

Cohen, C. C. D., & Clewell, B. C. (2007). *Putting English language learners on the educational map* (Policy brief). Washington, DC: Urban Institute.

Commission on No Child Left Behind. (2007). *Beyond No Child Left Behind: Fulfilling the promise to our nation's children.* Washington, DC: Aspen Institute.

Crawford, J. (1999). *Bilingual education: History, politics, theory, and practice* (4th ed.). Los Angeles: Bilingual Education Services.

Early Reading First, No Child Left Behind Act, Public Law No. 107-110, Title I, Part B, Subpart 2 (2001).

Elementary and Secondary Education Act of 1965, Title II, Public Law No. 89-10, 27 Stat. (1965).

Equal Educational Opportunities Act of 1974, Public Law No. 93-380, 88 Stat. 514 (1974).

Espinosa, L., & López, M. (2006). *Assessment considerations for young English language learners across different levels of accountability* [Prepared for the National Early Childhood Accountability Task Force]. Washington, DC: PEW Charitable Trusts.

Fry, R. (2007). *How far behind in math and reading are English language learners?* (Report). Washington, DC: PEW Hispanic Center.

Gandara, P., Moran, R., & García, E. E. (2004). Legacy of *Brown: Lau* and language policy in the United States. *Review of Research in Education, 28*(1), 27–46.

García, E. (2001a). *Hispanics education in the United States: Raices y alas.* Lanham, MD: Rowman & Littlefield.

García, E. (2001b). *Understanding and meeting the challenge of student diversity* (3rd ed.). Boston: Houghton Mifflin.

García, E. (2005). *Teaching and learning in two languages: Bilingualism and schooling in the United States.* New York: Teachers College Press.

García, E. E., & González, R. (1995). Issues in systemic reform for culturally and linguistically diverse students. *Teachers College Record, 96*(3), 418–431.

Guardians Association v. Civil Service Commission, 463 U.S. 582 (1983).

Hernandez, D. (2006). *Young Hispanic children in the United States: A demographic portrait based on Census 2000* [A report to the National Task Force on Early Childhood Education for Hispanics]. Albany: State University of New York.

Lau v. Nichols, 414 U.S. 563 (1974).

López, M., & Barrueco, S. (2006). *Latino infants and families: A national perspective of protective and risk factors for development* [A report to the National Task Force on Early Childhood Education for Hispanics]. Tempe, AZ: Arizona State University.

Moran, R. F. (2004, Summer). Undone by law: The uncertain legacy of *Lau v. Nichols. UC Linguistic Minority Research Institute Newsletter, 13,* 1–5.

National Institute of Child Health and Human Development. (2000). *Report of the National Reading Panel: Teaching children to read: An evidence-based assessment of the scientific research literature on reading and its implications for reading instruction* (NIH Publication No. 00-4769). Washington, DC: U.S. Government Printing Office.

Navarro, R. A. (1990). The problems of language, education, and society: Who decides. In E. E. García & R. V. Padilla (Eds.), *Advances in bilingual education research* (pp. 289–313). Tucson: University of Arizona Press.

No Child Left Behind Act, Public Law No. 107-110, 2001.

Otero v. Mesa County School District, No. 51, 408 F. Supp. 162 (1975).

Ramirez, J. D. (2001, May). *Bilingualism and literacy: Problem or opportunity? A synthesis of reading research on bilingual students.* Paper presented at the Research Symposium on High Standards in Reading for Students in Diverse Language Groups: Research, Policy, and Practice, Washington, DC.

Reading First, No Child Left Behind Act, Public Law No. 107-110, Title I, Part B, Subpart 1 (2001).

Rhodes, R. L., Ochoa, S. H., & Ortiz, S. O. (2005). *Assessing culturally and linguistically diverse students: A practical guide.* New York: Guilford Press.

Roos, P. (1984, July). *Legal guidelines for bilingual administrators.* Austin, TX: Society of Research in Child Development.

Snow, D., Burns, S., & Griffin, P. (1998). *Preventing reading difficulties in young children.* Washington, DC: National Academies Press.

U.S. Department of Education (2006). *Reading First implementation evaluation: Interim report.* Washington, DC: Author.

U.S. Department of Education. (2008). *Reading First*. Retrieved January 15, 2008, from *www.ed.gov/programs/readingfirstr/index.html*.

U.S. Department of Education, National Center for Education Statistics. (2006). *The condition of education 2006* [NCES Publication No. 2006-071]. Washington, DC: U.S. Government Printing Office.

U.S. Department of Education, National Center for Education Statistics. (2008). *The condition of education 2008* [NCES Publication No. 2008-031]. Washington, DC: U.S. Government Printing Office.

U.S. Department of Education, Office of Elementary and Secondary Education. (2002). *Outline of programs and selected changes in the No Child Left Behind Act of 2001*. Washington, DC: Author.

U.S. Government Accountability Office. (2006). *No Child Left Behind act: Assistance from education could help states better measure progress of students with limited English proficiency* [Publication No. GAO-06-815]. Washington, DC: Author.

Wiese, A., & García, E. E. (2006). Educational policy in the United States regarding bilinguals in early childhood education. In B. Spodek & O. N. Saracho (Eds.), *Handbook of research on the education of young children* (2nd ed., pp. 361–374). Mahwah, NJ: Erlbaum.

Zentella, A. C. (Ed.). (2005). *Building on strengths: Language and literacy in Latino families and communities*. New York: Teachers College Press.

# CHAPTER 3

# What Do We Know
# about the Discourse Patterns
# of Diverse Students in Multiple Settings?

ILIANA REYES, LEISY WYMAN, NORMA GONZÁLEZ,
ELIANE RUBINSTEIN- ÁVILA, KAREN SPEAR-ELLINWOOD,
PERRY GILMORE, *and* LUIS C. MOLL

In this chapter we present five case examples, all from recent empirical work that builds on research examining the discourse of children and youth in a variety of settings. Each example is abstracted from studies that provide insight into living and learning with language under particular social and cultural conditions, ranging from Mexican American preschoolers in the U.S. southwest to Yup'ik youth in Alaska, and from community settings to a virtual world in a computer. The researchers, the reader will note, are all professional colleagues and form part of a single academic unit at the University of Arizona. Although the studies were conducted independently, each study affirms a foundational principle of this line of research and the ethos of our unit: the inseparability of language and literacy development, and all other ways of meaning, from the details of social life.

A rich tradition of research addresses the sociocultural dynamics of language and literacy development in home and community settings. One might mention, for example, among several classic studies, Labov's work (1972) that challenges deprivation theories of African American speech patterns; Bernstein's (1971) analysis of social class relations, speech codes, and orientations to meanings; Heath's (1983) comparative ethnographic study of language and literacy among blacks and whites in the U.S. South; and Philips's (1983) analysis of participant structures organizing classroom and nonclassroom discourse in a Native American community.

In addition, heavily influenced by Hymes's notions of the ethnography of communication and communicative competence, edited volumes such as *Functions of Language in the Classroom* (Cazden, John, & Hymes, 1972), *Children in and Out of School* (Gilmore & Glatthorn, 1982), and *The Acquisition of Literacy: Ethnographic Perspectives* (Schieffelin & Gilmore, 1986) also marked new directions in the interdisciplinary ethnographic study of diverse discourses and competencies of children, both in and out of school settings. All of these are not simply landmark studies, but they represent, and helped to generate, programs of inquiry into the sociocultural dynamics of language and literacy acquisition, function, and use, all with implications on how we think about language in education. More recently, research on "funds of knowledge" and on the complexity of multimodal discourse communities extend these earlier studies and resist the easy dichotomy of a home–school discontinuity (e.g., González, Moll, & Amanti, 2005).

In the following discussion we explore the blurred borders and porous boundaries of these discourse communities, and present the examples in the following order:

• We start with a preschooler engaged in a bilingual school-related discourse practice in the context of a household setting. The example, by Iliana Reyes, captures how language socialization is a distributed phenomenon involving a range of family members, and introduces the term "hybrid practices" to capture this mix of multiple persons and experiences.

• We then turn to a different view of language socialization, by Norma González, that shows how language ideologies and policy play out in a school. The example captures a moment in history, the reaction and agency of school-children in a dual-language program to the new restrictive and punitive state law seeking to banish precisely the bilingual forms of schooling that have come to define them.

• The third example, by Leisy Wyman, takes us to Alaska, and the dramatic and complex struggles surrounding the survival and use of an indigenous language. It draws from a longitudinal study of the everyday linguistic practices and language ideologies of youth in a Yup'ik village of less than 700 residents during an early, yet uneven, phase of language shift to English. The work shows how youth navigate social learning in-the-moment, drawing on linguistic resources which shape and are shaped within complex cultural and linguistic ecologies.

• The next example, by Eliane Rubinstein-Ávila, takes us to an afterschool setting that facilitates, for adolescents who do not necessarily prosper in the context of formal schooling, multiple forms of assistance and displays of competence. In contrast to schools, this alternative setting does not shy away from controversial and contentious topics, such as race and class discrimination, but assists students in the careful scrutiny of these issues, challenging stereotypes held by others, and those in the mind of the beholder.

• The final example, by Karen Spear-Ellinwood, examines elements of doing an ethnographic analysis *of* and *in* a virtual world. The author herself is in the thick of the action, represented by an "avatar" who is computer savvy but a novice with the discourse practices in such a contrived "sociotechnical" setting. This example captures the constant mixing of fantasy and reality in these virtual worlds, where all is new and multiple languages coexist, but common social elements and cultural forms of interaction from the social world are replicated.

The examples in this chapter, each abstracted from full-fledged, individual studies, present multiple "voices" that deviate perhaps from the more unitary style that characterizes such chapters, even when coauthored. We think the diversity of presentations, however, is well worth any lack of cohesion in style; we hope our readers agree. We conclude with a discussion of the implications of the findings for the study of language in education.

## LEARNING LANGUAGES IN AN IMMIGRANT CONTEXT (ILIANA REYES)

A longitudinal study by Reyes (2006) and her colleagues on home literacy practices with first-generation Mexican families in the U.S. Southwest showed that extended family members play key roles in the development of two languages and biliteracy, benefiting not only the young child but also family members (Reyes, Alexandra, & Azuara, 2007). As Mexican families migrate to the north, they develop discourse varieties necessary to participate in their day-to-day activities. Reyes found that older siblings generally remain fluent speakers in varieties of Spanish, in this case from northern Mexico (Sonora and Sinaloa), and also acquire local, hybrid varieties from the U.S. Southwest, such as "Spanglish."

Younger siblings continue to develop a strong command of Spanish, but this becomes more limited as they continue their schooling predominantly in English. There are several pressures on them from school, peer culture, and popular media to embrace the dominant English language. Parents often want to support the development of literacy in both languages, but find themselves torn between competing home and school language practices. The U.S. educational system generally requires children to conduct their studies in English; however, hybrid interactional practices find their way into immigrant families, because it is impossible to shut down knowledge acquired in their countries of origin as they gain knowledge in their host community.

This point is illustrated by Alejandra, a 4-year-old girl whose learning is mediated by her mother, uncle, and aunt, all of whom play and help her learn the alphabet by trying to teach her in both languages. Her mother, her uncle, Andrés, and his wife, Aurelia, are talking in the living room. Alejandra brings an alphabet list she made as part of a school activity, and her mother tells Alejandra that she needs to practice the letters. Andres, the uncle, volunteers to help her. (All names are pseudonyms; translations are indicated in parentheses; A = Alejandra; M = Mother; U = Uncle Andrés; AU = Aunt Aurelia; R = Researcher.)

1 U: ¿Cuál es ésta, Alejandra? (Which [letter] is this, Alejandra?)

2 M: ¿Te gusta? Estan bonitos los colores ¿verdad? (You like them, the colors are pretty, right?)

3 U: Alejandra ¿Cuál es ...? (Which [letter] is ... ?) [Child does not respond.] Es la /a/. (It is the [letter] *a* [pronunciation in Spanish].)

4 A: /a/ [saying the English name of the letter]

5 U: Oh, si es cierto ... ¿Tiene que ser en inglés o en español? (Oh, that is right ... Does she have to learn them in English or in Spanish?)

6 M: Es bilingüe su clase. (Her class is bilingual.)

7 U: Esa es la /a/ [Spanish pronunciation of the letter.]

8 R: ¿La [escuela] Bonita Vista tambien va a ser bilingüe? (Is the Bonita Vista school going to be bilingual?)

9 M: Si pues, no te digo que todos los papeles los firme en español ... para que me la pongan en clase bilingüe. (Yes, haven't I told you that I signed all the papers in Spanish so she can attend a bilingual program.)

10 U: [He continues addressing Alejandra, saying the name of the letters of the alphabet in Spanish while pointing to each letter on the letter chart.] *la b* ... *la c* ... [continues]. (The *b* ... the *c* ... the. ...)

11 A: La /d/. (The *d*.)

12 U: La bolita hacia arriba y luego el palito. [Uncle Andrés explains to Alejandra how to write the letter *d*; "You draw the little circle up here and then the little stick"; the adults laugh; conversation continues.]

13 A: Díle con cosas, la /a/ de araña, si así se las aprende. (Tell her with things so it is easier to learn [and understand].) [Alejandra goes to sit with her mom.]

14 M: Ya no quiere. (She does not want to do it anymore.) [Adults keep laughing.]

15 M: A mi gorda no le gusta que se rian de ella. (My baby does not like others laughing about her.)
<skip 1 minute>

16 M: Aaapple ira aaapple /a/ /a/ /a/ [English pronunciation] /b/ [Spanish pronunciation of the letter] beisball [Spanish pronunciation] o ball [English pronunciation].

17 M and A: [Mom begins singing the ABC song in English and Alejandra repeats after her.] a b c de f g hi jk l mn op. [Both continue singing the whole alphabet song.]

18 M to A: ¿ya vez? Así se las tienes que decir a tu tío .. no tengas miedo mami no tengas miedo. (See? That's how you have to say them to your uncle ... don't be afraid, my baby, don't be afraid.)

19 M to U: ¿Ya vez? Si se las sabe. (See? She does know the letters.)

20 U: Yo pense que no te las sabias. (I thought you did not know [the letters].)

21 M: [en inglés] ... pero en español no se las sabe. ([in English] ... but in Spanish she doesn't know them.)

20 U to A: A ver, Alejandra. (Let's see, Alejandra.)

21 M to A: A ver cántaselo . . ahora cántalas en español. (Lets see, now sing them [the letters], sing them in Spanish.), a b c d e f g. [Mom starts singing the letters in Spanish with the English ABC song intonation.]

22 U: [singing in Spanish] Y sale la /a/ moviendo los pies. (And then the [letter] /a/ comes out moving her feet.) ¿Te acuerdas de la canción? (Do you remember that song?) [The uncle associates the singing in Spanish with a popular Latin American children's song in Spanish; the interaction continues for several minutes.]

The uncle supports Alejandra's development of biliteracy by reading the letters in the alphabet list in Spanish. He points to each letter and reads it in Spanish. He tells Alejandra how each letter is formed and draws their shapes in the air (see lines 1–12). Alejandra repeats after him, but after a minute or so, when Andrés asks her again to read each letter from the beginning, she appears not to remember the name of the letters in Spanish. This interaction goes on for several minutes, until the child is frustrated and does not want to repeat anymore. She goes to her mother instead (line 13). The mother insists that Alejandra does know the letters, but in English (lines 19 and 21). The mother starts reading the letters in English, makes associations of each letter with an object, a strategy suggested by the aunt (e.g., A for apple), and then starts singing the ABC song in English. Alejandra joins her with enthusiasm, and with no difficulty (line 17). At the end, the mother tells the uncle, 'See? She can do it," and insists for Alejandra to try in Spanish: "ahora cántalas en español" (line 21).

When they start singing the letters in Spanish, they adapt the song with the Spanish letters and the intonation of the ABC song; this triggers the uncle's association with one in Spanish made famous by Latin American children's songwriter Cri-Cri. The mother and uncle begin singing the song in Spanish that emphasizes the vowels (line 22). They talk about how, as young children, they learned the letters with this song and participated in a musical festival role-playing the letters. Alejandra watches her mother and uncle sing together.

The role of extended family members in literacy practices is highlighted by Alejandra's uncle, and in a more passive role, by her aunt, in helping Alejandra learn the alphabet in both Spanish and English. Latino immigrant parents rely on other family members to help support the development of biliteracy. Gregory,

Long, and Volk (2004) have observed a similar phenomenon with young children's grandparents in immigrant communities in London. Moreover, Alejandra's learning is enhanced by her mother and her uncle's use of hybrid literacy practices to adopt the learning of the alphabet in both languages according to the ways they learned when growing up in the north of Mexico.

## HOW CHILDREN ARE IDEOLOGICALLY FORMED THROUGH LANGUAGE (NORMA GONZÁLEZ)

Recent work on language socialization has focused on community and family discourse patterns, and has expanded to study larger institutional settings, such as schools, which are often sites for multiple layers of language ideologies (Budwig, 2001; Garrett & Baquedano-López, 2002; González, 2001; Lee, 1993; Mendoza-Denton, 2008). Such is the case with this example, taken from a dual-language immersion school in the borderlands of Arizona, a state that has passed English-only laws to govern schooling practices (González, 2005).

For the French philosopher Louis Althusser, nothing exists outside of ideology, and the school is a potent example of a dominant ideological state apparatus. Furthermore, ideology functions by naming and forming subject positions, "hailing" or "interpellating" them:

> Ideology "acts" or "functions" in such a way that it "recruits" subjects among the individuals (it recruits them all), or "transforms" the individuals into subjects (it transforms them all) by that very precise operation which I have called *interpellation* or hailing, and which can be imagined along the lines of the most commonplace everyday police (or other) hailing: "Hey, you there!" (1971, p. 174)

Thus, at the moment someone is "hailed" and acknowledges the identification, ideology has recruited the individual and transformed him or her into a subject constructed through ideologies. Within this framework, identity is formed as a subject of the ideological apparatus of the state. There is no room for the individual self outside of ideological formations, or for agency, because the interpellation project is ongoing and ever-present. Although this framework is excessively deterministic, it does foreground the structures and discourses that limit and/or enable particular linguistic and cultural practices.

Applied to language, this type of ideology is unconscious, but it maintains social stratification via particular speech practices. Thus, ideology implicates power, the exercise of power, and the reproduction of dominant and subordinate relations. This articulation between micro-level interaction and macro-level forces can be studied in schools by examining what children say, to whom they say it, and under what circumstances. Also crucial, on the other hand, are circulating metadiscourses about language, about the purpose and use of language, about learning languages, and about learning through one language or the other.

In the elementary school that is the site for this research, all students, regardless of language background, receive instruction through Spanish during their first 2 years (K–1), with an increase in English as the language of instruction in subsequent years, but never going below 70% Spanish. All students are immersed in literacy experiences in Spanish first. Most of the magnet students are English dominant, and 70% of the students are Latino, coming in as both students from the local *barrio* and magnet students from outside the immediate neighborhood. A significant percentage of the Latinos are third- or fourth-generation Mexican-origin children. They enroll for a variety of reasons, including the strong ancillary programs, but many families cite a desire for their children to recapture the Spanish language, often erased by English-only instruction. The faculty makes a conscious effort to privilege the minority language, so that students can exit the program fully proficient in two languages, going to extraordinary lengths to promote Spanish as the language of academic, administrative, and social interaction.

When we first conceptualized the study, we could not foresee a series of events that crystallized language ideologies within media and public discourses. This crystallization was marked by the passage, through popular vote, of Proposition 203, Arizona's version of California's antibilingual education initiative. The Proposition passed by a broad margin, underscoring how popular ideologies, this one about the absolute primacy of English, can drive classroom practices and pedagogical methodology.

What is the effect on children of such a volatile and contentious debate? To what discursive practices do children attend? During the course of our fieldwork, Proposition 203 led to alternate hardening and blurring of language ideologies as they met and collided within the school setting and the community. As implicit ideologies became explicit discourses, children found ways to talk back, to repel the interpellation of hailings and dominant discourses, and to constitute for themselves their own organic perspective of what the "fuss" was actually about.

In the following examples, children's voices come to the foreground in unexpected ways. Students in a classroom are discussing the concept of opposites. The teacher asks for a word in Spanish that means the opposite of the word that students are given, and students go around a circle. When the teacher says "Bilingüe," there's a moment's hesitation and thought before the student blurts out "tonto" (stupid or foolish), clearly refusing interpellations that construct bilinguals as being in need of remedial or compensatory programs. This child inverts the deficit discourse of bilingual education and recasts those students who do not have skills in more than one language as lacking academic achievement. Through the activity of articulation this child can subvert the rationale of hegemonic discourse and relocate an imposed negative identity.

The voices of the children plumb the depths of how adult discourses have the power to disrupt the only kind of schooling they know and love. Mariela, a second grader, expresses her fear concerning the possible passage of the proposition: "*Si pasa la ley, no vamos a poder hablar mas en español ...*" (If the law passes, we won't be able to speak Spanish anymore . . .) And then she adds: "*Porque no entienden*" (Because they don't understand). The subject "they" is not defined, but we can assume that she is referring to the persons who would vote in favor of the bill. *Porque no entienden* is a plaintive acknowledgment that as transparent as the issue is for her, her subjective understanding is not refracted onto dominant ideologies that seek to interpellate her as a subject of a monolingual state. Although, as a child, she is voiceless in terms of resisting the actual implementation of the law, she is not voiceless in apprehending the deeper structural/ideological current that has swept her and her classmates away. "[Ellos] *no entienden*" (They don't understand) how this school has created a space for children of both English-speaking and Spanish-speaking families to come together to attain high academic goals in not just one, but in two languages. Similarly, an English-dominant student laments, "Laura can get English anywhere, but I can only get Spanish here," incisively pinpointing an interpellation that the positionality of the minority language is circumscribed to a space outside of official discourses, and that without the protection and sustenance of a nascent second-language ability within the school site, the child will not attain another voice.

As the examples illustrate, the school site, rather than interpellating students through its ideological state apparatus, can instead be a space for counterinterpellations, as well as the formation of emergent subjectivities that can exercise a critical agency. In the borderlands, ideas about language and child rearing, or schooling, are neither uniform nor fixed (González, 2001), nor are they necessarily a coherent and integrated whole, and sometimes they produce contradictory sites for the push and pull of language in context.

For all teachers, and for those of us who study language socialization, listening to the voices of the children helps us look deeper and more closely into how language completes us as unfinished subjects.

## YOUTH DISCOURSES IN ENDANGERED LANGUAGE SETTINGS: A YUP'IK EXAMPLE (LEISY WYMAN)

In the current moment of worldwide language endangerment, dominant discourses of monolingualism frame the loss of minority languages as a natural, possibly regrettable, but unavoidable phenomenon and sanitize the histories of inequity that lead to endangerment (May, 2005). Stereotypical portrayals of youth as solely interested in global youth culture feed these discourses. Within indigenous communities, educators and community members may assume that youth simply choose to abandon their indigenous languages, because they no longer feel tied to indigenous identities or local places. Recent studies of indigenous youth in endangered language communities, however, show how youth produce discourses of language loss that are far more complex than previously assumed (Lee, 2007; McCarty, Romero-Little, & Zepeda, 2006; Meek, 2007). The following discussion illustrates these complexities. The data are drawn from a decadelong study of youth language and literacy practices conducted in Piniq (a pseudonym), a small and remote Yup'ik Eskimo village in Western Alaska (Wyman, 2004).

In 1980, Yup'ik (i.e., Central Alaskan Yup'ik Eskimo) was identified as one of only two indigenous Alaskan languages spoken by small children and most likely to survive. However, by 1995, the number of Yup'ik speakers had dropped from 13,000 to 10,000, indicating that Yup'ik, too, was facing possible language death (Krauss, 1997).

Language shift may appear to take root suddenly in a community, as families and whole communities appear quickly to "tip" into use of a dominant language within a generation's time (Dorian, 1989; Wong-Fillmore, 2000). Youth in endangered language communities add their own layer of complexity as they construct themselves in spontaneous and more enduring ways over time, using all that their complex linguistic and cultural repertoires have to offer.

This research examined two distinct, consecutive age cohorts of youth within a "cornerstone generation" (Gal, 1979; Kulick, 1992). Both groups of youth used bilingual skills to negotiate peer interaction and construct complex identities. Youth in the older group spoke Yup'ik as the predominant language of peer culture in the mid-1990s. In contrast, a majority of youth in the younger group spoke English as the predominant language of peer culture only 5 years later.

The local school was implicated in the language shift. A non-native administrator drastically reduced the local bilingual program in the 1980s. This policy was initiated even though the program had been considered a model one and was among the first of its kind in Alaska. The children who first used English as a peer language were those who were taught English, rather than Yup'ik, as a core language of instruction at the elementary level.

The weakening of the Yup'ik program in the local school coincided with an increase in urban-periphery and intervillage movement primarily for jobs and education. Increasing numbers of second-language speaking Yup'ik adults from urban spaces and English-speaking villages additionally moved into Piniq so that their children could grow up in what they perceived as a safe and strong traditional community. Most parents in Piniq started out speaking Yup'ik to their children, but many younger families used increasing amounts of English at home once their oldest children went to English-speaking school and played with English-speaking peers, mirroring patterns of family language loss in immigrant populations elsewhere (Dorian, 1989; Wong-Fillmore, 2000).

Overall the study documented how these combined changes produced uneven productive skills among youth in Piniq during early language shift, and how youth and adults interpreted changing patterns of bilingualism in ways that further intensified patterns of language shift. Young people were confronted regularly with ways they measured up to local adult expectations for heritage language use. They grew up with an overall sense of who was and was not "really speaking Yup'ik" according to local norms. In the younger group, it became increasingly common for youth to express linguistic insecurity in Yup'ik, or to self-identify as non-Yup'ik speakers.

Some youth critiqued how local schooling practices undermined their parents' efforts to maintain Yup'ik as a language of the home. These students described how they and their younger siblings first "tipped" into using English when they started attending the English-speaking local school. Many students, however, theorized their own positions and roles within language shift in ways that centered on single life events or contingencies unrelated to schooling. Consider the following informal interview in which I asked two youth what the village might be like in the future:

1 LTW: What kinds of things will be the same, what kinds of things will be different?

2 NATHAN: Our Yup'ik language might be the same, or might be different, I don't know.

3 MIKE: I heard one village lost their language.

4 LTW: What do people say about, like, Yup'ik and English?

5 NATHAN: When I used to be small, I used to speak Yup'ik language, but when they were [inaudible] we lost that language.

6 MIKE: Me, too.

7 NATHAN: When I played with…when my mom brought me to Anchorage, I forgot how.

8 MIKE: Me, I forgot how from, uh, playing with a boy who talked English too much. When I try speak Yup'ik I speak it wrong.

Both students echoed local concerns about imminent language loss (line 1), albeit indirectly. First is Nathan's reference to how "Our Yup'ik language … might be different" (line 2), then Mike's report about how "one village lost their language" (line 3). Mike and Nathan indirectly linked their individual trajectories of language socialization to the broader possibility of community language endangerment. Mike and Nathan described points in time when they themselves "knew" Yup'ik and were Yup'ik speakers, and explained why they no longer spoke Yup'ik, or why they felt insecure about their Yup'ik use. Nathan echoed collective understandings of language, identity, and shift as a one-way process with a discrete end point by briefly recapping how "we lost that language" (line 5). Both youth then relayed how single life contingencies, including Nathan's stint in a distant city (line 7) and Mike's local friendship with an English-speaking peer in the village (line 8), influenced their feelings of linguistic insecurity.

In doing so, they demonstrate their awareness of language socialization as a contingent accomplishment influenced by individual experiences (Bayley & Schecter, 2003; Wortham, 2005). By focusing solely on individual contingencies, however, Nathan and Mike partially erase the structural impact of changing school practices on collective resources for Yup'ik language learning and use in local peer culture. They seemingly distribute responsibility for supporting heritage language maintenance away from the local school, local adults, and themselves, precluding the collective envisioning, engagement, and activism necessary for reversing language shift (Fishman, 1991, 2001). At the same time, their slight softening from the verb "lost" to their descriptions of how "I forgot how" to speak Yup'ik (lines 7 and 8) leaves open the possibility that someday circumstances might allow them as individuals to "remember" what it feels like to be confident Yup'ik speakers.

Contextualizing Nathan's and Mike's self-descriptions with longitudinal data, ethnographic observations, and other moments in the interview, a more complicated picture of bilingualism emerges. In both older and younger groups in the study, youth like Nathan, who moved to urban areas or non-Yup'ik-speaking villages, then back to the village, typically spent years picking up receptive skills in Yup'ik. Many grew quite adept at "getting by" in the village by using simple statements and phrases in Yup'ik. Stories like Mike's, in contrast, first appeared and became increasingly common among members of the younger group over time as language shift took hold in the village, and as the "tipping" into English in local peer culture became a driving force of shift in itself.

Both boys' stories belied their own use of Yup'ik within their families. After returning from his stint in Anchorage, Nathan used Yup'ik at home to interact with his brothers, who never left Piniq, and with extended family members. As the younger child of a Yup'ik- and English-speaking family, Mike used some Yup'ik with relatives, and was observed translating for Yup'ik-speaking elders as they exchanged pleasantries with English-speaking teachers.

Like heritage language learners in nonindigenous communities documented elsewhere (Mertz, 1989; Zentella, 1997), Nathan and Mike used receptive skills, phrases, and simple statements in their heritage language to participate in their community. They also used Yup'ik to learn and to share traditional subsistence hunting and fishing practices that were intimately tied to a unique system of beliefs and practices specific to both the Yup'ik way of life and the mixed economy of their village.

Analyzing how young people's practices are situated in relation to historical and contemporary processes of schooling, as well as local activities and systems of learning, we can abandon stereotypes of youth in general and indigenous youth in particular as orienting simply toward local or global practices, heritage or dominant languages, or traditional versus modern worlds. Furthermore, we can bring into focus what languages mean to specific communities by identifying the dynamic ways that youth ideologize and use bilingualism within complex linguistic ecologies (Hornberger, 2002; McCarty et al., 2006). Finally, we can understand how youth may forge local continuities across boundaries of language and historical inequity, even as they interpret and enact their sometimes irreconcilable positions as agents of language loss.

## CREATING SPACES FOR YOUTH'S CRITICAL, MULTIMODAL LITERACIES AND AGENTIVE IDENTITIES (ELIANE RUBINSTEIN-ÁVILA)

Adolescent literacy development is commonly associated with continuous formal schooling. However, for nondominant youth (immigrant, poor, and/or youth of color), who are likely to attend overcrowded, underresourced, "low performing" public schools, classroom experiences do not tend to build on their "full repertoire of literacy practices" (Gutiérrez & Rogoff, 2003), or on their communities' "funds of knowledge" (González et al., 2005; Moll & González, 1994). Formal schooling, as a rule, does not encourage these students to read the word *through* their world (Freire & Macedo, 1987), or to cultivate agentive selfhood. Literacy instruction in most schools tends to focus on the narrow, more technical aspects of literacy development—a process that Freire called "banking education," and that Street (1995) described as "autonomous" literacy.

The research literature supports the assertion that, in general, schools fall short of providing nondominant youth the academic support they need to succeed, or encouraging the crafting of "their agentive selves" (Hull & Katz, 2006). In her exploration of schooling adaptation among immigrant students in secondary schools, Rubinstein-Ávila (2007b) found that even those who may have felt competent as students in their countries of origin were likely to feel confused and bewildered when faced with unfamiliar and unclear notions of what "counts" as literacy and as learning once they begin attending U.S. schools. As one young woman from the Dominican Republic expressed:

> In Santo Domingo, they expected us to learn and remember the information straight from the book, or from copying the teacher's notes [on the board], but *here* I am not so sure *what* exactly we should be learning. (adapted from p. 585)

Schultz and Hull (2002) have cautioned us against overemphasizing the school–out-of-school dichotomy, but Hull (2004) admits that schools are less likely than organized out-of-school programs to provide students with sustained attention to the visual aspect of new literacies. In fact, both authors claim that out-of-school learning contexts have contributed greatly to "widen[ing] the lens of what we consider literacy and literate activities" (Schultz & Hull, 2002, p. 11).

Although the broader goal of organized out-of-school youth programs is to support what have come to be known as the five C's of positive youth development—competence, confidence, connections, character, and caring (Hamilton & Hamilton, 2004)—numerous studies have reported on literacy-inspired programs beyond the walls of schools. These programs seem to have a common goal to engage youth with literacies and to provide spaces in which participating youth are supported through the complex negotiation of their overlapping identities (Blackburn, 2003, 2005; Hull, 2004; Rubinstein-Ávila, 2007a).

Youth in these programs are more likely to be considered a resource than a problem. They are viewed as knowledgeable and are encouraged to rely on their lived experiences, to express their opinions, and to share their feelings multimodally through an array of media, such as radio, zines, digital stories, books, magazines, and newspapers (Rubinstein-Ávila, 2007a). Moreover, these spaces often provide opportunities for diverse youth to reflect critically and "talk back" (hooks, 1989) to a wide audience.

These creative out-of-school spaces often demonstrate the potentially transforming power of "alternative pedagogies" (Chavez & Soep, 2005). Such pedagogies tend to rely on participatory approaches that focus on learners' agentive engagement and ownership of an array of modalities—print, oral, visual, and digital (Alvermann, Hagood, & Williams, 2001). In an ethnographic case study of an organization's program, Rubinstein-Ávila (2006) studied 20 participating youth throughout an 8-month cohort cycle. Four days a week, participating youth composed and eventually published a second annual issue of a 100+ glossy-page magazine, revealing the day-to-day hopes, dreams, and challenges faced by nondominant youth, their peers, and their communities. Through black-and-white photographs shot by the youth, and texts of various genres, the youth relied on their own inquiries and personal experiences to delve into an array of personal and social issues, including racial profiling of young Latino males by local police; health topics, such as eating disorders and the stigma around HIV testing; gentrification of their neighborhoods within the ongoing process of "urban revitalization"; and the complexities of growing into adulthood—and more specifically "manhood"—while still being financially dependent on one's extended family.

The 8-month multimodal literacy program provided its participating youth opportunities to get to know and collaborate with peers and mentors from ethnic groups and neighborhoods other than their own. Such opportunities provided a rich space for discourse patterns that deviated from the "color-blind" constraints of formal schooling. Gordo,[1] a young Mexican American man, had the opportunity to describe the racial profiling he experienced almost daily from the police. In an interview, excerpted below, Gordo talked about the gentrification of his neighborhood.

> I used to look at the world in a whole different way; you know what I mean? Like I don't know; this might sound racist, but I didn't really like white people. There's a lot of them [white people] in my neighborhood; you know what I mean? *Now there is*; and that's one of the reasons why I didn't like them. Because they came in and they took over; you know what I mean? They like buy everybody out (unintelligible); that's what pissed me off. ERA: And did that change with your participation in Equinox [the program]? Well, I got to know (the program's director) and (the two mentors), and some of the other guys here (participating youth) … you know what I mean? They're white, and … they're cool. But then you got your other white people that are just assholes, you know what I mean? I don't know; not *all* white people are bad, you know what I mean? I guess there's sometimes a couple of good apples in the bunch; you know what I mean?

Gordo's experience working intensively with an array of people, with whom he had only minimal prior contact and limited opportunities to dialogue, provided him an expanded lens from which to reflect on his ideas. Successful partnerships between formal and informal learning contexts can potentially expand interpersonal experiences of youth, and enrich their language, literacy practices, and discourses in and out of school. To create multimodal spaces in which students are encouraged not only to consume but also to produce knowledge critically and collaboratively, teachers, mentors, youth workers, and students have to be willing to engage in the ongoing process of learning across new modes of communication.

## The Discursive Construction of a Virtual World
## (Karen Spear-Ellinwood)

"Meaning in language," Gee (2001) has written, "is tied to people's experiences of situated action in the material and social world" (p. 715). Our social worlds, however, now include *virtual worlds*, where millions of people are creating new social networks in a collectively imagined space that becomes a part of real life, because, for the participants, these social relations have real meaning.

Second Life (SL), one such virtual world, has been touted by its creators as the beginning of the "metaverse" (Ondrejka & Rosedale, 2003), a universe that comprises intersecting technologies that traverse the real and virtual worlds (Smart, Cascio, & Paffendorf, 2007). SL emerged as a nongaming activity system; that is, there is no common purpose among all participants except the sustenance of the virtual world itself. However, a great variety of social and professional groups within the larger activity system define their own purposes of engagement. These in-world relationships and social networks are discursively constructed; that is, they are cogenerated by the integration, to varying degrees, of participants' talk and actions directed at a common purpose (Engestrom, Engestrom, & Kerosuo, 2003).

This virtual discourse in SL involves the combination of simulated, face-to-face interaction and the enactment of new literacies—posttypographic, electronic, or digitally mediated literacies (Goffman, 1967/1982, 1974; Lankshear & Knobel, 2003). New sets and forms of social practices have emerged in this new social space and continue to develop "at a rapid rate," tracking changes in technologies (Lankshear & Knobel, 2003, p. 16). As in the real world, these social practices are embedded in the "social languages"—genres of Discourse,[2] such as those found in professional disciplines, families, friends, various musical forms, and other "distinctive cultures or social groups" (Gee, 2001, p. 719). SL social groups and networks address a wide range of interests that one finds in the real world (e.g., book clubs, science centers, second-language learners, or people looking to make friends).

Although in 2007 the Linden Corporation, which owns SL, added voice as a means of communication, SL residents continue to use reading and writing to mediate conversation and to build social relations. As they get around in that virtual environment, they need to learn to create what Turkle (2005) calls a "second self," embodied in "avatars" that navigate this new sociotechnical environment. In learning how to develop full "digital citizenship" (Lankshear & Knobel, 2004) then, SL residents need to acquire a hybrid SL Discourse. Understanding what it is and how it can be learned opens up to researchers, literally, a whole new world of virtual ethnography.

What follows is an example from a study in SL (Spear-Ellinwood, 2007), in which three features of SL Discourse became apparent: (1) resident–artifact interaction and ambient artifact intrusion; (2) simulation of face-to-face interaction through the use of computer-animated gestures, facial expressions, or moods; and (3) information-related spaces, such as SL islands devoted to libraries and universities, where newcomers' SL Discourse is mediated by engaging in activities with more experienced residents, scripted objects, and textual artifacts. Below is a discussion of some data reflecting just one area, the simulation of interaction in the virtual discourse of SL.

While exploring one of the many SL "islands" or areas devoted to libraries and universities, Spear-Ellinwood was invited to join a book club discussion held in an outdoor amphitheater (see Figure 3.1). The discussion was remarkable for residents' efforts to simulate these features, as well as the dynamics and flow of real-life conversation. In addition, the exchanges were rather rapid considering that participants used the text-based chat feature.

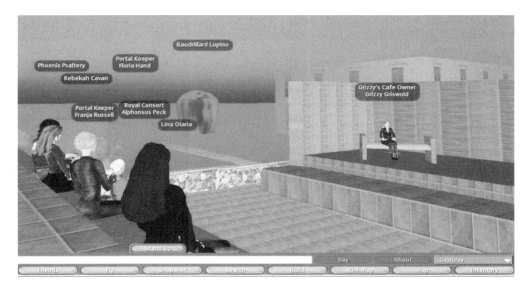

FIGURE 3.1. Second Life book discussion.

Spear-Ellinwood remained standing on the lawn just outside the amphitheater, not sure whether she should enter. She pointed her computer's mouse at the book club members and then at the moderator, which had the effect of moving her avatar's head as if she were looking around. The members continued their discussion, but one of the members interrupted the discussion to invite Spear-Ellinwood to join them. She initially indicated reluctance to join, because she had not read the book. But she was assured, "That's OK, some of us haven't. =)," combining a mixture of casual conversation and "emoticons" familiar to many with no SL experience through e-mail Discourse. After thanking the girl, Spear-Ellinwood sat down. The other residents turned their heads to look at her; some nodded, then returned their gaze to the next speaker.

Members seemed to coordinate their turns at talk as one would in a face-to-face encounter. Whenever someone spoke, others would turn their avatars' heads to face the speaker, displaying attentiveness, often nodding in agreement or acknowledgment. One resident "sipped" cappuccino, most participants sat in close proximity, and some used nicknames in referring to others, indicating prior familiarity. As for politeness, residents did not simply "disapparate," to use a Harry Potter term for magically disappearing, when they left the discussion. Instead, they waited for a pause and advised the group that they needed to leave, as one might expect in a real-life book club discussion at a local library. Upon leaving, residents indicated their enjoyment of the discussion and how good it was to visit with other members. One member even let others know that she would be away from her avatar for a moment by using an SL term, "*afk*, one sec," possibly not to seem rude.

Through these actions and talk, the book club participants discursively co-constructed a relaxed and respectful atmosphere that welcomed newcomers and return members alike. The residents in the book club discussion generally took turns at talk, and most often built on what others were saying. Consider the following exchange:

RC: If you have kids, you know that negative attention is better than no attention.

FR: Wouldn't they know they won't get the kind of attention that is worth getting?

GG [Moderator]: They can't do anything positive to get noticed so they do something negative.

[Karen]: When you respond to someone doing crazy things they get off on it.

FR: But they don't have power.

AP: They do, if you react to them.

PP: Exactly—it's the grown-up version of a temper tantrum.

Immediately following these exchanges, GG, the moderator, changed the topic abruptly—"Anyone familiar with the website *www.somthingawful.com*?"—

before the others were ready to surrender the floor. While FR, LO, and Karen wanted to complete their thoughts, PP assisted GG in taking the floor and changing the topic. When this did not work, the FH stepped in and threw the moderator a line to retake the floor and change the topic:

GG [Moderator]: <u>Anyone familiar with the website www.somethingawful.com?</u>

FR: They just have attention. They're different things.

PP: People have as much power as you give them.

LO: They have power to disrupt a study if you react to them.

FH: <u>Yes, Goss [shortened form of GG's name]</u>

GG <u>[Moderator]: They have a whole section dedicated to griefing sl.</u>

The underlined text is akin to shouting down other participants in conversations to ensure change in topic and confirm the moderator's line as manager of the discussion, having the right to change the topic. GG used the term "griefing" and later "griefer," referring to an experience unique to virtual Discourse and a group that these SL members perceive negatively. For the uninitiated, the conversation would not make sense. More experienced members advised that griefers are "ham avatars or a green cartoon duck in a Nazi uniform" that "cause trouble." When LO asked what a ham avatar is, GG responded, "They are hams with faces and arms and legs," a corollary to which can be found in another virtual medium, the cartoon.

The hybridity of virtual discourse allowed Spear-Ellinwood, from the beginning, to review the verbatim text of the conversation by opening up a small window called "chat history." In general, the chat feature was "successful at supporting interaction between strangers" and "a basic building block of online interaction—in a more natural way than other environments" (Brown & Bell, 2004, p. 357), such as asynchronous chat rooms. Overall these various encounters reflect what John-Steiner (2000) calls "distributed collaboration," which arises spontaneously and does not anticipate a long-term relationship or goals. The discourse work is aimed at accomplishing a specific objective, achievable in the immediate time period or short term.

The research literature has only begun to address the complexities of making and using technology to assist learning, which are pronounced more sharply in such online communities where "users are expected to virtually visit and interact with other users" in what is aptly described as "sociotechnical interaction networks," or STINs (Barab, Schatz, & Schekler, 2004, pp. 25–26). Virtual worlds represent limitless possibilities for building social networks, establishing sociotechnical practices for teaching and learning. Yet to take full advantage of these new spaces for research and learning, as virtual ethnographers, we need to become digital citizens to reach a more nuanced understanding of the role of real-life Discourse in developing communicative competence in *virtual* Discourse.

## IMPLICATIONS FOR RESEARCH AND PRACTICE

We started this chapter by seeking to provide examples of discourse patterns of diverse students (and others) in multiple settings, as the title indicates. However, in preparing the manuscript, we have come to a new understanding of what counts in this type of work. What counts are not necessarily the discourse patterns of diverse students per se, but the diverse range of discourses available to students, and those they create and participate in within the complex linguistic ecologies of their lives.

Like language itself, discourse patterns are never fixed and static but are continually changing and evolving, influenced by existing language policies and practices. These policies and practices both reflect and produce the discursive ideological positions, and the social and material conditions that surround and are embedded in them (Gilmore, 2008; Pennycook, 1998). Diverse discourses, each carrying unique sets of complex ideologies and identities, are ubiquitous in the linguistic landscapes. These discourses continually lure and repel potential participating members. Individuals continually negotiate their way through this multilayered language terrain, adopting and adapting their own blend of linguistic repertoires and discourse styles—constructing and reconstructing complex identities through their everyday language practices.

Each of the five excerpts of studies described in this chapter addresses this dynamic discursive process. Consider for example, Reyes's example about the "hybridity of practices" created from the family's combination of persons, codes, and experiences, and the children's necessities of schooling in a language that must also become their own. Note also how elementary school-age students in the González study attend to and explore competing discursive practices within a "volatile and contentious debate," which led to what she describes as the "alternate hardening and blurring of language ideologies." Wyman's study further illustrates how youth in endangered language communities construct themselves in complex ways over time "using all that their linguistic and cultural repertoires have to offer." And finally Rubinstein-Ávila and Spear-Ellinwood introduce the powerful "hail" of new (and yet to be fully explored) language practices in multimodal spaces and virtual discourse communities for the youth of today and the future.

The choice of discourse from any available array is always mediated by multiple factors, including omnipresent and competing language ideologies that, with differential success, "hail" children or youth toward, and away from, particular discourses and ways of understanding. These ideologies, we learn from the González and Wyman examples, are always implicated in the emergent subjectivities of children and youth; and these developing subjectivities always help to mediate the diffuse hailing of language ideologies toward one particular life with discourse or another. Both are also striking examples of the importance of schools as sociocultural institutions that may be deeply implicated in, say, the interpellation of choice to the detriment of the intergenerational survival of the indigenous language, in just a brief 5 years, in Wyman's case, or the resistance and counterpellation, presented by González, leading to student choice and agency in favor of bilingualism, even when constrained by the power of the state. Teachers must be keenly aware, through their theoretical development, that whatever language policy they choose or are forced to enact in their classrooms will have broader implications outside the classroom for the lives of students and families.

Finally, the last two examples illustrate the negotiation of discourse options, with strong implications for practice. The first example points to the development of what Rubinstein-Ávila calls creative spaces and alternative pedagogies that seek to support and expand development of multimodal discourses to produce knowledge that addresses problems that matter to youth. The contrast of action with the usual school-based practices is noteworthy, but so are the possibilities for creating a fusion of school and afterschool initiatives to develop an education that recruits rather than alienates youth from doing intellectual work with palpable consequences for their lives. The next example, by Spear-Ellinwood, also illustrating multimodal alternatives, brings us into the discourse practices of a virtual culture, the sort of space that is alluring to children and youth but generally excluded from classroom life. The point here is that adults in education must also engage the virtual, not just the material, if they are to discover its open-ended possibilities and exploit its potential for creativity and collaboration in thinking.

These examples point to the need for research on practices that allow students' agentive choices and blur boundaries between informal and formal modes of schooling. Teachers, too, need to be aware of their own agentive everyday language policy roles in the classroom, enacting practices that privilege a range of discourses and facilitate students' abilities to explore critically how they use and think about language, and how they exercise language choice, change, and possibility.

## NOTE

1. Participant's nickname is a pseudonym.
2. We follow Gee's (2001) convention of distinguishing between Discourse (with a capital *D*), to mean "forms of life" and discourse (with a small *d*) to denote "language use."

## REFERENCES

Althusser, L. (1971). Ideology and ideological state apparatuses. In *Lenin and philosophy and other essays* (pp. 127–186). New York: Monthly Review Press.

Alvermann, D. E., Hagood, M. C., & Williams, K. B. (2001). Image, language and sound: Making meaning with popular culture texts. *Reading Online, 4*(11). Retrieved March 3, 2007, from *www.reading.org/newliteracieslit_index. asp?href=?newliteacies/action/alvermann/index.html*.

Barab, S., Schatz, S., & Schekler, R. (2004). Using activity theory to conceptualize online community and using online community to conceptualize activity theory. *Mind, Culture, and Activity, 11*(1), 25–47.

Bayley, R., & Schecter, S. (Ed.). (2003). *Language socialization in bilingual and multilingual societies.* Clevedon, UK: Multilingual Matters.

Bernstein, B. (1971). *Class, codes and control: Vol. 1. Theoretical studies toward a sociology of language.* London: Routledge & Kegan Paul.

Blackburn, M. V. (2003). Disrupting the (hetero)normative: Exploring literacy performances and identity work with queer youth. *Journal of Adolescent and Adult Literacy, 46*(4), 312–324.

Blackburn, M. V. (2005). Exploring literacy performances and power dynamics at The Loft: Queer youth reading the world and the word. *Research in the Teaching of English, 37,* 467–490.

Brown, B., & Bell, M. (2004). CSCW at play: "There" as a collaborative virtual environment. In J. D. Herbsleb & G. Olson (Eds.), *Proceedings CSCW,* pp. 350–359.

Budwig N. (2001). Language socialization and children's entry into schooling (Preface to special issue). *Early Education Development, 12*(3), 295–302.

Cazden, C., John, V., & Hymes, D. (Eds.). (1972). *Functions of language in the classroom.* New York: Teachers College Press.

Chavez, V., & Soep, E. (2005). Youth radio and the pedagogy of collegiality. *Harvard Educational Review, 54*(4), 409–434.

Dorian, N. (Ed.). (1989). *Investigating obsolescence: Studies in language contact and death.* New York: Cambridge University Press.

Engestrom, Y., Engestrom, R., & Kerosuo, H. (2003). The discursive construction of collaborative care. *Applied Linguistics, 24*(3), 286–315.

Fishman, J. (1991). *Reversing language shift: Theoretical and empirical foundations of assistance to threatened languages.* Clevedon, UK: Multilingual Matters.

Fishman, J. A. (Ed.). (2001). *Can threatened languages be saved?* Clevedon, UK: Multilingual Matters.

Freire, P., & Macedo, D. (1987). *Literacy: Reading the word and the world.* New York: Bergin & Garvey.

Gal, S. (1979). *Language shift: Social determinants of linguistic change in bilingual Austria.* New York: Academic Press.

Garrett, P., & Baquedano-López, P. (2002). Language socialization: Reproduction and continuity, transformation and change. *Annual Review of Anthropology, 31,* 339–361.

Gee, J. P. (2001). Reading as situated language: A sociocognitive perspective. *Journal of Adolescent and Adult Literacy, 44*(8), 714–725.

Gilmore, P. (2008, April). *Creating and recreating language communities: Verbal practices transform social structure and reconstruct identities on a Kenya hillside and in the Alaska interior.* Paper presented at the Sociolinguistics Symposium 17 Micro and Macro Connections, Amsterdam, The Netherlands.

Gilmore, P., & Glatthorn, A. (1982). *Children in and out of school: Ethnography and education.* Norwood, NJ: Ablex.

Goffman, E. (1974). *Frame analysis: An essay on the organization of experience.* Cambridge, MA: Harvard University Press.

Goffman, E. (1982). *Interaction ritual.* New York: Pantheon Books. (Original work published 1967)

González, N. (2001). *I am my language: Discourses of women and children in the borderlands.* Tucson: University of Arizona Press.

González, N. (2005). Children in the eye of the storm: Language ideologies in a dual language school. In A. C. Zentella (Ed.), *Building on strength: Language and literacy in Latino families and communities* (pp. 162–174). New York: Teachers College Press.

González, N., Moll, L. C., & Amanti, C. (Eds.). (2005). *Funds of knowledge: Theorizing practices in household, communities, and classrooms*. Mahwah, NJ: Erlbaum.

Gregory, E., Volk, D., & Long, S. (2004). A sociocultural approach to learning. In *Many pathways to literacy: Young children learning with siblings, grandparents, peers and communities* (pp. 6–20). New York: Routledge Falmer.

Gutiérrez, K., & Rogoff, B. (2003). Cultural ways of learning: Individual traits or repertoires of practice. *Educational Researcher, 32*(5), 19–25.

Hamilton, S. F., & Hamilton, M. A. (Eds.). (2004). *The youth development handbook: Coming of age in American communities*. Thousand Oaks, CA: Sage.

Heath, S. B. (1983). *Ways with words: Language, life, and work in communities and classrooms*. New York: Cambridge University Press.

hooks, b. (1989). *Talking back: Thinking feminist, thinking black*. Boston: South End Press.

Hornberger, N. (2002). Multilingual language policies and the continua of biliteracy: An ecological approach. *Language Policy, 1*, 27–51.

Hornberger, N. (2007). Biliteracy, transnationalism, multimodality, and identity: Trajectories across time and space. *Linguistics and Education, 18*, 325–334.

Hull, G. (2004). AT LAST: Youth culture and digital media: New literacies for new times. *Research in the Teaching of English, 38*(2), 229–233.

Hull, G. A., & Katz, M. L. (2005). Crafting an agentive self: Case studies of digital storytelling. *Research in the Teaching of English, 41*(1), 43–81.

John-Steiner, V. (2000). *Creative collaboration*. New York: Oxford University Press.

Krauss, M. (1997). The indigenous languages of the north: A report on their present state. *Senri Ethnological Studies, 44*, 1–34.

Kulick, D. (1992). *Language shift and cultural reproduction: Socialization, syncretism and self in a Papua New Guinean village*. New York: Cambridge University Press.

Labov, W. (1972). *Language in the inner city: Studies in the Black English vernacular*. Philadelphia: University of Pennsylvania Press.

Lankshear, C., & Knobel, M. (2003). *New literacies: Changing knowledge and classroom learning*. New York: Open University Press.

Lee, C. (1993). *Signifying as a scaffold for literacy interpretation: The pedagogical implications of an African-American discourse genre*. Urbana, IL: National Council of Teachers of English.

Lee, T. (2007, Spring). "If they want Navajo to be learned, then they should require it in all schools": Navajo teenagers' experiences, choices, and demands regarding Navajo language. *Wicazo Sa Review*, pp. 7–33.

May, S. (2005). Language rights: Moving the debate forward. *Journal of Sociolinguistics, 9*(3), 319–347.

McCarty, T., Romero-Little, M. E., & Zepeda, O. (2006). Native American youth discourses on language shift and retention: Ideological cross-currents and their implications for language planning. *International Journal of Bilingual Education and Bilingualism, 9*(5), 659–677.

Meek, B. (2007). Respecting the language of elders: Ideological shift and linguistic discontinuity in a Northern Athapascan community. *Journal of Linguistic Anthropology, 17*(1), 23–43.

Mendoza-Denton, N. (2008). *Homegirls: Language and cultural practice among Latina youth gangs*. Malden, MA: Wiley Blackwell.

Mertz, E. (1989). Sociolinguistic creativity: Cape Breton Gaelic's linguistic "tip." In N. Dorian (Ed.), *Investigating obsolescence: Studies in language contact and death* (pp. 103–117). New York: Cambridge University Press.

Moll, L. C., & González, N. (1994). Lessons from research with language minority children. *Journal of Reading Behavior, 26,* 439–456.

Pennycook, A. (1998). *English and the discourses of colonialism.* London: Routledge.

Philips, S. U. (1983). *The invisible culture.* New York: Longman.

Reyes, I. (2006). Exploring connections between emergent biliteracy and bilingualism. *Journal of Early Childhood Literacy, 6*(3), 267–292.

Reyes, I., Alexandra, D., & Azuara, P. (2007). Home literacy practices in Mexican households. *Cultura y Educación, 19* (4), 395–407.

Rosedale, P., & Ondrejka, C. (2003). Enabling player-created online worlds with grid computing and streaming. Retrieved March 27, 2007, from *www.gamdsutra.com/resource_guide/20030916/rosedale_01.shtml.*

Rubinstein-Ávila, E. (2006). Publishing "Equinox": An ethnographic tale of youth literacy development after school. *Anthropology and Education Quarterly, 37*(3), 255–272.

Rubinstein-Ávila, E. (2007a). In their words, sounds and images: After-school literacy programs for urban youth. In B. Guzzetti (Ed.), *Literacy for a new millennium: Adolescent literacy* (pp. 239–250). Westport, CT: Praeger.

Rubinstein-Ávila, E. (2007b). What counts as literacy for Yanira Lara: From the Dominican Republic to Drew High. *Reading Research Quarterly, 42*(4), 568–589.

Schieffelin, B., & Gilmore, P. (Eds.). (1986). *The acquisition of literacy: Ethnographic perspectives.* Norwood, NJ: Ablex.

Schultz, K., & Hull, G. (2002). Locating literacy theory in out-of-school contexts. In G. Hull & K. Schultz (Eds.), *School's out!: Bridging out-of-school literacies with classroom practice* (pp. 11–31). New York: Teachers College Press.

Smart, E. J., Cascio, J., & Paffendorf, J. (2007). *Metaverse roadmap overview.* Retrieved February 27, 2008, from *www.metaverseroadmap.org/MetaverseRoadmapOverview.pdf.*

Spear-Ellinwood, K. (2007, October). *Learning to get around in Second Life (SL): Through the mediation of SL residents, TuringBots, and interactive scripted objects.* Paper presented at the XIV Research Conference on Sociocultural Theory and Second Language Learning, University of Arizona, Tucson.

Street, B. V. (1995). *Social literacies.* London: Longman.

Turkle, S. (2005). *The second self: Computers and the human spirit.* Cambridge, MA: MIT Press.

Wong-Fillmore, L. (2000). Loss of family languages: Should educators be concerned? *Theory Into Practice, 39*(4), 203–210.

Wortham, S. (2005). Socialization beyond the speech event. *Journal of Linguistic Anthropology, 15*(1), 95–112.

Wyman, L. (2004). *Language shift, youth culture and ideology: A Yup'ik example.* Unpublished doctoral dissertation, Stanford University, Graduate School of Education, Stanford, CA.

Zentella, A. (1997). *Growing up bilingual: Puerto Rican children in New York.* Oxford, UK: Blackwell.

# CHAPTER 4

# Family Literacy

## *Recognizing Cultural Significance*

Patricia A. Edwards, Jeanne R. Paratore, *and* Nancy L. Roser

Teachers, administrators, parents, and communities acknowledge the critical role that families play in children's literacy lives, and these stakeholders often unite to create partnerships to improve children's literacy learning (Edwards, 2004; Edwards & Turner, 2008; Risko & Bromley, 2001). Collaborations often are conceptualized as a type of "family literacy" program, intended specifically to improve children's opportunities for academic success. It is ironic, then, that family literacy has also become center stage for conflicts and controversies around the role of parents in children's literacy education (Edwards & Turner, 2008). Paratore (2001) illustrated the essence of these tensions within the field of family literacy when she noted that "[family literacy] is a complex and muddy arena—one in which there is wide disagreement about the goals, purposes, and potential effects on the lives of those the programs are intended to serve" (p. 100). Battle lines have been particularly drawn around culturally and linguistically diverse families. There have been heated debates in academic and political circles about what constitutes good parenting, appropriate parent involvement, and acceptable literacy practices in homes and families (Edwards & Turner, 2008). Because these tensions have been well documented elsewhere (Auerbach, 1995; Taylor, 1993, 1997), this chapter focuses instead on:

- Research that addresses the importance of the family in children's learning.
- Research that identifies the variety of structures, cultures, childrearing practices, values, and beliefs within culturally, linguistically, and economically diverse families, and the importance of recognizing and capitalizing on the social and cultural capital of each child.

- Research that delineates "the texts" of home and their availability, uses, and purposes in families' lives.
- Research that characterizes effective practices related to home–school partnerships in literacy.

Throughout this chapter, our focus is on children and families who are considered to be outside the "mainstream," that is, families and children who are economically poor or linguistically and culturally diverse.

## IMPORTANCE OF THE FAMILY IN LITERACY LEARNING

The importance of families in supporting literacy learning has long been recognized (Clark, 1984; Durkin, 1966; Ferreiro & Teberosky, 1982; Hoover-Dempsey & Sandler, 1995; Huey, 1908; Lareau, 1989; Leichter, 1984; Leseman & DeJong, 1998; Marvin & Wright, 1997). Some have cited the family as a single source of continuity as children progress from year to year. For example, Potter (1989) noted: "Children will have many teachers in their lives, but only one family. It must be the family who helps maintain the continuity of the child's education" (p. 28).

However, studies have shown that not all families are equal in this regard (e.g., Heath, 1983; Laosa, 1977; Lareau, 1987, 1989, 2003; Leichter, 1984). Children in mainstream families acquire cultural and social capital that make it easier for them to adapt to the literacy environment of school. Such knowledge and familiarity make learning the "new" substantially easier. Conversely, culturally, linguistically, and economically diverse families often have home literacy practices dissimilar from those of families within the American mainstream culture. Purcell-Gates (1995) described in poignant detail what happens to children who do not grow up with these experiences when they enter school:

> Their social and cultural lives do not support this effort but rather exist separately and often compete with it. From the beginning they are challenged to learn a code that some of them may not even have realized existed before. ... The language and purposes for print encountered through formal education are foreign. The vocabulary is too hard and removed from their daily lives; the conventional syntax of exposition and complex fiction is unfathomable. Without a great deal of support and motivation, their level of literacy skill attainment is bound to be low compared with that of their peers who are natives of the educated literate world. (p. 183)

Lapp, Fisher, Flood, and Moore (2002) emphasized that parents in culturally and linguistically diverse families are not unaware of or unconcerned with their children's academic needs, but many are unequipped to give their children the necessary economic, social, and cultural capital (Bourdieu, 1986; Compton-Lilly, 2007) to deal in the "marketplace" of schools (Compton-Lilly, 2003, 2007; Lareau,

1989, 2003). For many, this process requires not only acquisition of language registers and literacy practices that are not a "natural" or authentic part of home and family discourse (Auerbach, 1989; Taylor, 1997; Valdés, 1996; Yaden & Paratore, 2002), but also, in a larger sense, the social construction of a new identity or redefinition of self (Gallimore, Weisner, Kaufman, & Bernheimier, 1989; Super & Harkness, 1986).

As documented in numerous studies, differences in the ways children are socialized at home into the literacy and language discourses of schools are consequential. They influence the ways children understand and use language (Davidson & Snow, 1995; Delpit, 1995; DeTemple & Beals, 1991; Hart & Risley, 1995; Heath, 1983; Purcell-Gates, 1996), the ways children come to understand the purposes and practices of reading and writing (Anderson & Stokes, 1984; Barnett, 1998; Compton-Lilly, 2003, 2007; Delgado-Gaitan, 1990; Delpit, 1995; Gadsden, 1995, 1998; Gee, 1989, 1996; Heath, 1983, 1986; Purcell-Gates, 1995; Schieffelin & Cochran-Smith, 1984), and the available cultural and social resources— "survival skills" (Clark, 1983)—as children make their way through schooling (Bourdieu, 1986; Bronfenbrenner, 1979; Clark, 1983; Lareau, 1989, 2003). In the next section, we examine the nature of various home environments in which children are ushered into literacy learning.

## THE CONTEXTS FOR FAMILY LITERACY

Much of the significant research in this area began in the 1980s, and over time, ethnographic studies of culturally diverse families and communities (e.g., Heath, 1982, 1983; Li, 2006; Purcell-Gates, 1996; Taylor, 1993; Taylor & Dorsey-Gaines, 1988; Teale, 1986) have deepened understanding of the specific features of the home environment that serve as domains for literacy learning and development.

Shirley Brice Heath's (1983) seminal ethnography offered portraits of the cultural "ways" with language and literacy in two working-class communities in the Piedmont area of the Carolinas, where Heath lived and taught: Roadville (a white community) and Trackton (a black community). In both Roadville and Trackton, Heath showed how reading served (to different degrees) varied uses: instrumental (to achieve practical daily tasks); social-interactional (to reach others, to make plans); news-related (to learn about distant events), and confirmational (to gain support for attitudes and beliefs). In addition, Roadville residents sometimes used reading for recreational/educational purposes (for entertainment or for reading to preschoolers). Heath's study showed that the home literacy practices of children from Roadville prepared them for school literacy practices in a way that Trackton children's home literacy practices did not.

Anderson and Stokes (1984) observed the home environment of low-income families and cultural groups for the purposes of describing the literacy events that characterize their daily lives. After 2,000 systematic observations and many behavior samples, they concluded that "literacy events function not as isolated bits of human activity but as connected units embedded in a functional system of activity generally involving prior, simultaneously occurring, and subsequent units of action" (p. 26).

Leitcher (1984) focused on preschool children's literacy experiences. She categorized literacy events and interactions within three broad categories: physical, interpersonal, and emotional and motivational environments. In a later study, Stewart (1995) confirmed the central finding that literacy events within families are natural, purposeful, and embodied with individual meaning.

Taylor and Dorsey-Gaines (1988) studied low-income, African American families residing in the inner city. They, too, found that mothers and their children used literacy day in and day out to accomplish the routines of daily living. However, like Heath's (1983) children of Trackton, the ways these children used literacy differed from the uses of literacy in the classroom. Consequently, for many of them, schooling meant failure.

The outcomes in these studies are largely representative of other studies (Compton-Lilly, 2003; Goodman, 1986; Purcell-Gates, 1995; Teale, 1986; Voss, 1996); although they vary somewhat in the particular categories of literacy observed, these studies share two important characteristics. First, in the words of Teale (1986), "Virtually all children in a literate society such as ours have numerous experiences with written language before they ever get to school" (p. 191). Second, in culturally, linguistically, and economically diverse families, literacy experiences are fundamentally grounded in social and cultural (rather than academic) purposes.

## TEXTS IN HOMES: THEIR AVAILABILITY, TYPES, AND USES

There are some widely held notions about the available reading materials in the homes of this nation's poorest children. The first concerns sheer numbers (i.e., there are *fewer* texts when families are poor). A corollary of that assertion is that there are also fewer sources from which to purchase or borrow texts in high-poverty communities. The second notion concerns the types of texts that are present—with low-income families more likely to value "practical" forms (e.g., records, directions, news) over more school-related forms of print. The third contention is that the texts in high-poverty homes are referenced and invoked in ways that differ from those in middle-class families, and these differences have implications for schooling. We examine each of these assumptions below.

### Access to Texts

In a computer-linked and increasingly urban country, it may seem as though all children are within reach of inexpensive texts. However, Neuman and Celano (2001) challenged the assumption "that books and other literacy-related resources are easily and equally accessible to all children and their families" (p. 11). By examining the print environments of four Philadelphia neighborhoods, they were able to compare access to print for low- and middle-income families. They found no bookstores in either of the two low-income neighborhoods, compared with 10 bookstores in the higher-income communities. Only four shops in low-income neighborhoods stocked texts geared to children, compared with 24 shops in the middle-income neighborhoods. No middle-grade or young adult books were available for purchase in the lower-income neighborhoods. Because the research team counted the number of titles of available children's materials in each location, it was possible to calculate the ratio of book titles per child resident. In the two middle-income neighborhoods, those ratios were 13:1 and 1:3. In the two low-income communities, the ratios of different titles per child were 1:20 and 1:300 (the latter choice a coloring book). Not even the public library offerings escaped distinctions across economic levels: "Low-income communities had smaller overall collections in their public library, fewer books per child, and more limited nighttime hours than those in the middle-income communities" (p. 22).

Worthy and Roser (2004) studied text accessibility in a class of 18 fifth graders who spoke Spanish as their first language. Each of the children was either an immigrant or the child of an immigrant. There was no bookstore of any kind within 10 miles of the children's school and no nearby library. Some children found paperback books for purchase at "that little store, you know down at the corner" (attached to a gas station) or received books from a family member ("My uncle he gave it to me") (p. 186). Children's self-reports gathered through individual interviews led the researchers to conclude that each student's personal library averaged about eight books, most provided by Reading Is Fundamental.

Other studies have addressed more directly the quantity of texts in low-income homes. Zill, Moore, Smith, Stief, and Coiro (1997) analyzed data from the 1986 National Longitudinal Survey of Labor Market Experience of Youth (NLSY) to describe and compare the circumstances for children whose families were recipients of Aid to Families with Dependent Children (AFDC), and those who were not. The researchers found that in nonpoor families, 81% of children ages 3–5 had 10 or more books. In poor families, the proportion of children owning 10 books decreased to 51% for recipients of AFDC, and 59% of children whose families were poor but did not receive aid.

In a study of home storybook reading in 44 low socioeconomic scale (SES) families, Roberts (2008) indicated that one-third reported having no primary-level language books in the home, whereas three-fourths reported fewer than five books, a marked contrast with case studies of children's literacy growth in middle-class homes. Baghban (1984), for example, studying her daughter's literacy from birth to age 3, listed 74 titles that her child owned. White's (1954) reading diary with her daughter Carol, from ages 2 to 5, referenced 111 titles shared and talked over with her child, some of which were selected from the library.

It might be argued that scarcity of texts at home can be offset by library use. However, Hemmeter (2006) reported that library use is affected by distance, income, availability of relevant material, and patrons' needs.

## Types of Texts in Homes

As a partial test of her hypothesis that learning to read is related to the number of *responses* to literacy opportunities that children make prior to first grade, Almy (1949) interviewed parents of children who were completing first grade. The 106 families represented a range of economic levels, as gauged by the occupations of the fathers (from "well-to-do" to unskilled and unemployed) (p. 66). Based on parent reports, she concluded that most of these children had requested that someone read to them, and many were interested in numbers, letters, and words prior to first grade. Nearly 18% of the parents mentioned that reading, writing, and playing school were among their children's favorite play activities. Ninety-one percent responded positively when asked whether their children used print materials in their play. Among the print materials were pads, pencils, words, magazines, scrapbooks, blackboards, comics, and coloring books. Parents also mentioned the practices of drawing, making up stories, and reading pictures in books (p. 79).

A decade later (in 1958), Dolores Durkin studied the home-centered literacy opportunities that might be associated with children's early reading. Although Durkin did not set out specifically to document the texts in the homes of children who did and did not read early, it is possible to glean some of these details from her data. In the first of two studies, Durkin identified 49 first graders as "early readers" (representing Asian American, African American, and European American heritages). Over half of the children were subsequently described as representing "lower" classes (Durkin, 1966, p. 16). Through interviews, the children's parents alluded to the kinds of texts in their children's lives—those borrowed from libraries, used for "playing school," and independently constructed during siblings' homework sessions. All of the parents reported reading to their children, 78% indicated they had given their children an alphabet book or a picture dictionary, and 41% acknowledged providing school-type beginning basal readers. Durkin noted that in each of the 49 families that developed a successful early reader, a blackboard was made available (sometimes with alphabet letters on the perimeter), encouraging what she described as the pervasive "scribbling" of early readers (p. 57).

Durkin's second study allowed for comparisons of both early readers and non-early readers. Of the 60 families (30 early readers and 30 non-early) who provided interviews, only three were nonwhite. Approximately one-fourth of the interviewed sample was reported to be low SES. [None of the early readers' families was bilingual, whereas four non-early readers were]. Materials in the homes included texts owned by children, blackboards, and pencils and paper. In both groups (early and non-early readers), alphabet books were implicated as playing "an especially important role in stimulating early interest in letter names and, sometimes, in letter sounds" (Durkin, 1966, p. 108). Also named as providing help to learners were the presence of environmental print and the act of *rereading* stories.

The previously cited study by Heath (1983) is also instructive in a discussion of text accessibility. As in the Durkin study, it was not Heath's purpose to catalog the specific texts that served the mill communities she studied, but her thick descriptions allow us to glean the types of texts found in homes. Home texts in Trackton included greeting cards received from out of town, the drawings of older children, newspapers, car brochures, advertisements, and official school information. Every home had official documents, such as birth certificates, tax forms, and loan notes. There were few magazines and no books except for school texts, the Bible, Sunday School leaflets and photograph albums. Heath noted: "Expectant mothers [in Trackton] neither buy nor are given ... books as gifts" (p. 76). In fact, the books or toys that were present had likely been brought into the community by an outsider. She found that neither grown-ups nor siblings made stories for children, and adults did not read to children.

Expectant mothers in Roadville (the white community) received cloth books that were often kept on a bookshelf in the baby's room. The majority of the children's books were not plot-driven, but were instead nursery rhymes, alphabet, and label books. Some, however, were sustained narratives such as *Goldilocks and the Three Bears*, realistic fiction, or simplified stories from the Bible (Heath, 1983, p. 157), as well as coloring books (p. 226).

Roadville children watched cartoons and *Sesame Street*, and were given *Sesame Street* books and music as gifts. The Bible was acknowledged as a central source of guidance, and the children's Sunday School booklets reflected Biblical lessons (Heath, 1983, p. 147). Yet Roadville children had little exposure to "extended fictive or fanciful stories" (p. 161) before nursery school.

In addition to the scriptures, Roadville women read home and gardening magazines, true story and celebrity magazines, newsweeklies, denominational magazines, and paperback novels but the latter texts were not read publicly (Heath, 1983, pp. 155–156). There were also flyers and catalogs that arrived through the mail. As well, print materials might include football programs, how-to leaflets, warranties, clipped recipes, obituaries, and household hints, as well as Sunday School lessons (pp. 220–221). It is unclear whether children had access to these varied adult texts.

Teale's (1986) study revealed that literacy materials were both wide-ranging and varied across low-SES homes (with equal numbers of African Americans, Anglos, and Mexican Americans). Although some homes had fewer children's books or texts, many did have such materials, including magazines, newspapers, paperbacks, library books, religious material, and television guides. Four homes had a designated area for writing. Teale concluded that there is reason to question the assumption that low-SES children enter school with "a dearth of literacy experience" (p. 192).

In a study of children selected who had entered first grade not reading conventionally but exited reading at or above grade level, Roser, Hoffman, Kastler, and Sharp (1994) interviewed parents of 47 children drawn from 15 different first-grade classrooms. To conduct the interviews, researchers visited homes that spanned economic levels. Parents were asked to talk about the home literacy events that might help to explain the success of their children. Among the explanatory themes developed from parent interviews was "making text available" to children. Many of the children displayed battered cardboard boxes (or some other container) filled with their own books. Types of books included Dr. Seuss, Little Golden Books, wordless picture books, and children's magazines. Parents also provided (and showed) the materials and spaces their children used for creating texts—crayons, markers, magnetic letters, paper, and often a child-size table or desk.

Purcell-Gates (1996) described the range and frequency of literacy practices among 20 low-SES families residing in the Boston metropolitan area. The families in her study relied on print most frequently for entertainment (consulting the television schedule, checking the newspaper for movie times, playing board games that require reading, and reading books and magazines for pleasure). Families also frequently relied on print to accomplish daily tasks (reading coupons, ads, and text on containers).

Later, Duke and Purcell-Gates (2003) reanalyzed the field notes of Purcell-Gate's 1996 study of home literacy events to identify the specific genres of text that were present. They then compared these data with data drawn from Duke's (2000a, 2000b) study of print-centered activities in 10 first-grade classrooms, which allowed them to account for the genres used in home, school, and both. A Venn diagram of the resultant texts found in homes and/or schools appears in Figure 4.1.

In a review of literature on parenting and emerging literacy skills, Landry and Smith (2006) pointed to the need for more research, arguing that although there is evidence of the relation between parents' interactive strategies and children's language development, "less is known about relations between the home literacy environment and aspects of children's early literacy skills other than language" (p. 136). Even so, it is possible to draw a tentative conclusion, as did Teale (1986), that homes contain various texts.

## Texts in Use

Denny Taylor (1993) advised that differences in texts between homes of poverty and relative plenty should not lead to a deficit theory of literacy growth: "Sixteen years of ethnographic research in families and communities have taught me that sex, race, economic status, and setting cannot be used as significant correlates of literacy" (p. 551). Like Moll and Greenberg, (1990), Taylor cautioned those who would observe and interpret literacy environments not to be quick to dismiss the complex knowledge that families represent and transmit independently of wealth or schooling. Brooks (2006) offered an additional tenet: Even when children share membership in communities, one cannot assume commonalities in their experiences, knowledge, or interpretations. A similar argument was made by Compton-Lilly (2007) on the basis of her study of two economically poor Puerto Rican families.

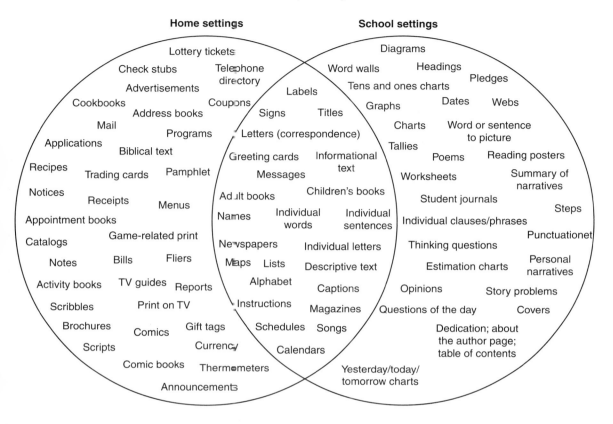

**FIGURE 4.1.** Comparison of text forms in home and school. From Duke and Purcell-Gates (2003). Copyright 2003 by the International Reading Association. Reprinted by permission.

Acknowledging the varied texts in children's lives, Teale (1986) described nine domains of family activity mediated by literacy. These practices included literacy related to "1) daily living routines; 2) entertainment; 3) school-related activities; 4) work; 5) religion; 6) interpersonal communication; 7) participation in information networks; 8) storybook time; and 9) literacy for the sake of teaching/learning literacy" (pp. 185–187). The patterns of literacy occurrence among these domains varied across the families he studied. Teale suggested that to understand the variability, it is necessary to "unpackage terms such as SES and ethnicity and keep at the forefront of our considerations that literacy is a social process and a cultural practice" (p. 193).

Further evidence of the diversity of texts in use in nonmainstream homes is drawn from a study by Melzi, Paratore, and Krol-Sinclair (2000). They studied 69 mothers, all of whom were immigrants to the United States and first-language Spanish speakers, representing 11 different countries. All mothers were participants in a family literacy program and were randomly selected to form two groups: high-education (9 to 12 years of schooling) and low-education (7 or fewer years of schooling). As part of their family literacy program classes, the mothers completed literacy logs each day, detailing literacy activities in which they engaged alone or with their children, and these logs provided the data source for the study. The authors analyzed and categorized 5,427 literacy log entries using the categories developed by Teale (1986). Across all participants, mothers were most likely to report on Literacy in Leisure activities (e.g., storybook time, entertainment, television viewing). They found no significant difference in the report of these types of activities by level of education. In addition to Literacy in Leisure activities, all mothers dedicated time and attention to Literacy for the Sake of Teaching or Learning. The data indicated that mothers spent more time with texts and activities related to their children's learning than to their own, with low-education mothers reporting more than three times as many child-related activities, and high-education mothers reporting more than five times as many child-related activities.

McTavish (2007), in a case study of the literacy support provided by a working-class family, also weighed the data against misconceptions about the literacy activities in low-income families (cf. Purcell-Gates, 2000; Taylor & Dorsey-Gaines, 1988). McTavish observed the focal child Katie being both initiated and instructed into purpose-filled literacy in her home through events such as helping to record upcoming events on the calendar, making a greeting card, copying a requested name, and selecting a television show using the onscreen guide. Katie was read to both in the afternoon and before bedtime, with her father the purveyor of information texts, and her mother of fiction. Katie owned a variety of books. She also produced her own lists and, when marketing, helped her mother read the adult-prepared shopping list, guided by her mother's cueing directives to use sounds associated with the initial letter. Furthermore, Katie was able to appropriate the models of reading that her parents, particularly her mother, provided.

Ultimately, it is not the differences in quantity, types, or access to texts that mark the essential messages to schools and teachers. Nor is it the simple listing of activities that involve reading and writing (Barton & Hamilton, 1998). Rather, the most successful portraits, practices, and programs must grow from the recognition of the literate practices in diverse home settings to build on those literacies in meaningful ways. But such efforts are neither readily conceived nor easily implemented (Allen, 2007; Goatley, 1997; McCarthey, 1997; Taylor & Dorsey-Gaines, 1988). In the next section, we present work that chronicles home–school partnerships that effectively join the literacies of home and school.

## SUPPORTING THE EXCHANGE OF INFORMATION BETWEEN PARENTS AND TEACHERS

Over the last two decades, motivated by growing evidence of the important role that parents play in children's academic success (Boethel, 2004; Henderson & Berla, 1994), both research and practice related to various forms of home–school partnerships have proliferated. Some research focuses specifically on intervention for children; other research, on improving both parent and child literacy; and still other research, on improving children's literacy learning opportunities by joining home and school literacies together in various ways. (See DeBruin-Parecki & Krol-Sinclair [2003] and Wasik [2004] for reviews of these various types of programs.) In this section, we limit our focus to the third type of program that takes a reciprocal approach to learning—one that is grounded in a belief that when teachers, parents, and children exchange and build on information about home and school literacy routines and practices, children's opportunities for literacy learning are enriched and expanded both at home and at school.

The work of Moll, González, and their colleagues has been especially instructive in understanding how to combine family and school resources (González, Moll, & Amanti, 2005; González et al., 1995; Moll, 1992; Moll, Amanti, Neff, & González, 1992). Their work is grounded in the importance of discovering *funds of knowledge,* "historically accumulated and culturally developed bodies of knowledge and skills essential for household or individual functioning and well-being" (González et al., 1995, p. 443). These researchers argued that learning about the funds of knowledge that exist in virtually every family creates instructional opportunities that not only acknowledge and honor what families know and do but also enrich and extend understanding of what it means to "do" literacy in and out of school.

A number of studies have built on the idea of uncovering and building on household funds of knowledge in various ways. For example, Paratore and her colleagues (Krol-Sinclair, Hindin, Emig, & McClure, 2003; Paratore, Hindin, Krol-Sinclair, & Durán, 1999; Paratore, Hindin, Krol-Sinclair, Durán, & Emig, 1999; Paratore et al., 1995) conducted two studies to examine effects of engaging parents in the construction of literacy portfolios on parents' and teachers' attitudes and actions. Working with low-income, immigrant Latino families enrolled in a family literacy program and teachers in an urban elementary school, the researchers taught parents how to observe and record their children's uses of literacy at home, and provided direction in the types of materials to collect. Parents were asked to bring the portfolios to regularly scheduled parent–teacher conferences, and teachers were asked to invite parents to share the samples and their understanding of their children's developing literacy. The researchers reported that with the home portfolios as a context, teachers and parents engaged in collaborative and connected conversations about children's learning.

Edwards, Pleasants, and Franklin (1999) interviewed parents to elicit their *stories*—"the narratives gained from open-ended conversations and interviews" (p. xvii) about traditional and nontraditional early literacy activities and experiences, as well as the ways they attempted to connect home and school. Much like the parents in the home portfolio studies cited previously, parents in this study (independent of their own literacy proficiency) became the "more knowledgeable other" (p. xxiv) as they shared information about their children, and described their home environments and the ways they worked and played with their children. In the families they studied, Edwards and colleagues found both significant strengths and needs—parents who were deeply committed to helping their children succeed in schools, while confronting harsh realities in their personal lives. The researchers noted that collecting parents' stories forced them to "envision other people's realities that do not fit into our schema of 'family,' 'child,' 'community,' or 'school'" (p. 61).

In another study, one acknowledging the significance of the church in the life of African American children, McMillon and Edwards (2008) examined literacy practices in the African American church environment and considered how these practices might connect with, reinforce, and support literacy practices within the school environment. Building on the Anderson and Stokes (1984) religion category, McMillon and Edwards identified literacy domains that crossed home and church settings. By uncovering the routine literacy events and interactions in the African American church, McMillon and Edwards hoped to establish among teachers of African American students awareness of an often unrecognized but fairly widely held "fund of knowledge" for many of their children.

Other studies have focused more narrowly on introducing parents to particular reading or writing skills, and on the types of interventions that influence teachers' understanding and use of family literacies. Krol-Sinclair (1996) taught immigrants with limited formal education effective storybook reading strategies and invited them to read aloud to children in elementary school classrooms. She examined the effects of parents' acquisition and use of reading strategies on their knowledge of classrooms and understanding of their role in children's learning, and of teachers' attitudes and perceptions of parents' knowledge about literacy and the role they play in their children's learning. She found that parents incorporated features into the read-aloud strategies that were not directly addressed in training—personal read-aloud strategies they added to those strategies that were directly taught. Moreover, their limited literacy skills did not prevent parents from successfully engaging in read-alouds of carefully selected and rehearsed books.

In a study involving children in two first-grade classrooms and their parents, Steiner (2008) studied the effects of an intervention that provided parents with information about how to support their children in school, and provided teachers with information about parents' home literacy practices. Steiner examined effects on three groups: children whose parents and teacher participated in the intervention; children for whom only the teacher participated; and a comparison group in which neither parents nor teachers participated. Parents in the treatment group showed statistically significant differences in the initiation of effective storybook reading strategies at the pre- and postreading stages. The intervention also promoted the treatment classroom teacher's knowledge and use of students' home literacy practices. The treatment classroom teacher incorporated specific opportunities to involve parents in children's literacy learning that led to an increase in parent–teacher collaboration. Results also indicated changes in the beliefs of parents and teachers about the role of parents in their children's literacy learning. Parents who participated in the intervention reported that they developed a stronger understanding of their children's literacy development and strengthened their relationships with the teacher as a result of their increased time spent in school. Finally, a combination of teacher and parent participation in the intervention led to statistically significant differences in students' scores on the Concepts about Print assessment compared to students in the control classroom (but no differences in their alphabet knowledge, phonemic awareness, or in-context reading).

Studies of this type are few and almost always limited by small sample sizes. Nonetheless, taken together, they provide evidence that such approaches, in which both parents and teachers assume roles of giving and receiving information, have the potential to increase children's opportunities to learn both at home and at school.

## SUMMARY OF MAJOR FINDINGS

Evidence related directly to understanding families and their interactions in children's literacy learning can be summarized as three major findings:

1. Low-SES and/or culturally/linguistically nonmainstream homes are not bereft of print, but they may have fewer school-like texts.
2. The literacy knowledge and abilities promoted by the parents and other caregivers in low-SES and/or culturally/linguistically nonmainstream homes may not be readily mapped onto the tasks and expectations of schools and classrooms.
3. Home–school partnerships based on exchanging information can help parents and teachers form positive and powerful relationships, and enable schools and families to see parent involvement as a shared responsibility.

## IMPLICATIONS FOR CLASSROOM PRACTICE

Acting on the evidence requires respectful collaboration with families and communities, marked by recognition of the funds of knowledge (González, Moll, & Amanti, 2005) available to all families. As Moll (1999) noted, "As educators we must not assume that we can only teach the families how to do school, but that we can learn valuable lessons by coming to know the families, and by taking the time to establish the social relationships necessary to create personal links between households and classrooms" (p. xiii).

The review of research leads us to three basic principles:

1. Collaborate based on shared knowledge. As teachers, we must take responsibility for establishing routines and procedures that not only help us get to know families but also help families get to know us. Studies indicate numerous ways to exchange information, including home visits, classroom visits, conferences, col-

lecting home literacy artifacts, and informational workshops. Of importance is the recognition that teachers and parents may be predisposed to particular types of interactions, and choosing those that "fit" both the setting and the individuals requires thoughtful consideration of factors that might influence participation and "disclosure" of useful information.

2.  Expand information and understanding by asking (and answering) important questions: How can we integrate and build on what we learn about children and their families as we teach the "required" curriculum in literacy and the language arts, and across the content areas? How can understanding of family discourse patterns influence classroom discourse and encourage children to engage with classroom activities? How can an understanding of family routines, responsibilities, and literacy practices influence choices of homework assignments?

3.  Support parents' interest and motivation for their children's academic success. Uncover resources for increasing accessibility to varied and appropriate texts, and establish programs that provide parents sustained instruction in supporting their children's literacy learning.

## IMPLICATIONS FOR FUTURE RESEARCH

Two decades ago, Taylor and Dorsey-Gaines (1988) put forth the following challenge to educators: "In trying to understand families' home literacy environments we must also try to understand ourselves, true and false, personal perceptions and deceptions, the ethnocentrism of our own mental baggage. It is here that we, as researchers, educators, and policymakers who wish to enhance the learning opportunities of young children, must begin" (pp. 202–203).

Unfortunately, we are still struggling to address this challenge. To continue this effort, we need to achieve the following:

1.  Develop understanding of how parents' beliefs correlate with children's beliefs (Sonnenschein et al., 1997).
2.  Examine how schools can build on the diverse abilities and beliefs that children bring to school, in an effort to achieve educational equality across class, race, and ethnicity (Purcell-Gates, 2000).
3.  Increase understanding of how teachers and parents can work together to create the most advantageous contexts for children (Edwards, 2004).
4.  Discover factors that influence parents' sense of self-efficacy in improving their children's educational outcomes (Lapp et al., 2002).

## CONCLUDING REMARKS

In 1978, Lightfoot recorded the following comment on the state of parent–teacher interaction:

There are very few opportunities for parents and teachers to come together for meaningful, substantive discussion. In fact, schools organize public, ritualistic occasions that do not allow for real contact, negotiation, or criticism between parents and teachers. Rather, they are institutionalized ways of establishing boundaries between insiders (teachers) and interlopers (parents) under the guise of polite conversation and mature cooperation. (pp. 27–29)

Three decades have passed, but there has been relatively little change in the routines schools enact to bring parents and teachers together to serve children better. Our review of the evidence convinces us that it need not be this way. Although there is much for us to learn about ways to bridge home and school literacy practices effectively, we know enough to do better than we are currently doing.

## REFERENCES

Allen, J. (2007). *Creating welcoming schools: A practical guide to home–school partnerships with diverse families.* New York: Teachers College Press.

Almy, M. C. (1949). *Children's experiences prior to first grade and success in beginning reading.* New York: Bureau of Publications, Teachers College, Columbia University.

Anderson, A., & Stokes, S. (1984). Social and institutional influences on the development and practice of literacy. In H. Goelman, A. Oberg, & F. Smith (Eds.), *Awakening to literacy* (pp. 24–37). Exeter, NH: Heinemann.

Auerbach, E. R. (1989). Toward a socio-cultural approach to family literacy. *Harvard Educational Review, 59,* 165–181.

Auerbach, E. R. (1995). Which way for family literacy?: Intervention or empowerment. In L. M. Morrow (Ed.), *Family literacy: Connections in schools and communities* (pp. 11–28). Newark, DE: International Reading Association.

Baghban, M. (1984). *Our daughter learns to read and write: A case study from birth to three.* Newark, DE: International Reading Association.

Barnett, W. S. (1998). Long-term effects on cognitive development and school success. In W. S. Barnett & S. S. Boocock (Eds.), *Early care and education for children in poverty: Promise, programs, and long-term results* (pp. 11–44). Albany: State University of New York Press.

Barton, D., & Hamilton, M. (1998). *Local literacy: Reading and writing in one community.* London: Routledge.

Boethel, M. (2004). *Readiness: School, family, and community connections.* Austin, TX: National Center for Family and Community Connections with Schools, Southwest Educational Development Laboratory.

Bourdieu, P. (1986). The forms of capital. In J. G. Richardson (Ed.), *Handbook of theory and research for the sociology of education* (pp. 241–258). New York: Greenwood Press.

Bronfenbrenner, U. (1979). *The ecology of human development: Experiments by nature and design.* Cambridge, MA: Harvard University Press.

Brooks, W. (2006). Reading representations of themselves: Urban youth use culture and African American textual features to develop literary understandings. *Reading Research Quarterly, 41*(3), 372–392.

Clark, M. M. (1984). Literacy at home and at school: Insights from a study of young fluent readers. In H. Goelman, A. Oberg, & F. Smith (Eds.), *Awakening to literacy* (pp. 122–130). Exeter, NH: Heinemann.

Clark, R. (1983). *Family life and school achievement: Why poor black children succeed or fail.* Chicago: University of Chicago Press.

Compton-Lilly, C. (2003). *Reading families: The literate lives of urban children.* New York: Teachers College Press.

Compton-Lilly, C. (2007). The complexities of reading capital in two Puerto Rican families. *Reading Research Quarterly, 42*(1), 72–98.

Davidson, R. G., & Snow, C. E. (1995). The linguistic environment of early readers. *Journal of Research in Childhood Education, 10,* 5–21.

DeBruin-Parecki, A., & Krol-Sinclair, B. (2003). *Family literacy from theory to practice.* Newark, DE: International Reading Association.

Delgado-Gaitan, C. (1990). *Literacy for empowerment: The role of parents in children's education.* New York: Falmer Press.

Delpit, L. (1995). *Other people's children: Cultural conflict in the classroom.* New York: New Press.

DeTemple, J. M., & Beals, D. E. (1991). Family talk: Sources of support for the development of decontextualized skills. *Journal of Research in Childhood Education, 6,* 11–19.

Duke, N. K. (2000a). 3.6 minutes per day: The scarcity of informational texts in first grade. *Reading Research Quarterly, 35*(1), 202–224.

Duke, N. K. (2000b). For the rich it's richer: Print experiences and environments offered to children in very low- and very-high socioeconomic status first-grade classrooms. *American Educational Research Journal, 37*(1), 441–478.

Duke, N. K., & Purcell-Gates, V. (2003). Genres at home and at school: Bridging the known to the new. *Reading Teacher, 57*(1), 30–37.

Durkin, D. (1966). *Children who read early: Two longitudinal studies.* New York: Teachers College Press.

Edwards, P. A. (2004). *Children literacy development: Making it happen through school, family, and community involvement.* Boston: Allyn & Bacon.

Edwards, P. A., Pleasants, H. M., & Franklin, S. H. (1999). *A path to follow: Learning to listen to parents.* Portsmouth, NH: Heinemann.

Edwards, P. A., & Turner, J. D. (2008). Family literacy and reading comprehension. In S. E. Israel & G. G. Duffy (Eds.), *Handbook of research on reading comprehension* (pp. 622–644). Mahwah, NJ: Erlbaum.

Ferreiro, E., & Teberosky, A. (1982). *Literacy before schooling.* Exeter, NH: Heinemann.

Gadsden, V. (1995). Representations of literacy: Parents' images in two communities. In L. M. Morrow (Ed.), *Family literacy: Connections in schools and communities* (pp. 287–304). Newark, DE: International Reading Association.

Gadsden, V. L. (1998). Family cultures and literacy learning. In J. Osborn & F. Lehr (Eds.), *Literacy for all: Issues in teaching and learning* (pp. 32–51). New York: Guilford Press.

Gallimore, R., Weisner, R., Kaufman, S., & Bernheimer, L. P. (1989). The social construction of ecocultural niches: Family accommodation of developmentally delayed children. *American Journal of Mental Retardation, 94*(3), 216–230.

Gee, J. P. (1989). What is literacy? *Journal of Education, 171,* 18–25.

Gee, J. P. (1996). *Social linguistics and literacies: Ideology in discourses* (2nd ed.). London: Taylor & Francis.

Goatley, V. J. (1997). Encouraging parent and teacher communication: Discourse to support students considered "at-risk." In C. K. Kinzer, K. A. Hinchman, & D. J. Leu (Eds.), *Inquiries in literacy theory and practice* (pp. 114–126). Chicago: National Reading Conference.

González, N., Moll, L. C., & Amanti, C. (2005). *Funds of knowledge: Theorizing practices in households, communities, and classrooms.* Mahwah, NJ: Erlbaum.

González, N., Moll, L. C., Tenery, M. F., Rivera, A., Rendon, P., Gonzáles, R., et al. (1995). Funds of knowledge for teaching in Latino households. *Urban Education, 29,* 443–470.

Goodman, Y. (1986). Children coming to know literacy. In W. Teale & E. Sulzby (Eds.), *Emergent literacy: Writing and reading* (pp. 1–14). Norwood, NJ: Ablex.

Hart, B., & Risley, T. R. (1995). *Meaningful differences in the everyday experiences of young American children.* Baltimore: Brookes.

Heath, S. B. (1982). What no bedtime story means: Narrative skills at home and school. *Language in Society, 11*(2), 49–76.

Heath, S. B. (1983). *Ways with words.* Cambridge, UK: Cambridge University Press.

Heath, S. B. (1986). What no bedtime story means: Narrative skills at home and at school. In B. B. Schieffelin & E. Ochs (Eds.), *Language socialization across cultures* (pp. 97–126). Cambridge, UK: Cambridge University Press.

Hemmeter, J. (2006). Household use of libraries and large bookstores. *Library and Information Science Research, 28*(4), 596–616.

Henderson, A. T., & Berla, N. (1994). *A new generation of evidence: The family is critical to student achievement.* Columbia, MD: National Committee for Citizens in Education.

Hoover-Dempsey, K. V., & Sandler, H. M. (1995). Parental involvement in children's education: Why does it make a difference? *Teacher's College Record, 97,* 310–331.

Huey, E. B. (1908). *The psychology and pedagogy of reading.* Cambridge, MA: MIT Press.

Krol-Sinclair, B. (1996). Connecting home and school literacies: Immigrant parents with limited formal education as classroom storybook readers. In D. J. Leu, C. K. Kinzer, & K. A. Hinchman (Eds.), *Literacies for the 21st century: Research and practice* (pp. 270–283). Chicago: National Reading Conference.

Krol-Sinclair, B., Hindin, A., Emig, J. M., & McClure, K. A. (2003). Using family literacy portfolios as a context for parent–teacher communication. In A. DeBruin-Parecki & B. Krol-Sinclair (Eds.), *Family literacy from theory to practice* (pp. 266–281). Newark, DE: International Reading Association.

Laosa, L. (1977). Socialization, education, and continuity: The importance of the sociocultural context. *Young Children, 32,* 21–27.

Lapp, D., Fisher, D., Flood, J., & Moore, K. (2002). "I don't want to teach it wrong": An investigation of the role families believe they should play in the early literacy development of their children. *National Reading Conference Yearbook, 51,* 276–287.

Landry, S. H., & Smith, K. E. (2006). The influence of parenting on emerging literacy skills. In D. K. Dickinson & S. B. Neuman (Eds.), *Handbook of early literacy research* (Vol. 2, pp. 135–148). New York: Guilford Press.

Lareau, A. (1987). Social class differences in family–school relationships: The importance of cultural capital. *Sociology of Education, 60,* 73–85.

Lareau, A. (1989). *Home advantage: Social class and parental intervention.* New York: Falmer Press.

Lareau, A. (2003). *Unequal childhoods: Class, race, and family life.* Berkeley: University of California Press.

Leichter, H. J. (1984). Families as environments for literacy. In H. Goelman, A. Oberg, & F. Smith (Eds.), *Awakening to literacy* (pp. 38–50). Portsmouth, NH: Heinemann.

Leseman, P. M., & DeJong, P. F. (1998). Home literacy: Opportunity, instruction, cooperation and social–emotional quality predicting early reading achievement. *Reading Research Quarterly, 33*(3), 294–318.

Li, G. (2006). *Culturally contested pedagogy: Battles of literacy and schooling between mainstream teachers and Asian immigrant parents.* Albany: State University of New York Press.

Lightfoot, S. L. (1978). *World apart: Relationships between families and schools.* New York: Basic Books.

Marvin, C. A., & Wright, D. (1997). Literacy socialization in the homes of preschool children. *Language, Speech, and Hearing Services in Schools, 28,* 154–163.

McCarthey, S. J. (1997). Connecting home and school literacy practices in classrooms with diverse populations. *Journal of Literacy Research, 29,* 145–182.

McMillon, G. M. T., & Edwards, P. A. (2008). Examining shared domains of literacy in the home, church and school of African American children. In J. Flood, S. B. Heath, & D. Lapp (Eds.), *Handbook of research on teaching literacy through the communicative and visual arts* (Vol. II, pp. 319–328). New York: Erlbaum.

McTavish, M. (2007). Constructing the big picture: A working class family supports their daughter's pathways to literacy. *Reading Teacher, 60*(5), 476–485.

Melzi, G., Paratore, J. R., & Krol-Sinclair, B. (2000). Reading and writing in the daily lives of Latino mothers who participate in a family literacy program. *National Reading Conference Yearbook, 49,* 178–193.

Moll, L. (1999). Foreword. In J. Paratore, G. Melzei, & B. Krol-Sinclair (Eds.), *What should we expect of family literacy?: Experiences of Latino children whose parents participate in an intergenerational literacy project.* Newark, DE: International Reading Association.

Moll, L., Amanti, C., Neff, D., & González, N. (1992). Funds of knowledge for teaching: Using a qualitative approach to connect homes and classrooms. *Theory Into Practice, 31,* 132–141.

Moll, L. C. (1992). Literacy research in community and classrooms: A sociocultural approach. In R. Beach, J. L. Green, M. L. Kamil, & T. Shanahan (Eds.), *Multidisciplinary perspectives in literacy research* (pp. 211–244). Urbana, IL: National Council of Teachers of English.

Moll, L. C., & Greenberg, J. B. (1990). Creating zones of possibilities: Combining social contexts for instruction. In L. C. Moll (Ed.), *Vygotsky and education: Instructional implications and applications of sociohistorical psychology* (pp. 319–348). Cambridge, UK: Cambridge University Press.

Neuman, S., & Celano, D. (2001). Access to print in low-income and middle-income communities: An ecological study of four neighborhoods. *Reading Research Quarterly, 36*(1), 8–26.

Paratore, J. R. (2001). *Opening doors, opening opportunities: Family literacy in an urban community.* Needham Heights, MA: Allyn & Bacon.

Paratore, J. R., Hindin, A., Krol-Sinclair, B., & Durán, P. (1999). Discourse between teachers and Latino parents during conferences based on home literacy portfolios. *Education and Urban Society, 32,* 58–82.

Paratore, J. R., Hindin, A., Krol-Sinclair, B., Durán, P., & Emig, J. (1999, December). *Deepening the conversation: Using family literacy portfolios as a context for parent–teacher conferences.* Paper presented at the National Reading Conference, Orlando, FL.

Paratore, J. R., Homza, A., Krol-Sinclair, B., Lewis-Barrow, T., Melzi, G., Stergis, R., et al. (1995). Shifting boundaries in home and school responsibilities: Involving immigrant parents in the construction of literacy portfolios. *Research in the Teaching of English, 29,* 367–389.

Potter, G. (1989). Parent participation in the language arts program. *Language Arts, 66*(1), 21–28.

Purcell-Gates, V. (1995). *Other people's words: The cycle of illiteracy.* Cambridge, MA: Harvard University Press.

Purcell-Gates, V. (1996). Stories, coupons, and the *TV Guide*: Relationships between home literacy experiences and emergent literacy knowledge. *Reading Research Quarterly, 31*(4), 406–429.

Purcell-Gates, V. (2000). Family literacy. In M. L. Kamil, P. B. Mosenthal, P. D. Pearson, & R. Barr (Eds.), *Handbook of reading research* (Vol. 3, pp. 853–870). Mahwah, NJ: Erlbaum.

Risko, V., & Bromley, K. (Eds.). (2001). *Collaboration for diverse learners: Viewpoints and practices.* Newark, DE: International Reading Association.

Roberts, T. A. (2008). Home storybook reading in primary or second language with preschool children: Evidence of equal effectiveness for second-language acquisition. *Reading Research Quarterly, 43*(2), 103–130.

Roser, N., Hoffman, J., Kastler, L., & Sharp, C. (1994). What parents tell us about children's emerging literacy. In S. Reifel (Ed.), *Advances in early education and day care: Topics in early literacy, teacher preparation, and international perspectives on early care* (Vol. 6, pp. 61–82). Greenwich, CT: JAI Press.

Schieffelin, B., & Cochran-Smith, M. (1984). Learning to read culturally: Literacy before schooling. In H. Goelman, A. Oberg, & F. Smith (Eds.), *Awakening to literacy* (pp. 3–23). Exeter, NH: Heinemann.

Sonnenschein, S., Baker, L., Serpell, R., Scher, D. Truitt, V. G., & Munsterman, K. (1997). Parental beliefs about ways to help children learn to read: The impact of an entertainment or a skills perspective. *Early Child Development and Care, 127*(1), 111–118.

Steiner, L. M. (2008). *Effects of a school-based parent and teacher intervention to promote first-grade students' literacy achievement.* Unpublished doctoral dissertation, Boston University.

Stewart, J. P. (1995). Home environments and parental support for literacy: Children's perceptions and school literacy achievement. *Early Education and Development, 6*(2), 97–125.

Super, C., & Harkness, S. (1986). The developmental niche: A conceptualization at the interface of child and culture. *International Journal of Behaviour Development, 9,* 1–25.

Taylor, D. (1993). Family literacy. Resisting deficit models. *TESOL Quarterly, 27*(3), 550–553.

Taylor, D. (Ed.). (1997). *Many families, many literacies.* Portsmouth, NH: Heinemann.

Taylor, D., & Dorsey-Gaines, C. (1988). *Growing up literate: Learning from inner-city families.* Portsmouth, NH: Heinemann.

Teale, W. H. (1986). Home background and young children's literacy development. In W. H. Teale & E. Sulzby (Eds.), *Emergent literacy: Writing and reading* (pp. 173–206). Norwood, NJ: Ablex.

Valdés, G. (1996). *Con respeto: Bridging the differences between culturally diverse families and schools.* New York: Teachers College Press.

Voss, M. M. (1996). *Hidden literacies: Children learning at home and at school.* Portsmouth, NH: Heinemann.

Wasik, B. H. (2004). *Handbook of family literacy.* Mahwah, NJ: Erlbaum.

White, D. (1954). *Books before five.* Christchurch, New Zealand: Whitcombe & Tombs.

Worthy, J., & Roser, N. (2004). Flood ensurance: When children have books they can and want to read. In D. Lapp, C. C. Block, E. J. Cooper, J. Flood, N. Roser, & J. V. Tinajero (Eds.), *Teaching all the children: Strategies for developing literacy in an urban setting* (pp. 179–192). New York: Guilford Press.

Yaden, D., & Paratore, J. R. (2002). Family literacy at the turn of the millenium: The costly future of maintaining the status quo. In J. E. Flood, D. Lapp, J. Jensen, & J. Squire (Eds.), *Research in English and the language arts* (pp. 532–545). Mahwah, NJ: Erlbaum.

Zill, N., Moore, K. A., Smith, E. W., Stief, T., & Coiro, M. J. (1997). The life circumstances and development of children in welfare families: A profile based on national survey data. In P. L. Chase-Lansdale & J. Brooks-Gunn (Eds.), *Escape from poverty: What makes a difference?* (pp. 38–62). Cambridge, UK: Cambridge University Press.

# CHAPTER 5

# Poverty and Its Relation to Development and Literacy

PEDRO PORTES *and* SPENCER SALAS

> Our task is to help replace their despair with opportunity.
> This administration today, here and now, declares
> unconditional war on poverty in America.
> —LYNDON B. JOHNSON (1964)

Almost half a century after the launching of the Great Society, over 40% of U.S. Latino, Native American, and African American children live in poverty compared to 14% of children from the dominant non-Hispanic white community. The developmental consequences of such economic group-based inequality (GBI) are vast and range from myriad health-related issues (Duncan & Brooks-Gunn, 2000) to exposure to communication patterns associated with future academic achievement (Hart & Risley 1995). Thus, a persistent and extraordinary gap in learning outcomes and academic development among ethnic groups is driven by disproportionate rates of poverty that befall families—posing a host of substantial risks for their children that are cumulative and interactive. In terms of school literacy, standardized test scores in math and reading indicate, for example, that, in general, a 13-year-old dominant-majority student's academic performance matches or exceeds that of a 17-year-old black or Latino high school senior (U.S. Department of Education, National Center for Education Statistics, 2004).

However reductive these measures of achievement may be, such measures still count tremendously in estimating how school-related literacy development influences the lives of U.S. children and their families living in poverty. Accordingly, our focus in this chapter is on generating a better understanding of why poverty and the social class differences it indirectly engenders appear to be impervious to change at the population level despite convincing evidence that, under certain conditions, the negative effects of poverty on school literacies can be moderated in socially organized circumstances involving psychological mediation (Kozulin, 1998; Portes, 2005; Ramey & Ramey, 2004).

In this chapter, we draw from cultural historical theory (Cole, 1996; Vygotsky, 1978) to hypothesize how the school literacies of poverty-bound children, particularly from nondominant communities, left behind by sustaining the present K–16 system, might be maximized through a systemic approach for equity in school literacy outcomes. The discussion that follows is framed around three key points:

- A synthesis of research on disciplinary perspectives of poverty, development, and literacy—and their combined interaction
- A cultural–historical theoretical framework for understanding GBI in terms of mediated learning and cultural history
- A lifespan model outline for sustainable praxis in dismantling the achievement gap

## POVERTY AND LITERACY(IES) ACROSS DISCIPLINARY DIVIDES: A SYNTHESIS OF RESEARCH

Understandings of "poverty" and "literacy," and their relationships, largely depend on the disciplinary traditions or "communities of practice" (Lave & Wenger, 1991) with which individuals identify. It is beyond the scope of this chapter to provide a historical account of literacy from the time before Cicero to the postdigital era— how that construct has unfolded, and the cultural tools and practices whereby it has been governed (see, e.g., Collins & Blot, 2003; Heath, 1991). That said, it is important to note that there exists across much of educational psychology a relatively high comfort level with the somewhat monolithic categories of "literacy" and "poverty"—and the postpositivist epistemologies wherein the lexis of the discipline is grounded.

From an educational psychologist's point of view, "literacy" is often simply a measure of what children (do not) learn in schools and, "poverty" is an income fault line below which various aspects of human development are compromised. Yet equity is a rather recent and complex value and goal in modern, developed countries. Bragging rights are forthcoming to societies that level group-based disparities in quality of life that are isomorphic with educational achievement. The number of societies that has achieved the latter remains limited with respect to systematic progress in leveling evitable gaps in children's development and economic well-being. If poverty saps human development, then a minimum level of income or labor remuneration is yet to be defined beyond government econometrics.

Though economists are not experts in human development, we rely on them to estimate minimum levels of subsistence above which comparable educational and economic opportunities operate unfettered. To do well for their people, Great Societies must work methodically to lessen constraints that interact with poverty in terms of opportunities to learn and develop essential psychological tools generally constituted through school-based teaching. The problem we see is that such teaching is neither sufficient nor designed to afford poor children comparable opportunities for the types of literacy that facilitate development and subsequent learning. In large part, this is due to differences in literacy support that lie outside schools' control. The paradox is that whereas these differences are largely a function of poverty and cultural history (Portes, 1996, 2005) the compensation required to level the field depends on restructuring the education now provided in terms of personnel, strategies, and school culture.

## "Ways with Words"

In contrast to the somewhat static understanding of literacy afforded by the educational psychology literature, growing numbers of researchers in language and literacy education conceptualize children's "ways with words" (Heath, 1983) as dynamic and interactive processes that shape thinking and emotions through repertoires of presupposed and popularly shared knowledge. In such scholarship, literacy is conceived of as "literacies" (see, e.g., Nocon & Cole, Chapter 1, this volume). Somewhere in between lies the concept of development, both individual and aggregated, in relation to quality of life.

We conceptualize literacy/literacies as the means whereby "culture(s)" come to be—and come to be shared. To that end, we reject the idea of an inherent superiority or inferiority of any one group and recognize the continued failure of public schools to take up the multiple and diverse literacies that children bring with them in ways that proactively challenge local orthodoxies and asymmetrical power relations whereby nondominant communities are marginalized. We also recognize that institutionalized construction of what it means to be literate, who has the right to decide, and who has the right to become literate are cultural productions of the dominant majority and the schools it has created to sustain and perpetuate those same cultural constructs (cf. Levinson, 2000; Levinson, Foley, & Holland, 1996).

Before embarking on another No Child Left Behind expedition[1] we, furthermore, acknowledge that interventions aimed at making "other people's children" literate in a dominant, middle-class sense of the term have not necessarily transformed the economic structures that—even after such interventions—still engulf children of poverty both in and outside the United States (see, e.g., Heath, 1983; Scribner & Cole, 1973, 1981). That said, in a K–12 context, we recognize an ethical obligation here in the United States to provide schooling that, at minimum, does not prevent future access to educational and economic opportunity structures such as postsecondary education.

## Meaningful Differences in Literacy Development

Even as contemporary U.S. society becomes more diverse and multivoiced, poverty remains a major instrumental constraint imposed unevenly upon large sectors of the population. The constraints are subtle and long-lasting over many generations. The relationship between economic status and school literacy represents a central focus of a substantial volume of research documenting myriad associations between the financial subsistence of U.S. families and their children's academic achievement and futures.

Quantitative examinations have scrutinized, among other things the relationships between poverty and cognitive test scores or standardized testing of verbal skills and reading achievement; tracking and grade retention; absenteeism; persistence; attrition, parental involvement, and more (Biddle, 2001; Bradley & Corwyn, 2002; D'Angiulli, Siegel, & Hertzman, 2004; Duncan & Brooks-Gunn, 2000; Duncan, Brooks-Gunn, Yeung, & Smith, 1998; Haveman & Wolfe, 1995; Mayer, 1997; Natriello, McDill, & Pallas, 1990; Pungello, Kupersmidt, & Vaden, 1996; Shonkoff & Phillips, 2000). Underlying these findings are critical differences in early literacy and cognitive–linguistic socialization (Hart & Risley, 1995) that today may still be traced to class-based patterns of adult–child interaction (Hess & Shipman, 1965; Portes, 1988).

*Children as capital* is yet another important concept related to any society's future. Literacy development and learning have been linked to the quality of teaching offered in school under five principles of/for effective teaching (Dalton, 2007; Tharp, Estrada, Dalton, & Yamauchi, 2000). Both concepts provide powerful lenses for understanding poverty in relation to the quality of education offered to children living in poverty and, as a result, their subsequent development.

In a landmark longitudinal study examining children's early family experience and their later intellectual growth, Hart and Risley (1995) identified five parenting features linked to future academic achievement: (1) language diversity; (2) feedback; (3) guidance style; (4) language emphasis; and (5) responsiveness in preschool.

Without belaboring the Hart and Risley (1995) findings, what strikes us is a continued lack of consensus for improving social policy—a decade after one of the most well-designed studies of young children's developmental environments provided evidence that the communication patterns of families in poverty may direct their children's development into paths that are not conducive to development of the communication patterns necessary for school success. The inertia that remains at a policy level is disturbing given that possible solutions do exist (Portes, 2005; Ramey & Ramey, 2004).

Unfortunately, in some cases, comparative research on literacy development has been exploited to forward a long-standing cultural deficit model, with the argument that if only poor and ethnic, racial, and linguistic minority caretakers acted "whiter," then their children would do better in schools (see, e.g., Rothstein, 2004). To that end, earlier federally funded evaluations of early intervention programs for the children of the poor leveled the blame for low academic achievement and other schooling issues on "pathological" families (Bereiter & Engelmann, 1966; Coleman, 1987, 1988).

Ethnicity was, and largely remains, a proxy for both economic and educational status differentials that are compounded by discrimination, resource allocation (Kozol, 1991), and language policy. Today, nondominant majority children's failure in schools is still too often conceived of as symptomatic of their inherently inferior home/community cultures and the languages spoken in those homes and communities (Rothstein, 2004). Or, as such "logic" would have it, intellectually and culturally flawed families in turn produce damaged children to be pitied as victims (see Scott, 1997, p. xiii). A historical awareness of mediated learning is still missing from such flawed analyses.

Public schools serving nondominant communities may be trying their best to promote students' literacy acquisition despite myriad systemic constraints. Yet far from being the great equalizer, public schools appear more and more the de facto societal mechanisms for institutionalizing GBI. As we have argued, pragmatically, whatever the measures employed in K–12 public schools to gauge literacy, be they adequate yearly progress (AYP) or end of grade (EOG) exams, such measures indicate the brands of literacy that schools sanction and privilege. Thus, an individual's achievement in U.S. schools remains a reductive gauge of schools' understandings of what constitutes achievement—a gauge that indirectly results in diminished literacy acquisition opportunities for students from nondominant communities. As such, developmental gaps prevail on both ends of the political economy of education—on the side of the educator/policy and on that of students placed at risk.

When literacy promotion programs designed for the "mainstream" students fail (once these are situated outside of the mainstream), such curricular interventions—driven by "scientific" evidence—are rarely challenged at a policy level. Ironically, when new programs succeed with students placed at risk, the learning generated from such "experiments" is often integrated or adopted wholesale for all students to the benefit of those already advantaged. For example, much of Tharp and Gallimore's (1989) work was soon adopted into professional development and preservice teacher education. Hence, the advantaged keep getting more advantages, even when the latter proceed from efforts to help *developing* populations.

What we currently witness remains a mindless political game of higher and higher stakes testing, evasive discourses blaming schools and teachers, and labeling of the victims of public education as "resistant" or "behavior disordered" and as being subject to less caring parents. Accordingly, many children's legal entitlement to quality public schooling continues to be routinely violated through underfunded, substandard, and visibly segregated schools, staffed with teachers inadequately prepared with knowledge, skills, or spirit to teach for diversity (Kozol, 1991, 2005; Olsen, 1997; Valdés, 1996, 2001). In this sense, schools frequently fail to provide optimal conditions for academic and intellectual development—by placing minority children at risk early and locking them there through tracking (Oakes, 1985) or other forms of "subtractive schooling" (Valenzuela, 1999) perpetuated by myopic curricula and sustained by "English only" language policies.

## The Genesis of Underachievement of Groups or Populations

Although academic disparity is not based on color or minority status per se (De Vos & Suárez-Orozco, 1990), discussions about GBI are often clouded by discourse about causality regarding color and race rather than an understanding of intergroup relations connected to mediational tools, access to those tools, and the making of minds (cf. Luria, 1976). The origins of disparity in quality of life sustained by differences in educational access are culturally and historically explained, with skin pigmentation remaining a correlate, depending on context and time.

Numerical contrasts of schooling outcomes and achievement patterns among groups require that attention be given to the particular cultural history of each group in interaction with others over generations. Undoubtedly, schooling and schools in high-poverty settings or those that serve largely nondominant majority students vary significantly from those found in middle- and upper-class neighborhoods with a majority of monolingual, European American, middle- and upper-class children. Over time, differing behaviors, beliefs, expectations, values, practices, and experiences are constructed and sustained by participants as individuals, and as members of groups—socialization patterns that may or may not be linked directly to what is required in school or to their potential to make successful adaptations to outside demands made by schools.

In some instances, we can expect an initial achievement gap for children of immigrants to disappear with a second generation; that is, despite a climate of discrimination, some immigrant students may nevertheless score above the norm in standardized achievement tests and other measures of achievement (see, e.g., Gibson, 1988; A. Portes & Rumbaut, 2001). In other instances, immigrant children risk a "downward assimilation" (A. Portes & Zhou, 1993) into marginalized subcultures of involuntary U.S. minorities, where, collectively, they are subject to massively disproportionate and long-standing measurable gaps in educational achievement shaping "group-based inequality" (Portes, 2005). In other cases and times, immigrants exceed the average status of even dominant groups.

The intergenerational trajectories of immigrant students depend on a confluence of contexts in which they initially find themselves (A. Portes & Rumbaut, 2001), and the support for literacy that follows in contexts of reception, acceptance, and encouragement. A gradual upward economic and social trajectory whereby immigrants quickly adopt the political and social mores of the dominant middle class may be associated with the social capital with which the immigrant family arrives and the mode of incorporation afforded by the receiving country. Possible modes of cultural adaptation that might encourage social adjustment and economic prosperity include receptive government policies, such as resettlement assistance, compatibility in political ideologies, and/or nonprejudiced societal reception or a sizable and economically diverse receiving community—as once afforded to Cuban exiles during the 1960s or to European immigrants today. More recently, members of certain social, economic, racial, ethnic, or linguistic categories who are repeatedly treated in ways perceived as unjust or inequitable, understandably, may choose to resist the status quo to which they and their communities are subjected—often historically (Matute-Bianchi, 1991; Ogbu, 1974, 1978, 2003; Valenzuela, 1999).

Such understandings of immigrants' trajectories also further our understanding of how cultural contexts and present educational structure govern the development of *nonimmigrant* students.

First, such structured economic unfairness erects oppositional habits of mind that are prone to resist short-term interventions and spell failure for a society. As identity politics play out, children's literacy development remains tied to family cultures that vary considerably based on parents' educational level. The determining factors most often noted in the literature come as no surprise in their prediction of literacy acquisition related to school and economic success. Such determining factors revolve around the activity affordances associated with educated parents who focus on mediating their children's development through multiple pathways. What remains most disturbing is that by now, our society should know better. Still, at a policy level, there is resistance to available research-based findings, options, and recommendations (see, e.g., Thomas & Collier, 1996). Ours is a society that encourages a multiplicity of viewpoints that vary in terms of scientific evidence and often result in gridlocks that seem inevitably to sustain the status quo.

## A Cultural–Historical Theoretical Framework for Understanding Group-Based Inequality in Terms of Mediated Learning and Cultural History

When over 20% of school-age children are born into and stranded in a cycle of poverty, overcoming the barriers imposed by the increased literacy demands of a global economy and high-stakes reform requires a systemic overhauling of the K–16 public education. Today however, many policymakers seem to endorse the idea that higher scores produced by more test-driven instruction will somehow mysteriously close the achievement gap between rich and poor. Based on cultural–historical activity theory, we argue that the roots of GBI are much deeper and dialectical in origin. Again, developmental gaps prevail on both sides of the dominant dialectic of the political spectrum.

### Whose Mind in Which Society?

Our understandings of the relationship between poverty and literacy, and its relationship to the construct of social capital and its distribution, are informed by a cultural–historical theoretical lens, as advanced by Portes (2005), with the aim of informing policy and practice (cf. Portes, Delgado-Romero, & Salas, in press; Portes, Gallego, & Salas, 2008; Portes & Salas, 2007).

Various sociocultural lenses for studying human development have drawn from the translated works of Vygotsky (1978, 1986) and contemporaries such as Luria (1976) and Bakhtin (1981, 1986), and the subsequent writings of their American translators and scholars (Cole, 1996; Lave & Wenger, 1991; Leont'ev, 1978, 1981; Scribner & Cole, 1981; Van der Veer & Valsiner, 1994; Wertsch, 1985, 1998, 2002). Tracing the latter is a difficult endeavor, beyond the scope of this chapter. Yet, as noted elsewhere, cultural–historical theory represents a rich metaparadigm that, unlike the other major forces in social science, resists reductionism in its plasticity (Portes, 1996, 1999; Portes et al., 2008).

### Helping Means and Mediating Processes

For Vygotsky and the interdisciplinary psychology he helped to inspire, higher mental functions in humans—memory, for example—are products of social interaction. Thus, human cultural development is a fundamental transformation of interpersonal processes into intrapersonal processes. Or as Vygotsky (1978) explains, "All the higher functions originate as actual relations between human individuals" (p. 57). "Higher functions" may be defined as the essence of literacy at its best; that is, logical thinking that can be decontextualized in time and space requires long, cumulative advances in concrete experiences and reflection, with more advanced peers and sources.

Similarly, central to the Russian cultural–historical school, and reflected in the hypothesis of the social nature of human cognitive development, is Vygotsky's "ur-characteristic of human mental and emotional activity" (Holland & Cole, 1995, p. 475), the use of material tools and symbolic artifacts to mediate thinking. Holland and Valsiner (1988) explain:

> He [Vygotsky] referred to these tools as "helping means" (in Russian *vspomogatel'nye sredstva*). These means (or activities, as Vygotsky with his emphasis on process might prefer) are psychological devices for mediating between one's mental states and processes and one's environment. (p. 248)

Illustrating "helping means" with the example of a woman tying a handkerchief into a knot around her arm to keep from forgetting, Vygotsky (1978) explains:

> She is, in essence, constructing the process of memorizing by forcing an external object to remind her of something; she transforms remembering into an external activity. ... The very essence of human memory consists in the fact that human beings actively remember with the help of signs. (p. 51)

Hence, for Vygotsky, handkerchiefs are mediating devices, whereby an elementary memory connecting event $A$ to event $B$ is replaced in the following equation: "$A$ to $X$ and $X$ to $B$, where $X$ is an artificial psychological tool—a knot in a handkerchief, a written note, or a mnemonic scheme" (Kozulin, 1984, p. 106). As such, human thought is "distributed" (Salomon, 1993) across the material tools, and social and cultural psychological devices that women and men have shaped over time and that have in turn shaped them (cf. Portes, 2005; Portes et al., 2008, in press; Portes & Salas, 2007).

## Literate Achievement and Cognitive Development

Literacy development is anchored in a child's facility with signs and symbols, and beliefs and expectations that in adolescence are progressively mediated by peer culture at a time of mental transformation. Still, the literature on literacy and development of children in poverty often misses the proverbial elephant standing in the middle of the room, namely, that the acquisition of literacy includes tools for thinking and critical strategies founded in discrete changes in cognition (Kohlberg, 1987; Piaget, 1832; Selman, 1980; Vygotsky, 1978, 1986).

Arguing that literate achievement is more than an "expansion of communicative or translation skills," Johnston (1999) writes:

> The literate interactions in which children participate are not simply a vehicle for learning, but also a major part of what they learn. Consequently, these must count as literate achievements with implications both for individual students and for the literate communities of which they are a part. (p. 4)

The transition from concrete forms of thought and literate interactions to what has been termed "formal" or "abstract" logical functions occurs only because certain social or cultural practices and interactions are available, taken up, and activated by individuals with others in zones of proximal development. To that end, economic poverty constrains certain opportunities to develop the structures that govern higher-level functioning and literate achievements observed inside and outside the classroom. Such constraints infringe on both the quality and number of what Johnston and others would count as literate interactions and achievements.

Contemporary U.S. demographic shifts are impacting views about literacy, poverty, language, and culture in ways that challenge the hegemony of traditional ethnocentric views about ways of learning to become literate in various sociocultural contexts with the role of norms and standards. Nevertheless, institutionalized constructs of literate achievement remain governed by political and economic power relations. Thus, despite efforts to associate high-quality education with diverse schools, both within-group segregation and radical differences in learning environments prevail (Kozol, 1991, 2005; Orfield & Chungmai, 2007).

Along with obvious differences in student populations, physical structures, and the communities surrounding them, are also significant variations at other levels, including the knowledge and dispositions of decision makers; resources allocated to students in poverty; teacher–student relations; quality and preparation of personnel, and their beliefs and goals; and the nature of pedagogical decisions based on the ways educators identify, evaluate, and respond to student cultural competencies. Thus, we reject the notion that socialization patterns associated and observed in certain cultures by educated parents are the sole causes of school or other achievement disparities any more than parental income or occupation. Rather, low academic achievement is often the long-term developmental product of forced adaptation to insensitive and inequitable sociohistorical conditions including but not limited to prejudice and poverty. The latter do in fact influence the various interactions, their intensity, and sustainability over time.

It is no secret that as task difficulty increases during schooling, intellectual demands placed on working-class and welfare parents, assuming that they are available, outstrip resources to which more advantaged children generally have access in a variety of ways. Hence, differentials in mediated activity (Kozulin, Gindis, Ageyev, & Miller, 2003; Wertsch, 1998) from the standpoint of the developmental pathways engulfing children's trajectories seem a more useful way than static factors to conceptualize literacy constraints (Portes & Vadeboncoeur, 2003).

## IMPLICATIONS FOR CLASSROOM PRACTICE: A LIFESPAN MODEL OUTLINE FOR SUSTAINABLE PRAXIS FOR DISMANTLING THE ACHIEVEMENT GAP

### Overcompensation

It may be precisely because of restrictions imposed on families and children's development that socialization practices evolve into dispositions that seem incompatible with those required in schools (Tharp, 1989). Early childhood interventions aimed at "normalizing" the development of children of the poor before they enter school have been the standard of national policies for the intergenerational dismantling of poverty (see, e.g., Aber, Bishop-Josef, Jones, Taaffe McLearn, & Phillips, 2006; Zigler, Gilliam, & Jones, 2006); promising gains appear to "wash out" in elementary schools as children move forward with less, if any, support (Portes, 2005). Thus, the achievement gap that begins in prekindergarten is sustained across children's K–12 trajectories, and into postsecondary education and other so-called "opportunity structures" vital to economic participation in a post–assembly line U.S. economy (Council of Economic Advisors, 2000; National Center for Public Policy and Higher Education, 2004). Thus, in a post-Fordist U.S. economy, although defining poverty and literacy, and how they interact, remains contested, less clear is the contemporary relationship between postsecondary education and individual lifetime earning power (Portes et al., in press).

To achieve a noteworthy and lasting effect on children's intellectual development that is sustainable at the group level, both individual and contextual supports need to be integrated into the lives of those placed at risk for school failure. Achieving comparable distributions and proportional achievement outcomes for students from nondominant communities categorized as "at risk" involves sustained, systematic overcompensation strategies with a high-intensity early start and continuity of culturally mediated experiences inside and outside of schools.

Overcompensation for the generations required to dismantle caste-like inequality for children should be additive and without detriment to native or home cultures. At issue is children's right to learn and to develop equitably. However, additive overcompensation efforts must show positive effects that truly narrow gaps in sustainable ways that move beyond celebrations of diversity and embrace the ethics of pursuing and effecting greater equity in quality of life for future generations of children across and eventually beyond U.S. society (Portes & Salas, 2007).

A social–linguistic support system of interwoven conditions for children reared in poverty needs to be in place to empower development in valued literacy or school content areas. Such a strategy would represent a departure from current stopgap, choral, restrictive approaches such as an English for speakers of other languages (ESOL) pullout or an "English only" curriculum in which ethnic groups are left to negotiate hostile school environments. School cultures surrounding the category of students placed at risk must involve "communities of learners" (Lave & Wenger, 1991) that activate continuous enrichment in the very ways that supportive, everyday classroom activities are mediated. Rigorous, challenging, academic environments designed for continuity need to be supplemented with human resources that are comparable to the other, more "established or institutionalized" programs, such as Special Education, Head Start, or even more expensive programs involving incarceration or alternative schools for minors. These programs need to reinforce the child's development in valued areas with respect to school success in both formal and informal settings. Such communities can promote self-regulation, motivation, higher-order thinking, and orient students placed at risk cumulatively toward grade-level academic learning.

A sociocultural model that promotes development for the most needy groups considers the application of primary intervention measures as a strategy for cultivating a level playing field for all children of poverty. Such a model necessarily employs an intergenerational historical lens to activate the critical issue of parent involvement. Our plan for providing and sustaining literacy supports and safeguarding cultural development is detailed elsewhere, as noted earlier. However, concepts of "enrichment" and "intellectual stimulation" need, for example, to be reexamined insofar as they concern the development of intelligence or school aptitude. We argue that such a reexamination of development needs to pay particular attention to the following network of principles and learning environment components:

• The input from the environment needs to be designed for continuity, challenging and reinforcing the child's development in various valued areas with respect to measures of school success. This can include life skills education for adolescents before they become parents rather than the test-dominated "drill and kill" menus now offered.

• These inputs need to be aligned with school curricula and to help foster proximal zones for development that are culturally prized and consonant with those from which intellectual assessments are made in relation to adult career roles, positive identities, and activities. The activities found in the environment that mediate development require particular attention to symbolic tools centered on language-mediated literacy, intellectual skills as well as beliefs, and expectations.

• The culture around children placed at risk for success in school requires continuous enrichment in the very ways that everyday activities are mediated. Before- and afterschool programs need to be systemic, with activities supplemented in ways comparable to the middle class's hidden curriculum.

• To structure comparable achievement or poverty distributions in the future, a strategy of overcompensation and enrichment for the first few generations of adolescents needs to be developed and sustained, until healthy community support levels and practices are established intergenerationally; that is, a social-cognitive support system needs to be in place long enough to influence future generations of families' school, socioeconomic, and culturally defined success.

• Innovative curricular strategies for teaching adult life skills in adolescence are needed to promote the formal operational thinking that is often constrained for teens in high-poverty schools. This counters the within-school segregation imposed on generations living in poverty and, just as important, the daunting challenge of how best to activate parent involvement to support children's school success.

• In summary, school-based activities need to be reorganized so that "basic skills" are not all that the child encounters: he or she also needs to learn higher-order skills. Too often we find that schooling, low expectations, and remedial classes fail to work within children's zones of proximal development and actually impede the development of their higher intellectual skills, motivation, and health (Portes, 2005).

## CONCLUDING REMARKS

Children in poverty develop literacy differently, as well as in different areas. A central issue for us in organizing this chapter was how best to present a balanced account of extant positions and policies in shaping a cogent argument for a meaningful systemic educational restructuring that aligns educational excellence (literacy development) and equity (opportunity to learn regardless of social status). As much as we would like to think that poor children's school lives have changed for the better, relatively small but cumulative differences in early literacy quickly burst into insurmountable learning and teaching shortfalls that render too many students susceptible to another generation of poverty by undereducation in a system remiss in developing healthy, "transcultural" (Suárez-Orozco & Suárez-Orozco, 2001), and productive citizens. A broader definition of literacy—one that is rich with many cultural tools—is long overdue regardless of the narrow political economy of tests that today leave important cultural values behind. Above all, the guarantee of a child's right to a grade-level education would prevent so much of the damage caused by poverty.

Given the data, it may be easy to accept an element of inevitability in the biblical dictum "The poor you will always have with you." However, what troubles us even more than poverty itself is that membership in an ethnic or racial category remains an almost statistical assurance for intergenerational economic privation via the educational system. From a cultural–historical tradition, the existing achievement gap for students placed at risk is a socially determined phenomenon compounded intergenerationally by poverty, fewer educational opportunities, and expectations that interact with and often define the meaning of ethnicity. Dismantling the achievement gap of students from nondominant communities requires bold, transformative, activity-rich policy strokes that depend on a substantial overcompensation strategy by the dominant communities and systemic reform of structures and policies that currently perpetuate the correlation between children's ethnocultural and economic history and their school achievement (Portes, 2005; Portes et al., 2008; Portes & Salas, 2007).

A developmentally sensitive and mediated learning approach can bring an ever more diverse society closer to equity in literacy, thus breaking down a powerful engine of group-based inequality and poverty. Our proposal is one of additive literacy, whereby culture-based differences are respected and all children are educated, at minimum, at grade level. Once that is achieved, overcompensation for children engulfed by poverty at the group level might be reduced, so that it is no longer significantly correlated with ethnicity.

We can transcend the statistical dimensions of group-based disproportionality that expose how too many children are deterred from reaching their potential in terms of a better understanding of historically determined pathways. It is in such historically, tool-assisted, co-constructed pathways that we might discover a way not only to win the war on poverty and finally erase its ethnic overtones, but also to maximize iteratively the cultural development of any society. Thus, in the case of the United States of America, the potential to become, if not a Great Society, a much better one for many more people's children remains an ethical imperative. Given our current know-how with respect to literacy development, the latter remains a viable, if not the most viable, direction for policy action.

## NOTE

1. By *expedition*, we refer back to earlier efforts to intervene in non-Western cultures to promote literacy education that did not prove successful (see, e.g., Scribner & Cole, 1973, 1981).

## REFERENCES

Aber, J. L., Bishop-Josef, S. J., Jones, S. M., Taaffe McLearn, K., & Phillips, D. A. (Eds.). (2006). *Child development and social policy: Knowledge for action.* Washington, DC: American Psychological Association.

Bakhtin, M. M. (1981). *The dialogic imagination: Four essays* (M. Holquist & C. Emerson, Trans.). Austin: University of Texas Press.

Bakhtin, M. M. (1986). *Speech genres and other late essays* (M. Holquist & C. Emerson, Trans.). Austin: University of Texas Press.

Bereiter, C., & Engelmann, S. (1966). *Teaching disadvantaged children in preschool.* Englewood Cliffs, NJ: Prentice-Hall.

Biddle, B. (2001). Poverty, ethnicity, and achievement in American schools. In *Social class, poverty, and education: Policy and practice* (pp. 1–29). New York: Routledge-Falmer.

Bradley, R. H., & Corwyn, R. F. (2002). Socioeconomic status and child development. *Annual Review of Psychology, 53,* 371–399.

Cole, M. (1996). *Cultural psychology: A once and future discipline.* Cambridge, MA: Belknap Press of Harvard University Press.

Coleman, J. S. (1987). Social capital and the development of youth. *Momentum, 18*(4), 6–8.

Coleman, J. S. (1988). Social capital and the creation of human capital. *American Journal of Sociology, 94,* S95–S120.

Collins, J., & Blot, R. (Eds.). (2003). *Literacy and literacies: Texts, power, and identity. Studies in the social and cultural foundations of language.* Cambridge, UK: Cambridge University Press.

Council of Economic Advisors. (2000). *Educational attainment and success in the new economy: An analysis of challenges for improving Hispanic student's achievement.* Washington, DC: Executive Office of the President.

Dalton, S. S. (2007). *Five standards for effective teaching: How to succeed with all learners, grades K–8.* San Francisco: Jossey-Bass.

D'Angiulli, A., Siegel, L. S., & Hertzman, C. (2004). Schooling, socioeconomic context and literacy development. *Educational Psychology, 24*(6), 867–883.

De Vos, G., & Suárez-Orozco, M. M. (1990). *Status inequality: The self in culture.* Newbury Park, CA: Sage.

Duncan, G., & Brooks-Gunn, J. (2000). Family, poverty, welfare reform, and child development. *Child Development, 71*(1), 188–196.

Duncan, G., Brooks-Gunn, J., Yeung, W.-J., & Smith, J. (1998). How much does childhood poverty affect the life chances of children? *American Sociological Review, 63,* 406–423.

Gibson, M. A. (1988). *Accommodation without assimilation: Sikh immigrants in an American high school.* Ithaca, NY: Cornell University Press.

Hart, B., & Risley, T. (1995). *Meaningful differences in the everyday experience of young American children.* Baltimore: Brookes.

Haveman, R., & Wolfe, B. (1995). The determinants of children's attainment: A review of methods and findings. *Journal of Economic Literature, 33,* 1829–1878.

Heath, S. B. (1983). *Ways with words: Language, life, and work in communities and classrooms.* New York: Cambridge University Press.

Heath, S. B. (1991). The sense of being literate: Historical and cross-cultural features. In R. Barr, M. Kamil, P. Mosenthal, & D. Pearson (Eds.), *Handbook of reading research* (Vol. 2, pp. 3–25). White Plains, NY: Longman.

Hess, R., & Shipman, V. (1965). Early experience and the socialization of cognitive modes in children. *Child Development, 36*(4), 869–886.

Holland, D. C., & Cole, M. (1995). Between discourse and schema: Reformulating a cultural–historical approach to culture and mind. *Anthropology and Education Quarterly, 26*(4), 475–489.

Holland, D. C., & Valsiner, J. (1988). Cognition, symbols, and Vygotsky's developmental psychology. *Ethos, 16*(3), 247–272.

Johnson, L. B. (1964). *President Lyndon B. Johnson's Annual Message to Congress on the State of the Union.* Retrieved January 10, 2008, from *www.lbjlib.utexas.edu/johnson/archives. hom/speeches.hom/640108.asp.*

Johnston, P. (1999). *Unpacking literate "achievement"* (No. CELA-R-12007). Albany, NY: National Research Center on Reading and Achievement.

Kohlberg, L. (1987). *Child psychology and childhood education: A cognitive-developmental view.* New York: Longman.

Kozol, J. (1991). *Savage inequalities.* New York: HarperPerennial.

Kozol, J. (2005). *The shame of the nation: The restoration of apartheid schooling in America.* New York: Crown.

Kozulin, A. (1984). *Psychology in utopia: Toward a social history of Soviet psychology.* Cambridge, MA: MIT Press.

Kozulin, A. (1998). *Psychological tools: A sociocultural approach to education.* Cambridge, MA: Harvard University Press.

Kozulin, A., Gindis, B., Ageyev, V., & Miller, S. (Eds.). (2003). *Vygotsky's educational theory in cultural context.* New York: Cambridge University Press.

Lave, J., & Wenger, E. (1991). *Situated learning: Legitimate peripheral participation.* Cambridge, UK: Cambridge University Press.

Leont'ev, A. N. (1978). *Activity, consciousness and personality.* Englewood Cliffs, NJ: Prentice-Hall.

Leont'ev, A. N. (1981). *Problems of the development of the mind.* Moscow: Progress Publishers.

Levinson, B. A. (2000). *Schooling the symbolic animal: Social and cultural dimensions of education.* Lanham, MD: Rowman & Littlefield.

Levinson, B. A., Foley, D. E., & Holland, D. C. (1996). *The cultural production of the educated person: Critical ethnographies of schooling and local practice.* Albany: State University of New York Press.

Luria, A. R. (1976). *Cognitive development, its cultural and social foundations.* Cambridge, MA: Harvard University Press.

Matute-Bianchi, M. E. (1991). Situational ethnicity and patterns of school performance among immigrant and nonimmigrant Mexican-descent students. In J. U. Ogbu & M. A. Gibson (Eds.), *Minority status and schooling: A comparative study of immigrant and involuntary minorities* (pp. 205–247). New York: Garland.

Mayer, S. (1997). *What money can't buy: The effect of parental income on children's outcomes.* Cambridge, MA: Harvard University Press.

National Center for Public Policy and Higher Education. (2004). *The educational pipeline: Big investment, big returns.* San Jose, CA: Author.

Natriello, G., McDill, E., & Pallas, A. (1990). *Schooling disadvantaged children: Racing against catastrophe.* New York: Teachers College Press.

Oakes, J. (1985). *Keeping track: How schools structure inequality.* New Haven, CT: Yale University Press.

Ogbu, J. U. (1974). *The next generation: An ethnography of education in an urban neighborhood.* New York: Academic Press.

Ogbu, J. U. (1978). *Minority education and caste: The American system in cross-cultural perspective.* New York: Academic Press.

Ogbu, J. U. (2003). *Black American students in an affluent suburb: A study of academic disengagement.* Mahwah, NJ: Erlbaum.

Olsen, L. (1997). *Made in America: Immigrant students in our public schools.* New York: New Press.

Orfield, G., & Chungmai, L. (2007). *Historic reversals, accelerating resegregation, and the need for new integration strategies.* Retrieved January 10, 2008, from *www.civilrights. org/assets/pdfs/aug-2007-desegregation-report.pdf.*

Piaget, J. (1832). *The language and thought of the child.* New York: Harcourt Brace.

Portes, A., & Rumbaut, R. G. (2001). *Legacies: The story of the immigrant second generation.* Berkeley: University of California Press.

Portes, A., & Zhou, M. (1993). The new second generation: Segmented assimilation and its variants. *Annals of the American Academy of Political and Social Science, 530,* 74–96.

Portes, P. R. (1988). Maternal verbal regulation and intellectual development. *Roeper Review, 11*(2), 106–110.

Portes, P. R. (1996). Ethnicity and culture in educational psychology. In D. Berliner & R. Calfee (Eds.), *The handbook of educational psychology* (pp. 331–357). New York: Macmillian.

Portes, P. R. (1999). Social and psychological factors in the academic achievement of children of immigrants: A cultural history puzzle. *American Educational Research Journal, 36*(3), 489–507.

Portes, P. R. (2005). *Dismantling educational inequality: A cultural–historical approach to closing the achievement gap.* New York: Peter Lang.

Portes, P. R., Delgado-Romero, E., & Salas, S. (in press). Latinos (not) in higher education and the continuum of group based inequality: A cultural historical perspective. In D. Sandhu, B. Hudson, & M. Taylor-Archer (Eds.), *A handbook of diversity in higher education.* New York: Nova Science.

Portes, P. R., Gallego, M. A., & Salas, S. (2008). Dismantling group based inequality in a NCLB era, effective practices, and Latino students placed at risk. In E. G. Murillo (Ed.), *Handbook of Latinos and education: Research, theory and practice.* Mahwah, NJ: Erlbaum.

Portes, P. R., & Salas, S. (2007). Dreams deferred: Why multicultural education has failed to close the achievement gap: A cultural historical analysis. *Cultura y Educacion, 19*(4), 365–377.

Portes, P. R., & Vadeboncoeur, J. A. (2003). Mediation in cognitive socialization: The influence of socioeconomic status: Vygotsky's theory of education in cultural context. In A. Kozulin, B. Gindis, V. Ageyev, & S. Miller (Eds.), *Vygotsky's theory of education in cultural context* (pp. 371–392). New York: Cambridge University Press.

Pungello, E. P., Kupersmidt, J. B., & Vaden, N. A. (1996). Environmental risk factors and children's achievement from middle childhood to early adolescence. *Developmental Psychology, 32,* 755–767.

Ramey, C., & Ramey, S. (2004). Early learning and school readiness: Can early intervention make a difference? *Merrill–Palmer Quarterly, 50*(4), 471–491.

Rothstein, R. (2004). *Class and schools: Using social, economic, and educational reform to close the achievement gap.* Washington, DC: Economic Policy Institute.

Salomon, G. (1993). *Distributed cognitions: Psychological and educational considerations.* Cambridge, UK: Cambridge University Press.

Scott, D. M. (1997). *Contempt and pity: Social policy and the image of the damaged Black psyche, 1880–1996.* Chapel Hill: University of North Carolina Press.

Scribner, S., & Cole, M. (1973). Cognitive consequences of formal and informal education: New accommodations are needed between school-based learning and learning experiences of everyday life. *Science, 182,* 553–559.

Scribner, S., & Cole, M. (1981). *The psychology of literacy.* Cambridge, MA: Harvard University Press.

Selman, R. (1980). *The growth of interpersonal understanding.* New York: Academic Press.

Shonkoff, J. P., & Phillips, D. A. (Eds.). (2000). *From neurons to neighborhoods: The science of early childhood development.* Washington, DC: National Academy Press.

Suárez-Orozco, C., & Suárez-Orozco, M. M. (2001). *Children of immigration.* Cambridge, MA: Harvard University Press.

Tharp, R. G. (1989). Culturally compatible education: A formula for designing effective classrooms. In H. T. Trueba, G. Spindler, & L. Spindler (Eds.), *What do anthropologists have to say about dropouts?* (pp. 51–66). New York: Falmer Press.

Tharp, R. G., Estrada, P., Dalton, S. S., & Yamauchi, L. A. (2000). *Teaching transformed: Achieving excellence, fairness, inclusion and harmony.* Boulder, CO: Westview Press.

Tharp, R. G., & Gallimore, R. (1989). *Rousing minds to life: Teaching and learning in social context.* New York: Cambridge University Press.

Thomas, W. P., & Collier, V. P. (1996). *Language minority student achievement and program effectiveness.* Fairfax, VA: Center for Bilingual/Multicultural/ESL Education, George Mason University.

U.S. Department of Education, National Center for Education Statistics. (2004). *The Condition of Education 2004* (NCES 2004-077). Washington, DC: U.S. Government Printing Office.

Valdés, G. (1996). *Con respeto: Bridging the distances between culturally diverse families and schools: An ethnographic portrait.* New York: Teachers College Press.

Valdés, G. (2001). *Learning and not learning English: Latino students in American schools.* New York: Teachers College Press.

Valenzuela, A. (1999). *Subtractive schooling: U.S.–Mexican youth and the politics of caring.* Albany: State University of New York Press.

Van der Veer, R., & Valsiner, J. (Eds.). (1994). *The Vygostky reader.* Oxford, UK: Blackwell.

Vygotsky, L. S. (1978). *Mind in society: The development of higher psychological processes* (M. Cole, V. John-Steiner, S. Scribner, & E. Souberman, Trans.). Cambridge, MA: Harvard University Press.

Vygotsky, L. S. (1986). *Thought and language* (A. Kozulin, Trans.). Cambridge, MA: MIT Press.

Wertsch, J. V. (1985). *Vygotsky and the social formation of mind.* Cambridge, MA: Harvard University Press.

Wertsch, J. V. (1998). *Mind as action.* New York: Oxford University Press.

Wertsch, J. V. (2002). *Voices of collective remembering.* Cambridge, UK: Cambridge University Press.

Zigler, E., Gilliam, W., & Jones, S. M. (Eds.). (2006). *A vision for universal preschool education.* Cambridge, MA: Cambridge University Press.

# CHAPTER 6

# Language, Literacy, and Content
## Adolescent English Language Learners

ROBERT T. JIMÉNEZ *and* BRAD L. TEAGUE

M any would argue that no other feature matters as much to the economic prospects and social integration of English language learners (ELLs) as does schooling (Portes & Rumbaut, 2001; Tienda & Mitchell, 2006). Others take a more critical stance vis-à-vis the relationship between schooling and later job prospects (Graff, 1981; Luke, 2004; Pennycook, 2001), arguing that other factors, such as race, gender, and language background, also influence one's life chances with respect to economic advancement or social mobility. These issues take on added urgency when one considers that the number of ELLs affected by the relationship between schooling and economic advancement is substantial and continues to grow. Children of immigrants currently comprise 20% of the student population, and this number is projected to more than double within the next 20 years (National Center for Education Statistics, 2005; Tienda & Mitchell, 2006). Importantly, 71% of students identified as ELLs from 2004 to 2007 were performing below grade level, and they continue to be among the nation's lowest-performing students (Short & Fitzsimmons, 2007). It is clear that the number of ELLs in the secondary grades is sizable, is growing, and that this population is not currently being well served.

In this chapter we use the concept of *segmented assimilation*, developed by Portes and Rumbaut (2001; Rumbaut & Portes, 2001), to frame our review. Segmented assimilation posits that the social adaptation outcomes of immigrants depend on the background features, or "human capital," that individuals possess in interaction with what these researchers term the "contexts of reception." These contexts include labor market conditions, the quality of available schooling, the discursive constructions of immigrants held by the host society, the policies of the host government, the attitudes of the native population, and the presence and size of a co-ethnic community (Portes & Rumbaut, 2001, p. 46). In accord with this framework, we use empirically derived findings to show how the academic outcomes of adolescent ELLs likewise involve a combination of background factors, such as prior schooling, first language (L1) literacy, and English language proficiency, as well as contextual factors, including the types of programs and instructional environments available to them in U.S. and Canadian schools. We argue that an accurate understanding of how these factors work together is essential for researchers, policymakers, and educators.

In this chapter we discuss:

- Research that illustrates the chances for academic success associated with particular background characteristics.
- Research that highlights the impact of particular types of English as a second language (ESL) and bilingual programs, as well as the issues of tracking and forms of inclusion–exclusion.
- Research that offers promising directions regarding instructional strategies that have been shown to be effective with adolescent ELLs.

## METHOD

### Search for Literature

For this work we initially generated a list of 15 key pieces of literature dealing with the experiences of secondary-age ELLs based on our knowledge of literacy, second-language (L2) acquisition, and ESL and bilingual education. We likewise located and reviewed all recent issues (since 2000) of the *Journal of Adolescent and Adult Literacy* for articles germane to our purpose. Moreover, we conducted an electronic search of the Education Resources Information Center (ERIC) using combinations of the following descriptors: ELLs, secondary education, adolescents, literacy, L2, ESL, and bilingual. As we reviewed this literature, we added works cited as references that seemed both scholarly (i.e., peer-reviewed, empirical) and directly relevant to our topic. We were especially interested in research published within the last 10 years.

Next, we searched the following online databases: Education Abstracts, ERIC, InfoTrac, Linguistics and Language Behavior Abstracts (LLBA), ProQuest, PsycINFO, and Sociological Abstracts. We also ran relevant articles through the Web of Knowledge database to locate additional pieces of literature.

### Criteria for Inclusion

When locating and retaining sources, we verified that they met a number of specific criteria. In particular, included studies needed to be:

1. *Focused on adolescent ELLs*. Previous reviews of the literature have focused primarily on ELLs at the elementary level.
2. *Empirical*. Studies included in the review are based on the collection and analysis of data dealing with the learning and teaching of adolescent ELLs.
3. *Conducted in Canada or the United States*. We have limited our review to studies carried out in the United States and Canada given our interest in secondary-age ELLs in these settings.
4. *Published as peer-reviewed articles*. Our review comprises mostly articles that have undergone peer review by experts in the field. In some instances we include discussion of other sources (e.g., book chapters, book-length manuscripts, and research reports), if they present relevant empirical data.

## BACKGROUND FACTORS

### Prior Schooling

Prior schooling, a factor that may appear self-evident in terms of its influence on the secondary school achievement of ELLs, includes all of the formal education completed by ELLs in their country of origin before enrolling in schools within one of the 50 U.S. states or Canada. Typically, this schooling takes place in a language other than English. Although it might seem obvious that the more prior schooling that students complete in their country of origin, the better they will perform in schools, there are some unresolved issues concerning social and academic practices, as well as content-specific differences found in subjects such as literature and history. Adolescent ELLs also vary a great deal in terms of the amount and quality of their prior schooling experiences.

We found three research studies that reported a relationship between prior schooling and academic achievement (Callahan, 2005; Gunderson & Clarke, 1998; Padilla & González, 2001). As Callahan (2005) points out:

> Recent immigrants with significant amounts of previous schooling have mastered grade-level academic content and often require instruction only in English literacy skills. Having missed more than 1 year of academic instruction in their home country, recent immigrants with limited schooling require literacy skill development *and* content-area instruction in order to access the high school curriculum. (p. 312, original emphasis)

Callahan examined student performance in a northern California high school, in which 355 students were ELLs from various language backgrounds (89% of her subjects were native Spanish speakers). Employing a series of linear regression models, Callahan examined the relationship between a student's grade, gender, ELL level, track placement, academic achievement data, generational cohort, years of U.S. residence, and previous schooling. She found that recent immigrant participants in her study with significant amounts of previous schooling attained higher GPAs than those without this background, and also that these learners enrolled in slightly higher-level content-area classes. She also reported, however, that only 2% of her sample completed a sufficient number of college preparatory courses to qualify for admission to postsecondary schooling. Although prior schooling clearly affects student outcomes, other forces (to be addressed later) also influence students' overall social mobility.

Padilla and González (2001) examined 2,167 cases of Mexican-origin high school students in three different community/school settings. Based on responses to a 300-item questionnaire, the researchers conducted *t*-tests and analyses of variance (ANOVAs) to examine relationships among place of birth, academic track placement, years of ESL/bilingual education, years of schooling in Mexico, gender, high school attended, parents' education, and Spanish proficiency. The researchers found that receiving schooling in Mexico resulted in higher grade point averages (GPAs) in U.S. schools in comparison to students who completed all of their schooling in the United States. In addition, they found that the greater the amount of schooling students received in Mexico, the higher their grades tended to be. Interestingly, this effect was noted even for those students who although born in the United States (*n* = 82) were raised and educated in Mexico and later returned to the United States. The researchers explain their findings by noting that students taught in Mexico receive a solid foundation in basic academic skills in their primary language that then transfers to English.

Gunderson and Clarke (1998) also reported a positive relationship between years of schooling in the country of origin and academic achievement, in their case, for high school ELLs in Vancouver, Canada. The researchers looked at data collected for a random sample of 55 students selected from a larger population of 24,987 school-age immigrants. These students came from a variety of national origin backgrounds, although the majority were from Asian countries (close to 70%). The researchers reported that the relationship between the number of years of L1 schooling and academic achievement, as reported by GPA, was as follows: English, .47; math, .44; social studies, .52; and English writing, .49. They concluded that the relationship of prior schooling to academic achievement was positive, but they also pointed out that over 90% of all the students were 2 or more years behind in their L2, or English, literacy skills.

Like Callahan's work (2005), Gunderson and Clarke's (1998) final observation indicates that these students are still experiencing serious academic problems, which may indicate that neither schools in Canada nor those in the United States are meeting the needs of adolescent ELLs.

To interpret these results within our *segmented assimilation* framework (Portes & Rumbaut, 2001; Rumbaut & Portes, 2001), students with more prior schooling possess human capital that they are able to convert into desirable academic outcomes. This finding, although based on very few studies, seems to be true for both Asian and native Spanish-speaking students. Specifically, content learned through one language is accessible through the second. Moreover, it is probably the case that ELLs who arrive with significant amounts of prior schooling are able to devote more of their attention to language learning as opposed to having to focus simultaneously on both language and content, which researchers (e.g., Short & Fitzsimmons, 2007) term "double the work."

## L1 Literacy

Another form of human capital that many ELLs possess includes developed literacy skills in their native language. We located five sources that spoke directly to the relationship between L1 literacy and the academic achievement of secondary-age ELLs (Buriel & Cardoza, 1988; Collier, 1987; García-Vázquez, Vázquez, López, & Ward, 1997; Reese, Gallimore, & Guthrie, 2005; Reese, Garnier, Gallimore, & Goldenberg, 2000). All of these studies reported a positive relationship.

Buriel and Cardoza (1988) analyzed data gathered for the High School and Beyond longitudinal study to draw conclusions about the academic achievement of three generations of Mexican American high school seniors. Their sample was drawn from a group of 11,300 students who had indicated some use of a non-English language. Interestingly, they found that the three groups of students did not differ on any of the three achievement tests of math, reading, and vocabulary. One of the few differences they discovered was that third-generation students who reported greater literacy skills in Spanish scored higher on their test of English reading. This was not true for the first and second generations. The researchers posited that some third-generation students in their senior year of high school might have been completing coursework in Spanish as a foreign language to fulfill higher-education admission requirements. As such, these students would be a select, college-bound group of higher than average achievers, whose study of Spanish interacts with their knowledge of English literacy.

Collier's (1987) study examined how long it took 1,548 ELLs to become proficient in academic English. In particular, the study focused on the relationship between length of residence and age on arrival, and grade-level performance, which included English reading outcomes. One of the groups she examined was students who arrived in the United States between the ages of 12 and 15. Collier found that these students experienced the most difficulty attaining grade-level performance, perhaps due to the advanced literacy demands of the curriculum. Her study suggests that whereas L1 literacy abilities can transfer across languages, ELLs also need to receive sustained instruction in academic English to prepare them to read and to understand conceptually complex texts in the later grades. Collier's work provides further support for Callahan's (2005) and Gunderson and Clarke's (1998) findings that ELLs at the secondary level experience notably high levels of academic stress.

Reese and colleagues (2000), in a longitudinal study of 121 Latino children in two school districts in California, looked at the antecedents of Spanish literacy and its effects on English reading outcomes. Specifically, these researchers followed a group of ELLs from kindergarten through middle school, and collected both quantitative and qualitative data on their backgrounds and progress.

These researchers found that early family literacy practices in Spanish and level of oral English proficiency—as measured when students were in kindergarten—predicted reading outcomes in English when students reached grade 7.

In a follow-up study, Reese and colleagues (2005) collected data on their original 121 subjects from kindergarten through grade 8. In addition, they evaluated the effects of an intensive Spanish literacy intervention in kindergarten with one-fourth of the students in this group. By the end of eighth grade, 91 students remained. The effects of this intervention were statistically significant through grade 3, and students still enjoyed a 9 percentile point advantage through grade 8. However, the researchers reported that, as a group, students performed about a half a standard deviation below the norm in their English reading throughout elementary and middle school, and also that as many as 33% of their entire sample (91 students) scored one or more standard deviations below national norms at the end of grade 8. These results are cause for concern, because one could interpret the middle school academic performance of these students as a predictor for dropping out of high school. At the same time, the results offer support for providing effective Spanish literacy instruction to native Spanish-speaking students in kindergarten.

García-Vázquez and colleagues (1997) looked at the relationship between English and Spanish proficiency and academic success. Specifically, they examined correlations between oral language, literacy, and scores on English academic achievement tests. Their participants included randomly selected Hispanic students (n = 151) in grades 6–12 in a Midwestern school district. They found significant correlations between proficiency in Spanish (based on standardized assessments) and English-language test scores. The strongest correlations existed between reading, writing, and vocabulary. They concluded that Spanish literacy clearly appears to have a positive influence on standardized achievement tests in English, especially skills such as "proofing, spelling, and grammar" (p. 343), which are evaluated on the tests in English. García-Vázquez and colleagues attributed their findings to the potential transfer of cognitive academic language proficiency (CALP; Cummins, 1979) between the two languages.

All of these studies offer support for Cummins's (1979, 1981) notions of "common underlying proficiency" and the "interdependence hypothesis." Cummins argued that the knowledge and skills acquired in one language, including many literacy abilities, are available for additional languages; that is, certain types of skills seem to transfer from one language to another, and, for this reason, all known languages become potential resources on which ELLs can draw for academic learning (see also Genesee, Lindholm-Leary, Saunders, & Christian, 2006). For the purposes of our analysis, we consider L1 literacy as a form of capital (Portes & Rumbaut, 2001; Rumbaut & Portes, 2001) that adolescent ELLs possess in different quantities. As was the case with prior schooling, the more of this type of capital they possess, the higher their predicted outcomes relative to academic achievement.

Nevertheless, it is worth noting that the findings reported by Buriel and Cardoza (1988), Collier (1987), and Reese and her colleagues (2000, 2005) either directly or indirectly suggest that all secondary-age ELLs still experience significant academic difficulties compared to their native English-speaking counterparts. Once again, this result is probably due to the enormous demands placed on them as they attempt to learn a new language in addition to a very conceptually dense curriculum. There may also be other factors associated with adolescence that have not been sufficiently addressed by these researchers, particularly those involving social factors. In Bourdieuian (1991, 1998) terms, (mis)recognition of their available capital probably accounts for at least some of the difficulties these students face.

### English Language Proficiency

Several of the studies also examined the influence of English language proficiency, both oral and literate, on students' learning. Reese and colleagues (2000) noted that students' English literacy in grade 7 was predicted by both their Spanish literacy abilities and their English oral proficiency, as measured in kindergarten. These researchers reported that the average length of U.S. residence for parents predicted their children's English oral proficiency and that this in turn predicted their English reading achievement in grade 7. García-Vázquez and colleagues (1997) found that as the English proficiency of their participants (ELLs in grades 6–12) increased, so did their achievement on standardized tests and their GPAs. Importantly, it was not how much English they learned as they worked their way through the grades but the amount of English they brought with them as they began their school careers that determined their later achievement levels. This finding suggests that many adolescent ELLs who arrive in the United States without this type of capital may not, under typical current conditions, ever have the opportunity to develop it in U.S. secondary schools. This finding fits well with Bourdieu's analysis of how schools favor individuals from privileged backgrounds because of their use of prestige language forms, especially in terms of diction and vocabulary (Swartz, 1997).

Watt and Roessingh (2001) examined a high school in Alberta, Canada, where 40% of the students were ELLs. They looked at two cohorts of students, the first ($n = 295$) of which had received more ESL instruction than the second ($n = 210$) because of budget cuts. They found that students' beginning English proficiency level was a powerful predictor of their educational outcomes, specifically among those students who had learned English in Canadian middle schools or in their home countries. Shockingly, almost 75% of students in both cohorts eventually dropped out of high school. Students who received less ESL instruction dropped out faster than those who had received more ESL instruction. The researchers found that, compared to their native English-speaking counterparts, these students had only a 1 in 10 chance of passing their grade 12 literature-based course, which is a university entrance requirement. Of concern is that only students who began their studies with high levels of English proficiency seemed to have had any hope of completing their high school education.

All of the previous studies point to English proficiency as a critical factor in the academic success of adolescent ELLs. English proficiency assumes the status of a highly valuable form of capital (Portes & Rumbaut, 2001; Rumbaut & Portes, 2001) that is either present or absent—dichotomous in nature—for the schools involved in the previous research studies. Students either begin their studies in possession of English proficiency or they do not, and high-quality instruction of academic English is not typically provided or available. Interestingly, Callahan (2005) concluded that prior schooling had more of an influence than English oral proficiency on her participants' GPAs. These discrepancies may be explained by the fact that Callahan looked at achievement in the content areas as an outcome, which requires substantial subject-matter knowledge, and at the effects of oral English proficiency, not at all aspects of language proficiency, including reading and writing abilities. Reese and colleagues (2000), on the other hand, focused on English reading, which, in most instances, can be considered more relevant than oral proficiency to school success.

Although high levels of proficiency in literacy do facilitate school success, it is theoretically and practically possible to divorce literacy from content-specific knowledge of subjects such as math and science. Even so, it seems possible that higher levels of literacy also spur content learning. Durán and Weffer (1992) reported that this was the case for adolescent ELLs in an afterschool science education program. That said, we recognize that the best academic outcomes are frequently the product of capital in the form of both strong language skills (including literacy) and highly developed content knowledge. An important finding of these studies is that ELLs in U.S. and Canadian schools are typically not given the English-language instruction they need to overcome initially low levels of English proficiency. It seems reasonable to ask how more effective language instruction might be made available.

## PROGRAMS

Recent research that looks at the types of programs available to secondary-level ELLs across the United States and Canada has informed our understanding of what seems to be most and least effective. This literature clusters around several major topics that include tracking, inclusion versus marginalization of ELLs within schools, high-quality versus poor ESL programs, and dual-language education. In this section we explore each of these issues in turn.

### Tracking

"Tracking" refers to the placement of students into different groups within schools based on their perceived academic abilities. Although it may be argued that tracking is beneficial in that it provides students with more individualized instruction in accordance with their needs, in secondary education this means that students receive differential preparation for college. Townsend and Fu (2001), citing the work of Oakes (1985), state that similar-grade classrooms in the same school may differ in their "selection of reading materials, classroom and homework requirements, academic expectations, and instructional approaches" (pp. 108–109). Unfortunately, ELLs are overrepresented in low-track classrooms.

Callahan (2005) found that track placement, coupled with previous schooling, correlated more highly with the academic success of ELLs than did English language proficiency. Of significance, she reports that around 98% of the ELLs in the northern California high school she studied were not enrolled in courses that would prepare them for 4-year colleges. Similarly, Padilla and González (2001) discovered that the average GPA of Mexican-origin students at the high school level was higher, regardless of age on arrival, for those who were enrolled in the college—as opposed to the general—track.

Other researchers who have considered the effects of tracking on ELLs are Harklau (1999) and Koyama (2004). Harklau, whose work focused on the learning environments of another U.S. high school, found that ELLs who were taking more high-track courses enjoyed "more copious linguistic interaction with academic, content-area material" (p. 52). These learners were likewise more active participants in class compared to those enrolled in lower-level tracks. In fact, Harklau wrote that ELLs in low-track courses were generally isolated and rarely had the opportunity to speak in class. She also found that the classes she studied differed in the kinds of activities engaged in by the students. For instance, high-level classes encouraged ELLs to "synthesize, analyze, and interpret reading material" (p. 54), practices that are valued in higher education. Low-level classes, in contrast, focused primarily on the development of basic skills, such as sight reading and vocabulary study.

Koyama (2004) conducted her study in a northern California high school. She looked specifically at the positioning and experiences of low-income, Mexican-origin ELLs who attended a predominantly non-Hispanic, white, middle- to upper-middle-class school. In her work she identified she existence of "two separate high schools," the mainstream "English-only" high school and the ELLs' school (p. 415). The latter was characterized by marginalization and expectations of failure. Also, Koyama noted that even though it was possible in theory to make the transition from ESL classes to the mainstream, in practice the "physical and linguistic isolation, the standardized testing, and the curricula made it almost impossible to do so" (p. 417), thus further constraining ELLs' effort and potential.

Together, these studies highlight the negative effects of tracking on the academic success of ELLs. Drawing on the segmented assimilation framework (Portes & Rumbaut, 2001; Rumbaut & Portes, 2001), we argue that tracking forms part of the "context of reception" that immigrant students encounter in the new country and school system. Placement in lower tracks within schools means that learners have a decreased chance of being adequately prepared for entry into 4-year colleges and universities. In this way, tracking placement interacts with the human capital students bring with them upon arrival.

## Inclusion versus Marginalization of ELLs

A few recently published studies shed light on the issue of the marginalization of ELLs within secondary school programs. Coulter and Smith (2006), for example, looked at the ways in which eight ELLs at an Alaskan high school confronted the traditional structure of the school. Over a 5-year period, the researchers concluded that (1) ELLs generally felt excluded from school functions and activities; (2) they were not given the same types of classrooms and materials as mainstream students; (3) their instruction was of lower quality; (4) they were tracked into remedial classes, which operated on low expectations; (5) they were isolated from native English speakers; (6) they were expected to assimilate; and (7) their native cultures and languages were devalued by the school.

Along the same lines, Gitlin, Buendía, Crosland, and Doumbia (2003) examined an ESL program for ELLs in a middle school located in the western United States. They set out to identify what, in addition to English, students acquired as part of their experiences in this setting. The school served students from Bosnian, Lebanese, Mexican, Sudanese, and Somali national origins, and also students from different Asian backgrounds. In short, the researchers found that whereas educators in the school officially espoused a welcoming policy of inclusion, a great many of the day-to-day practices stereotyped and excluded ELLs from true acceptance and inclusion into the broader school community. For instance, the school lacked appropriate ESL materials, many ELLs felt that their participation in school activities was limited, and local media discourses positioned low-income immigrants (particularly Hispanics) as problematic and unwanted. These conditions echo those described by Coulter and Smith (2006).

Reeves (2004, 2006) worked in a southeastern U.S. school district with 279 high school, subject-area teachers. Her study focused on teachers' attitudes and perceptions of ELLs in their classrooms. She found that even though the teachers expressed positive attitudes toward the inclusion of ELLs in their classes, their actual instructional practices reflected an assimilationist, English-only policy. Accordingly, these teachers did not view diversity as "legitimate vehicles for learning" (2004, p. 50), especially considering that the teachers generally lacked experience with diverse students. Reeves likewise reported that a number of problems interfered with her participants' abilities to improve their practice with ELLs, including a lack of willingness to change or to seek additional professional development, and even an unwillingness to recognize the need to modify instruction to better meet the needs of ELLs.

These three studies illustrate that although schoolwide programs and policies may superficially promote the inclusion of ELLs, actual practices tend to marginalize these learners in a number of ways. Portes and Rumbaut (2001) stress the impact of the host society and the ways in which it "receives" different immigrant populations. The researchers point out that minorities who are diverse in terms of their "physical appearance, class background, language, and religion" (p. 47) usually face more difficulties concerning their reception. We see similar processes at work in the studies just reviewed. In particular, school environments may include hidden obstacles with which certain groups of adolescent ELLs have to deal.

## Quality of ESL Programs

Research studies have reported mixed findings concerning the quality and usefulness of ESL programs at the secondary level. This issue is worthy of attention given the fact that ESL programs, which are (in theory) designed to support the learning of ELLs, too often fail to reach this goal. When poorly implemented, they can contribute to further isolation and underachievement.

Valdés (1998, 2001), whose work focused on the experiences of Hispanic-origin children in a California middle school, described the school's ESL program as comprising students of different ages and levels of proficiency, and as involving mostly the activities of copying vocabulary words and simple sentences. Moreover, the ELLs she studied had minimal contact with native speakers of English besides their teachers (often in large classes) and, even in the company of other ELLs, tended to work independently. Considering that the ESL instruction was inadequate and also that many of the mainstream teachers were not willing to work with students for whom English was a second language, most ELLs in this program were never transitioned into regular, content-area classrooms, thus remaining in what Valdés termed the "ESL ghetto." Valdés likewise found that the ESL teachers in this program did little to modify their speech to accommodate the needs of ELLs with lower levels of proficiency in English, and they rarely connected language lessons to meaningful content or communication.

Along similar lines, Godina (2004), through ethnographic research in a rural Midwestern high school, found that Mexican-background ELLs were often segregated from native English speakers and were relegated to low instructional tracks. There were very few qualified bilingual or ESL teachers in the school (only non-trained bilingual aides), and many of the classroom activities were decontextualized, in other words, focused on discrete language points as opposed to meaningful content. Godina also noted the teachers' low expectations and attitudes toward ELLs, their resistance toward allowing students to use their native languages as resources, and the lack of appropriate instructional materials. In another study, Ofelia García (1999) concluded that the ESL curriculum in two New York high schools serving large numbers of Dominican immigrants was "extremely easy and childish" (p. 72). More specifically, she observed that students were discouraged from using their L1 to aid in acquisition of English, they did not learn how to use English for authentic purposes, and teachers did not typically alter their instructional strategies to accommodate students' diverse linguistic needs (e.g., using gestures to communicate meaning). Furthermore, as in the Godina (2004) and Valdés (1998) studies, García discovered that ELLs spent a large part of their time copying and memorizing, without developing the ability actually to use their L2 for real-life purposes.

All three of these studies describe what can be considered poor ESL programs that do little to support secondary-age ELLs in their learning of English and grade-appropriate content. A few other researchers have reported on more promising ESL environments. Harklau (1999), for instance, found that the ESL classes she observed in a California high school seemed much more beneficial for the students than did their content-area classes. In particular, the ESL classes provided ELLs with plentiful opportunities for spoken interaction, meaningful practice in reading and writing, exposure to comprehensible input, and L2-learner-sensitive feedback. Additionally, in the ESL environment, students experienced a "haven for non-native speakers, where they could be among peers who understood the immigrant experience, what they had left behind and what they were going through at home and at school" (pp. 50–51).

Roessingh (2006), in a more recent publication, also documented a successful high school ESL program in Calgary, Canada. To determine the key features of this program, the researcher solicited the perspectives of 10 Asian-background, immigrant students who had already graduated and had since continued on to college. Based on student responses during interviews, Roessingh concluded that building trust with the ESL teacher contributed in large part to the success of the ESL program. Specifically, the teacher was highly trained, she cared about and was considered a "friend" to her students, and she provided a bridge between the families and the school. Other factors that played a role in the students' high level of achievement included high expectations for ELLs, a "family" of other ELLs, and ongoing communication among parents, students, and teachers. The author makes the point that when ESL programs are effective, as this one was, they are seen as valuable by both students and their parents.

The research reviewed in this section draws attention to the fact that ESL programs can be either beneficial or detrimental, depending on how they are conceptualized and implemented. Strong programs do the following: employ highly-trained teachers, encourage learners to engage with challenging yet appropriately adapted materials and activities, find ways to include parents and students in decision making, monitor student progress, allow opportunities for interaction and feedback (including with native English speakers), and focus on the development of the types of oral and written language valued by academic institutions. As was the case with tracking placement and inclusion–exclusion features, the quality of programs designed to support the learning of ELLs is an integral aspect of the context of reception available to adolescent newcomers. Those who have access to strong programs would be predicted to achieve on higher levels than those enrolled in lower-quality programs.

## INSTRUCTIONAL ACTIVITIES

We found seven studies dealing with the classroom instruction of secondary-level ELLs in North American contexts. This work serves to highlight the challenges facing ELLs who are learning English and content-area material simultaneously. These challenges boil down to providing these students with grade-appropriate content, as well as the tools to participate in common classroom activities. The authors of these studies often present ways to scaffold and support secondary-age ELLs in the process of learning challenging and conceptually dense curricula. Here we divide our discussion into general strategies and content-specific strategies.

### General Teaching Strategies

Three studies involved examinations of instruction that may be considered to possess cross-content-area applications, including a study of the use of cooperative learning (Jacob, Rottenberg, Patrick, & Wheeler, 1996), a study of cognitive learning strategies (O'Malley, Chamot, Stewner-Manzanares, Russo, & Kupper, 1985), and a study of vocabulary instruction (Carlo et al., 2004). Again, we feel that these findings are useful for understanding content-area learning in a variety of subject matters.

Jacob and colleagues (1996) focused on the use of cooperative learning in a sixth-grade classroom. Over the fall and spring semesters, she and her colleagues videotaped 12 cooperative learning groups, in which eight students were learning English. The study was not designed so much to speak to the efficacy of cooperative learning as to determine students' opportunities to acquire academic English as a result of their participation. These researchers found that ELLs did receive help from their English-only peers and from each other, particularly with academic terms and concepts, and written English. They also had opportunities to receive linguistic input and to produce oral English. Nevertheless, there were fewer such opportunities than expected. Jacob and her colleagues reported that they "found only 71 instances of positive opportunities over a total of 8¾ hours of interaction in the cooperative learning groups" (p. 268). These researchers conclude that cooperative learning "is a potentially powerful instructional strategy that requires careful attention" (p. 274). Significantly, for ELLs to benefit from cooperative learning activities, teachers need to provide more instruction and monitoring of student behavior during these sessions. It should be noted here that cooperative learning is a widely recommended technique to teachers of ELLs.

O'Malley and colleagues (1985) interviewed ELLs and their teachers to identify their use of cognitive strategies on a variety of common classroom tasks. They also taught strategies for vocabulary, listening, and speaking tasks to randomly selected students. Their participants for the first phase included 70 beginning- or intermediate-level ELLs in high school. All students were from Spanish-speaking backgrounds, with the exception of five students from Vietnam, and all were judged by their teachers to be of high academic ability. For the second phase of the study, the researchers' participants included 75 high school–age ELLs at an intermediate level. This time, one-third were Spanish speakers, another third were Asian, and the remainder came from other language backgrounds. The researchers reported limited success in teaching students to apply the vocabulary, listening, and speaking strategies identified in the first phase to typical learning tasks. This sort of outcome was typical of a great deal of the early research on cognitive and metacognitive strategies, and probably reflected technical difficulties of matching outcome measures to the constructs of interest. The researchers concluded that the application of strategies to new learning activities requires ongoing prompts and carefully guided direction.

Carlo and colleagues (2004) examined the results of an intervention designed to teach academic vocabulary to Latino students. Their study included 254 bilingual and monolingual children from nine fifth-grade classrooms in four schools in California, Virginia, and Massachusetts, and served students from Mexican American, Puerto Rican and Dominican, and other Caribbean and Central American backgrounds. Of the students, 142 were ELLs and 112 were English-only monolinguals (EOs). Ninety-four of the ELLs and 75 of the EOs participated in the intervention. The researchers found that students in the intervention showed greater gains on measures of word mastery, word association, and polysemy than did students in the comparison group. They concluded, "A challenging curriculum that focused on teaching academic words, awareness of polysemy, strategies for inferring word meaning from context, and tools for analyzing morphological and cross-linguistic aspects of word meaning did improve the performance of both ELL and EO fifth graders, to equal degrees" (p. 203). It may be concluded from this work that ELLs learn when vocabulary is taught to them explicitly and they benefit from learning about cross-linguistic relationships that include cognates and also retain more information when teachers highlight multiple aspects of vocabulary.

Obviously, the research in this area is thin and scattered over the early middle school grades and the latter high school years. These studies provide only brief glimpses of how instruction for secondary-level ELLs might be better designed to improve academic outcomes Still, it seems reasonable to conclude that focused instruction on cooperative learning, cognitive learning strategies, and vocabulary ought to be included in any program provided to these students. What is not known from this literature is what other, potentially beneficial cross-disciplinary instruction might be valuable.

## Content-Specific Teaching Strategies

Secondary-level ELLs face several specific challenges in terms of learning English and academic content. Duff (2001) conducted a 2-year study of the observed and reported challenges involving language, literacy, content, and culture facing ELLs in two grade 10 social studies classes (in Canada). The classrooms comprised 24 and 28 students, one of which included 17 ELLs, and the other 8 ELLs. There was a mixture of Cantonese and Mandarin speakers, with smaller numbers of Korean, Japanese, and Indonesian recent arrivals. Duff found that the teachers she observed often required the ELLs to become involved in a variety of activities, such as role plays, debates, poster making, and group presentations. All of these activities entailed various language, literacy, and interaction skills. However, these teachers, although clearly gifted in terms of the subject matter and with respect to their pedagogical skills, overlooked the specific language needs required to participate. For this reason, even when the ELLs were pushed to become involved, they responded with "brief, partially audible responses" (p. 116).

Nussbaum (2002) worked—over the course of a school year—in two sixth-grade urban classrooms that served 67 students from Latino (54%), African American (26%), and Asian (20%) backgrounds. He then selected four target students and analyzed their discourse in depth. According to the researcher, these target students, two African Americans and two Latinos, reflected a range of verbal Comprehensive Test of Basic Skills (CTBS) scores, proficiency levels in English, gender, and ethnicities. Recognizing that secondary ELLs need to learn how to participate appropriately in oral discussions of academic and social content, he had the focal students engage in *critical discussions*, that is, discussions of student-relevant topics (e.g., immigration) from a critical standpoint. Importantly, Nussbaum taught them the specific language (e.g., question formation) required to participate in these discussions. He found that the discussions allowed the learners both to resolve differences with others and to improve their language and content knowledge (p. 489). In particular, Nussbaum noted that this critical approach increased the amount of discourse produced by linguistic-minority students. He found it especially noteworthy for one male student, who gradually began asking more questions. The author's interpretation was that these questions involved him in more ongoing social interactions, which in turn allowed him to expand his linguistic knowledge. These findings are suggestive of the possibility that with engaging curriculum and explicit instruction on certain linguistic structures, ELLs can participate more actively in grade-level activities.

Similarly, Wolfe (2004) worked with adolescent ELLs in a large, inner-city high school in the Southwest (62% Latino, 11% Anglo, 24% African American), with the goal of helping them understand textual abstract literary concepts, such as *symbolism* and *theme*. Wolfe audio- and videotaped 30 literature study sessions for this work. The students, mostly immigrants from Mexico, had completed between 2 and 8 years of schooling in the United States. One of their assignments in an advanced ESL course was to read the novel *Bless Me, Última*. The teacher validated the contributions of all students even when their comments did not seem relevant to the discussion of the text. For example, while discussing the symbolism of the owl in the novel, one student mentioned that some pet shops in Mexico sell owls. Whenever possible, the teacher reformulated students' comments to approximate more closely those of scholarly literary analysis. Likewise, the teacher made an effort to connect complex ideas of *symbolism* and *theme* to concrete examples. These are important instructional techniques, because they involve students in discussion of grade-level literature. Moreover, they provide students with explicit models of how to analyze and deeply process texts. Wolfe claimed that the students in this class learned how to talk about books. She provides five detailed student responses as evidence that students achieved this goal. One of the significant contributions of Wolfe's work is that it provides specific guidance to English teachers regarding how to involve linguistic-minority students more effectively in learning about literacy concepts such as *symbolism* and *theme.*

Goldstein (2002) examined how to help high school–age ELLs represent their own language-learning experiences, and to research language and culture within their school communities. She did this by providing for students a play-writing workshop that comprised 12 sessions, three times a week, over a period of 4 weeks during the summer months (outside the regular school schedule). Fifteen students enrolled in grade 12 participated, and they were paid to complete reading and writing activities describing their own learning of English and how they negotiated linguistic differences in a Canadian school in Toronto. As part of the workshop, students had the opportunity to present their work to small, self-selected groups of students, to create videotapes of their plays, and to see demonstrations and hear lectures on how to write their plays. Goldstein concluded that these activities provided students with the instruction and practice they needed to present an oral presentation, an otherwise daunting task. She also pointed out that instruction for ELLs needs to go beyond the technical aspects of language learning to include political components as well.

## CONCLUSION AND IMPLICATIONS

### Implications for Instructional Practice

Our review of the literature suggests several implications for instructional practice. The findings reveal that students who begin studies with prior schooling in their countries of origin, who have previous knowledge of English, and who are literate in their native languages can expect to perform at higher levels in U.S. and Canadian schools. Even so, the Callahan (2005) and Gunderson and Clarke (1998) studies warn that most ELLs are not achieving in ways that allow for college admission. The implications are that instruction appears to require very careful examination of the sequence and content of teaching, as well as better monitoring of student progress.

The research by Reese and colleagues (2000, 2005) suggests that quality L1 literacy instruction in the early grades is beneficial to students' later academic achievement. For students without L1 literacy, who immigrate at ages later than the primary grades, our recommendation is that educators and school systems make intensive L1 literacy instruction available. This might be done through summer school instruction, afterschool lessons, or via community weekend schools of the type currently found in some ethnic communities (see Tse, 2001). Buriel and Cardoza's (1988) study suggests that Spanish-for-Spanish-speakers classes would be useful for many second- and third-generation immigrants. We recommend that such instructional provisions be combined with intensive L1 literacy instruction.

Perhaps the most obvious area of intervention is English instruction. Just as standards for student achievement have been carefully mapped by many states, a detailed and careful analysis of the English-language demands of each subject area is needed to provide teachers with specific guidance for instruction. Recommendations of this type have been made by experts in the field (e.g., Harper & de Jong, 2004). Indeed, all teachers of ELLs need to identify continuously the specific language demands of each content area vis-à-vis the perspective of an ELL.

ELLs should be able to obtain instruction that allows them to acquire the English they need to succeed in North American schools. As the research makes clear, however, they are not currently developing these proficiencies. This outcome appears to be the result of a lack of support provided to teachers. Indeed, many of the studies we reviewed indicate that teachers lack even basic curricular and material support for their efforts (Callahan, 2006; Gitlin et al., 2003; Valdés, 1998; Watt & Roessingh, 2001). In addition, very little programmatic support appears to be available to secondary-level ELLs in the form of bilingual and ESL instruction. We argue that any school that serves these students needs to analyze both instruction and content from the students' perspectives. Just as universities with study abroad programs think deeply and carefully about students' needs during their time outside the United States or Canada, the same consideration, planning, and thought needs to be invested in the programs and instruction offered to secondary-level ELLs.

One of the needs of secondary-level ELLs is to gain entry into the social and academic worlds of the schools in which they are enrolled. As anyone who has ever worked with students engaged in the process of learning English can attest, this is a difficult issue. Still, the research of Goldstein (2002), Nussbaum (2002), and Wolfe (2004) provide at least hints of how students can become actively involved in classrooms. Although we need to pay serious attention to the English-language needs of these learners, we need to pay equally serious attention to their content learning needs. The challenge here is to identify ways to help ELL students "get into the game," so that they are included as "legitimate" participants.

The instructional research that we examined recommends several key ideas. Instruction needs to be designed and structured with ELLs in mind. Students need to be able to participate in oral discussions, role plays, debates, poster making, and individual and group presentations (Duff, 2001; Goldstein, 2002; Nussbaum, 2002; Wolfe, 2004). Students need carefully designed instruction that provides the tools necessary to accomplish these tasks. Goldstein (2002) also recommends that teachers find ways to integrate the ELL experience into course content. This suggestion appears to have the added benefit of providing built-in motivation for students. Nussbaum (2002) provided recommendations and ideas for how ELLs can get involved in class discussion via engaging content and question-asking strategies. Engaging content that is culturally affirming and familiar has the potential to motivate students to "get into the game."

Finally, although L1 literacy is associated with improved academic performance, our interpretation of the literature is that the burden of transferring this knowledge to tasks involving English literacy is typically left to the students. Students with well-developed metalinguistic knowledge of how their two languages relate to each other and sophisticated understandings of the necessary conditional knowledge of what to access from their L1 literacy probably perform at higher levels than those without this knowledge (Jiménez, García, & Pearson, 1995, 1996). We encourage teachers to assume the role of comprehension monitor for the ELLs in their classrooms. It is important to remind learners when it makes sense to draw on their knowledge of L1 literacy, when cognate relationships might be appropriate, and when knowledge of content gained via their L1 may facilitate their academic content learning in English.

## Implications for Future Research

The need for more research in this area is almost limitless. Nevertheless, certain lacunae are prominent. We found little research, for example, on how to make science and math content more accessible to ELLs (Durán & Weffer, 1992). Also, although we did not include research on the professional development of teachers, it is clear that all teachers working with ELLs need guided and targeted professional development opportunities that focus on how simultaneously to make academic English and grade-appropriate content accessible to ELLs at the secondary level (Gitlin et al., 2003; Jiménez & Teague, 2007; Reeves, 2004, 2006; Teague, 2007).

We also need research that specifies what instructional and curricular modifications are beneficial and effective in helping ELLs learn academic English and attain grade-appropriate achievement. Research in this area should establish guidelines and procedures for student placements in different academic programs. We likewise need research that examines the role that supportive programs, such as ESL and bilingual instruction, might provide to secondary students. Studies might look at focused interventions designed to examine the role that hostile and marginalizing contexts play in influencing student achievement. Importantly, what difference would a highly supportive and positive environment play in facilitating student achievement? Also needed is research that collects survey data from students and their parents concerning their experience in various program options, and assesses how school climates affect their content-area knowledge and learning of English.

## Final Thoughts

Although there are clearly many challenges in terms of providing secondary-level ELLs with quality content-area instruction and opportunities to learn English, we believe that the literature in this area offers at least some hopeful directions. At minimum, this work will require thinking about such learners in more humane terms. In essence, we need to consider ELLs' specific needs and design our programs and instruction accordingly. Of course, such work will require adequate support in the way of material resources, funding for conceptual and empirical work, and the talent necessary to find solutions to these challenges.

## REFERENCES

Bourdieu, P. (1991). *Language and symbolic power.* Cambridge, MA: Harvard University Press.

Bourdieu, P. (1998). *Practical reason.* Stanford, CA: Stanford University Press.

Buriel, R., & Cardoza, D. (1988). Sociocultural correlates of achievement among three generations of Mexican-American high school seniors. *American Educational Research Journal, 25*(2), 177–192.

Callahan, R. M. (2005). Tracking and high school English learners: Limiting opportunity to learn. *American Educational Research Journal, 42*(2), 305–328.

Callahan, R. M. (2006). The intersection of accountability and language: Can reading intervention replace English language development? *Bilingual Research Journal, 30*(1), 1–21.

Carlo, M. S., August, D., McLaughlin, B., Snow, C. E., Dressler, C., Lippman, D. N., et al. (2004). Closing the gap: Addressing the vocabulary needs of English-language learners in bilingual and mainstream classrooms. *Reading Research Quarterly, 39*(2), 188–215.

Collier, V. (1987). Age and rate of acquisition of second language for academic purposes. *TESOL Quarterly, 21*(4), 617–641.

Coulter, C., & Smith, M. L. (2006). English language learners in a comprehensive high school. *Bilingual Research Journal, 30*(2), 309–335.

Cummins, J. (1979). Linguistics interdependence and the educational development of bilingual children. *Review of Educational Research, 49*(2), 222–251.

Cummins, J. (1981). The role of primary language development in promoting educational success for language-minority students. In California State Department of Education (Ed.), *Schooling and language minority students: A theoretical framework* (pp. 3–49). Los Angeles: National Dissemination and Assessment Center.

Duff, P. (2001). Language, literacy, content, and (pop) culture: Challenges for ESL students in mainstream courses. *Canadian Modern Language Review, 58*(1), 103–132.

Durán, B. J., & Weffer, R. E. (1992). Immigrants' aspirations, high school process, and academic outcomes. *American Educational Research Journal, 29*(1), 163–181.

García, O. (1999). Educating Latino high school students with little formal schooling. In C. Faltis & P. Wolfe (Eds.), *So much to say: Adolescents, bilingualism and ESL in the secondary school* (pp. 61–82). New York: Teachers College Press.

García-Vázquez, E., Vázquez, L. A., López, I. C., & Ward, W. (1999). Language proficiency and academic success: Relationships between proficiency in two languages and achievement among Mexican American students. *Bilingual Research Journal, 21*(4), 334–347.

Genesee, F., Lindholm-Leary, K., Saunders, W., & Christian, D. (2005). English language learners in U. S. schools: An overview of research findings. *Journal of Education for Students Placed at Risk, 10*(4), 363–385.

Gitlin, A., Buendía, E., Crosland, K., & Doumbia, F. (2003). The production of margin and center: Welcoming–unwelcoming of immigrant students. *American Educational Research Journal, 40*(1), 91–122.

Godina, H. (2004). The contradictory literacy practices of Mexican background students: Results from an ethnography in the rural Midwest. *Bilingual Research Journal, 28*(2), 153–180.

Goldstein, T. (2002). No pain, no gain: Student playwriting as critical ethnographic language research. *Canadian Modern Language Review, 59*(1), 53–76.

Graff, H. J. (1981). *Literacy and social development in the west.* New York: Cambridge University Press.

Gunderson, L., & Clarke, D. K. (1998). An exploration of the relationship between ESL students' backgrounds and their English and academic achievement. *National Reading Conference Yearbook, 47.* 264–273.

Harklau, L. (1999). The ESL learning environment in secondary school. In C. J. Faltis & P. Wolfe (Eds.), *So much to say: Adolescents, bilingualism, and ESL in the secondary school* (pp. 42–60). New York: Teachers College Press.

Harper, C., & de Jong, E. (2004). Misconceptions about teaching English language learners. *Journal of Adolescent and Adult Literacy, 48*(2), 152–162.

Jacob, E., Rottenberg, L., Patrick, S., & Wheeler, E. (1996). Cooperative learning: Context and opportunities for acquiring academic English. *TESOL Quarterly, 30*(2), 253–280.

Jiménez, R. T., García, G. E., & Pearson, P. D. (1995). Three children, two languages, and strategic reading: Case studies in bilingual/monolingual reading. *American Educational Research Journal, 32,* 31–61.

Jiménez, R. T., García, G. E., & Pearson, P. D. (1996). The reading strategies of bilingual Latino/o students who are successful English readers: Opportunities and obstacles. *Reading Research Quarterly 31,* 90–109.

Jiménez, R. T., & Teague, B. L. (2007). Legitimacy, recognition, and access to language and literacy: English language learners at the secondary school level. In L. S. Rush, A. J. Eakle, & A. Berger (Eds.), *Secondary school literacy: What research reveals for classroom practice* (pp. 165–183). Urbana, IL: National Council of Teachers of English.

Koyama, J. P. (2004). Appropriating policy: Constructing positions for English language learners. *Bilingual Research Journal, 28*(3), 401–423.

Luke, A. (2004). Teaching after the marketplace: From commodity to cosmopolitan. *Teachers College Record, 103*(7), 1422–1443.

National Center for Education Statistics. (2005). *Highlights from the 2003 International Adult Literacy and Lifeskills Survey.* Washington, DC: United States Department of Education.

Nussbaum, E. M. (2002). The process of becoming a participant in small-group critical discussions: A case study. *Journal of Adolescent and Adult Literacy, 45*(6), 488–497.

Oakes, J. (1985). *Keeping track: How schools structure inequality.* New Haven, CT: Yale University Press.

O'Malley, J. M., Chamot, A. U., Stewner-Manzanares, G., Russo, R. P., & Kupper, L. (1985). Learning strategy applications with students of English as a second language. *TESOL Quarterly, 19*(3), 557–584.

Padilla, A. M., & González, R. (2001). Academic performance of immigrant and U.S.-born Mexican heritage students  Effects of schooling in Mexico and bilingual/English language instruction. *American Educational Research Journal, 38*(3), 727–742.

Pennycook, A. (2001). *Critical applied linguistics: A critical introduction.* Mahwah, NJ: Erlbaum.

Portes, A., & Rumbaut, R. G. (2001). *Legacies: The story of the immigrant second generation.* Berkeley: University of California Press.

Reese, L., Garnier, H., Gallimore, R., & Goldenberg, C. (2000). Longitudinal analysis of the antecedents of emergent Spanish literacy and middle-school English reading achievement of Spanish-speaking students. *American Educational Research Journal, 37*(3), 633–662.

Reese, L. J., Gallimore, R., & Guthrie, D. (2005). Reading trajectories of immigrant Latino students in transitional bilingual programs. *Bilingual Research Journal, 29*(3), 679–697.

Reeves, J. (2004). "Like everybody else": Equalizing educational opportunity for English language learners. *TESOL Quarterly, 38*(1), 43–66.

Reeves, J. (2006). Secondary teacher attitudes toward including English language learners in mainstream classrooms. *Journal of Educational Research, 99,* 131–142.

Roessingh, H. (2006). The teacher is the key: Building trust in ESL high school programs. *Canadian Modern Language Review, 62*(4), 563–590.

Rumbaut, R. G., & Portes, A. (Eds.). (2001). *Ethnicities: Children of immigrants in America.* Berkeley: University of California Press.

Short, D., & Fitzsimmons, S. (2007). *Double the work: Challenges and solutions to acquiring language and academic literacy for adolescent English language learners—A report to Carnegie Corporation of New York.* Washington, DC: Alliance for Excellent Education.

Swartz, D. (1997). *Culture and power: The sociology of Pierre Bourdieu.* Chicago: University of Chicago Press.

Teague, B. L. (2007). *Preparing teachers to work with English language learners: A research synthesis.* Unpublished qualifying paper, Vanderbilt University, Nashville, TN.

Tienda, M., & Mitchell, F. (Eds.). (2006). *Multiple origins, uncertain destinies: Hispanics and the American future.* Washington, DC: National Academies Press.

Townsend, J. S., & Fu, D. (2001). Paw's story: A Laotian refugee's lonely entry into American literacy. *Journal of Adolescent and Adult Literacy, 45*(2), 104–114.

Tse, L. (2001). *"Why don't they learn English?": Separating fact from fallacy in the U.S. language debate.* New York: Teachers College Press.

Valdés, G. (1998). The world outside and inside schools: Language and immigrant children. *Educational Researcher, 27*(6), 4–18.

Valdés, G. (2001). *Learning and not learning English: Latino students in American schools.* New York: Teachers College Press.

Watt, D., & Roessingh, H. (2001). The dynamics of ESL drop-out: *Plus ça change . . . Canadian Modern Language Review, 58*(2), 203–222.

Wolfe, P. (2004). "The owl cried": Reading abstract literacy concepts with adolescent ESL students. *Journal of Adolescent and Adult Literacy, 47*(5), 402–413.

# PART II

# SPECIAL ISSUES CONCERNING LITERACY

# Academic English and African American Vernacular English

## *Exploring Possibilities for Promoting the Literacy Learning of All Children*

CYNTHIA H. BROCK, GWENDOLYN THOMPSON MCMILLON,
JULIE L. PENNINGTON, DIANNA TOWNSEND, *and* DIANE LAPP

A central concern facing educators, past and present, is how to promote students' academic success in American public schools (Dewey, 1938; Flood, Heath, & Lapp, 2008; Lave, 1996; Wertsch, 1998). Although promoting students' academic success is a complex undertaking that involves a plethora of different components and priorities, scholars (e.g., Corson, 1997; Edwards, 2007; Scarcella, 2003; Schleppegrell, 2004) increasingly are pointing to the important role that the acquisition of Academic English (AE) plays in students' overall academic success.

According to Scarcella (2003), AE is a variety of English associated with different academic disciplines and used in professional publications (like this one). However, rather than explore AE in general, we sought to explore AE as it pertains to a particular category of students (i.e., African American students who are speakers of African American Vernacular English [AAVE]). This focus on research pertaining to students who speak AAVE is also in keeping with the conceptual focus of this handbook on issues of equity and diversity. In short, the purpose of this chapter is to explore two strands of scholarship (i.e., AE and AAVE) and the extent to which they coalesce, intertwine, and/or overlap to inform our thinking about children's literacy learning. More specifically, we discuss the following research and scholarship:

- Key definitions of language and our theoretical framework
- AE and its history, definition, and positionality
- Current research involving AE and children's literacy learning
- AAVE and its history, definition, and positionality
- Current scholarship involving AAVE and children's literacy learning
- Pedagogical and theoretical implications

## SYNTHESIS OF THE RESEARCH

### Key Definitions

Because this chapter focuses on language and the different varieties of language (i.e., AAVE, AE, and Standard English [SE]), we draw on the scholarship of several linguists and sociolinguists to define key terms that relate to our work. Whereas there is general agreement among linguists that language is a system of sounds and a combination of thoughts, words, and feelings used for effective communication between people in specific contexts, there is less agreement about the ambiguous manner in which language actually functions within and across contexts (Crawford, 1993; Fillmore, 1986; Perez & McCarty, 2004; Smitherman, 1995).

Scholars such as Hymes (1974), Wardhaugh (1998), and Wolfram, Adger, and Christian (1999) use the term "language variation" to refer to the nonuniform nature of language. Wolfram and his colleagues note that language varies with respect to the "sociocultural characteristics of groups of people such as their cultural background, geographical location, social class, gender, or age" (p. 1). They also suggest that language variation can refer to the different ways that language users within or among groups employ language across contexts. In discussions among linguists these language varieties, often referred to as dialects, may refer to a type of language used by a particular group of people associated with geographical regions and/or social, cultural, and racial groups.

Believing that language, and language variation, are highly ideological and infused with issues of power and privilege (Lee, 2007; Wolfram & Schilling-Estes, 1998) we draw on the work of Wolfram and Schilling-Estes (1998) to illustrate this point. See Table 7.1 for an overview of Wolfram and Schilling-Estes's beliefs about how the general public views dialects and how linguists view dialects.[1]

Several points in Table 7.1 are worth noting. First, "pure" forms of language do not exist; rather, all users of language use varieties of languages that are constructed socially, culturally, and historically. Second, groups of language users assign "value" or "worth" to their own varieties of language and the varieties of language used by other groups. These notions of "worth" and "value" are social constructions; they are choices that groups make about their "versions" of language and the "versions" of language used by other groups. Third, assigning "value" and "worth" to varieties of language involves power, privilege, and position; that is, those in power in particular groups/cultures can assign more "worth" to some varieties of language and less "worth" to others. Languages and varieties of languages are created and used in broader social, cultural, and historical contexts.

**TABLE 7.1. Comparisons between the General Public's Conception of Dialects and Linguists' Conception of Dialects**

| General public's conception of dialects | Linguists' conception of dialects |
| --- | --- |
| "A dialect is something that SOMEONE ELSE speaks." | "Everyone who speaks a language speaks a dialect of the language; it is not possible to speak a language without speaking a dialect of the language." |
| "Dialects result from unsuccessful attempts to speak the 'correct' form of a language." | All speakers of languages speak dialects; moreover, "dialect speakers acquire their language by adopting the speech features of those around them, not by failing in their attempts to adopt standard language features." |
| "Dialects have no linguistic patterning in their own right; they are deviations from standard speech." | "Dialects, like all language systems, are systematic and regular; furthermore, socially disfavored dialects can be described with the same kind of precision as standard language varieties." |

*Note.* From Brock, Parks, and Moore (2004, p. 22; all quotes from Wolfram & Schilling-Estes, 1998, pp. 7–8). Copyright 2004 by The Guilford Press. Reprinted by permission.

## Theoretical Framework

To address the broader social, cultural, and historical contexts of which language is a part we explicate the theoretical work of Holland, Lachicotte, Skinner, and Cain (1998) as the chapter frame, because they discuss "figured worlds," which they define as conceptual and/or physical, culturally significant realities that rest on the interpretation of both community and individual relationships and positions. A figured world, then, for Holland and colleagues (p. 53) is a "socially and culturally constructed realm of interpretation in which particular characters and actors are recognized, significance is assigned to certain acts, and particular outcomes are valued over others." Drawing on these insights, as well as those of Bakhtin (1986) and Vygotsky (1978), we argue that the conceptual and/or physical realities (i.e., figured worlds) that individuals, institutions, and/or communities construct are both dialogic and developmental.

Dialogicality draws our attention to the manner in which utterances (those of individuals, communities, or institutions) come into contact with one another and the consequences that result (in terms of identity, power, and position) from those conversational encounters[2] (Bakhtin, 1986). "Development," for Vygotsky (1978), is broadly conceived, and refers to the conceptual growth of individuals and groups as they are situated institutionally, socially, and culturally across time.

Although the theoretical work of Holland and colleagues (1998), and the conceptual foundations on which it is based, is vast and complex, we tease out and draw on three central tenets from this work to frame our chapter: first, the importance of assuming a historical stance in any thoroughgoing analysis of phenomena; second, the role of identity as it relates to position and power; and third, ideas of empowerment, agency, and improvisation in the construction of figured worlds.

The first tenet, the role history plays in the construction of figured worlds, draws attention to the fact that figured worlds are socially are culturally constructed, and situated across time. Second, identities (those of individuals and groups) are "inextricably linked to power, status, and rank" (Holland et al., 1998, p. 271). Third, whereas individual and group identities are shaped and influenced by communities, institutions, and cultures, these relationships may also be reciprocal; that is, individuals and groups also shape communities, institutions, and cultures. This is where agency and empowerment come in to play.

Drawing on the figured worlds work of Holland and colleagues (1998), we now explore both the past and present conceptions of AE and AAVE. By situating these two strands of scholarship historically, as well as in the present, we offer a sense of how the "realities" of these two figured worlds came to be, and a sense of the identities of those individuals and groups who live and work within these figured worlds. We begin with an examination of AE, then move on to an examination of AAVE. As we discuss each strand of scholarship, we draw on our theoretical lens to examine issues of position, power, and agency with respect to each figured world.

## ACADEMIC ENGLISH: HISTORY, DEFINITION, AND POSITIONALITY

A broad definition of AE comes from Chamot and O'Malley (1994), the creators of the Cognitive Academic Language Learning Approach (CALLA). According to these researchers, who developed CALLA to improve students' academic language proficiency, AE is "the language that is used by teachers and students for the purpose of acquiring new knowledge and skills ... imparting new information, describing abstract ideas, and developing students' conceptual understanding" (p. 40). An earlier conceptualization of AE, and one that has been widely influential in research on the language development of English language learners (ELLs), was part of Cummins's BICS/CALP dichotomy (see Cummins, 1981). His explanation of CALP, or cognitive academic language proficiency, generally includes decontextualized and cognitively demanding language. BICS, or basic interpersonal communication skills, involves contextualized and cognitively undemanding language.

This BICS/CALP dichotomy has been challenged on a number of counts (for a review, see Aukerman, 2007; Cummins, 2000), primarily because it has been viewed as privileging CALP over BICS. Cummins (2000) responded to these criticisms by reiterating the purpose of creating the BICS/CALP framework, which emerged from empirical data and was intended "to warn against premature exit of ELL students (in the United States) from bilingual to mainstream English Only programs on the basis of attainment of surface level fluency in English" (p. 58).

A systemic functional linguistics (SFL) perspective is currently driving many discussions of AE (for a review of this perspective, see Schleppegrell, 2004). Rather than present AE as a variety of English that is more complex or less contextualized than other varieties of English, as the BICS/CALP framework would suggest, an SFL perspective recognizes that *all* language is contextualized. AE, then, is a variety of English used primarily in academic contexts, and AE has a set of linguistic features that help realize the norms of those academic contexts. Within academic contexts, AE may be cognitively demanding or it may be quite straightforward. An SFL perspective on AE research allows researchers and teachers to identify the specific linguistic features of AE and make them visible to students.

With the critiques of the BICS/CALP dichotomy and the influence of SFL, scholars have worked toward a better understanding of the components of AE. In this tradition, researchers have categorized the linguistic features of AE. Scarcella (2003) defines AE as "a variety or a register of English used in professional books and characterized by specific linguistic features associated with academic disciplines" (p. 19). She posits five linguistic components of AE: phonological, lexical, grammatical, sociolinguistic, and discourse. Bailey (2007) focuses on the lexical, grammatical, and discourse components of AE in her work on developing ways to assess AE. Inherent in the SFL perspective are answers to some sociocultural concerns. An SFL perspective posits that all registers are contextualized, and that knowledge of linguistic choices in particular contexts should help language users to navigate those contexts; thus, the more the structures and components of AE are made transparent to language users, the more language users have access to this variety of English.

Clearly, however, some populations of students have less familiarity with academic contexts and the linguistic options within them. AE presents more challenges to those students than do other, more familiar, varieties of language. As Corson (1997) suggests, "Depending on their linguistic or sociocultural position, children may acquire a lexicon–semantic range very different from that favored by the special literate culture of formal education" (p. 681). Similarly, educated people who find AE quite transparent may have difficulties in making the appropriate linguistic choices in other, unfamiliar contexts. Thus, although access to AE depends on a complex host of factors, including background and quality of educational opportunities to learn about and through AE, the importance of AE for academic success should not be underestimated (Corson, 1997).

## CURRENT RESEARCH INVOLVING AE
## AND CHILDREN'S LITERACY LEARNING

When we began this work, we sought studies in the AE literature that addressed children's literacy learning with respect to both AE and AAVE. Not only did we find a paucity of studies related to AE and children's literacy learning at the elementary level but we also found *no studies* in the literature that related to AE, AAVE, and children's literacy learning. The task we have set for ourselves in this literature review, however, is to discuss the work that has been done in K–6 literacy regarding AE and AAVE. Consequently, the studies we share that focus on AE are the studies we found that focus on AE at the elementary level.

Much of the recent increased attention on AE addresses the achievement gap between ELLs and native English speakers, particularly at the secondary level.

Efforts to better understand what challenges ELLs face in the classroom have pointed repeatedly to AE. Indeed, two important studies have shown that ELLs take two to three times as long to gain AE proficiency as they do to gain basic English proficiency (Cummins, 1981; Hakuta, Butler, & Witt, 2000). Additionally, a number of states now mandate that ELLs receive only 1 year of sheltered English support before they must enter mainstream classes. Guerrero (2004) explains how unlikely it is for ELLs to gain proficiency in AE in 1 year, yet many ELLs are transitioning, after just 1 year, to classrooms in which they are expected to adjust to the pace of an AE-intensive environment. Because AE is challenging to students who are not familiar with its linguistic features and the functions it serves, recent research has been directed at identifying the components of AE to provide professional development to teachers and to better determine appropriate assessments to monitor all students' growth in AE. However, most of this research has been conducted at the secondary and tertiary levels.

The few peer-reviewed studies involving AE that have been conducted at the K–6 level include Iddings's (2005) work with second graders, which suggested that bilingual students in English-only classrooms experienced partial exclusion from the academic community of practice. Gebhard, Harman, and Seger (2007) showed the effectiveness of using SFL as a tool to help teachers identify and explicitly teach the linguistic features of persuasive academic writing. In a related study, Zolkower and Shreyar (2007) demonstrated how SFL could be used to identify discourse patterns between teachers and students in a sixth-grade math classroom. In larger-scale assessment studies, Llosa (2007) found evidence for the validity of teacher judgment of the AE development of fourth-grade students. This study suggests that teachers are sensitive to their students who struggle with the AE demands of the classroom.

Studying third graders, Brown (2005) found that socioeconomic scale (SES) was the biggest predictor of performance on language-based math performance assessments for the native English-speaking students, but that a combination of factors, including SES and reading, had the most predictive value for the ELLs. This study highlights the importance of AE proficiency for all ELL students, and for all students from a low-SES background. These studies make a small but important contribution to our understanding of AE development. However, their variability strongly suggests that a more cohesive and systematic look at elementary-level AE is needed.

## African American Vernacular English: History, Definition, and Positionality

> No full understanding of the issues associated with language and the education of African American children can be gained unless the history of the role and dynamics of language in the context of oppression is developed.
> —Hilliard (1983, p. 24)

The history of education of African Americans in the United States is filled with victories, setbacks, hypocrisy and overt acts of racism (McMillon, 2001; Richardson, 2003). "Threads of racism have been interwoven in the institution of education in the United States from the beginning of the common school movement and remnants remain today" (Hilliard, 1983, p. 25). For example, working from a sociohistorical perspective (Holt, 1990) purports that blacks' traditional attitudes about education may be a cultural carryover sustained from African ancestors' views:

> African griots, the storytellers ... and other elders ... took responsibility for teaching young people ... included the history, values, and traditions of the family, of the clan, and of the nation. Education was intended to provide the young with a sense of ones place in that history and, thus, one's purpose in the world; a sense of obligation to kin and community, to one's ancestors and posterity. (p. 92)

This ideology is in stark contrast to the goals established by the forefathers of the Common School Movement in the United States, whose main goals, according to Church and Sedlak (1976, pp 55–56), were to

1. Provide a free elementary education for every white child living in the United States.
2. Create a trained educational profession.
3. Establish state control over local schools.

This example illustrates that from early on in the United States, education was never geared toward the needs, backgrounds, or experiences of African American children. This stark lack of attention to African American culture by white-dominant U.S. education was also manifest in perceptions about AAVE in the general public, as well as the institution of American education (both dominated by whites) (Perry & Delpit, 1998). In fact, little attention was given to AAVE by white-dominant America until the 1970s.

Although African Americans have spoken AAVE in the United States for centuries, Black English was not brought to the public or scholarly forefront and addressed from a sociopolitical perspective in America until the 1970s. In Detroit's *Bradley v. Miliken* (1977) case, the court stated:

> Children who have been thus educationally and culturally set apart from the larger community will inevitably acquire habits of speech, conduct, and attitudes reflecting their cultural isolation. They are likely to acquire speech habits, for example, which vary from the environment in which they must ultimately function and compete, if they are to enter and be a part of that community.

The political climate in the United States during the 1960s and 1970s had turned in favor of helping the disenfranchised. This favor was also displayed in the *Black*

*English Case* decision July 12, 1979 in Ann Arbor, Michigan, by Judge Charles W. Joiner, on the U.S. District Court of Michigan (*Martin Luther King Elementary School Children v. Ann Arbor School District Board*). The suit was filed on behalf of 15 black children living in a low-income housing project. The plaintiffs argued that the students did not have equal educational opportunities, because the school board had not considered the influence of the students' social, economic, cultural, and linguistic backgrounds when trying to teach them how to read in "Standard English" (Flood, Jensen, Lapp, & Squire, 1991; Smitherman, 1981). The judge ruled in favor of the plaintiffs, demanding that the students receive special treatment by teachers trained to address the issues.

Several sociolinguists have contributed to the literature concerning AAVE. After studying African American speech events in urban America, Labov (1972) defined AAVE as a viable and rule-governed symbol system.[3] He purported that Black English should not be viewed as "deficient," but rather as "different" from the variety of English valued in American public schools. Heath (1983) supports this view of "difference" in her study of families from black and white communities. The two communities (Roadville and Trackton) approached language "differently," but one approach could not be considered better than the other. However, the white usage of language was closer to school-based literacy.

While scholars such as Labov (1972) and Heath (1983) were beginning to identify the value and importance of AAVE, unstudied perceptions and beliefs rooted in ignorance and prejudice seemed difficult to dispel in education, and in society in general, in the United States. Writing over a quarter of a century ago, Torrey argued:

> My thesis is that the main impact of Afro-American dialect on education has not been its structural differences from Standard English, nor its relative intrinsic usefulness as a medium of thought, but its function as a low-status stigma and its association with a rejected culture. The attitudes of teachers toward this dialect and of dialect speakers toward the teachers' language have affected the social relationships of children with the schools in such a way as to make education of many children almost impossible. Black children of rural southern background have entered the urban schools to find that nearly everything they said was branded as "wrong." In order to be "right" they had to adopt forms that seemed alien even when they were able to learn how to use them. Their own spontaneous products were punished and treated as worthless, including the only language they knew really well. Because of this, they were almost forced to regard themselves and their society as bad, ugly, or even sinful. (1970, p. 257)

Over the years, several views have emerged to explain the language use and learning of African American children. Researchers supporting the "deficit" theory suggest that African American children are linguistically deprived, because the language that they speak is unstructured and underdeveloped (Bereiter & Englemann, 1966). They believe that Black English fails to provide an adequate foundation on which to build language skills in SE, and causes cognitive deficiency, which leaves these children unequipped for the abstract tasks exacted by the SE curriculum. However, other researchers have provided evidence that successfully disproved this theory (Baratz & Povich, 1967).

With many researchers maintaining that the language of black children is not deficient, the "difference" theory emerged (Baratz, 1969; Labov, 1965). Proponents believe that the language of African American children is highly structured, systematic, and logical; therefore, they are as linguistically capable as those who speak varieties of English sanctioned by white U.S. educators. Baratz (1969) and Labov (1965) insist that there are differences between the language of African American children, and the language that is privileged in schools populated primarily by white teachers and the curriculum they create, that may interfere with African American children's success in school.

From this very brief historical overview of African American language and culture, it should be clear that African Americans and their language have long been devalued by dominant white America. In fact, constituencies worked tirelessly to keep blacks from having access to education and to perpetuate feelings of racial inferiority (Harris, 1992). Thus, it should not be surprising to educators today when blacks show resistance or ambivalence, or when black educators question the intentions of those who develop programs specifically for urban schools. Noted intellectual and literary scholar, bell hooks (1994) states: "Standard English is not the speech of exile. It is the language of conquest and domination" (p. 168). She suggests that African American culture includes, among its characteristics, resistance to and distinction from the dominating culture (p. 171). In other words, some African American students are simply resistant learners rather than incapable of learning and using SE. They may consider changing the way they speak as surrendering or succumbing to a racist society that perpetuates inequities. Fordham and Ogbu (1986) affirmed this idea when they learned that some students consider speaking in SE as "acting white." They found that some students resist using SE as an act of resistance to society and allegiance to their own culture. Repeatedly, blacks have been promised social mobility and a better life based on educational opportunities; however, these promises often do not reflect students' daily lived experiences (Harris, 1992).

## CURRENT SCHOLARSHIP INVOLVING AAVE AND CHILDREN'S LITERACY LEARNING

Although earlier theories of AAVE and the literacy learning of African American children rested on deficit and difference perspectives about AAVE, a later theory looked to a different explanation—white teachers' attitudes toward children who speak AAVE (Cunningham, 1977; Simons & Johnson, 1974). Goodman and Buck (1973) pointed to the linguistic ignorance of many teachers regarding the ways they characterized their children's language. Researchers noted that white teachers and schools imposed disadvantages on speakers of low-status varieties of language, such as AAVE. Given that almost 90% of the teachers in U.S. public schools are monolingual and white, Dummett (1984) has argued, teachers' attitudes cannot be realistically changed without proposing changes to teacher education.

Considering the quickly changing demographics of the student population in America, white and minority educators concur that teachers need to acquire more knowledge about their students and develop racial, cultural, and linguistic awareness and sensitivity that fosters culturally relevant/responsive practice (Ball & Farr, 2003; Delpit, 1995; Cochran-Smith, 1995; Ladson-Billings, 1994; Lawrence & Tatum, 1997). In fact, many teacher education programs currently require courses that focus on helping teachers develop cultural understandings of the increasing minority student population (Lazar, 2004; McAllister & Irvine, 2002; Schmidt, 2001).

Another common belief among literacy researchers is that literacy practices in the home greatly influence literacy acquisition and development in school (Heath, 1983; Lapp, Fisher, Flood, & Moore, 2002: Moll, Amanti, Neff, & González, 1992; Purcell-Gates, 1995). Primary discourse patterns utilized in the home can be beneficial if they are similar to the discourse patterns used in the classroom environment. However, when the primary discourse patterns from home are different than the secondary discourse patterns in the classroom, miscommunication can occur (Delpit, 1995; Gee, 1991; O'Connor & Michaels, 1996). These differences in communication patterns can be one of the sources of negative teacher attitudes toward the linguistic abilities of students from nondominant backgrounds (Gutierrez, personal communication, August 2006), putting certain types of students, such as African Americans, at risk.

Because some African Americans have different language skills that are not necessarily valued in the school setting, researchers have attempted to develop ways to connect out-of-school literacy experiences with inschool classroom learning (Ball, 2000; Dyson, 2003; Foster, 2001; Lee, 1993; McMillon, 2001). Rickford (2003) outlined four major sociolinguistic approaches explaining how AAVE might be used to help blacks do better in school: (1) the linguistically informed approach; (2) contrastive analysis; (3) dialect readers; and (4) dialect awareness programs. Additionally, Alim (2004) has examined the possible use of hip-hop to improve literacy teaching and learning. Other scholars focus on cultural and social practices (Gee, 1996; Street, 1993) and how literacy events occur in everyday life (Hull & Schultz, 2002), and still others specifically address issues of power, dominance, and control (Ball & Freedman, 2004; Delpit, 1995; McMillon, 2001).

## IMPLICATIONS FOR CLASSROOM PRACTICE

When teachers understand, appreciate, and value the different varieties of language spoken by their students, they can provide higher-quality instruction for them. For example, Washington and Miller-Jones (1989) were interested in how teachers' knowledge of AAVE impacted children's learning opportunities in school. In an effort to study teachers' responses to students who demonstrated more and less use of AAVE during reading instruction, the researchers examined the classroom interactions of two second-grade teachers who had different knowledge and understanding about AAVE. The researchers found that the teacher who knew more about AAVE exhibited more positive behaviors in response to children's use of AAVE during reading instruction. The researchers suggested that it is essential for teachers to recognize dialectical influences on speech and reading, and to monitor the ways they respond to these dialectical differences. In short, teachers should value and accept the varieties of languages that students bring to the classroom, and draw on students' language and experiences as a foundation for teaching school-based varieties of AE.

In related work, Hollie (2001) discussed research that supported use of the Linguistic Affirmation Program (LAP). Hollie noted that this program was designed to help students acquire SE and simultaneously to value their home languages and cultures. Teachers who implemented the program with their children successfully employed some of the following strategies and approaches. First, they explicitly showed their students the differences between SE, as one variety of English, and other varieties of English, such as AAVE. (The ability to implement this approach depends, of course on teachers' understanding of varieties of English such as SE and AAVE.) Second, these teachers used second-language methodology (e.g., sheltered English) to help their students learn academic concepts, as well as the SE language to represent those concepts. Third, they employed active learning approaches, such as role-playing, reader's theater, and performance-type activities, in their lessons. They also used culturally relevant literature that included AAVE in their classrooms, such as works by Virginia Hamilton, Langston Hughes, and Julius Lester.

Ball (1992, 1995) conducted two studies that focused on students' use of, and preference for, different text design features, including SE expository-based or vernacular-based text structures. Ball's (1992) study included 102 students from grade 5 through high school, who represented a wide range of ethnicities. She sought to discern which oral and written text structures children of different ethnicities preferred. Results revealed that whereas elementary-level African American children did not show a clear preference for either type of text structure, African American high school students preferred using vernacular-based organizational patterns, including narrative interspersion and circumlocution, for both written academic work and conversations. Ball argues that children's discourse preferences are influenced by social and cultural experiences. Moreover, teachers should strive to understand and to take students' preferences into account when designing lessons for the students in their classrooms who speak and write different varieties of English.

Ball (1995) conducted a yearlong study to analyze the written discourse of four successful African American high school students. She found that the students in her study were effective code switchers; they could communicate well when speaking or writing AAVE and SE, depending on the nature of the writing task in which they were engaged. Ball asserts that, all too often, however, teachers do not recognize or appreciate students' unique linguistic abilities—such as fluency in both AAVE and SE. She asks teachers to acknowledge "the value in diverse voices" and to cultivate "a desire to actually hear those voices" in classroom work (p. 283).

Taken together, the studies reported in this section suggest important implications for classroom instruction. First, the goal of teachers, according to these scholars and others (e.g., Barwashi, 2003; Gadd & Arnold, 1998), should be to make explicit the many different ways that varieties of language are used with various intentions in various contexts. Second, teachers must value different language varieties, and they must demonstrate the manner in which they value language varieties through their words and actions in the classroom. Actions include, for example, using culturally relevant literature in the classroom that incorporates students' language—such as AAVE. Finally, teachers must be aware that understanding varieties of language gives students "flexible competencies" (Cazden, 1993), which allow students to communicate effectively across a host of cultural and linguistic contexts. Moreover, helping students learn to communicate across cultural and linguistic contexts should be an important instructional goal for teachers.

## IMPLICATIONS FOR FUTURE RESEARCH

In this review of the literature we sought to explore empirical work in two scholarly strands of literature: AAVE and AE. Prior to engaging in this work, we anticipated exploring studies that looked at both AAVE and AE; we found none. Consequently, in this chapter, we have shared the work we did find. Because we used figured worlds (Holland et al., 1998) as our theoretical framework, we attended (albeit briefly, due to space limitations) to the history of both AE and AAVE. The figured worlds theoretical framework also drew our attention to the ways that the identities of those individuals and groups who inhabit the figured worlds of AAVE and AE *are shaped by* the figured worlds they inhabit (and the roles that power and position play in this process). As well, the figured worlds theoretical framework we used in our work drew our attention to the ways that individuals and groups employ agency, empowerment, and improvisation, *to shape* the figured worlds of which they are a part.

The five of us who wrote this chapter had many conversations as we engaged in this work and sorted out our thinking about it over the last few months. Some of these conversations occurred face-to-face, others occurred over the phone, and still others occurred via e-mail. Most of this chapter represents a synthesis of our thinking and ideas about AAVE and AE. However, as we conclude this chapter and explore the implications of this work, as well as the manner in which the theoretical framework we employed shaped our thinking about this work, we shift to a dialogue format to share some central ideas from our many conversations. These ideas, we believe, are perhaps best represented by the individual voices we bring to this writing project. In the first part of this section, we discuss implications for future research and scholarship. Then we discuss implications for classroom practice.

DIANNA: AE, especially as it has been examined in the last 10–12 years, gives teachers tools for understanding the specific features of the language used in instructional materials and "teacher talk," so that they can make those features visible and explicitly teach them. Teachers who understand the specific features of AE, such as typical lexical items and grammatical structures, are better equipped to develop students' AE proficiency. To me, it seems that both areas of research, AAVE and AE, offer something essential to the scholarly discussion. The AAVE research we have reviewed here raises our awareness of how varieties of language represent power and identity. AE research gives teachers the tools to identify the language demands of school and to instruct students explicitly to meet those demands and build their AE proficiency.

However, AE research operates from the assumption that AE proficiency is necessary for academic (and, by default, life) success. AE researchers tend to be interested in helping *all* students access the curriculum and enjoy academic success. What AE research does not do is challenge the status quo or suggest alternative ways of being academically successful. Whereas AE scholarship recognizes the academic and assessment demands of school and work, and strives to help all students successfully participate in the current educational system, it also represents the language of power, the oppressors, and so forth. Therefore, it's very important for members of the mostly white teacher population to understand that the language they use and teach often represents cultural oppression and may invite resistance.

JULIE: Before we engaged in this work, I had not considered the differences between AE and SE. However, Dianna's earlier comments have merit. AE refers to the language variety that is used "academically" or "in school" in a more discrete way than just using SE. It makes sense to me that there would be a need for teachers and teacher educators focused on literacy to emphasize the importance of understanding not only how to teach but also the historical and current positioning of AE, SE, and AAVE. Ensuring that classroom teachers have these understandings may allow space for them to embrace multiple variations of language and to integrate what the children bring into their curriculum design and implementation.

DIANE: I continue to wonder how home–school language bridging can effectively become actual instructional practice. I am currently teaching 11th-grade students, many of whom speak AAVE as their home dialect. As I engage in conversations with them about many, many topics that fall within the subject of American English, I am awed by the wide range of topics on which they are conversant. Like other teachers, I want my students to have all of the knowledge they will need to succeed in any venture they attempt; and as their teacher I feel that one of my major tasks is to help them see beyond the experiential landscapes of their homes and school, and into a world full of new possibilities awaiting their exploration. The question of how to accomplish this must be situated in a sensitivity to the linguistic debates foregrounding the belief that success is tied to being able to give voice to one's ideas in an SE format, as well as to one's arguing that to expect SE usage of all students is promulgated racial discrimination (Baugh, 2000; Lee, 1993; Richardson, 2003; Wolfram et al. 1999). We believe the answer to this question is grounded in the work of the researchers we have studied in this chapter, who have illustrated that the focus of such instruction must be to teach students about language variation, without disparaging their homes and communities.

GWEN: Diane, Dianna, and Julie, you raise important issues here for us, as an academic community, to consider. As we examine the literature in AE and AAVE, the figured worlds framework forces us to recognize that we have come to a "pivotal place in the road." Holland and colleagues (1998) speak of "pivots of our lived worlds," in reference to the discursive relationship between societal influence and individual identity, as well as individual influence of society's identity. The notion of "standard" forms of English (i.e., AE, SE) as the norm—as the "required" language that is better than all other styles of talking (registers)—has been rejected by many minorities and even some whites. The white English "societal identity" of power has continuously challenged all to accept its influence or accept failure within the educational system and the Culture of Power. In other words, the message has been to minorities: Assimilate to "talking white" or fail. Some have resisted defiantly, held on to their own identities, and accepted "failure" in the educational system and the Culture of Power as a sort of "mantle" to prove that they held on to their dignity—their pride, their true selves, their identity. In my opinion, they are not bound by their own ideology to remain "free" from societal influences. Instead, they are bound by their own culture. Others have assimilated, submissively giving in and losing their own identities, accepting "success" in the educational system and the Culture of Power at all costs. They may feel that they have achieved the "American Dream," but it was at the risk of losing themselves. In my opinion, they are enslaved to society—trying to live by the standards of a culture that considered them less than human just a few hundred years ago. The persons who, I feel, are the most liberated are those who have developed a "double-consciousness" (DuBois, 1903). They move freely and efficiently in and out of their own culture with their African American brothers and sisters, and articulately present their arguments before white America. They represent their culture proudly, defending, protecting, and advocating for their own cultural values, and challenging society to change, develop, and improve in various ways. They sit at the table with decision makers and do not forget where they came from. This is the role for which

Diane and many other teachers are hoping to prepare their students. They push until they find a "pivot," and they force society to make the change. I see this happening with the issue of AE and AAVE. As an African American scholar, I understand the importance of AE, but I honor AAVE as being a part of my culture. I realize that I need to speak AE in certain contexts, but my ability to speak AAVE fluently in other contexts is just as valuable to me. In my figured world, AE is not valued over AAVE. They are both registers that I am able to utilize at various times, depending on the context. The ability to code-switch is vitally important to me. It is the "outcome" that I value over using AAVE and AE.

CINDY: Ladies, your comments here have helped me to see that teaching and learning different varieties of a language (AE, AAVE, SE, etc.) is complex and tricky business that has serious implications (for better or worse, as Gwen has pointed out) for the self-esteem and identity development of individuals, as well as groups. Given that we found no studies that focused on both AAVE and AE, one area of need in our field is that scholars with expertise in AAVE and AE could design and implement classroom studies that shed light on how educators might use these two varieties of language (and perhaps others) effectively in the classroom to promote children's literacy learning. While that concern addresses possible future research, it seems that educators might also act now to improve children's literacy learning, however. As we all know, almost 90% of the teachers teaching children in U.S. public schools are white women. Increasingly, the majority white teaching force is serving more and more children from nondominant (i.e., nonwhite) backgrounds. Gwen, could you share your thoughts as an African American scholar about how educators (who are mostly white) might engage effectively in this complex undertaking?

GWEN: I think that the dialogic issue of how AE and AAVE intersect or relate is left up to the individual, and his or her decision can be influenced greatly by teachers. If teachers of African Americans understand the sociocultural and historical issues related to AE and AAVE, they can assist them with successfully negotiating the cultural borders between AAVE (often their primary discourse) and AE (the secondary discourse needed to become successful at school and within the Culture of Power). Black students are less likely to resist the teachings of someone who has built a relationship of trust with them, and who honestly explains the benefits of learning how to use AE when needed. As Diane illustrates with her students, teachers who are able to do this provide students the skills necessary to become successful; they're teaching them how to "play the game." In order to "win," one must know the rules.

From a developmental prospective, as an African American scholar, I realize that my ideas have "matured" across time. I grew up in predominantly black schools, and we used terms like "talking white" when referring to AE. As a mother, however, my cue to my sons to code-switch was "use your college brain." Whenever I said that, they knew that I expected them to use AE, because we were in an environment where it was expected; or perhaps we were conversing with someone in a more formal way. This reminds me of my favorite quote by W. E. B. DuBois, which addresses the importance of having a "double-consciousness"—understanding the benefits of being black but embracing the positive that white America can teach:

> It is a peculiar sensation, this double-consciousness, this sense of always looking at one's self through the eyes of others, of measuring one's soul by the tape of a world that looks on in amused contempt and pity. One ever feels his two-ness—an American, a Negro; two souls, two thoughts, two unreconciled strivings; two warring ideals in one dark body, whose dogged strength alone keeps it from being torn asunder. The history of the American Negro is the history of this strife—this longing to attain self-conscious manhood, to merge his double self into a better and truer self. In this merging he wishes neither of the older selves to be lost. He wouldn't Africanize America, for America has too much to teach the world and Africa. He would not bleach his Negro soul in a flood of white Americanism, for he knows that Negro blood has a message for the world. He simply wishes to make it possible for a man to be both a Negro and an American, without being cursed and spit upon by his fellows, without having the doors of Opportunity closed roughly in his face. This then, is the end of his striving: to be a co-worker in the kingdom of culture, to escape both death and isolation, to husband and use his best powers and his latent genius. (1903, p. 23)

## Concluding Remarks

Our work on this project has made it clear that much work needs to be done with respect to designing curricula and research-related studies of SFL or AE at the elementary level. We, as a profession, need to explore what it means for elementary children to acquire proficiency in AE. In particular, we must address the following questions: How do we teach children to acquire proficiency in AE, and how do we assess their proficiency in AE? Additionally, we, as a field, must explore how the "variety" or register of AE relates to other varieties or registers, such as AAVE, that children come to school speaking. In particular, we must address how we can teach children school registers (e.g., AE), while also honoring and valuing children's home and community language registers. In conclusion, we believe that, as educational researchers, we must continue to study various instructional moves that suggest to students that there are different variations of English; that, for example, their home language of Black English Vernacular, which is rule-governed at the syntactic and semantic levels, has a long history of contributing to the artistic, literary, and political accomplishments of African American people. We must strive to convey and to study a model of difference but not deficit, so that each child's expanded knowledge of language will afford choices of the structures he or she selects to communicate ideas to various audiences.

## NOTES

1. Because of the popular misconceptions often associated with the term "dialect," some linguists prefer to avoid using the term altogether (Wolfram & Schilling-Estes, 1998). Thus, we primarily use the term "language variation" rather than "dialect" throughout our work.
2. Conversational encounters are not limited to oral conversations, but include all manner of communication (written, spoken, gestural, etc.).
3. Some scholars consider AAVE to be a variety of English, and others consider AAVE to be a separate language (Perry & Delpit, 1998; Rickford, 2003). For the purposes of our work here, we do not enter into this debate; rather, we acknowledge that the debate exists. The central point we draw on for our work here is that AAVE is a viable, rule-governed, symbol system.

## REFERENCES

Alim, H. (2004). Hip hop nation language. In E. Finegan & J. Rickford (Eds.), *Language in the USA: Perspectives for the 21st century* (pp. 387–409). Cambridge, UK: Cambridge University Press.

Alim, H. S. (2005). Critical language awareness in the United States: Revisiting issues and revising pedagogies in a resegregated society. *Educational Researcher, 34*(7), 24–31.

Aukerman, M. (2007). A culpable CALP. *Reading Teacher, 60*, 626–635.

Bailey, A. L. (2007). Introduction: Teaching and assessing students learning English in school. In A. L. Bailey (Ed.), *The language demands of school: Putting academic English to the test* (pp. 1–26). New Haven, CT: Yale University Press.

Bakhtin, M. M. (1986). *Speech genres and other late essays.* Austin: University of Texas Press.

Ball, A. (1992). Cultural preference and the expository writing of African-American adolescents. *Written Communication, 9*, 501–532.

Ball, A. (1995). Text design patterns in the writing of urban African American students: Teaching to the cultural strengths of students in multicultural settings. *Urban Education, 30*, 253–289.

Ball, A., & Farr, M. (2003). Language variations, culture and teaching the English language arts. In J. Flood, D. Lapp, J. Squire, & J. Jensen (Eds.), *Handbook of research on teaching the English language arts* (2nd ed., pp. 435–445). Mahwah, NJ: Erlbaum.

Ball, A. F. (2000). Empowering pedagogies that enhance the learning of multicultural students. *Teachers College Record, 102*(6), 1006–1034.

Ball, A. F., & Freedman, S. W. (Eds.). (2004). *Bakhtinian perspectives on language, literacy and learning.* New York: Cambridge University Press.

Baratz, J. C. (1969). Teaching reading in an urban Negro school system. In J. C. Baratz & R. W. Shuy (Eds.), *Teaching black children to read* (pp. 92–116). Washington, DC: Center for Applied Linguistics.

Baratz, J. C., & Povich, E. (1967, November). *Grammatical constructions in the language of the Negro preschool child.* Paper presented at the national meeting of the American Speech and Hearing Association, Washington, DC.

Baugh, J. (2000). *Beyond ebonics: Linguistic pride and racial prejudice.* New York: Oxford University Press.

Bawarshi, A. S. (2003). *Genre and the invention of the writer: Reconsidering the place of invention in composition.* Logan: Utah State University Press.

Bereiter, C., & Englemann, S. (1966). *Teaching disadvantaged children in preschool.* Englewood Cliffs, NJ: Prentice-Hall.

Bradley v. Miliken, 433 U.S. 267 (1977).

Brock, C. H., Parks, L. A., & Moore, D. K. (2004). Literacy, learning, and language variation: Implications for instruction. In F. B. Boyd, C. H. Brock, & M. S. Rozendal (Eds.), *Multicultural and mutilingual literacy and language: Contexts and practices* (pp. 15–32). New York: Guilford Press.

Brown, C. L. (2005). Equity of literacy-based math performance assessments for English language learners. *Bilingual Research Journal, 29,* 337–409.

Cazden, C. (1996, June). *A report on reports: Two dilemmas of genre teaching.* Paper presented at the Working with Genre Conference, Sydney, Australia.

Chamot, A. U., & O'Malley, M. (1994). *The CALLA handbook: Implementing the Cognitive Academic Language Learning Approach.* Reading, MA: Addison-Wesley.

Church, R. L., & Sedlak, M. (1976). *Education in the United States.* New York: Free Press.

Cochran-Smith, M. (1995). Color blindness and basket making are not the answers: Confronting the dilemmas of race, culture, and language diversity in teacher education. *American Educational Research Journal, 32,* 493–522.

Corson, D. (1997). The learning and use of academic English words. *Language Learning, 47,* 671–718.

Crawford, L.W. (1993). *Language and literacy learning in multicultural classrooms.* Boston: Allyn & Bacon.

Cummins, J. (1981). Age on arrival and immigrant second language learning in Canada. A reassessment. *Applied Linguistics, 2,* 132–149.

Cummins, J. (2000). *Language, power, and pedagogy.* Clevedon, UK: Multilingual Matters.

Cunningham, P. M. (1977). Teachers' correction responses to black-dialect miscues which are non-meaning-changing. *Reading Research Quarterly, 12*(4), 637–653.

Delpit, L. (1995). *Other people's children: Cultural conflict in the classroom.* New York: New Press.

Dewey, J. (1938). *Experience and education.* New York: Collier.

DuBois, W. E. B. (1903). *The souls of black folk.* Chicago: A. C. McClurg & Co.

Dummett, L. (1984). The enigma—The persistent failure of black children in learning to read. *Reading World, 24,* 31–37.

Dyson, A. H. (2003). *The brothers and sisters learn to write: Popular literacies in childhood and school cultures.* New York: Teachers College Press.

Edwards, P. A. (2007, December). *The education of African American students: Voicing the debates, controversies and solutions.* Presidential address to the National Reading Conference, Austin, TX.

Fillmore, L. (1997). *Language and education.* Paper presented at the Third Eastern States Conference on Linguistics, Pittsburgh, PA. (ERIC Document Reproduction Services No. ED 308 705)

Flood, J., Heath, S. B., & Lapp, D. (Eds.). (2008). *Handbook of research on teaching literacy through the communicative and visual arts* (Vol. II). New York: Erlbaum.

Flood, J., Jensen, J., Lapp, D., & Squire, J. (1991). *Handbook of research on teaching the English language arts.* New York: Macmillan.

Fordham, S., & Ogbu, J. (1986). Black students' school success: Coping with the "burden of 'acting white.'" *Urban Review, 18*(3), 176–206.

Foster, M. (2001). Pay Leon, pay leon, pay Leon, paleontologist: Using call-and-response to facilitate language mastery and literacy acquisition among African American students. In S. Lanehart (Ed.), *Sociocultural and historical contexts of African American English* (pp. 281–298). Philadelphia: Benjamins.

Gadd, N., & Arnold, J. (1998). Towards less humanistic English teaching, and towards more humanistic English teaching. *ELT Journal, 52*(3), 223–244.

Gebhard, M., Harman, R., & Seger, W. (2007). Reclaiming recess: Learning the language of persuasion. *Language Arts, 84,* 419–430.

Gee, J. (1991). What is literacy? In C. Mitchell & K. Weiler (Eds.), *Rewriting literacy: Culture and the discourse of the other* (pp. 3–12). New York: Greenwood.

Gee, J. P. (1996). *Social linguistics and literacies: Ideology in discourses.* London: Falmer.

Goodman, K., & Buck, C. (1973). Dialect barriers to reading comprehension revisited. *Reading Teacher, 27,* 6–12.

Guerrero, M. D. (2004). Acquiring academic English in one year: An unlikely proposition for English language learners. *Urban Education, 39,* 172–199.

Hakuta, K., Butler, Y. G., & Witt, D. (2000). *How long does it take English learners to attain proficiency?* Santa Barbara: University of California Linguistic Minority Research Institute.

Harris, V. (1992). African American conceptions of literacy: A historical perspective. *Theory Into Practice, 31*(4), 276–286.

Heath, S. B. (1983). *Ways with words: Language, life, and work in communities and classrooms.* Cambridge, UK: Cambridge University Press.

Hilliard, A. G. (1983). Psychological factors associated with language in the education of the African American child. *Journal of Negro Education, 52*(1), 24–34.

Holland, D., Lachicotte, W., Skinner, D., & Cain, C. (1998). *Identity and agency in cultural worlds.* Cambridge, MA: Harvard University Press.

Hollie, S. (2001). Acknowledging the language of African American students: Instructional strategies. *English Journal, 90*(4), 54–59.

Holt, T. (1990). Knowledge is power: The black struggle for literacy. In A. Lunsford, H. Moglen, & J. Slevin (Eds.), *The right to literacy* (pp. 91–102). New York: Modern Language Association.

hooks, b. (1994). *Teaching to transgress: Education as the practice of freedom.* New York: Routledge.

Hull, G., & Schultz, K. (Eds.). (2002). *School's out!: Bridging out-of-school literacies with classroom practice.* New York: Teachers College Press.

Hymes, D. (1974). *Foundations in sociolinguistics.* Philadelphia: University of Pennsylvania Press.

Iddings, A. C. D. (2005). Linguistic access and participation: English language learners in an English-dominant community of practice. *Bilingual Research Journal, 29,* 165–183.

Labov, W. (1972). *Language in the inner city: Studies in the Black English Vernacular.* Philadelphia: University of Pennsylvania Press.

Labov, W. A. (1965, April). *Linguistic research on nonstandard English of Negro children.* Paper presented to the New York Society for the Experimental Study of Education, New York.

Ladson-Billings, G. (1994). *The dreamkeepers: Successful teachers of African American children.* San Francisco: Jossey-Bass.

Lapp, D., Fisher, D., Flood, J., & Moore, K. (2002). "I don't want to teach it wrong": An investigation of the role families believe they should play in the early literacy development of their children. *Yearbook of the National Reading Conference*, pp. 275–286.

Lave, J. (1996). Teaching, as learning, in practice. *Mind, Culture, and Activity, 3*(3), 149–164.

Lawrence, S. M., & Tatum, B. D. (1997). White educators as allies: Moving from awareness to action. In M. Fine, L. Weiss, L. Powell, & M. Wong (Eds.), *Off white: Critical perspectives on race* (pp. 333–342). New York: Routledge.

Lazar, A. M. (2004). *Learning to be literacy teachers in urban schools: Stories of growth and change.* Newark, DE: International Reading Association.

Lee, C. D. (1993). *Signifying as a scaffold for literary interpretation: The pedagogical implications of an African American discourse genre.* Urbana, IL: National Council of Teachers of English.

Lee, C. D. (2007). *Culture, literacy and learning.* New York: Teachers College Press.

Llosa, L. (2007). Validating a standards-based classroom assessment of English proficiency: A multitrait–multimethod approach. *Language Testing, 24*, 489–515.

Martin Luther King Elementary School Children v. Ann Arbor School District Board, Civil Action No. 7-71861, 473 F. Supp. 1371 (1979).

McAllister, G., & Irvine, J. J. (2002). The role of empathy in teaching culturally diverse students: A qualitative study of teachers' beliefs. *Journal of Teacher Education, 53*(5), 433–443.

McMillon, G. M. T. (2001). *A tale of two settings: African American students' literacy experiences at church and at school.* Unpublished doctoral dissertation, Michigan State University, East Lansing.

Moll, L. C., Amanti, C., Neff, D., & González, N. (1992). Funds of knowledge for teaching: Using a qualitative approach to connect home and classrooms. *Theory Into Practice, 31*(2), 132–141.

O'Connor, M. C., & Michaels, S. (1996). Shifting participant frameworks: Orchestrating thinking practices in group discussion. In D. Hicks (Ed.), *Discourse, learning and schooling* (pp. 63–103). New York: Cambridge University Press.

Perez, B., & McCarty, T. L. (Eds.). (2004). *Sociocultural contexts of language and literacy* (2nd ed.). Mahwah, NJ: Erlbaum.

Perry, T., & Delpit, L. (Eds.). (1998). *The real ebonics debate: Power, language, and the education of African American children.* Boston: Beacon Press.

Purcell-Gates, V. (1995). *Other people's words: The cycle of low literacy.* Cambridge, MA: Harvard University Press.

Richardson, E. (2003). *African American literacies.* New York: Routledge.

Rickford, J. (2003, April). *Sociolinguistic approaches to working with vernacular varieties in schools.* Paper presented at the annual meeting of the American Educational Research Association, Chicago.

Scarcella, R. C. (2003). *Accelerating Academic English: A focus on English language learners.* Los Angeles: Regents of University of California.

Schleppegrell, M. J. (2004). *The language of schooling: A functional linguistics perspective.* Mahwah, NJ: Erlbaum.

Schmidt, P. R. (2001). Emphasizing differences to build cultural understandings. In V. J. Risko & K. Bromley (Eds.), *Collaboration for diverse learners: Viewpoints and practices* (pp. 210–227). Newark, DE: International Reading Association.

Simons, H. D., & Johnson, K. R. (1974). Black English syntax and reading interference. *Reading in the Teaching of English, 8*, 339–358.

Smitherman, G. (Ed.). (1981). *Black English and the education of black children and youth: Proceedings of the National Invitational Symposium on the King decision.* Detroit, MI: Wayne State University, Center for Black Studies.

Smitherman, G. (1995). Students' right to their own language. A retrospective. *English Journal, 84*(1), 21–27.

Street, B. (1993). *Cross-cultural approaches to literacy.* New York: Cambridge University Press.

Torrey, J. W. (1970). Illiteracy in the ghetto. *Harvard Educational Review, 40,* 253–259.

Vygotsky, L. (1978). *Mind in society: The development of higher psychological processes.* Cambridge, MA: Harvard University Press.

Wardhaugh, R. (1998). *An introduction to sociolinguistics.* Malden, MA: Blackwell.

Washington, V., & Miller-Jones, D. (1989). Teacher interaction with nonstandard English speakers during reading instruction. *Contemporary Educational Psychology, 14,* 280–312.

Wertsch, J. (1998). *Mind as action.* New York: Oxford University Press.

Wolfram, W., Adger, C., & Christian, D. (1999). *Dialectics in school and communities.* Mahwah, NJ: Erlbaum.

Wolfram, W., & Schilling-Estes, N. (1998). *American English.* Malden, MA: Blackwell.

Zolkower, B., & Shreyar, S. (2007). A teacher's mediation of a thinking-aloud discussion in a 6th grade mathematics classroom. *Educational Studies in Mathematics, 65,* 177–202.

# CHAPTER 8

# Engaging Diverse Students in Multiple Literacies in and Out of School

CHERYL A. MCLEAN, ERICA C. BOLING, *and* JENNIFER ROWSELL

In this chapter we review the range of ways in which literacy educators recognize and respond to the literacy practices and needs of diverse students. We use the following fields to focus on key approaches to engaging learners in school and out of school:

- Critical literacy and critical pedagogy
- New literacy studies
- Multimodality and multiliteracies

These three key areas offer us a lens through which to understand the evolving concept of literacy. They also provide a lens through which we reconsider the three fields of literacy research as "equity work"—ways of opening up a space to think about issues of access, voice, and participation within and outside of K–12 classrooms. Au and Raphael's (2000) definition of "education equity" informs our selection and discussion of these areas of literacy research. Au and Raphael define it as "the opportunity to participate successfully in schooling so that all students can become productive and contributing members of an evermore complex society" (p. 170). Thus, equity in literacy learning suggests the need to account for how an individual's race, culture, and socioeconomic background shape his or her understanding of texts and practices, how an individual positions him- or herself as learner, and how an individual's literacy practices are supported.

*A caveat*: In choosing to review the research in (1) critical literacy and critical pedagogy, (2) new literacy studies, and (3) multimodality and multiliteracies, we acknowledge the presence of other definitions, approaches, labels, and perspectives. We selected the works under review because they help us think about *diversity* in literacy theory and practice in terms of the range of perspectives (lenses), contexts (sites and communities), skills (strategies and tools), and groups (racial, cultural, social, academic, and communicational). In this chapter, the concept of diversity is reflected through traditional and alternative sites (inschool and out-of-school settings), the texts, and the geographic and social spaces in which research occurs.

## SYNTHESIS OF THE RESEARCH

### Critical Literacy

Critical literacy and critical pedagogy are important theoretical perspectives that inform literacy education. Critical literacy and critical pedagogy unite through the work and theory of critical theorist and Brazilian educator Paolo Freire, who advocated for a liberatory and participatory approach to education. Freire's view of literacy is grounded in the belief that if learners are to transform themselves and their environments, teaching and learning must directly reflect their words and worlds (Freire, 1998; Freire & Macedo, 1987). Furthermore, reading and writing are seen as platforms to develop and use critical consciousness to question, challenge, and critique the often inherited and oppressive beliefs, values, and ideologies of the language classroom (Freire & Macedo, 1995).

Thus, critical literacy attends to the politics of language and its implications for (re)defining power structures (Comber & Kamler, 1997; Giroux & McLaren, 1992). According to Beck (2005), critical literacy has as its goal the development of responsible citizens, able to confront social inequities and to take action against injustices. Comber and Kamler (1997) agree that although there is no widespread agreement on what critical literacy is, there are the following shared assumptions: (1) Literacy is a social and cultural construct; (2) its functions and uses are never neutral or innocent; and (3) the meanings constructed in text are ideological and involved in producing, reproducing, and maintaining arrangements of power that are unequal. Perhaps the most central focus of critical literacy is the transformation of social inequalities—of power and privilege, ideologies, and knowledge.

Critical literacy has been used by researchers and practitioners as a way to raise questions and confront social issues, and promote action against injustice. Schools and classrooms are seen as the sites for interrogating social conditions through open discussion, question, reflection, and action. In 2000, Linda Christensen, an English teacher, addressed issues of inequity in classrooms and education related to tracking and language. Christensen argued for critical literacy in the classroom, because the teaching of literacy is political, and all texts legitimate a "social blueprint" of what it means to operate in this world. Through texts such as cartoons and mass media, Christensen and her high school students used the tools of critical literacy as a way to expose, talk back to, and remedy any act of injustice or intolerance they witnessed.

Similarly, Janks's (2002) critical literacy work extends to curricular materials in schools as a direct way to effect social change. Janks's research in South Africa focuses on critical literacy education and language policy. Her work is located in a sociocultural theory of language, with a particular focus on the relationship between language and power. Janks states: "I saw my work in South Africa as both a moral and political project which valued education as an important factor in achieving a just society" (p. 7). In her case study research on female English students' engagements with advertising texts, Janks explored advertising texts and the media as a way to imagine new directions for pedagogy in the critical literacy classroom.

Dyson's (1999, 2001) ethnographic studies of the diversity in linguistic and symbolic resources appropriated by young students suggest that classrooms be revisioned to embrace the lived realities that young learners bring to their writing. Dyson, looking at the literacy and social practices of young students, argued that because children enter school with words and symbols from family and community contexts, learning reflects their recontextualization processes—the differentiation and translation of cultural materials across symbolic, social, and ideological borders. Using ethnographic research methods, Dyson (1999) examined first-grade students' appropriation of texts as acts of agency. In similar vein, Lee (1993) working with African American students, explored classroom language practices that are culturally responsive and open up opportunities for social engagement.

The complexity of the political work of language is evident in how young persons use "school" literacy practices in out-of-school settings to challenge social norms and resist oppression. Blackburn's (2003, 2005) work focuses on how youth in a youth-run center for lesbian, gay, bisexual, transgender, and questioning (LGBTQ) youth read and write words and worlds in ways that both contest and reinforce power dynamics. In her 2003 study on the literacy performance of young persons in a youth-run center, Blackburn made the point that their project of creating a glossary to distribute to outreach highlights how these young persons use language to define, destabilize, and challenge social boundaries and power dynamics. Though Blackburn uses a new literacy studies (NLS) framework, we mention her work in this section because of its potential for illuminating how youth can use literacy practices to reinforce *and* interrupt power dynamics through their agency as readers and writers.

Working out of Australia, Comber and Kamler (1997) examined the tensions of teachers negotiating the complexities and contradictions of critical literacy lessons in elementary school classrooms with students from diverse socioeconomic and cultural communities. More recently, in the United States, Jones (2006) used narratives to explore social class and literacy in her critical examination of poverty in the lives of a group of eight working-class girls. Critical literacy provides a framework for rethinking issues of class, and how socioeconomic status might frame what takes place in the elementary school classroom. The author offers critical literacy as a way to break the silence on the disconnection between poverty and how poverty is lived by young students attending school. "Critical literacy is building a way of life through active engagement *with* life—a way of noticing 'What's wrong with this picture?', a way of asking oneself, 'How is power exercised here and how does that shape what we're doing?'" (Jones, 2006, p. 68, original emphasis).

Coming out of this diverse body of research is the collective view that what a critical literacy perspective does offer teachers is a way to think about what it is that students are learning to read and write, what they do with that reading and writing, and what that reading and writing does to them and to their world (Comber & Kamler, 1997).

> To explore the social context of language practices is inevitably to explore the networks of power that are sustained and brought into existence by such practices. It is to explore how language practices are used in powerful institutions like the state, the school, the law, the family, the church, and how these practices contribute to the maintenance of inequalities and injustices. (p. 1)

Thus, the works of these and other researchers in the field of critical literacy suggest that a social view of reading is necessary, and that teachers who understand this perspective will pay more attention to the social and political contexts within reading, writing, and language broadly (Christensen, 2000; Jones, 2006).

## Critical Pedagogy

The terms "critical literacy" and "critical pedagogy" are often seen as interconnected and collaborative approaches to learning and teaching, because critical literacy offers a theory with *implications for practice* (Behrman, 2006). Critical literacy and critical pedagogy are intended to move pedagogues (teachers, teacher-educators, and researchers) toward creating a language of critique involving school, society, and the exercise of power. Shor (1992), one of the foremost proponents of critical pedagogy, argues for participatory classrooms that flatten classroom hierarchies and legitimize the voices and interests of students and teachers. Though the operationalization of a practice of resistance and critique focuses mainly on classrooms and curricula, there has been a broadening of sites to include digital spaces (Lankshear, Peters, & Knobel, 1996) and the media (Janks, 2000). Critical literacy and critical pedagogy bridge inschool and out-of-school practices because of the "political work" they engender through the shared understanding of sociocultural realities.

What does a critical pedagogy classroom look like? In this space, student interests, cultural resources, knowledge, and skills form not only the starting point but also the center of the curriculum. For example, in Christensen's (1999) classroom, students engaged in dialogue, learned to make connections, and questioned their lives, literature, and society. Using improvisation and dialogue journals Christensen created a democratic class, where students directed discussions, and where their questions and interests were supported. As Giroux and McLaren (1992) pointed out, for critical literacy to be effective, it must be embedded in the concrete lived conditions of the students themselves. "The critical literacy classroom is characterized by an emphasis on students' voices and dialogues as tools with which students reflect on and construct meanings from texts and discourses" (Beck, 2005, p. 394). Students are encouraged to critique their social conditions and to protest against them. According to Giroux and McLaren, critical pedagogical practices involve the following:

- Teaching students how to identify and challenge texts that position and create social identities and legitimate specific practices.
- Helping students learn to construct their individual voice.
- Considering often contradictory student needs and lived experiences so as to provide a better understanding of how students draw upon their own cultural resources to make meaning. (p. 8)

### New Literacy Studies

To reinforce the previous section on the emergence of critical literacy and our overarching definition of equity as an opportunity to participate successfully in schooling, so that all students can become productive, contributing members to a complex society, it is essential to present the emergence of two contemporaneous theories of literacy education: NLS and multimodality, which both emerged on the literacy scene around the same time but offer different perspectives. The two separate theoretical movements sparked "new" ways of defining literacy by arguing, first and foremost, that literacy happens everywhere, and that it is shaped by context, by the identity of the language user, and by practices involved in literate activity.

### The Emergence of NLS

Around two to three decades ago, several researchers were redefining literacy education by incorporating approaches to literacy from other, more disparate disciplines, such as anthropology, semiotics, linguistics, and sociology. Scholars researching in these disciplines worked together to forge an alternative approach to the ways we read and write. These more ideological concepts of literacy were fairly foreign at the time, when literacy education proper was predominantly approached with a cognitive perspective on literacy acquisition (Alexander & Fox, 2004).

In the 1980s and 1990s, there was a theoretical movement evolving within research into literacy, language, and linguistics. The origins of NLS grew from the work of Scribner and Cole and their research, outlined in *The Psychology of Literacy* (1981), which drew on their anthropological work with the Vai people in Liberia to explore what represents literacy practices in day-to-day life. Such a conception of literacy was radical at a time, when literacy sat primarily within schooling contexts. Scribner and Cole allowed us to see that viewing literacy solely in terms of schooling is a fairly limited way of seeing literacy education.

In 1983, Shirley Brice Heath published her ground-breaking study in *Ways with Words*, which featured the literacy practices of three communities in rural Carolinas: Trackton, Roadville, and Maintown. Over the course of a decade, Heath documented how these three communities spoke, lived, and communicated in different ways. Through ethnographic research methods, Heath recorded these ways of being and speaking, and identified that each community carried its own models of literacy development. Yet only one of the communities, Maintown, carried literacy practices that aligned with schooled literacy practices (Street, 1984). Both Roadville and Trackton children had distinctive ways with words, but they were not congruent with schooled literacy; hence, children from both communities underachieved in their literacy at school.

In conjunction with Heath's ethnography, Brian Street (1984) was conducting a longitudinal research study that also looked at three distinct types of literacy within the same community in Iran. Street's fieldwork in Iran brought a far more ideological approach to literacy development at the time. "Maktab" literacy occurred in the marketplace and street trading, and demanded a far more vernacular approach to literacy. Literacy practices that took place in the mosque were more reliant on oral language and the memorization of excerpts from the Koran. Finally, Standard English, as it was taught in the British schools in Iran, was yet another approach to literacy development. What is clear from Street's study is that each model carried its own set of practices, texts, concepts, and contexts in which they took place, and individuals, children, and adults all rendered them equally meaningful in fulfilling practices tied to reading, writing, speaking, and listening. Nonetheless, literacy in British schools was considered Standard English and carried more power than Maktab literacy and literacy practices at mosque.

In Pennsylvania, yet another ethnography was conducted by Del Hymes (1996), who immersed himself in the communicative practices of African Americans and Native Americans in the United States. Barton and Hamilton (2000) conducted a longitudinal study in Lancaster, England, that looked at and developed a language of description for literacy practices that crossed domains. Barton and Hamilton offered a rich account of textual practices, located these textual practices within particular contexts, and showed how context informs the nature of literacy practice. Around that time, James Paul Gee (1996) examined language practices of African American children and analyzed the need to situate everyday language across contexts, and how language is very much shaped by our identities. Gee is the theorist who coined the term "new literacy studies" to describe a social turn that took place over the 1980s and 1990s.

What emerges most strongly from the origins of NLS is a sociocultural, locally based account of the ways that we become literate. This standpoint was pivotal, because it illustrated that literacy does not just take place at school and in a vacuum; instead, literacy is shaped by the places in which we communicate, and our identities, texts, and practices inform the way that we understand language. Ethnography was the dominant methodology, because these studies were long term and involved a deeper understanding of people and their culture. The reflexivity of researchers also came to play a role in the nature of the studies, especially given their emphasis on identity, context, and practices. NLS also rests on the notion of power, and of certain kinds of literacy practice carrying more power than others, such as school literacy or, in the domain of multimodality, the written word.

More recently, studies built on the principles of NLS have explored how to invoke a more contextual, ideological understanding of literacy education. The work of Luis Moll and colleagues (Moll, Amanti, Neff, & González, 1992) examines how students in highly diverse places can use local, traditional, popular, and family knowledges and narratives as the bases of learning. The aim of such research is to develop understandings of the complex ways in which teachers design and enact a "permeable curriculum" (Dyson, 1993) that allows different children to negotiate meaningful trajectories with academic learning and school literacies through the diverse social worlds of their communities and classrooms, bearing in mind that the latter are often shaped or inflected by global media culture. The goal of studies that extend NLS is to address recent calls for "research and scholarship that documents and analytically explicates affirmative, emancipating and redressive texts and discourse practices" (Luke, 2004, p. 27). Hull and Schultz (2003) have conducted research and created a present-day compendium of NLS to illustrate what we can gain from a sociocultural approach to literacy development. Lankshear and Knobel (1997) have proposed a rereading of many of these studies to produce a new discourse of engagement, so that students understand their social positionings in terms of their identities. Their research on digital environments opened up NLS to alternative perspective on what *local* and *global* mean.

Opening up literacy to digital spaces introduced new ways of thinking through how we make meaning. Researchers such as Alvermann and Heron (2001), Carrington (2006), Davies (2006), Janks and Comber (2006), Knobel and Lankshear (2007), Marsh (2005, 2006), Merchant (2001), Pahl (2004), Pahl and Rowsell (2006), and Rowsell (2006) have illustrated the complementarity of NLS and work in digital and multimodal domains. There is a complementarity to NLS and multimodality, in that NLS can locate contexts, identities, texts, and practices within textual modalities. NLS has provided rich case studies of literacy in places, and multimodality has shown that physical features in texts point back to people and places.

## Multimodality

In 1978, Michael Halliday wrote *Language as Social Semiotic*, which revolutionized the way that we think about language in context. Halliday argued that there is a need to situate language in social context, and to apply social context to our understanding of texts. Gunther Kress, one of Halliday's students, took up Halliday's arguments about bringing semiotics into an understanding of language and literacy. In his early work, Kress focused on understanding signs in contexts and eventually came to a notion of "the motivated sign," which represents a belief that all signs or texts are motivated by the interests of sign makers. Kress illustrated in his research and writing that certain texts and drawings powerfully show what a child knows, yet they are (often) excluded from school literacy. In *Before Writing*, a seminal text on multimodality, Kress (1997) outlined a theory of language development, arguing that we need to find the principles of children's meaning making by accounting for all of the modes they use when they make meanings—everywhere (i.e., at school *and* at home). Kress opened up reading and writing by looking at how modes (that can be visual, written, tactile, interactive, spoken) work in concert with each other and are equally important, without one being more important than another (e.g., the written word). Another important work by Kress and Van Leeuwen, *Reading Images: A Grammar of Visual Design* (2006), provided a framework and terminology to describe the visual. In this popular text, they spotlight many genres of texts, from advertisements to textbooks to magazine layouts to works of art, to illustrate the grammar of the visual and to explain how we make meaning from the visual.

Over the years, Kress has extended his significant work in multimodality to technological shifts and digital texts as "our contemporary canvas" (Kress, 2003), and alongside research and writing with Carey Jewitt (Jewitt & Kress, 2003), he has created a robust theory of new communicational practice that contends we are no longer a monomedial society relying on one mode solely, but instead comprise a society that moves in and out of multimodality, and that we need to come to terms with multimodality, understand it, and have it as an informing principle of literacy pedagogy if we are to move forward.

Today multimodality is taking hold globally and is used as an informing principle in many research studies (Bearne, 2003; Carrington, 2004; Harste & Albers, 2007; Jewitt, 2005; Kendrick & McKay, 2004; Kenner, 2004; Lancaster, 2003; Leander, 2002; Rowsell & Pahl, 2007; Schwartz & Rubinstein-Ávila, 2006). Numerous studies that have taken up a multimodal framework to analyze texts and online environments have found multimodality useful in understanding children's text making. Multimodality has furnished a language of description for studies that apply an understanding of children's text making. In particular, there is a real strength in adopting a multimodal perspective to digital spaces such as blogs, wikis, and websites in general, because it is a theory that in looking at more than the written word, sees how modes work together. What is more, increased multimodality in our communicative landscape has changed the way that we read and write, and many current researchers find it helpful to look at texts with so many visuals, sounds, movement, animation, and so forth.

## Multiliteracies

What grew out of the traditions of multimodality and NLS was the field of multiliteracies. A historical event occurred in September 1994, in New London, New Hampshire, when a group of 10 scholars gathered to discuss what constitutes appropriate literacy teaching in the context of ever-changing forms of communication. Almost evenly split in terms of NLS and multimodal scholars, the group devised a conceptual framework for thinking about modern English in terms of design (design, available designs, and redesign), as well as a pedagogical framework that looks at multiliteracies strands (situated practice, overt instruction, critical framing, and transformed practice) as a pedagogy that better reflects modern communicational systems and practices. In light of the gathering, the New London Group (2000) began collaborative work that had two abiding goals: to create theory and pedagogy that engage with the multiplicity of communications channels and media; and to increase the salience of cultural and linguistic diversity (Cope & Kalantzis, 2000). Their work and resulting book catalyzed new ways of thinking about literacy in a modern age and of discussing new literacies in society.

With multiliteracies in mind, today's literacy practices are changing at an unprecedented pace (Alvermann, 2004). One of the reasons for this is because of the rapidly evolving technological advances that have forced individuals "to become readers of printed text, signs, and imagery" (Hagood, 2003, p. 390). Because new media and online literacies have become "part and parcel" of the day-to-day lives for many individuals, today's notions of text continually expand, extending beyond traditional print-based reading and writing (Hagood, 2003). According to Lemke (2006), today's text extends across multiple sites and media, allowing information to be easily exchanged and making our lives become more global and cross-cultural than ever before in human history. As communities are transformed by new communications and technology, they have the potential to represent a new literacy (Lemke, 2006). As information continues to be exchanged and our lives grow increasingly more global and cross-cultural, it will be even more important that individuals learn to communicate effectively with people who are different from themselves.

As we broaden our understanding of literacy and literacy education, the New London Group (2000, p. 9) argues that we need to take into consideration a "multiplicity of discourse." Cope and Kalantzis (2000) have used the term "multiliteracies" to describe "two important arguments we might have with the merging cultural, institution, and global order" (p. 7). This multiplicity involves extending the idea and scope of literacy pedagogy "to account for the context of our culturally and linguistically diverse and increasingly globalised societies" (New London Group, 2000, p. 9). This multiplicity also accounts for a pedagogy of literacy that speaks to the "burgeoning variety of text forms associated with information and multimedia technologies" (p. 9). As Cope and Kalantzis point out, what students need to learn is changing, and the main element of this change is that "there was no singular, canonical English that either could or should be taught any more" (p. 5). Because of cultural differences and the rapidly shifting communications media, the very nature of the subject of literacy pedagogy is also changing radically.

Although the development of new technologies may have helped to change literacy practices, as a community of teachers and researchers, we still have much to learn about the research and pedagogy of mutiliteracies. The extent to which new media and interactive communication technologies effectively support literacy teaching and learning in classrooms is unknown (Alvermann, 2004). Citing the work of Burbules and Callister (2000), Luke (2003) points out that we need to be mindful of the "risks and promises of information and communication technologies" while also investigating "whether equity promises are being realized in the alleged hierarchy-free zones of online communication" (p. 399).

When talking about the impact of new literacies and new technologies on education, Lemke (2006) and others described a need for a paradigm shift (Boling, 2008; Smolin & Lawless, 2003). Lemke (1998) argued that new information technologies will make it possible "for students to learn what they want, when they want, how they want, without schools" (paragraph 8). He also pointed out that not all students will have equal access to these technologies.

Regardless of viewing literacy from a critical, multimodal, NLS, or multiliteracies perspective, one of the fundamental questions that many educators must now confront is what do such changes in new literacies, new technologies, and our increasingly global world mean for literacy pedagogy. The New London Group (2000) states that if it were possible to define generally the mission of education, it could be said that "education's fundamental purpose is to ensure that all students benefit from learning in ways that allow them to participate fully in public, community, and economic life" (p. 9). It argues that pedagogy is a teaching and learning relationship that creates opportunities for building learning conditions that can lead to full and equitable social participation. Literacy pedagogy, specifically, is "expected to play a particularly important role in fulfilling this mission" (p. 9). Because of this, the New London Group argues, literacy pedagogy must move away from "formalized, monolingual, monocultural, and rule-governed forms of language" and begin to account for "the burgeoning variety of text forms associated with information and multimedia technologies" (p. 9).

## IMPLICATIONS FOR PRACTICE

When thinking about what these three evolving fields of literacy mean for schools and educational equity, we argue that we need to consider how critical readings on and conceptions of text and new information technologies may transform the teaching and learning that occurs in K–12 classrooms. What this calls for is a paradigm shift that requires educators to view learning, teaching, and knowledge through

- An interactive learning paradigm
- A reconceptualization of teacher philosophies, ideologies, and practices
- The valuing of youth popular culture and knowledges

Such a transformation, as argued by Lemke (1998), could allow us to move from a *curricular learning paradigm*, which currently dominates institutions such as schools and universities, to an *interactive learning paradigm*, which dominates institutions such as libraries and research centers. The curricular paradigm assumes that someone else decides what an individual needs to know, and arranges for an individual to learn in a fixed order and on a fixed schedule. The interactive learning paradigm, on the other hand, "assumes that people determine what they need to know based on their participation in activities where such needs arise, and in consultation with knowledgeable specialists" (Lemke, 1998, paragraph 3). The interactive learning paradigm is described as a paradigm of "access to information, rather than imposition of learning" and a paradigm of "how people with power and resources choose to learn" (paragraph 3).

We believe moving from a curricular to an interactive learning paradigm would be a positive move toward educating today's 21st-century students. We cannot ignore, however, the challenges that one might confront when attempting to do this. First, we recognize that there currently exists a "profound gap between the knowledge and skills most students learn in school and the knowledge and skills they need in typical 21st century communities" (Partnership for 21st Century Skills, 2003, p. 3). Although there has been an increased focus on technology in K–12 schools, research has shown that little technology is actually being used in classrooms in meaningful and transformative ways (Bruce & Hogan, 1998; Cuban, 2001). Instead of using technology to contribute to learner-centered teaching approaches that can improve learning (Askov & Bixler, 1998), many educators are using technology in ways that simply replicate what can be done with overhead projectors, televisions, or blackboards (Bruce & Hogan, 1998). Lemke (2006), Smolin and Lawless (2003), and others describe how we need a shift in educational philosophies if we hope to see changes in the ways technology and new media are used.

When promoting critical literacy, a NLS perspective, multimodal ways of thinking, and a multiliteracies approach that goes beyond conventional, print-based literacy practice, educators face a multitude of challenges. Encouraging changes in both teaching practices and philosophies can be quite daunting, especially when research studies have shown that prompting change in teacher beliefs can be extremely difficult (Borko & Putnam, 1996). However, a key challenge continues to exist. Many of today's classroom teachers do not know, or even consider worth knowing, the types of media and information communication technologies (ICTs) needed to participate in the 21st century (Alvermann, 2004).

Alvermann (2004) argued that if classroom teachers largely ignore "the influence of media and ICT literacies on youth's functioning both in and out of school," then they may fail to benefit "from insights that could be learned from tapping into literacies that count in today's youth culture" (p. 81). This becomes particularly problematic when many teachers and parents are concerned about "children's engagement with contemporary media culture—whether the Internet, online or console gaming, or television—and the practices of commodity consumption that tie popular and media culture together" (Luke, 2003, p. 398). Such concerns and anxieties over children's "alleged loss of innocence" and their "vulnerability to media and market seductions" make the new technologies easy targets "as they readily become objects of generational and political responses to the discourses and practices of new capitalism" (p. 398). Although the fundamental principles of reading and writing have not changed, Luke has described how the process has shifted "from the serial cognitive processing of linear print text to parallel processing of multimodal text–image information sources" (p. 399). As more texts become available in digital form, users access information in different ways that have potentially profound ramifications for reading and writing.

## CONCLUSION

The evolving notion of literacy has resulted in a gradual shift in researchers' and practitioners' understanding of the diverse texts, contexts, forms, and spaces of literacy learning and approaches to literacy instruction. With these shifts and evolving conceptions of texts and knowledge, we contend that if students are to participate meaningfully in our increasingly complex societies, as pedagogues, then we need to look at how different forms of texts lessen the gap between inside and outside school literacies, engage with new literacies by creating a space for multiple identities, and value literacy learners' funds of knowledge and the ways in which they can inform literacy teaching.

## REFERENCES

Alexander, P., & Fox, E. (2004). A historical perspective on reading research and practice. In R. Ruddell & N. Unrau (Eds.), *Theoretical models and processes of reading* (pp. 33–68). Newark, DE: International Reading Association.

Alvermann, D. E. (2004). Media, information communication technologies, and youth literacies: A cultural studies perspective. *American Behavioral Scientist, 48*(1), 78–83.

Alvermann, D. E., & Heron, A. H. (2001). Literacy identity work: Playing to learn with popular media. *Journal of Adolescent and Adult Literacy, 45,* 118–122.

Askov, E., & Bixler, B. (1998). Transforming adult literacy instruction through computer-assisted instruction. In D. Reinking, M. McKenna, L. Labbo, & R. Kieffer (Eds.), *Handbook of literacy and technology* (pp. 167–184). Mahwah, NJ: Erlbaum.

Au, K., & Raphael, T. (2000). Equity and literacy in the next millennium. *Reading Research Quarterly, 35*(1), 170–188.

Barton, D., & Hamilton, M. (2000). Literacy practices. In D. Barton, M. Hamilton, & R. Ivanic (Eds.), *Situated literacies: Reading and writing in context* (pp. 7–15). London: Routledge.

Bearne, E. (Ed.). (2003). *Classroom interactions in literacy education.* London: Open University Press.

Beck, A. (2005). A place for critical literacy. *Journal of Adolescent and Adult Literacy, 48*(5), 392–400.

Behrman, E. H. (2006). Teaching about language, power and text: A review of classroom practices that support critical literacy. *Journal of Adolescent and Adult Literacy, 49*(6), 490–498.

Blackburn, M. (2003). Exploring literacy performances and power dynamics at the Loft: Queer youth reading the world and the word. *Research in the Teaching of English, 37,* 467–490.

Blackburn, M. (2005). Disrupting dichotomies for social change: A review of, critique of, and complement to current educational literacy scholarship on gender. *Research in the Teaching of English, 39,* 398–416.

Boling, E. C. (2008). Learning from teachers' conceptions of technology integration: What do blogs, instant messages, and 3D chat rooms have to do with it? *Research in the Teaching of English, 43*(1), 74–100.

Borko, H., & Putnam, R. T. (1996). Learning to teach. In D. C. Berliner & R. C. Calfee (Eds.), *Handbook of educational psychology* (pp. 673–708). New York: Macmillan.

Bruce, B., & Hogan, M. (1998). The disappearance of technology: Toward an ecological model of literacy. In D. Reinking, M. McKenna, L. Labbo, & R. Kieffer (Eds.), *Handbook of literacy and technology* (pp. 269–281). Mahwah, NJ: Erlbaum.

Burbules, N., & Callister, T. (2000). *Watch IT: The risky promises and promising risks of new information technology in education.* Boulder, CO: Westview Press.

Carrington, V. (2004). Texts and literacies of the Shi Jurui. *British Journal of Sociology, 25*(2), 215–228.

Carrington, V. (2006). *Rethinking middle years: Digital technologies, youth culture.* Sydney: Allen & Unwin.

Christensen, L. (1999). Tales from an untracked class. In I. Shor & C. Pari (Eds.), *Education is politics: Critical teaching across differences, K–12* (pp. 178–191). Portsmouth, NH: Heinemann.

Christensen, L. (2000). *Reading, writing and rising up: Teaching about social justice and the power of the written word.* Milwaukee, WI: Rethinking Schools Publication.

Comber, B., & Kamler, B. (1997). Critical literacies: Politicising the language classroom. *Interpretations, 30,* 30–53.

Cope, B., & Kalantzis, M. (2000). Multiliteracies: The beginnings of an idea. In *Multiliteracies: Literacy learning and the design of social futures* (pp. 3–8). New York: Routledge.

Cuban, L. (2001). *Oversold and underused: Computers in the classroom.* Cambridge, MA: Harvard University Press.

Davies, J. (2006). Escaping to the Borderlands: An exploration of the Internet as a cultural space for teenaged Wiccan girls. In K. Pahl & J. Rowsell (Eds.), *Travel notes from the new literacy studies: Instances of practice* (pp. 57–72). Clevedon, UK: Multilingual Matters.

Dyson, A. H. (1993). *Social worlds of children learning to write in an urban primary school.* New York: Teachers College Press.

Dyson, A. H. (1999). Coach Bombay's kids learn to write: Children's appropriation of media material for school literacy. *Research in the Teaching of English, 33*(4), 367–402.

Dyson, A. H. (2001). Where are the childhoods in childhood literacy?: An exploration in outer (school) space. *Journal of Childhood Literacy, 1*(1), 9–39.

Freire, P. (1998). *Teachers as cultural workers: Letters to those who dare teach* (D. Macedo, D. Koike, & A. Oliveira, Trans.) Boulder, CO: Westview Press.

Freire, P., & Macedo, D. (1987). *Literacy: Reading the word and the world.* South Hadley, MA: Bergin & Garvey.

Freire, P., & Macedo, D. (1995). A dialogue: Culture, language and race. *Harvard Educational Review, 65*(3), 377–402.

Gee, J. P. (1996) *Social linguistics and literacies: Ideology in discourses* (2nd ed.). London: Taylor & Francis.

Giroux, H., & McLaren, P. (1992). Writing from the margins: Geographies of identity, pedagogy, and power. *Journal of Education, 174*(1), 7–30.

Hagood, M. C. (2003). New media and online literacies: No age left behind. *Reading Research Quarterly, 38*(3), 386–413.

Halliday, M. (1978). *Language as social semiotic: The social interpretation of language and meaning.* London: Arnold.

Harste, J., & Albers, P. (2007). The arts, new literacies, and multimodality. *English Education, 40*(1), 6–20.

Heath, S. B. (1983). *Ways with words: Language, life and work in communities and classrooms.* Cambridge, UK: Cambridge University Press.

Hull, G., & Schultz, K. (2003). *School's out: Bridging out-of-school literacies with classroom practice.* New York: Teacher's College Press.

Hymes, D. (Ed.). (1996). *Ethnography, linguistics, narrative inequality: Towards an understanding of voice.* London: Routledge.

Janks, H. (2000). Critical literacy: Beyond reason. *Australian Educational Researcher, 29*(1), 7–27.

Janks, H., & Comber, B. (2006). Critical literacy across continents. In K. Pahl & J. Rowsell (Eds.), *Travel notes from the new literacy studies: Instances of practice* (pp. 95–117). Clevedon, UK: Multilingual Matters.

Jewitt, C. (2005). *Technology, literacy, and learning: A multimodal approach.* London: Routledge.

Jewitt, C., & Kress, G. (Eds.). (2003). *Multimodal literacy.* New York: Peter Lang.

Jones, S. (2006). *Girls, social class and literacy: What teachers can do to make a difference.* Portsmouth, NH: Heinemann.

Kendrick, M., & McKay, R. (2004). Drawings as an alternative way of understanding children's constructions of literacy. *Journal of Early Childhood Literacy, 4,* 109–128.

Kenner, C. (2004). *Becoming literate: Young children learning different writing.* Stoke on Trent, UK: Trentham Books.

Knobel, M., & Lankshear, C. (2007). *A new literacies sampler.* New York: Peter Lang.

Kress, G. (1997). *Before writing: Rethinking the paths to literacy.* London: Routledge.

Kress, G. (2003). *Literacy in the new media age.* London: Routledge.

Kress, G., & Van Leeuwen, T. (2006). *Reading images: The grammar of visual design.* New York: Routledge.

Lancaster, L. (2003). Beginning at the beginning: How a young child constructs time multimodally. In C. Jewitt & G. Kress (Eds.), *Multimodal literacy* (pp. 107–122). New York: Peter Lang.

Lankshear, C., & Knobel, M. (1997). Different worlds?: Technology-mediated classroom learning and students' social practices with technologies in home and community settings. In C. Lankshear (Ed.), *Changing literacies* (pp. 164–187). Buckingham, UK: Open University Press.

Lankshear, C., Peters, P., & Knobel, M. (1996). Critical pedagogy and cyberspace. In H. Giroux, C. Lankshear, P. McLaren, & M. Peters (Eds.), *Counter narratives* (pp. 149–188). New York: Routledge.

Leander, K. M. (2002). Locating Letanya: The situated production of identity artifacts in classroom interaction. *Research in the Teaching of English, 37,* 198–248.

Lee, C. D. (1993). *Signifying as a scaffold for literacy interpretation: The pedagogical implications of an African American discourse genre.* Urbana, IL: National Council of teachers of English.

Lemke, J. (2006). Towards critical multimedia literacy: Technology, research, and politics. In M. McKenna, L. D. Labbo, R. D. Kieffer, & D. Reinking (Eds.), *International handbook of literacy and technology* (Vol. 2, pp. 3–14). Mahwah, NJ: Erlbaum.

Lemke, J. L. (1998). Metamedia literacy: Transforming meanings and media. In D. Reinking, M. McKenna, L. Labbo, & R. Kieffer (Eds.), *Handbook of literacy and technology: Transformations in a post-typographic world* (pp. 283–301). Mahwah, NJ: Erlbaum. Retrieved March 1, 2007, from *www-personal.umich.edu/~jaylemke/reinking.htm.*

Luke, A. (2004). Two takes on the critical. In B. Norton & K. Toolney (Eds.), *Critical pedagogies and language learning* (pp. 21–29). Cambridge, UK: Cambridge University Press.

Luke, C. (2003). Pedagogy, connectivity, multimodality, and interdisciplinarity. *Reading Research Quarterly, 38*(3), 397–403.

Marsh, J. (Ed.). (2005). *Popular culture, new media and digital literacy in early childhood.* London: Routledge/Falmer.

Marsh, J. (2006). Popular culture and literacy: A Bourdieuan analysis. *Reading Research Quarterly, 46*(2), 160–174.

Merchant, G. (2001). Teenagers in cyberspace: An investigation of language use and language change in Internet chatrooms. *Journal of Research in Reading, 24*(3), 293–306.

Moll, L., Amanti, C., Neff, D., & González, N. (1992). Funds of knowledge for teaching: Using a qualitative approach to connect homes and classrooms. *Theory Into Practice, 31,* 132–141.

New London Group. (2000). A pedagogy of multiliteracies designing social futures. In B. Cope & M. Kalantzis (Eds.), *Multiliteracies: Literacy learning and the design of social futures* (pp. 9–38). New York: Routledge.

Pahl, K. (2004). Narratives, artifacts and cultural identities: An ethnographic study of communicative practices in homes. *Linguistics and Education, 15*(4), 339–358.

Pahl, K., & Rowsell, J. (Eds.). (2006). *Travel notes from the New Literacy Studies: Instances of practice.* Clevedon: Multilingual Matters.

Partnership for 21st Century Skills. (2003). *Learning for the 21st century: A report and mile guide for 21st century skills.* Washington, DC: Author.

Rowsell, J. (2006). *Family literacy experiences.* Markham, ON, Canada: Pembroke.

Rowsell, J., & Pahl, K. (2007). Sedimented identities in texts: Instances of practice. *Reading Research Quarterly, 42*(3), 388–401.

Schwartz, A., & Rubinstein-Ávila, E. (2006). Understanding the manga hype: Uncovering the multimodality of comic-book literacies. *Journal of Adolescent and Adult Literacy, 50*(1), 40–49.

Scribner, S., & Cole, M. (1981). *The psychology of literacy.* Cambridge, MA: Harvard University Press.

Shor, I. (1992). *Empowering education: Critical teaching for social change.* Chicago: University of Chicago Press.

Smolin, L. I., & Lawless, K. A. (2003). Becoming literate in the technological and tools for teachers. *Reading Teacher, 56*(6), 570–578.

Street, B. V. (1984). *Literacy in theory and practice.* Cambridge, UK: Cambridge University Press.

# CHAPTER 9

# The New Literacies of Online Reading Comprehension and the Irony of No Child Left Behind

## Students Who Require Our Assistance the Most Actually Receive It the Least

DONALD J. LEU, J. GREGORY McVERRY, W. IAN O'BYRNE, LISA ZAWILINSKI, JILL CASTEK, *and* DOUGLAS K. HARTMAN

This chapter reviews research on the new literacies of online reading comprehension. Specifically, we address how the new literacies of online reading comprehension are related to issues of diversity, equity, and public policy. The review concludes that our current public policies in reading unwittingly ensure that the rich get richer and the poor get poorer in developing the new forms of online reading comprehension required for learning in the 21st century. It suggests that educators, researchers, and policymakers must begin to recognize the Internet as a reading comprehension issue, not a technology issue. Failing to recognize the Internet as a reading comprehension issue leads to the installation of public policies that actually hold back diverse literacy learners in economically challenged school districts. If we hope to prepare underserved populations for the reading and learning demands of the 21st century, we must begin to include the new literacies of online reading comprehension in our reading standards, assessments, curricula, and instructional practices. This chapter identifies a robust agenda for both instruction and research to ensure that diverse students in our most economically challenged school districts are fully prepared for their literacy future. This review of research is organized around several key ideas:

173

- The Internet is the defining technology for literacy and learning of our time.
- The Internet requires additional skills and strategies for successful online reading comprehension.
- Our failure to understand the Internet as a reading comprehension issue has produced policies that actually work to perpetuate achievement gaps among poor and diverse students.
- Important implications can be drawn from this perspective to inform research and classroom practice.

## THE INTERNET IS THE DEFINING TECHNOLOGY FOR LITERACY AND LEARNING OF OUR TIME

We begin this chapter with a central claim: The Internet has become the defining technology for literacy and learning in the 21st century (Friedman, 2005; International Reading Association, 2002; Partnership for 21st Century Skills, 2004). One way to understand this fundamental change may be seen in Table 9.1.

Put simply, literacy is rapidly shifting from page to screen. Table 9.1 shows that one-fifth of the world's population, 1.5 billion individuals, used the Internet in 2008 to read, write, communicate, learn, and solve important problems online (*Internet World Stats: Usage and Population Statistics*, n.d.). Moreover, the number of Internet users has increased by over 300% during the last 7 years. If this rate of increase continues, more than half of the world's population will be using the

**TABLE 9.1. Internet Usage Statistics as of November 20, 2008**

| World regions | Population (2008 est.) | Population % of world | Internet usage latest data | % Population (penetration) | Usage % of world | Usage growth, 2000–2007 |
|---|---|---|---|---|---|---|
| Africa | 955,206,348 | 14.3 | 51,065,635 | 5.3 | 3.5 | 1,031.2 |
| Asia | 3,776,181,949 | 56.6 | 578,538,527 | 15.3 | 39.5 | 406.1 |
| Europe | 801,401,065 | 12.0 | 384,633,765 | 48.1 | 26.3 | 266.0 |
| Middle East | 197,090,443 | 3.0 | 41,939,200 | 21.3 | 2.9 | 1,176.8 |
| North America | 337,167,248 | 5.1 | 248,241,969 | 73.6 | 17.0 | 129.6 |
| Latin America/ Caribbean | 576,091,673 | 8.6 | 139,009,209 | 24.1 | 9.5 | 669.3 |
| Oceania / Australia | 33,981,562 | 0.5 | 20,204,331 | 59.5 | 1.4 | 165.1 |
| World total | 6,676,120,288 | 100.0 | 1,463,632,361 | 21.9 | 100.0 | 305.5 |

*Note.* Data from *Internet World Stats: Usage and Population Statistics* (2008).

Internet in an additional 7 years, and nearly the entire world's population will be using the Internet 10–15 years from now. Never in the history of civilization have we ever seen a new technology for literacy adopted by so many, in so many different places, in such a short period of time (Coiro, Knobel, Lankshear, & Leu, 2008). This generation of educators, researchers, and policymakers has the important responsibility to help us successfully transition a period of profound change as literacy shifts from page to screen. Most importantly, we must do this is a manner that ensures equity for all segments of our society.

It is impossible to anticipate all of the changes in the social and cultural practices that will result from such an important shift in the contexts for literacy. Nevertheless, we know they will be profound, because we see the beginning of these changes in three areas that direct change throughout the world:

1. The reading habits of adolescents.
2. The technologies of literacy used in the workplace.
3. Public policy responses by nations outside the United States.

## *The Changing Nature in the Reading Habits of Adolescents*

Adolescents regularly signal important generational shifts in language, style, music, and other important aspects of culture (Estabrook, Witt, & Rainie, 2007; Jones & Madden, 2002; Lenhart, Madden, & Hitlin, 2005; Rainie, 2006). Perhaps more than any other age group, adolescents direct cultural change within societies; they are the harbingers of our future. We see this taking place now in the changing social practices of literacy as the Internet enters their lives (Lankshear & Knobel, 2006; Leander, 2008).

Adolescents, for example, read online at a rate far greater than other segments of the population (Roberts, Foehr, & Rideout, 2005). This trend represents an important divide in the generational privileging of texts, from those that appear offline to those that appear online. What is especially striking is that this pattern appears to be a global phenomenon. In Accra, Ghana, for example, more than half of 15- to 18-year-olds report having previously gone online (Borzekowski, Fobil, & Asante, 2006). In the United Kingdom, 74% of children and young people ages 9–19 have access to the Internet at home (Livingstone & Bober, 2005). In the United States, 87% of all students ages 12–17 report using the Internet, and nearly 11 million do so daily (Lenhart, Madden, & Hitlin, 2005).

In addition, adolescents in some nations use online information sources more than offline sources for school assignments, again signaling a shift in the generational privileging of texts. Seventy percent of students with home access to the Internet in the United States  for example, reported using the Internet in 2001 as the primary source for information on their most recent school report or project, but only 24% of these students reported using the library for the same task (Lenhart, Simon, & Graziano, 2001).

Perhaps the most telling change in the reading habits of adolescents is that many now spend more time reading online than offline. In the United States, for example, students ages 8–18 spend 48 minutes per day reading on the Internet and only 43 minutes per day reading offline (Roberts et al., 2005). Historically, this statistic may represent a singularly important tipping point for literacy because adolescents are likely to continue privileging online texts throughout their adult lives.

## The Changing Nature of Literacy in the Workplace

We also see the shift from page to screen occurring in the workplace. In just 1 year (August 2000–September 2001), use of the Internet at work to read, write, and communicate increased by nearly 60% among all employed adults age 25 and older in the United States (U.S. Department of Commerce, 2002).

Global economic competition is driving this transformation. As trade barriers have lowered, companies must increase their productivity to survive in a global and more competitive economy. Many of the productivity gains realized during the past decade in economies around the world are due to the rapid integration of the Internet into the workplace (Matteucci, O'Mahony, Robinson, & Zwick, 2005; van Ark, Inklaar, & McGuckin, 2003). It has been used widely to solve problems more effectively and to communicate with others.

Of course, effective online information use in the workplace will require that students become proficient in the new literacy skills of the Internet. As we become increasingly aware of this point, nations outside the United States are beginning to alter public policies to prepare workers for participation in an online information economy.

## Recent Public Policy Initiatives, as Nations Respond to the Shift from Page to Screen

Ireland was one of the first nations to expand its investment in education generally, and in the integration of the Internet into classrooms specifically (Leu & Kinzer, 2000). As a result, Ireland's graduates are being prepared in the new literacy skills demanded by a global information economy. Businesses that seek to increase productivity now have an important incentive to relocate to Ireland, whose workforce increasingly is skilled in the new forms of online reading, writing, communication, and problem solving. By attracting these companies, Ireland became one of the fastest-growing economies in the world. Ireland, for example, currently manufactures more software than the United States (hAnluain, 2001; Harris, 2003; Organization for Economic Development and Cooperation, 2004).

The changes taking place in the Irish economy have not gone unnoticed. Finland, for example, has developed a national training model to provide all teachers with 5 weeks of paid, release time for professional development to integrate the Internet into the classroom (Leu & Kinzer, 2000).

Japan, too, seeks to raise a new generation of citizens who are prepared for a global information economy. For $22 per month, Japan has broadband in nearly every home that is 16 times faster than the broadband in U.S. homes (Bleha, 2005). The government subsidizes these costs, knowing that students read far more outside of school than in school. Japan wants to make the information and learning potential of the Internet continuously available to every student.

Mexico is also responding to these changes. It has established a national policy, e-Mexico, to ensure that every citizen and every school has access to an Internet connection (Ludlow, 2006). The need to prepare students to compete in a global information economy drives Mexico's public policy initiatives in this area.

All of these events demonstrate that our literacy lives are changing in fundamental ways. The Internet makes our world flat, leveling the playing field for all nations (Friedman, 2005). This is especially true if we understand the Internet as a reading comprehension issue. The Internet, after all, is just the latest in a long line of technologies for information and communication, including cuneiform tablets, papyrus and ink, velum scrolls, codexes, and books. The skills required to obtain and use information on the Internet are no more technology skills than the skills required to read another technology, the book. The Internet is a reading comprehension issue, not a technology issue, for our schools. New literacies of online reading comprehension are necessary to take full advantage of information on the Internet.

## THE INTERNET REQUIRES ADDITIONAL SKILLS AND STRATEGIES FOR SUCCESSFUL ONLINE READING COMPREHENSION

To capture the changing nature of literacy online, many have begun to use the term *new literacies*. The term means many different things to many different people, however. To some, new literacies are seen as new social practices (Street, 1995, 2003). To others, new literacies are important new strategies and dispositions that are essential for online reading comprehension, learning, and communication (Coiro, 2003; Leu, Kinzer, Coiro, & Cammack, 2004). To still others, new literacies are new Discourses (Gee, 2003) or new semiotic contexts (Kress, 2003; Lemke, 2002). Still others see literacy as differentiating into multiliteracies (New London Group, 2000) or multimodal contexts (Hull & Schultz, 2002), or as a construct that juxtaposes several of these orientations (Lankshear & Knobel, 2006). When you include these different definitions of new literacies with terms such as "information and communication technology (ICT) literacy" (International ICT Literacy Panel, 2002) or "informational literacy" (Hirsch, 1999; Kuiper & Volman, 2008; Webber & Johnson, 2000), the construct of new literacies becomes even more challenging to understand.

To support better theory development and inform the broad sweep of new literacies research, a recent review (Coiro et al., 2008) concludes that most new literacies perspectives share four assumptions:

1. New literacies include the new skills, strategies, dispositions, and social practices that are required by new technologies for information and communication.
2. New literacies are central to full participation in a global community.
3. New literacies regularly change as their defining technologies change.
4. New literacies are multifaceted, and our understanding of them benefits from multiple points of view.

Although these are the common assumptions of a broad definition of new literacies, considerable work is taking place in many specific areas, each with its own additional assumptions, unique to separate areas of inquiry. This suggests that, from a theoretical viewpoint, we need to be precise about the specific form of new literacies to which we refer.

We use a new literacies theory of online reading comprehension (Castek et al., 2008; Coiro, 2003; Henry, 2006; Leu, Kinzer, et al., 2004; Leu, Zawilinski, et al., 2007) in this chapter to explore the changes in reading comprehension that take place as our reading world migrates from offline texts to the Internet. This perspective frames online reading comprehension as a process of problem-based inquiry involving the new skills, strategies, dispositions, and social practices that take place as we read on the Internet.

What differs from earlier models of traditional print comprehension is that the new literacies of online reading comprehension are defined around both a problem and a process of self-directed text construction (Coiro & Dobler, 2007). This self-directed text construction process occurs when readers navigate through an infinite information space to construct their own texts online as they read to solve problems. During this process, both new and traditional reading comprehension skills are required. This overlap between online and offline reading enriches, but also complicates, our understanding of reading comprehension in the 21st century.

Within this perspective, Leu, Kinzer, and colleagues (2004) define the new literacies of online reading comprehension around five processing practices in which we engage while reading on the Internet: (1) identifying important questions, (2) locating information, (3) critically evaluating information, (4) synthesizing information, and (5) communicating information. Within these five areas reside the skills, strategies, and dispositions that are distinctive to online reading comprehension, as well as other factors that are important for offline reading comprehension.

Online readers construct meaning in two different but intersecting ways. First, online readers construct mental models of meaning as they process the information they encounter. This is similar to what they do when reading offline (Bransford, Brown, & Cocking, 2000; RAND Reading Study Group, 2002). In addition, however, online readers also physically construct the texts they read according to the choices they make as they follow different links online to solve an information problem. We refer to these as "intertexts." Online readers dynamically construct the intertexts that they read as they move from site to site, whereas offline readers typically read the texts that others have constructed for them. Thus, the construction of meaning during online reading comprehension becomes much more complex, because the construction of a mental model taking place in our minds also directs our choices about the intertext we construct. This multiple-layered and transactional process of meaning construction, always driven by a question or problem, appears to be an important source of the differences between online and offline reading. What, specifically, takes place during each of the processing elements of online reading comprehension?

## Identifying Important Questions

Reading comprehension on the Internet always begins with a problem. It may be a relatively simple one, such as "What is the cheapest flight to California?" or "What would be a good recipe for dessert?" It may also be a complex one, such as "How can we end global conflict?" As a result, online reading comprehension may best be understood as a problem-based learning task situated within the social practices, texts, and contexts that define reading on the Internet. Taboada and Guthrie (2006) show that reading initiated by a question or problem differs in important ways from reading that does not. This is an important, initial source of the differences between online and offline reading comprehension.

## Locating Information

Beginning with a problem, then using a complex and infinite informational space to solve it, means that reading skills required to locate information become essential to online reading comprehension. New reading skills required to locate information are an important aspect of online reading comprehension, and we include these in our model. Some of these skills have been studied by scholars in information science or library and media studies (e.g., Bilal, 2000, Hsieh-Yee, 2001) and used by library media specialists.

Initial work (Henry, 2006; Leu, Reinking, et al., 2007) suggests that at least four general types of reading comprehension skills are associated with locating information on the Internet: (1) knowing how to read and use a search engine; (2) reading search engine results; (3) reading a Web page to locate information that might be present on that page; and (4) making an inference about where information is located by selecting a link at one site to find information at another site. Often these intersect.

Consider, for example, knowing how to read and to use a search engine to locate information. We frequently find students in economically challenged school districts who never use a search engine. Instead, they use what we call a "dot com" strategy within the address bar of a browser, inserting "www + topic + .com" to locate information through the browser window (Leu, Reinking, et al., 2007). This may be very effective when locating information on a favorite pop star (e.g., *www.britneyspears.com*) but it is usually ineffective for locating content-area information (e.g., *www.iraqwar.com*). We have also found that many students do not actually read search engine results (Zawilinski & Leu, 2008). Instead, they use a simple "click and look" strategy, beginning at the top of the search result list, clicking on each entry to see what it looks like. They do this rather than reading the summary of the result that appears below the link. Both "dot com" and "click and look" strategies make it difficult to locate useful information related to a specific question efficiently. They are typical unskilled online readers.

It is becoming clear that the skills required to locate information may be "circuit breaker" skills; having good online reading skills related to locating information leads to successful online reading comprehension, whereas lacking them often leads to failure. Put another way, if you cannot locate information related to your problem, you cannot determine the answer and, in essence, you cannot read online. There may be a useful analogy here to decoding skills during offline reading comprehension, where it is very difficult to comprehend offline text successfully without adequate decoding skills. Both decoding and locating skills can short-circuit the reading comprehension process.

## Critically Evaluating Information

Once you locate information, you need to know how much you can count on it. Is it accurate? Is it reliable? How was it shaped by the person who created it? Does it meet your needs? The range of potential sources online is so vast, and the range of perspectives is so diverse, that the ability to read and evaluate information critically becomes especially important. Although critical evaluation is a skill we want all readers to develop for both offline and online texts, it becomes especially important online, where increasingly sophisticated critical thinking is required.

## Synthesizing Information

Synthesis is a central component of online reading comprehension; it is also one of the most challenging to study. Much of synthesis takes place in the mind of the reader. The process happens so quickly and is extremely hard to observe in ways that provide visible patterns.

No two readers construct the same online intertext, even though they may have the same question or problem to solve. How they make decisions about which texts to connect and to read, and which links to follow as they seek an answer, is one aspect of synthesis that we need to understand better. When choosing texts to read offline, of course, this does not happen to nearly the same extent, with nearly the same speed, nor with units of text that are nearly so short. Intertextuality (Hartman, 1995, 2000) defines online reading; far too often, it is merely an offline possibility in school classrooms. We need much more work on the intertextual synthesis of meaning that occurs online during both the construction of mental models of meaning and the construction of intertext from the choices readers make online.

## Communicating Information

Finally, our model of online reading comprehension integrates reading and writing and, in an online context that is typically socially constructed, we frame writing as communication. Readers communicate with others as they read to answer a question, solve a problem, or share a solution. Many new communication tools are becoming available on the Internet. These tools are useful when one seeks to solve a problem, answer a question, or exchange ideas with others near or far. Each new tool requires its own set of strategies. Information networking sites, e-mail, text messaging, chats, blogs, wikis, discussion boards, and phone and video conferencing are just a few of the tools individuals use to read, communicate, and construct meaning on the Internet today. Each requires that we develop new skills and strategies to use them effectively.

## Recent Research Evidence on the Differences between Online and Offline Reading Comprehension

An emerging line of research has begun to illuminate our understanding of the differences between online and offline reading comprehension, first suggested by the RAND Reading Study Group (2002). This work indicates that (1) online reading comprehension is different from offline reading comprehension; (2) the online reading skills of locating and critically evaluating information appear to be especially important components; (3) there appear to be significant differences in the online reading comprehension skills of middle school students based on the socioeconomic level of their school district; and (4) integrating new literacies into content-area literacy classes may dissipate some of new teachers' traditional resistance toward integrating reading strategies while teaching subject-matter knowledge.

1. *Online reading comprehension is different from offline reading comprehension.* That online reading comprehension and offline reading comprehension are different is not a trivial matter. Learning is increasingly dependent on the ability to read and comprehend complex information at high levels (Alexander & Jetton, 2002; Bransford et al., 2000), and the Internet is now a central source of that information (Lyman & Varian, 2003).

What empirical evidence supports the conclusion that online and offline reading comprehension are different? One study (Leu et al., 2005) found no significant correlation among seventh-grade students between performance on a state reading comprehension assessment and an online reading comprehension assessment (ORCA-Blog) with good psychometric properties. These results suggest that new skills and strategies may be required during online reading.

Another result from this study was that, in classrooms with laptops, science-content learning actually decreased for 12 weeks, until students had acquired sufficient online reading comprehension skills to benefit from online information.

This, too, suggests that additional reading comprehension skills may be required on the Internet.

A final result from this study was that some of the lowest performing students on the state reading comprehension assessment were actually some of the highest performing students on the ORCA-Blog. This surprising finding also supports the conclusion that online and offline reading comprehension are somewhat different. (Video examples of online reading comprehension by these students may be viewed at *www.newliteracies.uconn.edu/reading.html.*)

A second study, conducted by Coiro and Dobler (2007), revealed that online reading comprehension shares a number of similarities with offline reading comprehension, but online reading comprehension also includes a number of important differences, making it more complex.

A third study (Coiro, 2007) used a regression model and found that offline reading comprehension was correlated with online reading comprehension, contributing a significant amount of variance to the prediction of online reading comprehension. However, it also found that an additional, unique, and significant amount of variance was contributed by knowing students' online reading comprehension ability. The results of this study are also consistent with the conclusion that new skills and strategies are required during online reading comprehension.

2. *The online reading skills of locating and critically evaluating information appear to be especially important components.* A preliminary study of think-aloud verbal protocols during online reading comprehension (Zawilinski & Leu, 2008) is beginning to outline the types of online reading comprehension skills that are distinctive and essential to successful online reading comprehension. This study shows that deficits in two areas in particular, locating and critically evaluating information, appear to impede successful online reading comprehension in important ways. If you cannot locate information related to your problem, you cannot read online. In addition, if you do not think critically about the information that you read online, it is easy to be led astray from effective solutions.

3. *There appear to be significant differences in the online reading comprehension skills of middle school students based on the socioeconomic level of their school district.* Henry (2007) found significant differences in online reading comprehension ability of middle school students according to the economic status of their school district. The same pattern was evident among the teachers of these students. Those in affluent school districts were more skilled at locating and critically evaluating information. Interviews with principals indicated that computers in schools not meeting adequate yearly progress indicators were used primarily for rote drill and skill (i.e., Accelerated Reader) activities in an attempt to increase offline reading achievement scores.

4. *Integrating new literacies into content-area literacy classes may dissipate some of the traditional resistance among new teachers to integrate reading strategies while they teach subject-matter knowledge.* A research project funded by the Carnegie Corporation of New York studied the integration of online reading comprehension

into preservice teacher preparation in secondary mathematics, science, English, and reading (Hartman, Leu, Olson, & Truxaw, 2005). Two findings stood out. First, a case study assignment comparing think-aloud data of their pupils' reading of content-area material in both online and offline contexts dissipated much of the traditional resistance among new teachers to integrating reading strategies while teaching subject-matter knowledge. New teachers became very interested in understanding more about reading from this experience. Second, the intervention altered how these new secondary teachers envisioned the role of reading comprehension in their future teaching.

5. *Some classroom contexts appear to be especially important in supporting the acquisition of online reading comprehension.* Castek (2008) examined the contexts and conditions that facilitated acquisition of online reading comprehension in a fourth- and fifth-grade combination classroom over the course of three instructional units lasting 15 weeks. Three elements were determined to be most supportive of students' new literacies acquisition: (1) extensive opportunities to apply new learning independently following teacher-guided instruction, (2) multiple opportunities to collaborate with other students with varying levels of skills and experience, and (3) integration of activities that consistently challenge learners to extend the boundaries of what they currently know and can do online. Both teacher–student and peer-to-peer scaffolding were needed for students to acquire online reading comprehension strategies. Although teacher scaffolding was most effective in the early stages of acquisition, peer-scaffolding played a more substantial role in supporting online student learning, once students acquired basic computer skills.

This study also investigated the extent to which 15 weeks of Internet integration increased students' content learning during an inquiry unit. Although a statistically significant difference was evident on a performance-based classroom project, over and above the performance of a control population, robust and lasting performance gains on a conceptual knowledge measure were not detected between groups. This finding suggests that instruction in online reading comprehension requires extended scaffolding, if it is to support content learning most effectively.

## Summary

One pattern in all of these studies is that online reading comprehension is not isomorphic with offline reading comprehension; new reading comprehension skills are required online. A second pattern is that the complexity of the online reading task appears to determine the extent to which online reading is either similar to or different from offline reading. Performance with simpler online reading tasks may correlate more with offline reading (e.g., Coiro, 2007); more complex online reading tasks do not (e.g., Leu et al., 2005). A third pattern is that online reading comprehension may have unexpected consequences, as well as opportunities. This appears to be the source of a tertiary gap between rich and poor school districts in online reading ability (Henry, 2007). It also appears to provide some special opportunities for the preparation of content-area teachers. Finally, we are also beginning to discover the different contexts that appear to support students in acquiring the new literacies of online reading comprehension.

### The Failure of State Standards and State Reading Assessments to Include the New Literacies of Online Reading Comprehension

It is increasingly clear that the Internet is a powerful new context for reading and learning. It is also clear that online reading comprehension is not the same as offline reading comprehension. Nevertheless, state reading standards and assessments have yet to include any of the new skills that are important to online reading comprehension. These continue to be based on the reading of paragraphs from traditional text sources, with traditional types of assessment tasks. Consider, for example, the following observations, which have not changed since they were first observed several years ago:

1. Not a single state in the United States measures students' ability to read search engine results during state reading assessments (Leu, Ataya, & Coiro, 2002).
2. Not a single state in the United States measures students' ability to evaluate critically information that is found online to determine its reliability (Leu et al., 2002).
3. Not a single state in the United States measures students' ability to compose clear and effective e-mail messages in their state writing assessment (Leu et al., 2002).
4. Few, if any, states in the United States permit all students to use a word processor on the state writing assessment (Leu et al., 2002).

The failure in the United States to include skills important to online reading comprehension in state reading standards and assessments is surprising given the rapid penetration of the Internet into our lives.

## THE RICH GET RICHER THE POOR GET POORER

Policies such as No Child Left Behind seek to close achievement gaps, especially in reading. Ironically, however, when these policies are combined with state standards and assessments that fail to include online reading comprehension skills, they actually increase achievement gaps between students. The cruelest irony of No Child Left Behind is that students who need to be most prepared at school for an online age of information are precisely those who are prepared the least.

How does this happen? First, consider children in our poorest school districts. These children have the least amount of Internet access at home. Cooper

(2004), for example, found that half of all households with incomes below $30,000 had no Internet at all at home, whereas half of all households with incomes above $75,000 had broadband. This is one aspect of a very real digital divide.

A second aspect results from the failure of schools in poorer districts to integrate the Internet into the curriculum. Unfortunately, our poorest schools are under the greatest pressure to raise scores on tests that have nothing to do with online reading comprehension. As a result, these schools focus instruction completely on offline reading skills. Why should they do anything else? Online reading comprehension is not tested; it contributes nothing to adequate yearly progress indicators in these poorer schools. Because instruction is increasingly driven by these state assessments, too few students in our poorest schools are being supported in developing the new literacies of online reading comprehension (Henry, 2007). In short, students in our poorest schools are doubly disadvantaged: They have less access to the Internet at home, and teachers do not prepare them for the new literacies of online reading comprehension at school.

Consider, on the other hand, students in our most privileged schools. Cooper (2004) indicates that most children from advantaged communities also have broadband Internet connections at home. As a result, teachers feel greater freedom to integrate the Internet into their curriculum and support their students with its use (Henry, 2007); it is easy to assign homework requiring Internet use when teachers know that their students have Internet access at home. Lazarus and Wainer (2005), for example, found that 63% of children from households earning more than $75,000 annually reported that they used the Internet at school, compared to only 36% of children from households earning less than $15,000 annually. Moreover, advantaged districts feel much less pressure in relation to test scores. Their students already perform at high levels on reading assessments. Thus, students in richer districts are doubly privileged: They have greater access to the Internet at home, and they use it more often at school.

This public policy failure has important consequences for education in the 21st century, in which the Internet is now a central source of information (Lyman & Varian, 2003) and learning is increasingly dependent on the ability to read and comprehend complex information at high levels (Alexander & Jetton, 2002; Bransford et al., 2000). As a result of our collective pubic policy failures, students who most require our support with the online reading comprehension skills required for the 21st century end up receiving it the least.

This failure is not inconsiderable, and it compounds the current reality. Eight million U.S. adolescents are considered illiterate (Biancarosa & Snow, 2004). Almost one-third of adolescents cannot read at basic levels (National Center for Education Statistics, 2003). Moreover, nearly twice the number of white, economically advantaged students perform above the basic level as their economically disadvantaged peers, those with the least Internet access at home (National Center for Education Statistics, 2003).

Given the new reading comprehension skills that the Internet requires, the compounded reading achievement gap between students in economically privileged and economically challenged districts will only get larger as online reading comprehension becomes more central to our lives. Each day that these policies remain unchanged, we deny the most vulnerable members of our societies important opportunities to learn skills and strategies that are central to success in an online age of information. Their full participation in our collective future is essential to build a world that is more thoughtful, more compassionate, and more connected, because the best solutions to problems appear to result from collaborative groups that bring diverse, multiple perspectives to the solution (Page, 2007). These outcomes will be essential to solve the important global problems of health, poverty, sectarian and religious strife, and, ultimately, war and peace.

## IMPLICATIONS FOR CLASSROOM PRACTICE

The conclusion that online reading comprehension requires additional skills, beyond those required for offline reading, suggests that there are important changes ahead for classroom instruction. We are only beginning to understand fully these classroom implications. What is clear is that educators need to recognize the Internet as an important text and context in all of our lives. They must begin to use the Internet as an important source of content for their curricula. Only then can educators begin to focus on what, and how, to teach and take full advantage of the information afforded by the Internet.

### What to Teach

The emerging research on online reading comprehension indicates that development of a number of new skills are important to prepare our students for the 21st century (Castek, 2008; Coiro, 2007; Coiro & Dobler, 2007; Henry, 2007; Leu, Reinking, et al., 2007). This is especially true for the diverse population of students in our most economically challenged schools. It is not that the skills required for offline reading comprehension no longer are necessary. Indeed, these will continue to be important during both offline and online reading comprehension. Recent research indicates, however, that additional reading comprehension skills are required online.

Take just one area of online reading comprehension: critical evaluation. Critical evaluation is important during offline reading, but it is even more essential during online reading, and new skills are required. In the online world, of course, anyone may publish anything. Thus, online reading comprehension requires our students to be especially skeptical about information they read, to think continuously about author, information, and motive. They also need to know how to locate the source of any information, and how to find out about any person, with the Internet, to see how that information is being shaped. This seldom happens, unfortunately. Approximately 75% of people in the United States do not regularly check the source of the health information they read online (Fox, 2006). New online reading comprehension skills and strategies are also required as readers use the Internet to define problems, then locate, synthesize, and communicate information. (See Leu et al., 2008, for a checklist of these skills.)

Although new skills are required during reading comprehension, new opportunities are also available. The Internet can be an especially powerful tool for English language learners (Castek et al., 2008), because students can find and read texts in both their languages, take advantage of online translators, and try out English conventions when communicating online.

### How to Teach

Emerging research on how to teach online reading comprehension (Leu & Reinking, 2005–2008) suggests that online reading comprehension might best be developed through problem-based activities in small groups within classrooms, often with one-on-one laptops, where students share and exchange successful strategies. One instructional model, Internet Reciprocal Teaching (Leu et al., 2008), is being developed around many of the principles on which reciprocal teaching is based, an instructional approach that appears to have the greatest effect size on comprehension outcomes (Rosenshine & Meister, 1994). Internet Reciprocal Teaching uses a three-phase instructional model:

- Phase 1: Direct instruction of essential and basic online reading comprehension skills and online tool use.
- Phase 2: Problem-based learning designed to extend online reading comprehension skills development. This includes daily, small-group activities in which students are given an information problem and asked to discover and exchange online reading comprehension strategies to solve each problem.
- Phase 3: Inquiry projects designed to extend further the development of new reading comprehension skills and strategies, and their exchange, in small groups.

Although a description of this instructional model is available (Leu et al., 2008) much remains to be learned about how best to teach online reading comprehension skills.

### The Opportunities That Diversity Provides: Beyond Online Reading Comprehension

Successful use of the Internet is much more than simply acquiring the comprehension skills that are important to reading on the Internet. These are necessary but not sufficient skills to be fully prepared for a lifetime of online literacy and learning. Although many other elements will be required, it is likely that an important element is to understand how best to take advantage of the opportunities that diversity provides in developing richer and better solutions to the complex problems we face in our world. Recent work (Page, 2007) indicates that better solutions emerge when different points of view, frequently from different cultural traditions, are brought to the same table to solve a problem. In a globalized world, it will be increasingly important that our students understand this lesson and have experience in working online with other students, from multiple cultural and linguistic traditions, around the world. It is likely that collaborative instructional models, such as Internet Project (Leu, Leu, & Coiro, 2004), may be especially useful. Online projects are increasingly available on the Internet at locations such as ePals (*epals.com*), GlobalSchool (*www.gsh.org*).Net, KidsProj (*www.kidlink.org/kidproj*), and other locations. These may be used to help us prepare our students for a diverse, online world that requires a deeper appreciation of issues, transcending different cultural, linguistic, and economic differences that students currently experience within a single nation's borders.

## IMPLICATIONS FOR RESEARCH

Perhaps the most obvious implication for research on the new literacies of online reading comprehension is that we need much more research very quickly, if we expect to chart our path forward with sufficient speed to keep up with the changes taking place in online technologies (Leu, 2000). Advances in Internet technologies and online information delivery systems wait for no one. While broad theoretical outlines about the nature of online reading comprehension are being resolved, the details of this process await additional work. These details will be essential to assessment, instruction, and research.

Most importantly, we need to understand more fully the apparent gap in the opportunities of students from rich and poor districts to develop online reading comprehension skills. Equity and diversity issues are paramount for societies that profess egalitarian ideals. In an age in which one's ability to use online information profoundly determines success in learning and life, it is a cruel irony, indeed, that policies organized around offline reading actually deny opportunities to students who most need our assistance with online reading.

A central line of research that needs to be carried forward rapidly is development of assessments of online reading comprehension that are reliable, valid, and easy to score. Current ORCAs (cf. Castek, 2008; Coiro, 2007; Leu et al., 2005; Leu & Reinking, 2005–2008) present online reading comprehension tasks within the open Internet and are typically based on rubric scoring procedures. This has proven useful for initial studies (Castek, 2008; Coiro, 2007) that have looked intensively at smaller numbers of students and in which the costs of labor-intensive scoring procedures were not prohibitive. As we scale up, we will require assessments of online reading comprehension administered across districts, states, and nations (Henry, 2007). This will require much less labor-intensive assessments than ORCA and that take place in a closed simulation of the Internet. These would be less subject to a small change on the Internet that could disrupt the design of an open Internet assessment.

Currently, several assessments have been developed like this. Educational Testing Service has developed the iSkills Assessment (*www.ets.org/ictliteracy*), and an assessment of online reading comprehension in closed environments is being developed for the Program for International Student Assessment (PISA) 2009. The United Kingdom appears to have developed something similar in their Key Stage 3 ICT assessment (see *www.naa.org.uk/naaks3/default.asp*), and the Progress in International Reading Study (PIRLS) may be considering the development of a similar assessment instrument (Kennedy, personal communication, October 22, 2007), again in a closed environment.

Two issues remain to be evaluated, however. First, do these assessments represent the essential elements of online reading comprehension? Because they have been developed in closed environments, and not the full complexity of the Internet, they have a tendency to be limited to tasks that fit best within bounded contexts, such as the reading of spreadsheet data sets or the evaluation of given Internet sites rather than the location and evaluation of information within the fully realized richness and complexity of the Internet. Second, to what extent does performance on more limited tasks such as these correlate with actual online reading comprehension performance?

Finally, important research must also be conducted to understand more completely instructional practices that support the development of online reading comprehension skills in classrooms. This line of research is likely to be extensive and demand extraordinary effort given the complexity of classroom contexts and the diverse needs of learners. Emerging work (Castek, 2008; Coiro, 2007; Dalton & Proctor, 2008; Henry, 2007) may provide useful initial direction. However, we need to expand rapidly these early efforts to understand more fully the potential of student online collaboration across national boundaries, especially if we hope to realize fully the potential of diversity for increasing literacy and learning opportunities for all students.

## SUMMARY AND CONCLUSION

The Internet is rapidly becoming a central context for literacy and learning. It also appears to require new literacies for proficient online reading comprehension and learning. Public policies in some nations appear to increase online reading achievement gaps between rich and poor, ironically, while they purport to close them. The literacy community must rethink what it means to be a reader in the 21st century if it hopes to prepare all students for the new literacies of online reading comprehension.

A second issue also arises: Unless the literacy community begins to rethink the nature of reading, literacy researchers and practitioners will become increasingly marginalized during the important public policy debates that lie ahead, losing the opportunity to influence events in school classrooms. Others, outside the literacy research community, will fill the vacuum and define online reading, writing, and communication for us and without us. Research communities in assessment (International ICT Literacy Panel, 2002), library and media studies (American Association of School Librarians and Association for Educational Communications and Technology, 1998), educational technology (International Society for Technology in Education, n.d.), and learning research communities (Partnership for 21st Century Skills, 2004) are already beginning to do so. If this trend continues, we will be left alone to study reading issues defined by our past, not our future, and the reading research community once again will be left out of important public policy decisions that profoundly affect issues of literacy and diversity for classrooms, teachers, and students. Clearly, we have much to do together.

## REFERENCES

Alexander, P. A., & Jetton, T. L. (2002). Learning from text: A multidimensional and developmental perspective. In M. L. Kamil, P. Mosenthal, P. D. Pearson, & R. Barr (Eds.), *Handbook of reading research* (Vol. 3, pp. 285–310). Mahwah, NJ: Erlbaum.

American Association of School Librarians and Association for Educational Communications and Technology. (1998). *Information power: Building partnerships for learning.* Chicago: American Library Association.

Biancarosa, G., & Snow, C. (2004). *Reading Next: A vision for action and research in middle and high school literacy: A report to the Carnegie Corporation of New York.* Retrieved April 15, 2008, from *www.all4ed.org/publications/readingnext.*

Bilal, D. (2000). Children's use of the Yahooligans! Web search engine: Cognitive, physical, and affective behaviors on fact-based search tasks. *Journal of the American Society for Information Science, 51,* 646–665.

Bleha, T. (2005, May/June). Down to the wire. *Foreign Affairs.* Retrieved December 15, 2005, from *www.foreignaffairs.org/20050501faessay84311/thomas-bleha/down-to-the-wire.html.*

Borzekowski, D., Fobil, J., & Asante, K. (2006). Online access by adolescents in Accra: Ghanaian teens' use of the Internet for health information. *Developmental Psychology, 42,* 450–458. Retrieved December 1, 2006, from *www.apa.org/journals/releases/dev423450.pdf.*

Bransford, J. D., Brown, A. L., & Cocking, R. R. (2000). *How people learn: Brain, mind, experience, and school* (expanded ed.). Washington, DC: National Academy Press.

Castek, J. (2008). *How are the new literacies of online reading comprehension acquired by 4th and 5th grade students?: Exploring the contexts that facilitate learning.* Unpublished doctoral dissertation, University of Connecticut, Storrs.

Castek, J., Leu, D. J., Jr., Coiro, J., Gort, M., Henry, L. A., & Lima, C. (2008). Developing new literacies among multilingual learners in the elementary grades. In L. Parker (Ed.), *Technology-mediated learning environments for young English learners: Connections In and out of school* (pp. 111–153). Mahwah, NJ: Erlbaum.

Coiro, J. (2003). Reading comprehension on the Internet: Expanding our understanding of reading comprehension to encompass new literacies. *Reading Teacher, 56,* 458–464. Retrieved November 1, 2006, from *www.readingonline.org/electronic/elec_index.asp?href=/electronic/rt/2-03_column/index.html.*

Coiro, J., & Dobler, E. (2007). Exploring the online reading comprehension strategies used by sixth-grade skilled readers to search for and locate information on the Internet. *Reading Research Quarterly, 42,* 214–257.

Coiro, J., Knobel, M., Lankshear, C., & Leu, D. (2008). Central issues in new literacies and new literacies research. In J. Coiro, M. Knobel, C. Lankshear, & D. Leu (Eds.), *Handbook of research on new literacies* (pp. 25–32). Mahwah, NJ: Erlbaum.

Coiro, J. L. (2007). *Exploring changes to reading comprehension on the Internet: Paradoxes and possibilities for diverse adolescent readers.* Unpublished doctoral dissertation, University of Connecticut, Storrs.

Cooper, M. (2004). *Expanding the digital divide and falling behind on broadband: Why telecommunications policy of neglect is not benign.* Washington, DC: Consumer Federation of America. Retrieved April 17, 2007, from *www.consumerfed.org/pdfs/digitaldivide.pdf.*

Dalton, B., & Proctor, P. (2008) The changing landscape of text and comprehension in the age of new literacies. In J. Coiro, M. Knobel, C. Lankshear, & D. Leu (Eds.), *Handbook of research on new literacies* (pp. 297–324). Mahwah, NJ: Erlbaum.

Estabrook, L., Witt, E., & Rainie, L. (2007). *Information searches that solve problems.* Washington, DC: Pew Internet and American Life Project. Retrieved December 20, 2007, from *www.pewinternet.org/pdfs/pip_online_health_2006.pdf.*

Fox, S. (2006). *Health search 2005.* Washington, DC: Pew Internet and American Life Project. Retrieved April 15, 2008, from *www.pewinternet.org/pdfs/pip_online_health_2006.pdf.*

Friedman, T. L. (2005). *The world is flat: A brief history of the twenty-first century.* New York: Farrar, Straus & Giroux.

Gee, J. P. (2003). *What video games have to teach us about learning and literacy.* New York: Palgrave/Macmillian.

hAnluain, D. O. (December 5, 2001). Irish betting on biotech. *Wired.* Retrieved October 15, 2005, from *www.wired.com/news/medtech/0,1286,48632,00.html.*

Harris, W. C. (2003). Foresight predicates commitment. *FST Journal, 18*(2). Retrieved October 15, 2005, from *www.foundation.org.uk/pdf18/fst18_2.pdf.*

Hartman, D., Leu, D. J., Olson, M. R., & Truxaw, M. P. (2005). *Reading and writing to learn with the "new literacies": Preparing a new generation of teachers and researchers to develop literate American adolescents.* A research grant funded by Carnegie Corporation of New York.

Hartman, D. K. (1995). Eight readers reading: The intertextual links of proficient readers reading multiple passages. *Reading Research Quarterly, 30,* 520–561.

Hartman, D. K. (2000). What will be the influences of media on literacy in the next millennium? *Reading Research Quarterly, 35,* 280–282.

Henry, L. A. (2006). SEARCHing for an answer: The critical role of new literacies while reading on the Internet. *Reading Teacher, 59,* 614–627.

Henry, L. A. (2007). *Exploring new literacies pedagogy and online reading comprehension among middle school students and teachers: Issues of social equity or social exclusion?* Unpublished doctoral dissertation, University of Connecticut, Storrs.

Hirsh, S. G. (1999). Children's relevance criteria and information seeking on electronic resources. *Journal of the American Society for Information Science, 50,* 1265–1283.

Hsieh-Yee, I. (2001). Research on Web search behavior. *Library and Information Science Research, 23,* 167–185.

Hull, G., & Schultz, K. (Eds.). (2002). *School's out!: Bridging out-of-school literacies with classroom practice.* New York: Teachers College Press.

International ICT Literacy Panel. (2002, May). *Digital transformation: A framework for ICT literacy.* Retrieved May 1, 2007, from *www.ets.org/media/tests/information_and_communication_technology_literacy/ictreport.pdf.*

International Reading Association. (2002). *Integrating literacy and technology in the curriculum: A position statement.* Newark, DE: International Reading Association.

International Society for Technology in Education. (n.d.). *National foundation standards for all students.* Retrieved December 5, 2005, from *www.cnets.iste.org/currstands/cstands-netss.html.*

*Internet world stats: Usage and population statistics.* (n.d.). Retrieved March 15, 2008, from *www.internetworldstats.com/stats.htm.*

Kress, G. (2003). *Literacy in the new media age.* London: Routledge.

Kuiper, E., & Volman, M. (2008). The Web as a source of information for students in K–12 education. In J. Coiro, M. Knobel, C. Lankshear, & D. Leu (Eds.), *Handbook of research on new literacies* (pp. 241–266). Mahwah, NJ: Erlbaum.

Lankshear, C., & Knobel, M. (2006). *New literacies, Second Edition.* Maidenhead, UK: Open University Press.

Lazaras, W., & Wainer, A. (2005). *Measuring digital opportunity for America's children: Where do we stand and where do we go from here.* Washington, DC: The Children's Partnership.

Leander, K. M. (2008). Toward a connective ethnography of online/offline literacy networks. In J. Coiro, M. Knobel, C. Lankshear, & D. Leu (Eds.), *Handbook of research on new literacies* (pp. 33–66). Mahwah, NJ: Erlbaum.

Lemke, J. L. (2002). Travels in hypermodality. *Visual Communication, 1,* 299–325.

Lenhart, A., Madden, M., & Hitlin, P. (2005). *Teens and technology.* Washington, DC: Pew Internet and American Life Project. Retrieved April 15, 2008, from *www.pewinternet.org/pdfs/PIP_Teens_Tech_July2005web.pdf.*

Lenhart, A., Simon, M., & Graziano, M. (2001). *The Internet and education: Findings of the Pew Internet and American Life Project.* Washington, DC: Pew Internet and American Life Project. Retrieved April 15, 2008, from *www.pewinternet.org/report_display.asp?r=39.*

Leu, D., Castek, J., Hartman, D., Coiro, J., Henry, L., Kulikowich, J., et al. (2005). *Evaluating the development of scientific knowledge and new forms of reading comprehension during online learning* [Final report presented to the North Central Regional Educational Laboratory/Learning Point Associates]. Retrieved May 15, 2006, from *www.newliteracies.uconn.edu/ncrel.html.*

Leu, D. J., Jr. (2000). Literacy and technology: Deictic consequences for literacy education in an information age. In M. L. Kamil, P. Mosenthal, P. D. Pearson, & R. Barr (Eds.), *Handbook of reading research* (Vol. 3, pp. 743–770). Mahwah, NJ: Erlbaum.

Leu, D. J., Ataya, R., & Coiro, J. (2002). *Assessing assessment strategies among the 50 states: Evaluating the literacies of our past or our future?* Paper presented at the 18th National Reading Conference, Miami, FL.

Leu, D. J., Coiro, J., Castek, J., Hartman, D. K., Henry, L. A., & Reinking, D. (2008). Research on instruction and assessment in the new literacies of online reading comprehension. In C. C. Block & S. R. Parris (Eds.), *Comprehension instruction: Research-based best practices* (pp. 321–346). New York: Guilford Press.

Leu, D. J., Jr., & Kinzer, C. K. (2000). The convergence of literacy instruction and networked technologies for information and communication. *Reading Research Quarterly, 35,* 108–127.

Leu, D. J., Jr., Kinzer, C. K., Coiro, J., & Cammack, D. (2004). Toward a theory of new literacies emerging from the Internet and other information and communication technologies. In R. B. Ruddell & N. Unrau (Eds.), *Theoretical models and processes of reading* (5th ed., pp. 1568–1611). Newark, DE: International Reading Association.

Leu, D. J., Jr., Leu, D. D., & Coiro, J. (2004). *Teaching with the Internet: New literacies for new times* (4th ed.). Norwood, MA: Christopher-Gordon.

Leu, D. J., & Reinking, D. (2005–2008). *Developing Internet comprehension strategies among adolescent students at risk to become dropouts.* A research grant funded by the U.S. Department of Education, Institute of Education Sciences.

Leu, D. J., Reinking, D., Carter, A., Castek, J., Coiro, J., Henry, L., et al. (2007, April). *Defining online reading comprehension: Using think aloud verbal protocols to refine a preliminary model of Internet reading comprehension processes.* Paper presented at the American Educational Research Association, Chicago.

Leu, D. J., Zawilinski, L., Castek, J., Banerjee, M., Housand, B., Liu, Y., et al. (2007). What is new about the new literacies of online reading comprehension? In L. Rush, J. Eakle, & A. Berger, (Eds.) *Secondary school literacy: What research reveals for classroom practices* (pp. 37–68). Urbana, IL: National Council of Teachers of English.

Livingstone, S., & Bober, M. (2005). *UK children go online: Final report of key project findings* [Project report]. London: London School of Economics and Political Science.

Ludlow, A. (2006, March 2). *Rolling out the national e-Mexico system.* Paper presented at the Digital Cities Convention, Houston, TX. Retrieved March 15, 2006, from *www.w2idigitalcitiesconvention.com/02282006/e_s/emexico.html.*

Lyman, P., & Varian, H. R. (2003). *How much Information 2003?* Berkeley: University of California. Retrieved April 1, 2008, from *www.sims.berkeley.edu/research/projects/how-much-info-2003.*

Matteucci, N., O'Mahony, M., Robinson, C., & Zwick, T. (2005). Productivity, workplace performance and ICT: Industry and firm-level evidence for Europe and the US. *Scottish Journal of Political Economy, 52,* 359–386.

National Center for Education Statistics. (2003). *The nation's report card: Reading highlights 2003.* Washington, DC: U.S. Department of Education. Retrieved October 15, 2004, from *nces.ed.gov/pubsearch/pubsinfo.asp?pubid=2004452.*

New London Group. (2000). A pedagogy of multiliteracies designing social futures. In B. Cope & M. Kalantzis (Eds.), *Multiliteracies: Literacy learning and the design of social futures* (pp. 9–37). London: Routledge.

Organization for Economic Development and Cooperation. (2004). *OECD Information Technology Outlook.* Turpin, UK: Author. Retrieved October 15, 2005, from *www.oecd.org/dataoecd/20/47/33951035.pdf.*

Page, S. E. (2007). *The difference: How the power of diversity creates better groups, firms, schools and societies.* Princeton, NJ: Princeton University Press.

Partnership for 21st Century Skills. (2004). *Learning for the 21st century.* Retrieved August 15, 2006, from *www.21stcenturyskills.org/reports/learning.asp.*

Rainie, L. (2006). *Digital natives invade the workplace.* Washington, DC: Pew Internet and

American Life Project. Retrieved January 15, 2008, from *www.pewinternet.org/ppt/new%20workers%20--%20pewresearch.org%20version%20_final_pdf.*

RAND Reading Study Group. (2002). *Reading for understanding: Toward an R&D program in reading comprehension.* Santa Monica, CA: Author.

Roberts, D. F., Foehr, U. G., & Rideout, V. (2005). *Generation M: Media in the lives of 8–18 year olds.* Menlo Park, CA: Kaiser Family Foundation. Retrieved January 28, 2008. from *www.kff.org/entmedia/7251.cfm.*

Rosenshine, B., & Meister, C. (1994). Reciprocal teaching: A review of the research. *Review of Educational Research, 64,* 479–530.

Street, B. (2003). What's "new" in new literacy studies? Critical approaches to literacy in theory and practice. *Current Issues in Comparative Education, 5,* 77–91.

Street, B. V. (1995). *Social literacies: Critical approaches to literacy in development, ethnography and education.* London: Longman.

Taboada, A., & Guthrie, J. (2006). Contributions of student questioning and prior knowledge to construction of knowledge from reading information text. *Journal of Literacy Research, 38,* 1–35.

U.S. Department of Commerce, National Telecommunications and Information Administration. (2002). *A nation online: How Americans are expanding their use of the Internet.* Washington, DC: Author.

van Ark, B., Inklaar, R., & McGuckin, R. H. (2003). ICT and productivity in Europe and the United States: Where do the differences come from? *CESinfo Economic Studies, 49,* 295–318.

Webber, S., & Johnson, B. (2000). Conceptions of information literacy: New perspectives and implications. *Journal of Informational Science, 26,* 381–397.

Zawilinski, L., & Leu, D. J. (2008, March). *A taxonomy of skills and strategies from verbal protocol of accomplished adolescent Internet users.* Paper presented at the American Educational Research Association Conference, New York.

# CHAPTER 10

# Roles of Engagement, Valuing, and Identification in Reading Development of Students from Diverse Backgrounds

JOHN T. GUTHRIE, ROBERT RUEDA, LINDA B. GAMBRELL, AND DANETTE A. MORRISON

This chapter explores the issue of reading and literacy development among diverse readers through the perspective of engagement in literacy. We adopt an embracing view of engagement that includes motivational goals and beliefs, behavioral predispositions and practices, and social interaction patterns. Because we are addressing reading development through engagement, our first aim is to examine studies on how processes of engagement connect to reading development for diverse populations of students. We first inquire into the extent that engagement is associated with achievement for African American, Hispanic, and European American students. We next examine motivational variables related to reading achievement, such as valuing of achievement and identification with schooling. Finally, we examine instructional studies that have attempted to increase reading engagement and achievement, including social structures for learning and culturally responsive teaching.

We emphasize studies that have been conducted with carefully defined participants who represent specific ethnic groups and subgroups (while still recognizing the significant within-group variability that may be included in these labels). In this way, we avoid overreliance on a few individuals who may be atypical of their age, gender, achievement level, or ethnic group. For this discussion, we do not include studies that aggregate diverse individuals into heterogeneous groups, or that relate engagement or instruction to achievement of the heterogeneous groups. We rely on indicators or measures of reading achievement, engagement, and identification that are available in the professional literature. We use evidence about individuals and groups that is publicly reproducible through common tools and shared procedures. In other words, we rely on studies in the confirmation tradition to identify findings that form a base for building beneficial classroom practices. Finally, although we recognize that socioeconomic status is a potentially important variable that merits consideration in the body of research to be discussed, the separate analysis that is needed awaits future work and is beyond the scope of this chapter.

Organizational subjects are as follows:

- Contributions of engagement and motivation to reading development of African American and European American students
- Valuing achievement
- Disidentification with schooling
- Engagement perspective on disidentification theory
- Educating for engagement of diverse students
- Implications for teaching
- Implications for research

## CONTRIBUTIONS OF ENGAGEMENT AND MOTIVATION TO READING DEVELOPMENT OF AFRICAN AMERICAN AND EUROPEAN AMERICAN STUDENTS

As we attempt to understand how to foster reading development among diverse students, we begin by locating the characteristics of individuals that are most highly associated with reading achievement. At any point in time, the overwhelmingly most powerful predictor of reading achievement is previous achievement. After admitting this obvious point, we seek the ethnic variations in the motivations of learners that impact their literacy development. Several studies show that the characteristic of individual learners most strongly associated with reading achievement is reading engagement. It is crucially important to recognize that this finding is sustained for both African American and European American students.

One study of the contribution of reading engagement to reading achievement in grade 4 for African American and European American students was reported by Voelkl (1997), who investigated 1,335 African American and European American eighth-grade youngsters in 104 urban, suburban, rural, and intercity schools in one state. Students' engagement in this investigation was termed "classroom participation," based on a 14-item teacher rating of individual student learning behaviors. Teachers observed students to indicate the extent to which they "paid attention in class" and "did more than just the assigned work," showing their initiative. Likewise, negative forms of disengagement were observed, such as "needs to be reprimanded" and "interferes with peers' work." Their engagement scale provided a measure of students' involvement, participation, and commitment to reading activities within the classroom. The authors reported that the students' levels of reading engagement correlated substantially with their achievement in grade 7. The correlations of .45 for African American students and .47 for European American students were both highly statistically significant. Reading engagement was substantially associated with levels of tested achievement for both African American and European American students.

To investigate the identification with school among these eighth graders, the levels of students' sense of belongingness and valuing of school were ascertained in a self-report questionnaire. Items for belongingness were exemplified by the following statements: "I feel proud of being part of my school" and "School is one of my favorite places to be." The students' valuing was represented by the following statements: "School is more important than most people think" or its reverse, "Most of the things we learn in class are useless." A student who was highly affirming of the importance of belonging and valuing was likely to be a relatively higher achiever. However, this relationship was relatively weak. Among European American students, the association of identification and achievement was .13, which was substantially lower than the association of engagement and achievement. For African American students, the association of identifications with school and achievement was not statistically significant (the correlation was not different from zero). It appears that the relationship of classroom engagement to achievement was dramatically higher than the relationship of identification with achievement at grade 8 for both African American and European American students. Based on this investigation, if one were to attempt to design an intervention to increase achievement, one would target the variables of engagement and class participation rather than the variable of identification with schooling.

Engagement in reading for diverse students may be viewed from the teacher's perspective, as shown in the previous study, or it may be viewed from the individual student's perspective. Smalls, White, Chavous, and Sellers (2007) reported on student engagement from the students' perspective. They worked with 390 self-identified African American middle and high school students (grades 7–10) from a Midwestern school. Their indicator of engagement represented students' attention, participation, effort, and persistence when presented with new reading material in the classroom. Sample items from the students' self-report questionnaire included "If I can't get a problem right the first time I just keep trying" and "When I do badly on a test I work harder the next time." For this sample of African American students, the student self-report of engagement correlated .20 with their grade point averages (GPAs) in English, science, and social studies, which were statistically significant. At the same time, an indicator of disengagement included undesirable school behaviors, such as skipping a class without a valid excuse, fighting in school, being sent to the principal's office, and cheating on tests and exams. This scale represents extreme forms of disengagement, which may be associated with affects such as hostility and anxiety. The disengagement scale correlated −.26 with GPA, which was highly significant. Not only did the more highly engaged African American students achieve more, but also the disengaged students achieved less than their peers.

In this investigation of self-reported engagement, the investigators inquired into several student beliefs regarding ethnic identity and its relation to schooling. Specifically, the investigators identified (1) the extent to which students believed that their ethnic identity was central to their view of themselves (centrality), (2) the extent to which the students believed that African Americans should assimilate to be successful in society (assimilation), (3) the extent to which students believed that similarities across races were most important (humanism), (4) the extent to which individuals shared a mutual experience with oppressed groups (minority), and (5) the extent to which students stressed the importance of the uniqueness of being African American in society (nationalism). All of these ethnic values were associated weakly with achievement. The median correlation of .09 was not statistically significant. One implication from this finding for schooling and classroom practices is that targeting engagement is more likely to impact students' reading development than targeting students' beliefs about ethnicity and diversity in a sociocultural framework.

Yet another perspective on the engagement of learners may be drawn by an outside observer of classroom interactions. Hall, Merkel, Howe, and Lederman (1986) reported classroom observations of European American and African American students in five middle schools in Northeastern medium-size cities. Observers were trained to detect the extent to which students were *attending, on-task, participating*, and *highly active* in the academic activities of the classroom. Engaged students were viewed as actively observing, preparing, discussing, and reacting to text materials. Students' achievement in this study comprised reading and math scores that reflected simple comprehension of text. According to the observers, indicators of engagement (i.e., grades in school) correlated .72 for African American males, .56 for European American males, .66 for African American females, and .81 for European American females. All of these associations of engagement and achievement were highly significant, and the ethnic differences were not statistically significant. These findings show that, according to observers in the classroom, active learning behaviors were associated with achievement as highly for African American students as for European American students in these middle school grades. In multiple regression analyses, engagement in learning predicted the outcome of grades even when gender, race, and ability levels of students were accounted for statistically. In other words, engagement, rather than the demographic characteristics of learners, was most markedly associated with achievement.

Primary school students are just as likely as elementary and middle school students to be characterized by an association of engagement and achievement. In a study of 443 first-grade students in a small Southern urban center, Hispanic, African American, and European American students were rated for their engagement in reading (Hughes & Kwok, 2007). Teachers rated students on a 10-item scale that included statements such as "is a reliable worker" and "perseveres until the task is finished," or their reverse "is easily distracted." In addition, indicators of engagement such as "sets and works toward goals" or "turns in homework" were utilized to show academic behaviors in a social framework that contribute to measureable achievement in reading. Students' achievement was indicated by the Woodcock–Johnson III Test of Reading, which included letter–word identification, reading fluency, and paragraph comprehension. In this investigation, students' level of engagement, according to teacher ratings, had a positive correlation of .36 with their growth in reading from the beginning to the end of first grade; that is, the most effortful, conscientious, and actively participating students in classroom reading activities increased their word level and reading comprehension abilities during grade 1. Benefits of engagement were equal for European American and African American students in this investigation. However, the European American students entered first grade at a higher level of reading engagement than did African American students. Although engagement benefited both ethnic groups, the engagement level of African Americans was lower at the outset; consequently, the reading achievement of African Americans was lower at the end of first grade than that of European American students.

Engagement in schooling in the form of commitment to hard work is highly associated with achievement for African American students according to an in-depth interview study by Sanders (1997). She identified high-, medium-, and low-achieving African Americans in an Eastern urban school. After interviewing these 40 middle school adolescents, the three achievement levels were associated with three degrees of awareness of barriers to success and commitment to engagement in school. One of the highly engaged students stated, "I want to come to school so I can get an education, and make the white man know that just because he says that black people are not going to succeed does not make it so. I want to show him different." Another highly committed, highly engaged African American male stated, "I see black men everywhere. They are there, making it, regardless of what people say, and I see getting there as a challenge. I know that it is going to be hard because boys and girls have the same dreams inside, but boys have more pressure." These high-achieving African American students were committed to their schooling, engaged in school activities, and aware of the potential racial barriers. The authors concluded that these high-achieving students "did not consciously or subconsciously withdraw from school. Instead, they exerted more academic effort ... which was generally reflected in their above-average grades" (p. 90).

## VALUING ACHIEVEMENT

In this section, we examine the extent to which valuing achievement is associated with success in school, as indicated by grades, test scores, and teacher appraisals. This positive association refers to the finding that students who possess high positive values for achievement are likely to be relatively successful in school, whereas students who possess lower values, or more negative values, are likely to be less successful in vitally important school outcomes. These findings are based largely on studies of African American students and are valid for this population, although the investigations often confirmed the finding for Hispanic and European American students as well.

We investigate the term "valuing achievement" using slightly different terms and procedures for research. Despite these differences, the qualities of the individuals' motivations for achievement fit comfortably under the umbrella of valuing achievement. For example, Chavous and colleagues (2003) refer to "valuing" in terms of the importance of school. Their questionnaire included the phrase "Being successful in school is important to me." Students who agreed with this statement were viewed as valuing achievement, and those who disagreed were viewed as devaluing achievement. These investigators examined a similar construct of relevance, which referred to questionnaire items such as "Learning in school is valuable later in life." Both of these constructs may be subsumed within the frame of valuing achievement.

Hwang and Echols (2002) referred to "valuing" as the affirmation that education is the key to success in life and in getting a job. This construct assumes that students' efforts in education are rewarded with indicators of accomplishment, and that this school success leads to benefits in life after school. Ford and Harris (1996) referred vaguely to students' positive attitudes toward other students who were high achievers. Valuing achievement in their study was represented by students' affirmation of the positive qualities of high achievers and the negative attributes of low-achieving learners. In the investigations of Taylor and Graham (2007), "valuing achievement" refers to students' statements about who they admired and emulated in school. High valuing of achievement was represented by the nomination of admirable students who were high achievers. Students who were viewed as devaluing achievement were those who nominated low achievers as individuals they admired. Mickelson (1990) referred to "valuing" in two forms, abstract and concrete. In this discussion we examined the "concrete" form of valuing, which refers to students' perceptions that education improves the likelihood of success in life for them and for members of their family or immediate community. Finally, in more than one investigation, devaluing of achievement was central. For example, Long, Monoi, Harper, Knoblauch, and Murphy (2007) examined the extent to which students agreed with statements such as "I want to do as little work as possible in school." Although this construct has been termed "work avoidance" by Meece and Holt (1993), it also represents devaluing, because an individual who wants to do little work holds low values for schooling, whereas an individual who is willing to work hard holds higher values for schooling.

Using the term "valuing achievement," as synthesized from the previously presented studies, we illustrate the nature of the evidence that valuing achievement is associated with relatively successful school performance. Mickelson (1990) studied 1,193 high school seniors from eight public high schools in the Los Angeles area, who were evenly divided between white and black students. The measure of achievement consisted of students' GPAs, although similar findings were obtained from two standardized test scores and rank in the graduating class. The result was that valuing achievement was associated with school success for both black and white students, even after the investigators controlled for mothers' and fathers' occupation, education, and gender. Although the correlation was higher for whites than for blacks, the association was statistically significant for both groups, after extensive controls for background variables for both black and white students. Ford and Harris (1996) documented that valuing achievement was associated with school success for younger black students. They examined 75 fifth graders and 73 sixth graders, and showed that those students' valuing of achievement was associated with their tested achievement levels. In this study, the most high-achieving black students held more positive perceptions of successful students than did lower achievers. Similarly, devaluing achievement was associated with lower success. The lowest-achieving students in the group perceived the highest achievers to be "nerds," or some other negative descriptor.

The role of devaluing achievement was emphasized by Long and colleagues (2007). In a study of Midwestern urban students consisting of 222 African Americans, 25 European Americans, and 7 other (Hispanic, Native American, and Asian), these investigators documented that devaluing school was associated with low academic achievement in the form of standardized test scores and grades. For ninth-grade students, devaluing was highly associated (–.217) with low school success, even when the other variables of gender, learning orientations, level of interest in subject matter, and self-efficacy were statistically controlled. It should be noted that self-efficacy was positively associated (.204) with achievement for these African American students at a relatively high level, which is similar to the pattern found for European American students in other investigations (Schunk & Zimmerman, 2007).

The developmental course of achievement valuing was examined by Graham, Taylor, and Hudley (1998). They found that for sixth- to eighth-grade students, 145 African American males and 149 females' values for achievement did not correlate to school success. This finding was based on peer nominations, in which students nominated individuals they admired or wished to emulate, and the characteristics of the most frequently nominated students were inspected. For African American males, the most frequently nominated students were low achievers who wore "cool" clothing and participated in sports. This finding occurred for both male and female nominators. Among African American females, the most frequently nominated individuals were high achievers who were sharp dressers and active in sports. Taylor and Graham (2007) found that this devaluing of achievement among African American males was present for students in grade 7, but not for younger students in grades 2 and 4. In the elementary grades, the African American males and females valued achievement highly. Their peer nominations occurred more frequently for high-achieving than for low-achieving learners.

Among black college students, valuing achievement was associated with school success. Hwang and Echols (2002) found that students in a major Southeastern university who identified themselves as black or African American, and had a GPA above 3.5, were inclined to value academic achievement highly. A majority of these students reported that they studied for high grade performance and attempted to prepare for each class conscientiously. They stated that they enjoyed acquiring knowledge and believed it would reward them with future career opportunities. Nearly half of the students stated that they had an interest in learning, and that their intentions were to master the content for its own sake.

Not all studies confirmed the principle that achievement valuing is associated with school success. In a longitudinal study of 606 African American students in grade 12, Chavous and colleagues (2003) reported that valuing achievement in the form of perceived importance of school and the relevance of education was not predictive of GPA for the total group. However, a subgroup of students, who believed that society valued African Americans, rated the usefulness of school and the importance of school learning higher than did other students. In other words, for students with strong African American identities, who believed that society affirmed this ethnic group, the valuing of achievement was relatively high.

## DISIDENTIFICATION WITH SCHOOLING

One prominent viewpoint regarding the sources of the achievement gap between African American and European American students centers on the concept of students' disidentification with success in academics. As articulated by Steele and Aronson (1995) and Ogbu (2003), among others, leading authors have argued that factors inherent in U.S. society prevent students of color from identifying with schooling and succeeding in the educational system. Concretely, Osborne (1997) stated, "The concept of identification with academics has emerged as an important contribution to the racial achievement gap" (pp. 732–733).

In this line of thinking, "identification with academics" refers to viewing school as central to one's self-concept. When a domain is central to one's sense of self, feedback about success or failure in that domain is likely to be connected to one's self-worth. If being an athlete is a valued activity, then success in athletics will reflect positively on one's self-worth. Likewise in academics, if being successful in school is important to the individual, then feedback about accomplishments in school will be important and associated with self-esteem.

Theorists who advocate the importance of disidentification as an explanation of the achievement gap for African American and European American students suggest that when an individual believes that racial barriers prevent opportunity for success and advancement in society, schooling is likely viewed as having little potential benefit. Under these conditions, they argue, individuals will disidentify with schooling. They will disconnect their view of their self-worth and their sense of self-esteem from school achievement. Such disidentification protects students' self-worth from being eroded by low achievement. Disidentification with schooling, then, leads to lower achievement, because these students do not commit effort to education. Theorists claim that the inequitable opportunity structure in society leads students to be skeptical about the potential benefits of education; consequently, they retreat from a commitment to schooling. As students devalue the hard work and effort required in school, they experience reductions in achievement.

Several forms of evidence have been offered in support of this view about the contributions of disidentification to the achievement gap. Most prominently, Ogbu (2003) conducted extensive interviews with African American students who were both high and low achievers. He reported several poignant cases of individuals who said that they chose not to work hard in school, because hard work would not benefit them.

The process of disidentifying with school is best shown in the correlations between achievement and self-esteem for diverse racial groups of both genders across time. In a study of 24,599 eighth-grade students representing 1,052 schools in the United States, Osborne (1997) investigated the association between academic outcome (in the form of grades in math, English, history, and science) and self-esteem, according to the Rosenberg Self-View Inventory. Items within the inventory include "I take a positive attitude toward myself," "I am able to do things as well as most people," and "At times I feel I am no good at all." The correlation between achievement and self-esteem was observed to be .25 for all groups of white males, white females, black males, black females, Hispanic males, and Hispanic females. This correlation decreased to near zero by 10th grade for black males and was slightly negative by 12th grade. Thus, in this national sample, black males disconnected their self-esteem from their schooling achievement between grades 8 and 10, with further declines in grades 10–12. It is noteworthy that black females did not display this disassociation, and neither male nor female Hispanics showed the trend of the black males. Thus, disidentification was uniquely evident for black males during the 8th- to 10th-grade period.

An additional source of evidence regarding disidentification was provided by Sandoval, Gutkin, and Naumann (1997). They reasoned that African American adolescents might form clusters in their self-perceptions about their identity, and that these clusters might be related to achievement in different ways. Working with African American students in grades 10–12 from a predominantly European American Midwestern city, they observed three types of group identity: *preencounter, immersion*, and *internalization*. In the *preencounter* group, the African American students adopted an ethnically biased view, which stated that European Americans were expected to excel, and that African Americans were not expected to be successful in school or other endeavors. This view was significantly and negatively correlated with reading achievement according to standardized test scores. The *immersion* group identified with their own "blackness" and believed that African American students who strive for academic success are attempting to "act White" (p. 5). This identity was significantly and negatively correlated with GPA and a composite of reading and math standardized test scores. The *internalization* group viewed themselves as self-reliant, competent, and achieving, to the extent that they committed themselves to educational goals. Within this internalization group, scores were associated positively and correlated significantly with GPA as an outcome of schooling.

Based on the findings of Sandoval and colleagues (1997), it is conceivable that self-esteem assumes different forms for different subgroups. Thus, students with some forms of self-esteem (internalization) will have a positive correlation of identification with achievement, whereas other forms of self-esteem (preencounter or immersion) will have a negative correlation between their self-esteem level and achievement. This finding does not undermine the results of Osborne (1997) regarding the disidentification process, but it indicates that the forms of self-esteem that are negatively associated with achievement are more typical of African American students than are other forms.

## ENGAGEMENT PERSPECTIVE ON DISIDENTIFICATION THEORY

Our view of the processes of motivation and reading development for diverse learners are represented in Figure 10.1. At the top of the figure is the process of Engagement in Reading, which refers to students' internally motivated dispositions to use cognitive strategies and knowledge during reading activities. Next in the circle of Figure 10.1 is Competence in Reading, which refers to students' achievement according to grades or standardized test scores. This may comprise word-level skills for primary students, simple comprehension for elementary students, or higher-order reading comprehension for secondary students. Next in the circle is Valuing Reading Achievement, which refers to the construct of valuing, as expressed previously in this chapter. This includes viewing school as important and perceiving reading as beneficial to one's present and future goals. Next in the circle is Identification with Reading Achievement. Allied to identification with academics, this refers to the students' view that reading is central to their sense of self-concept, and achievement in reading is linked to their self-worth. The pathways between these processes are labeled with the letters A through D.

Figure 10.1 represents the principles presented previously in this chapter. First, we describe pathway A, indicating that students' engagement and their competency in reading are highly associated, and that this connection is equally

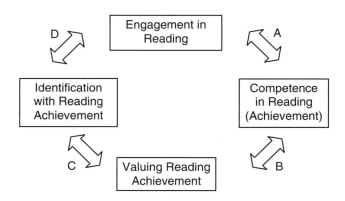

FIGURE 10.1. Engagement perspective on disidentification in reading.

strong for African American and European American students. Furthermore, this linkage is substantial from primary grades through high school. The pathway is known to be bidirectional in the sense that higher engagement increases competence in reading, and higher competence fosters deeper engagement (Morgan & Fuchs, 2007). Second, pathway B depicts the bond between competence in reading and the valuing of it, as shown in the previous section in this chapter. For both African American and European American students, it is evident that students who value schooling are higher achievers than students who devalue schooling. We make the extension here from schooling to reading for purposes of this conceptualization, because reading is integral to all types of subject matter and educational programs. Although empirical studies have not examined the issue, we expect that valuing reading and competence in reading are reciprocally determined, showing that each causes acceleration of the other during the course of schooling. Pathways C and D have not been studied with suitably designed scientific investigations. However, we hypothesize that students who value reading increase their identification with reading achievement. When students perceive that reading is of benefit, enabling them to know valuable things and enjoy new, aesthetic experiences, they slowly adopt reading into their lifestyle and, as a result, into their self-concept. Likewise, we hypothesize that pathway D is highly functional. As individuals grow in their internalization of reading as part of who they are, their engagement in reading widely and frequently becomes more extensive. One might ask about other pathways in Figure 10.1, such as the relation between valuing reading and engagement in reading. The reviewed studies, which emphasized data on African American students, did not present information on this or other possible connections. Although plausible, there is no evidence from confirmatory research on these points.

Although Figure 10.1 displays a positive set of processes of engagement (competence, valuing, and identification), it is also possible to conceive of these in undermining terms. One may view this as a dynamic. Disengagement from reading leads to less competence and lower reading achievement. Lower competence is associated with devaluing of reading achievement and eventuates in disidentification with reading. Disassociation of reading from the sense of self is likely to produce more extreme forms of disengagement, including opposition and hostility to reading.

We may view the major processes in Figure 10.1 as correlated constructs; that is, engagement, valuing, and identification are associated with achievement and with each other. A crucially important question is "Which comes first in a child's development?" It is extremely unlikely that a child will enter first grade in a state of disidentification with academics. The process of disidentification requires reasoning, knowledge, experiences, and self-reflection that are improbable for the large majority of 6-year-olds. However, it is extremely possible, and it has been empirically documented, that some first graders may come to school with relatively low levels of engagement in reading. These students have relatively less interest, less participation, and less commitment, and are less likely to enjoy reading in school than other individuals in grade 1, as documented by Hughes and Kwok (2007) and Hamre and Pianta (2005). Because it is known that lower engagement induces lower competence, and lower competence generates lower valuing of reading, it is highly plausible that initial disengagement of students as they begin school might result in disidentification from reading and schooling by the end of middle school.

The processes of disengagement from reading in the primary grades that lead to lower achievement, then to disidentification can and do occur in students of all ethnic groups. These processes may be attributable to variations in language and literacy practices in the home and community that do not map well to the conventions of academic reading in school. These variations may also be exacerbated for some students by differences in the quality and experience of schooling. Because African American students are more likely to experience this set of processes than are European American students (Hamre & Pianta, 2005; Hughes & Kwok, 2007), it seems potentially valuable to recognize this need for engagement and to address it explicitly in classrooms and schools. The potential for engagement is undoubtedly equal across all students, and the contexts of schooling and home are the most potent sources of variation for diverse groups.

One advantage of taking the engagement perspective on disidentification is that engagement in reading is substantially determined by the classroom conditions and teaching practices within schools. As shown in a broad spectrum of research from primary to secondary school, more engagement in reading increases achievement, according to multiple criteria (Guthrie, McRae, & Klauda, 2007). One major environmental force influencing identification and achievement in schooling is under the control of teachers and school administrators. To the extent that the achievement gap is fueled by disidentification, which is impacted by disengagement from reading, educators are in a strong position to address the achievement gap. Practices that impact engagement, in both the short and the long term, impact the achievement gap.

Sociological analyses that emphasize opportunity structure in society and poverty in our urban centers may certainly reveal valid sociological patterns. However, these analyses do not identify educational actions that can address the achievement gap. It is evident that poverty is associated with lowered educational opportunity for reading activities and quality of schooling in the United States. Addressing sources of poverty and their effects on learning is a political issue that merits the attention of all citizens. Unfortunately, educators are not empowered to impact the societal and political forces that drive poverty. On the other hand, educators are uniquely empowered to improve classrooms, schools, and reading engagement. In our view, educators should step beyond the sociological view of disidentification as a major contributor to the achievement gap and focus on the educational processes of engagement in reading, and the classroom practices that inspire achievement (Fink & Samuels, 2007). Educational researchers should study how to assemble the building blocks of achievement, such as engagement, rather than focus on the sociological barriers to achievement, which, by definition, cannot advance the progress of diverse students.

## EDUCATING FOR ENGAGEMENT OF DIVERSE STUDENTS

To increase achievement for diverse students we first affirm that reading engagement is integrally linked to reading achievement, and just as tightly for African American as for European American students. Accepting this, our challenge becomes how to guide the classroom engagement of diverse learners. Do studies support the suggestion that increasing engagement will improve the reading development of both African American and European American students? Essentially we asked whether the known principles of classroom instruction for engagement (relevance for interest, autonomy support for ownership, success for self-efficacy, thematic units for mastery learning goals, and collaborative structures for social motivation) (Taboada, Guthrie, & McRae, 2007) apply explicitly to minority groups. The only principle that had been investigated with confirmatory research is social interaction and collaboration as an engagement support.

Burchinal, Peisner-Feinberg, and Pianta (2002) documented that primary age children's personal relationship with the teacher is an extremely important quality of classrooms that increases literacy engagement. Teachers who were able to interact personally, emotionally, and affectively in affirming terms increased the reading engagement of individuals in the classroom. Remarkably, this strong teacher–student relationship was more beneficial for African American students than for European American students. African American children who enjoyed a strong personal relationship with the teacher grew more rapidly in reading engagement and reading achievement than did European American children. Thus, social relations with the teacher, although helpful for both ethnic groups, were even more likely to contribute to engagement and success in reading for African American than for European American students.

In a related finding, Hughes and Kwok (2007) documented that teacher support for children's interests, security, and need for intimacy led to clear gains in engagement and achievement for African American and European American children during first grade. In a longitudinal, quantitative design using structural equation modeling, the authors showed that students who experienced a close, affirming relationship with the teacher had greater participation and literacy activity than students who experienced a supportive but less positively affective relationship with the teacher. Teacher support for students' interests and social needs facilitated engagement equally in both African American and European American students. Furthermore, the rise in reading engagement generated equal gains in achievement for the two ethnic groups.

For African American students who are 10 to 11 years old, Dill and Boykin (2000) showed the advantages of collaborative learning environments over individual learning environments. A collaborative (or communal) learning setting increased the recall of stories read during collaborative interactions compared to individual readings. More centrally, collaborative learning structures accelerated enjoyment of the learning activity, and the desire to participate in similar activities in the future, for the African American students. One source of such a benefit may be elaborated discussion. There is evidence that African American students respond to collaborative learning opportunities by discussing text in relatively elaborate ways. In an experimental study, Webb and Farivar (1994) showed that African American students who were taught communication and helping skills in small-group work during the reading of story problems had more elaborate and rich discussions than did comparison groups. On the other hand, European American students did not benefit from the training in communication skills. Thus, African Americans were cognitively responsive in social interactions around text, thus gaining cognitive competencies in these settings.

Further evidence that teacher–student relationships in the classroom may be important to engagement and achievement in literacy was presented by Decker, Dona, and Christenson (2007), who examined the associations between teacher–student relationship and outcomes for African American students who were behaviorally at risk for referral to special education. Students were identified by their teachers as having behavior problems. Participants were 44 students and 25 teachers from two suburban and three urban elementary schools in a Midwestern state. A multirater, multimethod approach was used. As both teacher and student reports of teacher–student relationship quality increased, there were also increases in positive social, behavioral, and engagement outcomes. Additional analyses of teacher–student relationship patterns indicated that as the relationship pattern improved, there were increases in positive social, behavioral, and engagement outcomes for students. Especially intriguing was the finding that as kindergartners' reports of wanting to be closer to their teachers increased, their letter-naming fluency increased.

### Fostering Engagement through Culturally Responsive Teaching

Significant evidence amassed over several decades (Cazden, 1986; Heath, 1983; Phillips, 1972, 1983), as well as more recently (Tudge et al., 2006; Tyler, Boykin, Miller, & Hurley, 2006), indicates that for some students of diverse groups, home cultural values, beliefs, and practices differ from those typically found in most American classrooms (e.g., see Lee [2005] for a comprehensive review of this perspective for African American students). Although much of this evidence has been qualitative (ethnographies, case studies, etc.), there are quantitative examples as well. Suizzo (2007), for example, examined quantitatively multiple dimensions of interdependence and independence in parents' long-term goals and values for their children across different ethnic groups. Ethnicity explained differences in all five scales examined in the study, which controlled for parental education level. Similarly, Reese and Gallimore (2000) employed data from a 12-year longitudinal study of immigrant Latino families and their children. They found that parents' use of textual material with their children at home was guided by widely shared, implicit notions—cultural schemas or models—about how and under what conditions literacy develops. Thus, according to one hypothesis, classrooms that provide a closer match to conditions with which students are familiar or comfortable improve students' engagement and produce better achievement.

Evidence for this hypothesis is suggestive, but it is not confirmed with quantitative procedures and data. The best-known example of this latter type of study was based on attempts to design a culturally sensitive educational program to improve literacy and reading achievement in the Kamehameha Early Education Program (KEEP) (Au & Mason, 1981; Tharp, 1982). This work is unique because of the long period of empirical documentation of native Hawaiian culture and the deliberate attempt to use this empirical base systematically to introduce culturally relevant interactional patterns into the classroom. Examples of these factors included self-selected turns by students, overlapping speech (characteristic of out-of-school narratives), and absence of the teacher's explicit and overt control of the interaction.

Au and Mason (1981) found that when classroom instructional interaction is compatible with interaction patterns in Hawaiian children's native culture, the students demonstrate higher levels of achievement-related behaviors than when instructional patterns conform to typical U.S. classroom patterns. Areas in which differences in students' behavior were noted during reading lessons included (1) academic engagement, (2) ownership of reading, (3) topical and correct responses, (4) number of idea units expressed, and (5) logical inferences. One issue with this study is that multiple factors were operational during the intervention, including active, direct teaching of comprehension; cooperative learning structures; frequent assessment of student progress; extensive teacher support; and positive classroom management strategies. Given these factors, it is difficult to separate the effects of culturally specific factors in affecting student behavior.

## The Role of Culturally Relevant Text and Text-Related Factors

It has been suggested that use of culturally relevant text for instructional purposes may be a way to improve reading outcomes for students from diverse backgrounds (Freeman & Freeman, 2004). Some notable contradictions to the hypothesis that culturally relevant text is engaging have been reported. For example, Holmes, Powell, Holmes, and Witt (2007) sought to determine the effect of race in a book's primary characters on the reading motivation of third-grade students in Mississippi. Students ($n = 35$) from two third-grade classrooms chose books with covers that depicted main characters who were either black or white. The authors sought to determine whether books in which the race of the principal characters was identical with that of the readers motivated students' reading. Results did not support such a conclusion. Instead, data suggested that students often chose books with characters that had racial backgrounds different from their own. Although this study sample was small, it does run counter to the hypothesis.

Though it was not a direct test of the effects of culturally relevant text on motivation or engagement, Goldenberg, Gallimore, and Reese (2001) conducted a study that illustrates the sometimes complex relationships between text and cultural practices. These authors reported on a yearlong series of case studies of Hispanic kindergartners, in which the types of materials sent home were varied (meaningful, short, narrative stories or *libritos*, or more traditional worksheets). The results suggested a complex interaction. Although children who used the *libritos* produced better test results than those using worksheets, the use of worksheets but not *libritos* at home was significantly related to literacy development in kindergarten. They explained these findings by noting that the use of standard "homework sheets" at home was associated with higher scores, because they were more consistent with these low-income parents' views of how children learn to read; therefore, they were used in a way that was more meaningful to both parents and children.

Addressing identification processes as a basis for building engagement and achievement in reading, Powers (2006) conducted an exploratory study of cultural identity and culture-based educational programs using survey data collected from 240 urban Native American students. Specifically, the impact of culture-based and universally accepted, effective practices in education on Native American educational outcomes was examined. The results indicated that the effect of culture-based programs was largely indirect, affecting students' educational outcomes via universal constructs, such as a safe and positive school climate, parent involvement in school, and instruction quality. Furthermore, individual students' cultural identification appeared to moderate the effects of cultural programs. Cultural programming appeared to have greater influence on urban Native American students who were most strongly identified with their Native American culture. Unfortunately, the outcome measures were more general academic indicators and did not include direct assessments of reading or literacy-related variables.

## IMPLICATIONS FOR TEACHING

The review of the research presented in this chapter focused on the roles of engagement, valuing, and identification in reading development of students from diverse backgrounds. This literature documents that reading engagement correlates with school reading achievement in grades 1–12 for both African American and European American students. This is the first case in which studies have been synthesized to document this finding. The review reveals that teachers' support for engagement in reading through strong interpersonal relationships with students appears to be especially powerful for African American and European American students. A number of studies have documented this finding with strong quantitative designs that give scientific evidence for supporting the notion that engagement in reading is strengthened when teachers foster strong interpersonal relationships with their students.

To form positive interpersonal relationships with students, we need to understand their lives outside of school. Although the demographic composition of a particular classroom may vary from year to year, teachers may be fairly assured that the students in their classrooms will be somewhat reflective of the school's community. Knowledge of the surrounding community, its ethnic and socio-economic characteristics, and the types of prevalent businesses and community events should indicate which cultural influences students bring to the classroom. Therefore, teachers are well advised to become familiar with the community and to be aware of the cultural influences that are displayed, particularly if they differ from the communities in which teachers live or were brought up.

Although the community is reflected in the classroom through its influence on the students, the classroom can also reach out to connect with the surrounding area through service, learning, or other cooperative ventures. These connections bring relevance and authenticity to student learning as teachers make use of the familiar in teaching novel material. In communities where the influences are diverse or pluralistic, providing a variety and choice of projects may positively influence student engagement and participation. If community service projects are not a viable option, bringing materials and texts from the community into the classroom for learning, such as local newspapers, community center brochures, or the work of local writers and artists, can also connect the classroom to the communities and neighborhoods where students live.

Another way to connect with students and to gain insight into their background knowledge is to reach out to their families. In doing so, teachers can discover family members' expectations regarding teacher–student and school–home relationships, as well as their livelihoods and hobbies. Particularly in early elementary and primary classrooms, parent involvement in classrooms provides valuable insights into cultural influences and funds of knowledge that can enhance instruction. By becoming familiar with community and parental influences, teachers may avoid the pitfall of assuming the stereotypical characteristics or expectations of various ethnic or socioeconomic groups. Rather, involvement with communities and parents reveals points at which cultures interact, influence, or isolate from each other. This knowledge is valuable to teachers, because it reveals much about what students and their families already know and value. This is the beginning of all good teaching.

Teachers who provide a variety of options for learning and expressing knowledge have a greater chance of connecting with the students they teach. Although some students may choose tasks based on their cultural background, they may be just as likely to pursue their personal interests and learning goals. Unless teachers provide choices of topic and product, the things that naturally motivate students may remain unrevealed and cannot be of assistance to the teacher in future instructional planning. If, for example, through providing choices to students in completing an English project, a teacher discovers that several students are quite artistic and enjoy representing knowledge in visual form, or that other students exhibit a keen interest in their family culture through their choice of texts, that teacher gains valuable insights that can be useful in exploring new topics. Becoming alert to the interests and preferences of students is important to developing the type of student–teacher relationship that enhances engagement outcomes.

Although there is a strong evidence base for the teachers' interpersonal support for engagement, some classroom practices that are widely advocated in the literature are not clearly supported by confirmatory investigations. For example, although the use of culturally relevant text is advocated as a way to increase engagement, evidence supporting this practice is extremely thin. However, providing a one-size-fits-all curriculum with uniform materials often suits no one and may result in students disengaging from what they view as "teacher tasks." As the review by Taboada and colleagues (2007) suggests, fostering students' individuality by providing choice and control can improve instruction. These practices are more likely to engage students, because they connect them to the learning at hand. On the other hand, closed tasks, in which the teacher controls the materials and products of learning, may be seen as irrelevant, therefore isolating students from the learning process. The key issue is to identify choices that reflect students' experience, knowledge, and interests, while maintaining a reasonable alignment with the school's curricular goals. The Taylor, Pearson, and Peterson (2003) study of teaching practices supports this emphasis on microchoices to encourage active versus passive learner involvement.

## IMPLICATIONS FOR RESEARCH

To better understand how, and whether, to afford students instructional accommodations related to gender, income, ethnicity, or cultural variations, we must first discover how these background factors influence an individual student's engagement in learning. Although we are learning more about elements of instruction that are engaging to most students, such as providing choice and using relevant and authentic tasks, we are just beginning to develop an understanding of how these factors influence instruction for diverse ethnic groups, such as African American students. Some schools present a homogeneous student population, whereas others serve students who represent a greater diversity of ethnic, socioeconomic, and linguistic backgrounds. How to shift instruction for the degree of heterogeneity in the classroom is a challenge. Our schools and classrooms are not uniform across cities, regions, or states; therefore, how do we discover the elements that are the *sine qua non* of effective and engaging instruction, and those that can be tailored to suit particular contexts?

It is promising to place the student in the center of the research lens. In this approach, we seek to explain student variation as the starting point of inquiry into teaching diverse populations. What characteristics of the individual students are related to their engagement in the classroom? If boys show different engagement patterns than girls, then we may support their engagement differently. If individuals from one ethnic group show unique patterns, then we may need to identify unique support for that group. For example, initial evidence suggests that intrinsic motivation (reading for enjoyment and interest) is much more highly correlated with achievement for European American than for African American students (Long et al., 2007). African American students are not necessarily less motivated for reading, but their intrinsic motivation is less connected to their achievement than that of European American students. This is sufficiently important to be examined more fully.

Preliminary evidence with strong quantitative measures suggests that avoidance of reading is more highly associated with achievement for African American than for European American students (Guthrie et al., 2007), which is consistent with qualitative case studies by Ogbu (2003) on the academic disengagement of African American students. When African American students avoid reading, their achievement drops quickly, and when they devote themselves to reading, their achievement rises quickly. These processes are more prominent for African American than for European American students. If this is confirmed, fostering devotion of African American students, and helping them to reduce reading avoidance, will be a relatively powerful form of engagement support. Although European American students may benefit from such an emphasis, it may not be as valuable for them. We should embrace the investigative challenge of how to adapt engagement-supporting patterns to students from diverse populations.

Beginning with students as the starting point of investigation we may identify aspects of culture associated with their engagement and achievement. For example, Smalls and colleagues (2007) reported in the *Journal of Black Psychology* that African American students who experience racism frequently are more likely to be academically disengaged than are students who experience racism less often. Experiencing racism is an aspect of some African American students' community life, and this dimension of culture is connected to academic engagement for some subsets of this ethnic group. It is important to identify other dimensions of culture that are linked to reading engagement, which may be accomplished by fusing qualitative inquiries with generalizable, replicable studies.

## REFERENCES

Au, K., & Mason, J. M. (1981). Social organizational factors in learning to read: The balance of rights hypothesis. *Reading Research Quarterly, 17*, 115–152.

Burchinal, M. R., Peisner-Feinberg, E., & Pianta, R. (2002). Development of academic skills from preschool through second grade: Family and classroom predictors of developmental trajectories. *Journal of School Psychology, 40*, 415–436.

Cazden, C. B. (1986). Review of adult–child interaction and the process of language acquisition. *PsycCRITIQUES, 31*, 467–468.

Chavous, T. M., Bernat, D. H., Schmeelk-Cone, K., Caldwell, C. H., Kohn-Wood, L., & Zimmerman, M. A. (2003). Racial identity and academic attainment among African American adolescents. *Child Development, 74*, 1076–1090.

Decker, D. M., Dona, D. P., & Christenson, S. L. (2007). Behaviorally at-risk African American students: The importance of student–teacher relationships for student outcomes. *Journal of School Psychology, 45*, 83–109.

Dill, E., & Boykin, A. W. (2000). The comparative influence of individual, peer tutoring, and communal learning on text recall of African American children. *Journal of Black Psychology, 26*, 65–78.

Fink, R., & Samuels, S. J. (2007). *Inspiring reading success: Interest and motivation in an age of high-stakes testing.* Newark, DE: International Reading Association.

Freeman, Y., & Freeman, D. (2004). Connecting students to culturally relevant text. *Talking Points, 15*, 7–11.

Ford, D. Y., & Harris, J. J. (1996). Perceptions and attitudes of black students toward school, achievement, and other educational variables. *Child Development, 67*, 1141–1152.

Goldenberg, C., Gallimore, R., & Reese, L. (2001). Cause or effect?: A longitudinal study of immigrant Latino parents' aspirations and expectations, and their children's school performance. *American Educational Research Journal, 38*, 547–582.

Graham, S., Taylor, A. Z., & Hudley, C. (1998). Exploring achievement values among ethnic minority early adolescents. *Journal of Educational Psychology, 90*, 606–620.

Guthrie, J. T., McRae, A., & Klauda, S. L. (2007). Contributions of Concept-Oriented Reading Instruction to knowledge about interventions for motivations in reading. *Educational Psychologist, 42*, 237–250.

Hall, V. C., Merkel, S., Howe, A., & Lederman, N. (1986). Behavior, motivation, and achievement in desegregated junior high school science classes. *Journal of Educational Psychology, 78*, 108–115.

Hamre, B. K., & Pianta, R. C. (2005). Can instructional and emotional support in the first-grade classroom make a difference for children at risk of school failure? *Child Development, 76*, 949–967.

Heath, L. (1983). Testing social interventions. *PsycCRITIQUES, 28*, 291–292.

Holmes, K., Powell, S., Holmes, S., & Witt, E. (2007). Readers and books characters: Does race matter? *Journal of Educational Research, 100*, 14–19.

Hughes, J., & Kwok, O. (2007). Influence of student–teacher and parent–teacher relationships on lower achieving readers' engagement and achievement in the primary grades. *Journal of Educational Psychology, 99*, 39–51.

Hwang, Y. S., & Echols, C. (2002). Multidimensional academic motivation of high achieving African American students. *College Student Journal, 36*, 544–555.

Lee, C. D. (2005). The state of knowledge about the education of African Americans. In J. E. King (Ed.), *Black education: A transformative research and action agenda for the new century* (pp. 45–72). Mahwah, NJ: Erlbaum.

Long, J. F., Monoi, S., Harper, B., Knoblauch, D., & Murphy, P.K. (2007). Academic motivation and achievement among urban adolescents. *Urban Education, 42*, 196–222.

Meece, J. L., & Holt, K. (1993). A pattern analysis of students' achievement goals. *Journal of Educational Psychology, 85*, 582–590.

Mickelson, R. A. (1990). The attitude–achievement paradox among black adolescents. *Sociology of Education, 63*, 44–61.

Morgan, P. L., & Fuchs, D. (2007). Is there a bidirectional relationship between children's reading skills and reading motivation? *Exceptional Children, 73*, 165–183.

Ogbu, J. U. (2003). *Black American students in an affluent suburb: A study of academic disengagement.* Mahwah, NJ: Erlbaum.

Osborne, J. W. (1997). Race and academic disidentification. *Journal of Educational Psychology, 89*, 728–735.

Phillips, B. N. (1972). School-related aspirations of children with different socio-cultural backgrounds. *Journal of Negro Education, 41*, 48–52.

Phillips, B. N. (1983). Law-related training in school psychology: A national survey of doctoral programs. *Journal of School Psychology, 21*, 253–259.

Powers, K. M. (2006). An exploratory study of cultural identity and culture-based educational programs for urban American Indian students. *Urban Education, 41*, 20–49.

Reese, L., & Gallimore, R. (2000). Immigrant Latinos' cultural model of literacy development: An evolving perspective on home–school discontinuities. *American Journal of Education, 108,* 103–134.

Sanders, M. G. (1997). Overcoming obstacles: Academic achievement as a response to racism and discrimination. *Journal of Negro Education, 66,* 83–93.

Sandoval, S. R., Gutkin, T. B., & Naumann, W. C. (1997). Racial identity attitudes and school performance among African American high school students: An exploratory study. *Research in the Schools, 4,* 1–8.

Schunk, D. H., & Zimmerman B. J. (2007). Influencing children's self-efficacy and self-regulation of reading and writing through modeling. *Reading and Writing Quarterly, 23,* 7–25.

Smalls, C., White, R., Chavous, T., & Sellers, R. (2007). Racial ideological beliefs and racial discrimination experiences as predictors of academic engagement among African American adolescents. *Journal of Black Psychology, 33,* 299–330.

Steele, C. M., & Aronson, J. (1995). Stereotype threat and the intellectual test performance of African Americans. *Journal of Personality and Social Psychology, 69,* 797–811.

Suizzo, M. A. (2007). Parents' goals and values for children: Dimensions of independence and interdependence across four U.S. ethnic groups. *Journal of Cross-Cultural Psychology, 38,* 506–530.

Taboada, A., Guthrie, J. T., & McRae, A. (2007). Building engaging classrooms. In R. Fink & S. J. Samuels (Eds.), *Inspiring reading success: Interest and motivation in an age of high-stakes testing* (pp. 141–166). Newark, DE: International Reading Association.

Taylor, A. Z., & Graham, S. (2007). An examination of the relationship between achievement values and perceptions of barriers among low-SES African American and Latino students. *Journal of Educational Psychology, 99,* 52–64.

Taylor, B. M., Pearson, P. D., & Peterson, D. S. (2003). Reading growth in high-poverty classrooms: The influence of teacher practices that encourage cognitive engagement in literacy learning. *Elementary School Journal, 104,* 3–28.

Tharp, R. G. (1982). The effective instruction of comprehension: Results and description of the Kamehameha Early Education Program. *Reading Research Quarterly, 17,* 503–527.

Tudge, J. R. H., Doucet, F., Odero, D., Sperb, T. M., Piccinini, C. A., & Lopes, R. S. (2006). A window into different cultural worlds: Young children's everyday activities in the United States, Brazil, and Kenya. *Child Development, 77,* 1446–1469.

Tyler, K. M., Boykin, A. W., Miller, O., & Hurley, E. (2006). Cultural values in the home and school experiences of low-income African American students. *Social Psychology of Education, 9,* 363–380.

Voelkl, K. E. (1997). Identification with school. *American Journal of Education, 105,* 294–318.

Webb, N. M., & Farivar, S. (1994). Promoting helping behavior in cooperative small groups in middle school mathematics. *American Educational Research Journal, 31,* 369–395.

# CHAPTER 11

# Robust Informal Learning Environments for Youth from Nondominant Groups

## *Implications for Literacy Learning in Formal Schooling*

KRIS GUTIÉRREZ *and* CAROL D. LEE

In this chapter, we discuss how informal learning ecologies can serve as productive learning environments for students from nondominant communities. To do so, we draw from two complementary bodies of empirical work that illustrate the affordances of ratcheting up learning environments in which all students can be smart. Our common focus has been on developing more robust notions of learning that move us away from deficit perspectives of cultural communities, their members, and practices, and on challenging reductive notions of what counts as learning. There is a long history of empirical work in this tradition. In particular, our work concerns how the social organization of robust learning environments supports expansive learning opportunities in disciplinary domains, particularly literacy. In this chapter, we bring together two related lines of work, sociocultural approaches to informal learning and cultural modeling approaches, which have informed our theoretical and empirical work. We discuss the following:

- A cultural–historical view of learning
- Culturally organized robust literacy learning in informal settings
- Examples of school-based projects that take up what we have learned from robust informal settings: the Cultural Modeling Project and the Funds of Knowledge Project
- Implications for future research

Formal education has much to learn from informal learning environments. This is particularly the case for those settings in which teachers work with youth from low-income minority communities. Research has documented the positive outcomes for these youth as a result of their participation in a variety of arts-related organizations (Fisher, 2003, 2004; Halverson, 2005; Heath, 2004; Heath & M. M. McLaughlin, 1994 Heath & M. W. McLaughlin, 1993; Jocson, 2008; McLaughlin, 1993; McLaughlin, Langman, & Irby, 1994). Although personnel in these organizations typically do not explicitly teach literacy skills, youth engage in many authentic acts of reading, writing, and speaking. Many studies describe the social organization of these settings, as well as the kinds of activities in which youth engage. However, there is a need to understand the fundamental principles that guide the organization of these settings. In this chapter, we examine generative propositions about robust learning in such settings that have implications for teaching and learning in schools.

## A CULTURAL–HISTORICAL VIEW OF LEARNING

There is a long history, particularly in the cross-cultural literature, of empirical work in informal learning environments, especially in settings where schooling has not been prevalent (Greenfield, 2004; Rogoff, 2003; Scribner & Cole, 1973). Cross-cultural research, such as Jean Lave's (1988) study of tailors in Liberia, Barbara Rogoff's (2003) long-term studies in San Pedro, Guatemala, and Sylvia Scribner and Michael Cole's (1981) literacy work in Liberia, document the ways that *learning is related to participation in the valued practices of which people are a part.* In this way, *learning is continuous with experiences encountered in everyday life.* Thus, the knowledge and skills that people acquire through participation across activity settings have *a highly positive social value to participants because they are linked to practices and valued relationships in which learning is not the primary reason for engagement.* In contrast to solo or discovery learning, in which learning is an individual accomplishment, the social organization of informal learning is integrated into community activities, where learning is neither hidden nor the object of activity.

Understanding what makes some learning environments and their practices more meaningful to people has been foundational to new lines of work focused on designing robust and meaningful learning ecologies for students from nondominant communities. One salient example advanced by Rogoff, Paradise, Arauz, Correa-Chávez, and Angelillo (2003) is the notion of intent community participation, in which children and youth are incorporated into the community's practices, with the ongoing expectation that they will be full participants in the endeavor. For example, learning is a shared endeavor, with assistance readily available to ensure both participation and understanding of the task and practice at hand. Here, the emergent, collective, and distributed nature of learning is key. There are important implications for learning in such communities.

In our own work, cross-cultural research on informal learning has helped us understand the cultural dimensions of learning, particularly how individuals learn the valued practices, forms of participation, and ways of learning in communities (Gutiérrez & Rogoff, 2003). A brief discussion of the instrumental view of culture as central to a cultural–historical approach to learning is warranted here, because it undergirds our work developing innovative learning ecologies for students from nondominant communities. "Culture" within this perspective is a verb, as Brian Street (1993) once noted; that is, it involves what people do; how they live; or what values, beliefs, and meanings are ascribed to particular practices. Culture, then, should not be conflated solely with race and ethnicity—a notion that can lead to viewing culture as a trait of an individual by virtue of membership in a particular community. In educational contexts, making "culture" simply synonymous with "race" and "ethnicity" also makes it easier to attribute a learning style to members of communities (Gutiérrez & Rogoff, 2003). As we have argued, it is both more productive and more accurate to focus on people's repertoires of practice, and this includes ways of engaging in activities stemming from participation in a range of cultural practices (Nasir, Rosebery, Warren, & Lee, 2006). We characterize people's repertoires in terms of their familiarity with engaging in particular practices, on the basis of what is known about their own and their community's history (Gutiérrez & Rogoff, 2003). And because the valued practices of communities are indexed with histories and meanings that have sustained some resilience over time, we can look to these to understand what is cultural in what people do in everyday activity (Lee, 2008; Lee, Spencer, & Harpalani, 2003).

At the same time, cultural practices are not static, and they change in important ways, influenced by the affordances and constraints of the local ecological niche, larger historical forces, and individual life histories. In the domain of literacy, this instrumental view of culture helps us to conceive of literacy practices as part of a toolkit that is socially and culturally shaped as individuals participate in a range of practices across familiar, new, and hybrid contexts and tasks. Thus, literacy learning is not an individual accomplishment; instead, it is built on a history of relationships and influences, both local and distal.

Of significance, learning among individuals in communities is organized in ways that have been effective and valued for many generations, and it helps account for the sustainability of practices or elements of practices in families and across generations. And whereas change in these practices and their participants is ongoing, we have been interested in understanding what is cultural about the enduring, hybridized, or transformed practices of nondominant communities (Lee, 2007). From an activity-theoretical perspective (Cole & Engeström, 1993; Engeström, 1996), the emphasis in informal learning is on recognizing/using the horizontal or everyday expertise that learners acquire across quotidian activity toward some meaningful personal or community goal. Similarly, our work has recognized the importance of organizing learning around the horizontal knowledge to expand students' school-based and disciplinary knowledge (Gutiérrez, 2008; Lee, 2007).

This focus on horizontal knowledge is central to a cultural approach to learning. Within this approach, learning is oriented toward shared practices that are historically and locally situated, and organized around students' repertoires of practices—that is, practices developed in the movement and flow as youth move across everyday settings and practices. This approach works against the traditional dichotomies that often characterize research in cultural communities (home–school, inside–outside school, etc.). Our own approach to learning brings together both horizontal *and* vertical, or school-based, knowledge to expand students' repertoires of practice to include disciplinary knowledge and expertise.

## CULTURALLY ORGANIZED ROBUST LITERACY LEARNING IN INFORMAL SETTINGS

For example, if we are interested in understanding the literacy practices of migrant students in California, as in the work of Gutiérrez (2008), a cultural–historical view pushes us to consider an ecological view of students' learning to understand how repertoires of practice develop, as well as how students' environments and practices also are the consequence of globalization, transmigration, and the intercultural experiences of their everyday lives. In this way, rather than focusing on immigrant students' "linguistic deficiencies," we focus on the sociohistorical influences on their language and literacy practices, and on their social, economic, and educational realities—factors mediated by proximal and historical influences (Gutiérrez, 2004).

As in the work on informal learning, this requires characterizing people's experience and initiative in cultural activities across the lifespan. In doing so, we would find that culture is not practiced in uniform or necessarily harmonious ways within and across families in communities. For this reason, we have been careful in our design and study of robust learning ecologies to seek accounts of the regularity and variance in the ways people live culturally. For example, in work with high school students from migrant farmworker backgrounds, Gutiérrez (2008) focused on students' history of involvement with literacy practices, and the influences on those practices, rather than focusing solely or primarily on students' unfamiliarity with school-based practices.

We would want to understand migrant students' language and literacy practices across a minimum of several activity settings and a range of practices (Engeström, 2005); this would help us avoid analyses that tend to dichotomize home and school, and inschool and out-of-school practices, and to oversimplify or romanticize the literacy practices of these youth. In contrast, our analyses would focus on the expertise that youth develop as they move within and across tasks and contexts, and spatial, linguistic, and sociocultural borders. And we would not attribute observed regularities in migrant students to their membership in Mexican-origin communities but to their history of participation in familiar cultural practices, and to public schooling experiences in California that restrict engagement and limit the use of cultural resources that are part of their repertoires. As previously noted (Gutiérrez, 2007), these regularities also could be understood in part as a historical consequence of colonizing practices of which students have been a part as migrants, immigrants, and members of indigenous communities.

Utilizing what we have learned from sociocultural studies of informal learning, cultural–historical approaches to learning and development (Cole, 1996), and cultural, ethnic, and literacy studies, as well as critical approaches to pedagogy, robust learning ecologies for K–5 and high school students have been developed in an afterschool computer-mediated learning club, *Las Redes*, and a summer residential program for high school students from migrant farmworker backgrounds (Gutiérrez, 2008; Nixon & Gutiérrez, 2007). These are hybrid spaces that bring together horizontal forms of learning, students' linguistic and sociocultural repertoires, and everyday ways of learning and being with vertical forms of learning that include academic literacy and its practices, new texts, discourses, and identities. Such programs, then, cannot be defined by a specific curricular program but by their focus on designing particular ecologies that are tool-saturated and carefully scaffolded with varying forms and networks of support, as well as new and familiar ways of organizing learning, participation, and communication.

Like the informal learning environments described earlier, learning is contiguous with participation in meaningful and challenging practices with peers and adults. Here the focus is on creating learning ecologies where cultural amplification (Cole & Griffin, 1980) and expansive learning (Engeström, 1987) are in sync and mutually reinforcing. In the afterschool and migrant program, the object is to help students develop new identities as meaning makers, learners, and knowledgeable consumers of their own and larger cultural practices and histories. Toward this end, these learning ecologies are designed to help students develop toolkits that support critical understandings of texts, ideas, and histories, the use and function of everyday and technical or academic languages and practices, and the social world around them.

Of relevance for this largely immigrant student population, these hybrid learning environments privilege joint activity and shared practice in which hybrid language practices are normative—in which students can use their full linguistic toolkit in the service of learning (Gutiérrez, Baquedano-Lopez, & Alvarez, 1999). Organized around the leading activities of play and the imaginary situation, peer relations, and learning (Griffin & Cole, 1984), motivation for learning and engagement is enhanced. In this specific context, using play and the imaginary situation in the form of *teatro*, metaphorical thinking (e.g., collective dreaming for a better future for their communities) opens up opportunities for students to reframe the outcomes of education and to develop agentic identities.

Organizing for transformative learning allows us to highlight the practices of reasoned questioning, taking critical stances, identifying contradiction, and emphasizing historicity—hallmark characteristics of expansive learning ecologies. As others (Engeström, 2005) have also argued, students should understand the schooling practices in which they participate, including the history of those practices. This understanding is critical to the development of a *sociocritical liter-*

*acy* (Gutiérrez, 2008). For example, the approach used with migrant farmworker and elementary school students utilizes hybrid language practices and extends students' repertoires to include academic literacy that in other settings privileges English. Clearly these two practices are in tension in an English-only state such as California. Rather than ignoring this tension, the Migrant Program, for example, makes this contradiction the object of study and discussion, including issues of power, inequity, and the history of such inequitable practices. Such learning practices promote generative thinking that engages youth in deep learning and the development of powerful literacies.

## IMPLICATIONS FOR ROBUST LITERACY LEARNING IN FORMAL SCHOOL SETTINGS

Informal learning ecologies perhaps offer such important lessons for formal schooling in part because they are not constrained by the deficit assumptions that often characterize schools. The best informal learning ecologies have positive outcomes for youth, particularly youth from nondominant groups living in low-income communities, because they include the following characteristics of robust learning environments (Nasir et al., 2006):

- Address cognitive, social, and emotional needs in a holistic manner.
- Position the learner as competent.
- Make evident the social good or utility of the activity.
- Make problem solving explicit and provide guided timely support.
- Situate evaluation in terms of publicly understood criteria rather than as a measure of finite ability.
- Engage youth directly in wrestling with issues of identity, societal racism, poverty, and power.
- Integrate literacy (i.e., reading, writing, and speaking) into the practical goals of the activities rather than as a decontextualized goal.

We have illustrated how literacy is integrated into the social organization of these informal settings and have emphasized the ways in which cultural resources are leveraged to address the holistic needs of youth, including working with youth to make sense of the daily microaggressions they experience as a consequence of the institutionalization of racism and poverty.

Schools as organizations typically struggle to have the same degrees of freedom as community organizations. High-stakes accountability, state requirements for the credentialing of teachers, and district mandates that often focus on basic skills place severe constraints on classroom teaching. In addition, commercial curricula, particularly at the middle and high school levels, rarely situate the learning of content areas within community funds of knowledge or community-based and generational goals in part, as a consequence of these structural constraints and the fact that teacher preparation programs typically do not help teacher candidates understand how to link in-classroom instruction, and social, emotional, and cognitive development, or to address social justice goals. Thus, we have many instances of youth who thrive in their participation in community-based organizations but fail in the contexts of school. The success of these organizations indicates clearly that there is much for schools to learn from these institutions.

We offer here several examples of programs of research inside schools that institutionalize the principles we have described for robust learning environments that meet the triple quandary faced by youth from nondominant groups. We have selected examples with an explicit focus on literacy: the Cultural Modeling Project and the Funds of Knowledge Project.

At least three conceptual links need to be made for school-based, content-area instruction to meet the criteria we have raised. We focus broadly on content-area instruction, because it always involves reading, writing, and speaking. The first is how to conceptualize links between disciplinary knowledge taught in schools and everyday knowledge, particularly everyday knowledge constructed out of experiences in cultural communities of nondominant groups. The second is how to address the issue of language variation, particularly in terms of language practices in communities of nondominant groups, and assumptions about academic language. The third is how to integrate a holistic focus on social, emotional, and cognitive development within the constraints of K–12 schooling, particularly at the level of classroom instruction. Each of the two programs of research we describe here addresses some or all of these conceptual challenges. These examples are not meant to be exhaustive, but are illustrative of the ways to adapt what we have learned from the successes of informal learning environments in formal schooling for nondominant groups.

## The Cultural Modeling Project

The Cultural Modeling Project (CMP) addresses each of the three challenges we have raised: (1) linking disciplinary and everyday knowledge; (2) scaffolding everyday and academic language; (3) addressing the holistic needs of youth from nondominant groups. The CMP has focused explicitly on skills required for students to engage in complex reasoning about literary texts at the high school level, and composing at the elementary level (Lee, 1993, 1995, 2000, 2001, 2007). Here we draw on the high school work in literary reasoning. In many respects, CMP represents an expanded conceptualization of learning in this domain and shares with the informal learning settings we have described an incorporation of intergenerational, community-based cultural tools as resources for learning. The CMP has been implemented in high schools with predominantly African American students who live in low-income communities and are predominantly speakers of African American English (AAE).

The foundational research that informs cultural modeling (CM) is based on decades of research on the structure and pragmatics of AAE (Makoni, Smitherman, Ball, & Spears, 2003; Mufwene, Rickford, Bailey, & Baugh, 1998; Smitherman, 1977) and literary and psychological studies of literary reasoning (Booth, 1974, 1983; Culler, 1975; Jones, 1991; Purves, 1991; Scholes, 1985; Trabasso & van den Broek, 1985; van den Broek, 1996). Literary reasoning as a goal of instruction is particularly well positioned for the pursuit of knowledge that has personal and practical benefits for students. Recall that one of the features of the successful informal learning environments we have described is that they position literacy tasks inside practical, goal-directed, socially valued activities. Literature, especially great literature, provides a medium in which readers wrestle with the big and enduring questions of what it means to be human. Works of literature, especially those by the great writers representing the cultural and historical conversations of those now positioned as nondominant groups in the United States, pose conundrums, and offer critical insights and life scenarios that can help young people better understand the vicissitudes and opportunities of their lives. However, two limitations of typical literature instruction, particularly in high schools in low-income communities, help to explain why most high school graduates, regardless of socioeconomic status (SES) or ethnicity, come to hate the very literature that English teachers want them to love. The first is constraint on the range of cultural traditions represented in the literature that is taught. Applebee (1993) has documented the conservative nature of the secondary literature curriculum. Thus, students are asked to identify with characters and life events that they perceive as unconnected to the worlds they know. The second limitation is that the secondary literature curriculum does not teach students the generative skills they need as novice and often struggling readers to tackle the problems they will meet in great literature (Lee, 2007; Smith & Hillocks, 1988).

The CMP addresses these two limitations. Lee (2007) has identified prototypical kinds of problems that the novice reader will meet across a wide range of literary texts and heuristics, as well as strategies for identifying and tackling these problems. These interpretive problems include symbolism, satire, irony, and problems of narration, including unreliable narration (Smith, 1989, 1991a, 1991b). By identifying these problem types and strategies in the canonical literature, Lee has been able to examine sources of overlap with reasoning about similar problems in the everyday practices of African American youth and youth culture broadly speaking. Through the use of what Lee calls "cultural data sets" and "metacognitive instructional conversations," youth who more often than not are disengaged from canonical literature in the contexts of schooling examine how they identify and make sense of these interpretive problems in their everyday routine practices. Such practices, now institutionalized in cultural data sets, include stretches of signifying talk in AAE, rap lyrics and videos, covers of rap CDs, clips from popular films, television programs, and advertising. Students examine these interpretive problems as they present themselves in these everyday texts (Morrell, 2002; Morrell & Duncan-Andrade, 2002). Through "metacognitive instructional conversations," students make public the thinking that is typically tacit in the everyday context, now made explicit and communicated in the language of academic abstraction as rules of thumb that subsequently are then applied to canonical works. Through such instructional conversations, students are able to see how what they are being asked do with the canonical works is similar to what they already do and value. In this way, students are able to see the social good of this practice of literary reasoning, not only in terms of the outcome of what they come to understand about life from reading such texts but also in terms of their value and the appreciation of the process (i.e., attending to language play as an aesthetically pleasing end in itself). This initial focus on examining cultural data sets also reorganizes the status relations between teachers and students, because students often have greater prior knowledge of content of these everyday texts than teachers, connecting what we have described earlier as horizontal and vertical forms of learning. The students understand the content, and the teacher understands the process. This more horizontal relationship between teachers and students is also characteristic of many of the successful informal learning environments we have described. Thus, in CM, the conceptual link between the disciplinary and the everyday literature is addressed head on. Although literature is clearly an optimal candidate for such links, similar conceptualizations can be found in science education, with the CheChe Konnen Project (Rosebery, Warren, Ballenger, & Ogonowski, 2005; Rosebery, Warren, & Conant, 1992; Warren, Ballenger, Ogonowski, Rosebery, & Hudicourt-Barnes, 2001), and in mathematics, with the Algebra Project (Moses, 1994; Moses & Cobb, 2001; Moses, Kamii, Swap, & Howard, 1989) and research emanating from the Center for Mathematics Education of Latino Students (CEMELA). In these projects, literacy in science and mathematics is integrated in ways that capture the features of robust learning we have described as ecologies. We describe the ecologies of these projects because they effectively link learning across home and school.

The second conceptual link addresses connections between academic and everyday language (Gutiérrez, Baquedano-Lopez, & Alvarez, 1999; Gutiérrez, Baquedano-Lopez, & Tejada, 1999; Lee, 1997). In CM classrooms where students are speakers of AAE, AAE is the medium of instructional talk. In both the academy and policy debates, AAE has been vilified as detrimental to academic learning (Perry & Delpit, 1998). However, rather than viewing AAE as a barrier, CM views it as a linguistic resource. Classroom discussions in which students use AAE discourse norms provide resources for thinking and for participating. Learning how to engage in classroom talk is a common barrier in opportunity to learn. The expectation that Standard English must be the medium of communication is not a characteristic of successful informal learning environments. Lee has documented how African American rhetorical features, engaging in sustained multiparty, overlapping talk, have characterized those instances of deepest engagement with texts among AAE speakers in CM classrooms (Lee, 2005a, 2005b, 2006). There is no problem with what Lee calls AAE instructional discourse in itself. The challenges come in the ability of students to reason and to translate these canonical texts into academic writing genres (Ball, 1995, 1999, 2002; Ball & Farr,

2003). But Lee (2007) argues that students are highly unlikely to care about these problems of translation if they have not already developed deep affiliations with the texts themselves, such that the students have something important to say about the texts.

The third conceptual challenge has to do with seamlessly integrating the social, emotional, and cognitive needs of students. The best informal learning environments are successful in such integration. The CMP addresses this integration in several ways. Complex learning always has social, emotional, and cognitive dimensions. Complex learning typically involves coordination with other people, in which self-presentation, reading the internal states of others, and coordinating personal and group goals are necessary (Flavell & Miller, 1998; Kunda, 1999). The emotional dimension has to do with perceptions of the self, the task, and others (peers, teachers, etc.) (Eccles, Wigfield, & Schiefele, 1998; Spencer, 2006). It is the learner's response to these perceptions that counts in terms of goals and effort. The substantive body of research on stereotype threat has shown that such perceptions matter for nondominant youth (Steele, 2004). Lee (2007) argues that the ways that CM makes the task salient to the goals and prior experiences/knowledge of learners, and structures and makes visible the problem-solving process— including guided support while students engage in literary reasoning—influence the effort that students are willing to put forth. The availablity of culturally congruent discourse norms structures roles for participation that are familiar. These efforts together position the learner as competent and enhance the likelihood that youth will see the task as relevant and doable, themselves as competent for the task, and the teacher and peers as supportive (Lee, 2007).

Finally, holistic development is further addressed by the selection of texts initially that embody character types and life experiences closer to students' life experiences, and themes that address in complex and nuanced ways those life challenges they currently face, or anticipate facing, as they move toward adult roles. Such selection and sequencing of texts function as a platform for racial socialization, identity work, and life course developmental issues (Brown, 2008; Caughy, O'Campo, Randolph, & Nickerson, 2002; Murray & Mandara, 2003). With African American students, after extensive examination of cultural data sets, canonical texts begin with texts from the African American literary tradition, then sequence to texts whose life worlds are further removed from students' everyday experience. These initial cultural texts are selected for not only their common themes but also a common set of interpretive problems they pose.

On pre-, post-, and quarterly assessments in literature classrooms, students who are often in the bottom quartile in terms of standardized reading assessments demonstrate complex reasoning about canonical literary texts that has not been taught directly in the instructional units (Lee, 1995, 2007).

We offer this case as an example of the ways that literacy instruction in school contexts can be informed by characteristics that have been found in successful informal learning environments for nondominant youth.

## The Funds of Knowledge Project

The Funds of Knowledge Project (FOK) illustrates another set of important ways in which schools may take up features of robust learning ecologies in informal settings (González, Moll, & Amanti, 2004; Moll & González, 2004; Moll & Greenberg, 1990). One huge barrier to the transformation of schools in ways that support the kind of robust and expansive learning we have described is the lack of any significant formal relations between schools and local communities. Few school personnel are poised to actually learn from the communities they serve. The FOK has developed tools to facilitate learning from the community in ways that help to transform teachers' perceptions and knowledge of youth from nondominant groups and to support teachers in reconceptualizing their practice. Issues of language are central to this work and, as such, inevitably influence what counts as literate practices in FOK schools.

FOK has operated for over a decade in schools in Arizona, California, and New York. Students in these schools are largely of Hispanic—particularly Mexican American—Native American, and African American backgrounds. The term "funds of knowledge" refers to the knowledge and skills developed in families and communities that sustain the functioning and well-being of households. This includes knowledge of finance, business, trade, farming and animal husbandry, construction, plumbing, and so on (Civil, 2001, 2002). These bodies of knowledge are often related to the immigrant origins of a given household and/or community. Families use this accumulated, intergenerational knowledge to acquire goods and services within the community and, as a consequence, build and sustain social networks (Moll & Greenberg, 1990). Children are observers and often participants in these household activities. These everyday practices entail multiple literacies that involve reading, writing, speaking, mathematics, science, history, and politics. These everyday practices often involve hybrid language practices, including children translating for parents (Orellana, 2009; Orellana, Reynolds, Dorner, & Meza, 2003; Valdés, 2002), as well as answering questions about the political and economic issues affecting family and community life.

The FOK has developed tools and training for teachers to go into households and conduct family interviews. They have used the tools of ethnography as a resource for teacher learning (González, 2004). The goals of these ethnographic interviews conducted by classroom teachers are to expand their understanding of and attitudes toward community knowledge, and to facilitate relationship building among teachers, families, and communities, or *confianza* (i.e., mutual trust) (Mercado & Moll, 1997). In addition to conducting family interviews, teachers also explore neighborhoods to identify sites of knowledge building and exchange, as well as relationship building (community gardens, community art on walls and buildings, informal sites of automobile repair, yard sales, sibling child care, language code switching, etc.). The project is based on the theory that student interest and motivation will be enhanced by connecting school and everyday knowledge that is valued in the practices of students' families and communities.

Study groups of teachers, both within and across schools, meet with the support of both FOK facilitators and community members to engage in joint inquiry about how to incorporate these community funds of knowledge into classroom instruction (González, 1995; Moll, 2000). The instruction that evolves from these efforts often involves community members as direct resources in classrooms and expanded tools for speaking, reading, and writing. Teachers come to value the multiple-language resources that youth bring and the importance of drawing upon the expanded social networks in children's lives. For example, upon learning about a group of children's experiences in selling candy from Mexico in the United States, the teacher invited a parent who knew how to make the candy. From the learning activities embedded in this investigation, children learned mathematical, science, health, and consumer education concepts. Literacy is then embedded in reading, writing, thinking, and speaking about topics that are not only salient in students' family and community lives, but that also enlist expanded social networks to support learning in schools.

## IMPLICATIONS FOR FUTURE RESEARCH

To expand opportunities for rich literacy learning with students from nondominant populations, additional research needs to examine the range of reading, writing, and linguistic practices in which youth engage (Moje, Young, Readence, & Moore, 2000). We have learned from research on effective informal learning environments how the holistic needs of youth—cognitive, social, and emotional—are addressed through relationship building and a focus on how learning goals are connected with the social, political, and economic circumstances of youths' lives. Further research on cultural and ecological influences on motivation is also needed, including research on how these influences can be recruited in classroom instruction. Finally, additional research is needed to expand our conceptualization of pathways to disciplinary literacy that leverage the knowledge and dispositions that youth develop through valued everyday and community practices.

## CONCLUSION

Examinations of the social organization of robust learning environments for youth from nondominant groups in informal settings have revealed the following characteristics:

- An expanded conception of culture as lived practices that are central to people's functioning in the world.
- The importance of learning embedded in the valued practices of communities.

- Reorganization of learning in terms of horizontal, as opposed to purely vertical, relationships.
- The capacity to draw on the full linguistic repertoires of learners.

We have illustrated both how these characteristics play out in informal settings and the implications of how these features of robust learning may be central to school-based learning. Robust literacy learning across these informal and formal settings expands what counts as worthwhile knowledge, including knowledge that helps youth examine the social, political, and economic ecologies of their lives in ways that build identity and resilience.

## REFERENCES

Applebee, A. (1993). *Literature in the secondary school: Studies of curriculum and instruction in the United States* (NCTE Research Report No. 25). Urbana, IL: National Council of Teachers of English.

Ball, A. (1995). Text design patterns in the writing of urban African-American students: Teaching to the strengths of students in multicultural settings. *Urban Education, 30,* 253–289.

Ball, A. (1999). Evaluating the writing of culturally and linguistically diverse students—the case of the African American English speaker. In C. R. Cooper & L. Odell (Eds.), *Evaluating writing* (pp. 225–248). Urbana, IL: National Council of Teachers of English.

Ball, A. (2002). Three decades of research on classroom life: Illuminating the classroom communicative lives of America's at-risk students. In W. Secada (Ed.), *Review of research in education* (Vol. 26, pp. 71–112). Washington, DC: American Educational Research Association.

Ball, A., & Farr, M. (2003). Language varieties, culture and teaching the English language arts. In J. Flood, D. Lapp, J. Squire, & J. Jensen (Eds.), *Handbook of research on teaching the English language arts* (2nd ed., pp. 435–445). Mahwah, NJ: Erlbaum.

Booth, W. (1974). *A rhetoric of irony.* Chicago: University of Chicago Press.

Booth, W. (1983). *A rhetoric of fiction.* Chicago: University of Chicago Press.

Brown, D. L. (2008). African American resiliency: Examining racial socialization and social support as protective factors. *Journal of Black Psychology, 34*(1), 32–48.

Caughy, M. O., O'Campo, P. J., Randolph, S. M., & Nickerson, K. (2002). The influence of racial socialization practices on the cognitive and behavioral competence of African American preschoolers. *Child Development, 73,* 1611–1625.

Civil, M. (2001). Mathematics instruction developed from a garden theme. *Teaching Children Mathematics, 7*(7), 400–405.

Civil, M. (2002). Culture and mathematics: A community approach. *Journal of Intercultural Studies, 23*(2), 133–148.

Cole, M. (1996). *Cultural psychology: A once and future discipline.* Cambridge, UK: Belknap Press of Harvard University Press.

Cole, M., & Engeström, Y. (1993). A cultural-historical approach to distributed cognition. In G. Salomon (Ed.), *Distributed cognitions: Psychological and educational considerations* (pp. 47–87). New York: Cambridge University Press.

Cole, M., & Griffin, P. (1980). Cultural amplifiers reconsidered. In D. Olson (Ed.), *Social foundations of language and thought.* New York: Norton.

Culler, J. (1975). *Structuralist poetics: Structuralism, linguistics, and the study of literature.* New York: Cornell University Press.

Eccles, J. S., Wigfield, A., & Schiefele, U. (1998). Motivation to succeed. In W. Damon & N. Eisenberg (Eds.), *Handbook of child psychology* (5th ed., Vol. 3, pp. 1017–1096). New York: Wiley.

Engeström, Y. (1987). *Learning by expanding: An activity-theoretical approach to developmental research.* Helsinki, Finland: Oriento-Konsultit Oy.

Engeström, Y. (1996). Development as breaking away and opening up: A challenge to Vygotsky and Piaget. *Swiss Journal of Psychology, 55,* 126–132.

Engeström, Y. (2005). Knotworking to create collaborative intentionality capital in fluid organizational fields. In M. M. Beyerlein, S. T. Beyerlein, & F. A. Kennedy (Eds.), *Collaborative capital: Creating intangible value* (p. 307). Amsterdam: Elsevier.

Fisher, M. T. (2003). Open mics and open minds: Spoken word poetry in African Diaspora Participatory Literacy Communities. *Harvard Education Review, 73*(3), 362–389.

Fisher, M. T. (2004). "The song s unfinished": The new literate and the literary and their institutions. *Written Communication, 21,* 290–312.

Flavell, J. H., & Miller, P. H. (1998). Social cognition. In W. Damon, D. Kuhn, & R. Siegler (Eds.), *Handbook of child psychology* (5th ed., Vol. 2, pp. 851–898). New York: Wiley.

González, N. (1995). The funds of knowledge for teaching project. *Practicing Anthropology, 17*(3), 3–6.

González, N. (2004). Disciplining the discipline: Anthropology and the pursuit of quality education. *Educational Researcher, 33*(5), 17–25.

González, N., Moll, L., & Amanti, C. (Eds.). (2004). *Funds of knowledge: Theorizing practices in households, communities, and classrooms.* Mahwah, NJ: Erlbaum.

Greenfield, P. (2004). *Weaving generations together: Evolving creativity in the Maya of Chiapas.* Santa Fe, NM: School of American Research Press.

Griffin P., & Cole, M. (1984). Current activity for the future: The zo-ped. In B. Rogoff & J. V. Wertsch (Eds.), *Children s learning in the zone of proximal development* (New Directions for Child Development, No. 23). San Francisco: Jossey-Bass.

Gutiérrez, K. (2004). *Intersubjectivity and grammar in the third space.* Paper presented at the annual meeting of the American Educational Association, Montreal.

Gutiérrez, K. (2007). Commentary. In C. Lewis, P. E. Enciso, & E. B. Moje (Eds.), *Reframing sociocultural research on literacy: Identity, agency, and power* (pp. 115–120). Mahwah, NJ: Erlbaum.

Gutiérrez, K. (2008). Developing a sociocritical literacy in the third space. *Reading Research Quarterly, 43*(2), 148–164.

Gutiérrez, K., Baquedano-Lopez, P., & Alvarez, H. (1999). A cultural–historical approach to collaboration: Building a culture of collaboration through hybrid language practices. *Theory Into Practice, 38*(2), 87–93.

Gutiérrez, K., Baquedano-Lopez, P., & Tejada, C. (1999). Rethinking diversity: Hybridity and hybrid language practices in the Third Space. *Mind, Culture, and Activity, 6*(4), 286–303.

Gutiérrez, K. D., & Rogoff, B. (2003). Cultural ways of learning: Individual traits or repertoires of practice. *Educational Researcher, 32*(5), 19–25.

Halverson, E. (2005). InsideOut: Facilitating gay youth identity development through a performance-based youth organization. *Identity: An International Journal of Theory and Research, 5*(1), 67–90.

Heath, S. B. (2004). Risks, rules, and roles: Youth perspectives on the work of learning for community development. In A. N. Perret-Clermont, C. Pontecorvo, L. B. Resnick, T. Zittoun, & B. Burge (Eds.), *Joining society: Social interaction and learning in adolescence and youth* (pp. 41–70) New York: Cambridge University Press.

Heath, S. B., & McLaughlin, M. M. (1994). The best of both worlds: Connecting schools and community organizations for all day, all year learning. *Educational Administration Quarterly, 30*(3), 278–300.

Heath, S. B., & McLaughlin, M. W. (1993). Ethnicity and gender in theory and practice: The youth perspective. In *Identity and inner-city youth: Beyond ethnicity and gender* (pp. 13–35). New York: Teachers College Press.

Jocson, K. (2008). *Youth poets: Empowering literacies in and out of schools.* New York: Peter Lang.

Jones, G. (1991). *Liberating voices: Oral tradition in African American literature.* New York: Penguin Books.

Kunda, Z. (1999). *Social cognition: Making sense of people.* Cambridge, MA: MIT Press.

Lave, J. (1988). *Cognition in practice: Mind, mathematics and culture in everyday life.* Cambridge, UK: Cambridge University Press.

Lee, C. D. (1993). *Signifying as a scaffold for literary interpretation: The pedagogical implications of an African American discourse genre.* Urbana, IL: National Council of Teachers of English.

Lee, C. D. (1995). A culturally based cognitive apprenticeship: Teaching African American high school students' skills in literary interpretation. *Reading Research Quarterly, 30*(4), 608–631.

Lee, C. D. (1997). Bridging home and school literacies: A model of culturally responsive teaching. In J. Flood, S. B. Heath, & D. Lapp (Eds.), *A handbook for literacy educators: Research on teaching the communicative and visual arts* (pp. 330–341). New York: Macmillan.

Lee, C. D. (2000). Signifying in the zone of proximal development. In C. D. Lee & P. Smagorinsky (Eds.), *Vygotskian perspectives on literacy research: Constructing meaning through collaborative inquiry* (pp. 191–225). New York: Cambridge University Press.

Lee, C. D. (2001). Is October Brown Chinese?: A cultural modeling activity system for underachieving students. *American Educational Research Journal, 38*(1), 97–142.

Lee, C. D. (2005a). Culture and language: Bi-dialectical issues in literacy. In P. L. Anders & J. Flood (Eds.), *Literacy development of students in urban schools: Research and policy* (pp. 241–274). Newark, DE: International Reading Association.

Lee, C. D. (2005b). Double voiced discourse: African American Vernacular English as resource in cultural modeling classrooms. In A. F. Ball & S. W. Freedman (Eds.), *New literacies for new times: Bakhtinian perspectives on language, literacy, and learning for the 21st century.* New York: Cambridge University Press.

Lee, C. D. (2006). Every good-bye ain't gone: Analyzing the cultural underpinnings of classroom talk. *International Journal of Qualitative Studies in Education, 19*, 305–327.

Lee, C. D. (2007). *Culture, literacy and learning: Taking bloom in the midst of the whirlwind.* New York: Teachers College Press.

Lee, C. D. (2008). The centrality of culture to the scientific study of learning and development: How an ecological framework in educational research facilitates civic responsibility. *Educational Researcher, 37*(5), 267–279.

Lee, C. D., Spencer, M. B., & Harpalani, V. (2003). Every shut eye ain't sleep: Studying how people live culturally. *Educational Researcher, 32*(5), 6–13.

Makoni, S., Smitherman, G., Ball, A., & Spears, A. (Eds.). (2003). *Black linguistics: Language, society, and politics in Africa and the Americas.* New York: Routledge.

McLaughlin, M. W. (1993). Embedded identities: Enabling balance in urban contexts. In S. B. Heath & M. W. McLaughlin (Eds.), *Identity and inner-city youth: Beyond ethnicity and gender* (pp. 36–68). New York: Teachers College Press.

McLaughlin, M. W., Langman, J., & Irby, M. (1994). *Urban sanctuaries: Neighborhood organizations in the lives and futures of inner-city youth.* San Francisco: Jossey-Bass.

Mercado, C. I., & Moll, L. (1997). The study of funds of knowledge: Collaborative research in Latino homes. *CENTRO, Journal of the Center for Puerto Rican Studies, 9*(1), 27–42.

Moje, E. B., Young, J. P., Readence, J. E., & Moore, D. W. (2000). Teenagers in new times: A new literacy studies perspective. *Journal of Adolescent and Adult Literacy, 43*(5), 412–422.

Moll, L. (2000). Inspired by Vygotsky: Ethnographic experiments in education. In C. D. Lee & P. Smagorinsky (Eds.), *Vygotskian perspectives on literacy research: Constructing meaning through collaborative inquiry* (pp. 256–268). New York: Cambridge University Press.

Moll, L. C., & González, N. (2004). Engaging life: A funds-of-knowledge approach to multicultural education. In J. Banks & C. A. M. Banks (Eds.), *Handbook of research on multicultural education* (2nd ed., pp. 699–715). New York: Jossey-Bass.

Moll, L., & Greenberg, J. B. (1990). Creating zones of possibilities: Combining social contexts for instruction. In L. Moll (Ed.), *Vygotsky and education: Instructional implications and applications of sociohistorical psychology* (pp. 319–348). New York: Cambridge University Press.

Morrell, E. (2002). Toward a critical pedagogy of popular culture: Literacy development among urban youth. *Journal of Adolescent and Adult Literacy, 46*(1), 72–78.

Morrell, E., & Duncan-Andrade J. (2002). Promoting academic literacy with urban youth through engaging hip-hop culture. *English Journal, 91*(6), 88–93.

Moses, R. P. (1994). The struggle for citizenship and math/sciences literacy. *Journal of Mathematical Behavior, 13,* 107–111.

Moses, R. P., & Cobb, C. E. (2001). *Radical equations: Math literacy and civil rights.* Boston: Beacon Press.

Moses, R. P., Kamii, M., Swap, S. M., & Howard, J. (1989). The Algebra Project: Organizing in the Spirit of Ella. *Harvard Educational Review, 59*(4), 423–443.

Mufwene, S., Rickford, J., Bailey, G., & Baugh, J. (1998). *African-American English: Structure, history and use.* New York: Routledge.

Murray, C. B., & Mandara, J. (2003). An assessment of the relationship between racial socialization, racial identity and self-esteem in African American adolescents. In D. A. Azibo (Ed.), *Africa-centered psychology* (pp. 293–325). Durham, NC: Carolina Academic Press.

Nasir, N. S., Rosebery, A. S., Warren, B., & Lee, C. D. (2006). Learning as a cultural process: Achieving equity through diversity. In K. Sawyer (Ed.), *The Cambridge handbook of the learning sciences* (pp. 489–504). New York: Cambridge University Press.

Nixon, A. S., & Gutiérrez, K. (2007). Digital literacies for young English learners: Productive pathways toward equity and robust learning. In C. Genishi & A. L. Goodwin (Eds.), *Diversities in early childhood education: Rethinking and doing* (pp. 121–135). New York: Routledge.

Orellana, M. (2009). *Translating immigrant childhoods: Children's work as culture and language brokers.* New Brunswick, NJ: Rutgers University Press.

Orellana, M., Reynolds, J., Dorner, L., & Meza, M. (2003). In other words: Translating or "paraphrasing" as a family literacy practice in immigrant households. *Reading Research Quarterly, 38*(1), 12–34.

Perry, T., & Delpit, L. (1998). *The real Ebonics debate: Power, language and the education of African-American children.* Boston: Beacon Press.

Purves, A. (1991). *The idea of difficulty in literature.* New York: State University of New York Press.

Rogoff, B. (2003). *The cultural nature of human development.* Oxford, UK: Oxford University Press.

Rogoff, B., Paradise, R., Arauz, R. M., Correa-Chávez, M., & Angelillo, C. (2003). Firsthand learning through intent participation. *Annual Review of Psychology, 54,* 175–203.

Rosebery, A. S., Warren, B., Ballenger, C., & Ogonowski, M. (2005). The generative potential of students' everyday knowledge in learning science. In T. Romberg, T. Carpenter, & D. Fae (Eds.), *Understanding mathematics and science matters* (pp. 55–80). Mahwah, NJ: Erlbaum.

Rosebery, A. S., Warren, B., & Conant, F. R. (1992). Appropriating scientific discourse: Findings from language minority classrooms. *Journal of the Learning Sciences, 2*(1), 61–94.

Scholes, R. (1985). *Textual power, literary theory and the teaching of English.* New Haven, CT: Yale University Press.

Scribner, S., & Cole, M. (1973). Cognitive consequences of formal and informal education: New accommodations are needed between school-based learning and learning experiences of everyday life. *Science, 182,* 553–559.

Scribner, S., & Cole, M. (1981). *The psychology of literacy.* Cambridge, MA: Harvard University Press.

Smith, M. (1989). Teaching the interpretation of irony in poetry. *Research in the Teaching of English, 23,* 254–272.

Smith, M. (1991a). Constructing meaning from text: An analysis of ninth-grade reader responses. *Journal of Educational Research, 84*(5), 263–271.

Smith, M. (1991b). *Understanding unreliable narrators: Reading between the lines in the literature classroom.* Urbana, IL: National Council of Teachers of English.

Smith, M., & Hillocks, G. (1988, October). Sensible sequencing: Developing knowledge about literature text by text. *English Journal,* pp. 44–49.

Smitherman, G. (1977). *Talkin and testifyin: The language of Black America.* Boston: Houghton Mifflin.

Spencer, M. B. (2006). Phenomenology and ecological systems theory: Development of diverse groups. In W. Damon & R. M. Lerner (Eds.), *Handbook of child psychology* (6th ed., Vol. 1, pp. 829–893). New York: Wiley.

Steele, C. M. (2004). A threat in the air: How stereotypes shape intellectual identity and performance. In J. Banks & C. Banks (Eds.), *Handbook of research on multicultural education* (2nd ed., pp. 682–698). San Francisco: Jossey-Bass.

Street, B. V. (1993). *Cross-cultural approaches to literacy.* Cambridge, UK: Cambridge University Press.

Trabasso, T., & van den Broek, P. (1985). Causal thinking and the representation of narrative events. *Journal of Memory and Language, 24,* 612–630.

Valdés, G. (2002). *Expanding the definitions of giftedness: The case of young interpreters from immigrant countries.* Mahwah, NJ: Erlbaum.

van den Broek, P. (1996). Causal inferences in the comprehension of literary texts. In R. J. Kreuz & M. S. MacNealy (Eds.), *Empirical approaches to literature and aesthetics.* Norwood, NJ: Ablex.

Warren, B., Ballenger, C., Ogonowski, M., Rosebery, A. S., & Hudicourt-Barnes, J. (2001). Rethinking diversity in learning science: The logic of everyday sense-making. *Journal of Research in Science Teaching, 38,* 529–552.

# CHAPTER 12

# Assessing Student Progress
# in the Time of No Child Left Behind

GEORGIA EARNEST GARCÍA AND EURYDICE B. BAUER

Under the No Child Left Behind Act (NCLB, 2001), the role of assessment has changed, so that formal literacy assessments no longer sample student performance but now play a major role in defining student progress (National Clearinghouse for English Language Acquisition, 2006). Teachers are supposed to use data from students' test performance to inform their literacy instruction, and educators and policymakers are supposed to use student test performance to evaluate instruction. The types of formal tests emphasized have changed from norm-referenced assessments, which are designed to sort and rank student performance according to the performance of other students, to standards-based assessments.

Standards-based assessments are designed so that there is for each domain a range of test items that, when aggregated, are supposed to characterize student performance according to certain levels of performance-based expectations or standards (e.g., needs improvement, basic, proficient, advanced). Student performance is evaluated according to the attainment of the standard, and every student whose performance meets the same standard receives the same score. Because the test items on standards-based assessments are supposed to be drawn from the domain being taught and, therefore, "aligned" with instruction, student performance on the assessment also is supposed to be used to evaluate and inform instruction.

According to the American Psychological Association, assessments should be evaluated according to their validity (e.g., Does the content of the assessment adequately reflect the construct being measured?), reliability (Are the results of the assessment consistent with those of other assessments that measure the same construct for the same students?), and fairness (Are the test construction, scoring, and reporting procedures free from linguistic and cultural biases?) (Messick, 1994; National Clearinghouse for English Language Acquisition, 2006). Several assessment experts have warned that "consequential validity" also should be considered (Linn, Baker, & Dunbar, 1991), which involves examining how test results differentially affect the education and lives of diverse groups of test takers (García & Pearson, 1994).

The purpose of this chapter is to review research relevant to the current and future literacy assessment situation in the United States. Although changes in NCLB are likely to occur when Congress reauthorizes the legislation, the focus on standards and the use of formal assessments to evaluate student performance and monitor student progress, as well as inform instruction, are expected to continue. Therefore, we have chosen to focus our review on the types of assessments required by NCLB (2001) for students enrolled in Reading First (grades 1–3), students receiving Title I services in grades 3–8, and English language learners (ELLs; grades 1–8) funded through Title III. Our emphasis is on the use of assessments with students from diverse backgrounds: students who attend schools of poverty and students who are ELLs. We have organized the chapter to focus on the following topics:

- The role of assessment in NCLB
- Historical research on formal literacy assessments
- Research on literacy assessments used in Reading First
- Research on literacy assessments used in Title I (grades 3–8)
- Research on language and literacy assessments used with ELLs in grades 1–8 (Title III)

We conclude the chapter by discussing implications for classroom practice and future research.


## THE ROLE OF ASSESSMENT IN THE NCLB LEGISLATION

In one of the most sweeping reforms of education in the United States, in 2002, President George W. Bush signed into law the No Child Left Behind Act of 2001. A major goal of the law is to pressure school districts across the country to narrow the gap between "disadvantaged and minority students and their peers" (*www.ed.gov/programs/readingfirst/legislation.html*). There are four guiding principles: stronger accountability for results, increased flexibility and local control, expanded parent options, and an emphasis on proven teaching methods.

To receive federal funds, states and school districts have to provide instruction based on "scientifically based reading research" and use specific types of assessments. For example, low-income, low-performing schools with students in grades 1–3 may receive federal funding under Reading First, an initiative of

NCLB, if they provide students with reading instruction and assessments that the federal government views as representative of scientifically based research. Under Title I, NCLB requires all states to select or design a standards-based reading/ language arts assessment that is administered annually to every student in grades 3–8 and once in high school. In addition, under Title III, all ELLs in grades 1–8 have to participate in specific types of language and literacy assessments. Below we describe the NCLB literacy assessment requirements for Reading First, Title I, and Title III.

## Reading First

The goal of Reading First is to ensure that all children read at or above grade level by the end of third grade. Reading First provides grants to states with low-performing schools, and the states fund individual school districts through sub-grants. To receive Reading First funds, school districts have to propose and implement a research-based pedagogical plan designed to raise the performance of all K–3 students to grade-level performance. The district plans have to address the five components of the National Reading Panel's report on early reading: phonemic awareness, phonics, vocabulary, fluency, and reading comprehension (National Institute of Child Health and Human Development, 2000). Reading First funds may be spent on curricula and instructional materials, interventions for struggling readers, professional staff development and training, and assessments for the screening and diagnosis of early reading difficulties and monitoring of student progress (Institute of Education Sciences [IES], 2008). Progress monitoring has to occur at least three times per year, so that students' instruction is adjusted appropriately. To make sure that all student groups benefit, assessment results have to be disaggregated and reported according to income, racial groups, ELLs, and special education populations at the school, district, and state levels.

## Title I (Students in Grades 3–8)

All students in grades 3–8 who attend public schools in states that receive federal funding must participate on a yearly basis in a standards-based reading/language arts assessment to show their annual progress and attainment of reading/ language arts, including ELLs who have been in U.S. schools for longer than 12 months. States may choose or develop their own assessment, but the assessment has to be based on state literacy standards. School and district reports, along with individual student reports, have to show the annual test results. In the school and district reports, the test data have to be disaggregated and reported according to "gender, each major racial and ethnic group, migrant status, students with disabilities, students with limited English proficiency, and economically disadvantaged students" (U.S. Department of Education, 2003, p. 11). In addition, an "academic indicator" other than the "proficiency targets" on the state test also has to be defined and met (IES, 2007, p. 4).

The assessment is called "high stakes" because by 2013–2014, the federal government requires that 100% of the students in each school meet or exceed the state literacy standards. To show their progress in meeting the state standards, schools have to establish baseline data for each of the subgroups and set annual measurable achievement objectives (AMAOs). To demonstrate that the school is making adequate yearly progress (AYP) toward meeting the 100% goal in 2014, 95% of all the students in each subgroup must participate in the annual assessment, and each subgroup has to meet the prespecified AMAOs. If either of the two conditions is not met for every school subgroup, the school is evaluated as failing to make AYP (U.S. Department of Education, 2003). Schools not making AYP for 2 consecutive years must implement required interventions, which includes offering students the option of transferring to a different school. Those not making AYP 5 years in a row must choose from a number of high-stakes options, which include the replacement of all or most of their staff, reopening as charter schools, or state takeover (IES, 2007).

School districts may receive funds under Title I for schoolwide improvements when not less than 40% of the children in the attendance area are from low-income families, or not less than 40% of the school enrollment is from low-income families (NCLB, Title I). Schools receiving Title I funds may use other assessments, in addition to the mandated state tests, to monitor their progress toward attaining AYP.

## English Language Learners

Title III of NCLB specifies procedures for evaluating the English proficiency and language arts/reading performance of ELLs. The AYP results are to be disaggregated according to gender, the native languages spoken by the children, their socioeconomic status, and whether the children are disabled.

To determine the English language proficiency of all entering ELLs, school personnel are supposed to ask the children's parents or legal guardians to complete a home language survey to indicate the languages spoken in the home and whether the children speak a language other than English. If the survey indicates that the children may be ELLs, then school personnel are required to give the children a standards-based language proficiency test to determine whether they are limited English proficient (LEP). Children classified as LEP are supposed to receive appropriate services to help them attain English proficiency (e.g., placement in a bilingual education or English as a second language [ESL] program; National Clearinghouse for English Language Acquisition, 2006).

For all students classified as LEP, and for those who for 2 previous years were classified as LEP, district personnel have to administer an annual standards-based language proficiency test to determine the students' English attainment and AYP (U. S. Department of Education, 2006). The standards-based language proficiency test has to be based on English language proficiency standards developed by the respective states; evaluate students' "level of comprehension, speaking, listening, reading, and writing skills in English"; and evaluate whether students have the conversational and academic language proficiencies needed to perform on grade level in all-English classrooms (NCLB, Title III, p. 1702). In addition, the assessment is supposed to indicate the student's stage of English language proficiency development. To help determine when students are ready to leave the bilingual or ESL program and be placed in an all-English classroom, districts may administer other types of assessments, including classroom-based assessments or academic, norm-referenced assessments.

Under Title I, ELLs in grades 3–8 also have to participate in a standards-based reading/language arts assessment that is different from the standards-based language proficiency test described earlier. They may participate in the same standards-based English reading/language arts assessment administered to everyone in the school, a standards-based English reading/language arts assessment designed just for ELLs, or a standards-based reading/language arts assessment in the home language "until such students have achieved English language proficiency" (NCLB, Title 1, p. 115, Stat. 1451). If students have been in the United States for at least 3 years, then they have to participate in a standards-based reading/language arts assessment in English. However, schools still may test the latter children for up to 2 more years in the native language "on an individual case-by-case basis" if they think the data will be "more accurate and reliable" (p. 115, Stat. 1451). When ELLs are given the same English assessment as everyone else in the school, then testing accommodations may be used, such as providing additional time to complete the assessment, simplified instructions, or audiotaped instructions in English or in the native language.

## HISTORICAL RESEARCH ON FORMAL LITERACY ASSESSMENT

### Problems with Reading Comprehension Assessment

Unfortunately, the movement to standards-based assessments progressed much more rapidly than the ability of test developers or literacy researchers to design the types of reading comprehension measures requested by many literacy experts. For example, the RAND Reading Study Group's report on reading comprehension (2002; Snow, 2003) called for the development of a comprehensive assessment system that would be standards based, inform instruction, and improve student comprehension performance. This assessment system was to include "accountability-focused" assessments and classroom teachers' assessment of reading skills, so that teachers could "adapt and individualize teaching" to "improve outcomes" (Snow, 2003, p. 192). The RAND Reading Study Group (2002) recommended that the assessments in the system should be valid and reliable, "reflect progress toward reading benchmarks" and be closely tied to the curriculum being taught (Snow, 2003, p. 193). The group wanted a set of assessments that could evaluate different aspects of the reading comprehension process, such as "strategic, self-regulated reading"; "motivation and engagement"; and fluency; as well as evaluate the effectiveness of specific types of instruction with different types of readers (Snow, 2003, pp. 200–201).

The RAND Reading Study Group (2002; Snow, 2003) acknowledged that the field of reading assessment still had to confront major challenges in evaluating students' reading comprehension, including how to capture the complexity of the reading comprehension process in an assessment system; how to design test items for a comprehension assessment, so that they are not "unduly simple" and narrow; and how to identify when a student's performance reflects specific comprehension breakdowns (e.g., poor inferencing, lack of key vocabulary, lack of word recognition or decoding). The RAND Reading Study Group also warned against using assessments that would "narrow the curriculum" and not capture essential outcomes of effective reading, such as "comprehension for engagement, for aesthetic response, for purposes of critiquing an argument or disagreeing with a position" because such neglect could lead to classroom instruction that would not develop such outcomes (Snow, 2003, p. 195).

## Biases in the Development of Formal Assessments

In 1994, García and Pearson published a historical review of the assessment literature from a diversity perspective. In their review, they observed that the historical development of formal assessments, such as IQ tests, was based on the assumption that for the tests to sort the performance of U.S. participants effectively, they should result in high scores for the types of individuals that U.S. society viewed as being successful. In the early 1900s, the favored population was Anglo-Saxon, Protestant, middle- and upper-class males. When test items resulted in a higher performance of women, as compared to men, the items that favored women were disregarded and eliminated (Mercer, 1989). Karier (1973) revealed that this type of cultural bias also occurred with an IQ test in the 1960s, when students were asked to select the drawing that was prettier, that of a Nordic/Anglo female (the answer considered to be correct) or that of a Mexican American/southern European.

Although standards-based tests are not designed to sort students according to a bell curve (García & Pearson, 1994), they still are designed according to the performance expectations for a "typical" student at the various proficiency levels. García and Pearson (1994) explain that "a test is considered biased when it over- or under-predicts the performance of particular groups in relation to the performance of the mainstream group" (p. 344). The expected alignment of standards-based tests with teachers' instruction and use of curricular materials may help to decrease the amount of topical or content bias on standards-based tests. However, other cultural and linguistic testing issues need to be considered, such as the point of view or interpretation expected on the test, the familiarity of the language and vocabulary employed on the test, and the extent to which students from diverse groups find the test to be engaging or motivating. Finally, the extent to which standards-based tests accurately reflect the performance of readers (high, average, and low) from diverse backgrounds still needs to be determined.

## Problems with Assessments for ELLs

Two sets of reviewers have identified a number of problems, in addition to the previously mentioned biases, that still occur when assessing the language or literacy performance of ELLs (García, McKoon, & August, 2006, 2008; García & Pearson, 1994). First, due to differences in the development of receptive (reading and listening) and productive skills (writing and speaking), ELLs often demonstrate more comprehension of English reading when they are allowed to respond in their dominant language. Second, because ELLs tend to process text in their second language, and in some cases in both languages, more slowly than monolinguals, they may need more time than monolinguals to complete written tests. Third, their limited English proficiency may mean that they will miss identifying the correct answers on a formal reading test due to unfamiliar English vocabulary in the test instructions or in the test items. Fourth, their vocabulary knowledge sometimes is underestimated, because they know some vocabulary concepts in one language and different vocabulary concepts in another language.

The available language proficiency assessments have been criticized (García et al., 2008), because they tend to sample language skills related to oral language development (e.g., phonology, syntax, morphology, and lexicon) rather than evaluate how students use language in real-life settings. More importantly, they often focus on social language rather than the type of academic language that ELLs need to understand instruction in English and to learn new concepts from written texts in English.

Knowing when ELLs are proficient enough in English to participate in an English assessment normed on or designed for monolingual English speakers is a question that still has not been answered (García et al., 2008; Hakuta & Beatty, 2000). According to the Standards of Educational and Psychological Testing (American Educational Research Association, American Psychological Association, and National Council on Measurement in Education, 1999), when examinees "do not speak the language of the test as their primary language," then "the test user should investigate the validity of the score interpretations ... [because] the achievement, abilities, and traits of [such] examinees ... may be seriously mismeasured by the test" (p. 118). Similarly, "test norms based on native speakers of English either should not be used with individuals whose first language is not English or such individuals' test results should be interpreted as reflecting in part current level of English proficiency" (p. 91).

A major problem in using formal assessments with ELLs is that they "highlight what students cannot do while ignoring and failing to build upon what students can do" (Ivey & Broaddus, 2007, p. 541). Bernhardt (2003) warns that it is especially difficult to use assessments to diagnose ELLs individually when the assessments do not consider the students' performance from a native-language perspective and take into account differences between English and the native language in lexicon, morphology, phonology, semantics, and syntax.

Solano-Flores and Trumbell (2003) contend that current assessment practices for ELLs do not acknowledge students' bilingualism and "the complex nature of language, including its interrelationship with culture" (p. 3). They argue that assessment practices for ELLs should take into account contextual factors that may affect test item interpretation (e.g., cultural and linguistic scripts or frames); that consider the concept of validity from a "sociocultural view of cognition," in which "culture and society shape minds" or thinking (p. 4); and that is based on continua of bilingual proficiency, in which test performance reflects varied "patterns of language dominance," and "strengths may be expressed differently in different contexts (e.g., home or school) and in the written and oral modes" (p. 4).

## RESEARCH ON ASSESSMENTS AND READING FIRST

The assessment tool that most often is used in Reading First is the Dynamic Indicators of Basic Early Literacy Skills (DIBELS; Good & Kaminski, 2002), also available in Spanish. DIBELS was developed at the University of Oregon to facilitate "early and accurate identification of students (K–3) in need of intervention" and to predict future reading difficulty (Riedel, 2007, p. 546). The assessment may be downloaded at no cost, but schools must pay to have their student data analyzed (see *dibels.uoregon.edu*). The DIBELS maps onto the Reading First early reading requirements and includes 1-minute subtests administered to students individually: Letter Naming Fluency (LNF), Initial Sound Fluency (ISF), Phoneme Segmentation Fluency (PSF), Nonsense Word Fluency (NWF), Oral Reading Fluency (ORF), Retell Fluency (RF), and Word Use Fluency (WUF).

Several researchers have voiced concerns about DIBELS due to its pervasiveness, narrow reading focus, and influence on the curriculum (Allington & Nowak, 2004; Goodman, 2006). According to the DIBELS website, over 14,000 schools reported using the data system for the 2007–2008 school year (*dibels. uoregon.edu/data/index.php*). Although supporters and critics of DIBELS agree that reading comprehension is the ultimate goal of reading, Riedel (2007) reports that not all of the subtests (e.g., LNF and PSF) have predicted students' comprehension on other types of reading comprehension measures, even though students' scores on the early subtests may significantly correlate with their ORF scores.

Riedel (2007) conducted a study to investigate how well several of the subtests (LNF, PSF, NWF, ORF, RF) administered to urban, predominantly African American first graders (*n* = 1,518) at the beginning, middle, and end of first grade predicted students' reading comprehension and vocabulary on other formal measures at the end of first and second grade. He reported that the ORF administered in the middle and end of first grade was the best predictor of students' comprehension test performance at the end of first grade on the Group Reading Assessment and Diagnostic Evaluation (GRA+DE, 2008; Williams, 2001), and at the end of second grade on the Terra Nova (CTB/McGraw-Hill, 2003). GRA+DE is a standardized reading assessment that at the primary level includes receptive vocabulary measures, in which students select pictures to match written words and identify the words read by the teacher, and a sentence comprehension measure, in which students select the best words to complete the sentences, and a passage comprehension measure. The ORF scores predicted the first and second graders' reading comprehension status accurately 80 and 71% of the time, respectively, with the PSF and NWF scores at the end of first grade misjudging students' comprehension 47% and 32% of the time, respectively. ORF scores at the end of first grade also were strong predictors of comprehension on the GRA+DE for the 59 ELLs who participated in the study, with the PSF again the weakest. Riedel concluded that by the middle of first grade, there was no reason to administer any of the DIBELS subtests other than ORF.

Riedel (2007) questioned whether the ORF can indicate the type of intervention needed for struggling readers, because it does not provide any diagnostic information. He noted that 15% of the students who scored satisfactorily on the ORF had poor comprehension and vocabulary skills on the GRA+DE, and he wondered whether the latter students would have benefited from a vocabulary intervention. Samuels (2007) also observed that the ORF's focus on fluency is faulty, because it only measures the number of words read correctly in 1 minute and does not measure both decoding and comprehension.

Clearly, administration of DIBELS to students from diverse backgrounds, especially those who speak African American Vernacular English or ESL, does not address the bias issues we addressed previously in this chapter. Riedel (2007) points out that DIBELS is normed on a homogeneous population, and Goodman (2006) warns that it overemphasizes children's correct pronunciation of English.

Several critics have voiced serious concerns about the type of instruction and interventions that students in Reading First receive (Allington & Nowak, 2004; Stewart, 2004; Teale, Paciga, & Hoffman, 2007). For example, the required sequential administration of subtests on the DIBELS means that students who do not do well on one of the "stepping-stone" subtests are kept at that level until they demonstrate mastery of the skill (Institute for Development of Educational Achievement, *idea.uoregon.edu*), narrowing students' exposure to other aspects of reading instruction. Teale and his colleagues (2007) observe that due to the type of professional staff development provided to teachers and the types of assessments employed, reading instruction for young children in schools funded by Reading First is only "about children learning phonological awareness, how to decode, and how to read words accurately and fluently" (p. 345).

Stewart (2004) explains that although Reading First does not mandate the use of specific curriculum programs, Congressional regulations that interpret the law do specify that school districts must use a portion of the Reading First funds to purchase a comprehensive, published program. She questions whether a "one-size-fits-all" practice, in which common assessments and a commercial reading curriculum are implemented so that all students at the same grade level are on the same page, will result in improvements in student motivation and engagement. Based on a review of effective classrooms, Stewart states that students are motivated and engaged readers when teachers implement student-centered instruction to "hook [the] learner in multiple ways" (p. 734). According to Stewart, effective teachers are "dynamic—adjusting to the needs of their students" and will have "different teaching styles, personalities, and beliefs" (p. 734).

After conducting classroom visits and interviews with literacy leaders in urban schools, Teale and colleagues (2007) concluded that the implementation of Reading First has led to a curriculum gap for K–3 children in low-income schools. They warn that the assessment and instructional emphases on phonics and word recognition skills have resulted in teachers in Reading First emphasizing short-term goals and ignoring long-term goals, such as postponing comprehension instruction, and exposing students to high-quality text beyond their actual decoding levels. They point out that teachers' instruction in low-income schools is ignoring a key question (p. 345): "What is going to make young children be readers, now and when they are teenagers and adults?"

A recent evaluation (IES, 2008) revealed that Reading First instruction did not result in increased percentages of first, second, or third graders with reading comprehension test scores at or above grade level. In fact, at each of the grade levels, "fewer than half of the students in the Reading First schools were reading at or above grade level" (p. 6). These findings were in spite of the fact that first- and second-grade teachers in Reading First spent increased class time on the five essential components of reading instruction required by Reading First. According to the *Washington Post* (Glod, 2008), Dr. Grover J. Whitehurst, director of the IES, offered two explanations for the evaluation findings: "It's possible that, in implementing Reading First, there is a greater emphasis on decoding skills and not enough emphasis, or maybe not correctly structured emphasis, on reading comprehension." Also, it is possible that the Reading First program helps children to establish the building-block skills but does not "take children far enough along to have a significant impact on comprehension" (p. A01).

## RESEARCH ON THE USE OF LITERACY ASSESSMENTS FOR TITLE I (GRADES 3–8)

In 2005–2006, every state used a standards-based reading/language arts test for students in grades 3–8 as prescribed by NCLB, with 24 of the states receiving federal approval of the tests (IES, 2007). However, 20 states still had to revise or improve their standards-based assessment. In 2004–2005, schools with high percentages of poor and minority students, and those in urban areas, were more likely to be identified as schools not meeting their AYP and needing improvement (32% of high-poverty schools and 31% of high-minority schools) compared to schools with lower percentages of poverty and minority students, and in nonurban areas (4%) (IES, 2007).

Because the states do not use the same sets of standards for their assessments, critics have warned that states can skew the performance of their students by setting their standards too low. The Title I evaluation (IES, 2007) indicated that those states less likely to meet AYP in 2004–2005 were the ones that had set "more challenging proficiency standards than other states" and had "further to go to reach the NCLB goal of 100 percent proficient" (p. 13). For example, states with high standards had to increase their students' performance by 81% compared to states with moderate standards (an increase of 59%) and low standards (an increase of 49%).

Although all public schools with federal funding have to show AYP, those with Title I funding are more influenced by the NCLB requirements than those without Title I funding. In 2004–2005, Title I funds went to 56% of U.S. public schools, with 72% going to elementary schools (pre-K–6). Two-thirds of the student participants were minority students (IES, 2007). Title I funds may be used for curriculum, computers, and instructional services and resources, including salaries for teachers and aides. Similar to Reading First, curricula and instructional methods have to be consistent with "scientifically based research" (IES, 2007).

The actual percentage of students who qualify for free and reduced lunch often influences the approach taken by the district to address student needs. For example, if a school has 40% or more students who qualify for free and reduced-price lunch, the district may decide to implement a schoolwide assessment and instructional program. In cases where the percentage may be below 35%, schools may choose to target their assistance only to students in need.

About one-third of the elementary schools needing improvement in 2004–2005 reported that they increased the amount of daily instructional time in reading by 30 minutes, and three-fourths of them offered afterschool or extended-time instructional programs (IES, 2007). The extent to which such efforts are improving student's reading performance is uncertain. An evaluation of four popular supplementary programs (Corrective Reading, Failure Free Reading, Spell Read P. A. T. [Phonological Auditory Training], and Wilson Reading) was conducted 1 year after the programs had been implemented with third and fifth graders in a school district in Pennsylvania, in which 45% of the students qualified for free or reduced lunch, and 28% were African American and 72% were European American (Torgensen et al., 2006, as cited in IES, 2007). Only the word level plus comprehension program (Failure Free Reading) had an impact on the third graders' reading comprehension, in addition to an impact on phonemic decoding, word reading accuracy, and fluency. The other three programs, which were considered word level programs, impacted the third graders' word attack and identification performance but did not have any impact on their reading comprehension, as measured by commercial reading comprehension tests. Very few of the programs had any impact on the fifth graders' performance, with the word level programs only improving the fifth graders' performance on the phonemic decoding measures. None of the programs resulted in improved performance of the third graders on the state assessment (Pennsylvania System of School Assessment), whereas the performance of the fifth graders actually decreased on the state assessment.

The high-stakes nature of the required literacy assessment in grades 3–8 means that schools often use a range of assessments, in addition to the required state standards assessment, to monitor student progress and guide teachers' instruction. Among others, these include DIBELS, commercial curriculum and district-generated exams, and the Developmental Reading Assessment (DRA and DRA2) (Beaver, 2006). For example, several school districts in the Midwest use the ORF and the RF from the DIBELS with fourth and fifth graders at the beginning of the school year to place students in reading groups and at the end of the school year to determine student progress. Although we searched for information on the validity, reliability, and usefulness of curriculum and district-generated assessments with students from diverse backgrounds, no empirical research was found.

The DRA is a criterion-based performance assessment for students in grades K–8. According to Beaver (2006), the DRA helps students become proficient, enthusiastic readers who read for a variety of purposes. It "assesses student performance in … reading engagement, oral reading fluency, and comprehension" (p. 6). A more recent version, the revised DRA2 (Beaver, 2006), is described as evaluating how well students read orally and comprehend fiction and nonfiction in Benchmark Assessment Books ranging from Level A (emerging reader) to Level 40 (fourth grade). Teachers record individual students' reading engagement; oral reading fluency; the number of miscues not self-corrected; how students retell the text, paying attention to key events from the beginning, middle, and end of a story; and students' reflections on the text. Student scores from the oral reading fluency and comprehension components determine students' independent, instructional, and advanced reading levels. Teachers' evaluations of individual students are guided by fiction and nonfiction continua that are linked to the level of the text being read and the type of reading behavior teachers should see in their students.

The validity and reliability of the DRA are fairly strong for evaluating students' reading comprehension, making it a much better reading comprehension assessment than the DIBELS for middle-class, native-English-speaking students. Williams (1999) reported that student DRA scores from a large urban school district significantly correlated with their vocabulary, reading comprehension, and total reading scores on the Iowa Test of Basic Skills at the .01 level, with the highest correlation for total reading ($r = .70$). Williams also reported that the inter-rater reliability for two teacher raters was strong ($r = .80$), although this reliability declined when three raters were used. However, the validity and reliability of the DRA with students from diverse backgrounds generally is not known. Similarly, use of the DRA or DRA2 to inform teachers' reading instruction of students from diverse backgrounds has not been evaluated.

Findings on the success of NCLB are mixed, depending on the evaluation metric and timing of the implementation. For example, Title I evaluation results for states that had 3-year trend data (2002–2003 and 2004–2005) showed that "the percentage of [elementary] students achieving at or above the state's proficient level rose for most subgroups in a majority of the states" (IES, 2007, p. 8). Low-income students in 27 of 35 states showed achievement gains on the state reading assessment in fourth grade "or an adjacent elementary grade" (p. 8). These gains occurred in all of the low-income subgroups (e.g., 77% of black students, 80% of Hispanic students, 77% of LEP students, and 71% of white students). However, the rates of change were not large enough for the states to meet the 100% proficient target in 2013–2014. Also, eighth graders did not make gains in reading on any of the state tests. Perhaps, most importantly, the amount of time that had elapsed between the time of NCLB implementation and the evaluation was too short to determine whether improvements were due to NCLB or to other factors (IES, 2007).

The National Assessment of Educational Progress (*nces.ed.gov/nationsreportcard*) trend data, based on the same type of assessment since the 1970s, showed that black and Hispanic fourth graders had made significantly greater gains in reading than white students between 1992 and 2005, although some of the yearly changes from 2002 to 2005 were not statistically significant. Whether these gains were due to the implementation of NCLB is uncertain. Also, even though black and Hispanic students made gains, their 2005 average scale scores still were 29 and 27 points, respectively, below those of white students.

## RESEARCH ON THE USE OF LANGUAGE
## AND LITERACY ASSESSMENTS WITH ELLs

Although NCLB requires schools to use standards-based language proficiency assessments to evaluate the English language proficiency of all students classified as LEP, and to use such assessments, along with other types of assessments, to determine the appropriate placement and exit of LEP students from bilingual or ESL services, we do not know very much about the standards-based language proficiency assessments being developed or used (García et al., 2008). From a national evaluation of Title I (IES, 2007), we know that in 2004–2005, all of the states were implementing some type of ESL proficiency assessment, although 44 of them reported that they were planning to revise what they were using. Also, only 20 states said that they had ESL proficiency assessments that met current NCLB requirements. A serious problem that all the states face is the NCLB requirement that the language proficiency assessments should identify stages of language development of ELLs, a task that even commercial test developers have not been able to accomplish (García & DeNicolo, in press). Given the problems that commercial developers of language proficiency assessments face, the probability of states developing standards-based language proficiency measures that meet all of the NCLB conditions, including the evaluation of academic language proficiency, is highly questionable.

One set of researchers has investigated how well an English standards-based state reading test (in Kansas, and developed prior to NCLB) reliably predicted the performance of ELLs (Asian and Hispanic) compared to native-English speakers, and former ELLs (Asian and Hispanic) (Pomplun & Omar, 2001). Compared to a commercial standardized test of reading, the authors report that the state test had fewer but longer authentic passages and some constructed responses. They also found that the reliability of the standards-based state test was high for all of the learners, but there were some differences in the narrative scores of the ELLs and native-English speakers that may be due to differences in the students' cultural and linguistic backgrounds.

Although NCLB allows use of testing accommodations when ELLs are given reading/language arts assessments in English, almost all of the testing accommodation research has occurred with assessments in mathematics and science (García et al., 2006, 2008). García and DeNicolo (in press) point out that the reading construct itself (with its emphasis on vocabulary and syntax) makes the use of testing accommodations from mathematics and science assessments—such as simplified syntax, simplified vocabulary, glossaries or bilingual dictionaries, and dual-language tests—problematic. However, without effective accommodations, it will be difficult to know whether the test scores of ELLs on English reading tests reflect their LEP status or actual reading ability (Butler & Stevens, 2001).

When ELLs are included in English assessments developed for native-English speakers, such as DIBELS, the DRA, curriculum and district-generated assessments, and state standards-based tests, it is important to remember the previously discussed linguistic and cultural biases. For example, a key component of DIBELS is speed for accomplishing tasks on the subtests, yet research findings have shown that ELLs often need more time to process English, their second language, than do native-English speakers (García, 1991). Bauer's (in progress) work with her young German/English bilingual daughter revealed that when her daughter had to identify letters of the alphabet, she could identify most of the letters that were common across the two languages (i.e., /m/), but she was uncertain when the letters had two different names across the two languages (i.e., i = /e/ in German, and i = /i/ in English). She took longer to identify the letters with different names than she did for the letters with the same names.

Questions about the use of NCLB assessments and instructional practices with ELLs also have been raised. In a formative experiment in an ESL language arts classroom of immigrant ELLs (seventh and eighth graders), Ivey and Broaddus (2007) concluded that it is difficult to address ELL students' reading engagement and motivation, and the state literacy standards in 1 year. They warn that relegating struggling adolescent readers to low-level skills work "may be at odds with what engages students" (p. 518). They found that the typical assessments administered in middle school classrooms (Qualitative Reading Inventory—III, 2001; Standardized Test for the Assessment of Reading [STAR], 2003; as well as developmental spelling inventories in English and Spanish, and a writing sample) indicate very little useful information about ELL students' English literacy performance and the type of instruction that would be beneficial. The authors discovered that small-group guided-reading lessons, choral reading, and echo reading—techniques often used with young, struggling readers—did not result in increased reading or engagement. Effective intervention required the use of teacher readalouds and book talks to familiarize students with books, helping individual students to identify books in English and Spanish that they could comprehend, oral reading of complete books to individual students, the use of sheltered English with individual students to explain unfamiliar concepts or wording, and provision of class time for students to read. Student writing increased with dictations and the Language Experience Approach, in which students write in Spanish with English translation, mix Spanish and English, or write in English, along with the explicit use of writing models and patterns.

In addition to the problems that English assessments and instruction designed for native-English speakers pose for ELL students, other issues complicate the learning environment. Reflecting on the prohibition of bilingual education in Arizona and California, and how these policies have intersected with NCLB assessment and instructional requirements, Gutiérrez and her colleagues (2002) warn that there has been a "drastic increase in the implementation of mandated scripted reading programs at the expense of known effective instructional practices for second-language learners" (p. 334). Wright (2005) explains that even though states may require that ELLs participate in the state language arts assessment in English, they do not always report their annual progress. For example, the state of Arizona does not require schools to report the AYP of ELLs when there are less than 30 students enrolled in a single school. The end result is that the public does not know how ELLs are performing in many of the Arizona schools. The latter particularly is problematic given that bilingual education for ELLs younger than age 10 generally does not exist in Arizona. Wright explains that "the elimination of bilingual education (and ESL) and the imposition of the ill-defined SEI [Sheltered English Instruction] model, and the efforts to legally legitimize the placing of ELL students in mainstream classrooms will have a negative impact on the academic achievement of ELL students. The exclusion of ELL scores from the accountability program will help mask this failure" (p. 19).

## IMPLICATIONS FOR CLASSROOM PRACTICE

Given the limitations already noted in the required NCLB assessments for students from diverse backgrounds, it is important for school districts and teachers to know how to implement authentic classroom assessments to inform student instruction and monitor student progress, and to add information about the students' literacy development. García and Pearson (1994) characterize authentic classroom assessment as being "situated in the classroom, designed by the teacher, and used to evaluate student performance within the classroom curriculum context" (p. 357). Because authentic classroom assessments are supposed to be integrated with teachers' classroom instruction (García & DeNicolo, in press), these assessments should not reduce the time that teachers need to administer mandated NCLB assessments. Given the narrow focus on reading emphasized in Reading First, and the serious questions that the national evaluation of Reading First raised, the use of authentic assessments should allow teachers to go beyond the limited curricular emphasis in Reading First to focus on features of early reading instruction that have been found to be effective with students from diverse backgrounds in low-income schools (August et al., 2008; Goldenberg, Rueda, & August, 2008; Taylor, Pearson, Clark, & Walpole, 2000).

Authentic assessments also should allow schools and teachers to adapt assessment practices so that they are more fair, reliable, and valid for ELLs by allowing students to retell or answer comprehension questions about English texts in their dominant language, giving them more time to process assessment measures in English, and clarifying key vocabulary that may get in the way of understanding comprehension questions. Furthermore, if ELLs are given authentic assessments in their native language, then information that has been shown to predict their English reading performance (e.g., phonological awareness in the native language, a uniform view of reading across the two languages, cross-linguistic transfer of knowledge and strategies, reading level in the native language; García, 2003) can be obtained and used to evaluate student progress.

Bauer and Garcia (2002) report on a second-grade teacher who used authentic assessments over a school year to provide effective reading instruction to her students, some of whom were low-performing and from diverse backgrounds. Through the use of student-centered portfolios, she encouraged students to self-evaluate, enhanced her knowledge of individual students, and developed a keener awareness of what was needed to support each student's literacy development. The teacher held individual reading and writing conferences (four per month), in which she asked each student to discuss student-selected text and personal writing, to evaluate his or her progress, and to set literacy goals for each month. Because students' voices were heard and their ideas were honored, they became more engaged and enthusiastic. Assessment clearly influenced classroom instruction, because the teacher used what she learned from each student conference to inform her subsequent conferences and group reading instruction.

The employment of authentic assessments is consistent with the recommendation of Ivey and Broaddus (2007) that "formative assessments" (authentic assessments that change in the process of being implemented in the classroom to document student progress and inform effective instruction) should precede summative assessments (e.g., the assessments required by NCLB). Through the iterative process of the formative experiment, they were able to "determine the instructional strategies and reading materials" that led to improvements in the ELL students' reading engagement, reading performance, and oral English development, which changed the "context of instruction so that students operate[d] more strategically, enthusiastically, and productively" (p. 541). Effective use of authentic classroom assessments should help to supplement the information obtained through the required NCLB assessments and improve the quality of instruction that students from diverse backgrounds receive.

## IMPLICATIONS FOR FUTURE RESEARCH

Whether NCLB has resulted in high-quality literacy instruction for students from diverse backgrounds is an extremely important question that just now is being investigated. Considerably more research is needed to investigate the usefulness of DIBELS for the assessment and prediction of early reading difficulties in children from diverse backgrounds and the value of instruction derived from this type of assessment. Similarly, we need to know the extent to which states are developing valid, reliable, and fair language proficiency tests that capture the oral and academic language proficiency of ELL students and whether standards-based reading/language arts tests administered in English to ELLs are valid, reliable, and useful in informing their instruction. However, the field cannot wait too long for this type of research to occur, because the consequential validity issues are too serious. Teale and colleagues (2007) warn that for students in grades K–3, the combined impact of the required reading/language arts standards-based state test administered in third grade, along with the screening and progress-monitoring assessments used for Reading First, have "reinforced instructional practices focused on a limited set of foundational literacy skills" (p. 345). The poor Reading First evaluation results highlight the urgency with which literacy assessment and instructional research with students from diverse backgrounds needs to proceed.

Sadly, the literacy achievement gap between low-income and high-income children, which NCLB was designed to eradicate, continues to exist (Haycock, 2007). According to Teale and colleagues (2007), a "literacy achievement gap" occurs when a designated group of students scores significantly lower than another group. They point out that there has been a historical literacy achievement gap between low-income children and middle- and high-income children, and between African American and Latina/o children and European American children on the NAEP (2005). Furthermore, they point out that the two gaps are interrelated with NAEP studies of fourth- and eighth-grade reading achievement showing that the gaps in 2005 and 2003, respectively, were larger for students in urban schools than for those in other types of schools.

One of the problems with the standards-based state tests is that the standards do not tell us how to instruct students from diverse backgrounds so that the literacy gap can be resolved. Gutiérrez and her colleagues (2002) point out that low school resources in high-poverty schools are still an unresolved issue. We need high-quality research on the following:

- Reading and language assessments that take into account the concerns of the RAND Reading Study Group (2002), the linguistic and cultural biases reported for students from diverse backgrounds (García & Pearson, 1994), and the recommendations put forward for the improved language and literacy assessment of ELLs (García et al., 2006, 2008).
- The types of instruction and resource support that will result in higher literacy performance for *all* students in U.S. schools, recognizing that it is very likely that the type of instruction that works for one group of students may not work for another.
- The closure and eradication of the literacy gap between students from low-income families and those from middle- or upper-income families; students enrolled in urban, suburban, and rural schools; students from diverse ethnic/racial groups and language backgrounds; and students with and without disabilities.

## Concluding Remarks

To close and to eradicate the literacy performance gap between students from diverse backgrounds and their peers, it is imperative for policymakers to rely on more inclusive views of literacy, instructional research, and language and literacy assessments. In particular, we strongly encourage policymakers, and educators who implement the policies, to heed the warnings of reading researchers about the challenges of developing reading comprehension assessments that are too narrow and that do not focus on the multiple purposes and aspects of reading that may be motivating and engaging to students from diverse backgrounds. We urge policymakers and educators to pay attention to the types of instruction that have been found to be effective with students from diverse backgrounds, and to use these findings to inform instructional policies and practices. To avoid the use of biased and uninformative assessments, we recommend that policymakers fund the development and testing of language and literacy assessments that are valid and reliable, and linguistically and culturally fair for students from diverse backgrounds.

We also question whether one or two types of assessments can serve multiple purposes (e.g., determine student progress, evaluate student performance, inform student instruction, and evaluate teacher and school effectiveness). The weight and influence of only one or two assessments for such a range of purposes are too great, especially in the time of NCLB, to rely on only a few assessments for such important decisions. We recommend that educational personnel use a range of assessments, formal and classroom-based, for the varied purposes, and that policymakers accept their use.

To avoid issues of consequential validity, we strongly advise policymakers to vet proposed policies widely, taking into account the opinions of the critics, as well as the promoters and advocates. Finally, if the goal is to improve the educational lives and success of students from diverse backgrounds, then it is important that required programs and polices undergo periodic review, so that when ineffective assessments and instructional programs or methods are identified, they can be adjusted in a timely manner.

## REFERENCES

Allington, R., & Nowak, R. (2004). "Proven programs" and other unscientific ideas. In D. Lapp, C. C. Block, E. J. Cooper, J. Flood, N. Roser, & J. V. Tinajero (Eds.), *Teaching all the children: Strategies for developing literacy in an urban setting* (pp. 93–102). New York: Guilford Press.

American Educational Research Association, American Psychological Association, & National Council on Measurement in Education. (1999). *Standards for educational and psychological testing 1999.* Washington, DC: American Educational Research Association Publications.

August, D., Beck, I. L., Calderón, M., Francis, D. J., Lesaux, N. K., Shanahan, T., et al. (2008). Instruction and professional development. In D. August & T. Shanahan (Eds.), *Developing reading and writing in second language learners: Lessons from the Report of the National Literacy Panel on Language Minority Children and Youth* (pp. 131–250). New York: Routledge, Center for Applied Linguistics, and International Reading Association.

Bauer, E. B., & García, G. E. (2002). Lessons from a classroom teacher's use of alternative literacy assessment. *Research in the Teaching of English, 36,* 462—494.

Beaver, J. (2006). *Developmental Reading Assessment, K–3* (2nd ed.). Lebanon, IN: Celebration Press, Pearson Education.

Bernhardt, E. (2003). Challenges to reading research from a multilingual world. *Reading Research Quarterly, 38*(1), 112–117.

Butler, F. A., & Stevens, R. (2001). Standardized assessment of the content knowledge of English language learners K–12: Current trends and old dilemmas. *Language Testing, 18*(4), 409–427.

CTB/McGraw-Hill. (2003). *TerraNova Second Edition: California Achievement Tests technical report.* Monterey, CA: Author.

García, G. E. (1991). Factors influencing the English reading test performance of Spanish-speaking Hispanic children. *Reading Research Quarterly, 26*(4), 371–392.

García, G. E. (2003). The reading comprehension development and instruction of English language learners. In A. P. Sweet & C. E. Snow (Eds.), *Rethinking reading comprehension* (pp. 30–50). New York: Guilford Press.

García, G. E., & DeNicolo, C. P. (in press). Making informed decisions about the language and literacy assessment of English language learners. In L. Helman (Ed.), *Literacy development with English learners: Research-based instruction in grades K–6.* New York: Guilford Press.

García, G. E., McKoon, G., & August, D. (2006). Language and literacy assessment of language-minority students. In D. August & T. Shanahan (Eds.), *Developing literacy in second-language learners: Report of the National Literacy Panel on Language-Minority Children and Youth* (pp. 597–624). Mahwah, NJ: Erlbaum.

García, G. E., McKoon, G., & August, D. (2008). Language and literacy assessment. In

D. August & T. Shanahan (Eds.), *Developing reading and writing in second language learners: Lessons from the Report of the National Literacy Panel on Language Minority Children and Youth* (pp. 251–274). New York: Routledge, Center for Applied Linguistics, and International Reading Association.

García, G. E., & Pearson, P. D. (1994). Assessment and diversity. In L. Darling-Hammond (Ed.), *Review of research in education* (Vol. 20, pp. 337–392). Washington, DC: American Educational Research Association.

Glod, M. (2008, May 2). Study questions No Child Act's reading plan: Lauded program fails to improve test scores. *Washington Post*, p. A01.

Goldenberg, C., Rueda, R. S., & August, D. (2008). Sociocultural contexts and literacy development. In D. August & T. Shanahan (Eds.), *Developing reading and writing in second language learners: Lessons from the Report of the National Literacy Panel on Language Minority Children and Youth* (pp. 95–130). New York: Routledge, Center for Applied Linguistics, and International Reading Association.

Good, R. H., & Kaminski, R. A. (2002). *Dynamic Indicators of Basic Early Literacy Skills* (6th ed.). Eugene, OR: Institute for the Development of Educational Achievement.

Goodman, K. (2006). *The truth about DIBELS: What it is and what it does.* Portsmouth, NH: Heinemann.

*Group Reading Assessment and Diagnostic Evaluation (GRA+DE).* (2008). Retrieved June 8, 2008, from *www.pearsonlearning.com/content/file/grade*.

Gutiérrez, K. D., Asato, J., Pacheco, M., Moll, L. C., Olson, K., Horng, E. L., et al. (2002). "Sounding American": The consequences of new reforms on English language learners. *Reading Research Quarterly, 37*(3), 328–343.

Hakuta, K., & Beatty, A. (2000). *Testing English language learners in U. S. schools.* Washington, DC: National Academy Press.

Haycock, K. (2007, October). *Raising achievement and closing the gap for all groups of kids.* Paper presented at the Celebrate our Rising Star Summit, the Education Trust, Washington, DC. Retrieved May 31, 2008, from *www.edtrust.org*.

Institute of Education Sciences (IES). (2007, October). *National assessment of Title I: Final report: Summary of key findings.* Washington, DC: National Center for Education Evaluation and Regional Assistance, U.S. Department of Education.

Institute of Education Sciences (IES). (2008, April). *Reading First impact study: Interim report: Executive summary.* Washington, DC: National Center for Education Evaluation and Regional Assistance, U.S. Department of Education.

Ivey, G., & Broaddus, K. (2007). A formative experiment investigating literacy engagement among adolescent Latina/o students just beginning to read, write, and speak English. *Reading Research Quarterly, 42*(4), 512–545.

Karier, C. J. (1973). Testing for order and control in the corporate liberal state. *Educational Theory, 22*, 159–180.

Linn, R. L., Baker, E. L., & Dunbar, S. B. (1991). Complex, performance-based assessment: Expectations and validation criteria. *Educational Researcher, 20*(8), 15–21.

Mercer, J. (1989). Alternative paradigms for assessment in a pluralistic society. In J. A. Banks & C. A. Banks (Eds.), *Multicultural education: Issues and perspectives* (pp. 289–304). Boston: Allyn & Bacon.

Messick, S. (1994). The interplay of evidence and consequences in the validation of performance assessments. *Educational Researcher, 23*(2), 13–23.

National Clearinghouse for English Language Acquisition. (2006). *Resources about assess-*

*ment and accountability for ELLs.* Washington, DC: Author. Retrieved November 13, 2007, from *www.ncela.gwu.edu/resabout/assessment/index.html.*

National Institute of Child Health and Human Development. (2000). *Report of the National Reading Panel: Teaching children to read: An evidence-based assessment of the scientific research literature on reading and its implications for reading instruction* (NIH Publication No. 00-4769). Washington, DC: U.S. Government Printing Office.

No Child Left Behind Act of 2001, 20 U. S. C. 6301 et seq., Pub. L. No. 107-110 (2002).

Pomplun, M., & Omar, M. H. (2001). The factorial invariance of a test of reading comprehension across groups of limited English proficient students. *Applied Measurement in Education, 14*(3), 261–283.

RAND Reading Study Group. (2002). *Reading for understanding: Toward an R&D program in reading comprehension.* Santa Monica, CA/Washington, DC: RAND Corporation.

Riedel, B. W. (2007). The relation between DIBELS, reading comprehension, and vocabulary in urban first-grade students. *Reading Research Quarterly, 42*(4), 546–562.

Samuels, S. J. (2007). The DIBELS tests: Is speed of barking at print what we mean by reading fluency? *Reading Research Quarterly, 42*(4), 563–566.

Snow, C. E. (2003). Assessment of reading comprehension: Researchers and practitioners helping themselves and each other. In A. P. Sweet & C. E. Snow (Eds.), *Rethinking reading comprehension* (pp. 192–206). New York: Guilford Press.

Solano-Flores, G., & Trumbell, E. (2003). Examining language in context: The need for new research and practice paradigms in the testing of English-language learners. *Educational Researcher, 32*(3), 3–13.

Stewart, M. T. (2004). Early literacy instruction in the climate of No Child Left Behind. *Reading Teacher, 57*(8), 732–743.

Taylor, B. M., Pearson, P. D., Clark, K., & Walpole, S. (2000). Effective schools and accomplished teachers: Lessons about primary grade reading instruction in low-income schools. *Elementary School Journal, 101,* 121–166.

Teale, W. H., Paciga, K. A., & Hoffman, J. L. (2007). Beginning reading instruction in urban schools: The curriculum gap ensures a continuing achievement gap. *Reading Teacher, 61*(4), pp. 344–348.

U.S. Department of Education. (2003). *Standards and assessment: Non-regulatory guidance.* Washington, DC: Author.

U.S. Department of Education. (2006, September 13). Secretary Spellings announces final limited English proficiency regulations [Press release]. Retrieved October 25, 2007, from *www.ed.gov/adminis/lead/accfount/lepfactsheet.html.*

Williams, E. J. (1999). *Developmental reading assessment reliability study.* Retrieved November 19, 2008, from *www.pearsoned.com/new_research.html.*

Williams, K. T. (2001). *Technical manual: Group Reading Assessment and Diagnostic Evaluation.* Circle Pines, MN: American Guidance Service.

Wright, W. E. (2005). English language learners left behind in Arizona: The nullification of accommodations in the intersection of federal and state policies. *Bilingual Research Journal, 29*(1), 1–29.

# CHAPTER 13

# Meeting the Needs of Diverse Learners

## Effective Management
## of Language Arts Instruction

D. RAY REUTZEL, LESLEY MANDEL MORROW,
*and* HEATHER CASEY

Effective management of the classroom environment is one of the principal concerns for classroom teachers (Morrow, Reutzel, & Casey, 2006). Little research has focused specifically on understanding how to manage language arts classrooms with diverse populations. As a result, this chapter synthesizes research describing effective management and from these studies draws implications for meeting the needs of diverse learners in language arts classrooms.

Classroom management may be thought of as a collection of actions teachers take, which includes organizing classroom space and resources; allocating instructional time; developing positive relationships with students; grouping students and teaching them procedures, so that an orderly and positive classroom atmosphere is maintained. This facilitates quality literacy instruction (Reutzel & Cooter, 2008). As Brophy and Evertson (1976) stated decades ago, "A teacher, who is grossly inadequate in classroom management skills, is probably not going to accomplish much" (p. 127). Studies of teacher effectiveness assessed by surveys or direct observations report that classroom management is central to student learning (Morrow et al., 2006; Wong & Wong, 1998).

In this chapter, we review research related to five aspects of classroom management and how these affect the literacy development of diverse groups of children: (1) student engagement, (2) access, (3) classroom environment, (4) effective instruction, and (5) teacher–student relationships.

## RESEARCH ON MANAGEMENT IN LANGUAGE ARTS CLASSROOMS FOR HELPING ALL STUDENTS LEARN

Wang, Haertal, and Walberg (1994) created a knowledge base comprising 11,000 statistical findings addressing the question "What helps students learn?" Using meta-analysis, Wang and colleagues found that classroom management ranked as the most influential on a scale of 1–70, with a score of 64.8 in 28 categories of direct and indirect influences on student learning. The classroom management category included active student participation, learner accountability, effective questioning strategies, smooth transitions between activities, and teacher "with-it-ness." In contrast, ineffectively managed classrooms evidenced negative learning and behavioral consequences for all students (Milner, 2006; Strickland, 2001). Brophy and Evertson (1976) found that "low SES [socioeconomic status] children ... usually needed more restrictions on movement about the classroom and more structure concerning assignments" (p. 59). The most successful teachers of low-SES children provided structure and restrictions.

## STUDENT ENGAGEMENT IN DIVERSE LANGUAGE ARTS CLASSROOMS

Prior to discussing the effects of teachers' effective management of diverse language arts classrooms on students' engagement, we need to define what we mean by the term "student engagement." It is typically understood to be the conditions and elements that relate to and support students' active involvement with ongoing teaching and learning activities in the classroom. Two elements associated with student engagement external to a student's direct control are the use of *time* and *access* to necessary materials and supplies that support language arts teaching and learning activities. Later, we address internal aspects of engagement that students control, such as choices and teacher–peer relationships.

### What Does the Research Say about Time Management in Diverse Language Arts Classrooms?

Time is an important factor affecting students' learning (Black, 2002). During the early 1990s, the National Education Commission on Time and Learning (1994) found that the amount of time available in the traditional school day was alarmingly brief. Much of the time allocated to language arts instruction was lost to class openings, closings, directions, discipline, and poorly executed procedures and transitions between learning activities that restricted class time available for instruction. When it comes to children learning in diverse classrooms, a critical issue facing low-SES and low-achieving schools is the allocation of time and the fact that these students often need more time to learn (Canady & Retting, 1995; Marzano, 2000).

In a research project known as Beating the Odds, which helped to teach children at risk for failure to read, the most effective teachers allocated 134 minutes per day, compared with less effective teachers' allocation of 113 minutes per day for language arts instruction (Taylor, Pearson, Clark, & Walpole, 2000). Shanahan (2003), in his work with the Chicago schools, documented the need for 120 minutes per day for language arts instruction.

In the 1970s, Fisher and colleagues (1978), working on the Beginning Teacher Evaluation Study (BTES), described what was then a new outcome variable for documenting student engagement—academic learning time (ALT). This has since been shown to predict student achievement (Fisher et al., 1978). ALT not only represented the amount of time allocated to instruction but also described classroom management practices that optimized the amount of time students were actively involved in teaching and learning activities. Research has shown that ALT is highly correlated with students' levels of achievement and engagement (Gettinger & Kohler, 2006; National Education Commission on Time and Learning, 1994). Taylor and colleagues (2000) found that very effective grade 1–3 teachers have higher ratings, an average of 96% of their students' on-task during language arts instruction, than do moderately effective teachers, 84% on-task, or less effective teachers, 61% on-task. Teddlie, Kirby, and Stringfield (1989) found that ineffective teachers were characterized by lower rates of student time on-task.

Taylor and colleagues (2000) found that student achievement may be predicted by time allocation, ALT, and how time is distributed among several different learning and teaching activities. An average of 25 minutes per day was spent in whole-class, teacher-led, explicit instruction on core language arts skills, strategies, and concepts. On the other hand, *more than* 25 minutes per day in whole-class instruction was associated with the least accomplished language arts teachers. In the classrooms with the most accomplished language arts teachers, 48–60 minutes per day were spent in small-group instruction, with the remaining allocated instructional time of 134 minutes per day spent engaging children in independent reading practice. The National Reading Panel (2000) questioned the value of independent reading practice compared with oral, guided, repeated reading practice with adequate teacher monitoring. More recently, Reutzel, Fawson, and Smith (2008) found that independent reading can be adapted, using a scaffolded silent reading (ScSR) approach that it is effective with low-SES third-grade students.

To allocate learning time more effectively, Canady and Rettig (1996, 2001) developed a scheduling technique called "parallel block scheduling" (PBS), in which children received 90 minutes of daily, explicit, teacher-directed instruction in small groups focused on the language arts. One-half of students receive 45 minutes of instruction from the classroom teacher, and the other half go to a center for 45 minutes of small-group reading and language arts instruction. After each 45-minute period, the groups switch. According to its authors, PBS increased ALT and instructional time spent in small-group settings. Unlike classrooms in which children do independent seatwork or work in centers, where teacher supervision is minimal, children in PBS received daily double-doses of teacher-directed instruction that is continually monitored and adjusted to their needs.

How ALT is distributed goes beyond grouping strategies, teacher instruction, or independent student practice. The 2000 report of the National Reading Panel (NRP) identified essential elements of reading instruction, including writing that should be taught—phonemic awareness, alphabetic awareness, phonics, fluency, vocabulary, and comprehension. The implications from the NRP are that time should be distributed among essential instructional elements. Although the NRP reading instruction essentials have been criticized as incomplete (Allington, 2002; Pressley, 2002), it is hard to conceive of effective language arts instruction without daily time devoted to these essentials (Shanahan, 2004).

In addition to managing time well, as already described, research shows that effective language arts teachers are exceptionally skilled at establishing rules, routines, and procedures (Evertson & Emmer, 1982). Jones and Jones (2001) found that even in well-managed classrooms, noninstructional activities consumed 50% of the time available for instruction. Classroom rules for student conduct need to be taught explicitly and be sufficiently concrete and of high utility. Classroom rules should be integrated into the very fabric of the classroom routine (Reutzel & Morrow, 2007). Classroom procedures comprise ways to take care of repetitive classroom actions, such as lining up, taking restroom breaks, movement among activities, or when a student may sharpen a pencil. Key to teaching rules and procedures is a teacher's monitoring and enforcing compliance (Brophy & Evertson, 1976; Kounin, 1970).

Routines are established when procedures, rules, and schedules are taught and rehearsed over and over again. Yinger (1979, 1980) states that routinization of classroom rules and procedures leads to fewer interruptions of the flow and sequence of classroom events and interactions. According to Doyle (2006), "Routines provide a continuous signal for organizational and interpersonal behavior" (p. 108). Finally, transition times between activities in the classroom need to be minimized to maximize learning time through teaching and rehearsing transition procedures. According to Doyle (1984), skilled teachers clearly signal the onset of transitions, actively structure and monitor transitions, and strive to reduce the time involved in transitions to minimize the loss of instructional momentum in the classroom. In one study, Ardoin, Martens, and Wolfe (1999) found that the use of three rapidly presented directions (touch your nose, scoot in your chair, walk quietly to the rug) with which children can easily comply is helpful in achieving maximum compliance from children during transitions. In summary, research seems to indicate that to optimize the use of time in managing diverse language arts classrooms, Brophy and Evertson's (1976) assertion that "low SES children . . . usually needed more restrictions on movement about the classroom" (p. 59) seems to be worth repeating.

Managing time well in diverse language arts classrooms means that teachers need to pay attention to the psychological climate and to communicate high expectations and personal warmth (Pressley et al., 2003). Teachers need to express to verse students that they can and are expected to perform well (Brophy & Good, 1986). These students need to feel accountable for doing their best work (Brophy, 2006). According to research, many diverse children who live in poverty or lack resources in their lives often do not receive positive reinforcements and praise in their out-of-school lives. Hart and Risley (1995) found that the average child in a professional family received 32 affirmations and 5 prohibitions per hour, resulting in a ratio of 6 encouragements to 1 discouragement per hour. On the other hand, a child in a welfare family accumulated 5 affirmations and 11 prohibitions per hour—a ratio of 2 discouragements to 1 encouragement per hour. Teachers of diverse children need to engage regularly in communicating praise, compliments, encouragement, warmth, care, and concern (Pressley et al., 2003). When children feel worthwhile, encouraged, and accountable in their classroom, they are motivated to respond more appropriately, which results in less instructional time wasted in behavioral interruptions.

### What Does the Research Say about Access to Print in Diverse Language Arts Classrooms?

Research in the past decade has demonstrated that access to print is unevenly distributed across socioeconomic levels in the United States. Neuman (1999) showed that providing access to books in large urban preschools had a salutary effect on students' early literacy development. With greater access to books, children in the intervention group scored statistically significantly higher than the control group on four of six early literacy assessment measures. Six months later, these gains in early literacy skills were still evident. Findings from this research provide support for the positive effects on literacy development when children have easy access to books.

Neuman and Celano (2001) investigated access to print in low- and middle-income neighborhoods in a large eastern city. Using a group of trained researchers, they carefully documented and reported the availability of print in these communities. In so doing, these researchers described the likelihood that children would be able to access books and other print resources in their communities. They carefully quantified and qualified print in signs and logos; access to public spaces conducive to reading, to books in preschools, and to books in school and public libraries; and places where books could be purchased. Results of this yearlong study showed striking differences in access to print between low- and middle-income neighborhoods. Middle-income children had access to a large variety of print resources, whereas low-income children had much less access to print materials in their communities. Even in public institutions, such as libraries and schools, this uneven distribution of access to printed materials was found. A prevailing assumption among many policymakers and the public is that books and other literacy-related resources are easily and equally accessible to all children and their families. This research challenges that assumption. Without equal access to print, books, environmental print, and adult models of literate behavior, children in poverty are placed at greater risk of developing reading problems (Juel, Griffith, & Gough, 1986).

The problem of access goes even deeper than mere access to books and print. Stories or narratives abound in the early literacy experiences of children in diverse language arts classrooms. However, many children of diversity are unable to see themselves in the stories they read in books at school (Mason & Schumm, 2003). Hefflin and Barksdale-Ladd (2001) found that roughly 3% of children's books feature African Americans as main characters. Only 2% of these books are written by African American authors. Even fewer storybooks featuring African Americans as the main characters were judged to be of high literary quality.

Mohr (2003) conducted a study of 190 first-grade children's book preferences in a diverse school setting in Texas. When asked to choose from among nine quality picture books of various genres, including multicultural story texts in a single book that students would like to keep, 84% of these children chose an information book entitled *Animals Nobody Loves* (Simon, 2001). Although access to multicultural literature may be important for children of diversity, Mohr's research seems to demonstrate these "data do not support the claim that some advocates make—that students want to see themselves in their books" (p. 174). It may be the case that when narratives are storied accounts embedded in culture, diverse children like seeing themselves in book. When given the choice among narrative and informational texts, however, children view books more as windows to their world rather than as mirrors of themselves, and they prefer information texts.

Duke (2000) found that first-grade children read or wrote information texts an average of only 3.6 minutes per day in 20 first-grade classes in low- and high-SES school districts. She also found those first-grade children in *low*-SES school districts averaged only 1.9 minutes per day reading and writing information texts. Thus, the information books that diverse children find appealing and that may increase their acquisition of knowledge and engagement are the least accessible books in many of their classrooms. Similarly, Worthy, Moorman, and Turner (1999) examined the reading preferences and access to reading materials of sixth graders from three middle schools in a diverse Southwestern school district. Access to the most popular books in classrooms among this age group of diverse students was also limited, prompting the title of the study What Johnny Likes to Read Is Hard to Find in School.

Au (2006) expressed concern that access to technology may be contributing to a widening of the achievement gap among students from diverse languages and cultures. Leu (2002) indicated that technology has the potential to open venues for students to read and write in ways that can increase cultural understandings. Several technology projects (La Clase Mágica, Dreamweaver, and Searider Productions) have shown the potential of culturally sensitive technological formats to motivate increased reading and writing among diverse students. But, at present, there is little research demonstrating that diverse students have access to culturally appropriate uses of technology in their classrooms or that having such access results in higher achievement for them.

These finding suggest that diverse students have limited access to books, print, and possibly technology they find interesting or relevant. Lack of access to these materials may not only lead to problems in engaging diverse students' interests and preferences for reading and writing but may also suppress diverse students' acquisition of knowledge and widen the achievement gap. Neuman (2001) summarized it well when she stated, "Today in the U.S., economic differences between the haves and have-nots are greater than at any other time in history since 1929. . . . Teachers must ensure that children develop factual knowledge that has coherence and depth. All of our children, rich and poor and in between deserve no less" (pp. 470–471).

## CLASSROOM ENVIRONMENT
## AND DIVERSE LANGUAGE ARTS LEARNERS

An important aspect of classroom management involves designing and organizing the physical environment. Barker (1968, 1978) was one of the first researchers to discuss and investigate human behavior relative to setting, ecology, or environment. He put forth three generalizations that may be viewed within the context of the classroom: (1) Human behavior changes from setting to setting to meet the conditions of each setting; (2) behavior of individuals and groups in any setting is more alike than different; and (3) individual behavior tends to be consistent over time in the same or similar settings. Early studies of classroom environments largely substantiated Barker's claims (Oxford, Morrison, & McKinney, 1979; Smith & Connolly, 1980; Stodolsky, 1988).

Research has documented the coercive effect of environment, or what is also called "environmental press," on the literacy learning outcomes and behaviors of students in preschool and primary grades. A number of researchers have described how the manipulation of various physical aspects within the classroom environment affects youngsters' play behaviors and overall reading and writing development (Christie & Enz, 1992; Morrow, 1990; Roskos & Neuman, 2001; Vukelich, 1994; Zill & Resnick, 2006). Teachers in diverse communities need to plan carefully the physical design of their language arts classrooms. This is effectively accomplished through careful design and teacher modeling, which have been shown to "enliven and invigorate children's literacy learning in the classroom" (Roskos & Neuman, 2001, p. 290).

Designing classroom space to support effective language arts instruction involves (1) the structure of space, (2) selection of materials and furnishings for the environment, and (3) the literacy activities to be carried out (Wolfersberger, Reutzel, Sudweeks, & Fawson, 2004). Although some classroom teachers design the space in their rooms with the intent to support literacy learning, research often is not used to inform their decisions (Neuman & Fischer, 1995). Studies have shown that when language arts classrooms are partitioned into smaller spaces, such as learning centers or activity areas, small-group discussion increases. When classroom space was partitioned into smaller spaces, verbal interaction among peers increased, enhancing cooperative and associative learning (Morrow, 1990; Rivlin & Weinstein, 1984). A review of ecological studies of play and cognitive performance validated environmental factors that promoted literacy learning in varied settings, such as centers, play areas, and so forth. The most important factors were (1) organization of settings, (2) procedures, (3) familiarity of objects, (4) meaningfulness of activities, and (5) social interactions (Neuman & Roskos, 1997). Cambourne (2002) suggests that when teachers organize classroom settings, they make important decisions about which literacy tools, props, and objects to purchase; when and how these objects will be used, and by whom and for how long; and how they will be accessed and stored. They also decide what print will be displayed within the classroom, how furniture is arranged, and so forth.

Children demonstrate more advanced thinking when familiar literacy objects, activities, and independent literacy center areas are available for use in language arts classrooms. Meaningful literacy experiences, familiarity with learning tasks, and procedures to follow help children to demonstrate their competence in literacy. Authentic literacy learning that reflects what children have experienced in their lives should be present in the classroom. Lave (1988) maintains that children need to be presented *authentic dilemmas* that offer them opportunities to use literacy tools and objects to create problem-solving situations and experiment with a variety of solutions. Examples of such settings include a post office, a restaurant, a travel agency, a supermarket, or a gas station (Morrow, 2008). Children use these centers and participate in literacy activities they see in their everyday lives. The relevance of classroom literacy experiences with children from urban settings is very important. If school experiences relate to children's real-life situations, school will have meaning for them.

## EFFECTIVE INSTRUCTION IN DIVERSE LANGUAGE ARTS CLASSROOMS

Researchers who focus on exemplary language arts instruction want to know about methods for instruction, interactions between children and teachers, scheduling routines, design of environments, and how the classroom community affects student achievement (Genishi, Ryan, Ochsner, & Yarnall, 2001; Pressley, Rankin, & Yokoi, 1996; Roehler & Duffy, 1984). Researchers have identified exemplary teachers as those who (1) have students with excellent literacy achievement scores over a period of time; (2) have children with test scores above those expected from children considered "at risk"; and (3) are recommended by administrators, peers, parents, and students.

In one large-scale study, researchers questioned students in grades K–12 about the characteristics of their influential literacy teachers, in an attempt to build a model of effective literacy instruction (Ruddell, 1995; Ruddell & Harris, 1989). The results indicated that influential literacy teachers (1) use highly motivating teaching strategies; (2) build strong, effective relationships with their students; (3) create excitement about what they are teaching; (4) adjust instruction to meet the individual needs of their students; (5) create rich physical environments to support their teaching; and (6) have strong organization and management skills.

In another study of exemplary practice, Metsala and Wharton-McDonald (1997) described data from surveys and interviews of exemplary teachers. Data indicated the most important literacy practices and routines of these 89 K–3 regular education and 10 special education teachers. They were described by their peers and supervisors as masterful classroom managers of time, materials, and student behavior. They had high expectations, direction, and objectives for their students. Exemplary teachers cited a literate classroom environment as an important classroom characteristic for the support of effective early literacy instruction. Effective teachers provided explicit instruction in reading and writing skills and strategies, used contextualized and isolated skills and strategy instruction, provided access to varied reading materials, and varied ways to engage students in reading and writing. They also adapted instruction to the needs of their students, worked at motivating students to want to read and write, and monitored students' literacy progress through systematic accountability (Wharton-McDonald, Pressley, Rankin, & Mistretta, 1997).

Morrow, Tracey, Woo, and Pressley (1999) observed six exemplary teachers from three school districts, both urban and suburban. Approximately 25 hours of observation were completed for each of the six teachers, as well as interviews. These six exemplary teachers had created "literacy-rich classroom environments." They utilized a variety of learning settings, such as whole-group, small-group, one-on-one, teacher-directed centers, and social interactions with adults and peers. They provided a rich variety of print and print-producing materials for children to use daily. They employed various types of instructional approaches (e.g., spontaneous, authentic, explicit, direct, systematic, meaning-oriented, problem-solving, and open-ended). They engaged children daily in shared, guided, oral, silent, independent, and collaborative reading and writing. They offered regular writing, word analysis, and comprehension instruction. And they made consistent efforts to connect reading and writing instruction to content taught through themes and at other times of the day. Many of these same practices and instructional routines were also reported and confirmed by Cantrell (1999) in her study of the effects of literacy instruction on primary students' reading and writing achievement.

More recently, Morrow (2008) surveyed 150 classroom teachers in urban settings to determine what they felt was most important to make their teaching more effective. The most frequent responses were as follows: (1) knowing more about how to motivate children to read; (2) learning more about the multiple cultures of students in their classrooms to select appropriate materials and understand them better; (3) instruction for English language learners; (4) differentiating instruction in small groups to meet individual needs; (5) enhancing parent involvement, and (6) knowing more about organization and management, so that their daily routines would run smoothly.

## What Does the Research Say about Differentiating Instruction in Diverse Language Arts Classrooms?

Effective teachers can negotiate content and pedagogy in diverse contexts across grade levels (Allington, Johnston, & Day, 2002; Taylor, Peterson, Pearson, & Rodriguez, 2002). Effective teachers are described as having an understanding of content and pedagogy, consistently mediating the two in response to the needs of the students with whom they work. Decisions about curriculum, content, and pacing evolve in response to students' needs and interests. Differentiation of instruction offers a framework for organizing and managing diverse language arts classrooms (Taylor et al., 2000).

Differentiating instruction has traditionally been understood as the teacher's capacity to pair students' cognitive abilities with instructionally appropriate processes, products, and assessments mediated by students' interests, abilities, and readiness levels (Tomlinson, 2001). Teachers who differentiate instruction use multiple assessment tools to understand students' needs, make use of multiple grouping structures to support learning objectives, draw on a variety of materials to support reading and writing development, and consider students' interests and experiences when designing instructional plans. These teachers are master "organizers and managers" as they integrate structures for learning and expectations for students (Casey, 2007).

Differentiation has traditionally been presented as negotiating multiple academic demands in heterogeneous classrooms. However, there needs to be consideration for not only academic differences but also differences in cultural, economic, and linguistic diversity in classrooms (MacGillivray & Rueda, 2004). In a study of effective schools, Sailors, Hoffmann, and Matthee (2007) studied primary and intermediate classrooms in low-SES settings that "beat the odds." The teachers in these classrooms were described as scaffolding learners through reading and writing events, and co-constructing print-rich environments with students that motivated and supported learning across content areas (p. 379). These teachers responded to individual students' diverse linguistic and academic needs, and had a strong awareness of the larger community in which their classrooms were positioned. It is this awareness of community, and its linguistic and economic diversity, that guided teachers' decisions about curriculum, content, and pacing. This view of differentiation suggests that effective teachers organize and manage instruction through balancing the needs of students with arrangement of physical space, discourse-mediated learning, the larger community in which the school is positioned, and artifacts surrounding these events (Street, 2005).

## What Does the Research Say about the Effect of Small-Group Instruction on Teacher and Diverse Student Behaviors in Language Arts Classrooms?

A major challenge in the organization and management of a language arts program in an urban setting is the use of small-group instruction. When teachers create space and time for small-group learning, it is designed for a variety of reasons and for the most part has positive effects (Bansberg, 2003; Cambourne, 2002; Moore, 1986; Reutzel & Cooter, 1991; Taylor & Pearson, 2002). One type of small-group work is to engage children productively and independently of the teacher. Children work alone or in collaboration with others. Teachers create areas they call centers for this type of collaborative work. The centers are used predominantly during guided reading instruction, when the teacher works with a small reading group for specific skills development. These centers engage students in practicing the work that had been introduced to them, while the teacher works with another group of students. Examples of well-known centers found in K–6 classrooms include (1) a word study center, (2) a library corner, (3) a writing center, (4) a listening/comprehension center, and (5) a literacy-enriched play area. The activities encourage collaborative work with others, which benefits productivity.

Another type of small-group work is guided reading. For this type of instruction, the teacher needs a table and chairs to accommodate up to seven students and him- or herself (Fountas & Pinnell, 1996). These should be placed in a quiet part of the room, but where the teacher can see the rest of the children. The guided reading area is designed so that the teacher can assess and teach a small group of children to meet their individual needs. Materials for guided instruction include many sets of leveled books or basal stories of different levels of difficulty, white dry erase boards, magnetic letters, markers and paper, and so forth. Teachers have easels and a pocket chart for working with story structure, sentences, phrases, and words (Reutzel & Cooter, 2004). Students in guided reading are grouped by ability. Teaching and materials are geared to their needs.

Grouping students to meet their individual needs is considered important. Yet research varies widely for this type of organizational practice. Most studies reveal that high-achieving children do better in reading ability groups than they would do if not grouped. The data were not as clear in groups of middle- and low-achieving students. Grouping did not seem to help or hurt middle achievers; however, the data about low achievers were not consistent. Some studies found that low achievers did not do better in small-ability groups for instruction; other studies found that they did better (Eder, 1981; Hiebert, 1983; Lou, Abrami, & Spence, 1996).

Observations of what happens in small-ability groups during reading instruction help to explain the findings about grouping and achievement. High-ability groups read more text than do children in the low-ability groups. Children in high-ability groups were asked analytical questions and received lots of praise. Those in low-ability groups spent less time reading, and read segmented text rather than whole texts; teachers had low expectations for these students. Children recognized when they were in the low-ability groups and had negative feelings about it (Allington, 1984; Grant & Rothenberg, 1986).

Students who participated in ability groups during language arts instruction had both positive and negative comments about this type of instruction. On the positive side, students felt that they read more in small-group instruction; they had more positive interactions with the teacher, and with each other, and they felt that independent work during small-group instruction was productive (Hiebert, 1983). Negative comments about ability groups included the following: Once a group is formed there is fixed membership, and students cannot move; and there is a disproportionate number of children of color in low-ability groups. Most of the negative comments about grouping came from children in the low-ability groups (Allington, 1984; Grant & Rothenberg, 1986).

Teachers questioned about grouping for instruction said that they could attend to more individual differences in small-group instruction, and that students had more positive attitudes about themselves and what they were learning (Kulik & Kulik, 1982). Teachers grouped students according to ability level to meet individual needs, but they also had heterogeneous groups in their rooms for other, collaborative projects and for a writing workshop (Allington et al., 2002; Cambourne, 2002; Cantrell, 1999; Morrow, 2002, 2005; Robb, 2008). Expert management of small-group instruction is one of the characteristics of exemplary language arts classrooms and is considered a difficult task for many teachers.

## TEACHER–STUDENT RELATIONSHIPS IN DIVERSE LANGUAGE ARTS CLASSROOMS

Wells (1999) suggests that language, what Cole (1996) described as the "master tool," mediates learning. It is through using this "master tool" to explain, question, and invite collaboration that teachers carve out the relationships that permit them to mentor their students' learning. Classroom discussions within this contextualized frame suggest that "teacher talk" should be responsive to the culture of the classroom and the context in which an explanation occurs (Cazden, 2001). Gee (1996) describes the larger cultural discourse ("big D") that surrounds diverse contexts, as well as the focused exchanges that map specific learning events ("little d"). Discourse in classrooms structures the relationships, while it describes the learning. This linguistic composition is framed around a view of communication as social activity (Street, 2005; Wells, 1999). Wells offers the IRF model as the dominant mode of exchanges in classrooms. The teacher is positioned as the Initiator of discussion, the students Respond, and the teacher retains control by offering Feedback. Cazden (2001) describes open exchanges as "discourse intensive." Open exchanges involve more student-to-student feedback and are not controlled or directed by the teacher.

In a study of four teachers' diverse classrooms, the content of exchanges was considered along a continuum of curricular, co-curricular, and procedural discourse (Casey, 2006). Procedural exchanges between teachers and students are intended to organize instruction, the design of the learning environment, and other aspects of the classroom management system. Procedural exchanges include communications that monitor the progress of individual students and groups of students, as well as classroom planning decisions.

Casey (2006, 2007) reported several case studies describing the efforts of effective seventh-grade language arts teachers from multiple socioeconomic contexts motivate struggling readers and writers. One important finding focused on how relationships between teachers and students in diverse classrooms are built through discourse practices that derive from procedural exchanges around organization and management decisions.

Teachers and students in these case studies engaged in procedural exchanges around the students' progress and products. In more affluent classrooms with limited cultural diversity, procedural exchanges were tightly controlled by the teacher and fell into Well's description (1999) of *triadic dialogue*. In contrast, procedural exchanges in culturally diverse, lower-SES classrooms were open, and emerged as an evolving discussion, with teachers and students sharing power (Cazden, 2001). In the diverse classroom cases, students worked collaboratively in heterogeneous groups, although it should be noted that all teachers consciously and continuously shifted the physical space to support learning objectives.

The tone and tenor of the discourse practices fostered positive relationships in all of these teachers' classrooms with all students, regardless of their academic need. Johnston (2004) reminds us that "the social relationships within which they [children] learn are fundamentally social" (p. 65). Teachers who effectively organize and manage instruction in diverse classrooms attend to both the physical and discursive spaces of practice.

Research on diverse classroom settings also suggests that the structures we use to monitor, motivate, and engage students should be equally diverse (Robb, 2008). Learning is both individual and collective. A teacher engages with students both individually and as part of a shared community. Sociocultural theory posits that students and teachers are constantly drawing on shared experiences and prior instructional episodes to shape understanding (Cazden, 2001; Street, 2005). Describing diversity is complicated, because once a demographic category is invoked (i.e., urban, suburban, racial) a stereotype is often brought into play. Our classrooms include teachers and students who are diverse intellectually, racially, culturally, economically, linguistically, and digitally (Rowsell & Pahl, 2007). Addressing this diversity is complex; even within similar demographic groupings, multiple layers of diversity exist. As teachers organize and manage diverse students within the classroom space, so that they include diverse identities, foster the temporary communities that are co-constructed within these shared physical and virtual spaces, and respond both to the curricular demands that exist within the school community and to those imposed by outside agencies, they increase the likelihood of also fostering increased language arts achievement and engagement (Afflerbach, 2005).

## IMPLICATIONS FOR FUTURE RESEARCH

Effective classroom management is an absolute *necessity*, but it is also an insufficient condition for providing diverse learners with effective language arts instruction. Researchers have undeniably documented how the elements of an effectively managed classroom can positively affect teachers' abilities to teach and students' abilities to learn in traditional language arts classrooms. However, many questions remain unanswered when it comes to effective classroom management in today's increasingly diverse classroom communities:

- How much of diverse children's language arts achievement is directly attributable to elements associated with classroom management?
- How does providing diverse learners increased access to culturally relevant print materials and technology impact their language arts achievement and engagement?
- How does providing increased access to information and technology impact diverse learners' knowledge acquisition, language arts achievement, and engagement?
- What effective classroom management procedures and routines promote diverse students' learning in language arts classrooms?
- What are effective ways to motivate diverse learners to want to read and write?
- How can teachers effectively be helped to know how to select appropriate materials to support the multiple cultures found in today's classrooms?
- What aspects of classroom management facilitate or inhibit positive relationships between teachers and diverse learners?

## CONCLUDING REMARKS

Classroom management has been a primary concern of teachers and administrators. When good management is lacking, the supportive conditions necessary for effective instruction can be undermined. Classroom management includes effective planning for motivating students to engage in the language arts activities. Effective management focuses on optimal use of time; students access to abundant, challenging, culturally relevant print; and technologies to promote language arts learning. A well-designed classroom environment has been shown to undergird the success or failure of a language arts classroom. The quality of instruction, which includes attention to monitoring individual students' progress and providing targeted, differentiated instruction in small groups, has been shown to be an effective classroom management procedure that benefits all students but especially diverse language arts learners. Creating discourse-rich, open exchanges between students and teachers, in which they negotiate the curriculum together, discuss events beyond the classroom, and develop explicit but sensitive exchanges, has the potential to build positive relationships that promote diverse students' motivation to read and write. Appropriate attention to planning and designing effective classroom management can help to promote student engagement and achievement in language arts.

## REFERENCES

Afflerbach, P. (2005). National reading conference policy brief: High stakes testing and reading assessment. *Journal of Literacy Research, 37,* 151–162.

Allington, R. L. (1984). Content coverage and contextual reading in reading groups. *Journal of Reading Behavior, 16,* 85–96.

Allington, R. L. (2002). *Big brother and the national reading curriculum: How ideology trumped evidence.* Portsmouth, NH: Heinemann Educational Books.

Allington, R. L., Johnston, P. H., & Day, J. P. (2002). Exemplary fourth-grade teachers. *Language Arts, 79*(6), 462–466.

Ardoin, S. P., Martens, B. K., & Wolfe, L. A. (1999). Using high-probability instruction sequences with fading to increase student compliance during transitions. *Journal of Applied Behavior Analysis, 32,* 339–351.

Au, K. H. (2006). Diversity, technology, and the literacy achievement gap. In M. McKenna, L. Labbo, R. Kieffer, & D. Reinking (Eds.) *International handbook of literacy and technology* (Vol. II, pp. 363–368). Mahwah, NJ: Erlbaum.

Bansberg, B. (2003). Applying the learner-centered principles to the special case of literacy. *Theory Into Practice, 42*(2), 142–150.

Barker, R. G. (1968). *Ecological psychology.* Stanford, CA: Stanford University Press.

Barker, R. G. (1978). Stream of individual behavior. In R. Barker & Associates (Eds.), *Habitats, environments, and human behavior* (pp. 3–16). San Francisco: Jossey-Bass.

Black, S. (2002). Time for learning. *American School Board Journal, 189,* 1–6.

Brophy, J. (2006). History of research on classroom management. In C. Weinstein & C. Evertson (Eds.), *Handbook of classroom management: Research, practice, and contemporary issues* (pp. 17–43). Hillsdale, NJ: Erlbaum.

Brophy, J., & Good, T. (1986). Teacher behavior and student achievement. In M. Wittrock (Ed.), *Handbook of research on teaching* (3rd ed., pp. 328–375). New York: Macmillan.

Brophy, J. E., & Evertson, C. M. (1976). *Learning from teaching: A developmental perspective.* Boston: Allyn & Bacon.

Cambourne, B. (2002). Conditions for literacy learning. *Reading Teacher, 55*(4), 358–360.

Canady, R. L., & Retting, M. D. (1995). The power of innovative scheduling. *Educational Leadership, 53,* 4–10.

Canady, R. L., & Retting, M. D. (2001). Block scheduling: The key to quality learning time. *Principal, 80,* 30–34.

Cantrell, S. C. (1999). The effects of literacy instruction on primary students' reading and writing achievement. *Reading and Research Instruction, 39*(1), 3–26.

Casey, H. (2006). *Making room for the middle: Understanding effective middle school teachers and their work with struggling readers and writers.* Unpublished doctoral dissertation, Rutgers University, New Brunswick, NJ.

Casey, H. (2007). Making room for the middle grades: High-stakes teaching in an era of high-stakes testing. *Journal of Curriculum and Instruction, 1*. Retrieved September 1, 2007, from *www.joci.ecu.edu/index.php/joci/article/view/34*.

Cazden, C. (2001). *Classroom discourse: The language of teaching and learning* (2nd ed.). Portsmouth, NH: Heinemann.

Christie, J. F., & Enz, B. (1992). The effects of literacy play interventions on preschoolers' play patterns and literacy development. *Early Education and Development, 3*, 205–219.

Cole, M. (1996). *Cultural psychology: A once and future discipline*. Cambridge, MA: Harvard University Press.

Doyle, W. (1984). How order is achieved in classrooms: An interim report. *Journal of Curriculum Studies, 16*(3), 259–277.

Doyle, W. (2006). Ecological approaches to classroom management. In C. M. Evertson & C. S. Weinstein (Eds.), *Handbook of classroom management: Research, practice, and contemporary issues* (pp. 97–125). Hillsdale, NJ: Erlbaum.

Duke, N. K. (2000). 3.6 minutes per day: The scarcity of informational texts in first grade. *Reading Research Quarterly, 35*(2), 202–224.

Eder, D. (1981). Ability grouping as a self-fulfilling prophecy: A micro-analysis of teacher–student interaction. *Sociology of Education, 54*, 151–162.

Evertson, C. M., & Emmer, E. T. (1982). Preventive classroom management. In D. L. Duke (Ed.), *Helping teachers manage classrooms* (pp. 2–31). Alexandria, VA: Association for Supervision and Curriculum Development.

Fisher, C. W., Filby, N. N., Marliave, R., Cahen, L. S., Dishaw, M. M., Moore, J. E., et al. (1978). *Beginning Teacher Evaluation Study* (Technical Report, V-1). San Francisco: Far West Laboratory.

Fountas, I. C., & Pinnell, G. S. (1996). *Guided reading instruction: Good first teaching for all children*. Portsmouth, NH: Heinemann.

Gee, J. (1996). *Social linguistics and literacies: Ideology in discourses* (2nd ed.). London: Falmer Press.

Genishi, C., Ryan, S., Ochsner, M., & Yarnall, M. M. (2001). Teaching in early childhood education: Understanding practices through research and theory. In V. Richardson (Ed.), *Handbook of research on teaching* (pp. 1175–1210. Washington, DC: American Education Research Association.

Gettinger, M., & Kohler, K. M. (2006). Process–outcome approaches to classroom management and effective teaching. In C. Weinstein & C. Evertson (Eds.), *Handbook of classroom management: Research, practice, and contemporary issues* (pp. 73–95). Hillsdale, NJ: Erlbaum.

Grant, L., & Rothenberg, J. (1986). The social enhancement of ability differences: Teacher–student interactions in first-and second-grade reading groups. *Elementary School Journal, 87*, 30–49.

Hart, B., & Risley, T. R. (1995). *Meaningful differences in the everyday experience of young American children*. Baltimore: Brookes.

Hefflin, B., & Barksdale-Ladd, M. (2001). African American children's literature that helps students find themselves: Selection guidelines for grades K–3. *Reading Teacher, 54*, 810–819.

Hiebert, E. H. (1983). An examination of ability grouping for reading instruction. *Reading Research Quarterly, 28*, 231–255.

Johnston, P. (2004). *Choice words*. Portland, ME: Stenhouse.

Jones, V., & Jones, L. (2001). *Comprehensive classroom management* (6th ed.). Boston: Allyn & Bacon.

Juel, C., Griffith, P., & Gough, P. (1986). Acquisition of literacy: A longitudinal study of children in first and second grade. *Journal of Educational Psychology, 78*, 243–55.

Kounin, J. S. (1970). *Discipline and group management in classrooms.* New York: Holt, Rinehart & Winston.

Kulik, C. C., & Kulik J. A. (1982). Research synthesis on ability grouping. *Educational Leadership, 39*, 619–621.

Lave, J. (1988). *Cognition in practice.* New York: Cambridge University Press.

Leu, D. J. (2002). The new literacies: Research on reading instruction with the Internet. In A. E. Farstrup & S. J. Samuels (Eds.), *What research has to say about reading instruction* (3rd ed., pp. 310–336). Newark, DE: International Reading Association.

Lou, Y., Abrami, P. C., & Spence, J. C. (1996). Effects of within-class grouping on student achievement: An exploratory model. *Journal of Educational Research, 94*, 101–113.

MacGillivray, L., & Rueda, R. (2004). Listening to inner city teachers of English language learners: Differentiating literacy instruction. In R. Robinson, M. McKenna, & J. Wedman (Eds.), *Issues and trends in literacy education* (pp. 99–102). Boston: Pearson.

Marzano, R. (2000). Optimizing teachers' use of instructional time. In *A new era of school reform: Going where the research takes us.* Aurora, CO: Mid-Continent Research for Education and Learning. (ERIC Document Reproduction Services No. ED454255)

Mason, P. A., & Schumm, J. S. (2003). *Promising practices for urban reading instruction.* Newark, DE: International Reading Association.

Metsala, J. L., & Wharton-McDonald, R. (1997). Effective primary-grades literacy instruction = balanced literacy instruction. *Reading Teacher, 50*(6), 518–521.

Milner, H. R. (2006). Classroom management in urban classrooms. In C. Weinstein & C. Evertson (Eds.), *Handbook of classroom management: Research, practice, and contemporary issues* (pp. 491–522). Hillsdale, NJ: Erlbaum.

Mohr, K. A. J. (2003). Children's choices: A comparison of book preferences between Hispanic and non-Hispanic first-graders. *Reading Psychology: An International Quarterly, 24*, 163–176.

Moore, G. (1986). Effects of the spatial definition of behavior settings on children's behavior: A quasi-experimental field study. *Journal of Personality and Social Psychology, 6*, 205–231.

Morrow, L. M. (1990). Preparing the classroom environment to promote literacy during play. *Early Childhood Education Research Quarterly, 5*, 537–554.

Morrow, L. M. (2002). *The literacy center: Contexts for reading and writing* (2nd ed.). Portland, ME: Stenhouse.

Morrow, L. M. (2005). *Literacy development in the early years: Helping children read and write* (5th ed.). Needham Heights, MA: Allyn & Bacon.

Morrow, L. M. (2008). *Literacy development in the early years: Helping children read and write* (6th ed.). Needham Heights, MA: Allyn & Bacon.

Morrow, L. M., Reutzel, D. R., & Casey, H. (2006). Organizing and managing language arts teaching: Classroom environments, grouping practices, exemplary instruction. In C. Weinstein & C. Evertson (Eds.), *Handbook of classroom management: Research, practice, and contemporary issues* (pp. 559–581). Hillsdale, NJ: Erlbaum.

Morrow, L. M., Tracey, D. H., Woo, D. G., & Pressley, M. (1999). Characteristics of exemplary first-grade literacy instruction. *Reading Teacher, 52*(5), 462–476.

National Education Commission on Time and Learning. (1994). *Prisoners of time: Report of the National Education Commission on Time and Learning.* Washington, DC: U.S. Government Printing Office.

National Reading Panel. (2000). *Report of the National Reading Panel: Teaching children to read.* Washington, DC: National Institute of Child Health and Human Development.

Neuman, S. B. (1999). Books make a difference: A study of access to literacy. *Reading Research Quarterly, 34,* 286–311.

Neuman, S. B. (2001). The role of knowledge in early literacy. *Reading Research Quarterly, 36,* 468–475.

Neuman, S. B., & Celano, D. (2001). Access to print in low-income and middle-income communities: An ecological study of four neighborhoods. *Reading Research Quarterly, 36,* 8–26.

Neuman, S. B., & Fischer, R. (1995). Task and participation structures in kindergarten using a holistic literacy teaching perspective. *Elementary School Journal, 95,* 325–337.

Neuman, S. B., & Roskos, K. (1997). Literacy knowledge in practice: Contexts of participation for young writers and readers. *Reading Research Quarterly, 32*(1), 10–33.

Oxford, R. L., Morrison, S. B., & McKinney, J. D. (1979). Classroom ecology and off-task behavior of kindergarten students. *Journal of Classroom Interaction, 15*(1), 34–40.

Pressley, M. (2003). *Beginning reading instruction: The rest of the story from research.* Washington, DC: National Education Association. Retrieved from *www.nea.org/reading/images/beginning reading.pdf.*

Pressley, M., Dolezal, S. E., Raphael, L. M., Mohan, L., Roehrig, A. D., & Bogner, K. (2003). *Motivating primary-grade students.* New York: Guilford Press.

Pressley, M., Rankin, J., & Yokoi, L. (1996). A survey of instructional practices of primary teachers nominated as effective in promoting literacy. *Elementary School Journal, 96*(4), 363–383.

Reutzel, D. R., & Cooter, R. B. (1991). Organizing for effective instruction: The reading workshop. *Reading Teacher, 44,* 548–554.

Reutzel, D. R., & Cooter, R. B. (2004). *Teaching children to read: Putting the pieces together* (4th ed.). Upper Saddle River, NJ: Prentice-Hall/Merrill.

Reutzel, D. R., & Cooter, R. B., Jr. (2008). *Teaching children to read: The teacher makes the difference* (5th ed.). Columbus, OH: Merrill/Prentice-Hall.

Reutzel, D. R., Fawson, P. C., & Smith, J. A. (2008). Reconsidering silent sustained reading: An explorative study of scaffolded silent reading (ScSR). *Journal of Educational Research, 102*(1), 37–50.

Reutzel, D. R., & Morrow, L. M. (2007). Promoting and assessing effective literacy learning classroom environments. In J. R. Paratore & R. L. McCormick (Eds.), *Classroom literacy assessment: Making sense of what students know and do* (pp. 33–49). New York: Guilford Press.

Rivlin, L., & Weinstein, C. (1984). Educational issues, school settings, and environmental psychology. *Journal of Environmental Psychology, 4,* 347–364.

Robb, L. (2008). *Differentiating reading instruction: How to teach reading to meet the needs of each student.* New York: Scholastic Teaching Resources: Theory and Practice.

Roehler, L. R., & Duffy, G. G. (1984). Direct explanation of comprehension process. In G. G. Duffy, L. R. Roehler, & J. Mason (Eds.), *Comprehension instruction: Perspectives and suggestions* (pp. 265–280). New York: Longman.

Roskos, K., & Neuman, S. B. (2001). Environment and its influences for early literacy teaching and learning. In S. B. Neuman & D. K. Dickinson (Eds.), *Handbook of early literacy research* (Vol. 1, pp. 281–294). New York: Guilford Press.

Rowsell, J., & Pahl, K. (2007). Sedimented identities in texts: Instances of practice. *Reading Research Quarterly, 42,* 388–405.

Ruddell, R. B. (1995). Those influential literacy teachers: Meaning negotiators and motivation builders. *Reading Teacher, 48*(6), 454–463.

Ruddell, R. B., & Harris, P. (1989). A study of the relationship between influential teachers' prior knowledge and beliefs about teaching effectiveness: Developing higher order thinking in content areas. In S. McCormick & J. Zutell (Eds.), *Cognitive and social perspectives for literacy research and instruction* (pp. 461–472). Chicago: National Reading Conference.

Sailors, M., Hoffman, J., & Matthee, B. (2007). South African schools that promote literacy learning with students from low-income communities. *Reading Research Quarterly, 42,* 364–387.

Shanahan, T. (2003, November). *A framework for improving reading achievement.* Paper presented at the National Conference on Family Literacy and the California Family Literacy Conference, Long Beach, CA.

Shanahan, T. (2004). Critiques of the National Reading Panel report: Their implications for research, policy, and practice. In P. McCardle & V. Chhabra (Eds.), *The voice of evidence in reading research* (pp. 235–268). Baltimore: Brookes.

Simon, S. (2001). *Animals nobody loves.* San Francisco: SeaStar Books.

Smith, P. K., & Connolly, K. J. (1980). *The ecology of preschool behavior.* Cambridge, UK: Cambridge University Press.

Stodolsky, S. S. (1988). *The subject matters.* Chicago: University of Chicago Press.

Street, B. (Ed.). (2005). *Literacies across educational contexts: Mediating learning and teaching.* Philadelphia: Caslon.

Strickland, D. S. (2001). Early intervention for African American children considered to be at risk. In S. B. Neuman & D. K. Dickson (Eds.), *Handbook of early literacy research* (Vol. 1, pp. 322–332). New York: Guilford Press.

Taylor, B. M., & Pearson, P. D. (2002). *Teaching reading: Effective schools, accomplished teachers.* Mahwah, NJ: Erlbaum.

Taylor, B. M., Pearson, P. D., Clark, K., & Walpole, S. (2000). Effective schools and accomplished teachers: Lessons about primary-grade reading instruction in low-income schools. *Elementary School Journal, 101*(2), 121–165.

Taylor, B. M., Peterson, D. S., Pearson, P. D., & Rodriguez, M. C. (2002). Looking inside classrooms: Reflecting on the "how" as well as the "what" in effective reading instruction. *Reading Teacher, 56*(3), 270–279.

Teddlie, C., Kirby, P. C., & Stringfield, S. (1989). Effective versus ineffective schools: Observable differences in the classroom. *American Journal of Education, 97*(3), 221–236.

Tomlinson, C. (2001). *How to differentiate instruction in mixed-ability classrooms* (2nd ed.). Alexandria, VA: Association for Supervision and Curriculum Development.

Vukelich, C. (1994). Effects of play interventions on young children's reading of environmental print. *Early Childhood Research Quarterly, 9*(2), 153–170.

Wang, M. C., Haertal, G. D., & Walberg, H. J. (1994). What helps students learn? *Educational Leadership, 51*(4), 74–79.

Wells, G. (1999). Language and education: Reconceptualizing education as dialogue. *Annual Review of Applied Linguistics, 19,* 135–155.

Wharton-McDonald, R., Pressley, M., Rankin, J., & Mistretta, J (1997). Effective primary-grades literacy instruction equals balanced literacy instruction. *Reading Teacher, 50*(6), 518–521.

Wolfersberger, M., Reutzel, D. R., Sudweeks, R., & Fawson, P. F. (2004). Developing and validating the Classroom Literacy Environmental Profile (CLEP): A tool for examining the "print richness" of elementary classrooms. *Journal of Literacy Research, 36*(2), 211–272.

Wong, H. K., & Wong, R. T. (1998). *How to become an effective teacher: The first days of school.* Mountain View, CA: Wong.

Worthy, J., Moorman, M., & Turner, T. (1999). What Johnny likes to read is hard to find in school. *Reading Research Quarterly, 34*, 12–27.

Yinger, R. J. (1979). Routines in teacher planning. *Theory Into Practice, 18*(3), 163–169.

Yinger, R. J. (1980). A student of teacher planning. *Elementary School Journal, 80*, 107–127.

Zill, N., & Resnick, G. (2006). Emergent literacy of low-income children in Head Start: Relationships with child and family characteristics, program factors, and classroom quality. In S. B. Neuman & D. K. Dickinson (Eds.), *Handbook of early literacy research* (Vol. 2, pp. 347–371). New York: Guilford Press.

# PART III

# STRATEGIES FOR TEACHING

# Cross-Language Transfer of Phonological, Orthographic, and Semantic Knowledge

MARÍA S. CARLO

Proponents of bilingual education have long argued that instruction in the mother tongue can, in addition to promoting academic learning among bilingual children, facilitate their acquisition of academically mediated skills in the second language. Empirical tests of this notion have been conducted ever since the first federally funded bilingual education programs were implemented across the United States (e.g., Kaufman, 1968). Yet it was not until the late 1970s that a testable hypothesis about the relationship between first and second language development was proposed (Cummins, 1979). A significant number of studies has been conducted since to probe the developmental interdependence hypothesis proposed by Cummins. The purpose of this chapter is to review the research evaluating the relationship between first- and second-language early reading development and the notion that development of literacy in the mother tongue can be beneficial to the development of these skills in the second language. This chapter provides the following:

- A discussion of the developmental interdependence hypothesis and of the theoretical framework on which it is based.
- A review of early studies that evaluated transfer effects using comparison-group designs and/or global measures of reading performance, and a discussion of methodological issues that make problematic the interpretation of language transfer in these studies.
- A review of recent studies evaluating cross-language transfer of phonological, orthographic, and lexical sources of knowledge in the development of second-language reading abilities.

## THE DEVELOPMENTAL INTERDEPENDENCE HYPOTHESIS

Cummins (1984) proposed a theoretical framework concerning the relationship between second-language development and academic achievement that has significantly influenced the way educators think about instructional experiences designed to benefit second-language learners. One important premise guiding this framework involves the idea that academically mediated language skills can be transferred across languages in a manner that facilitates the acquisition of these skills in the second language (Cummins, 1978, 1979, 1980, 1984). This notion was formalized into the developmental interdependence hypothesis (DIH), which states that

> the level of L2 [second language] competence which a bilingual child attains is partially a function of the type of competence the child has developed in L1 [mother tongue] at the time when intensive exposure to L2 begins. (Cummins, 1979, p. 233)

As stated, the DIH assumes that growth in second-language competence is mediated by learners' competence in the primary language. When applied to reading, one would expect that learners with well-developed reading skills in the primary language would develop stronger reading skills in the second language than learners with poorly developed reading skills in the first language.

It is important to note that Cummins's broader theoretical framework restricts the applicability of the DIH only to language competencies that involve cognitive academic language proficiency (CALP), as opposed to those involving basic interpersonal communication skills (BICS). Within Cummins's framework, BICS refers to language skills used in the context of face-to-face communication. He defines BICS as those language skills used for communicative events that make low cognitive demands and provide high contextual support. On the other hand, CALP refers to language skills used for communicative events that make high cognitive demands on the interlocutors and provide low contextual support. The DIH would not predict transfer for general language skills that are outside the realm of CALP.

## EARLY STUDIES ON CROSS-LANGUAGE TRANSFER

Researchers have studied language transfer from a variety of methodological approaches. Some of the early research studies addressed the question of transfer through comparison group designs conducted in the context of program evaluation studies. The general approach involved comparing achievement on global measures of language proficiency of bilingually instructed L2 learners to monolingually instructed L2 learners. The findings from these studies can be summarized as follows:

- Elementary school students who have learned to read in the native language have better performance and/or are more likely to be judged as competent readers in the second language than students who learned to read only in the second language (Kaufman, 1968; Modiano, 1979; Rosier & Farella, 1976).
- Elementary school students in French immersion programs in Canada can perform at the level of the average student in English programs on measures of word reading skills after only minimal instruction in English (Kendall et al., 1987; Lambert & Tucker, 1972).
- Spanish-speaking children participating in a Spanish-language preschool program show an advantage in terms of their readiness for school over students participating in an English-only preschool program (Campos, 1985).

Although these findings are certainly consistent with a transfer interpretation, methodological limitations in the design of these studies also make the findings consistent with several alternative interpretations. With one notable exception involving an experimental design with random assignment (Kaufman, 1968), practical and ethical reasons have required that research on transfer use quasi-experimental designs, often involving intact classrooms. Thus, these studies are vulnerable to the threats to internal validity that typically accompany such designs (Campbell & Stanley, 1963). Research based on comparisons of potentially nonequivalent groups does not offer strong support for cross-language transfer, because it becomes impossible to determine whether differences between the groups are due exclusively to the effects of native-language instruction, or whether they are attributable to the effects of systematic differences between the groups.

Correlational designs have provided an alternative to the problem of comparisons across nonequivalent groups for researchers interested in understanding the nature of the relationship between first- (L1) and second-language (L2) reading competencies. These designs have allowed researchers to relate differences in the outcome variables (i.e., English reading comprehension) to levels of reading proficiency in the L1 (i.e., Spanish reading comprehension) (e.g., Cummins et al., 1984; Escamilla, 1987; Royer & Carlo, 1991). However, these early studies using correlational designs also have a number of problems related to interpretation of the causes of facilitation in reading performance. One of these problems relates to an inability to differentiate between effects of general ability factors and factors specific to reading in explaining the relationships between native-language and L2 reading achievement (Deacon, Wade-Woolley, & Kirby, 2007). Indeed, a more parsimonious interpretation of the Cummins and colleagues (1984), Escamilla (1987), and Royer and Carlo (1991) findings would be that high-ability children are better literacy learners in any language; thus, the correlation between performance on reading comprehension measures in L1 and L2 is due to general ability.

Studies of language transfer based on correlational designs have varied in terms of their ability to rule out general ability factors as mediators of the relationships observed between L1 and L2 reading abilities. A great deal of improvement in the quality of research on language transfer was achieved by the incorporation of nonverbal ability measures as control variables in the analyses and/or the use of longitudinal designs that accounted for initial L2 performance in the prediction of L2 outcomes. Another important development that has led to improvements in the quality of the research stems from the adoption of component process theories of reading to guide questions about transfer.

## CROSS-LANGUAGE TRANSFER WITHIN COMPONENTS OF READING

Contemporary reading theories describe the reading process in terms of cognitive components in interaction (Gough, 1971; LaBerge & Samuels, 1974; Perfetti, 1988). More recent studies of transfer have adopted this view of the reading process and have used it to guide study design. The general practice has been to attempt to isolate one or more of the components that underlie reading and to test the nature of the relationship for particular components across languages. This section reviews studies on transfer from sources of first-language knowledge that are believed to be fundamental to the development of early reading competencies (e.g., Snow, Burns, & Griffin, 1998). A substantial number of studies have been published following the National Literacy Panel's (NLP) review of language transfer research (August & Shanahan, 2006). Thus, this review focuses on studies published after 2003, the final year of research included in the NLP study. For in-depth reviews of studies published prior to 2003, the reader may consult Dressler and Kamil (2006) and Genesee and Geva (2006).

### Transfer of Phonological Awareness

Research on reading development of monolingual children points to the importance of phonological awareness as a predictor of early reading achievement (NRP, 2000). "Phonological awareness," or awareness that speech comprises smaller units of sound, is believed to facilitate the understanding of the relationship between sounds and symbols in alphabetic languages. Results from studies investigating the cross-language relationship for performance on phonological awareness tasks suggest that development of these skills in the L1 and L2 is interrelated (Cisero & Royer, 1995; Comeau, Cormier, Gradmaison, & Lacroix, 1999; Durgunoglu, Nagy, & Hancin-Bhatt, 1993; Gottardo, 2002; Gottardo, Yan, Siegel, & Wade-Woolley, 2001; Harrison & Krol, 2007; Quiroga, Lemos-Britton, Mostafapour, Abbott, & Berninger, 2002; Schiff & Calif, 2007). The investigators in the vast majority of these studies employ control variables that strengthen the credibility of a transfer interpretation and argue against an interpretation of the cross-language correlations in terms of the influence of general ability factors.

Three recent studies contribute new, relevant information to understanding the conditions under which transfer of phonological awareness emerges (Branum-

Martin et al., 2006; Cardenas-Hagan, Carlson, & Pollard-Durodola, 2007) and the manner in which children may exploit phonological knowledge available to them through analysis of the first language, while performing a phonological awareness task in the second language (San Francisco, Carlo, August, & Snow, 2006).

In what constitutes perhaps the largest-scale longitudinal study on cross-language transfer available to date, Cardenas-Hagan and colleagues (2007) have reported on the relationship between initial phonological awareness performance in Spanish and performance on a parallel English phonological awareness task a year later in a sample of over 1,000 Spanish–English bilingual kindergarten students, sampled from schools in two districts in Texas and one district in California. The students were enrolled in one of three models of language instruction: English language immersion, transitional bilingual, and dual-language. Consistent with previous studies, Cardenas-Hagan and colleagues found evidence of transfer across phonological awareness performance in Spanish and English, but the effect emerged only in students who were receiving Spanish instruction. Specifically, Spanish phonological awareness at the beginning of kindergarten predicted English phonological awareness at the beginning of first grade, after researchers controlled for English kindergarten performance on the same task. However, this effect emerged only for the Spanish-instructed students. The contribution of Spanish to English phonological awareness was not significant for English-instructed Spanish–English bilingual kindergarteners.

Martin and colleagues (2006) conducted analyses on a subsample of the sample reported by Cardenas-Hagan and colleagues (2007). Martin and colleagues used a multilevel-model confirmatory factor analysis to evaluate the extent to which phonological awareness tasks in Spanish and English were indicative of language-specific constructs or of a unitary phonological awareness construct. The multilevel latent variable model allowed the researchers to contrast the two hypothesized models, while controlling for measurement error and distinguishing individual and classroom effects. This analysis was performed on data obtained from over 800 Spanish–English bilingual kindergarten students sampled from 71 classrooms across 23 schools. All students were sampled from schools that were implementing a transitional bilingual education program. The results suggested that the measures of nonword blending, segmenting, and phoneme elision in Spanish and English formed a single factor within each language at both the student and the classroom level. The Spanish and English phonological awareness factors were highly related to one another at both the individual and the classroom level. The authors interpreted these findings as being indicative that the development of Spanish and English phonological awareness is interrelated at the student level, yet "classrooms, as aggregations of students with a given teacher, [can differ] in these phonological outcomes in consistent ways with each language" (p. 179).

San Francisco and colleagues (2006) also obtained evidence consistent with transfer of phonological awareness skills that is conditional on language of instruction. In this study, English monolingual and Spanish–English bilingual kindergartners and first graders receiving either English or Spanish literacy instruction were assessed in English phonological awareness and in English and Spanish vocabulary, as appropriate. The findings indicated that Spanish-instructed bilinguals were more likely than either English-instructed bilinguals or English monolinguals to treat English diphthongs as two separate phonological units, reflecting their application of Spanish phonology and orthography in the analysis of English words. Moreover, better performance on the English phonological awareness task was related to bilingual status; that is, unbalanced bilinguals who were dominant in either English or Spanish scored better on English phonological awareness tests than children with approximately equal scores on the English and Spanish vocabulary tests. The authors interpreted this finding as consistent with previous research on monolingual speakers relating the emergence of phonological awareness to the development of vocabulary breadth (Snow et al., 1998).

## Transfer of Orthographic Skills

A significant number of studies has demonstrated transfer from L1 phonological and orthographic skills to performance on measures that involve orthographic processes in L2 reading as it develops (Abu-Rabia, 1997; da Fontoura & Siegel, 1995; Durgunoglu et al., 1993; Gholamain & Geva, 1999). Dressler and Kamil's (2006) in-depth reviews of each of these studies show the influence of L1 phonological and orthographic skills in predicting isolated word reading performance in the second language. Here I review new evidence on transfer of orthographic skills that, although consistent with the previous findings, also point to conditions that appear to limit the transfer of orthographic skills because of either basic differences in the manner in which the writing system codes speech or developmental constraints related to task performance.

The study by Cardenas-Hagan and colleagues (2007) suggests that individual differences in L2 orthographic knowledge may constrain the effect of transfer from the first language. As reported earlier, their large-scale study systematically tested phonological and orthographic transfer over time and as a function of language of instruction. Their data suggest that the emergence of a transfer effect depends on the level of development of orthographic skills in the second language. They showed that performance on English letter name and letter–sound identification skills was predicted by Spanish performance on the letter name and letter–sound identification task measured a year earlier, and on control of initial English performance on the same task. But this effect emerged only for those students with poor performance on the initial measures of orthographic knowledge in English. Thus, a transfer effect was present only under conditions in which students had insufficient knowledge of English orthography and compensated by relying on their knowledge of Spanish orthography. Thus, these findings suggest that Spanish-speaking students may exploit their knowledge of Spanish orthography during the initial stages of acquisition of English orthography, and that their knowledge of Spanish orthography becomes less useful to them as they develop greater amounts of knowledge about English orthography.

A study by Deacon and colleagues (2007) also suggests that degree of transfer from L1 skills that predict L2 word-reading changes over the course of literacy development. Deacon and colleagues analyzed longitudinal data collected from first-grade native-English speakers in a French immersion program in Canada. Word-reading ability and awareness of inflectional morphology was measured in French and English, in addition to general ability, breadth of English vocabulary, and English phonological awareness. Deacon and colleagues evaluated the extent to which morphological awareness performance predicted reading ability across languages and controlling for general ability, vocabulary, and phonological awareness. These researchers also evaluated the extent to which the cross-language prediction remained stable over each year of the study. The results indicated that English morphological awareness at grade 1 predicted French word reading in grades 1–3; however, English morphological awareness at grade 2 predicted French word reading only at grade 2. English morphological awareness was not predictive of grade 3 French word reading.

Transfer of morphological awareness in French to English word reading was also evaluated. The pattern of results was reversed. French morphological awareness did not reliably predict English word reading in grades 1–3, but French morphological awareness in second grade was predictive of second- and third-grade English word reading. Grade 3 French morphological awareness predicted English word reading in grade 3. The authors summarized the results, stating that "morphological awareness seems to teeter-totter in its relationship with reading: as contributions from the first language decrease those from the second language increase" (p. 741).

A recent study by Schiff and Calif (2007) also highlights the manner in which individual differences in knowledge about orthographic patterns in the L1 and L2 can impact the extent to which transfer processes operate during L2 reading. Schiff and Calif tested 57 native speakers of Hebrew in their fourth year of English instruction. On average, the students were approximately 10 years of age at the time of the study. The study was designed to test the influence of orthographic–phonological and morphological awareness in Hebrew and English on students' ability to read isolated words in English. Through a series of regression analyses, the researchers examined the extent to which performance on the Hebrew tasks predicted English task performance. The findings showed a relationship across Hebrew and English performance on the orthographic–phonological and morphological awareness tasks. However, the prediction of English word reading revealed a more complex relationship across the tasks in the two languages. The results indicated that performance in English word reading was predicted by performance on the English and Hebrew orthographic–phonological and morphological awareness tasks, by the Hebrew word-reading task, and by a three-way interaction of the three Hebrew tasks, such that the cross-language relationship between English and Hebrew word reading was "only indicated when either or both Hebrew orthographic–phonological and morphological-awareness scores [were] deficient" (p. 291).

Wang, Cheng, and Chen (2006) also examined the influence of phonological processing and morphological awareness in measured in Chinese and English on both English word reading and Chinese character reading. The subjects were 64 Chinese immigrant students in grades 1–5 (U.S. school system) who also attended grades 2 and 4 at a Chinese school on weekends. In this study, Chinese phonological and morphological awareness scores did not contribute significantly to the prediction of English word-reading performance over and above the effects of the same variables in English. But English phonological and morphological awareness performance did contribute to the prediction of Chinese character reading over and above the effects of the same variables in Chinese. Similarly to studies reviewed earlier, these results suggest asymmetrical transfer, such that the stronger developed reading skills appear to compensate for low levels of performance in the weaker language. Because these students presumably were receiving more reading instruction in English than in Chinese, the weaker language for literacy purposes was Chinese.

The next set of studies provides evidence suggesting that cross-language transfer of orthographic knowledge may be limited to languages based on similar writing systems. Previous studies have shown transfer of L1 orthographic skills to L2 word reading for alphabetic languages, regardless of similarity in script (Wagner, Spratt, & Ezzaki, 1989). The next set of studies evaluates transfer of orthographic knowledge across different writing systems: alphabetic and logographic.

In a study with some similarities to the Gottardo and colleagues (2001) study, Wang, Perfetti, and Liu (2005) tested whether word and pseudoword reading performance in English could be predicted from measures of phonological and orthographic processing in Chinese. Gottardo and colleagues showed that Chinese rhyme detection predicted English word and pseudoword reading accuracy among native speakers of Cantonese in grades 1–8. Wang and colleagues demonstrated similar results among native Mandarin speakers learning to read English in grades 2 and 3, who were also receiving Mandarin reading instruction on the weekends. The results showed that English word and pseudoword accuracy was predicted by a measure of accuracy in Chinese tone matching; however, no predictive relationship was obtained for a task measuring orthographic skills in Chinese. Thus, the evidence for transfer from Mandarin phonological and orthographic processing to English orthographic processing was restricted to the phonological processing in Mandarin.

Wang and colleagues (2005) also tested whether Chinese character reading could be predicted from the English phonological and orthographic tasks. These analyses yielded no significant results, suggesting that transfer of phonological skills was occurring from the stronger to the weaker of the two languages.

A study by Cheung, Chan, and Chong (2007) provides similar results. They indicate that a task measuring children's ability to use phonetic radicals to derive Chinese character pronunciations was a significant predictor of isolated word reading and of reading comprehension performance in English. However, tasks that measured ortho-semantic processing in Chinese were not predictive of performance on either of the English reading tasks.

## Transfer of Vocabulary Knowledge

The transfer of vocabulary knowledge and its effect on reading has been studied most frequently in relation to bilingual students' ability to recognize semantic similarities among "cognates," words that because of common etymology have similar spellings and/or pronunciations in the two languages. These studies have consistently shown that students exploit knowledge of cognates in the first language to infer the meaning of the unfamiliar English forms (García, 1991; Hancin-Bhatt & Nagy, 1994; James & Klein, 1994; Jiménez, García, & Pearson, 1995; Nagy, García, Durgunoglu, & Hancin-Bhatt, 1993; Saville-Troike, 1984; see Dressler & Kamil [2006] for an in-depth review of these studies). Whereas all the studies reviewed by Dressler and Kamil (2006) indicate that students use knowledge of the first language to benefit their performance in the second language, a study by Cunningham and Graham (2000) shows transfer effects for cognates in the opposite direction. These investigators showed that students can use knowledge of cognates learned in a foreign language to benefit performance in the mother tongue. Cunningham and Graham examined the effects of reversed transfer (from the L2 to the L1) among fourth- to sixth-grade native English-speaking children in a Spanish immersion setting. The study involved a comparison of Spanish immersion students and nonimmersion students on measures of vocabulary knowledge. The results revealed that the immersion students outperformed nonimmersion students on the English Peabody Picture Vocabulary Test (PPVT) items that were cognates, but not on the noncognates. The immersion students also outperformed the nonimmersion students on a measure that tested examinees' knowledge of cognate words that were of low frequency in English and high frequency in Spanish (e.g., *edifice, corridor, infirm, comestibles,* etc.).

More recent research on transfer of vocabulary knowledge has begun to consider transfer of morphological knowledge and its relationship to L2 reading. One of the first research efforts to study transfer of morphological awareness was conducted by Hancin-Bhatt and Nagy (1994), who examined students' knowledge of cognate relations in the context of the development of their knowledge of derivational morphology. The subjects were Spanish–English bilinguals in the fourth, sixth, and eighth grades. The students' cognate knowledge was assessed by means of a translation task that required them to provide a Spanish translation for cognate and noncognate English words that appeared in a sentence context. Students' knowledge of morphological relations across languages was assessed by means of a matching task. This task required that students match an English word, such as *novelty*, to one of four derivationally related Spanish translations. The results indicated transfer of students' ability to recognize morphological relationships across languages. Students were more likely to be able to extract the stem from a derived word containing a cognate stem, such as *naturally*, than from a derived word with a noncognate stem, such as *daintily*.

More recently, Wang and colleagues (2006) have examined the effects of transfer of morphological awareness on reading in a second language. Wang and colleagues examined the influence of transfer of morphological awareness on reading comprehension as part of the earlier reported cross-language transfer of phonological and morphological awareness to word reading in Chinese and English. The same pattern of asymmetrical transfer was obtained as in the analyses for isolated word reading among the sample of Chinese immigrant students who also attended Chinese schools on weekends. Chinese phonological and morphological awareness scores did not contribute significantly to the prediction of English reading comprehension; yet English phonological and morphological awareness performance did contribute to the prediction of Chinese reading comprehension, over and above the effects of the same variables in Chinese.

The last study reviewed in this section examined the contribution of breadth of vocabulary in the first language to reading comprehension performance in the second language. Proctor, August, Carlo, and Snow (2006) examined the contribution of vocabulary, oral comprehension, and orthographic skills in Spanish and English to the prediction of English reading comprehension among 135 Spanish–English bilingual fourth graders. The results revealed a significant main effect for Spanish vocabulary knowledge and an interaction between Spanish vocabulary and English fluency. Plots of this interaction revealed that faster English readers benefited more from Spanish vocabulary knowledge than did their less fluent counterparts. The authors characterized these results as consistent with LaBerge and Samuels's (1974) claim that with more efficient decoding skills, readers could devote greater attention resources to creating meaning from text. They argued that in the bilingual situation, as L2 lexical access requires decreasing attention (i.e., as fluency increases), the bilingual reader is able to devote more cognitive resources to meaning-making strategies that make use of semantic information available in both languages.

## IMPLICATIONS FOR CLASSROOM PRACTICE

Research on cross-language transfer has the potential to contribute to decisions about how to design instruction that maximizes opportunities for L2 learning. It can contribute by identifying not only those domains of language and literacy learning in which transfer is occurring but also those domains in which transfer in unlikely. For example, in a fourth-grade classroom of Spanish-literate students, an English as a second language (ESL) teacher might allocate more of the time available to preteaching high-utility academic English words that do not have Spanish cognates, knowing that the high-utility Academic English words that are cognates to Spanish can be taught in less time, and by reference to the words that the students already know in Spanish.

Research on transfer can also help to optimize learning by identifying those sources of positive transfer that benefit from direct instruction. One of the faulty assumptions that often guided the implementation of transition plans for students entering English-only classrooms, after having "graduated" from transitional bilingual education programs, was the idea that students would be able to figure out, on their own, how the skills they had developed in their first language could be useful in learning English in the mainstream classroom. Instruction that promotes transfer needs to be explicit about how previously acquired knowledge applies to the new learning situation. Knowledge about addition transfers to learning multiplication. Good math instruction makes this relationship explicit to learners even though some may figure it out on their own. Likewise, good ESL literacy instruction should be explicit (in a developmentally appropriate way) about how learning to read English might be similar to reading Arabic for a young Arabic reader, or different from reading Mandarin for a young Mandarin speaker. Instruction might make explicit to Spanish readers who are beginning English reading instruction that many of the consonant letters and their sounds are similar in Spanish and English, but that the vowels are rather different—or, in the case of a more advanced English learner, the reminder that the phonology and spelling of the cognate *confiado* can help to disambiguate the spelling of the schwa in confident.

Research that speaks to the developmental parameters governing transfer can help to guide decisions about the appropriate timing of instruction that promotes transfer. For example, with adequate knowledge about the time course for the development of derivational morphology in the first language, one could make more informed decisions about the timing and appropriateness of instruction about English affixation as a source of information for inferring the meaning of unknown L2 words. A 7-year-old native-English speaker learning French as a foreign language would not benefit from such instruction as much as would an 11-year-old given what we know about the development of derivational morphology knowledge among English speakers (Anglin, 1993).

Finally, research on cross-language transfer also has the potential to guide teacher-educators about the depth of knowledge of applied linguistics that teachers need to be able to identify and correct errors in students' work that stem from the misapplication of knowledge transferred from the first language.

## IMPLICATIONS FOR FUTURE RESEARCH

Research on transfer is important for the contribution it can make to our understanding of L2 and literacy development, and to the development of educational interventions that optimize the conditions that support L2 and literacy development. As studies of cross-language transfer continue, a number of theoretical and methodological issues are in need of further clarification.

As previously stated, research on transfer in reading benefited by the shift to a components process approach to understanding reading. The use of global measures of language and or reading performance did not promote the nuanced understanding of transfer that is needed to make predictions about the locus, timing, conditions, and mechanisms that support it. As should be evident in this review, a substantial number of studies have helped to identify the locus of transfer effects for early reading. The most recent studies appear to signal both an interest and a need for further research that addresses questions about developmental, educational, and linguistic parameters that either constrain or promote transfer. Additionally, cross-language transfer research needs to attend more explicitly to questions about what transfers, and about the cognitive mechanisms that enable transfer. Researchers have implicitly defined what transfers by the choice of measures they have employed. The research reviewed here draws from a broad set of measures of language and literacy that ranges from assessments of metalinguistic and metacognitive processes (e.g., phonemic awareness, cognate awareness, morphological awareness), assessments of declarative knowledge (e.g., letter–sound identification; receptive or productive vocabulary), and even assessments of procedural knowledge (i.e., response time measures of phonological and lexical processing). Decisions about the choice of measures in transfer research need to be tied more deliberately and systematically to hypotheses about the nature of the cognitive operations (i.e., the cognitive mechanisms) that enable transfer. Research on the development of expertise has a long tradition of this in its investigations of transfer of knowledge across domains of expertise (Singley & Anderson, 1989). Research on cross-language transfer might achieve greater theoretical coherence by adopting a similar approach.

## CONCLUDING REMARKS

My purpose in this chapter was to review research evidence that evaluates the relationship between L1 and L2 early reading development. The chapter also has explored the notion that learning to be literate in the mother tongue can be beneficial to the development of these skills in the second language. One of the greatest challenges we face in the United States is cross-language transfer. On a daily basis, children from all over the world come to our schools. Multiple languages are spoken in one classroom. There are many simple, practical suggestions for helping students, such as having a child who speaks both Spanish and English become the buddy of a student who only speaks Spanish. The intent is for the student who speaks both languages to help the other child learn English. But what do we do when there is not a buddy who speaks the language of a child who has just arrived? Having literature and print in the room in languages spoken by the children is another practical idea. But when 10 different languages are spoken in one classroom, this can be difficult to achieve. This chapter has some research-based answers to the issues set forth, but more are needed. Learning to speak and to read English is necessary to succeed in this country, and maintaining literacy in one's first language is also crucial.

# REFERENCES

Abu-Rabia, S. (1997). Verbal and working memory skills of bilingual Hebrew–English speaking children. *International Journal of Psycholinguistics, 13*, 25–40.

Anglin, J. M. (1993). Vocabulary development: A morphological analysis. *Monographs of the Society for Research in Child Development, 58*(10), Serial No. 238.

August, D., & Shanahan, T. (2006). *Developing literacy in second language learners. Report of the National Literacy Panel on Minority-Language Children and Youth.* Mahwah, NJ: Erlbaum.

Bialystok, E. (1997). Effects of bilingualism and biliteracy on children's emerging concepts of print. *Developmental Psychology, 33*(3), 429–440.

Branum-Martin, L., Mehta, P. D., Fletcher, J. M., Carlson, C. D., Ortiz, A., & Carlo, M. S. (2006). Bilingual phonological awareness: Multilevel construct validation among Spanish-speaking kindergarteners in transitional bilingual education classrooms. *Journal of Educational Psychology, 98*(1), 170–181.

Campbell, D. T., & Stanley, J. C. (1963). *Experimental and quasiexperimental designs for research.* Chicago: Rand McNally.

Campos, J. (1985). *A Spanish language preschool program: Carpinteria Unified School District.* (ERIC Document Reproduction Service No. ED 283369)

Cardenas-Hagan, E., Carlson, C., & Pollard-Durodola, S. D. (2007). The cross-linguistic transfer of early literacy skills: The role of initial L1 and L2 skills and language of instruction. *Language Speech and Hearing Services in Schools, 38*(3), 249–259.

Cheung, H., Chan, M., & Chong, K. (2007). Use of orthographic knowledge in reading by Chinese-English bi-scriptal children. *Language Learning, 57*, 469.

Cisero, C. A., & Royer, J. M. (1995). The development and cross-language transfer of phonological awareness. *Contemporary Educational Psychology, 20*(3), 275–303.

Comeau, L., Cormier, P., Grandmaison, E., & Lacroix, D. (1999). A longitudinal study of phonological processing skills in children learning to read in a second language. *Journal of Educational Psychology, 91*, 29–43.

Cummins, J. (1978). Educational implications of mother tongue maintenance in minoritylanguage groups. *Canadian Modern Language Review, 35*, 395–416.

Cummins, J. (1979). Linguistic interdependence and the educational development of bilingual children. *Review of Educational Research, 49*(2), 222–251.

Cummins, J. (1980). The crosslingual dimensions of language proficiency: Implications for bilingual education and the optimal age issue. *TESOL Quarterly, 14*(2), 175–187.

Cummins, J. (1984). *Bilingualism and special education: Issues in assessment and pedagogy.* San Diego, CA: College Hill Press.

Cummins, J., Swain, M., Nakajima, K., Handscombe, J., Green, D., & Tran, C. (1984). Linguistic interdependence among Japanese and Vietnamese immigrant students. In C. Rivera (Ed.), *Communicative competence approaches to language proficiency assessment: Research and application.* Clevedon, UK: Multilingual Matters.

Cunningham, T. H., & Graham, C. R. (2000). Increasing native English vocabulary recognition through Spanish immersion: Cognate transfer from foreign to first language. *Journal of Educational Psychology, 92*(1), 37–49.

da Fontoura, H. A., & Siegel, L. S. (1995). Reading, syntactic, and working memory skills of bilingual Portuguese-English Canadian children. *Reading and Writing: An Interdisciplinary Journal, 7*, 139–153.

Deacon, S. H., Wade-Woolley, L., & Kirby, J. (2007). Crossover: The role of morphological awareness in French immersion children's reading. *Developmental Psychology, 43*, 732–746.

Dressler, C., & Kamil, M. (2006). First- and second-language literacy. In D. August & T. Shanahan (Eds.), *Developing literacy in second language learners. Report of the National Literacy Panel on Minority-Language Children and Youth* (pp. 197–239). Mahwah, NJ: Erlbaum.

Durgunoglu, A. Y., Nagy, W. E., & Hancin-Bhatt, B. J. (1993). Cross-language transfer of phonological awareness. *Journal of Educational Psychology, 85*(3), 453–465.

Escamilla, K. (1987). *The relationship of native language reading achievement and oral English proficiency to future achievement in reading English as a second language.* Unpublished doctoral dissertation, University of California, Los Angeles.

García, G. E. (1991). Factors influencing the English reading test performance of Spanish-speaking Hispanic children. *Reading Research Quarterly, 26*(4), 371–392.

Genesee, F., & Geva, E. (2006). Cross-linguistic relationships in working memory, phonological processes, and oral language. In D. August & T. Shanahan (Eds.), *Developing literacy in second language learners. Report of the National Literacy Panel on Minority-Language Children and Youth* (pp. 175–184). Mahwah, NJ: Erlbaum.

Gholamain, M., & Geva, E. (1999). Orthographic and cognitive factors in the concurrent development of basic reading skills in English and Persian. *Language Learning, 49*(20, 183–217.

Gottardo, A. (2002). Language and reading skills in bilingual Spanish-English speakers. *Topics in Language Disorders, 23*, 42–66.

Gottardo, A., Yan, B., Siegel, L. S., & Wade-Woolley, L. (2001). Predictors of English reading in children with Chinese as a first language. *Journal of Educational Psychology, 93*, 530–542.

Gough, P. B. (1971). One second of reading. In J. Kavanaugh & I. Mattingly (Eds.), *Language by ear and by eye* (pp. 331–358). Cambridge, MA: MIT Press.

Hancin-Bhatt, B., & Nagy, W. (1994). Lexical transfer and second language morphological development. *Applied Psycholinguistics, 15*(3), 289–310.

Harrison, G. L., & Krol, L. (2007). The relationship between L1 and L2 word-level reading and phonological processing in ESL adults. *Journal of Research in Reading, 30*(4), 379–393.

James, C., & Klein, K. (1994). Foreign language learners' spelling and proof-reading strategies. *Papers and Studies in Contrastive Linguistics, 29*, 31–46.

Jiménez, R., García, G., & Pearson, P. (1995). Three children, two languages, and strategic reading: Case studies in bilingual/monolingual reading. *American Educational Research Journal, 32*, 67–97.

Kaufman, M. (1968). Will instruction in reading Spanish affect ability in reading English? *Journal of Reading, 11*(6), 521–527.

Kendall, J., Lajeunesse, G., Chmilar, P., Rauch Shapson, L., & Shapson, S. M. (1987). English reading skills of French immersion students in kindergarten and grades 1 and 2. *Reading Research Quarterly, 22*(2), 135–154.

LaBerge, D., & Samuels, S. J. (1974). Toward a theory of automatic information process in reading. *Cognitive Psychology, 6*, 293–323.

Lambert, W. E., & Tucker, G. R. (1972). *Bilingual education of children: The St. Lambert experiment.* Rowley, MA: Newbury House.

Modiano, N. (1979). The most effective language of instruction for beginning reading: A field study. In H. T. Trueba & C. BarnettMizrahi (Eds.), *Bilingual multicultural education and the professional: From theory to practice.* Rowley, MA: Newbury House.

Nagy, W., García, G. E., Durgunoglu, A. Y., & Hancin-Bhatt, B. (1993). Spanish–English bilingual students' use of cognates in English reading. *Journal of Reading Behavior, 25*(3), 241–259.

Perfetti, C. A. (1988). Verbal efficiency in reading ability. In G. E. MacKinnon, T. G. Waller, & M. Daneman (Eds.), *Reading research: Advances in theory and practice* (Vol. 6, pp. 109–143). New York: Academic Press.

Proctor, C. P., August, D., Carlo, M. S., & Snow, C. E. (2006). The intriguing role of Spanish language vocabulary knowledge in predicting English reading comprehension. *Journal of Educational Psychology, 98*(1), 159–169.

Quiroga, T., Lemos-Britton, Z., Mostafapour, E., Abbott, R. D., & Berninger, V. W. (2002). Phonological awareness and beginning reading in Spanish-speaking ESL first graders: Research into practice. *Journal of School Psychology, 40*(1), 85–111.

Rosier, P., & Farella, M. (1976). Bilingual education at Rock Point—some early results. *TESOL Quarterly, 10*(4), 379–388.

Royer, J. M., & Carlo, M. S. (1991). Using the sentence verification technique to measure transfer of comprehension skills from native to second language. *Journal of Reading, 34*(6), 450–455.

San Francisco, A. R., Carlo, M., August, D., & Snow, C. E. (2006). The role of language of instruction and vocabulary in the English phonological awareness of Spanish-English bilingual children. *Applied Psycholinguistics, 27,* 229–246.

Saville-Troike, M. (1984). What really matters in second language learning for academic achievement? *TESOL Quarterly, 17,* 199–219.

Schiff, R., & Calif, S. (2007). Role of phonological and morphological awareness in L2 oral word reading. *Language Learning, 57*(2), 271–298.

Singley, M. K., & Anderson, J. R. (1989). *The transfer of cognitive skill.* Cambridge, MA: Harvard University Press.

Snow, C., Burns, M. S., & Griffin, P. (1998). *Preventing reading difficulties in young children.* Washington, DC: National Academy Press.

Wagner, D. A., Spratt, J. E., & Ezzaki, A. (1989). Does learning to read in a second language always put the child at a disadvantage?: Some counterevidence from Morocco. *Applied Psycholinguistics, 10,* 31–48.

Wang, M., Cheng, C., & Chen, S. (2006). Contribution of morphological awareness to Chinese-English biliteracy acquisition. *Journal of Educational Psychology, 98*(3), 542–553.

Wang, M., Perfetti, C. A., & Liu, Y. (2005). Chinese-English biliteracy acquisition: Cross-language and writing system transfer. *Cognition, 97,* 67–88.

# CHAPTER 15

# Learning to Read in English

*Teaching Phonics to Beginning Readers
from Diverse Backgrounds*

Linnea C. Ehri

Learning to read in an alphabetic writing system is not possible without phonics. The term "phonics" has two meanings. It refers to beginning reading *instruction* that is designed to teach letter–sound relations and their use in reading words in or out of text. It also refers to the *knowledge and skills* that are learned. Most children require explicit instruction to acquire phonics knowledge and skills. This is particularly true in a nontransparent, complex writing system, such as English. The purpose of this chapter is to review theory and research to clarify the phonics knowledge and skills that beginning readers need to acquire and the forms of instruction that facilitate acquisition in English, giving special consideration to the needs of beginning readers of low socioeconomic status (SES) and to language-minority (LM) children from families whose primary language is not English.[1] The major topics considered are as follows:

- Phonemic awareness and instruction
- Letter knowledge and instruction
- Word reading skills and beginning reading instruction

## PREVIEW OF PHONICS KNOWLEDGE AND SKILLS

Phonics instruction provides foundational knowledge of the writing system and its application to reading. This includes concepts about print, such as left-to-right orientation. It includes "phonemic awareness," which is the ability to distinguish and manipulate the smallest sounds in spoken words called "phonemes" (e.g., four phonemes in *s-t-o-p*; three phonemes in *ch-e-ck*). It includes 52 letter shapes, their names, and the major grapheme–phoneme correspondences. Phonics instruction teaches word reading skills. This includes two print-based strategies to decode words: "phonological recoding," which involves transforming graphemes into phonemes and blending them to form recognizable words, and "analogizing," which involves applying letter patterns from known words to read new words. This includes a text-based strategy involving prediction to identify or confirm the pronunciations and meanings of written words. It includes building a sight vocabulary. This involves fully analyzing *specific* written words by computing grapheme–phoneme (GP) mapping relations that connect letters in the spellings of words to phonemes detected in their pronunciations. Application of GP knowledge enables beginners to remember how to read words that they practice and also to spell words. A growing memory bank of sight words combined with strategies for decoding unknown words enables beginners to read text independently.

## BEGINNING READERS FROM DIVERSE BACKGROUNDS

Of special concern are the needs of low-SES children and LM children, many of whom are also low in SES (August & Shanahan, 2006). LM children include bilinguals and English language learners. These children are more likely to enter school with little foundational knowledge in reading. Frequently they join kindergarten and first-grade classmates who already have letter knowledge, phonemic awareness, and even some reading ability. This creates large disparities in students' response to formal reading instruction. Whereas well-prepared children may scarcely be affected by instruction that slights foundational and word reading skills, ill-prepared children may find it devastating and may make little progress. Thus, it is especially important for teachers and teacher educators to understand fully the foundational and word reading skills that are important and how to teach them. Studies indicate that many teachers lack an adequate understanding of reading acquisition processes, particularly phonemic awareness (McCutchen et al., 2002; Moats, 1994; Scarborough, Ehri, Olson, & Fowler, 1998). Instructional shortcomings that result from either less effective beginning reading curricula or poorly trained teachers hit hardest those children who are least prepared in literacy when they enter school.

Approaches to reading instruction that are effective with native-English speakers have also been found to be effective with LM and low-SES students. The same foundational skills, word reading strategies, and accumulation of sight words in memory are required. Across several studies, findings indicate that LM students and native English-speaking students learn to read in similar ways. When LM students from preschool through second grade received explicit, high-quality phonics instruction, they were able to acquire word recognition and spelling skills as well as children learning in their first language (Geva & Siegel, 2000; Lesaux

& Siegel, 2002; Roberts & Neal, 2004; Stuart, 1999). These findings are not surprising. The words and meanings that readers encounter in beginning-level texts are basic, so at least some knowledge of English vocabulary and syntax may be sufficient for reading comprehension. The difficult part for beginners involves learning letters and the writing system. Acquisition of these skills is influenced primarily by the quality of classroom instruction rather than by students' oral language proficiency (Ehri & Roberts, 2006).

Although the phonics skills to be acquired are the same, some adjustments to instruction for LM and low-SES students may be necessary (August & Shanahan, 2006). More extensive attention to oral language, articulatory accuracy, and vocabulary growth is important, particularly as these children move beyond second grade and encounter less common words in the texts they read (Hart & Risley, 1995; Roberts, 2005). Also, because languages differ in the sounds that are phonemically distinct, LM children need to learn those phonemic categories that exist in English but not in their first language. LM students who have already learned to read a nonalphabetic language, such as Chinese, may have more trouble acquiring phonemic awareness and working out GP mapping relations in English words than LM students who are accustomed to reading an alphabetic script (August & Shanahan, 2006). Systematic phonics instruction is likely to be more effective if it addresses these special needs.

## The English Writing System

In contrast to other writing systems, such as Spanish or Finnish, with highly predictable mappings between graphemes and phonemes in the spellings of words, the English writing system lacks transparency and is complex (Seymour, Aro, & Erskine, 2003). However, it is not hopelessly irregular (Moats, 2000; Venezky, 1999). The spellings of words are standardized. They comprise graphemes (one or more letters) representing phonemes (smallest sounds) in spoken words. For example, graphemes in the word *ship* comprise the digraph SH plus two single letters, each representing a separate phoneme. GP relations may be variable, with the same letter representing more than one phoneme (e.g., C representing /k/ or /s/),[2] and single phonemes represented by alternative graphemes (e.g., /j/ written J, G, or DG). As a result, reading and spelling English words require knowledge of the writing system combined with memory for specific word forms. Readers apply their general knowledge of GP mapping relations to specific words to remember which of the possible ways those words are written. For example, although /sIti/ might be spelled *sitty* or *sittie* or *citty* or *cittie*, the correct spelling to be remembered is *city*. Multiple experiences with the correct word form establish GP connections between its spelling and pronunciation, along with its meaning in memory.

Spelling regularities in English also exist at the grapho-syllabic and morphographic levels. Syllabic and subsyllabic segments map onto spelling units larger than grapho-phonemic units such as *-ing*, *-ake*, or *-tion*, that recur in many different words. The rime spelling pattern in monosyllabic words is a source of regularity. The rime unit comprises the vowel plus the consonants that follow it, for example, *-ide* in *side*, *ride*, *hide*, and *tide*. Spellings of a limited number of rimes, as few as 37 patterns, recur in over 500 words (Stahl, Osborn, & Lehr, 1990). Words may share common roots or morphemes that are spelled consistently in derived forms of the words, such as *sign*, *signal*, and *signature*, or *cite*, *city*, *citizen*, and *citadel*. For the beginning reader, the main problem is to acquire knowledge of the writing system at the GP level. Then as this knowledge is applied in learning to read and spell words, the larger spelling units are formed out of these smaller units (Ehri, 2005; Seymour, 2005).

Although the writing system is variable and includes irregularities such as the *AI* in *said* and the *F* in *of*, the focus of systematic phonics instruction is on teaching beginners to expect and to seek regularities as they encounter and learn new words. LM students who are already literate in a transparent writing system may have an advantage in holding a set for regularity when they learn to read English. Moreover, LM students may detect regularities from "cognates," that is, words whose spellings and meanings bear a resemblance in both languages (e.g., Spanish cognates *bank* vs. *banco*, *reason* vs. *razonar*).

## PHONEMIC AWARENESS

Phonemes are the smallest sounds comprising spoken language. English comprises 41–44 phonemes depending on one's dialect. "Phonemic awareness" (PA) refers to the ability to shift attention away from meaning, and to focus on and manipulate phonemes in spoken words. PA is different from "phonological awareness," which is a more encompassing term that refers not only to phonemes but also to awareness of larger spoken units, such as syllables and rhyming words. Instruction typically begins by teaching children to distinguish and manipulate these larger units in words (Adams, Foorman, Lundberg, & Beeler, 1998). However, the most important skill that prepares beginners for reading is PA (Liberman, Shankweiler, Fisher, & Carter, 1974).

Several types of tasks have been used to assess and teach PA: (1) phoneme *isolation*, which requires extracting and identifying single phonemes in words, such as the beginning or ending sound; (2) phoneme *identity*, which requires identifying the common phoneme in two or more different words; (3) phoneme *categorization*, which requires identifying from a set of three or four words the word that does not share phonemes with the other words (e.g., *bat*, *bag*, *top*); (4) phoneme *blending*, which requires listening to a sequence of separately articulated phonemes and combining them to form a recognizable word; (5) phoneme *segmentation*, which requires dividing a word into its constituent phonemes; and (6) phoneme *deletion* or *substitution*, which requires identifying what new word remains when a specified phoneme is removed (e.g., "Say *black* without /b/), or when one phoneme is substituted for another phoneme (e.g., "Take away the /k/ sound from *cat* and put in the /m/ sound"). It is important to note that the concept of PA pertains to spoken language, not to letters, although its purpose is to enable beginners to map phonemes onto graphemes in learning to read and spell.

Many studies have shown the importance of PA in learning to read and spell (Ehri, Nunes, Willows, et al., 2001). When measured at the beginning of kindergarten, it is one of two best predictors of how well children will learn to read during the first 2 years of reading instruction (Share, Jorm, Maclean, & Matthews, 1984). (The other predictor is letter knowledge.) Phoneme blending skill enables students to combine phonemes into a recognizable pronunciation when decoding unfamiliar written words. Phoneme segmentation skill enables students to distinguish the separate phonemes in spoken words to generate plausible spellings. Also, phoneme segmentation skill enables students to connect graphemes to phonemes within the pronunciations of specific words to retain them in memory for reading and spelling (Ehri, 1992, 1998). These processes are discussed further below.

One reason why PA is especially important to teach explicitly is that phonemic constituents are not obvious to preliterate children, whose focus is on the meaning of language rather than its formal properties. Children are not used to treating language as an object that can be inspected. Another reason is that speech is a continuous stream of sound. Separate phonemes are hard to distinguish, because the sounds overlap and are folded into each other, without any breaks signaling where one phoneme ends and the next begins. Moreover, in a language such as English, with an opaque writing system, the mapping relations between graphemes and phonemes within the spellings of some words are less obvious. In a meta-analysis of experiments that examined the contribution of PA instruction in various languages, results showed that PA instruction in English produced a greater boost to reading than PA instruction in other languages (Ehri, Nunes, Willows, et al., 2001). This occurred presumably because mapping graphemes onto phonemes is harder to figure out in English than in more transparent languages (Share, 2008).

It has been proposed that children who learn English as a second language may have an advantage in PA tasks. Knowing two languages may enhance awareness because it draws children's attention to the formal properties of language as distinct from semantic properties. Bialystok, Majumder, and Martin (2003) examined this possibility by recruiting English-speaking first and second graders, and comparing monolinguals to bilinguals whose first language was French, Spanish, or Chinese. They administered various PA tasks. Across three studies, they failed to find consistent differences favoring the bilinguals. In fact, in one of the studies, Spanish bilinguals outperformed monolinguals, but Chinese bilinguals did worse than monolinguals on a phoneme segmentation task. They conclude that bilingual children do not acquire PA more easily than do monolingual children.

## Instruction

PA may be taught in several different ways. One factor influencing the tasks chosen is the skill level of the student. Those who are prereaders, with little reading or spelling ability and little insight about phonemes, require easier PA tasks, such as phoneme isolation or phoneme identity, to get started (Byrne, 1992; Stahl & Murray, 1994). Also, the words being manipulated make a difference. Words with fewer phonemes, only two or three, and words lacking consonant clusters (e.g., *bl-, st-, -mp, -nd*) are easier for beginners to blend and segment (Uhry & Ehri, 1999).

The research of Byrne and Fielding-Barnsley (1995) illustrates how an easier form of PA, phoneme identity, can be taught effectively. To teach 4-year-olds to recognize when the same phoneme recurred in different words, children were shown pictures of a variety of objects and were taught to select those whose names began with the same first sound (e.g., *sea, seal, sailor, sand*). They were also taught to identify pictures whose names ended with the same sound. One phoneme in one position was taught to small groups in each session. The letter representing the target phoneme was included as well. The control group engaged in story reading and meaning-based activities using the same pictures. After completing 12 training sessions, posttests were given. The PA-trained children outperformed the control group on initial and final phoneme identity tasks with taught phonemes as well as phonemes that were not taught. Also, the PA group did better at matching written and spoken words. Some long-term benefits of PA instruction on reading were observed 3 years later.

Although PA involves analyzing phonemes in spoken words, research has shown that providing learners with concrete visual markers facilitates the acquisition of PA. One reason is that speech is ephemeral, making it hard to analyze. Sounds disappear as soon as they are spoken, whereas visual markers have permanence. Elkonin (1973) was among the first to study this effect. He taught Russian children to break words apart into their constituent phonemes by pronouncing each phoneme as they moved a cardboard counter into a row of horizontal boxes, as shown in Figure 15.1, for *hat* and *desk*. He found that children who were trained in this way learned to segment words better than did children trained without counters or boxes.

Another way to make phonemes concrete is by teaching children to monitor the articulatory gestures involved in pronouncing words. Mouth positions are easier to hold still and analyze than sounds, which are short-lived and fleeting. This approach is used in the Lindamood Phoneme Sequencing (LIPS) program, designed to teach struggling readers to read and spell (Lindamood & Lindamood, 1998). Castiglioni-Spalten and Ehri (2003) tested this approach with kindergartners who could name many alphabet letters but had not acquired PA. They were taught to associate phonemes with pictures of mouth positions depicting those phonemes, as shown in Figure 15.2. For example, a picture of closed lips was taught as the gesture for /m/, /p/, and /b/, and a picture of lips slightly open in a

**FIGURE 15.1.** Elkonin boxes into which children move cardboard counters as they pronounce phonemic segments in *hat* and *desk*.

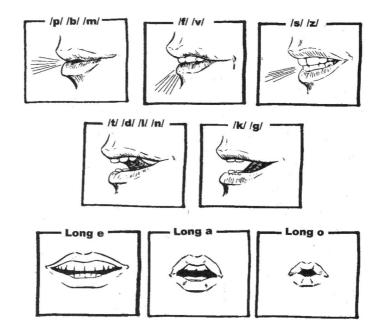

**FIGURE 15.2.** Mouth pictures depicting 13 consonant and 3 vowel phonemes used to teach children to segment words into a sequence of articulatory gestures. Mouth drawings from Lindamood and Lindamood (1975). Copyright 1975 by C. and P. Lindamood. Reprinted by permission.

smile was taught as the gesture for /i/ (i.e., long *e* as in *beet*). They used mirrors to compare the pictures to their own mouth positions. Then they practiced using these pictures to track their mouth movements in pronouncing words, for example, *meat*, depicted with three mouth pictures, lips closed for /m/, smile for /i/, and lips open and tongue up for /t/ (see Figure 15.2). It was not difficult to teach children to select mouth pictures as they segmented the sounds in words, and they were intrigued by the process. A control group was taught to segment the same words using blocks without mouth pictures. Both groups were taught PA to a criterion of mastery. Also, a no-treatment control group was included. Findings on posttests showed that both forms of PA training enabled children to segment sounds in words and to spell the sounds better than the no-treatment control group. However, only articulatory instruction enhanced children's word reading processes. These findings suggest the value of teaching beginners to monitor not only sounds that they hear but also sounds that they feel their mouths making.

Another form of materialization involves teaching PA with letters, once children know the letters. Hohn and Ehri (1983) compared two ways of teaching phoneme segmentation. One group learned to segment words into phonemes using blank counters, and the other group learned with counters displaying letters. The children were kindergartners who knew the names of letters but lacked phoneme segmentation skill and were nonreaders. Results at the end of training indicated that both PA-trained groups could segment words better than a no-treatment control group, indicating that both methods taught the children to segment. However, children who were trained with letters segmented words better than did children trained with blank markers on posttests, where segmentation was performed without letters. The explanation is that letters provided concrete symbols for the phonemes, thus helping children focus on and distinguish them in words.

Teaching phonemic segmentation with letters is the equivalent of teaching students to invent spellings of words by segmenting pronunciations into sounds, and writing letters for those sounds. This is a commonly used writing activity in kindergarten. However, for children to progress in their phonics skills, it is important that teachers extend children's analyses by providing explicit instruction in how to segment words into phonemes, and how to select letters for those phonemes rather than leave children to invent on their own.

The National Reading Panel (2000) conducted a meta-analysis of many experiments that compared the performance of groups who received PA instruction and control groups that did not receive PA instruction (Ehri, Nunes, Willows, et al., 2001). The studies were coded so that those with certain characteristics could be compared, including the SES levels of participants and whether PA was taught orally or with letters. Results confirmed the value of PA instruction for teaching low-SES students PA and for improving their reading and spelling skills. PA instruction was more effective when taught with letters than without letters. PA instruction proved especially valuable when taught early to preschoolers. Instruction did not have to be lengthy (i.e., longer than 20 hours total) to be maximally effective.

To summarize, PA is an important foundational skill that is part of phonics instruction. It enables students to access the smallest sounds in spoken words, a skill that is not easy but is necessary for learning to read and spell words. Various forms of instruction are effective for teaching PA. Instruction can be enhanced by materializing phonemes with markers, articulatory pictures, or letters. The goals of PA instruction are to enable students to blend phonemes in decoding words, to segment phonemes in spelling words, and to clarify the phonemes in pronunciations that map onto graphemes in the spellings of specific words.

## Alphabet Letters

The most important foundational skill in learning to read is learning the shapes, names, and sounds of letters. Learning letters typically begins very early at home or preschool, when children learn letters in their own names (Bloodgood, 1999; Levin & Ehri, in press; Treiman & Broderick, 1998). Mastery and even overlearning of letters are thought to be important prerequisites for making good progress in learning to read (Adams, 1990). Seymour, Duncan, Aro, and Baillie (2007) found that children needed to know at least 80% of the letters in English before their reading skills took off.

Letter-name knowledge is one of the best predictors of how well children learn to read when formal reading instruction begins (Share et al., 1984). One reason is that most of the names contain relevant sounds, either at the beginning or end of the names, for example, *tee* containing /t/, *em* containing /m/. Although the letter *H* represents the sound /h/ not found in its name, its name *aich* contains the relevant sound /č/ found in GP mappings of words, such as *check*. When children first begin analyzing the sounds in words and picking letters to spell them, they consult sounds in letter names, for example, using YL to spell *while*, and HK to spell *chicken* (Read, 1971; Treiman, 1993). Also, beginners who know letter names are able to use these names to remember how to read simplified spellings of words. Several studies have shown that prereaders can remember how to read words, such as JL for *jail*, GRF for *giraffe*, and LFT for *elephant*, better than spellings that are visually distinctive but nonphonetic, for example, XYP for *giraffe* (De Abreu & Cardoso-Martins, 1998; Ehri & Wilce, 1985; Roberts, 2003; Scott & Ehri, 1989; Treiman & Rodriguez, 1999). In contrast, children who do not know letters learn the visual forms better than they learn the phonetic forms. This shows that letter knowledge influences word reading processes as soon as letter name or letter–sound associations are learned.

Another advantage of knowing letters names is that they provide a way of talking about letters as objects in discussing the spellings of words. This function of letter names is particularly important in a less transparent orthography such as English, where there is much ambiguity about how to spell words correctly. I am told that if someone asks a Spanish speaker how to spell a word, the answer may be a single letter, because there is only one letter that is ambiguous in that word's spelling. In contrast, such a question about the spelling of an English word elicits the names of all the letters, because many letters may be ambiguous.

Various factors influence the learning of letters. Working with low-SES 4-year-olds, Justice Pence, Bowles, and Wiggins (2006) identified four factors. Children were more likely to know the letters in their personal names, letters closer to the beginning of the alphabet, letters whose names contain sounds that are symbolized by those letters in the writing system, and consonant letters whose sounds are known to emerge earlier during the course of phonological development. Treiman, Levin, and Kessler (2006) analyzed the letter errors that 4- and 5-year-olds made in an attempt to identify factors that created confusion and slowed down learning. Names of letters were mixed up with names of numbers. Letters with similar shapes were commonly confused (i.e., *S* vs. *Z*, *U* vs. *V*). The confusion was greater when both the shapes and the names were similar (i.e., *b* /bi/ and *d* /di/). Letters that were adjacent in the alphabet sequence were sometimes mistaken for each other.

Kindergartners differ greatly in their knowledge of letter names when they enter school. Bowey (1995) found that 5-year-olds from low-SES homes knew only half as many letter names as children from high-SES homes. This makes a big difference in the ease of learning letter–sound relations. In an experiment, Share (2004a) found that letter–sound learning was much faster when children already knew the names of letters containing those sounds than when they did not. This finding carries an important implication for classroom instruction. Students who enter school already knowing most letters will have a decided edge over those who do not know letters. Teachers need to identify such disparities by assessing children's letter knowledge, then providing effective instruction to make sure that those without such knowledge catch up. Otherwise, when confronted with further instruction in reading, students with holes in their GP mapping capabilities will struggle.

## Instruction

Analysis of letter learning reveals three parts: stimulus learning (shapes), response learning (names and sounds), and associative learning. The shapes of uppercase and lowercase letters must be learned so that students can recognize, distinguish among, and write them from memory. The shapes must be associated with names and sounds. Mnemonic devices can contribute to letter learning by making the information more memorable and reducing learning time. Various types of mnemonics have been studied (Ehri & Roberts, 2006).

To teach students the names of letters and their alphabetic order, a commonly taught mnemonic is the alphabet song. Although students learn to recite all the names, they may not recognize where one name ends and the next begins. For example, *elemenopee*, may be regarded as one nonsense word rather than five letter names. Additional instruction is needed to break apart the names. A benefit is that the song familiarizes students with the set of letter-name responses that need to be associated with letter shapes.

Most studies and instructional schemes involving mnemonics have focused on teaching GP associations. Marsh and Desberg (1978) compared two types, first-sound mnemonics involving pictures whose names began with the sound of the letter (e.g., *pumpkin* for /p/), and action mnemonics involving pictures depicting an action that produces the sound (e.g., a boy blowing out a candle and saying /p/). Control groups were shown no pictures or irrelevant pictures. Results indicated that mnemonic-trained children could produce the sounds better than controls when the pictures were in view, but *not* when the pictures were removed and only the letters were shown. Perhaps more practice was needed for these mnemonics to become associated with the letters themselves.

Letter-shape learning and associative learning are more effectively taught with embedded picture mnemonics. In this case, links between letter shapes and their phonemes are mediated via objects that resemble letter shapes and have names beginning with the letters' sounds. Examples are shown in Figure 15.3. Ehri, Deffner, and Wilce (1984) examined the value of embedded picture mnemonics. They selected children who did not know the names or sounds of the letters that were taught. First, children were taught phoneme isolation to enable them to segment initial sounds in the names of the mnemonic objects (e.g., /s/ in *snake*). Second, the treatment group was taught letter–sound associations, with letters that were drawn to assume the shapes of familiar objects, for example, *s* was drawn as a snake, *h* was drawn as a house with a chimney, *w* was drawn as wings on an insect. Children were taught to look at the letters, remember the objects resembling the shapes of the letters, and produce the first sound in those

**FIGURE 15.3.** Integrated picture menmonics to teach the grapheme–phoneme relations for *a, c, k,* and *z*. From Wendon (2007). Copyright 2007 by L. Wendon. Reprinted by permission. See *www.letterland.com*.

objects' names (i.e., *S, snake, /s/*). Two control conditions were included. In one, children were taught the same associations, but the drawings of objects did not resemble letter shapes, called "disassociated mnemonics." For example, the snake was stretched out rather than wavy. In the other control condition, children practiced associating the shapes, sounds, and object names, but without any pictures. Results showed that children took less time to learn the letter–sound associations with embedded mnemonics than in the other conditions, and they remembered them better.

Findings were replicated in a study teaching Hebrew letter–sound relations to English-speaking children (Shmidman, 2008). For example, the Hebrew letter ש was embedded in a drawing of a ship with three sails to teach the association between the letter's shape, the mnemonic word *ship*, and the initial sound /š/. In this study, findings showed that embedded mnemonics enabled children to learn letter–sound relations more quickly, they improved children's memory for the shapes of the letters and their association to sounds, and they reduced confusion among similarly shaped letters. In addition, in tasks where children read and spelled English words using Hebrew letters, those who had learned with embedded mnemonics outperformed those who had learned letters with disassociated mnemonics.

Embedded letter mnemonics to teach letter–sound relations have been incorporated into several commercial programs, such as Letterland (Wendon, 1992, 2007). (See Figure 15.3.) Although mnemonics may not be needed by children who already know letters containing the relevant sounds in their names, mnemonics can still help them learn the sounds of letters not present in names. These include the five short vowels (i.e., vowels in *at, Ed, it, on, up*), as well as the consonants *C* for /k/, *G* for /g/, *H* for /h/, *W* for /w/, *Y* for /y/, and the consonant digraphs *CH*, *TH*, and *SH*. Also, embedded mnemonics can reduce confusion when letters have similar shapes (i.e., *b/d, p/q, n/u, m/w, s/z*), and when the names of letters begin with another letter's sound at the beginning of the alphabet name (i.e., *c, f, g, h, l, m, n, q, r, s, w, x*, and *y*).

To summarize, mastery of letter shapes, names, and GP relations is fundamental in learning to read and spell. The first letters that children learn are those in their personal names. Children who already know letter names have an easier time learning sounds when the names contain these sounds compared to children who do not know letter names. Once children learn letters, they can perform reading and spelling tasks using this knowledge. Mnemonic devices are useful for teaching letter–sound relations, particularly embedded picture mnemonics.

## WORD READING SKILLS

Words are the basic units of written language. Becoming a skilled reader requires learning to read words automatically, in or out of context. Reading words entails recognizing their pronunciations, meanings, and function in sentences (Ehri,

1980, 1991, 1992). There are various ways that readers might read words. If they have never read the words before, they might apply the following strategies to figure out their identities:

1. *Phonological recoding.* Reading words by recoding or decoding involves transforming graphemes into phonemes and blending them to form spoken words with recognizable meanings. It also involves blending larger syllabic spelling units. This decoding strategy is the hallmark of synthetic phonics instruction.
2. *Analogizing.* Reading words by analogy involves applying parts of known words to read new words, for example, reading *faint* by analogy to *paint* (Gaskins, Ehri, Cress, O'Hara, & Donnelly, 1996–1997; Goswami, 1986). To facilitate analogizing, a set of key words containing common spelling patterns may be taught as the analogues.
3. *Prediction.* Predicting words involves combining letter cues with cues from the surrounding context to anticipate a word's pronunciation and meaning (Tunmer & Chapman, 2006). Although this strategy helps readers identify words that are too difficult to decode, the downside is that it limits new word learning if readers guess words and ignore their written forms (Rosenthal & Ehri, 2008b). Proponents of systematic phonics instruction regard prediction as a backup strategy to *confirm* the identities of unfamiliar words, once their spellings have been decoded.

Whereas readers apply these strategies to figure out unknown words, they read words they have read before by accessing them in memory, also referred to as "reading words by sight" (Ehri, 1992, 2005). The process of retaining sight words in memory does not involve memorizing the shapes or other strictly visual features of words, without regard to GP mappings within the words. Rather, sight word learning requires readers to form connections between graphemes in spellings and phonemes in pronunciations to retain the words in memory. PA and knowledge of the alphabetic system enable readers to form these connections. The connections provide the "glue" that secures specific written words in memory for reading and for spelling. This connection-forming process applies to all words, not just regularly spelled words. Even irregularly spelled words contain some graphemes that map onto phonemes within the words, for example, all letters but the *W* in *sword*, two letters *S* and *D* in *said*, and *W* and *S* in *was*. Although *F* in the word *of* (/ʌv/) is considered irregular, the expected sound of *F* is articulated in the same place as /v/. Rack, Hulme, Snowling, and Wightman (1994) showed that beginning readers could use such articulatory similarities to remember how to read words.

When readers encounter an unfamiliar written word, they may determine its spoken identity and meaning by applying strategies such as phonological recoding, analogizing, or prediction, or by asking someone. When the word is seen and pronounced, connections are activated between spelling units and sounds along with meanings. Reading the word one or more times in this way secures it in memory, so that it can be read by sight. All words, once they have been practiced, are read from memory by sight. Several studies have documented this connection-forming process in students learning to read words (Ehri & Saltmarsh, 1995; Ehri & Wilce, 1985; Rack et al., 1994; Share, 1999, 2004b).

Acquiring a growing memory of sight words that can be recognized automatically, without expending any attention or effort, is essential for becoming a skilled reader (LaBerge & Samuels, 1974). When readers' eyes land on words that they know automatically, they recognize them as single units rather than as a sequence of graphemes and phonemes (Ehri & Wilce, 1983), and their pronunciations and meanings are activated immediately in memory (Guttentag & Haith, 1978). It is this capability that enables readers to read text efficiently and to concentrate on the meaning, without having to shift attention to figure out individual words.

Learning to spell is intertwined with learning to read words (Ehri, 1997; Morris & Perney, 1984). Both capabilities require letter knowledge, PA, and GP associations. These skills are applied to retain correct spellings of words in memory. If correct spellings of words are unknown, these skills are recruited to devise plausible spellings. The correlations between word reading and word spelling skills are very high, with r's averaging around .84, indicating that the same learning processes are involved and are mutually supportive. Training studies have shown that teaching beginners to spell words enhances their word reading ability (Ehri & Wilce, 1987; Uhry & Shepherd, 1993). Thus, learning to spell is an important component of phonics instruction.

The course of development in learning to read words from memory has been portrayed as a series of phases, each labeled to reflect the involvement of alphabetic knowledge in the connection-forming process (Ehri, 2005). The "prealphabetic phase" refers to the earliest period, when children lack much letter knowledge and phonemic awareness, so by default they memorize visual or contextual cues to "read" words. For example, the golden arches are used to read *McDonalds*. The "partial alphabetic phase" emerges when children know several letter names or sounds and have some PA. They use this knowledge to remember how to read words by forming partial connections, linking some of the graphemes in spellings to phonemes in pronunciations, and storing these connections along with meanings in memory. Typically, beginning and ending graphemes are connected to phonemes in pronunciations, but middle letters are slighted. At this point, children lack much ability to recode unfamiliar words phonologically or to read them by analogy. However, they can use prediction to guess unfamiliar words. They have difficulty remembering correct spellings of words, because their knowledge of the spelling system is not fully formed.

The "full alphabetic phase" emerges when children acquire knowledge of the major GP mapping relations and phonological recoding skill. They can use this knowledge and strategy to read unfamiliar words and to connect spellings more completely to pronunciations in memory. The recoding strategy serves as a self-teaching device to build a sight vocabulary as words are read in text (Share, 1999, 2004b). As beginners' repertoires of sight words grow, they can use these known words to read unfamiliar words by applying an analogy strategy. The "consolidated alphabetic phase" emerges as children learn larger spelling patterns that they can use to form connections for reading and spelling words. Knowing syllabic and morphemic letter patterns as units eases the task of reading multisyllabic words and retaining them in memory.

An important goal of phonics instruction taught in kindergarten and first grade is to enable students to reach the full alphabetic phase. LM students may face an extra source of difficulty in learning English GP mapping relations. This is because some of the phonemic categories in their first language may be discrepant with those in English. For example, Spanish speakers may fail to distinguish /š/ and /č/ as two different phonemes, so *ship* and *chip* sound like the same word. Japanese and Chinese speakers may fail to distinguish /l/ and /r/, as in *lake* and *rake*. Also LM children must learn to articulate the pronunciations of English words accurately to make better sense of the GP mapping relations in these words (Roberts, 2005). In turn, once they learn how English graphemes represent phonemes, the spellings of words can help to clarify how the words are pronounced (Ehri, 1984).

Acquisition of GP mapping skill to retain words in memory has implications for vocabulary learning, which is especially important for LM and low-SES children known to have below-average vocabularies (Hart & Risley, 1995). Rosenthal and Ehri (2008a) conducted a study with low-SES second and fifth graders, who were taught new vocabulary words in one of two ways. In both conditions, students heard and practiced saying the pronunciations and meanings of several unfamiliar words. In addition, in one condition but not the other, students saw the *spellings* of words as they practiced their pronunciations and meanings. However, spellings were not present when students recalled the words during the test. Results showed that students learned both the pronunciations and meanings more rapidly, and remembered the words better, when they had seen spellings than when they had not. The explanation is that spellings helped to secure the pronunciations of words, along with their meanings in memory, by activating connections between graphemes and phonemes, and establishing this spelling-based representation in memory.

The value of orthographic representations of words for helping LM students build their English vocabularies has been recognized by researchers studying second-language acquisition. Hatch and Brown (1995) have suggested that English language learners need to retain clear images of written words in memory to combat semantic confusions among similarly sounding words misinterpreted as cognates (e.g., *happened* vs. *happy*). In their studies, many second-language learners reported heavy reliance on spellings to learn vocabulary words. Sparks and colleagues (1997), who examined high school students learning a foreign language, found that word decoding skill was the best predictor of year-end foreign language *oral proficiency*, better even than students' grades in their foreign language class the previous year. This indicates the utility of spellings for building representations of spoken vocabulary words in memory.

Most sight words and new vocabulary words are learned in the course of reading text through self-teaching (Share, 1999, 2004b); that is, to accumulate new words in memory, students need to stop and decode unfamiliar words as they read text. This activates the GP connections that secure the words' spellings, pronunciations, and meanings in memory. However, context cues may allow students to slight unfamiliar words and substitute synonyms to comprehend the meanings of sentences. Such a strategy undermines sight word, as well as new vocabulary, learning. Rosenthal and Ehri (2008b) found that vocabulary learning was enhanced when students were required to stop and orally pronounce new words that were underlined as they read text silently, compared to a condition in which students read the words silently. Slighting words was especially likely among poorer readers when they read text silently. Poorer readers benefited substantially in learning new words, even more than the better readers, when they had to decode the words aloud.

Tunmer and Chapman (2006) compared the contribution of print-based and text-based word reading strategies to reading achievement. Print-based strategies involved reading unfamiliar words by phonological recoding or analogizing. The text-based strategy involved 'prediction," defined as students' success using limited context clues to read correctly words that they could not read in isolation, for example, reading *glove* in isolation as /glōv/ with a long *O*, but then reading the word correctly in the sentence "He lost his glove." They examined the contribution of print-based and context-based strategies to students' reading comprehension. Two other skills were examined for their contribution as well: phonemic segmentation and grammatical sensitivity, the latter assessed in tasks requiring students to complete cloze sentences and to reorder words to form grammatical sentences. Beginners were followed as they learned to read during the first and second years in school. The setting was New Zealand, where teachers adhered to a whole-language philosophy that involved less systematic phonics instruction. Path analyses were used to determine relationships as reading skills developed.

Results showed that both print- and text-based word reading strategies contributed significantly to students' reading comprehension at the end of grade 2, with print-based processing contributing more than context processing. In addition, Tunmer and Chapman (2006) found that each skill contributed to growth in the other skill as reading developed. Moreover, at earlier points in time, phonemic segmentation skill contributed to the development of print-based strategies, and grammatical sensitivity contributed to the development of a text-based strategy. They assert that these are the two major word learning strategies that contribute to reading achievement during the early grades. They interpret findings to suggest that when beginners encounter unfamiliar words in text, they should be taught to apply print-based strategies first, then to use context to confirm the identities of the words they have decoded. Students should be discouraged from using context to guess words and ignoring their written forms.

*Beginning Reading Instruction*

The preceding discussion makes it apparent that some form of systematic phonics instruction is needed by children learning to read in an alphabetic writing system. Alternative approaches have been developed (Stahl, Duffy-Hester, & Stahl, 1998). Synthetic phonics programs teach children a phonological recoding strategy to read words. Analytic phonics avoids having children pronounce phonemes in isolation to figure out words, and teaches children to analyze GP relations once a word is identified. Analogy phonics teaches children to use parts of written words they already know to identify new words. Also, there are phonics-through-spelling programs, phonics-in-context programs, and other varieties and hybrids that combine approaches.

Educators have disagreed about how to structure phonics instruction (Adams, 1990; Stahl et al., 1998). One issue has been whether instruction in whole-word memorization should precede phonics instruction. Another is whether phonics should be taught systematically or casually, on an as-needed basis, as in whole-language programs. Another is about the most effective form of phonics instruction: whether it should be synthetic or analytic or analogy phonics. Also debated are whether beginners need to read decodable texts that give them practice using the letter–sound relations they have learned and how decodable the texts should be. Another issue has centered on whether all students need a full dose of explicit, systematic phonics instruction.

Several issues were addressed by the National Reading Panel (2000), who conducted a meta-analysis of many studies comparing systematic phonics instruction to other forms of instruction involving less systematic phonics or no phonics. "Systematic phonics" was defined as explicit instruction that taught children a set of prespecified associations between letters and sounds, and how to use them to read words. The panel limited attention to experiments with control groups. The studies were coded for various characteristics. Results were interpreted to indicate whether systematic phonics instruction surpassed other forms of instruction in helping children learn to read under various conditions (Ehri, Nunes, Stahl, & Willows, 2001). Findings in the National Reading Panel report included the following:

1. Systematic phonics instruction was significantly more effective than other forms of instruction involving less or no phonics approaches, which included whole-word and whole-language approaches.
2. Although various types of systematic phonics instruction were more effective than approaches involving less or no phonics, they did not differ among themselves in their effectiveness. The types distinguished were synthetic phonics; larger-unit phonics, including an analogy approach; and miscellaneous approaches that included phonics through spelling. This suggests that the use of some form of systematic phonics to teach reading is more important than the particular approach that is adopted.

3. Phonics instruction that began early in kindergarten or first grade showed significantly larger effects than phonics instruction that began after first grade. This supports the value of teaching foundational phonics skills to children at the earliest point in learning to read.

4. Systematic phonics instruction was more beneficial than less phonics or no-phonics approaches for low-SES students and for beginning readers at risk of developing reading difficulties. "At risk" was defined as poor letter knowledge, poor PA, poor reading skills, or enrollment in low-achieving schools.

A common component of systematic phonics instruction is a scope and sequence chart that identifies the major GP correspondences to be taught and the order in which they are introduced. However, programs have differed in the particular GP correspondences taught and their sequence (Adams, 1990). Also programs have differed in whether letter names are taught along with GP correspondences (Adams, 1990). Opposition to the teaching of letters names has been especially strong among proponents of synthetic phonics, which requires students to operate with letter–sound relations when words are sounded out and blended. The argument is that letter names get in the way and are confusing.

Another point of contention among phonics proponents is whether phonemes should be pronounced in isolation. This is regarded as a problem for synthetic phonics instruction. Phonological recoding requires children to merge stop consonants, such as /b/ pronounced "buh," with other sounds to form a blend, such as "bat," which does not include the schwa vowel "uh." Otherwise the sounds are blended as "buhatuh," which is unrecognizable. Other stop consonants creating this blending problem are /d/, /g/, /j/, / č/ /k/, /p/, and /t/.

An approach that eliminates this problem and helps to clarify the blending process involves teaching blending first with continuant phonemes, such as /s/, /m/, /n/, /f/, /l/, /r/, /v/, /w/, /y/, or /z/. These phonemes can be spoken and extended without adding schwa vowels that have to be deleted during blending. For example, the phonemes /s/ - /ae/ - /m/ can be blended to read *Sam*, without any extra vowels, and in fact without breaking the stream of speech (Adams, 1990; Moats, 2000). This suggests that scope and sequence charts should begin with continuants before introducing stops.

Another component of systematic phonics instruction that has stirred debate is the inclusion of decodable books. Juel and Roper-Schneider (1985) compared two groups of first graders (mostly Mexican American children in Texas). Both groups entered school as nonreaders, and both received phonics instruction. One group practiced reading preprimer-level text that emphasized regular, decodable patterned words, thus allowing children to use their phonics knowledge and strategies. The other group read preprimer text that included a mix of high-frequency words and irregularly spelled words, along with some regularly spelled words. Results showed that the decodable text group implemented a phonological recoding strategy earlier and more lastingly, whereas the other group employed a visual strategy and relied on cues such as word length. The decodable group also acquired implicit knowledge of uninstructed patterns from their text reading, whereas the other group did not. The authors interpret their findings to suggest that the types of words that appear in beginning-level texts may exert a more powerful influence than the method of reading instruction.

However, Jenkins, Peyton, Sanders, and Vadasy (2004) conducted a study comparing the contribution of high- versus low-decodable text with two groups of at-risk first graders. Both groups received phonics instruction in their classrooms. One group received tutoring on highly decodable text and the other, on low decodable text. Results revealed no differences between the groups on reading measures either during or at the end of the school year. What might explain the discrepancy in outcomes of the two studies remains unclear and leaves open the issue regarding the contribution of decodable text. Its value may be limited to the beginning months of instruction, before students have learned all the major GP relations. In the Juel and Roper-Schneider (1985) study, the advantages were greater during the first part of the school year.

Another issue surrounding phonics instruction is whether all students need a full dose. Children entering kindergarten and first grade typically vary widely in their literacy skills. From the previous discussion, it is apparent that if children who begin formal reading instruction already possess some foundational and reading skills, they may require little instruction in these components and may be ready for more advanced instruction. In contrast, students who enter school lacking this knowledge will need to start from zero.

Juel and Minden-Cupp (2000) studied four low-SES first-grade classrooms that differed in the reading instruction that teachers provided to their students. Three levels of beginning readers were identified at the start of school: a low group, with little PA and letter–sound knowledge and no word reading skill; a middle group, with letter knowledge, some PA, and the ability to read a couple words; and a high group, reading at or above a first-grade level. Results on measures of reading at the end of the year suggested that the middle and high groups "did exceptionally well in a classroom that included a less structured phonics curriculum and more reading of trade books and writing of text" (p. 484), whereas the low group grew the least in this classroom. The low group made the most progress in the classroom that taught students to sound out and blend phonemes; that provided the most practice doing this, including spelling practice that involved writing sounds in words; and that taught students to decode using larger onset and rime units, as well as graphemes and phonemes. Phonics was taught first and rapidly in this classroom, so that by midyear, when students had acquired word reading skills, instruction shifted to include work on vocabulary and reading comprehension. These findings support the conclusion that students who have already acquired foundational knowledge benefit more from instruction that gives them practice using their skills to read text, whereas students who lack foundational knowledge need to acquire this before they can benefit from text-reading practice.

Connor, Morrison, and Katch (2004) have studied larger samples of classrooms and readers and have found similar interactions between the skill levels of students and the characteristics of effective reading instruction. Students who began first grade with weak letter knowledge and word reading skills made better progress in reading when they spent more time in explicit phonics instruction that was managed by the teacher. In contrast, students who began with above-average reading skills showed greater growth on word reading measures when they received less time in explicit, teacher-managed phonics activities. Also children's vocabulary level interacted with instruction, such that those with larger vocabularies made greater gains in reading when they spent more time in meaning-focused, student-managed activities, such as independent reading. In contrast, those with weaker vocabularies benefited most from a combination of instructional types that began with phonics activities, then shifted to meaning-focused instruction as the year progressed.

These findings serve to temper blanket claims that all kindergartners and first graders need to receive systematic phonics instruction that starts with letter–sound instruction and PA. Rather, how much and which phonics components need to be taught and practiced appear to depend on which phonics components the children have already learned and how well they have mastered them. Note that this does not challenge the claim that all students must acquire *phonics knowledge and skills* to become proficient readers. It only questions the *dose of phonics instruction* needed to make the most progress in reading growth during a school year. Children who enter school without any preparation absolutely require a full dose, or else they will falter. Children who have already acquired some reading-related skills when they enter school will make more progress during the year if instruction addresses what they have not yet learned or practiced.

The means of enabling all students to progress at comparable rates within one classroom involves implementing differentiated instruction. This approach requires regular assessment that begins at the start of the school year and recurs as skills develop in response to instruction. Student performance guides the forms of instruction that students receive, and reveals when they have acquired skills and are ready to move on. Connor, Morrison, Fishman, Schatschneider, and Underwood (2007) have developed an algorithm that enables teachers to manage differentiated phonics instruction of this sort. Students' scores are entered into Web-based software and guide teachers in what type, when, and how much instruction to provide. In a study evaluating the effectiveness of this approach, findings revealed that when first-grade teachers were taught how to plan and implement individualized reading instruction using the algorithm over the course of a year, students grew more in reading than did a control group of students whose teachers taught reading for the same length of time per day (90 minutes) but did not implement this individualized program. Such an approach appears promising as a means of providing effective reading instruction to children entering kindergarten or first grade with a wide range of prereading and reading skills.

To summarize, learning to read requires learning various strategies for reading unfamiliar words, including phonological recoding, analogizing, and text-based prediction strategies. Application of these strategies enables students to build a sight vocabulary of familiar words. GP mapping relations secure specific words in memory for reading and spelling, and also for vocabulary learning, which is an especially important accomplishment for low-SES and LM students. Word reading skills develop in phases from a prealphabetic level to partial, full, and consolidated alphabetic levels. Systematic phonics instruction, whether it involves synthetic phonics, analogy phonics, or phonics through spelling, is especially effective for teaching foundational and word reading skills, particularly when taught in kindergarten and first grade. However, whether a full dose of phonics instruction enables beginners to make maximal progress during a school year depends on what students already know about letters, PA, and the writing system. Because low-SES and LM students are the least likely to enter school with foundational knowledge, they have the greatest need for a full dose supplemented by extra work in oral vocabulary instruction. Once students learn the GP mapping system, spellings of words can facilitate vocabulary growth.

## Directions for Further Research

Many of the studies described here were conducted as experiments with individual students. This allowed researchers to control the effects of extraneous factors to observe the reading acquisition processes of interest. Further studies might examine these processes when adapted for classroom instruction delivered to small groups or whole classes. The utility of articulatory pictures to teach PA and its impact on helping students learn to read and spell is one direction to pursue. The effectiveness of embedded picture mnemonics to help children learn GP relations when these are incorporated into classroom activities is another direction for study. It is especially important to examine the contribution to vocabulary learning that results from showing students the written forms of new vocabulary words as their meanings are explained and discussed, and teaching students to spell new words by emphasizing the connections between graphemes and phonemes within the words. These instructional activities are especially promising as a means of helping low-SES and LM students build their vocabularies.

Letter knowledge is fundamental in learning to read and spell. However, it is unclear whether some aspects of letter knowledge are more important than others, or whether all aspects need to be mastered. Candidates include naming the shapes of letters, producing their sounds, writing them from memory, mastering all the letters in their uppercase and lowercase forms, and overlearning these skills so that they can be performed quickly. How do these different levels of knowledge influence beginners' ability to perform reading and writing tasks? Understanding how well letters must be known and the contribution of the various letter skills may be worth studying.

Researchers have identified various factors influencing which letters pre-schoolers know. The next step in these studies might be to determine whether instruction that takes into account these factors might facilitate letter learning. For example, teaching letters that appear in students' own names and those of their classmates might facilitate acquisition compared to teaching letters in isolation, unconnected to these contexts. Spending extra time to teach letters at the end of the alphabet might improve letter learning compared to spending equal time on all the letters.

Additional investigation of the interaction between text reading and word learning during the beginning years is needed. Further study of the value of decodable text merits attention. How beginners process less decodable text, and the knowledge and strategies that enable them to add words to their sight vocabularies with texts that are less decodable, deserve investigation.

Although many studies of phonics and phonics instruction have included children from low-SES backgrounds, relatively few have focused on LM children (August & Shanahan, 2006). More research is needed to determine what sorts of adjustments to instruction make a difference in how easily LM children learn to read in English. Developing low-SES and LM children's oral vocabularies is important. Ways to enrich phonics programs by including more information about the meanings of words that appear in workbook exercises and text should prove beneficial. These, as well as other processes involved in reading acquisition and instruction, need to be studied.

## IMPLICATIONS FOR INSTRUCTION

This chapter has focused on processes that enable children to learn to read during the early years and on the types of instruction that facilitate learning. The biggest hurdle for beginners involves learning how the writing system represents their knowledge of spoken language. Instruction is effective to the extent that it enables learners to form this connection between written and spoken language. The connection is secured primarily at the level of words. These are the most reliable units linking print and speech. However, effective instruction does not develop word reading skill directly through simple exposure and practice. Rather, specific foundational knowledge and skills are needed for children's minds to retain connections between written and spoken words in memory, as this chapter has shown.

Teachers of beginning reading need to make sure that they provide adequate instruction to teach the following knowledge and skills to students who lack them:

- Concepts about print, including the left-to-right reading direction
- Mastery of letter shapes and names
- Phonemic awareness, enabling beginners to distinguish phonemic units in spoken words

- Knowledge of the major grapheme–phoneme connections
- Strategies for figuring out unfamiliar words, including phonological recoding, analogizing, predicting, and confirming words from context cues
- Exposure to text that provides practice in applying these skills to support the growth of a sight word vocabulary
- Memory for the spellings of words

In addition, beginning readers from lower-SES and LM families are likely to need extra attention directed at the meanings of English words to build their spoken vocabularies and to make sure that they understand the words and sentences in the texts they read.

Children enter kindergarten and first grade with widely varying skills. This requires that teachers assess what their students know to provide differentiated instruction. It is especially important to make sure that students at the lowest skill levels receive a full dose of instruction in foundational skills. Often the low-SES and LM students are at higher risk of reading difficulties, if instruction is inadequate.

Many instructional recommendations and implications are woven into the present chapter. A few of these can be reiterated. To teach letter–sound relations, I have recommended the use of embedded pictorial mnemonics that have proven effective for teaching letter shapes and their connections to sounds. Beginning reading programs typically include letter–sound instruction. Criteria can be applied to evaluate the quality of the mnemonics provided. To teach letter shapes, a mediating object must resemble the letter's shape, so that its essential features are remembered. To teach the connection between letters and sounds, the mediating object must not only resemble the letter's shape but also have a name that begins with the sound of the letter. The connection must be salient enough that sight of the bare letter activates the object's shape and name in memory.

To teach PA, I have recommended tailoring instruction to the learner. The first step for preliterate children who know few letters is teaching them to segment beginning sounds in familiar words. Once children learn the names or sounds of letters, they can use these as concrete markers to segment and spell the sounds they hear in words. With instruction, their spelling can become more refined phonetically. Another aid in segmenting words into phonemes involves drawing attention to the articulatory movements involved in pronouncing words. It is easier to analyze mouth positions than to analyze sounds. Providing pictures of mouth positions may be incorporated into phonemic segmentation tasks. However, extensive PA instruction may not be necessary once children gain insight and are able to represent phonemes in words with letters. Spelling instruction can take over as a means of teaching mapping relations between phonemes and graphemes.

To teach word reading strategies, a distinction should be maintained between primary and backup strategies. After children acquire knowledge of GP relations, they can be taught to recode words phonologically by sounding out and blending.

Instruction, however, should begin with continuant phonemes in initial positions of words, followed by vowels. Blending words with consonant clusters should come later. Once children learn some basic written words with generalizable spelling patterns, they can be taught to use these words to read new words by analogy. Because context cues are available when words are read in text, some of the words can be predicted. However, children should be taught to apply their GP knowledge to decode letters and confirm that the spelling matches the predicted word. Guessing words without attending to constituent GP mappings limits growth in sight word learning and promotes a bad habit.

In conclusion, teachers who come to understand the processes discussed in this chapter, and how to teach them effectively, are in a strong position to help all of their students make progress in learning to read.

## NOTES

1. It is gratifying that a wealth of studies exist on these topics but frustrating that there is insufficient room to consider many of them. For more depth, readers should refer to the articles cited, as well other relevant work found in many journals and books but not cited here.
2. Symbols between slash marks indicate International Phonetic Alphabet symbols for phonemes.

## REFERENCES

Adams, M. (1990). *Beginning to read: Thinking and learning about print.* Cambridge, MA: MIT Press.

Adams, M., Foorman, B., Lundberg, I., & Beeler, T. (1998). *Phonemic awareness in young children: A classroom curriculum.* Baltimore: Brookes.

August, D., & Shanahan, T. (2006). *Developing literacy in second-language learners: Report of the National Literacy Panel on language minority children and youth.* Mahwah, NJ: Erlbaum.

Bialystok, E., Majumder, S., & Martin, M. (2003). Developing phonological awareness: Is there a bilingual advantage? *Applied Psycholinguistics, 24,* 27–44.

Bloodgood, J. W. (1999). What's in a name?: Children's name writing and literacy acquisition. *Reading Research Quarterly, 34,* 342–367.

Bowey, J. (1995). Socioeconomic status differences in preschool phonological sensitivity and first-grade reading achievement. *Journal of Educational Psychology, 87,* 476–487.

Byrne, B. (1992). Studies in the acquisition procedure for reading: Rational, hypotheses and data. In P. Gough, L. Ehri, & R. Treiman (Eds.), *Reading acquisition* (pp. 1–34). Hillsdale, NJ: Erlbaum.

Byrne, B., & Fielding-Barnsley, R. (1995). Evaluation of a program to teach phonemic awareness to young children: A 2- and 3-year follow-up and a new preschool trial. *Journal of Educational Psychology, 87,* 488–503.

Castiglioni-Spalten, M., & Ehri, L. (2003). Phonemic awareness instruction: Contribution of articulatory segmentation to novice beginners' reading and spelling. *Scientific Studies of Reading, 7*, 25–52.

Connor, C., Morrison, F., Fishman, B., Schatschneider, C., & Underwood, P. (2007). The early years: Algorithm-guided individualized reading instruction. *Science, 315*, 464–465.

Connor, C., Morrison, F., & Katch, L. (2004). Beyond the reading wars: Exploring the effect of child–instruction interactions on growth in early reading. *Scientific Studies of Reading, 8*, 305–336.

De Abreu, M., & Cardoso-Martins, C. (1998). Alphabetic access route in beginning reading acquisition in Portuguese: The role of letter-name knowledge. *Reading and Writing, 10*, 85–104.

Ehri, L. (1980). The development of orthographic images. In U. Frith (Ed.), *Cognitive processes in spelling* (pp. 311–338). London: Academic Press.

Ehri, L. (1984). How orthography alters spoken language competencies in children learning to read and spell. In J. Downing & R. Valtin (Eds.), *Language awareness and learning to read* (pp. 119–147). New York: Springer-Verlag.

Ehri, L. (1991). Development of the ability to read words. In R. Barr, M. Kamil, P. Mosenthal, & P. Pearson (Eds.), *Handbook of reading research* (Vol. 2, pp. 383–417). New York: Longman.

Ehri, L. (1992). Reconceptualizing the development of sight word reading and its relationship to recoding. In P. Gough, L. Ehri, & R. Treiman (Eds.), *Reading acquisition* (pp. 107–143). Hillsdale, NJ: Erlbaum.

Ehri, L. (1997). Learning to read and learning to spell are one and the same, almost. In C. Perfetti, L. Rieben, & M. Fayol (Eds.), *Learning to spell* (pp. 237–269). Hillsdale, NJ: Erlbaum.

Ehri, L. (1998). Grapheme–phoneme knowledge is essential for learning to read words in English. In J. Metsala & L. Ehri (Eds.), *Word recognition in beginning literacy* (pp. 3–40). Mahwah, NJ: Erlbaum.

Ehri, L. (2005). Development of sight word reading: Phases and findings. In M. Snowling & C. Hulme (Eds.), *The science of reading: A handbook* (pp. 135–154). Oxford, UK: Blackwell.

Ehri, L., Deffner, N., & Wilce, L. (1984). Pictorial mnemonics for phonics. *Journal of Educational Psychology, 76*, 880–893.

Ehri, L., Nunes, S., Stahl, S., & Willows D. (2001). Systematic phonics instruction helps students learn to read: Evidence from the National Reading Panel's meta analysis. *Review of Educational Research, 71*, 393–447.

Ehri, L., Nunes, S., Willows, D., Schuster, B., Yaghoub-Zadel, Z., & Shanahan, T. (2001). Phonemic awareness instruction helps children learn to read: Evidence from the National Reading Panel's meta-analysis. *Reading Research Quarterly, 36*, 250–287.

Ehri, L., & Saltmarsh, J. (1995). Beginning readers outperform older disabled readers in learning to read words by sight. *Reading and Writing, 7*, 295–326.

Ehri, L., & Wilce, L. (1983). Development of word identification speed in skilled and less skilled beginning readers. *Journal of Educational Psychology, 75*, 3–18.

Ehri, L., & Wilce, L. (1985). Movement into reading: Is the first stage of printed word learning visual or phonetic? *Reading Research Quarterly, 20*, 163–179.

Ehri, L., & Wilce, L. (1987). Does learning to spell help beginners learn to read words? *Reading Research Quarterly, 22*, 47–65.

Ehri, L. C., & Roberts, T. (2006). The roots of learning to read and write: Acquisition of letters and phonemic awareness. In D. K. Dickinson & S. B. Newman (Eds.), *Handbook of early literacy research* (Vol. 2, pp. 113–131). New York: Guilford Press.

Elkonin, D. (1973). U.S.S.R. In J. Downing (Ed.), *Comparative reading* (pp. 551–579). New York: Macmillan.

Gaskins, I. W., Ehri, L. C., Cress, C., O'Hara, C., & Donnelly, K. (1996–1997). Procedures for word learning: Making discoveries about words. *Reading Teacher, 50*, 312–328.

Geva, E., & Siegel, L. (2000). Orthographic and cognitive factors in the concurrent development of basic reading skills in two languages. *Reading and Writing: An Interdisciplinary Journal, 12*, 1–30.

Goswami, U. (1986). Children's use of analogy in learning to read: A developmental study. *Journal of Experimental Child Psychology, 42*, 73–83.

Guttentag, R., & Haith, M. (1978). Automatic processing as a function of age and reading ability. *Child Development, 49*, 707–716.

Hart, B., & Risley, T. (1995). *Meaningful differences in the everyday experiences of young American children.* Baltimore: Brookes.

Hatch, E., & Brown, C. (1995). *Vocabulary, semantics, and language education.* Cambridge, MA: Cambridge University Press.

Hohn, W., & Ehri, L. (1983). Do alphabet letters help prereaders acquire phonemic segmentation skill? *Journal of Educational Psychology, 75*, 752–762.

Jenkins, J., Peyton, J., Sanders, E., & Vadasy, P. (2004). Effects of reading decodable texts in supplemental first-grade tutoring. *Scientific Studies of Reading, 8*, 53–85.

Juel, C., & Minden-Cupp, C. (2000). Learning to read words: Linguistic units and instructional strategies. *Reading Research Quarterly, 35*, 458–492.

Juel, C., & Roper-Schneider, D. (1985). The influence of basal readers on first grade reading. *Reading Research Quarterly, 20*, 134–152.

Justice, L., Pence, K., Bowles, R., & Wiggins, A. (2006). An investigation of four hypotheses concerning the order by which 4-year old children learn the alphabet letters. *Early Childhood Research Quarterly, 21*, 374–389.

LaBerge, D., & Samuels, J. (1974). Toward a theory of automatic information processing in reading. *Cognitive Psychology, 6*, 293–323.

Lesaux, N., & Siegel, L. (2002). The development of reading in children who speak English as a second language. *Developmental Psychology, 39*, 1005–1019.

Levin, I., & Ehri, L. (in press). Young children's ability to read and spell their own and classmates' names: The role of letter knowledge. *Scientific Studies of Reading.*

Liberman, I., Shankweiler, D., Fisher, F., & Carter, B. (1974). Reading and the awareness of linguistic segments. *Journal of Experimental Child Psychology, 18*, 201–212.

Lindamood, C., & Lindamood, P. (1975). *The A.D.D. Program: Auditory discrimination in depth.* Boston: Teaching Resources Corporation.

Lindamood, P., & Lindamood, C. (1998). *The Lindamood phoneme sequencing program for reading, spelling and speech*: The LIPS Program. Austin, TX: Pro-Ed.

Marsh, G., & Desberg, P. (1978). Mnemonics for phonics. *Contemporary Educational Psychology, 3*, 57–61.

McCutchen, D., Abbott, R. D., Green, L. B., Beretvas, S. N., Cox, S., Potter, N. S., et al. (2002). Beginning literacy: Links among teacher knowledge, teacher practice, and student learning. *Journal of Learning Disabilities, 35*, 69–86.

Moats, L. (1994). The missing foundation in teacher education: Knowledge of the structure of spoken and written language. *Annals of Dyslexia, 44*, 81–102.

Moats, L. (2000). *Speech to print: Language essentials for teachers.* Baltimore: Brookes.

Morris, D., & Perney, J. (1984). Developmental spelling as a predictor of first grade reading achievement. *Elementary School Journal, 84*, 441–457.

National Reading Panel. (2000). *Report of the National Reading Panel: Teaching children to
read: An evidence-based assessment of the scientific research literature on reading and its
implications for reading instruction: Reports of the subgroups*. Rockville, MD: National
Institute of Child Health and Human Development Clearinghouse.

Rack, J., Hulme, C., Snowling, M., & Wightman, J. (1994). The role of phonology in young
children's learning of sight words: The direct-mapping hypothesis. *Journal of Experimental Child Psychology, 57*, 42–71.

Read, C. (1971). Pre-school children's knowledge of English phonology. *Harvard Educational Review, 41*, 1–34.

Roberts, T. (2003). Effects of alphabet letter instruction on young children's word recognition. *Journal of Educational Psychology, 95*, 41–51.

Roberts, T. (2005). Articulation accuracy and vocabulary size contributions to phonemic
awareness and word reading in English language learners. *Journal of Educational
Psychology, 97*, 601–616.

Roberts, T., & Neal, H. (2004). Relationships among preschool English language learners' oral proficiency in English, instructional experience and literacy development.
*Contemporary Educational Psychology, 29*, 283–311.

Rosenthal, J., & Ehri, L. (2008a). The mnemonic value of orthography for vocabulary
learning. *Journal of Educational Psychology, 100*, 175–191.

Rosenthal, J., & Ehri, L. (2008b). *Pronouncing new words aloud during the silent reading
of text facilitates fifth graders' vocabulary learning*. Manuscript submitted for publication.

Scarborough, H., Ehri, L., Olson, R., & Fowler, A. (1998). The fate of phonemic awareness
beyond the elementary school years. *Scientific Study of Reading, 2*, 115–142.

Scott, J., & Ehri, L. (1989). Sight word reading in prereaders: Use of logographic vs. alphabetic access routes. *Journal of Reading Behavior, 22*, 149–166.

Seymour, P. (2005). Early reading development in European orthographies. In M. Snowling & C. Hulme (Ed.), *The science of reading: A handbook* (pp. 296–315). Oxford, UK:
Blackwell.

Seymour, P., Aro, M., & Erskine, J. (2003). Foundation literacy acquisition in European
orthographies. *British Journal of Psychology, 94*, 143–174.

Seymour, P., Duncan, L., Aro, M., & Baillie, S. (2007). *Learning to read in Finland, Scotland
and England: Effects of language, orthography and culture on foundation literacy acquisition*. Manuscript submitted for publication.

Share, D. (1999). Phonological recoding and orthographic learning: A direct test of the
self-teaching hypothesis. *Journal of Experimental Child Psychology, 72*, 95–129.

Share, D. (2004a). Knowing letter names and learning letter sounds: A causal connection.
*Journal of Experimental Child Psychology, 88*, 213–233.

Share, D. (2004b). Orthographic learning at a glance: On the time course and developmental onset of self-teaching. *Journal of Experimental Child Psychology, 87*, 267–298.

Share, D. (2008). On the Anglocentricities of current reading research and practice: The
perils of over-reliance on an "outlier" orthography. *Psychological Bulletin, 134*, 584–
615.

Share, D. L., Jorm, A. F., Maclean, R., & Matthews, R. (1984). Sources of Individual differences in reading acquisition. *Journal of Educational Psychology, 76*, 1309–1324.

Shmidman, A. (2008). *Integrated pictorial mnemonics in English help preschoolers learn*

*Hebrew letter–sound relations*. Unpublished doctoral dissertation, Graduate Center of the City University of New York.

Sparks, R., Ganschow, L., Patton, J., Artzer, M., Siebenhar, D., & Plageman, M. (1997). Prediction of foreign language proficiency. *Journal of Educational Psychology, 89*, 549–561.

Stahl, S., Duffy-Hester, A., & Stahl, K. (1998). Everything you wanted to know about phonics (but were afraid to ask). *Reading Research Quarterly, 33*, 338–355.

Stahl, S., & Murray, B. (1994). Defining phonological awareness and its relationship to early reading. *Journal of Educational Psychology, 86*, 221–234.

Stahl, S., Osborn, J., & Lehr, F. (1990). *Beginning to read: Thinking and learning about print by Marilyn Jager Adams: A summary*. Urbana–Champaign, IL: Center for the Study of Reading.

Treiman, R. (1993). *Beginning to spell*. New York: Oxford University Press.

Treiman, R., & Broderick, V. (1998). What's in a name?: Children's knowledge about the letters in their own names. *Journal of Experimental Child Psychology, 70*, 97–116.

Treiman, R., Levin, I., & Kessler, B. (2006). Learning of letter names follows similar principles across languages: Evidence from Hebrew. *Journal of Experimental Child Psychology, 93*, 139–165.

Treiman, R., & Rodriguez, K. (1999). Young children use letter names in learning to read words. *Psychological Science, 10*, 334–338.

Tunmer, W., & Chapman, J. (2006). Metalinguistic abilities, phonological recoding skill, and the use of context in beginning reading development: A longitudinal study. In R. Joshi & P. Aaron (Eds.), *Handbook of orthography and literacy* (pp. 617–635). Mahwah, NJ: Erlbaum.

Uhry, J., & Ehri, L. (1999). Ease of segmenting two- and three-phoneme words in kindergarten: Rime cohesion or vowel salience? *Journal of Educational Psychology, 91*, 594–603.

Uhry, J., & Shepherd, J. (1993). Segmentation/spelling instruction as a part of a first-grade reading program: Effects on several measures of reading. *Reading Research Quarterly, 28*, 218–233.

Venezky, R. L. (1999). *The American way of spelling: The structure and origins of American English orthography*. New York: Guilford Press.

Wendon, L. (1992). *First steps in Letterland*. Cambridge, UK: Letterland, Ltd.

Wendon, L. (2007). *Letterland ABC*. Cambridge, UK: Letterland, Ltd.

# CHAPTER 16

# Vocabulary Instruction for Diverse Students

SUSAN WATTS TAFFE, CAMILLE L. Z. BLACHOWICZ, *and* PETER J. FISHER

In this chapter we examine the research on vocabulary instruction and learning with students from diverse populations. Whenever we use the term "vocabulary," unless it is otherwise defined, we are referring to meaning vocabulary. We recognize that teaching academic English vocabulary involves significant issues related to power, domination, and inclusion. However, we feel that it is not our charge here to address these issues. In this chapter we write from our perspective as teacher-educators working with preservice and inservice teachers who struggle with the appropriate pedagogy for teaching word meanings in diverse settings. Our chapter addresses the following topics:

- Background on vocabulary instruction in relation to reading development
- Vocabulary instruction for economically disadvantaged students
- Vocabulary instruction for English language learners

## BACKGROUND ON VOCABULARY INSTRUCTION IN RELATION TO READING DEVELOPMENT

Knowledge of meaning vocabulary has long been recognized as one of, if not *the*, most important correlate to reading comprehension (Davis, 1944; Terman, 1916). Yet because it is not print-bound, it affects much more than reading performance. Vocabulary knowledge, or the lack thereof, impacts social interaction, participation in classroom academic routines, and learning in the content areas. In short, vocabulary knowledge is intimately connected to academic achievement in all areas, and particularly reading comprehension, for both native and non-native

English speakers (Beck, Perfetti, & McKeown, 1982; Carlo, August, & Snow, 2005; Nation, 2001; Stahl & Nagy, 2006).

As we all know, every classroom in the United States is diverse in that it comprises separate and unique individuals (the teacher included) who bring to school each day their own distinctive experiences with language, learning, and the world. When it comes to vocabulary development, two particular dimensions of diversity (both of which have cultural implications) have been shown to make a difference: socioeconomic status (SES) and English language proficiency. Several studies point to differences between the vocabularies of economically advantaged and economically disadvantaged children (Becker, 1977; Coyne, Simmons, & Kame'enui, 2004; Hart & Risley, 1995; White, Graves, & Slater, 1990). Studies have also shown that these differences are detectable as early as the preschool years and persist across the grades (Biemiller, 2001; Juel, Biancarosa, Coker, & Deffes, 2003). Furthermore, differences in English vocabulary knowledge play a significant role in the discrepancy in reading performance between native English speakers and English language learners (ELLs), even when the ELL students possess strong knowledge of their native-language vocabulary (García, 1991; Goldenberg, Rezaei, & Fletcher, 2005). Many refer to these differences in vocabulary knowledge as "the vocabulary gap."

Another way to look at "the vocabulary gap" is to consider the gap that too often exists between what we know to be high-quality instruction and what teachers actually practice. Observational research on classroom vocabulary instruction suggests that nonproductive approaches of the "write 'em down, look 'em up" variety have prevailed for decades (Blachowicz, 1987; Scott, Jamieson-Noel, & Asselin, 2003; Watts, 1995). The problem of moving more vocabulary research into practice is compounded by the fact that students in economically disadvantaged settings often have less exposure to and experiences with print that parallel school-based literacy practices and expectations. Duke's (2000) conclusion that "schools may contribute to relatively lower levels of literacy achievement among low-SES children" (p. 470) may be particularly true in the area of vocabulary instruction, where teachers appear to implement a relatively small portion of research-based practices.

In this chapter we examine vocabulary teaching and learning for students often considered "at risk"—students who are economically disadvantaged and those who have not yet achieved English language proficiency. Our review indicates that what we have learned from research on exemplary vocabulary instruction in general also applies to students of diversity; they, like all our students, need the best instruction possible (August & Shanahan, 2006). However, our review indicates that, given the best instruction, they need *more* of it; they need it *sooner*; and they need it with more *intentional supports and scaffolds*.

The report of the National Reading Panel (2000) states that both direct and indirect instruction are needed to maximize vocabulary learning, with the most effective approaches utilizing multiple methods. Graves (2006) and others suggest that a substantive vocabulary program includes four parts: providing rich and varied language experiences, teaching individual words, teaching word learning strategies, and fostering "word consciousness" (keen interest in and awareness of words and their meanings). For this review we have combined word consciousness with a word-rich environment and present our findings using the following categories of effective approaches to vocabulary instruction:

1. Students learn in an environment that is concept-rich, language-rich, and word-rich.
2. Students are taught the meanings of individual words, with a focus on deep understanding and lasting retention.
3. Students are taught strategies for becoming independent word learners.

We believe this understanding of what constitutes exemplary instruction for all students is required to determine what constitutes exemplary instruction for students of diverse backgrounds, and to begin to develop high-quality vocabulary programs in all classrooms and schools. At the same time, it is important to note that these are not mutually exclusive categories. In some cases, studies reported within a particular category also include an approach that might fall into another category.

## Synthesis of Research on Vocabulary Instruction for Economically Disadvantaged Students

In identifying students for federal and other funding, economic disadvantage, typically indicated by eligibility for free or reduced lunch, is an important correlate of students being considered "at risk." In this section, we examine research-based strategies for enhancing the vocabularies of these students.

### Building Concept-Rich, Language-Rich, and Word-Rich Learning Environments

An exciting avenue for enhanced word learning is increasing students' exposure to, and use of, rich discussion and book language through scaffolded read-alouds using conceptually rich texts. Reading aloud to students has been examined as an important curricular practice to affect vocabulary learning positively (Dickinson & Smith, 1994). Because children's books present more advanced, less familiar vocabulary than is typically used in everyday speech (Cunningham & Stanovich, 1998), teacher read-alouds and shared book reading help students to extend their existing oral vocabularies. Teacher elaboration and discussion after shared storybook reading gives students opportunities to use new vocabulary in new language contexts (Snow, 1991). Weizman and Snow (2001) found that even small amounts of elaborated language use by low-income parents have increased the school vocabularies of their children.

DeTemple and Snow (2003) draw an important contrast between talk around shared storybook reading that is cognitively challenging and talk that is not. There has been substantial research on the nature and effects of storybook reading, both in home and school settings, that supports the notion that cognitively challenging tasks, coupled with scaffolding, maximize vocabulary learning from read-alouds for young students (Neuman & Dickinson, 2001). Involving students in discussions during and after reading a book to them has produced significant word learning, especially when the teacher scaffolds this learning by asking questions, adding information, or prompting students to describe what they heard. Whitehurst and his associates (1994, 1999) have called this process "dialogic reading."

Since children with less rich initial vocabularies are less likely to learn new vocabulary incidentally, a well-designed approach that includes both scaffolding and follow-up is needed to maximize vocabulary learning from shared storybook reading (Robbins & Ehri, 1994; Schwanenflugel et al., 2005; Sénéchal, Thomas, & Monker, 1995). Teacher scaffolding and follow-up may include highlighting of words; explicit instruction of words; relating word meanings to existing student knowledge; and charting, sorting, writing, and other methods that help the students make deeper semantic connections to the words, including activities that require use and manipulation of words and their meanings in multiple contexts (Beck & McKeown, 2007; Stahl & Fairbanks, 1986).

In a recent study, Beck and McKeown (2007) found that kindergarten and first-grade students in a low–SES school learned sophisticated words found in trade books after being told explicitly the word's meaning, being given examples of the word in contexts other than the one used in the story, then engaging in rich and varied activities in which they themselves determined what constituted further examples of the word and also constructed their own examples. In a second, related study the researchers found that providing this instruction with greater frequency and longer duration nearly doubled the gains.

In a series of studies, Scott, Flinspach, and Samway (2007) investigated the effects of encouraging students to analyze authors' word choices in their independent reading, as well as in their own writing relative to vocabulary development. Their belief is that approaching vocabulary development through explicit attention to word use in children's literature, and integrating this word study into writing workshops, will develop word consciousness, leading to greater vocabulary knowledge, and enhanced reading and writing abilities.

## Teaching Individual Words for Deep Understanding and Lasting Retention

Numerous studies have supported the notion that utilizing and building prior knowledge can help students to learn more easily new, related concepts and vocabulary. Stevens (1982) used easier texts to present essential topics and exposure to vocabulary with urban 10th graders. She found that this "jump-starting" allowed students to better comprehend information and vocabulary in their more difficult textbooks. Another way to build background knowledge is through "vocabulary visits" (Blachowicz & Obrochta, 2007), in which students participate in scaffolded, content-focused read-alouds, followed by semantically focused activities. In addition to building prior knowledge, it is important to ascertain and utilize the prior knowledge that students may already have.

It is important to note that the goal of explicit instruction is not rote memorization. Stahl and Fairbanks (1986) and Kolich (1991) have determined that word learning is enhanced if definitions of words are combined with contextual information, as well as usage examples. Scott and Nagy (1997) found that the inclusion of sample sentences in the introduction of words is an important component of effective instruction. Bos and Anders (1990) found that instruction in vocabulary for at-risk learners in junior high school was most effective when the instruction included semantic manipulation of the words being learned, a study confirmed by a multitude of strategies developed for classifying words or visually representing their relationships. A recent study by Ehri and Rosenthal (2007) indicated that second- and fifth-graders' word learning was positively influenced by explicit attention to the spelling and pronunciation of the word in addition to its meaning. Finally, no matter what the approach to teaching individual words, multiple contextual exposures to words learned are necessary for retention (Stahl & Fairbanks, 1986; Wasik & Bond, 2001).

Pressley, Disney, and Anderson (2007) suggest that the question of which words to teach is a pressing one. Current lists indicating the frequency with which various words appear in texts at various grade levels have yet to be published. However, our recent knowledge that it is less familiar, sophisticated vocabulary that prompts further vocabulary learning, coupled with research by Beck and McKeown (2007) and others showing that diverse students are capable of learning sophisticated words, leads us to believe that word sophistication is an important consideration. Another is the power of self-selection, as indicated by Ruddell and Shearer (2002), who found that student self-selection resulted in durable word learning among middle school students. Working with at-risk middle graders, Jiménez, García, and Pearson (1996) and Harmon, Hedrick, Wood, and Gress (2005) found, respectively, that self-selection was a powerful motivator for word learning, and that students were able to select important words.

### Teaching Strategies for Independent Word Learning

Teaching students how to use "morphology" (the study of word structure), "context" (the ability to infer word meaning from the meaning of surrounding text), and the dictionary are critical to strategic vocabulary learning (Baumann, Kame'enui, & Ash, 2003; Carlisle & Katz, 2007; Graves, 2006; Nagy & Scott, 2000). Baumann, Ware, and Edwards (2007) report positive effects from teaching a list of common prefixes and suffixes in conjunction with the type of language- and word-rich activities previously discussed.

Teaching students to use visual–verbal associations, as well as morphology, has been shown to impact vocabulary acquisition. Hopkins and Bean (1999) found that specific words were better learned and retained when at risk adolescent students were encouraged to make a visual–verbal association. They used a "four-square" process for learning affixes and affixed vocabulary. In one quadrant of the square, the word or word part was registered. A meaning was entered in the second quadrant; a visual association was placed in the third, and a verbal association in the fourth.

Using the box format popularized by Elkonin (1963) for registering decoding "chunks," Ogle and Correa (2007) show promising initial results working with middle graders to use the boxes to assess their knowledge of word parts. Students' placement of word parts in frames provides both diagnostic information for the teacher and scaffolded frameworks for analyzing new words. For example, students working with the word *disability* would be given two boxes as a physical cue to chunk the word into its component parts, dis + ability. Then, below each box, they would register a meaning for each chunk, constructing a definition. Finally, they would use the dictionary to refine their meaning and give a personal sentence.

## SYNTHESIS OF RESEARCH ON VOCABULARY INSTRUCTION FOR ELLs

Research on vocabulary instruction for ELL students is still in its early stages. The recent report of the National Literacy Panel on Language-Minority Children and Youth (August & Shanahan, 2006) reviews our current knowledge of literacy instruction for such students. This section draws on that report and additional research in relation to vocabulary learning and instruction.

### Building Concept-Rich, Language-Rich, and Word-Rich Learning Environments

As with native English speakers, the importance of metalinguistic awareness to word learning in a second language is supported by various studies. Carlisle, Beeman, and Shah (1996) and Carlisle, Beeman, Davis, and Spharim (1999) found that the ability to provide formal and informal definitions of nouns in both languages contributed to reading comprehension. Ordonez, Carlo, Snow, and McLaughlin (2002) found that cross-language effects, a function of the use of cognates, as addressed in the next section, were more likely for higher- than for lower-order vocabulary knowledge. This research mirrors that on the transfer of metacognitive knowledge of reading comprehension strategies from one language to another (August & Shanahan, 2006).

Various cognitive models of instruction have been tried with ELL students. Carlo and her associates (2004, 2005) used a long-term approach that incorporated seeing, hearing, spelling, and using strategies to analyze word structure and meaning. Words were encountered in multiple content-area contexts and Spanish language texts were used to support English language texts. Cognate words, as well as noncognate words, were learned, and the researchers focused on creating relational sets of words by looking at synonyms, antonyms, and multiple meanings. There were significant effects for both a more comprehensive and a less comprehensive approach to word learning. Therefore, it appears that comprehensiveness of instruction and use of the native language in support text and cognates are tools for increasing the vocabulary of ELL students.

Calderón and colleagues (2005) researched the teaching of vocabulary in Success for All schools. Their findings suggest that teaching words as part of such a comprehensive program may be helpful, although greater success was achieved with decoding skills than with word learning. This result mirrors the findings of several studies reviewed by Shanahan and Beck (2006) in relation to reading comprehension. They concluded that the advantages of comprehensive programs were greater for preliteracy skills and decoding than for reading comprehension. Clearly, the nature of comprehensive programs varies, as does the emphasis on the various components of literacy, so the important factors in such programs need further exploration.

Many authors draw a distinction between cognitive strategy instruction and sociocultural factors in learning (Freeman & Freeman, 2003; Moje, Dillon, & O'Brien, 2000; Rueda, August, & Goldenberg, 2006). Because the educational context determines the relative contributions of various cognitive and sociocultural factors, positivistic studies often fail to capture the complexity of the learning process. Various ethnographic studies have shown the importance of process approaches to literacy learning that allow students to express themselves first in their native language, and allow opportunities to experiment with English (Hornberger, 1990; Jiménez & Gersten, 1999; Martinez-Roldan, 2003; Moll, Saez, & Dworin, 2001). Clearly, vocabulary is learned well when students are allowed to practice and to use it. Classrooms structured to allow this are word- and language-rich environments.

## Teaching Individual Words for Deep Understanding and Lasting Retention

Some researchers argue that command of the basic, most frequent words in English is essential for starting to learn in that language (Cummins, 2003; Nation, 2001). A general Teaching English to Speakers of Other Languages (TESOL) list (West, 1953) forms the basis for many other lists that suggest 2,000–2,500 words as a basic vocabulary (Folse, 2004). Such lists may help students get started, but they do not provide "school" words that help them, particularly older students, advance academically (Cummins, 2003). Nation (1993) suggests four categories of words for instruction: (1) the high-frequency words just mentioned; (2) general academic vocabulary comprising about 800 word families; (3) technical vocabulary from the content areas, estimated to be about 2,000 words per subject area;

and (4) high-frequency words not in common use. August, Carlo, Dressler, and Snow (2005) have adapted this categorization for instruction using Beck, McKeown, and Kucan's (2002) three-tier concept of word type. The presupposition of many of these lists is that students already have knowledge of basic concepts in their native language, so word study becomes largely a matter of translation.

Shanahan and Beck (2006) argue that pedagogy that is effective for teaching individual words to native English-speaking students is also generally effective for ELL students. Findings of research with ELL students suggest that for students to retain the meanings of words, instruction should encourage deep processing and involve repetition of the target vocabulary in different contexts. Graves (2006), in his review of the research, reached similar conclusions.

Beyond the acquisition of basic vocabulary, Collins (2004, 2005) found that ELL preschoolers with varying levels of English language vocabulary knowledge were able to learn sophisticated words as a part of storybook reading. In this study, between five and nine sophisticated words were inserted into the storybooks, which were read three times in a 3-week period. Each reading was followed by rich explanation, along with an association between the target word and an illustration in the storybook.

## Teaching Strategies for Independent Word Learning

A specific type of morphological analysis that allows ELL students to draw upon their first-language skills is the use of "cognates," which are words in their native languages that are similar to English forms of words (e.g., *excelente* [Spanish] and excellent [English]) (García, 1991; Jiménez et al., 1996; Nagy, García, Durgunoglu, & Hancin-Bahtt, 1993). In their review of the research, Dressler and Kamil (2006) argue:

> In summary, transfer between cognates occurs optimally between closely related first and second languages, and in learners possessing high levels of reading proficiency, cognitive flexibility and metalinguistic awareness. (p. 215)

How do they come to this conclusion? Much of the research has been done with Spanish–English cognates. Being Romance languages, they share common etymology in terms of Latin roots. In English, these multisyllabic words occur in academic English more than in conversational English. It is posited, therefore, that use of cognates is a more effective strategy in the later grades. Further evidence comes from a study by James and Klein (1994) comparing the use of English–German cognates. Basic terms in English are often of Germanic, not Latinate, origin, so use of cognates is more effective for words that occur frequently in conversational English (e.g., house/*haus*). We know that native English speakers are more likely to use morphology as an aide to word learning as they become older and more proficient readers. Jiménez and colleagues (1996) found that poorer readers view languages as more dissimilar than alike so they are less likely to look for cognates.

In terms of instruction, García (1998) found that middle-grade Spanish-speaking students were able to learn how to use Spanish cognates to figure out English words. However, ELL students often (and understandably) rely on phonological similarity to identify cognates (Dressler & Kamil, 2006; James & Klein, 1994). So, although it appears that specific instruction in use of cognates may be useful, most authors caution that there are many "false cognates."

## SEVEN IMPLICATIONS FOR CLASSROOM PRACTICE WITH AT-RISK LEARNERS

We now turn our attention to recommendations for those who truly have the capacity to facilitate vocabulary growth among our children. Because many U.S. classrooms include a wide array of students, we list recommendations that apply both to economically disadvantaged students and to ELL students.

- *Commit to gaining an in-depth understanding of what constitutes effective instruction for all students to understand what constitutes exemplary practices for students of diverse backgrounds.* We cannot emphasize enough the importance for teachers, as well as instructional leaders in school buildings and districts, to become increasingly familiar with what has been learned from research over the past 20–30 years. We encourage educators to take advantage of some of the excellent compilations of research findings and practical classroom ideas, such as those offered by Beck and colleagues (2002; Beck, McKeown, & Kucan, 2008), Blachowicz & Fisher (2009), Blachowicz, Fisher, Ogle, and Watts-Taffe (2006), Hiebert and Kamil (2005), Graves (2006), Scott, Skobel, and Wells (2008), and Stahl and Nagy (2006), as well as teaching techniques described in journals such as *The Reading Teacher* and the *Journal of Adolescent and Adult Literacy*.

- *Allocate time for vocabulary instruction.* Vocabulary instruction has long been an instructional consideration only insofar as it has related to decoding and comprehension of specific texts. With the knowledge that vocabulary learning for the sake of vocabulary learning is vital for school success, it is important for teachers, as well as those responsible for supporting teachers in their ongoing professional development, to move vocabulary teaching to the forefront of their instructional priorities. One of the ways to do this and still teach "everything else" is to plan ways to integrate vocabulary instruction into "everything else," from read-alouds to content-area lessons.

- *Teach sophisticated words.* We now know that knowledge of sophisticated words, rather than basic words, propels future word learning. Beck and her colleagues (2002) define "sophisticated words" as those that are found in written language (i.e., well-written narrative and expository text) and the oral vocabularies of more mature language users. Recent research indicates that very young children, even those with limited English language proficiency, are capable of learning sophisticated words when they are taught in accordance with principles of effective vocabulary instruction. Although students may also need to learn the meanings of more basic words, these should be taught along with, not in lieu of, sophisticated words.

• *Provide scaffolding in moving students to independence.* Teachers should provide students with a clear, user-friendly definition, and if the word can be illustrated, demonstrated, or otherwise shown, they should do so. Also students should be provided with contextual information, so that they get a sense of two or three situations to which the word would apply. Providing examples and non-examples is another way to provide contextual information. Teachers should then shift the cognitive work of articulating and manipulating semantic information from themselves to their students. Engaging students in games, questions, writing, dramatics, and other experiences requires them to make sense of and practice their sense of the word's meaning. Finally, teachers should provide multiple exposures to the new word and multiple opportunities to practice its meaning.

• *Build on the foundation of prior knowledge.* Always find ways for students to mingle the knowledge they already have with the new knowledge they are gaining. Both economically disadvantaged students and ELL students may use vocabulary or language styles that are unfamiliar but integral to the communities in which they live or the countries from which they hail. By engaging children in conversation rather than inundating them with a preponderance of teacher talk, teachers convey both their own belief that students are capable language users and their interest in supporting connections between home (and home knowledge) and school (and school knowledge).

• *Engage students in rich conversations.* It is clear that children from diverse backgrounds benefit greatly from large quantities of language input. In addition, engaging students in discussion allows them to do the important cognitive work of "semantic manipulation"—figuring out how new word meanings fit with their prior knowledge and with the meanings of other words. Rich conversations, which can easily be integrated into establishing and maintaining classroom academic routines, shared reading experiences, social interactions, and content-area learning also assist teachers in scaffolding student learning. When student talk reveals a misunderstanding, teachers may use that information as a guide to elaborate further a word's meaning to correct the misunderstanding.

• *Start young and continue through the grades.* It is clear that the effects of rich word-learning experiences take hold in the preschool years, with continuous impact as children advance through school. Therefore, it is critical to prioritize vocabulary instruction in early childhood, the elementary and middle grades, and high school. As children get older and move squarely into "reading to learn" territory, they are called upon to gain more word knowledge independently, with an emphasis on more complex, content-specific and academic vocabulary. Such words are problematic for all learners, not just those in low-income settings and those who speak English as a second language. Vocabulary instruction is as much a concern of the high school mathematics teacher as of the preschool teacher. It requires the attention and focus of all educators.

## IMPLICATIONS FOR FUTURE RESEARCH

Here we pose four questions that are worthy of future research efforts:

• *What are the characteristics of integrated, comprehensive approaches to instruction that enhance vocabulary learning?* Recent studies point to the great potential of instruction that is integrated into activities such as shared book reading, literature study and writing, and content-area instruction (Baumann et al., 2007; Schwanenflugel et al., 2005; Scott et al., 2007). More research in this area will benefit those who are concerned with curricular alignment, both within and across grades.

• *Is it effective to teach a list of "basic words" to ELL students?* So far, this recommendation lacks a research base. It would be immensely helpful to know whether ELL students who are taught a set of basic English words before engaging in further learning in English experience significant benefits. If so, it would also be extremely important to know which words comprise this basic list.

• *In what ways do new technologies impact word learning?* To date, studies of computer-assisted instruction have produced mixed results. Often carried out with students receiving special educational services (many of whom are economically disadvantaged and/or ELLs), these studies point to a differentially positive impact on students with mild disabilities (Marston, Deno, Kim, Diment, & Rogers, 1995; Montali & Lewandowski, 1996) and with learning disabilities (MacArthur & Haynes, 1995). In a recent study by Proctor, Dalton, and Grisham (2007), fourth-grade ELL students made gains in vocabulary knowledge as a result of engaging in various activities associated with an online reading environment. Working with economically disadvantaged students, Labbo, Love, and Ryan (2007) found that engaging learners in a vocabulary flood as part of a digital language experience resulted in vocabulary gains. In addition to research focused on the assistive features of new technologies, future research might compare and contrast the vocabulary demands of digital text with those of print text.

• *What are the characteristics of effective teacher professional development for vocabulary teaching?* Having previously discussed the importance of bridging the gap between theory and practice in the vocabulary instruction that occurs in most classrooms (Blachowicz et al., 2006), we are interested in the ways in which researchers, teachers, and professional development facilitators (e.g., literacy coaches, teacher-educators, instructional specialists) might build collaborative knowledge in this area. As Pressley and his colleagues (2007) point out, we need to be equally concerned with getting research-based approaches into practice and getting teachers' day-to-day instructional contexts into research.

## Concluding Remarks

None of the instructional practices described here can be categorized as rote teaching for superficial learning and short-term retention, as is too often the case for students classified as "at risk." Instead, the evidence-based approaches described in this chapter call for high degrees of learner engagement within contexts of high-quality instruction that starts early and continues throughout the grades. The approaches we have described can be used with all learners, with variations of instructional intensity and word selection based on the strengths, interests, and needs of specific groups of students. In this, we agree with Vygotsky (1978, p. 88): "Children grow into the intellectual life around them." We believe that research points to the need for richer and more intense vocabulary work for at-risk students, with an enhanced environment for word learning to help structure this intellectual life.

## References

August, D., Carlo, M., Dressler, C., & Snow, C. E. (2005). The critical role of vocabulary development for English language learners. *Learning Disabilities Research and Practice, 20*(1), 50–57.

August, D., & Shanahan, T. (Eds.). (2006). *Developing literacy in second-language learners: Report of the National Literacy Panel on Language-Minority Children and Youth.* Mahwah, NJ: Erlbaum.

Baumann, J., Ware, D., & Edwards, D. C. (2007). "Bumping into spicy, tasty words that catch your tongue": A formative experiment on vocabulary instruction. *Reading Teacher, 61,* 108–122.

Baumann, J. F., Kame'enui, E. J., & Ash, G. E. (2003). Research on vocabulary instruction: Voltaire redux. In J. Flood, D. Lapp, J. R. Squire, & J. M. Jensen (Eds.), *Handbook of research on teaching the English language arts* (2nd ed., pp. 752–785). Mahwah, NJ: Erlbaum.

Beck, I., McKeown, M., & Perfetti, C. (1982). The effects of long-term vocabulary instruction on lexical access and reading comprehension. *Journal of Educational Psychology, 74,* 506–521.

Beck, I. L., & McKeown, M. G. (2007). Increasing young low-income children's oral vocabulary repertoires through rich and focused instruction. *Elementary School Journal, 107,* 251–271.

Beck, I. L., McKeown, M. G., & Kucan, L. (2002). *Bringing words to life: Robust vocabulary instruction.* New York: Guilford Press.

Beck, I. L., McKeown, M. G., & Kucan, L. (2008). *Creating robust vocabulary: Frequently asked questions and extended examples.* New York: Guilford Press.

Becker, W. C. (1977). Teaching reading and language to the disadvantaged—what we have learned from field research. *Harvard Educational Review, 47,* 518–543.

Biemiller, A. (2001). Teaching vocabulary: Early, direct, and sequential. *American Educator, 25*(1), 24–28, 47.

Blachowicz, C., & Fisher, P. J. (2009). *Teaching vocabulary in all classrooms* (4th ed.). Upper Saddle River, NJ: Pearson.

Blachowicz, C. L. Z. (1987). Vocabulary instruction: What goes on in the classroom? *Reading Teacher, 41*(2), 132–137.

Blachowicz, C. L. Z., Fisher, P. J. L., Ogle, D., & Watts-Taffe, S. (2006). Vocabulary: Questions from the classroom. *Reading Research Quarterly, 41*, 524–539.

Blachowicz, C. L. Z., & Obrochta, C. (2007). "Tweaking practice": Modifying read-alouds to enhance content vocabulary learning in grade 1. In D. W. Rowe, R. Jiménez, D. Compton, D. Dickson, Y. Kim, K. Leander, et al. (Eds.), *Fifty-seventh Yearbook of the National Reading Conference* (pp. 140–150). Oak Creek, WI: National Reading Conference.

Bos, C. S., & Anders, P. L. (1990). Effects of interactive vocabulary instruction on the vocabulary learning and reading comprehension of junior-high learning disabled students. *Learning Disability Quarterly, 13*, 31–42.

Calderón, M., August, D., Slavin, R., Duran, D., Maddan, N., & Cheung, A. (2005). Bringing words to life in classrooms with English-language learners. In E. H. Hiebert & M. Kamil (Eds.), *Teaching and learning vocabulary: Bringing research to practice* (pp. 115–136). Mahwah, NJ: Erlbaum.

Carlisle, J. F., Beeman, M., & Shah, P. P. (1996). The metalinguistic capabilities and English literacy of Hispanic high school students: An exploratory study. In D. J. Leu, C. K. Kinzer, & K. A. Hinchman (Eds.), *45th Yearbook of the National Reading Conference* (pp. 306–316). Oak Creek, WI: National Reading Conference.

Carlisle, J. F., Beeman, M. M., Davis, L.-H., & Spharim, G. (1999). Relationship of metalinguistic capabilities and reading achievement for children who are becoming bilingual. *Applied Psycholinguistics, 20*(4), 459–478.

Carlisle, J. F., & Katz, L. A. (2006). Defining lexical quality as a factor in reading derived words. *Reading and Writing: An Interdisciplinary Journal, 19*, 669–693.

Carlo, M. S., August, D., McLaughlin, B., Snow, C. E., Dressler, C., Lipman, D. N., et al. (2004). Closing the gap: Addressing the vocabulary needs of English-language learners in bilingual and mainstream classes. *Reading Research Quarterly, 39*, 188–215.

Carlo, M. S., August, D., & Snow, C. E. (2005). Sustained vocabulary-learning strategies for English language learners. In E. H. Hiebert & M. Kamil (Eds.), *Teaching and learning vocabulary: Bringing research to practice* (pp. 137–153). Mahwah, NJ: Erlbaum.

Collins, M. F. (2004, May). *The contribution of storybook reading to second language acquisition.* Paper presented at the annual convention of the International Reading Association, San Antonio, TX.

Collins, M. F. (2005). IRA outstanding dissertation award for 2005: ESL preschoolers' English vocabulary acquisition from storybook reading. *Reading Research Quarterly, 40*, 406–408.

Coyne, M. D., Simmons, D. C., & Kame'enui, E. J. (2004). Vocabulary instruction for young children at risk of experiencing reading difficulties: Teaching word meanings during shared storybook readings. In J. F. Baumann & E. J. Kame'enui (Eds.), *Vocabulary instruction: Research to practice* (pp. 41–58). New York: Guilford Press.

Cummins, J. (2003). Reading and the bilingual student: Fact and friction. In G. G. García (Ed.), *English learners: Reaching the highest level of English literacy* (pp. 2–33). Newark, DE: International Reading Association.

Cunningham, A. E., & Stanovich, K. E. (1998). What reading does for the mind. *American Educator, 22*(1–2), 8–15.

Davis, F. B. (1944). Fundamental factors of comprehension in reading. *Psychometrika, 9,* 185–197.

DeTemple, J. M., & Snow, C. E. (2003). Learning words from books. In A. van Kleeck, S. A. Stahl, & E. B. Bauer (Eds.), *On reading books to children: Parents and teachers* (pp. 16–36). Mahwah, NJ: Erlbaum.

Dickinson, D. K., & Smith, M. W. (1994). Long-term effects of preschool teachers' book readings on low-income children's vocabulary and story comprehension. *Reading Research Quarterly, 29,* 104–122.

Dressler, C., & Kamil, M. L. (2006). First- and second-language literacy. In D. August & T. Shanahan (Eds.), *Developing literacy in second-language learners: Report of the National Literacy Panel on Language-Minority Children and Youth* (pp. 197–238). Mahwah, NJ: Erlbaum.

Duke, N. (2000). For the rich it's richer: Print experiences and environments offered to children in very low- and very high-socioeconomic status first-grade classrooms. *American Educational Research Journal, 37,* 441–478.

Ehri, L. C., & Rosenthal, J. (2007). Spellings of words: A neglected facilitator of vocabulary learning. *Journal of Literacy Research, 39,* 389–409.

Elkonin, D. B. (1963). The psychology of mastering elements of reading. In B. Simon (Ed.), *Educational psychology in the U.S.S.R.* London: Routledge & Kegan Paul.

Folse, K. S. (2004). *Vocabulary myths: Applying second language research to classroom teaching.* Ann Arbor: University of Michigan Press.

Freeman, Y., & Freeman, D. (2003). Struggling English language learners: Keys for academic success. *TESOL Journal, 12*(3), 5–10.

García, G. E. (1991). Factors influencing the reading test performance of Spanish speaking Hispanic children. *Reading Research Quarterly, 26*(4), 371–392.

García, G. E. (1998). Mexican-American bilingual students' metacognitive reading strategies: What's transferred, unique, problematic? In T. Shanahan & F. V. Rodriguez-Brown (Eds.), *47th Yearbook of the National Reading Conference* (pp. 253–263). Oak Creek, WI: National Reading Conference.

Goldenberg, C., Rezaei, A., & Fletcher, J. (2005, May). *Home use of English and Spanish and Spanish-speaking children's oral language and literacy achievement.* Paper presented at the annual convention of the International Reading Association, San Antonio, TX.

González, N., Moll, L. C., & Amanti, C. (2005). Funds of knowledge: Theorizing practices in households and classrooms. Mahwah, NJ: Erlbaum.

Graves, M. F. (2006). *The vocabulary book: Learning and instruction.* New York: Teachers College Press.

Harmon, J. M., Hedrick, W. B., Wood, K. D., & Gress, M. (2005). Vocabulary self-selection: A study of middle-school students' word selections from expository texts. *Reading Psychology, 26,* 313–333.

Hart, B., & Risley, T. R. (1995). *Meaningful differences in the everyday experience of young American children.* Baltimore: Brookes.

Hiebert, E. H., & Kamil, M. L. (2005). *Teaching and learning vocabulary: Bringing research to practice.* Mahwah, NJ: Erlbaum.

Hopkins, G., & Bean, T. W. (1999). Vocabulary learning with the verbal–visual word association strategy in a Native American community. *Journal of Adolescent and Adult Literacy, 42*(4), 274–281.

Hornberger, N. (1990). Creating successful learning contexts for bilingual literacy. *Teachers College Record, 92*(2), 212–229.

James, C., & Klein, K. (1994). Foreign language-learners' spelling and proof-reading strategies. *Papers and Studies in Contrastive Linguistics, 29*, 31–46.

Jiménez, R. T., García, G. E., & Pearson, P. D. (1996). The reading strategies of bilingual Latina/o students who are successful English readers: Opportunities and obstacles. *Reading Research Quarterly, 31*, 90–112.

Jiménez, R. T., & Gersten, R. (1999). Lessons and dilemmas derived from the literacy instruction of two Latino/a teachers. *American Educational Research Journal, 36*(2), 265–301.

Juel, C., Biancarosa, G., Coker, D., & Deffes, R. (2003). Walking with Rosie: A cautionary tale of literacy instruction. *Educational Leadership, 60*(7), 12–18.

Kolich, E. M. (1991). Effects of computer-assisted vocabulary training on word knowledge. *Journal of Educational Research, 84*, 177–182.

Labbo, L. D., Love, M. S., & Ryan, T. (2007). A vocabulary flood: Making words "sticky" with computer-response activities. *Reading Teacher, 60*, 582–588.

MacArthur, C. A., & Haynes, J. B. (1995). Student Assistant for Learning from Text (SALT): A hypermedia reading aid. *Journal of Learning Disabilities, 28*, 150–159.

Marston, D., Deno, S. L., Kim, D., Diment, K., & Rogers, D. (1995). Comparison of reading intervention approaches for students with mild disabilities. *Exceptional Children, 62*, 20–37.

Martinez-Roldan, C. M. (2003). Building worlds and identities: A case study of the role of narratives in bilingual literature discussions. *Research in the Teaching of English, 37*, 491–526.

Moje, E. B., Dillon, D. R., & O'Brien, D. (2000). Reexamining the roles of learner, text, and context in secondary literacy. *Journal of Educational Research, 93*, 165–180.

Moll, L. C., Saez, R., & Dworin, J. (2001). Exploring biliteracy: Two student case examples of writing as a social practice. *Elementary School Journal, 101*, 435–449.

Montali, J., & Lewandowski, L. (1996). Bimodal reading: Benefits of a talking computer for average and less skilled readers. *Journal of Learning Disabilities, 29*, 271–279.

Nagy, W. E., García, G. E., Durgunoglu, A. Y., & Hancin-Bahtt, B. (1993). Spanish–English bilingual students' use of cognates in English reading. *Journal of Reading Behavior, 25*, 241–259.

Nagy, W. E., & Scott, J. A. (2000). Vocabulary processes. In M. L. Kamil, P. B. Mosenthal, P. D. Pearson, & R. Barr (Eds.), *Handbook of reading research* (Vol. 3, pp. 269–283). Mahwah, NJ: Erlbaum.

Nation, I. S. P. (2001). *Learning vocabulary in another language.* Cambridge, UK: Cambridge University Press.

Nation, P. (1993). Vocabulary size, growth, and use. In R. Schreuder & B. Weltens (Eds.), *The bilingual lexicon* (pp. 115–134). Amsterdam: Benjamins.

National Reading Panel. (2000). *Report of the National Reading Panel: Reports of the subgroups.* Washington, DC: National Institute of Child Health and Human Development Clearinghouse.

Neuman, S. B., & Dickinson, D. K. (Eds.). (2001). *Handbook of early literacy research* (Vol. 1). New York: Guilford Press.

Ogle, D., & Correa, A. (2007). *Building morphological skills: Presentation to the Chicago Public Schools Striving Readers Project.* Chicago: Chicago Public Schools.

Ordonez, C. L., Carlo, M. S., Snow, C. E., & McLaughlin, B. (2002). Depth and breadth of vocabulary in two languages: Which vocabulary skills transfer? *Journal of Educational Psychology, 94*(4), 719–728.

Pressley, M., Disney, L., & Anderson, K. (2007). Landmark vocabulary instructional research and the vocabulary instructional research that makes sense now. In R. K. Wagner, A. E. Muse, & K. E. Tannenbaum (Eds.), *Vocabulary acquisition: Implications for reading comprehension* (pp. 205–232). New York: Guilford Press.

Proctor, C. P., Dalton, B., & Grisham, D. L. (2007). Scaffolding English language learners and struggling readers in a Universal Literacy Environment with embedded strategy instruction and vocabulary support. *Journal of Literacy Research, 39*, 71–93.

Robbins, C., & Ehri, L. C. (1994). Reading storybooks to kindergarteners to help them learn new vocabulary words. *Journal of Educational Psychology, 86*, 54–64.

Ruddell, M. R., & Shearer, B. A. (2002). "Extraordinary," "Tremendous," "Exhilarating," "Magnificent": Middle school at-risk students become avid word learners with the Vocabulary Self-Collection Strategy (VSS). *Journal of Adolescent and Adult Literacy, 45*, 352–363.

Rueda, R. S., August, D., & Goldenberg, C. (2006). The sociocultural context in which children acquire literacy. In D. August & T. Shanahan (Eds.), *Developing literacy in second-language learners: Report of the National Literacy Panel on Language-Minority Children and Youth* (pp. 319–339). Mahwah, NJ: Erlbaum.

Schwanenflugel, P. J., Hamilton, C. E., Bradley, B. A., Ruston, H. P., Neuharth-Pritchett, S., & Retrepo, M. A. (2005) Classroom practices for vocabulary enhancement in pre-kindergarten: Lesson plans from PAVEd for success. In E. H. Hiebert & M. L. Kamil (Eds.), *Teaching and learning vocabulary: Bringing research to practice* (pp. 155–178). Mahwah, NJ: Erlbaum.

Scott, J. A., Flinspach, S., & Samway, K. D. (2007, April). *Linking word knowledge to the world: The VINE project.* Paper presented at the annual meeting of the American Educational Research Association, Chicago.

Scott, J. A., Jamieson-Noel, D., & Asselin, M. (2003). Vocabulary instruction throughout the day in twenty-three Canadian upper elementary classrooms. *Elementary School Journal, 103*, 269–286.

Scott, J. A., & Nagy, W. E. (1997). Understanding the definitions of unfamiliar verbs. *Reading Research Quarterly, 32*, 184–200.

Scott, J. A., Skobel, B. J., & Wells, J. (2008). *The word-conscious classroom: Building the vocabulary readers and writers need.* New York: Guilford Press.

Sénéchal, M., Thomas, E., & Monker, J. (1995). Individual differences in 5 year olds' acquisition of vocabulary during storybook reading. *Journal of Educational Psychology, 87*, 218–229.

Shanahan, T., & Beck, I. L. (2006). Effective literacy teaching for English-language learners. In D. August & T. Shanahan (Eds.), *Developing literacy in second-language learners: Report of the National Literacy Panel on Language-Minority Children and Youth* (pp. 415–488). Mahwah, NJ: Erlbaum.

Snow, C. (1991). The theoretical basis of the Home–School Study of Language and Literacy Development. *Journal of Research in Childhood Education, 6*, 5–10.

Stahl, S., & Fairbanks, M. (1986). The effects of vocabulary instruction: A model-based meta-analysis. *Review of Educational Research, 56*, 72–110.

Stahl, S. A., & Nagy, W. E. (2005). *Teaching word meanings.* Mahwah, NJ: Erlbaum.

Stevens, K. C. (1982). Can we improve reading by teaching background information? *Journal of Reading, 25*, 326–329.

Terman, L. M. (1916). *The measurement of intelligence.* Boston: Houghton Mifflin.

Vygotsky, L. S. (1978). *Mind in society.* Cambridge, MA: Harvard University Press.

Wasik, B. A., & Bond, M. A. (2001). Beyond the pages of a book: Interactive book reading and language development in preschool classrooms. *Journal of Educational Psychology, 93,* 243–250.

Watts, S. M. (1995). Vocabulary instruction during reading lessons in six classrooms. *Journal of Reading Behavior, 27,* 399–424.

Weizman, Z. O., & Snow, C. E. (2001). Lexical input as related to children's vocabulary acquisition: Effects of sophisticated exposure and support for meaning. *Developmental Psychology, 37,* 265–279.

West, M. (1953). *A general service list of English words.* London: Longmans, Green & Company.

White, T. G., Graves, M. F., & Slater, W. H. (1990). Growth of reading vocabulary in diverse elementary schools: Decoding and word meaning. *Journal of Educational Psychology, 82,* 281–290.

Whitehurst, G. J., Epstein, J. N., Angell, A. L., Payne, A. C., Crone, D. A., & Fischel, J. E. (1994). Outcomes of an emergent literacy intervention in Head Start. *Journal of Educational Psychology, 86,* 542–555.

Whitehurst, G. J., Zevenberg, A. A., Crone, D. A., Schultz, M. D., Velting, O. N., & Fischel, J. E. (1999). Outcomes of an emergent literacy intervention from head Start through second grade. *Journal of Educational Psychology, 91,* 261–272.

# CHAPTER 17

# Comprehension

## The Means, Motive, and Opportunity
## for Meeting the Needs of Diverse Learners

SUSIE M. GOODIN, CATHERINE M. WEBER, P. DAVID PEARSON,
and TAFFY E. RAPHAEL

We have adapted the guiding metaphor for this chapter from the television program *Law and Order*. If we were sufficiently persistent in our historical scholarship on crime drama, we would likely find that Perry Mason and Sherlock Holmes were even earlier custodians of the tradition from which we have so liberally (and literally) borrowed. When detectives investigate a case, such as a missing person, they look for the reasons the person has "gone missing," as well as the means, motive, and opportunity that help them to explain and to resolve the case. The *means* are the tools used to "disappear" the person. The *motive* is the "rationale," the purpose that compels the crime. Opportunity reflects being at the right place at the time to remove the "missing" from circulation. We find the components of this metaphor to be particularly useful in our review of research on comprehension instruction for diverse learners. Whereas so much is known about comprehension and comprehension instruction, achievement levels at the national and state levels suggest that something is missing, creating challenges to many students' success in reading.

Borrowing from the metaphor, we ask, "What can the research literature suggest to us regarding diverse learners' means, motives, and opportunities to experience high-quality, effective comprehension instruction and, in parallel, to engage independently in successful meaning making?" That is, pedagogical practices are effective to the degree that they provide learners with the means, motive, and opportunity to learn. The "means" are the student skills and strategies that teachers help their diverse learners develop through high-quality pedagogical practices. "Motive" refers to providing and supporting students with good reasons for pursuing the means, applying what they are learning to meet a broad array of goals: "If you learn and use *X*, you will . . .

> be able to read books on your own.
> find out fascinating and important information about the world.
> figure out new words on your own.
> have more fun in and outside of school.
> be able to participate more fully in classroom and nonschool activities.
> get better grades."

Opportunity in reading development includes (1) interesting activities within which students can practice taught strategies and skills, while engaged in real reading with real texts; (2) contexts in which students can practice when their teacher is available to coach them through the tough bits, at least until they have them under control; and (3) equal access to reading a wide range of interesting texts in all formats. So opportunity includes guided practice with teacher support and independent practice while engaging in everyday reading of diverse texts. We do not want to see means, motives, and/or opportunities "missing in action" from today's classroom for any of our students, but particularly those students who depend on school for their literacy and language development.

The overarching question for the chapter, "What do we know about comprehension instruction for diverse learners?," and its primary subquestion, "What can we do to be more effective in applying what we know to support diverse learners more effectively?," are examined in light of four areas of investigation:

1. What have we learned from over three decades of research about comprehension and instruction?
2. What do we know about comprehension instruction in learners with diverse language, culture, race, and/or economic levels?
3. What do we know about current practices in teaching comprehension?
4. What are illustrative, successful projects for teaching diverse learners comprehension strategies and skills?

We summarize these areas in terms of their implications for classroom practice and conclude the chapter with remarks on policy and a view toward future research.

## Understanding Comprehension Instruction: Means and Motives for Creating Learning Opportunities

The past three decades have provided educators with a plethora of knowledge about comprehension strategies, skills, and frameworks to enhance students' understandings of text and their abilities to think critically about the texts they encounter. Prior to the 1980s, the "means" for developing comprehension strategies with students were largely nonexistent. Until Durkin's (1978–1979) publication of a study about reading comprehension instruction in schools, the topic was not at the forefront of reading researchers' minds. Durkin based her study on questions raised within the Center for the Study of Reading:

1. Can reading comprehension be taught?
2. What does comprehension instruction look like in current classrooms?
3. What should it look like?

Researchers associated with the Center were beginning research on comprehension instruction at this time and Durkin (1978–1979, 1981) provided important baseline data about classroom instructional practices and the nature of comprehension instruction in the teachers' guides for the prevalent basal reading programs.

Durkin used existing research to describe the then-current state of reading comprehension instruction in U.S. classrooms. In her large-scale observational study, Durkin gathered data during reading and social studies instruction in 24 classrooms led by teachers whom administrators had identified as their best. The study was to document the degree to which comprehension instruction was occurring in elementary classrooms, and the amount of time devoted to it. Durkin coded observations in terms of instruction, review, application, the assignment, help with the assignment, preparation for reading, assessment, and prediction. The study revealed that less than 1% of instructional time focused on comprehension and, during that time, little instruction took place. Out of three participating schools, "two schools gave no time to comprehension instruction while the third spent a total of four minutes on it" (Durkin, 1978–1979, p. 508). Durkin's observational data revealed trends of quick, unexplained instructional shifts; questions generally from the basal text comprehension assignments focused on cloze exercises; and assignments primarily comprised of workbooks and worksheets. Furthermore, observations during social studies instruction revealed that teachers viewed this as a time to cover content, not to help with reading.

Similarly, Quirk, Trismen, Weinberg, and Nalin (1975) observed 156 second-through sixth-grade classrooms and found only slightly higher percentages of attention to comprehension—12% related to comprehension activities, divided fairly evenly (6 and 4%, respectively) between teacher and student talk. However, comprehension was not the focus of instruction or learning. Findings from Durkin's (1981) study of basal reading textbooks were consistent with her earlier work and with that of Quirk and colleagues (1975), revealing a lack of any guidance in the teacher manuals that might help teachers with comprehension instruction. A common theme across the basal texts was the idea that children "understand by doing, not by receiving, direct, explicit instruction that is complemented with application and practice" (Durkin, 1981, p. 525). The analyses revealed that most of the basal texts were filled with opportunities for comprehension practice and assessment, but few, if any, explicit means for teaching comprehension strategies.

Durkin's revealing studies about the lack of comprehension instruction in class-rooms, or the means for teaching it in textbooks, contributed to expanding the field of comprehension research. The 1980s proved to be a pivotal time, in which the focus of comprehension instruction shifted from a collection of subskills to be mastered to a set of strategies to be learned.

The early 1980s was characterized by a focus on identifying the components of successful instruction. For example, within the process–product tradition, Rosenshine (1983) reviewed successful teacher training and student achievement programs to determine common features. He concluded that "basic skills are taught hierarchically so that success at any level requires application of knowl-edge and skills mastered earlier" (p. 337), and he promoted the concept of over-learning low-level, or basic, skills through direct instruction as prerequisite to learning higher cognitive functions. He identified six instructional functions: (1) review of the previous day's work; (2) presentation of new content/skills; (3) ini-tial student practice; (4) feedback and correctives; (5) independent practice; and (6) weekly and monthly reviews.

Within a constructivist perspective, Pearson and Dole (1987) offered a more holistic view of reading comprehension instruction, one based in the metaphor of a scaffold (Wood, Bruner, & Ross, 1976), with instruction characterized in terms of *temporary, adjustable support*. This support varies as responsibility for using and controlling strategies taught is gradually released from teacher to learner through a process of (1) direct explanation and/or modeling of comprehension strategies, (2) guided practice, (3) consolidation, (4) independent practice, and (5) applica-tion of knowledge to new material. Using this model, teachers maintain control of the learning environment but take into consideration students' initial knowledge and ability levels as they adjust the amount of support provided. Rather than an emphasis on speed and accuracy, the emphasis is on successful application of taught strategies in a variety of text situations. Students are given more respon-sibility to monitor their own comprehension of the text and to use strategies to solve problems.

With the new attention to *how* to teach comprehension came a parallel focus on *what* to teach. Throughout the 1980s and early 1990s, studies of instruction and use of single strategies dominated the research literature. Findings have been reviewed in myriad articles and chapters, including those by Dole, Duffy, Roeh-ler, and Pearson (1991), Liang and Dole (2006), Pearson and Fielding (1991), Raphael, Weber, George, and Nies (2008), and Tierney and Cunningham (1984). Comprehension strategy instruction focused on teaching students to incorporate their own knowledge and experiences to help them understand text (e.g., Han-sen & Pearson's [1983] study of inference training) and to think metacognitively about strategy use (e.g., Raphael & Pearson's [1985] study of question–answer relationship). As Paris, Lipson, and Wixson (1983) described the importance for strategic readers to have both the "skill" (i.e., the means or the knowledge of strat-egy and how it works) and the "will" (i.e., the motive or knowledge of when and why a strategy should be used), they detailed the importance of "declarative" (i.e., what the strategy is designed to accomplish), "procedural" (i.e., how it works), and "conditional" (i.e., when and why to use it) knowledge.

Over three decades, research on individual strategies was extended in new and more complex directions. Raphael and colleagues (2008) characterized three waves: (1) individual strategy research, (2) frameworks for multiple strategy use, and (3) cross-grade coherence in strategy instruction. Individual strategy research focused on identifying the strategies and evaluating their effectiveness. Frameworks for multiple strategy use focused on settings in which students could use multiple strategies in tandem to comprehend a variety of texts for various purposes. The third wave focuses on the current decade and the need to bring coherence across classrooms within a school to reach all students effectively. It marks a shift from individual teachers' comprehension instruction to a schoolwide effort to meet the needs of diverse learners.

In the first wave of comprehension research, single strategies were explored and tested. Researched strategies included summarizing (Berkowitz, 1986; Taylor & Beach, 1984; Winograd, 1984), questioning (Raphael & Pearson, 1985; Raphael & Wonnacott, 1985), monitoring reading (Paris, Saarino, & Cross, 1986), making inferences (Hansen & Hubbard, 1984; Hansen & Pearson, 1983), and identifying important information (Ogle, 1986; Schwartz & Raphael, 1985). These initial studies of comprehension were foundational in the field, because they helped to define comprehension and provided us with effective strategies for teaching it.

In the second wave of research, comprehension instruction moved from teaching individual strategies to teaching students "to coordinate a repertoire of strategic processes" (Pressley et al., 1992, p. 515) through use of multiple strategies, such as SAIL (Students Achieving Independent Learning), many of which trace their roots to the classic studies of reciprocal teaching by Palincsar and Brown (1984; Palincsar, 1986). Within the multistrategy framework, students developed metacognitive awareness about strategy application, discussed text with the teacher and with other students, built a broad base of knowledge, and were motivated to use reading strategies for pleasure reading. Of particular interest was the shift in the role of the teacher from deliverer of knowledge to collaborator in the learning experience. Researchers found that students who generated questions along with the teacher performed better on comprehension tasks than did students who simply answered teacher-generated questions (Dole et al., 1991).

We examine the third wave of comprehension research, schoolwide coherence in comprehension instruction, later in this chapter as we consider successful models for meeting the needs of diverse learners.

## Considering Diverse Learners

With a foundation of knowledge documenting effective instructional approaches to reading comprehension, research attention turned to considerations for learners who are diverse with regard to home language, economic background, race, and ethnicity (e.g., Au, 1995; Englert & Palincsar, 1991; Gallimore, Tharp, & Rueda, 1989; Goatley, Brock, & Raphael, 1995; Jiménez, García, & Pearson, 1996; Lapp, Fisher, Flood, & Moore, 2002; Moll, 1992). Although we know much about effective comprehension instruction with mainstream students, we must develop a deeper understanding about how this research translates into practice for students with diverse backgrounds. There is mounting evidence that diversity *does* matter in literacy development; decades of research provide clues for piecing together the impact of student differences in their literacy learning. Seeing diversity as a resource in combination with, and enlarging upon, solid pedagogical practices, as described in the previous section, we proceed to describe the means, motives, and opportunities for comprehension growth revealed through the "expert testimony" of research.

## Means

A growing body of research evidence on effective comprehension instruction for diverse learners provides insights into practices that have demonstrated success (see August & Shanahan, 2006; García, 2003). We know that community differences exist in practices and ways of using oral and written texts, and modes of participation in classrooms (Au & Kaomea, 2008; Heath, 1982, 1983), and that poverty impacts and constrains a sense of literacy possibilities (Berliner, 2005; Hicks, 2004). We know that, as educators, we have a responsibility to help all of our learners access the conventions of the language of power to build economic equity and full participation in society (Delpit, 2001; Jiménez, 2004b). We know that differences in knowledge and vocabulary (Lesaux, Koda, Siegel, & Shanahan, 2006; Proctor, August, Carlo, & Snow, 2005) speak to the heart of comprehension instruction for all students, and that a nuanced understanding of the contributions from all literacy practices enriches instruction. Keeping in mind the array of contributions to the construct of diverse learners and the importance of differentiated instruction, we begin by noting the foundations of good instruction for all learners.

Both quantitative and qualitative research consistently demonstrate that effective instruction for increasing reading comprehension across diverse student populations includes the following:

- Practice in oral language proficiency, especially for English language learners (ELLs), along with attention to building background knowledge and deep vocabulary understandings.
- Instruction in the use of code-switching, cognates, code-mixing, and cross-linguistic transfer (García, 2003).
- Phonics instruction (see August & Shanahan, 2006), embedded in the context of vocabulary and comprehension work in meaningful content, and connected to ongoing oral language development.

Lesaux and colleagues (2006) reported that comprehension difficulties for ELL students start by second grade and resemble those of non-ELL students. Though their study was based on a small number of studies on text-level comprehension skills, they concluded that taking a situational perspective and attending to individual differences is essential:

> With regard to reading comprehension, unlike the findings of studies on word-level tasks, these students [ELL] experience difficulties as compared with their native-speaking peers. Such difficulties may be related to oral proficiency, lack of exposure to print, limited opportunities to learn and poor quality of literacy instruction, and inability to navigate complex text and draw inferences from prior knowledge. Thus, the difficulties of language-minority children should not necessarily be attributed to a learning disability. Instead, research should focus on optimal educational interventions for these children that consider both contextual and child-level factors. (p. 114)

Proctor and colleagues (2005) studied 135 bilingual fourth-grade students in three urban sites, comparing progress in reading development when initial instruction occurred in either English or Spanish, using the same reading program. They recorded a huge range in comprehension scores for *both* modes of instruction (with grade equivalent scores ranging from pre-K to 16 year, 9 month levels on the battery of tests). They found a significant difference favoring initial English instruction on reading comprehension. Noting that vocabulary knowledge impacted both listening and reading comprehension, the authors referred to Coady's "beginner's paradox," inherent to ELL vocabulary learning: " 'How can they learn enough words to learn vocabulary through extensive reading when they do not know enough words to read well?' " (Coady, 1997, cited in Proctor et al., 2005, p. 254). Given that even 2% unknown words in a text may negatively impact comprehension, vocabulary knowledge is crucial but hard to get through extensive reading in a second language (L2). So, if incidental vocabulary learning through extensive reading is not the answer for L2 readers, what is? Their findings suggest that focusing on literacy engagements that embed vocabulary tasks to develop a depth and breadth of word knowledge, teaching cognate strategies, and providing a wide range of interesting texts to read may be productive practices (Proctor et al., p. 254).

We present further evidence from two studies providing clues to what works pedagogically for diverse populations. In the first, Saunders and Goldenberg (1999) examined the efficacy of separate components of literature-based instruction in a program for transitional bilingual education. They studied the instruction with 116 fourth- and fifth-grade students from a largely Hispanic, ELL, and urban-poor population. They tested two instructional components (literature logs, instructional conversations) combined into four treatment conditions (including both treatments, a single treatment, or neither treatment component) to determine what most effectively increased reading comprehension. Their analysis of pre-

and posttest results showed that the treatment groups (ELL *and* fluent English students) using *both* literature logs and instructional conversations scored significantly higher on factual and interpretive comprehension questions in comparison to the control group.

The second study (Jiménez et al., 1996) compared the reading strategies of eight bilingual Latina/o students proficient in English reading to the strategies of three successful monolingual English readers and three less successful bilingual readers of English to uncover any qualitatively different student approaches. They found that the successful bilingual English readers were unique in accessing cognates and in using cross-linguistic transfer to understand text and their primary language skills to make meaning. Finding that the successful Anglo readers used comprehension strategies less frequently, the authors suggested that strategy use for successful readers was needs based and not recognized as helpful by the less successful Latina/o readers, who focused on merely finishing the text rather than understanding it. The study provided further evidence that poor readers approach texts in similarly unsuccessful ways, making few adjustments in their approach to texts to make meaning.

It is sensible to conclude that although strategy instruction provides *means* for all students to take responsibility for constructing understanding of texts, adjustments must be made for unique populations, depending on the strengths they bring to the reading table. Overall, students are more similar than different in their need for good strategy instruction, but situational sensitivity should direct the specific emphasis in instruction.

### Motives

Teachers' motives for striving in reading comprehension instruction may, of necessity, be tightly bound to current accountability mandates and interests in equity, but we focus here on teachers' motivational classroom practices as they apply to students' motives and reading comprehension. Guthrie and Humenick (2004) conducted a meta-analysis of 22 experiments and quasi-experiments focused on studies with students, ages 8–14, that highlighted the importance of four key components of instruction on students' reading motivation and reading achievement.

First, the authors found that helping students to *define clear goals* for content knowledge acquisition—for a purpose based on understanding the content rather than achieving better test scores—enabled students to become more deeply engaged in reading. Some practices that worked to the students' advantage included connecting the material to students' prior knowledge and experience, designing hands-on activities, modeling the stance of a curious reader, using thematic units, connecting to real-world tasks, and working in collaborative modes.

Second, Guthrie and Humenick (2004) examined the influence of *choice* on students' motivation and performance. "Choice" may refer to selecting the book, genre, response type, and site for reading, resulting in a substantial impact on students' higher intrinsic motivation to read and higher reading comprehension achievement. Their findings echoed Morrow's (1992) study of literature-based programs on literacy practices with children from minority backgrounds. The use of literature with second graders in both collaborative and independent work, balanced with traditional work in basal instruction in two groups, was compared with a control group that focused solely on basal instruction. Findings for the groups using literature-based instruction included significantly elevated performance on three comprehension measures: probed recall comprehension, oral and written story retellings, and enhanced story creation and vocabulary development. Though no difference between groups was reported for scores on a standardized test of reading, student interviews revealed heightened interest in reading and more actual reading of books in the literature-based groups. Importantly, comparisons made across diverse racial backgrounds indicated that concerns that minority students might not benefit from literature-based, "progressive" instruction were unfounded.

Third, Guthrie and Humenick (2004) investigated the effect of *access to interesting texts* on student engagement and performance. They found that students' memory and comprehension of texts improved as they engaged with texts that called on children's background knowledge, included good visual assets, and connected to concrete experiences. These effects in turn led to higher intrinsic motivation to read and higher reading comprehension performance.

Fourth, Guthrie and Humenick's (2004) meta-analysis investigated the role of *social collaboration in reading*. Although findings were limited by fewer available studies, they reported that cooperative work appeared to increase overall willingness to work on academic tasks. Morrow (1992) found a similar advantage in collaborative work on second graders' motivation to read and comprehension capacity.

Although the Guthrie and Humenick (2004) meta-analysis showed clear effects of instructional practices on students' motivation, Arzubiaga, Rueda, and Monzó (2002) argued that motivation theory should also include sociocultural influences. Previous work on motivation and engagement has focused on individual responses and ignored social contexts; Arzubiaga and colleagues use an ecological perspective to address that gap. They argued that adding an ecocultural lens to the traditional cognitive framework, to view learners within their social contexts, provides a more accurate picture of literacy attainment. This approach recognizes the complexity of literacy practices within cultural groups, noting how varying practices mediate literacy development in varied ways based on diverse opportunities, values, and constraints in everyday family practices.

Arzubiaga and colleagues (2002) interviewed 18 Latino families in the urban Southwest and administered a reading survey to the elementary school–age children enrolled in the third and fourth grades in a school with 100% of students qualifying for free lunch. The students completed an extensive questionnaire addressing their self-concept as readers and the value of reading. Both measures showed high variability within this population. Results also showed a high negative correlation between children's value of reading and parents' domestic *workload* feature. As workload increased, children's reading motivation decreased, except where child care activity was part of the workload. The *nurturance* feature correlated with children's valuing of reading, indicating that "the more time a family spends together the more children value reading and that as families promote values and identity, children's self-concept as reader also increases" (p. 238). The *culture and language* feature revealed that religious activity correlated to children's self-concept as readers. More of such studies have the potential to address the gap in research on sociocultural influences on literacy development.

These findings were complemented by an extensive analysis of research completed by Goldenberg, Rueda, and August (2006) on sociocultural influences on literacy attainment. The authors reviewed the hard-to-define sociocultural framework of home influences on students' school performance, taking on an ecological point of view and a stance that included student outcomes beyond standardized test scores. They found that the immigrant student population is not the homogenous group so often portrayed, and that immigration status is not predictive of children's reading motivation or reading self-concept. Furthermore, they reported that literacy attainment by Southeast Asian refugees was explained by parent education, the age of the student upon arrival, and the number of years in the United States, rather than on immigration factors alone. Consistent with other researchers (e.g., Au, 1980; Au & Mason, 1981), Goldenberg and colleagues found an influence of varied cultural discourse patterns: Interaction patterns compatible with students' native culture led to higher levels of achievement-related behaviors than when instruction mirrored more traditional patterns. There was a modest impact on reading achievement, but the authors noted that generally better instruction could have caused this effect.

Overall, Goldenberg and colleagues (2006) concluded that evidence of the impact of sociocultural factors on reading and literacy development generally is weak but there is some consistency in findings that language-minority students' reading comprehension improves with the use of culturally familiar texts. However, text language is an even stronger predictor for reading achievement. Together, these studies (Arzubiaga et al., 2002; Goldenberg et al., 2006) explored the assumptions behind students' motivations for reading and literacy attainment, arguing that everyday social routines and family environments impact literacy development. Their work supports a more complex view of diverse groups: There are wide differences in literacy practices within populations otherwise thought of as homogenous.

Closely related to motivation research is research that focuses on children's interests in text. Extensive research reviews on the subject (e.g., Galda, Ash, & Cullinan, 2000; Guthrie & Greaney, 1991) note that, at the elementary school level, whereas interests vary according to age, sex, and reading ability, they reliably indicate preferences for humor, nonsense and rhyme, and action-packed narratives. Middle grade preferences revealed an expansion in topics of interest, including reading books in a series. Both sets of researchers reported that boys prefer science, sports, and transportation, whereas girls prefer realistic fiction and fantasy, with boys moving even more toward nonfiction by the end of elementary school. Boys enjoy comics more than girls, until high school. By secondary school there is an overall decline in interest in independent reading, more interest in periodicals, and increased interest in access to adult best-sellers. Overall, there was little interest in poetry, though this may be a result of generational differences due to current elevated interest in song lyrics and zine production. Broad consistency across large studies over time has, at the same time, uncovered individual differences driven by individual abilities and sociocultural influences. Information about students' reading preferences contributes to the likelihood that we, as practitioners, will engage students in reading texts that may advance their reading comprehension capacities.

Finally, a survey of diverse sixth-grade students' classroom reading preferences (Ivey & Broaddus, 2001) affirmed the importance of a wide range of interesting texts to students' motivation to read. We can conclude that attending to broad issues of motivation and choice in instructional practices makes a substantial contribution to *all* children's motivation to read and reading comprehension achievement.

## Opportunity

Beyond instruction that develops the *means* and *motives* for students' reading comprehension growth, instruction must also provide equitable access to texts. Common sense tells us that text availability and the *opportunity* to read self-selected texts of interest to (1) apply comprehension skills, (2) practice comprehension strategies as needed, and (3) acquire new ideas incidentally through reading are essential to successful reading outcomes, although we readily admit that the research base is less definitive on this score than we would like. The practice effect, dubbed the "Matthew effect" of reading (Stanovich, 1986), assumes a positive relationship between reading volume and reading competence. In a series of studies reporting the impact of students' independent reading, correlational evidence supports the effect of practice on students' motivation and comprehension (Anderson, Wilson, & Fielding, 1988; Cullinan, 2004; Lonsdale, 2003; Taylor, Frye, & Maruyama, 1990).

## Underrepresented Evidence about Opportunity from Library Research

Delving more widely into available evidence, we find an underreported research base in the field of school librarianship that is pertinent to reading achievement. Research on the effect of school libraries on student reading achievement includes over 75 studies in the past few decades; in this review, we focus on key studies since 1990. The bulk of library effectiveness studies tests the new "participatory" and collaborative school library/librarianship model (American Association of School Librarians, 1998; Giorgis & Peterson, 1996) for its impact on student achievement. As a group, the studies show cohesion on the value of school library programs for reading achievement from a range of research designs completed in a range of geographical and social contexts by at least 11 different research teams (19 U.S. states have been assessed recently). The studies point toward a significant positive impact, even if the cause of that impact is not yet fully understood.

In two studies on the effectiveness of Colorado school libraries (Lance, Rodney, & Hamilton-Pennell, 2000; Lance, Welborn, & Hamilton-Pennell, 1993), data included a collection of variables connected to *program development* (e.g., ratios of library staff hours per student, print volumes and other materials, library expenditures, visits to the library), *collaboration with teachers* (e.g., hours of lesson design, professional development, instruction in information literacy, leadership capacity in the school community), and *technology leadership* (e.g., computer–pupil ratios, networking capacities, remote access). These factors were correlated with standardized test results and controlled for a variety of school and community differences, including characteristics of teachers (education, experience, compensation), teacher–pupil ratio and expenditures per pupil, and community factors, such as poverty levels, minority demographics, and adult educational attainment.

The findings of the Lance groups and other, subsequent researchers working in different states suggest that students in schools with higher-level school libraries have achievement test scores that are 10–18% higher than those in schools with lower-level library programs. And even when all socioeconomic differences are controlled, school libraries still account for up to 8% of the variation in standardized test achievement (Lance, 2004).

In another example, Baughman (2000) conducted a statistical survey similar to the Lance groups' surveys, mailing 1,818 questionnaires to schools at the elementary, middle/junior high, and high school levels in Massachusetts. On the basis of the school library statistical samples and correlation with data on the National School Lunch Program, Baughman found a clear positive relationship between access to school library services and achievement on the Massachusetts Comprehensive Assessment System (MCAS). Percentage differences on gains made on the MCAS—7.3% at the elementary level, 4.5% at the middle/junior high level, and 1.5% at the high school level—were connected to various factors of library service. Summarizing the findings for K–8 schools, Baughman claimed that libraries with more books, more open hours, and staffing by a teacher-librarian and paraprofessional had higher achievement scores. As Baughman noted, lower levels of access, print experience, and library service may have a powerful negative cumulative impact on a student's achievement over the course of a school career—an effect consistent with the Matthew effect of reading (Stanovich, 1986).

In a final example from the school library effectiveness studies, Smith's (2001) survey of a random sample of 600 Texas school libraries correlated survey findings with state data on school characteristics, community economic data, and student performance on the reading section of the Texas Assessment of Academic Skills (TAAS). The study was designed to assess characteristics of school libraries, relate the findings to reading achievement on TAAS, and highlight best practices in high-performing schools. The study found that at all school levels, students performed better on TAAS in schools with a teacher-librarian than in schools without a teacher-librarian: "Over 10 percent more students in schools *with* librarians than in school *without* librarians met minimum TAAS expectations in reading. On average, 89.3 percent of students in schools with librarians compared with 78.4 percent in school without librarians met minimum TAAS expectations in reading" (Smith, 2001, p. 1).

School library effectiveness studies rarely are cited within reviews read by the reading research community, yet they can serve as a valuable part of the knowledge base driving whole-school reform efforts in regard to literacy instruction. The critical finding for all schools—elementary, middle, and high schools—has been the distinct, positive difference made by well-resourced collections and professionally credentialed teacher-librarians in regard to student reading achievement. Although the variation between state studies is notable, the commonality of strong student achievement in schools with strong library programs is clear, even after a large percentage of the reading test score variation is accounted for by socioeconomic status (SES) factors, including the school percentage of students in the National School Lunch Program (Lance, 2004; Lonsdale, 2003). It is important to note that in these studies the single biggest factor in explaining test score variation, *after* SES has been accounted for, is the activity of a credentialed teacher-librarian, and that even in the best of school circumstances related to these statistical data on staffing, most schools were understaffed in terms of recommended student–librarian ratios (Baughman, 2000; Lance et al., 1993, 2000; Smith, 2001).

To summarize, providing equitable access to instruction that attends to motives, means, and opportunity matters in our diverse school populations. This attention includes access to appropriate texts and, especially in relation to student engagement and print volume, connects to school library effectiveness literature. Best practices determined by research call for a combination of effective instructional techniques, modified to suit individual differences, in concert with equitable access to resources and time to read. We conclude this segment with a quote from Guthrie and Greaney (1991, p. 90) that illustrates the reciprocal nature of reading instruction, reading practice, and successful reading:

> The amount of independent reading for both boys and girls is positively correlated with the availability of printed material, ownership of a library card, reading achievement level, methods of reading instruction, recreational interests, language/literacy interactions, parental example and home values. Children's self-generated purposes for reading have been classified as utilitarian, diversionary, and enjoyment. The amount of reading for enjoyment is influenced by achievement level.

With a clearer set of findings about what works in reading comprehension instruction, we now turn our investigation to searching out clues on the present state of instruction.

## OPPORTUNITY FOR RICH INSTRUCTION: WHAT DO WE KNOW ABOUT CURRENT PRACTICES IN TEACHING COMPREHENSION?

Extensive research during the 1980s and 1990s provided teachers with the means to teach reading comprehension explicitly. It also provided samples of the opportunities to apply strategies for effective comprehension. Dole and her colleagues (1991), in their review of comprehension research, identified two major factors that, unlike our earliest studies of comprehension, are taken as "givens" today. The first factor is the importance of students' prior knowledge (about topic, general world knowledge, and/or organization of text) for successful comprehension. The second is the need to understand the effective use of strategies for successful comprehension. The extant body of research details five categories of strategies that correlate to increased capacity to comprehend:

1. Determining importance (e.g., gist, topic sentences, thesis, theme, interpretation)
2. Summarizing information (e.g., differentiate important from unimportant information, sift through text, synthesize ideas)
3. Drawing inferences (e.g., elaborate on what is read, fill in details omitted from the text)
4. Generating questions (e.g., ask questions of the text and/or author)
5. Monitoring comprehension (e.g., control and adapt strategic processes while reading)

Whereas Dole and colleagues (1991) noted *strategies* that have been shown to be effective for improving comprehension when taught explicitly and used to guide students during independent practice, Pressley (2000) identified five *components* of reading instruction that affect comprehension: decoding, vocabulary, prior knowledge, wide reading, and monitoring for meaning. Our concern, as a nation, that students' reading comprehension levels are still not yet where we want them to be may reflect lack of time spent teaching instructional strategies, lack of balance in addressing the different components, some combination of the two, or even lack of attention to the changing nature of literacy.

Just as the nature of literacy is changing, methods for teaching comprehension must similarly shift (New London Group, 1996; Unsworth, 2002, 2006). Perhaps the challenge that Pressley raised about comprehension not being taught is more a challenge that comprehension is not being taught in a manner that reflects the changing nature of text that students encounter today. We need to incorporate multiple types of "texts" (e.g., graphics, color, sound) into our comprehension instruction to equip our students sufficiently to be high achievers. According to Dole and colleagues (1991), it is crucial that students understand the types and purposes of different texts, as well as be able to negotiate across texts strategically. This is more pertinent today than ever, because students are required to navigate multiple modalities and need to be able to do so critically. Students are bombarded with so much information from so many sources—some credible, some not—that they must learn to apply comprehension strategies to new situations and information (Coiro, 2003; Leu, Kinzer, Coiro, & Cammack, 2004).

Because the nature of text itself is changing and a much wider array of sources exist for producing text, the demands for critical reading across contexts are increasingly challenging (Lankshear & Knobel, 2007). Particularly in diverse settings, educators must engage in systematic, meaningful strategy instruction that enables students to develop the skills necessary to comprehend complex texts.

Students from diverse backgrounds consistently score lower than their mainstream peers on standardized tests in reading (National Assessment of Education Progress, 2002). To ensure high levels of reading achievement for diverse learners, we must engage them in targeted comprehension strategy instruction that focuses on analyzing sources of information, synthesizing across texts, critiquing arguments, and formulating stances (Henry, 2006; Leu et al., 2004). We must also give students the opportunity to engage in substantive work around high-level questioning (Taylor, Pearson, Peterson, & Rodriguez, 2004). Equipping students with these skills will develop them into as strategic readers who are capable of meeting the literacy demands of the 21st century.

Although we are fully aware of the means for teaching comprehension effectively and we have the motivation to do so, we question whether all students have equal opportunity to engage in substantive comprehension instruction.

## LOOKING AHEAD TO SUCCESSFUL MODELS OF INSTRUCTION

We close on a more optimistic note by examining successful school programs that work to overcome barriers to effective reading pedagogy. Although we have learned much about comprehension instruction over the past three decades of research, the question remains: Is comprehension being taught in a systematic way in all schools?

To be successful in and out of school, students need consistent, high-quality instruction that builds in a coherent manner from year to year. This is true for all students; however, the issue is increasingly important for students from diverse backgrounds. It is the responsibility of the entire school to provide students with the highest quality comprehension instruction. Raphael and colleagues (2008) describe this as the third wave of comprehension research, in which schoolwide coherence is key to ensuring high levels of achievement for all learners.

We explore the intersection between comprehension instruction and schoolwide reform to understand better how to build coherence across classrooms and grade levels. The school reform literature, coupled with what we know about comprehension, enables us to create contexts in which diverse learners are able to receive high-quality instruction year after year. In reviewing the literature about comprehensive school reform efforts, several themes emerged as critical for this work to be successful: (1) common vision and clear goals (Au, 2005), (2) distributed leadership (Mason, Mason, Mendez, Nelsen, & Orwig, 2005), (3) ownership and buy-in (Advanced Reading Development Demonstration Project, 2008), (4) targeted professional development (Au, Raphael, & Mooney, 2008b), and (5) coherent, coordinated curriculum (Au, Raphael, & Mooney, 2008a).

Teachers and administrators must communicate with one another about expectations and goals for student learning. They must agree upon a *common vision and clear goals* to reach that vision (Au, 2005; Bryk, Rollow, & Pinnell, 1996; Copland, 2003; Pressley, Mohan, Raphael, & Fingeret, 2007; Purkey & Smith, 1983; Rowan, 1990). All teachers in a school must work collaboratively to create clear expectations for students, so that the curriculum reflects a developmental progression from grade to grade in terms of comprehension strategies and skills. Additionally, expectations should build on the belief that all students are capable of learning and reaching high levels of comprehension (Taylor et al., 2004).

Several initiatives across the United States are successfully addressing the barriers to comprehension instruction by engaging entire school faculties in shared decision making around data-driven instruction. Here we describe two illustrative examples, including the Bay Area School Reform Collaborative (BASRC) in California, and the Standards-Based Change Process (SBCP), with sister sites in both Hawaii and Chicago.

Au and her colleagues (Au, 2005; Au, Hirata, & Raphael, 2005) describe the centrality of a shared vision and common goals in their work with schools in the SBCP in both Hawaii and Chicago. The SBCP is iterative in nature, meaning that the process is revisited on a regular basis to ensure rigor and continuous improvement. It is guided by a nine-item To-Do List, which allows schools to improve comprehension instruction in a systematic manner. The To-Do List comprises the following: (1) developing the school philosophy; (2) creating a school literacy vision; (3) defining end-of-year targets for student learning; (4) developing goals into student-friendly "I can" statements; (5) gathering evidence; (6) creating or modifying scoring tools (rubrics, rating scales, etc.); (7) creating bar graphs that represent students' progress toward year-end goals; (8) reporting evidence to the whole school faculty; and (9) making wise instructional decisions based on data.

*Distributed leadership* is key to building coherence schoolwide and improving comprehension instruction in every classroom; thus, it is the foundation of the SBCP. Members of school faculties engage in substantive conversations about shared goals, assessments, instructional practices, and desired student outcomes (Au, 2005; Mason et al., 2005). Teachers, administrators, students, and parents have ownership of the process and agreed-upon goals, because they all contribute to the schoolwide effort to improve comprehension teaching and learning.

Because of the importance of *ownership* and involved stakeholders, school leaders must be proactive in engaging each member of the school community in efforts to improve comprehension for every student. Research has shown that efforts to improve teaching and learning are more likely to be successful if the entire school is engaged in the work (Bryk et al., 1996; Purkey & Smith, 1983). To address effectively the barriers to comprehension instruction, schools must build communities of teachers and learners that rally around a common purpose and vision.

The BASRC is an example of a project that explored schoolwide improvement through distributed leadership. Researchers worked with 86 leadership schools for varying lengths of time, between 3 and 5 years. Entire school faculties engaged in ongoing cycles of inquiry that focused on student learning, standards, and instructional practices. Faculty members worked together to identify challenges and barriers to the schools' progress. School teams created action plans and engaged in group problem solving to address the identified impedances and move the school forward.

Distributed leadership is crucial for successful development of schools in which the entire community is focused on improving comprehension teaching and learning (Au, 2005; Bryk et al., 1996; Purkey & Smith, 1983). Teachers and key leaders must work in tandem to identify and address instructional needs in an effective manner. Key leaders may include, but are not limited to, the principal, a literacy coordinator, a curriculum coordinator, and/or a bilingual lead teacher. School leaders must create time and space for teachers to meet. They must also facilitate conversations among staff to make meeting time productive and effective. Additionally, school leaders are instrumental in supporting instructional improvement, teacher development, and curricular coherence (Louis, Marks, & Kruse, 1996; Purkey & Smith, 1983; Rowan, 1990). The principal is often the person who initiates efforts for improvement but must rely on teachers and other leaders to improve comprehension instruction successfully across the entire school (Au, 2005; Bryk et al., 1996; Pressley et al., 2007).

For schools to improve comprehension instruction systematically, teachers must have the knowledge base necessary to do so. *Professional development*, a key component to improving teaching and learning schoolwide, needs to be strategically planned, goal-oriented, aligned with schoolwide foci, and connected in a coherent manner over time, so that it supports both teacher and student learning (Au, 2005; Louis et al., 1996; Newmann, Smith, Allensworth, & Bryk, 2001; Pressley et al., 2007; Purkey & Smith, 1983; Strahan, 2003). Professional development time should be used to learn new strategies and skills pertaining to comprehension instruction, and focus on inquiry about students' and schools' progress toward their vision (Au, 2005; Au et al., 2005; Bryk et al., 1996; Copland, 2003). Professional development activities may include looking at student work samples and/or assessments, discussing curricular goals within and across grade levels, or co-constructing standards and data-collection procedures.

In addition, strategic efforts must be made to *coordinate curricular materials*, instructional strategies, and assessment practices within and across grade levels, so that improvements in comprehension teaching and learning align horizontally and vertically (Au et al., 2005, 2008b; Purkey & Smith, 1983). Teachers in the SBCP (Au, 2005; Au et al., 2005) systematically assess students three times per year to monitor progress toward year-end benchmarks. School personnel create a schedule for administering and collectively scoring the student data, then report the results to their colleagues. This enables teachers to hear about grade-level expectations, assessments, and instructional plans across the entire school. Conversations about curricular coherence can take place and teachers are able to critique whether goals are rigorous enough and/or develop in a staircase across grades (Newmann et al., 2001).

These successful projects demonstrate how the means, motive, and opportunity of effective comprehension instruction can positively impact student learning.

## IMPLICATIONS FOR PRACTICE: TAKING THE MYSTERY, NOT THE COMPLEXITY, OUT OF INSTRUCTION

Although research findings may seem far removed from the classroom contexts that comprise most teachers' days, we believe that attending to the ways in which research translates to everyday practice helps to promote reading comprehension instruction. So, what can practitioners derive from the research evidence on implementing effective reading comprehension instruction for all of our students?

Reviewing the clues gathered in the preceding sections, we propose the following thematic issues for schools and educators to consider that tie the findings together:

- Intentional development of *access*, including both physical access to texts and choices of texts, and access to the best instruction utilizing what we know about successful comprehension pedagogy.
- Adoption of *collaborative practices* in regard to the whole learning community as all enter into a complex balance of recommended practices.
- Ongoing discussion of *accountability and appropriate assessment* as a part of implementation issues, and *professional development* connected to current constraints in teaching explicit comprehension strategies.

Recent reports help to enumerate the principles and site-specific practices that work to build the literacy reform capacity of schools (Biancarosa & Snow, 2006). The overarching principle is that effective instructional decisions situated in a particular school may benefit from the coordinated elements we saw manifested in our successful school projects: collaborative visioning; distributed leadership; shared goals; ongoing professional development; and alignment of curriculum, instruction, and assessment.

Expert advice at the classroom level from Allington (2001) and Pearson, Raphael, Benson, and Madda (2007) has focused on best practices and a balanced approach to reading instruction. Their examinations speak directly to the accumulated research impacting comprehension instruction that we described in preceding sections. Allington recommends that students complete a large volume of reading of diverse texts, appropriately matched to their reading level, as well as extensive practice in writing. Extensive practice must be accompanied by expert vocabulary pedagogy and comprehension instruction in strategies for developing "thoughtful literacy" that go beyond mere remembering: These comprehension strategies include activating prior knowledge, summarizing, story grammar work, imagery formation, question generation, and think-alouds with texts.

Likewise Pearson and colleagues (2007) have championed the notion of ecological balance in reading instruction as a system with multiple dimensions that works to support the reader's growth. It is "grounded in the belief that ownership of literacy is central to students' lifelong success" (p. 47). The instructional areas to be held in balance include comprehension strategies, composition, literary aspects, and language conventions. Balance is seen in intersecting dimensions along continua of *context of work* and *content of instruction*. Balance within reading instruction, then, includes attention to lower processes, such as phonemic awareness and phonics, as well as to more complex areas of vocabulary and comprehension instruction. These balance points should attend to the context of instruction by including rich conversations about text, strategy instruction, and word meanings. Each of the areas describes a model of gradual release of responsibility for teachers' roles.

An accompanying sensibility is that drawing students into productive engagement with texts requires a schoolwide, concerted effort to coordinate access to a range of texts and the time to read them with instructional support. The implication is that schools may need to develop classroom and school libraries to provide students with equitable access to resources.

Furthermore, Gersten and colleagues (2007) have provided expert consensus on best practices for ELLs at the elementary level. Their practice guide recommends an "actionable" and "coherent" set of guidelines for practitioners, and in this sense it is well suited for our purposes. The five recommendations for ELLs include (1) using formative assessments to identify at-risk students, (2) providing intensive small-group interventions, (3) providing research-based vocabulary instruction throughout the day, (4) developing academic English, and (5) devoting at least 90 minutes a week to peer-assisted instruction. Although Gersten and colleagues acknowledge a scarcity of research and pay scant attention to separate comprehension instruction, the practices they prescribe impact comprehension. Overall, their recommendations posit that ELLs may be taught with the same thoughtful, evidence-based strategies as native English speakers, paying special attention to vocabulary instruction, pacing, language proficiency, and extensive professional development for schoolwide coherence in instructional practices. Attending to the issues of best practice without a focus on text types, access to texts, and meaning making as central to successful reading instruction provides an incomplete picture that we have amended with other research, as noted earlier.

For students who may need supplementary aid, effective instruction also means making accommodation that departs from a deficit model, and instead perceives of linguistic differences as resources to be embedded in everyday pedagogy. Adjusting our perspective to *include difference* through enriched, hybrid, and inclusive practices opens the classroom door to multivoiced, diverse expressions, providing equitable possibilities for growth and learning by consulting cultural and linguistic differences (Gutiérrez, Baquedano-Lopez, & Tejada, 1999). The "funds of knowledge" that students bring to school need to be accounted for in our pedagogical practices if we are to succeed with all students (Moll, Amanti, Neff, & González, 1992).

## IMPLICATIONS FOR PRACTICE: BARRIERS TO EXPLORE

Studies indicate that enacting an ambitious comprehension curriculum is easier said than done (e.g., Benson-Griffo, Kohansal, & Pearson, 2007; Hacker & Tenent, 2002). Rounding up suspects that may impede comprehension instruction leads us to see themes of best practices and the barriers to those practices as parallel topics: What is recommended, when lacking, becomes a barrier. These barriers constitute issues of equity and include integrated and embedded explicit strategy instruction, access and opportunity to work with diverse texts, collaborative teaching and learning structures, and appropriate assessments driving curriculum. All constitute potential areas for future research.

The first potential suspect in the barrier search is encapsulated, or nonintegrative, instruction: Comprehension strategy instruction may be neglected for specific skills work, and may not be part of a balanced reading program. Furthermore, attention to reading instruction may be done at the expense of content-area knowledge development. This in turn has a snowballing, deleterious effect on knowledge development that supports comprehension. Paris (2005) argues that attention to reading skills should be considered in a developmental trajectory, with an understanding that some skills, like phonemic awareness, are usually constrained in their learning time frame, whereas others, like fluency, vocabulary growth and comprehension, are developed over a long period of time. Understanding the nature of the skills and their placement in students' reading growth complex mediates against exaggerated attention to early skills and a bits-and-pieces approach to reading instruction.

Excessive attention to basic skills work may take the place of explicit, embedded strategy instruction in many classrooms in which comprehension instruction is not occurring (Pressley & Wharton-McDonald, 2002). Compounding the impact of a skew toward skills instruction over comprehension instruction is the notion that knowledge construction is shorted in the content areas as English language arts (ELA) takes precedence over science and social studies in the curriculum. The Center on Education Policy (2008), revealed that for districts reporting change in instructional time, there was an average shift in instructional time of 43% toward ELA and math; in 80% of those districts, instructional time increased from 75 to 150 minutes a week. The increased time devoted to ELA and math was accompanied by decreased time spent on other subjects, a decrease of 75 minutes per week or more. The narrowing of the curriculum is visible in the statistics reported, with deep cuts to many areas, especially social studies, science, and the arts.

The second suspected barrier to implementation of comprehension instruction is access, specifically, a lack of access to diverse texts, and the opportunity to choose and to read appropriate independent reading texts may accompany a lack of enriched instruction for comprehension. We know from repeated research efforts that access to texts at appropriate levels, with support for selection by students, is an equity issue (Constantino, 2005; Neuman, 1999; Neuman & Celano, 2001; Smith, Constantino, & Krashen, 1997; Worthy, 1996). These studies confirm that students from low-income homes, schools, and neighborhoods have markedly fewer print resources available than their middle-class counterparts, which impacts their access to interesting and diverse texts. It appears that what students want to read is not well accommodated in middle-school classrooms (Ivey & Broaddus, 2001), and that access to and use of nonfiction texts are extremely limited in early primary classrooms (Duke, 2000). These access issues limit students' reading practice and comprehension growth.

The third suspect is the lack of collaborative teaching and learning structures and practices, in spite of ongoing calls for them (DiPardo, 1999; Lieberman & Miller, 1999). A professional community is considered an important element for improved instruction, but it remains elusive because sole practitioners or small "goer" groups with few followers lead the way on reform pedagogy. Halting progress in reform efforts may in part be a result of endemic problems in the structure of schools, with scant incentive to work outside the autonomous classroom, where the singleton teacher wields some decision-making control (Huberman, 1993; Kennedy, 2005; Little, 1990).

Finally, we suspect that inappropriate assessment and, perhaps more commonly, the inappropriate *uses* of assessment contribute to a narrow and ineffective reading curriculum. When assessment focuses on narrowly defined and highly specific skills, as do some in current usage, the main purpose of reading for meaning may get lost in the drive to improve test scores on very specific skills tests. This may in turn impact curricular decisions that attend to piecemeal skills acquisition rather than the broader purposes of reading instruction: engaging students in authentic texts and tasks that lead to deep and important meaning making about the world. Also of concern is the circumscribed nature of many assessments; they offer limited information about the students' learning patterns and needs. Both Dressman, Wilder, and Connor (2005) and Jiménez (2004a) have argued that standardized tests must be supplemented by investigations into the particular circumstances of a struggling student's literacy development. In this more complex notion of assessment, students might be seen through multiple lenses, by a focus on the multiple literate interests, engagements, and life skills that contribute to a total picture of literacy growth. Assessment in quantitative terms only informs on one level of student performance, but the lack of particularity in finding ways to address reading failure may misguide the teacher and direct attention away from comprehension instruction.

## Concluding Remarks

In a cautionary note, we argue that using research as a guide to sorting out the complexity of instruction at the local site "must inform teaching, but should not determine it" (Dudley-Marling, 2005, p. 128), because no single strategy or approach has been proven to work with all students all of the time (Pearson, 2007). The networks of practices and partners involved in expert reading comprehension instruction pose a challenge to policymakers as they seek to establish programs and guidelines that encourage all the staff at all schools to engage in collaborative practices. But whereas policy development may emerge from a research base, it cannot override the on-the-ground wisdom of practitioners situated at school sites. We suggest that the teaching team at each site be supported in inquiry-based, ongoing professional development programs through dynamic, shared leadership, recognizing that solving the case of missing reading comprehension instruction is an evolving process that utilizes all available expertise.

In the end, it is a commitment to equity that must drive our new endeavors in regard to reading comprehension instruction—a commitment that ensures avoidance of differentiated instruction and resource allocation based on social status. This "pedagogical divide" can be avoided by using a broad swath of research about how people learn, as well as a focus on language processes at the heart of literacy instruction (Cummins, 2007). Furthermore, Ladson-Billings (2006) asks us to conceive of the equity issue in education in terms of an "education debt," one that has accrued over the long term through recurrent deficits in expenditures for minority and disadvantaged students. It is time to do business in education with a different imperative, one informed by an accumulation of historic, moral, and economic components that are far more descriptive than the widely named "achievement gap."

## References

Advanced Reading Development Demonstration Project. (2008). Partnerships for Improving Literacy in Urban Schools: Advanced Reading Development Demonstration Project. *Reading Teacher, 61*(8), 674–680.

Allington, R. L. (2001). *What really matters for struggling readers: Designing research-based programs.* New York: Longman.

American Association of School Librarians. (1998). *Information power: Building partnerships for learning.* Chicago: American Library Association.

Anderson, R. C., Wilson, P. T., & Fielding, L. G. (1988). Growth in reading and how children spend their time outside of school. *Reading Research Quarterly, 23*(3), 285–303.

Arzubiaga, A., Rueda, R., & Monzó, L. (2002). Family matters related to the reading engagement of Latino children. *Journal of Latinos and Education, 1*(4), 231–243.

Au, K. H. (1980). Participation structures in reading lessons: Analysis of a culturally appropriate instructional event. *Anthropology and Education Quarterly, 11*, 91–115.

Au, K. H. (1995). Critical issues: Multicultural perspectives on literacy research. *Journal of Reading Behavior, 27*(1), 85–100.

Au, K. H. (2005). Negotiating the slippery slope: School change and literacy achievement. *Journal of Literacy Research, 37*(3), 267–288.

Au, K. H., Hirata, S. Y., & Raphael, T. E. (2005). Inspiring literacy achievement through standards. *California Reader, 39*(1), 5–10.

Au, K. H., & Kaomea, J. (2008). Reading comprehension and diversity in historical perspective. In G. G. Duffy & S. E. Israel (Eds.), *Handbook of research on reading comprehension* (pp. 1197–1230). New York: Erlbaum/Taylor & Francis.

Au, K. H., & Mason, J. M. (1981). Social organizational factors in learning to read: The balance of rights hypothesis. *Reading Research Quarterly, 17*(1), 115–152.

Au, K. H., Raphael, T. E., & Mooney, K. (2008a). Improving reading achievement in elementary schools: Guiding change in a time of standards. In S. B. Wepner & D. S. Strickland (Eds.), *Supervison of reading programs* (4th ed., pp. 71–89). New York: Teachers College Press.

Au, K. H., Raphael, T. E., & Mooney, K. (2008b). What we have learned about teacher education to improve literacy achievement in urban schools. In V. Chou, L. Morrow, & L. Wilkinson (Eds.), *Improving the preparation of teachers of reading in urban settings: Policy, practice, pedagogy* (pp. 159–184). Newark, DE: International Reading Association.

August, D., & Shanahan, T. (Ed.). (2006). *Developing literacy in second-language learners: Report of the National Literacy Panel on Language Minority and Youth.* Mahwah, NJ: Erlbaum.

Baughman, J. C. (2000, October). *School libraries and MCAS scores.* Paper presented at a symposium sponsored by the Graduate School of Library and Information Science, Boston.

Benson-Griffo, V., Kohansal, R., & Pearson, P. D. (2007). Curriculum reform in the context of a state mandate. In *56th Yearbook of the National Reading Conference* (pp. 323–337). Milwaukee, WI: National Reading Conference.

Berkowitz, S. J. (1986). Effects of instruction in text organization on sixth-grade students' memory for expository reading. *Reading Research Quarterly, 21*(2), 161–178.

Berliner, D. (2005). *Teachers College Record.* Retrieved December 27, 2005, from *www.tcrecord.org.*

Biancarosa, G., & Snow, C. E. (2006). *Reading Next—A vision for action and research in middle and high school literacy: A report from Carnegie Corporation of New York.* Washington, DC: Alliance for Excellent Education.

Bryk, A. S., Rollow, S. G., & Pinnell, G. S. (1996). Urban school development: Literacy as a lever for change. *Educational Policy, 10*(2), 172–201.

Center on Education Policy. (2008). *Instructional time in elementary schools: A closer look at changes for specific subjects.* Washington, DC: Author.

Coiro, J. L. (2003). Reading comprehension on the Internet: Expanding our understanding of reading comprehension to encompass new literacies. *Reading Teacher, 56,* 458–464.

Constantino, R. (2005). Print environments between high and low socioeconomic (SES) communities. *Teacher Librarian, 32*(3), 22–25.

Copland, M. A. (2003). Leadership of inquiry: Building and sustaining capacity for school improvement. *Educational Evaluation and Policy Analysis, 25*(4), 375–395.

Cullinan, B. E. (2004). *Independent reading and school achievement.* Retrieved April 12, 2005, from *www.ala.org/aasl/slmr/vol3/independent/independent.html.*

Cummins, J. (2007). Pedagogies for the poor?: Realigning reading instruction for low-income students with scientifically based reading research. *Educational Researcher, 36*(9), 564–572.

Delpit, L. (2001). The politics of teaching literate discourse. In E. Cushman, E. Kintgen, B. M. Kroll, & M. Rose (Eds.), *Literacy: A critical sourcebook* (pp. 545–554). Boston: Bedford/St. Martin's Press.

DiPardo, A. (1999). *Teaching in common.* New York: Teachers College Press.

Dole, J. A., Duffy, G. G., Roehler, L. R., & Pearson, P. D. (1991). Moving from the old to the new: Research in reading comprehension instruction. *Review of Educational Research, 61*(2), 239–264.

Dressman, M., Wilder, P., & Connor, J. (2005). Theories of failure and the failure of theories: A cognitive/sociocultural/macrostructural study of eight struggling students. *Research in the Teaching of English, 40*(1), 8–61.

Dudley-Marling, C. (2005). The complex relationship between reading research and classroom practice. *Research in the Teaching of English, 40,* 127–130.

Duke, N. K. (2000). 3.6 minutes per day: The scarcity of informational texts in first grade. *Reading Research Quarterly, 35*(2), 202–224.

Durkin, D. (1978–1979). What classroom observations reveal about readingcomprehension instruction. *Reading Research Quarterly, 14*(4), 481–533.

Durkin, D. (1981). Reading comprehension instruction in five basal reader series. *Reading Research Quarterly, 16,* 515–544.

Englert, C. S., & Palincsar, A. S. (1991). Reconsidering instructional research in literacy from a sociocultural perspective. *Learning Disabilities Research and Practice, 6*(4), 225–229.

Galda, L., Ash, G. E., & Cullinan, B. E. (2000). Children's literature. In M. L. Kamil, P. Mosenthal, P. Pearson, & R. Barr (Eds.), *Handbook of reading research* (Vol. 3, pp. 361–379). Mahwah, NJ: Erlbaum.

Gallimore, R., Tharp, R., & Rueda, R. (1989). *The social context of cognitive functioning in the lives of mildly handicapped persons.* London: Falmer Press.

García, G. E. (2003). The reading comprehension development and instruction of English-language learners. In A. P. Sweet & C. E. Snow (Eds.), *Rethinking reading comprehension* (pp. 30–50). New York: Guilford Press.

Gersten, R., Baker, S., Shanahan, T., Linan-Thompson, S., Collins, P., & Scarcella, R. (2007). *Effective literacy and English language instruction for English learners in the elementary grades: A practice guide* (No. NCEE 2007-4011). Washington, DC: National Center for Education, Evaluation and Regional Assistance, Institute for Education Sciences, U.S. Department of Education. Retrieved from *www.ies.ed.gov/ncee.*

Giorgis, C., & Peterson, B. (1996). Teachers and librarians collaborate to create a community of learners. *Language Arts, 73,* 477–482.

Goatley, V. J., Brock, C. H., & Raphael, T. E. (1995). Diverse learners participating in regular education "Book Clubs." *Reading Research Quarterly, 30*(3), 352–380.

Goldenberg, C., Rueda, R. S., & August, D. (2006). Sociocultural influences on the language attainment of language-minority children. In D. August & T. Shanahan (Eds.), *Developing literacy in second-language learners: Report of the National Literacy Panel on Language Minority and Youth*. Mahwah, NJ: Erlbaum.

Guthrie, J. T., & Greaney, V. (1991). Literacy acts. In R. Barr, M. Kamil, P. Mosenthal, & P. D. Pearson (Eds.), *Handbook of reading research* (Vol. 2, pp. 68–96). Mahwah, NJ: Erlbaum.

Guthrie, J. T., & Humenick, N. M. (2004). Motivating students to read. In P. McCardle & V. Chhabra (Eds.), *The voice of evidence in reading research* (pp. 329–354). Baltimore: Brookes.

Gutiérrez, K. D., Baquedano-Lopez, P., & Tejada, C. (1999). Rethinking diversity: Hybridity and hybrid language practices in the third space. *Mind, Culture, and Activity, 6*(4), 286–303.

Hacker, D. J., & Tenent, A. (2002). Implementing reciprocal teaching in the classroom: Overcoming obstacles and making modifications. *Journal of Educational Psychology, 94*(4), 699–718.

Hansen, J., & Hubbard, R. (1984). Poor readers can draw inferences. *Reading Teacher, 37*(7), 586–589.

Hansen, J., & Pearson, P. D. (1983). An instructional study: Improving the inferential comprehension of good and poor fourth-grade readers. *Journal of Educational Psychology, 75*, 821–829.

Heath, S. B. (1982). What no bedtime story means: Narrative skills at home and school. *Language in Society, 11*, 49–76.

Heath, S. B. (1983). *Ways with words: Language, life and work in communities and classrooms*. Cambridge, UK: Cambridge University Press.

Henry, L. A. (2006). SEARCHing for an answer: The critical role of new literacies while reading on the Internet. *Reading Teacher, 59*(7), 614–627.

Hicks, D. (2004). Coming of age in working-poor America. In D. S. Strickland & D. E. Alvermann (Eds.), *Bridging the literacy achievement gap, grades 4–12* (pp. 30–42). New York: Teachers College Press.

Huberman, M. (1993). The model of the independent artisan in teachers' professional relations. In J. W. Little & M. W. McLaughlin (Eds.), *Teachers work: Individuals, colleagues, and contexts* (pp. 11–50). New York: Teachers College Press.

Ivey, G., & Broaddus, K. (2001). "Just plain reading": A survey of what makes students want to read in middle school classrooms. *Reading Research Quarterly, 36*(4), 350–377.

Jiménez, R. T. (2004a). More equitable literacy assessments for Latino students. *Reading Teacher, 57*(6), 576–578.

Jiménez, R. (2004b). Reconceptualizing the literacy learning of Latino students. In D. S. Strickland & D. E. Alvermann (Eds.), *Bridging the literacy achievement gap, grades 4–12* (pp. 17–29). New York: Teachers College Press.

Jiménez, R., García, G. E., & Pearson, P. D. (1996). The reading strategies of bilingual Latina/o students who are successful English readers: Opportunities and obstacles. *Reading Research Quarterly, 31*(1), 90–112.

Kennedy, M. M. (2005). *Inside teaching: How classroom life undermines reform*. Cambridge, MA: Harvard University Press.

Ladson-Billings, G. (2006). Presidential address: From the achievement gap to the education debt: Understanding achievement in U.S. schools. *Educational Researcher, 35*(7), 3–12.

Lance, K. C. (2004). Libraries and student achievement. Retrieved November 12, 2004, from *www.ciconline.org*.

Lance, K. C., Rodney, M. J., & Hamilton-Pennell, C. (2000). *How school librarians help kids achieve standards: The second Colorado Study (Executive summary).* Retrieved April 24, 2000, from *www.lrs.org/impact.asp*.

Lance, K. C., Welborn, L., & Hamilton-Pennell, C. (1993). *The impact of school library media centers on academic achievement.* Castle Rock, CO: HiWillow Research & Publishing.

Lankshear, C., & Knobel, M. (2007). Sampling "the new" in new literacies. In C. Lanshear & M. Knobel (Eds.), *A new literacies sampler* (pp. 1–24). New York: Peter Lang.

Lapp, D., Fisher, D., Flood, J., & Moore, K. (2002). "I don't want to teach it wrong": An investigation of the role families believe they should play in the early literacy development of their children. In D. Shallert, C. Fairbanks, J. Worthy, B. Maloch, & J. Hoffman (Eds.), *51st Yearbook of the National Reading Conference* (pp. 275–287). Chicago: National Reading Conference.

Lesaux, N., Koda, K., Siegel, L., & Shanahan, T. (2006). Development of literacy. In D. August & T. Shanahan (Eds.), *Developing literacy in second-language learners: Report of the National Literacy Panel on Language Minority and Youth.* Mahwah, NJ: Erlbaum.

Leu, D. J., Jr., Kinzer, C. K., Coiro, J., & Cammack, D. W. (2004). Toward a theory of new literacies emerging from the Internet and other communication technologies. In R. Ruddell & N. Unrau (Eds.), *Theoretical models and processes of reading* (5th ed., pp. 1570–1613). Newark, DE: International Reading Association.

Liang, L. A., & Dole, J. A. (2006). Help with teaching reading comprehension: Comprehension instructional frameworks. *Reading Teacher, 59*(8), 742–752.

Lieberman, A., & Miller, L. (1999). *Teachers—transforming their world and their work.* New York: Teachers College Press.

Little, J. W. (1990). The persistence of privacy: Autonomy and initiative in teachers' professional relations. *Teachers College Record, 991*(4), 509–536.

Lonsdale, M. (2003). *Impact of school libraries on student achievement: A review of research.* Cambenwell, Victoria: Australian Council for Educational Research.

Louis, K. S., Marks, H. M., & Kruse, S. (1996). Teachers' professional community in restructuring schools. *American Educational Research Journal, 33*(4), 757–798.

Mason, B., Mason, D. A., Mendez, M., Nelsen, G., & Orwig, R. (2005). Effects of top-down and bottom-up elementary school standards reform in an underperforming California district. *Elementary School Journal, 105*(4), 353–376.

Moll, L. C. (1992). Literacy research in community and classrooms. In R. Beach, J. L. Green, M. L. Kamil, & T. Shanahan (Eds.), *Multidisiplinary perspectives on literacy research* (pp. 211–244). Urbana, IL: National Conference on Research in English/National Council of Teachers of English.

Moll, L. C., Amanti, C., Neff, D., & González, N. (1992). Funds of knowledge for teaching: Using a qualitative approach to connect homes and schools. *Theory Into Practice, 31*(2), 132–141.

Morrow, L. M. (1992) The impact of a literature-based program on literacy achievement, use of literature, and attitudes of children from minority backgrounds. *Reading Research Quarterly, 27*(3), 250–275.

National Assessment of Educational Progress. (2002). *The nation's report card: Reading 2002.* Retrieved May 31, 2008, from *nces.ed.gov/nationsreportcard/pdf/main2002/2003521. pdf.*

Neuman, S. B. (1999). Books make a difference: A study of access to literacy. *Reading Research Quarterly, 34*(3), 286–311.

Neuman, S. B., & Celano, D. (2001). Access to print in low-income and middle-income communities: An ecological study of four neighborhoods. *Reading Research Quarterly, 36*(1), 8–26.

New London Group. (1996). A pedagogy of multiliteracies: Designing social futures. *Harvard Educational Review, 66*(1), 60–91.

Newmann, F. M., Smith, B., Allensworth, E., & Bryk, A. S. (2001). Instructional program coherence: What it is and why it should guide school improvement policy. *Evaluation and Policy Analysis, 23*(4), 297–321.

Ogle, D. M. (1986). K-W-L: A teaching model that develops active reading of expository text. *Reading Teacher, 39*(6), 564–570.

Palincsar, A. S. (1986). The role of dialogue in providing scaffolded instruction. *Educational Psychologist, 21*(1–2), 73–98.

Palincsar, A. S., & Brown, A. L. (1984). Reciprocal teaching of comprehension-fostering and comprehension-monitoring activities. *Cognition and Instruction, 1*(2), 177–175.

Paris, S. G. (2005). Reinterpreting the development of reading skills. *Reading Research Quarterly, 40*(2), 184–202.

Paris, S. G., Lipson, M. Y., & Wixson, K. K. (1983). Becoming a strategic reader. *Contemporary Educational Psychology, 8*, 293–316.

Paris, S. G., Saarnio, D. A., & Cross, D. R. (1986). A metacognitive curriculum to promote children's reading and learning. *Australian Journal of Psychology, 38*(2), 107–123.

Pearson, P. D. (2007). An endangered species act for literacy education. *Journal of Literacy Research, 39*(2), 145–162.

Pearson, P. D., & Dole, J. A. (1987). Explicit comprehension instruction: A review of research and a new conceptualization of instruction. *Elementary School Journal, 88*(2), 151–165.

Pearson, P. D., & Fielding, L. (1991). Comprehension Instruction. In R. Barr, M. L. Kamil, P. Mosenthal, & P. D. Pearson (Eds.), *Handbook of reading research* (Vol. II, pp. 819–860). New York: Longman.

Pearson, P. D., Raphael, T. E., Benson, V. L., & Madda, C. L. (2007). Balance in comprehensive literacy instruction: Then and now. In L. B. Gambrell, L. M. Morrow, & M. Pressley (Eds.), *Best practices in literacy instruction* (3rd ed., pp. 30–54). New York: Guilford Press.

Pressley, M. (2000). What should comprehension instruction be the instruction of? In M. L. Kamil, P. B. Mosenthal, P. D. Pearson, & R. Barr (Eds.), *Handbook of reading research* (Vol. III, pp. 545–561). Mahwah, NJ: Erlbaum.

Pressley, M., El-Dinary, P. B., Gaskins, I., Scuder, T., Bergman, J., Almasi, J., et al. (1992). Beyond direct instruction: Transactional instruction of reading comprehension strategies. *Elementary School Journal, 92*, 513–555.

Pressley, M., Mohan, L., Raphael, L. M., & Fingeret, L. (2007). How does Bennett Woods Elementary School produce such high reading and writing achievement? *Journal of Educational Psychology, 99*(2), 221–240.

Pressley, M., & Wharton-McDonald, R. (2002). The need for increased comprehension instruction. In M. Pressley (Ed.), *Reading instruction that works* (pp. 236–288). New York: Guilford Press.

Proctor, C. P., August, D., Carlo, M., & Snow, C. (2005). Native Spanish-speaking children reading in English: Toward a model of comprehension. *Journal of Educational Psychology, 97*(2), 246–256.

Purkey, S. C., & Smith, M. S. (1983). Effective schools: A review. *Elementary School Journal, 83*(4), 426–452.

Quirk, T. J., Trismen, D. A., Weinberg, S. F., & Nalin, K. B. (1975). The classroom behavior of teachers during compensatory reading instruction. *Journal of Educational Research, 68*(5), 185–192.

Raphael, T. E., & Pearson, P. D. (1985). Increasing student's awareness of sources of information for answering questions. *American Educational Research Journal, 22,* 217–236.

Raphael, T. E., Weber, C. M., George, M. A., & Nies, A. (2008). Approaches to teaching reading comprehension. In G. G. Duffy & S. E. Israel (Eds.), *Handbook of research on reading comprehension* (pp. 449–469). New York: Erlbaum/Taylor & Francis.

Raphael, T. E., & Wonnacott, C. A. (1985). Heightening 4th grade students' sensitivity to sources of information for answering comprehension questions. *Reading Research Quarterly, 20,* 282–296.

Rosenshine, B. (1983). Teaching functions in instructional programs. *Elementary School Journal, 83*(4), 335–351.

Rowan, B. (1990). Commitment and control: Alternative strategies for organizational design of schools. *Review of Research in Education, 16,* 353–389.

Saunders, W. M., & Goldenberg, C. (1999). Effects of instructional conversations and literature logs on limited- and fluent-English-proficient students' story comprehension and thematic understanding. *Elementary School Journal, 99*(4), 277–301.

Schwartz, R. M., & Raphael, T. E. (1985). Concept of definition: A key to improving students' vocabulary. *Reading Teacher, 39*(2), 198–205.

Smith, C., Constantino, R., & Krashen, S. (1997). Differences in print environment for children in Beverly Hills, Compton and Watts. *Emergency Librarian, 24,* 8–9.

Smith, E. G. (2001). *Texas school libraries: Standards, resources, services, and students' performance.* Austin, TX: Texas State Library and Archives Commission.

Stanovich, K. E. (1986). Matthew effects in reading: Some consequences of individual differences in the acquisition of literacy. *Reading Research Quarterly, 21*(4), 360–407.

Strahan, D. (2003). Promoting a collaborative professional culture in three elementary schools that have beaten the odds. *Elementary School Journal, 104*(2), 127–146.

Taylor, B. M., & Beach, R. W. (1984). The effects of text structure instruction on middle-grade students' comprehension and production of expository text. *Reading Research Quarterly, 19*(2), 134–146.

Taylor, B. M., Frye, B. J., & Maruyama, G. M. (1990). Time spent reading and reading growth. *American Educational Research Journal, 27*(2), 351–362.

Taylor, B. M., Pearson, P. D., Peterson, D. S., & Rodriguez, M. C. (2004). The CIERA school change framework: An evidence-based approach to professional development and school reading improvement. *Reading Research Quarterly, 40*(1), 40–69.

Tierney, R. J., & Cunningham, J. W. (1984). Research on teaching comprehension. In P. D. Pearson, R. Barr, M. L. Kamil, & P. Mosenthal (Eds.), *Handbook of reading research* (pp. 609–655). New York: Longman.

Unsworth, L. (2002). Changing dimensions of school literacies. *Australian Journal of Language and Literacy, 25*(1), 62–77.

Unsworth, L. (2006). Towards a metalanguage for multiliteracies education: Describing the meaning-making resources of language–image interaction. *English Teaching: Practice and Critique, 5*(1), 55–76.

Winograd, P. W. (1984). Strategic difficulties in summarizing texts. *Reading Research Quarterly, 19*(4), 404–425.

Wood, D., Bruner, J. S., & Ross, G. (1976). The role of tutoring in problem solving. *Journal of Child Psychology and Psychiatry, 17*, 89–100.

Worthy, J. (1996). Removing barriers to voluntary reading for reluctant readers: The role of school and classroom libraries. *Language Arts, 73*, 483–492.

# CHAPTER 18

# Helping Diverse Learners to Become Fluent Readers

MELANIE R. KUHN AND TIMOTHY RASINSKI

M odels of literacy development and instruction (e.g., Chall, 1996) suggest that fluency is an essential element of skilled reading, combining the ability to decode accurately and automatically with the use of prosodic elements, such as appropriate phrasing and expression. However, for struggling readers and English language learners (ELLs), the transition to fluent reading is often difficult to achieve. In this chapter, we discuss the theoretical underpinnings of fluency as it relates to diverse learners; specifically, we look at how fluency contributes to comprehension, and how fluency-oriented instruction can expand learners' exposure to a range of vocabulary, concepts, and text structures. We further argue that such instruction is especially critical for closing the achievement gap between skilled readers and their struggling peers (e.g., Stanovich, 1986), both by exposing learners to a broad range of reading materials, and by providing them with the necessary tools to develop as independent readers. In this chapter, we present our answers to the following questions in the hope that we can contribute to the ongoing dialogue around the construct of fluency and its role in the overall reading process:

- What is fluency and why is it important?
- What does research say about fluency and diverse learners?
- What are the implications of fluency research for classroom practice?
- What are the areas in which future research should focus?

In exploring these questions, we hope that fluency instruction will become a foundational element for effective literacy instruction for all learners.

## WHAT IS FLUENCY AND WHY IS IT IMPORTANT?

Fluent reading is considered by many to be a bridge or link between decoding and comprehension (e.g., Pikulski & Chard, 2005). It is the process that allows learners to move from laborious and monotonous reading to smooth and expressive reading, and it is typically defined as accurate, automatic word recognition, coupled with the appropriate use of prosody (Kuhn & Stahl, 2003; National Reading Panel, 2000). Furthermore, fluency is a critical element in readers' comprehension of text, both because automatic word recognition frees up readers' attention, allowing them to focus on the sense of what is written, and because the appropriate use of expression and phrasing helps them to determine and construct shades of meaning (inferential comprehension) (e.g., Rasinski & Hoffman, 2003).

### Automaticity and Reading Fluency

According to automaticity theorists, reading is a complex task that involves the integration of multiple elements, including decoding and comprehension (LaBerge & Samuels, 1974). However, despite the fact that complex tasks, including that of reading, make multiple demands on individuals, a limited amount of attention or cognitive resources is available to process the various facets of these tasks. As a result, in the case of reading, attention that learners devote to word recognition and lower-level reading tasks is necessarily attention that is unavailable for comprehension. In other words, when initially learning to read, students expend significant amounts of attention identifying the words. However, this means that there is less attention left for determining the meaning of units beyond the word level (i.e., phrases, sentences or paragraphs). As a result, these learners have difficulty making sense of the text as a whole.

Fortunately, as learners' decoding ability becomes automatic, the amount of attention required for word identification lessens; this results in the freeing-up of cognitive resources for the construction of meaning. The questions then become, how do learners shift from slow, intentional decoding to automatic word recognition, and how can teachers help to facilitate this process? According to automaticity theorists, the most effective way for students to do so is through practice (Adams, 1990; Samuels, 1979; Stanovich, 1984). Such practice provides learners with extensive exposure to print and allows them to develop their familiarity with a written language's orthographic patterns, and phonological and morphological representations. This in turn allows learners to recognize the phonological and morphological representation of words with increasing accuracy and automaticity, permitting them to focus on a text's meaning rather than on simply determining the words.

However, all practice is not created equal. To maximize the transition to automaticity, students should engage in practice that is scaffolded, or supported, (Rasinski, 2003), and that involves reading connected text rather than words in isolation (e.g., Fleisher, Jenkins, & Pany, 1979–1980). Finally, this scaffolded practice of reading connected text should make use of a range of materials, from instructional to challenging (Kuhn, 2009), and should involve the repeated reading of a given text (e.g., Dowhower, 1989) or the single reading of a wide range of materials[1] (e.g., Kuhn & Schwanenflugel, 2008).

### Prosody and Reading Fluency

In addition to accurate and automatic word recognition, prosody plays an important role in fluent reading (e.g., Erekson, 2003; Schwanenflugel, Hamilton, Kuhn, Wisenbaker, & Stahl, 2004). Prosody is comprised of those elements that allow oral reading to sound like oral language or speech; these include stress, intonation, and suitable phrasing (Hanks, 1990; Harris & Hodges, 1981, 1995). Prosody is important for two reasons. First, readers' ability to apply prosodic elements to text serves as an indicator that they have achieved a basic understanding of a passage and are able to represent this understanding through their use of appropriate expression and phrasing (Dowhower, 1991; Schreiber, 1980, 1987, 1991; Schreiber & Read, 1980). In fact, recent research has suggested that prosody's role in fluent reading may be an indicator that a child has achieved automaticity in text reading (Miller & Schwanenflugel, 2006; Schwanenflugel et al., 2004). Second, prosody adds to the enjoyment of both the reader and the listener, since plodding, monotonous reading adds little to a learner's desire to continue with the task of reading (e.g., Erekson, 2003; Rasinski, 2003).

It is important, however, to note that the exact role of prosody in reading comprehension is not entirely clear (e.g., Kuhn et al., 2006). There are three distinct possibilities. The first is that prosodic elements can only be applied after an individual has grasped the meaning of a text. The second is that a reader has to apply prosodic elements to be able to construct meaning from a text. The third and final possibility is that prosody's role in comprehension is an interactive one that both contributes to and results from the comprehension of a text. Although we consider this later position to be most likely, the question is open to further research (e.g., Cowie, Douglas-Cowie, & Wichmann, 2002; Levy, Abello, & Lysynchuck, 1997; Schwanenflugel et al., 2004). Nevertheless, it is clear that whether prosody is a precursor or product of comprehension, focusing students' attention on prosody in reading simultaneously focuses their attention on and fosters textual comprehension.

### WHAT DOES RESEARCH SAY ABOUT FLUENCY AND DIVERSE LEARNERS?

In light of the previous discussion of fluency's role in skilled reading, it seems reasonable to argue that fluency is a central element in the reading development of all learners. In fact, three major reviews of the literature have indicated that fluency is indeed a critical component of the overall reading process (e.g., Kuhn

& Stahl, 2003; National Reading Panel, 2000; Rasinski & Hoffman, 2003). How-ever, it is often the case that struggling readers (e.g., Shanahan, 2006) and ELLs (e.g., Montero & Kuhn, in press) experience difficulties in making the transition to fluent reading. There are myriad reasons for these difficulties, from the amount of oral language to which children are exposed, to a lack of familiarity with vari-ous aspects of English (e.g., vocabulary, syntax, prosody), to a lack of knowledge regarding concepts of print, phonemic awareness, and letter–sound correspon-dences. What is important to us as authors of this chapter, however, is not just that some learners experience difficulties with the transition from slow, monoto-nous reading to smooth and expressive rendering of text, but that research indi-cates instruction targeted toward improving students' fluency can help them to become skilled readers.

One of the key differences between students who experience success in their literacy learning and those who experience difficulties has to do with the sheer amount of reading that they undertake. According to Stanovich (1986), who labeled this phenomenon the Matthew effect, students who initially experience success in reading, enjoy reading and, therefore, welcome opportunities to read. As a result, they read more, become increasingly familiar with English orthog-raphy, are exposed to a broad vocabulary, and are introduced to an extensive number of concepts, all of which lead to improved fluency, enhanced comprehen-sion, and a further increase in their enjoyment of reading. Students who initially experience difficulties with their reading, on the other hand, begin to dislike reading and tend to avoid it whenever possible. Because they read less, they do not have the opportunity to develop comfort with letter–sound correspondences, to expand their vocabulary through texts, or to learn about new concepts through their reading. Therefore, their reading improves at a much slower rate than that of their peers, leading to a difference in reading ability that increases over the course of their schooling.

Given this understanding, if we are to help learners who experience reading difficulties become skilled readers, then it is critical that we, as educators, find instructional approaches that provide them with access to many texts in a vari-ety of genres and forms, and at a variety of reading levels. One way to do this is through effective fluency instruction. Because reading instruction, like reading itself, is multifaceted, we are not proposing that fluency instruction is the only means of increasing students' reading ability and achievement. What we are pro-posing, however, is that fluency instruction is a valuable piece of the broader lit-eracy curriculum, and one that research indicates is important to learners' overall reading development.

Although it may sometimes appear that fluency has received significant amounts of attention only as a result of the publication of the National Reading Panel report in 2000, there is actually a significant body of research, stretching back to the 1970s and earlier, regarding its importance (Rasinski & Hoffman, 2003; Rasinski & Mraz, 2008). Much of this work focuses on the fluency develop-ment of struggling readers; unfortunately, however, little of this research looks specifically at ELLs (Montero & Kuhn, in press), a point we address directly in the section on future research. The main body of research regarding fluency development in struggling readers has involved the concept of textual repetition (e.g., Dowhower, 1989; Samuels, 1979), which is considered to be a key means of developing struggling readers' automaticity. As we mentioned in the previous section, to become skilled readers, students' word recognition needs to become automatic, and the best way to develop such automaticity is through practice.

When we consider what we know about practice in areas other than reading (e.g., tennis, playing the piano, learning to drive), it is usually the case that an individual moves from novice to expert in part through the repetition of a given task. However, when thinking about the way that reading is generally taught, Samuels (1979) realized that most students have only one opportunity to read a given text before they are expected to move on to a new selection. He posited that, as is the case with other skills, learners who experience difficulty with word recognition might become proficient more quickly if they had the opportunity to practice reading a selection, or a passage from a selection, several times rather than just once. Furthermore, because a large percentage of the words in any given text consist of a limited number of high-frequency words, such as *the, it,* and *of*, it seemed likely that a word learned in one context would be more readily recognized in another, previously unpracticed, context.

### Repetition or Supported Reading of Multiple Texts?

Over the past three decades, the vast majority of research on fluency development has made use of some form of repetition, and, when looking at these studies as a body, there is a clear trend indicating that repetition does indeed lead to improvements in reading fluency in terms of not only developing students' automatic word recognition but also, where measured, their prosody and comprehension (Kuhn & Stahl, 2003). These studies used a variety of designs and instructional approaches. However, it is critical to note that one group of studies had more nuanced results; that is, when students using repeated readings were compared to students using the supported reading of an equivalent amount of text, students in both conditions tended to make similar gains. As a result, recent research has focused on the relative effectiveness of repetition and the scaffolded reading of a wide range of text. Importantly, research designed specifically to look more closely at these two approaches has indicated that whereas both types of instruction led to significant gains in students' reading, supported reading of a wide range of texts (e.g., using echo, choral, or partner reading) actually led to somewhat greater growth than did repeated reading (e.g., Kuhn, 2005; Mostow & Beck, 2005; Schwebel, 2007), although there is a possibility that repetition may be more beneficial for those who are experiencing the greatest degree of difficulty in establishing automaticity (Kuhn, Schwanenflugel, Morrow, & Bradley, 2006).

One basis for these results may be found in Logan's (1997) instance theory of automaticity, which puts forward the argument that each time a learner reads a word or phrase, a trace of that word or phrase is left in his or her memory. Therefore, it may be that repeated reading of a given text serves to deepen a limited number of traces, whereas the scaffolded reading of a wider range of texts provides a broader, albeit more shallow, number of traces. Because there is a significant amount of overlap in the number of words used in written materials, at least at the primary level, it may be that students learn a new word more easily by encountering it in a number of different contexts rather than by seeing it repeatedly in one text (Mostow & Beck, 2005). For example, it is possible that students learn the word *snow* more readily if they practice the word in three distinct phrases (e.g., the falling *snow*, a *snow* globe, and the white *snow*), and forms (e.g., *snow, snowing, snowball, snowfall, snowed*), than if they practice reading the same word or phrase three times (e.g., the falling *snow*).

One reason for the lack of robust findings for repeated readings in some studies may be the purpose for which repeated readings have been employed. In a number of commercial programs employing repeated readings, students are asked to read texts repeatedly, without an authentic purpose for the repeated readings. In these programs, reading speed has been used as the primary criterion for success; students are asked to read a text repeatedly, until they achieve a predetermined reading rate. Such a purpose seems to lack authenticity: It is rare in real life that a person is asked to read a text for the main purpose of reading it quickly.

Repeated readings (rehearsals) are very often used in real life for performance activities; that is, actors and other performers rehearse or practice to be able to provide a masterful performance for an audience. This is clearly a more authentic employment of repeated readings. Classroom-based studies that have employed repeated readings in this way (using the repeated reading of scripts, poetry, songs, etc.) have demonstrated gains in readers' fluency and comprehension that have exceeded normal expectations (e.g., Griffith & Rasinski, 2004; Martinez, Roser, & Strecker, 1999), especially for students who previously have struggled in reading.

## Challenging Material

Although both repeated and wide-reading approaches to fluency instruction require some form of scaffolding (whether this involves a skilled reader serving as a model or is based on the repetition itself; e.g., Dowhower, 1989; Kuhn, 2005), such support is most necessary when the material is at an appropriate level of challenge. Looking over the reviews of the literature (Kuhn & Stahl, 2003; National Reading Panel, 2000; Rasinski & Hoffman, 2003) along with more recent research, it becomes apparent that a significant part of what makes these approaches successful is the amount of scaffolding they employ; in fact, it is this support that allows students to use texts that would otherwise be considered to be frustration level (i.e., between an 85 and 90% accuracy level on the first reading; Stahl & Heubach, 2005). However, it is important to note that the amount of scaffolding required is dependent on the challenge presented by the material; that is, the more challenging the text, the more extensive the support needs to be.

## WHAT ARE THE IMPLICATIONS OF FLUENCY RESEARCH
## FOR CLASSROOM PRACTICE?

Given what we know about fluency, it is important to think about the construct in terms of implications for classroom practice. For example, what can we, as educators, do to ensure that students become fluent readers? We would argue that, based on our previous discussion, at least three factors would allow this to occur. First, students need extensive opportunities to read connected text. Second, these texts need to be challenging. Third, to ensure that students are able to use these texts successfully, their reading needs to be scaffolded and supported by knowledgeable teachers.

When considering the question of reading development, Stanovich (1986) considered it critical that, in order to become skilled readers, students have extensive opportunity to read connected texts. For those students who seem to experience reading success from the start, this is not a difficult requirement; they enjoy reading and often choose to engage in reading, both in and out of school. For others, however, learning to read is problematic almost from the beginning; such students are not likely to choose to read, and they may even actively avoid it. One way to help such struggling readers is to support them in their reading of challenging texts. This provides them with opportunities to read extensively in material that would not otherwise be accessible; that is, in texts that not only are beyond their independent level but also are beyond what we traditionally think of as their instructional level. However, with sufficient scaffolding (support and practice), whether through repeated, echo, choral, or partner reading (e.g., fluency-oriented reading instruction [FORI] and wide reading: Kuhn, Schwanenflugel, Morrow, et al., 2006; fluency development lesson: Rasinski, Padak, Linek, & Sturtevant, 1994), along with a focus on word study as necessary, it is possible for students to read such texts successfully. Importantly, such instruction allows struggling readers to read the same variety of books as their more skilled peers. As such, they are being introduced to a more extensive range of concepts and vocabulary than they would be otherwise. Finally, such instruction also provides struggling readers with greater opportunities to familiarize themselves with written orthography and syntax, thereby increasing the likelihood that they will develop automaticity, and gives them access to models of skilled readers, which in turn are likely to help them to integrate prosodic elements into their reading.

For students who struggle with reading fluency and with their overall reading development, we recommend that a specific instructional portion of the daily reading curriculum be devoted to fluency instruction and development. Daily instructional routines devoted to fluency development should be implemented with students (e.g., FORI and wide reading: Kuhn, Schwanenflugel, Morrow, et al., 2006; fluency development lesson: Rasinski et al., 1994). Knowledgeable teachers can also develop their own fluency routines that comprise the elements of effective fluency instruction presented earlier in this chapter. The key is to make fluency instruction a regular and integral part of the overall reading curriculum, especially for struggling readers.

In short, we feel that students need a wide range of supported instructional experiences in their literacy education to develop fluency and overall reading proficiency. They need to read widely and deeply (repeated reading). They need to read material that ranges in difficulty from independent through challenging, with varying levels of support commensurate with the difficulty of the passages. Their fluency instruction needs to be aimed at the development of automaticity and prosody, and, of course, always focused on meaning-making (comprehension). They need to read a variety of text types—from informational and narrative texts that support the development of content knowledge, to poetry, scripts and plays, oratory and rhetoric, and other voiced texts that support the development of automatic and prosodic performance of texts through supported rehearsal (repeated readings). And all fluency instruction needs to be integrated into methods and activities that students find engaging, authentic, and enjoyable. Most definitely this is a challenge. However, we feel that this challenge will pay large dividends in terms of students' literacy development.

## WHAT ARE THE AREAS IN WHICH FUTURE RESEARCH SHOULD FOCUS?

Given all that we have learned about fluency over the past 30 or so years, what areas do we feel are in need of future research? Although we consider numerous questions to be worthy of continued study, among the most pressing are the following:

- What texts (and features of texts) lend themselves to the development of automaticity and prosody?
- What is the relationship between prosody and comprehension, and how can it best be fostered in literacy instruction?
- How does oral reading contribute to the development of children's oral language and vice versa?
- What approaches most benefit ELLs, and at what point in their reading development?
- Under what conditions is repeated reading most effective for students, especially struggling readers? And is wide reading more effective for developing readers than for older, struggling readers?
- What level of challenge is most effective for building the fluency of struggling readers? What kinds and what levels of support are most beneficial for struggling readers?
- How effectively do fluency strategies assist students in developing their understanding of content-area subjects?

- At what point in reading development should students be introduced to fluency activities? For example, are these approaches appropriate for first graders?
- At what point in students' reading development should fluency instruction cease, if at all? For example, are fluency activities appropriate for students in secondary and adult literacy education?
- Are there specific fluency approaches that better lend themselves to developing students' comprehension, as well their automaticity and prosody?
- What is the relationship between silent reading, fluency, and overall reading proficiency? Does guided silent reading improve fluency and overall reading proficiency? Does independent silent reading improve fluency and overall reading proficiency?

We believe that research in these areas will further improve our understanding of fluency and fluency instruction, which we feel are important as part of a broader and balanced approach to reading instruction. We hope that this chapter has led you to the same conclusions.

## NOTE

1. By *wide reading* we do not mean the cursory reading of a single text once over the course of a week, followed by unconnected literacy activities. Rather, we consider wide reading to involve the scaffolded reading of a number of challenging texts over the course of a week (e.g., 20–40 minutes of daily choral, echo, or partner reading) accompanied by supportive activities, built around the selections and designed to develop students' word recognition, vocabulary, comprehension, and writing.

## REFERENCES

Adams, M. J. (1990). *Beginning to read: Thinking and learning about print*. Cambridge, MA: MIT Press.

Chall, J. S. (1996). *Stages of reading development* (2nd ed.). Fort Worth, TX: Harcourt Brace.

Cowie, R., Douglas-Cowie, E., & Wichmann, A. (2002). Prosodic characteristics of skilled reading: Fluency and expressiveness in 8–10 year old readers. *Language and Speech, 45*, 47–82.

Dowhower, S. L. (1989). Repeated reading: Theory into practice. *Reading Teacher, 42*, 502–507.

Dowhower, S. L. (1991). Speaking of prosody: Fluency's unattended bedfellow. *Theory Into Practice, 30*(3), 158–164.

Erekson, J. (2003, May). *Prosody: The problem of expression in fluency*. Paper presented at the annual meeting of the International Reading Association, Orlando, FL.

Fleisher, L. S., Jenkins, J. R., & Pany, D. (1979–1980). Effects on poor readers' comprehension of training in rapid decoding. *Reading Research Quarterly, 15*, 30–48.

Griffith, L. W., & Rasinski, T. V. (2004). A focus on fluency: How one teacher incorporated fluency with her reading curriculum. *Reading Teacher, 58,* 126–137.

Hanks, P. (Ed.). (1990). *The Collins English dictionary.* Glasgow: William Collins.

Harris, T. L., & Hodges, R. E. (1981). *A dictionary of reading and related terms.* Newark, DE: International Reading Association.

Harris, T. L., & Hodges, R. E. (Eds.). (1995). *The literacy dictionary: The vocabulary of reading and writing.* Newark, DE: International Reading Association.

Kuhn, M. R. (2005). A comparative study of small group fluency instruction. *Reading Psychology, 26,* 127–146.

Kuhn, M. R. (2009). *The hows and whys of fluency instruction.* Boston: Allyn & Bacon.

Kuhn, M. R., & Schwanenflugel, P. J. (Eds.). (2008). *Fluency in the classroom.* New York: Guilford Press.

Kuhn, M. R., Schwanenflugel, P. J., Morris, R. D., Morrow, L. M., Woo, D., Meisinger, B., et al. (2006). Teaching children to become fluent and automatic readers. *Journal of Literacy Research, 38,* 357–387.

Kuhn, M. R., Schwanenflugel, P. J., Morrow, L. M., & Bradley, B. A. (2006, May). *The development of fluent and automatic reading: Scaling up—year 2.* Poster presented at the annual meeting of the International Reading Association, Chicago.

Kuhn, M. R., & Stahl, S. (2003). Fluency: A review of developmental and remedial strategies. *Journal of Educational Psychology, 95,* 3–21.

LaBerge, D., & Samuels, S. J. (1974). Toward a theory of automatic information processing in reading. *Cognitive Psychology, 6,* 293–323.

Levy, B. A., Abello, B., & Lysynchuck, L. (1997). Transfer from word training to reading in context: Gains in reading fluency and comprehension. *Learning Disability Quarterly, 20,* 173–188.

Logan, G. D. (1997). Automaticity and reading: Perspectives from the instance theory of automaticity. *Reading and Writing Quarterly: Overcoming Learning Difficulties, 13,* 123–146.

Martinez, M., Roser, N., & Strecker, S. (1999). "I never thought I could be a star": A Readers Theatre ticket to reading fluency. *Reading Teacher, 52,* 326–334.

Miller, J., & Schwanenflugel, P. J. (2006). Prosody of syntactically complex sentences in the oral reading of young children. *Journal of Educational Psychology, 98,* 839–853.

Montero, K., & Kuhn, M. R. (in press). Fluency and English language learners: What we know and what we need. In L. Helman (Ed.), *Literacy instruction with English learners in the elementary grades: What, why, and how?* New York: Guilford Press.

Mostow, J., & Beck, J. (2005, June). *Micro-analysis of fluency gains in a reading tutor that listens.* Paper presented at the Society for the Scientific Study of Reading annual meeting, Toronto, ON, Canada.

National Reading Panel. (2000). *Teaching children to read: An evidence-based assessment of the scientific research literature on reading and its implications for reading instruction: Reports of the subgroups.* Bethesda, MD: National Institutes of Health. Retrieved May 30, 2000, from *www.nichd.nih.gov/publications/nrp.*

Pikulski, J. J., & Chard, D. J. (2005). Fluency: Bridge between decoding and reading comprehension. *Reading Teacher, 58,* 510–519.

Rasinski, T. V. (2003). *The fluent reader: Oral reading strategies for building word recognition, fluency, and comprehension.* New York: Scholastic Professional Books.

Rasinski, T. V., & Hoffman, J. V. (2003). Oral reading in the school curriculum. *Reading Research Quarterly, 38,* 510–522.

Rasinski, T. V., & Mraz, M. (2008). Fluency: Traversing a rocky road of research and practice. In M. J. Fresch (Ed.), *As essential history of current reading practices* (pp. 106–119). Newark, DE: International Reading Association.

Rasinski, T. V., Padak, N. D., Linek, W. L., & Sturtevant, E. (1994). Effects of fluency development on urban second-grade readers. *Journal of Educational Research, 87,* 158–165.

Samuels, S. J. (1979). The method of repeated readings. *Reading Teacher, 32,* 403–408.

Schreiber, P. A. (1980). On the acquisition of reading fluency. *Journal of Reading Behavior, 12,* 177–186.

Schreiber, P. A. (1987). Prosody and structure in children's syntactic processing. In R. Horowitz & S. J. Samuels (Eds.), *Comprehending oral and written language* (pp. 243–270). New York: Academic Press.

Schreiber, P. A. (1991). Understanding prosody's role in reading acquisition. *Theory Into Practice, 30,* 158–164.

Schreiber, P. A., & Read, C. (1980). Children's use of phonetic cues in spelling, parsing, and—maybe—reading. *Bulletin of the Orton Society, 30,* 209–224.

Schwanenflugel, P. J., Hamilton, A. M., Kuhn, M. R., Wisenbaker, J., & Stahl, S. A. (2004). Becoming a fluent reader: Reading skill and prosodic features in the oral reading of young readers. *Journal of Educational Psychology, 96,* 119–129.

Schwebel, E. A. (2007). *A comparative study of small group fluency instruction—a replication and extension of Kuhn's (2005) study.* Unpublished master's thesis, Kean University, Union, NJ.

Shanahan, T. (2006). *Teaching fluency and the precursors of fluency to young children (pre–K–3).* Paper presented at the International Reading Association Preconference Institute #4, Chicago.

Stahl, S. A., & Heubach, K. (2005). Fluency-oriented reading instruction. *Journal of Literacy Research, 37,* 25–60.

Stanovich, K. E. (1984). The interactive–compensatory model of reading: A confluence of developmental, experimental, and educational psychology. *Remedial and Special Education, 5*(3), 11–19.

Stanovich, K. E. (1986). Matthew effects in reading: Some consequences of individual differences in the acquisition of literacy. *Reading Research Quarterly, 21,* 360–407.

# PART IV

# PREPARING TEACHERS TO TEACH LITERACY TO DIVERSE STUDENTS

# Teacher Knowledge in Culturally and Linguistically Complex Classrooms

## Lessons from the Golden Age and Beyond

DJANGO PARIS *and* ARNETHA F. BALL

A review of the literature on approaches to serving the educational needs of culturally and linguistically nondominant students (CLNS) in U.S. schools reveals that numerous perspectives have guided the development of curriculum and pedagogy over the past two decades. In this chapter we provide an overview of those perspectives before discussing what we see as the most relevant contemporary research in the current decade concerning resource perspectives on serving the educational needs of CLNS. This review highlights the following:

- Research that illuminates changing perspectives on approaches to serving the educational needs of CLNS.
- Research concerning the ways in which changing pedagogical and curricular approaches have worked hand in hand with changing notions of the teacher knowledge necessary to teach in culturally and linguistically complex classrooms.
- Research on the importance of connecting teacher knowledge and the knowledge that CLNS bring into the classroom.

We conclude the chapter with a discussion of the critical role of teachers' generative knowledge in addressing the challenges of serving the educational needs of CLNS in our changing and segregated urban schools.

## Language and Literacy Pedagogy in a Resource Era

Educational research has for decades focused on the failure of our schools to meet the needs of students of color from nondominant ethnic and language groups. Although not always couched in these terms (the focus has more often been the failure of students to meet the needs of schooling), the overarching goal of this research has been to expose and eradicate barriers to educational access and achievement. Steeped in a history of various forms of institutionalized discrimination against different ethnic groups of color, this research has often had competing visions of the cultural and linguistic practices that students bring to school from their home communities. Much of the research leading into the civil rights decades was squarely positioned in deficit thinking. In fact, scholarly work well into the 1960s held firm to deficit perspectives (Jensen, 1969). This research viewed the cultural practices and languages that students brought into the classroom as deficient. The goal was to find ways to replace these deficiencies with the superior ways of the school.

Following seminal work in sociolinguistics and educational anthropology during the 1970s and 1980s (Heath, 1983; Labov, 1972; Smitherman, 1977), researchers began to view the language and literacy practices of ethnically marginalized students as equal but different and, more progressively, as resources to be used in learning the school's dominant, European American, middle-class ways of acting and using language. Such work explored the cultural mismatches between home and school and often attempted to create alternative models to help teachers and students bridge home and school practices.

Important work during this era focused on the language practices of urban African American communities. Labov's (1972) early sociolinguistic research on African American Vernacular English (AAVE) in urban African American communities, for example, soundly refuted deficit thinking, providing evidence of the systematic grammar and complex pragmatics of AAVE. With these findings in hand, other researchers, such as Smitherman (1977) and Heath (1983), set about extending the understanding of AAVE grammar and literate practices in communities speaking AAVE, and developing education programs that used AAVE language as a basis for school literacy acquisition.

What have we learned about using the language and literacy practices of CLNS as resources for literacy learning in the decades following the seminal work of the 1970s and 1980s? Specifically, what have we learned about the teacher knowledge necessary to work from resource perspectives in classrooms serving CLNS? Have we moved beyond simply seeing nondominant language and literacy practices as an examination of school ways? Have we moved beyond celebrating nondominant ways, with little pedagogical attention to issues of power? Finally, are current conceptions of teacher knowledge adequate for our increasingly culturally and linguistically complex classrooms?

## The Golden Age of Resource Pedagogies: Research and Teacher Knowledge

One of the earliest and most important studies that brought together sociolinguistic, pedagogical, and curricular concerns was Shirley Brice Heath's (1983) landmark book *Ways with Words*. In a multiyear ethnographic study, Heath documented the ways in which language, literacy, and culture impacted the classroom learning of poor, linguistically marginalized black and white students in the rural Southeastern United States. Heath researched ways that teachers and students can build cultural and linguistic bridges between the school's mode of knowing and ways with language, and those of the students it serves. Heath was one of the earliest researchers to note that for many children born into the dominant culture, the transition to school is rather seamless. The dominant cultural behaviors and Dominant American English language and literacy required in school were a part of their upbringing. For many CLNS, however, Heath portrayed school as a place where the ways of doing and knowing associated with home were no longer acceptable.

Heath's (1983) study represented a major shift in research about language and literacy among CLNS. She began to ask "what reading and writing are for, how they are conducted, and how they are judged" (cited in Collins & Blot, 2003, p. 35). In addition, Heath sought to understand the pedagogical value of these socioculturally situated notions of literacy; that is, Heath was interested in how teachers could use the knowledge of how language and literacy worked in the home lives of their students as resources for school learning. Although Heath and the teachers in her work did not necessarily build critical understanding about power, race, and language, in themselves or their students, her work marked a fundamental shift toward resource approaches in language and literacy instruction. How this shift would play out in communities of other CLNS and in conceptions of teacher knowledge would slowly build over to the next decade.

García's (1993) fine review capitalized on the shift toward understanding resource approaches by summarizing the research literature at the intersection of language, culture, and education at the beginning of the 1990s. In his review, García pointed to research documenting a cultural difference or mismatch in a variety of U.S. communities of color. The research he cited spans the decades from the 1970s to the 1990s and explores the mismatch between home and school cultures for African American, Hawaiian American, Native American, Mexican American, and Vietnamese American students (among others). Looking over a large body of research, García saw that "in essence, these researchers have suggested that without attending to the distinction between home and school culture and language, educational endeavors aimed at these distinct students are likely to fail" (p. 54). To avoid this failure, García prescribed a rather clear resource perspective approach: "Observe, come to understand, and appropriate into the schooling contexts these attributes of culture and language that characterize the student" (p. 89).

We see García's (1993) review as marking the beginning of what we call the "golden age" of research on resource approaches to language and literacy instruction for CLNS. In essence, the review revealed what until then had been several loosely connected areas of inquiry to be part of a larger field of language and literacy education for equity in nondominant communities. There followed a period of unprecedented knowledge building about pedagogical methods using the nondominant languages and literacies of CLNS inside the classroom to foster academic achievement. This period of knowledge building was both practical and theoretical. It produced seminal studies, lasting theoretical contributions, and the future leaders of the field. And, not at all coincidentally, it marked a time when female and male scholars of color, and others committed the cultural ways of CLNS, had reached the professorate levels and graduate schools in critical numbers. We place the epicenter of this age at the mid-1990s and see it leading up to the brink of the 21st century. In the following section we review several research contributions to language and literacy instruction that mark this period for CLNS from various ethnic backgrounds.

### Research in the Golden Age

The golden age found an early and lasting theoretical framework in the work of Moll (1992; Moll & González, 1994). Moll and his collaborators' conception of *funds of knowledge* offered researchers and teachers a way to view the resources of students from an additive perspective. Working in mainly Mexican American communities in the Southwest, Moll and his collaborators produced a body of research focusing on instructional practices for maintaining cultural competence in nondominant language and literacy, while simultaneously gaining dominant skills. Moll and González (1994), for example, documented teachers who capitalize on the funds of knowledge that students bring into the classroom from their homes and communities. These funds include linguistic and other cultural practices, and are used simultaneously with mainstream materials in the curriculum. Students in these classrooms read, write, and speak in both Spanish and English to accomplish school tasks as they expand their literacy skills in both languages. For Moll and González, there is no need to sacrifice learning and literacy in the home language to become competent in the dominant one.

In another landmark contribution from the mid-1990s, Lee (1995) investigated the purpose of using African American language practices as a resource for literature learning. Lee documented instruction that coupled the reading of African American literature and the African American linguistic practice of signifying.[1] Lee's study focused on the use of classic pieces of modern and contemporary African American literature as a way to bridge the linguistic skills of her students with those found in Dominant American English (DAE). Lee capitalizes on students' cultural and linguistic knowledge of figurative language by analyzing figurative language used by novelists Zora Neale Hurston, Toni Morrison, and Alice Walker. Students gained complex skills of literary analysis using their own linguistic resources as a foundation. These critical literary analysis skills, gained through culturally relevant literacy instruction, are important in any literature classroom.

Whereas Lee's (1995) study focused on using African American language practices in reading instruction at the secondary level, Ball (1995) focused on the way such practices were used in writing. She analyzed the formal and informal writing of AAVE-speaking students and found that certain *text design patterns* showed up in both classroom and informal texts, depending on topics and audience. Her work uncovered uses of folk idioms, patterns of repetition, and narrative interspersions in student writing that are characteristic of African American discourse. Ball also found that effective teachers who encouraged a range of topics and audiences allowed students to use these resources in their school writing, though these characteristic text patterns were often seen as random or poorly constructed by less effective teachers. As a result of these findings, Ball argued that teachers must be taught "to see each student's culturally influenced styles of expression as resources and to encourage the maintenance of such styles as students gain proficiency in the use of other discourse patterns" (p. 281).

While Moll (1990) and Moll and González (1994) were researching how to use the funds of knowledge of bilingual Latino students, and Lee (1995) and Ball (1995) were investigating bridges between the literate practices of bidialectal African American youth and dominant school literacy, other important researchers also reported on educational studies emerging from Native American communities. In a themed issue of the *Bilingual Research Journal*, researchers investigated ways to support "indigenous literacies" (McCarty & Zepeda, 1995). Such literacies necessarily bring home and school practices of young Native Americans into productive contact. Much like the other research of this era, the themed issue centers on ways that successful programs for Native American students "systematically utilize local cultural and linguistic knowledge" (p. 1).

Research in the mid-1990s moved forward from the work Heath (1983) and others reviewed by García (1993) to demonstrate that resource approaches to language and literacy instruction were successful and necessary for CLNS from a variety of backgrounds.[2] Yet an important question remained. Each of the researchers, teachers, or teacher-researchers in this golden age work was versed in the funds of knowledge of the communities in which they taught. They knew about the historic and continuing marginalization of the languages and literacies they attempted to use as resources in the classroom. Whether they themselves were members of those communities, whether they gained these understandings of the linguistic and literate practices through research, or both, the fact remains that they recognized repertoires of teacher knowledge that needed coherent vision and theory. A central question guided much of this research: What did teachers need to know and to be able to do to meet the demands of resource pedagogies for CLNS?

### Teacher Knowledge in the Golden Age

One seminal message that emerged in the literature on the teacher knowledge necessary to successfully integrate the home practices of CLNS in classroom learning was Ladson-Billings's (1995) notion of *culturally relevant pedagogy*. As is evident from the work we have reviewed to this point, several such notions of pedagogy were prevalent in the decades preceding the 1990s, and Ladson-Billings's contribution is one of these. During the previous 15 years, researchers had used the terms "culturally appropriate" (Au, 1980), "culturally responsive" (Cazden & Legget, 1976), "culturally synchronic" (Irvine, 1990) and, finally, "culturally relevant" (Ladson-Billings, 1994) to describe educational programs that attempted to match closely school culture and students' home culture to promote academic success.[3]

Ladson-Billings (1995) offered a coherent theoretical statement that encompassed the resource approach research from her own work among successful teachers of African American students, as well as previous work with CLNS. She proposed three elements of culturally relevant pedagogy. Such pedagogy must "produce students who can achieve academically, produce students who demonstrate cultural competence, and develop students who can both understand and critique the existing social order" (p. 474). The first two tenets were, in effect, guiding the seminal research of the golden age. Researchers were interested in ways to help students achieve without reducing competence in their own cultures; they were interested in marrying the home and school in additive ways. The third tenet of critical consciousness is one that, we believe, continues to be lacking to date in much of the current resource approach pedagogy. Although some of the golden age research did encourage such a critique of power and inequity, it was not usually the emphasis. We return to this critical element in the third section of this chapter.

Still, in the mid-1990s, researchers and teacher-educators faced the challenge of connecting knowledge and theory produced through research to the professional development of teachers for work with CLNS. How could we help teachers gain what was necessary for culturally relevant teaching? Cochran-Smith (1995) provided important work on this topic, building on her own teaching and research in teacher education. She proposed a model of teacher knowledge demanding that teachers "explore and reconsider their own assumptions, understand the values and practices of families and cultures different from their own, and construct pedagogy that takes these into account in locally appropriate and culturally sensitive ways" (p. 495). Such a model forced teachers and teacher-educators to center teacher learning in the culture of the actual school and community. This required teachers to engage in research projects and ethnography not unlike the ethnographic and social language research conducted by the leading scholars of the golden age; that is, it requires teachers to observe and understand the funds of knowledge of particular communities before developing pedagogies and curricula for those communities. Cochran-Smith detailed several of these teacher inquiries and the culturally relevant knowledge and pedagogy teachers gained through the process.

By the end of the 1990s, evidence had amassed from the golden age. From research on various nondominant communities to theories of teaching, to models of teacher education, it was clear that basing the teaching and learning of CLNS in a dialogue between nondominant and dominant ways was crucial to cultural maintenance and academic achievement. It was also clear that teacher knowledge needed to be cultivated locally and grounded in the linguistic and cultural practices of nondominant students to achieve this dialogue. As leading educational reform scholars Darling-Hammond and McLaughlin (1999) noted at the close of the century:

> As schools become more socioeconomically and ethnically diverse ... policies must be sensitive to the fact that standardized practices will not allow teachers to address differences among students, and that strategies for doing so are a major area of needed learning. (p. 381)

What have we learned about the strategies necessary to work successfully with the resources of CLNS since the golden age? In the next section we look at the ways recent researchers have learned from this vital period and have worked to bolster evidence for resource approaches.

## RESOURCE PEDAGOGY IN THE NEW CENTURY

In this first decade of the new century, researchers have continued to grapple with how to bridge the language and literacy practices of CLNS from various ethnic backgrounds with the dominant practices demanded for school success. This contemporary research, of course, owes much to those before and during the golden age, who provided solid evidence for the merits of culturally relevant language and literacy pedagogy. Our review here is not exhaustive; rather, it highlights studies focused on using nondominant practices in language and literacy instruction, and the teacher knowledge necessary to carry out such instruction. In addition, we seek to explore studies that move us beyond simply using student resources to mainstream CLNS, and into the realms of critical consciousness and cultural maintenance that are key to Ladson-Billings's (1995) conception of culturally relevant pedagogy. It is our contention that much of the resource approach work today fails in these regards, regressing into the less progressive difference perspectives of past decades.

Many contemporary studies build directly on work of the 1990s, attempting to bolster what we gained in those extremely productive years. Moje and her collaborators (2004) build explicitly on Moll's (1992) *funds of knowledge* and the concept of the *third space* advanced by Gutiérrez, Baquedano-Lopez, Tejada, and Riveria (1999) during the late 1990s. In a multiyear ethnographic study of the funds of knowledge of 30 Latino middle school students, the research team found that a complex web of funds outside the school could be used in the literacy curriculum, specifically in science literacy instruction. The funds these researchers uncover are vast, from home funds centered on knowledge about parents' work lives to those from peers, popular culture, and other countries of family origin. The challenge of using these everyday resources in productive dialogue with academic funds is the heart of Gutiérrez's (2008) use of the "third space" concept: How can researchers and teachers gain knowledge about these funds and connect them to classroom learning so that neither is lost, but that instead a space of shared, or hybrid, practice is created? This is where Moje and her collaborators (2004) find great challenge. They hearken back to Lee's (1995) study of African American signifying and literary analysis as a model of the way systematically to bridge the home and school, and work to push their own work toward such a third space.

Another study that explicitly uses the *funds of knowledge* concept is Dworn's (2006) investigation of biliteracy development among fourth-grade Latino students. Dworn documents a "family stories project," in which students investigated family histories in their home communities, then wrote and translated stories in Spanish and English. His major findings echo those of Moll (1990) and García (1993)—that bringing the languages and experiences of bilingual students into their language and literacy work, with attention to the development of both languages, is a key to fostering biliteracy and academic achievement. We should note that the teacher knowledge necessary for Moje and her team (2004) to use community funds in the classroom was uncovered through long-term ethnographic research, whereas the funds in Dworn's (2006) work came from his own membership in the bilingual Latino community, as well as through the pedagogical strategy of having his students investigate their homes and families.

Research in predominantly African American communities that seeks to use the linguistic traditions and features of AAVE has also continued in the vein of the golden age work. One example is Williams's (2006) case study of an African American teacher's use of multiple literacies instruction. Williams analyzes the practices of an eighth-grade language arts teacher who supports the critical use of both AAVE and DAE in her formal and informal lessons. Whether in oral or written language, the teacher in Williams's study sees both language varieties as useful and works to contrast them with students. Although this teacher was a native speaker of AAVE, others have researched how such linguistic knowledge can be brought to non-AAVE-speaking teachers preparing to teach in urban schools (Ball & Lardner, 2005; Fogel & Ehri, 2006; Redd & Webb, 2005; Richardson, 2003; Thompson, 2004). Teacher knowledge about AAVE, then, may be part of the instructor's everyday repertoire, may be studied in teacher education and professional development classes, or may be studied *and* be a part of the teacher's repertoire.

Other researchers working from a resource approach and emphasizing AAVE linguistic features have increasingly looked to hip-hop as one vital resource for classroom learning. As Mahiri (2001) puts it, many rap artist have become "public pedagogues—educators with degrees in street knowledge and a lyrical curriculum for raising consciousness" (p. 382). Using the language and critical content of rap music as a key component of the curriculum for AAVE speakers and other urban youth can provide rich linguistically and culturally relevant texts for literacy learning. Past simple consumption, students can also write and perform rap and spoken-word poetry that challenges systems and histories of inequality. It is these *critical pop culture pedagogies* and curricula that Mahiri espouses for urban youth.

Teacher-researchers Morrell and Duncan-Andrade (2002) provide an example of using hip-hop in the secondary English curriculum. Like others before them, these researchers see the need to bring out-of-school literacy practices of CLNS into the classroom as a means to overcome the irrelevance and inaccessibility of traditional literature courses. Morrell and Duncan-Andrade describe a poetry unit in which they explicitly place hip-hop music alongside different historical periods of poetry. Students read canonical poems from various periods, then read rap lyrics from critical hip-hop artists. Students were then asked to interpret the canonical poems and the rap lyrics, and to draw connections between the language, content, and historical periods represented in the texts. Capitalizing on the linguistic and cultural resource of rap, these researchers simultaneously foster a critical consciousness about history, writing, and dominant literacy. Other important researchers on hip-hop and AAVE as a critical resource for classroom learning include Alim (2004) and Kirkland (2008). Critical resource approaches to using the spoken word as part of this pop culture pedagogy have also begun to emerge in the literacy research (Fisher, 2005; Jocson, 2004).

The current decade has seen more resource approach literacy work among Asian American and immigrant Asian students.[4] In a qualitative study of an after-school book club, Vyas (2004) focused on the bicultural identity development of three immigrant youth: one from Tawain, one from South Korea, and one from Nepal. Through reading of Asian American literature, the teacher-researcher was able to encourage these youth to explore their struggles with cultural negotiation. Both the literature *and* the researcher's own experiences as a bicultural Asian American helped to bring students' bicultural experiences to the surface for discussion and writing. Contrast this with Townsend and Fu's (2001) case study of a Laotian refugee's painful struggle toward English literacy, without such a sympathetic and knowledgeable teacher and literature, and Vyas's rather straightforward findings seem all the more important.

This attention to finding appropriate literature and encouraging reflection on critical bicultural development is also part of White-Kaulaity's (2007) work in developing stages of reading development for Native American students. Working from interviews, conversations, essays by Native American authors, and personal experiences, White-Kaulaity contrasts the reading development of Native Ameri-

cans with the stages developed by Donelson and Nilsen (2005). Although she
finds much overlap, White-Kaulaity also notes important differences in Native
American families' and communities' ways with words that must be taken into
account in supporting students through stages of reading development. Among
the resources that Native American children bring with them is a rich oral tradition that can be bridged to print literacy. She suggests that teachers must become
knowledgeable about oral literacies if they are to teach Native American children
successfully. White-Kaulaity, like Vyas (2004), also finds the importance of choosing Native American–authored texts in motivating the people in her work to read.
She sees, like many scholars before her working on issues of literacy instruction
for CLNS, that the students in her community come with different and valuable
tools and experiences that teachers must understand and learn to use.

## IMPLICATIONS FOR PRACTICE: STRATEGIES FOR GAINING TEACHER KNOWLEDGE

In each of these studies, as well as in those from the 1990s, teachers had or needed
to acquire significant cultural and linguistic knowledge about the learners with
whom they worked. This knowledge was gained in several different ways, from
the teacher inquiry that Cochran-Smith (1995) proposed, to use of students as
inquirers themselves in gathering their own funds of knowledge for use in the
classroom. The following list suggests some of the ways that teachers can access
the cultural and linguistic knowledge necessary to bridge nondominant and dominant skills and knowledge in the classrooms of CLNS. We do not see these as
mutually exclusive or hierarchical, and we realize that in many successful studies,
teachers use more than one strategy.

- *Community cultural and linguistic membership.* The teacher shares ethnic
  and/or linguistic background with students, and may have access to and
  knowledge of students' resources, or the teacher and students do not share
  a background and move into other ways of understanding.
- *Inquiry projects by teachers.* The teacher conducts research with or about his
  or her students and communities to make differences and resources visible
  to all parties.
- *Book and classroom learning.* The teacher studies literature (fiction, nonfiction, research) about the cultural resources of his or her students inside
  and/or outside the classroom setting.
- *Students as experts and researchers.* The teacher encourages students to
  gather information and to create projects to bring their resources from outside the classroom for the learning of both teacher and student.

Some of these are pedagogical strategies, others are stances toward teaching,
and still others are ways of being in the world that come from our own cultural

communities. As teacher-educators, we believe that each of these strategies can and should be central to literacy education classes for practicing and prospective teachers. In our own teacher education literacy classes, we require that teacher candidates use all four strategies for gaining teacher knowledge. Simply put, the vast evidence of success using resource approaches demands that we help teachers acquire the skills and knowledge needed to use nondominant resources in their classrooms, regardless of their ethnic and linguistic backgrounds.

## IMPLICATIONS FOR FUTURE RESEARCH

Knowledge about how to access and work with the cultural and linguistic resources of CLNS in instruction has grown considerably since Heath's (1983) landmark study and García's (1993) important review. However, we see two areas that need research. The first is the need for more critical resource approaches to literacy instruction. We are concerned that the third tenet of Ladson-Billings's (1995) culturally relevant pedagogy—critical consciousness about the power relationships in culture, language, and race—is absent from too much current research. Although resources are often seen as a bridge to biliteracy and biculturalism, it is not always the case that teachers and students gain an awareness of why the tensions and struggles between home and school ways continue in their lived experience. In preparing teachers for 21st-century classrooms and beyond, we believe it is crucial to note not only differences in cultural practices to be addressed in instruction but also power differentials based in historic and continuing discrimination. For teachers and for students, this means investigations into critical pedagogies (Freire, 1970), in addition to social and cultural understandings.

A second area in need of future research is multiethnic and multilingual contexts. The vast majority of research on CLNS has taken place with one nondominant group (e.g., Latino, African American, or Native American). There is good reason for this. There are many areas in which such monoethnic, nondominant communities remain the norm, where all of the students share certain cultural and linguistic ways that differ from the academic language and literacy practices required by the school.[5] In addition, we continue to need to update and understand the literacy experiences of particular ethnic groups in particular communities, and to understand the teacher knowledge necessary to serve students in these communities from a resource perspective.

However, current demographic shifts across the nation (Klein, 2004; Smelser, Wilson, & Mitchell, 2001), coupled with continuing segregation of schools and communities of color, have made schools serving more than one group of CLNS increasingly common. In Paris's (2008) current work in the urban West, for example, it is common to have Latino, African American, Pacific Islander, and Southeast Asian students in the same classrooms. Paris has documented the language and literacy practices in such high schools. Findings suggest that oral and written discourse in AAVE and Spanish, as well as student understandings of ethnicity,

often challenge dominant notions of who speaks, writes, and is a member of a particular group. Latino and Pacific Islander students participate in oral and written
AAVE, and African American students employ Spanish for communicative effect.
These emergent findings challenge us to look at the various funds of knowledge
in such multiethnic and multilingual settings. We cannot identify linguistic or
cultural practices by ethnicity alone, nor can we predict the hybrid language and
literacies that emerge within such contexts.

We know very little about the literacy resources available in such deeply culturally and linguistically complex classrooms (Ball, 2009). Future research must
apply the lessons from the golden age and from the current decade in these contexts. This is not an easy task. Yet the work over two decades of language and
literacy researchers has shown what can be achieved when students and teachers
share, bridge, and blend the cultural knowledge of community and school. We
have little choice but to equip our teachers to work in ever more complex classrooms. To do so will take research into the resources students that bring and
create in such multiethnic and multilingual schools. To meet the challenges of
these 21st-century culturally and linguistically complex classrooms, we must also
revise our training and development of teachers. We end our chapter by considering what such changes will require.

Ball (2009) reports on research designed to advance knowledge concerning
*what* and *how* teachers must learn from professional learning to teach CLDS successfully in these contexts. Ball concludes that generativity plays a critical role
in the preparation of teachers to work with CLNS. Ball uses the term "generativity" to refer to teachers' ability to add to their understanding by connecting
their personal and professional knowledge with their students' knowledge in ways
that produce new knowledge that is useful to them in curricular planning and
pedagogical problem solving to meet the educational needs of their students. She
argues that, through such generativity, teachers must envision their classroom
as "communities of change," in which transformative learning and emancipatory
teaching take place. Such learning has the purpose of educating a generation of
students that will itself become generative in thinking and literacy practices. Such
learning necessarily incorporates the critical consciousness element of Ladson-
Billings's (1995) pedagogy as a crucial part of teacher and student knowledge.

This work requires moving beyond simplistic notions of learning communities and toward notions of dynamic learning environments in which generative thinkers engage with new perspectives. It requires a research agenda that
focuses specifically on preparing teachers for work with CLNS, and for preservice
and inservice programs that envision culturally and linguistically complex classrooms as communities of change. And it requires the development of rigorous
programs that focus on the acquisition of knowledge needed to live and work in
a multicultural society, participate in a democratic society, and engage in critical
discourse about competing ideas. To accomplish this, Ball (2009) has proposed
a model of generative change that should be used in teacher education programs
and replicated in the classrooms of teachers serving CLNS.

The model in Figure 19.1 depicts the process of preparing teachers for CLNS, which begins with an emphasis on reflective writing used to facilitate teachers' increased metacognitive awareness concerning the critical role of literacies in their own lives and in the lives of students from culturally and linguistically diverse backgrounds. Next, the model encourages teacher education programs to emphasize the use of guided introspective writing, which requires teachers to look closely within themselves to determine the role they play in the education of CLNS. It also requires that teachers be introduced to new theoretical perspectives to facilitate the process of ideological becoming and an increased sense of agency. During the third phase of the model, teachers are required to write critiques of course readings as they complete action research projects selected to increase a sense of advocacy and the development of plans of action that they can later implement in their teaching. The fourth phase of the model represents the point at which teachers are encouraged to combine theory, best practices, and actual work with CLNS to facilitate the development of generative thinking skills, theory posing, and the development of their own voices on approaches to teaching CLNS.

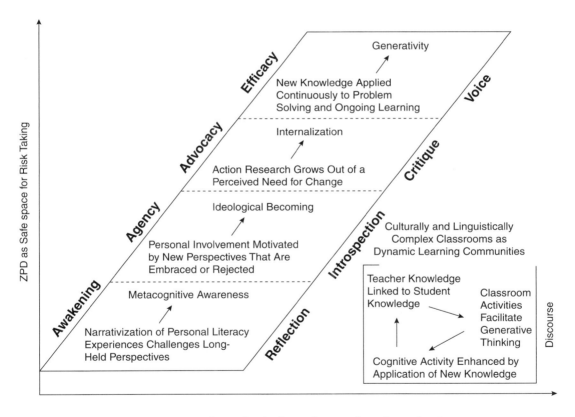

**FIGURE 19.1.** The processes through which teachers and students develop voice, generativity, and efficacy in their thinking and practice. From Ball (2009). Copyright 2009 by the American Educational Research Association. Reprinted by permission.

Historically, teacher education has focused too narrowly on the teacher learning that occurs away from the school site and in the teacher-education classroom. It has not given adequate attention to the learning that must occur with the learners in the school community. This model calls for a change in this conception, so that teacher learning is seen to occur when teachers combine the knowledge they gain from teacher education programs and personal experiences, and the knowledge their CLNS bring into the classroom. Teachers must use generative thinking to combine this knowledge to meet the learning needs of their students and to educate students to become generative thinkers as well. A unique challenge facing teachers in culturally and linguistically complex classrooms is the demand to make the appropriate curricular and pedagogical adjustments to work from a resource perspective with their students. Because many of the teachers in these classrooms come from very different cultural, linguistic, and socioeconomic backgrounds than their students, it is imperative that they become generative in their curricular problem-solving skills, so they can link the knowledge they have with the knowledge their students bring into the classroom. A critical key to achieving our goal of preparing teachers is the facilitation of teachers' internal change concerning issues of equity and the development of teachers as generative practitioners.

This model attempts to draw together the learning about critical resource approaches to teaching CLNS from the 1990s through the present. We believe the elements of this model were present in much of the research, teaching, and conceptions of pedagogy in the golden age, and that they continue to the present in the current research we review in this chapter. However, the elements of this model remain marginal in teacher education to date; they have not been coherently drawn together for teacher-educators. It is our hope that future teacher education research and future teacher-educators can lead a new vision of teacher learning.

Achieving this vision requires changes in teachers' conceptions of themselves as teachers and as learners, and changes in teacher education programs as well. Remember that the vast bulk of the research we have reviewed in this chapter is reports of successful resource curricula and pedagogy, but much work is needed to illuminate how teachers acquire knowledge of these resources. Drawing on this model, teacher education programs can design instruction that helps teachers to recognize the need to modify their own pedagogical practices and instructional organization in response to the information they gain in their courses, and in response to the information they gain from the students they teach. Teachers can subsequently use this model as a tool to help them arrive at solutions to the day-to-day challenges they face in their classrooms.

We have learned much since the phenomenal work of the 1990s about successful literacy instruction for CLNS. The current decade has carried this work considerably further. It is time for teacher knowledge in today's multicultural and multilingual classrooms to catch up to what research has shown for decades now. We see teacher education as one major lever to equip teachers for the culturally and linguistically complex classrooms, where they will spend their professional lives working to equip our young people with the critical literacy skills they need to flourish in a multicultural society.

## NOTES

1. "Signifying" is a discourse practice that employs figurative language to criticize, instruct, or inform (Lee, 1995).
2. There was very little research in this area during this time for Asian American students, though Cai (1999) provides an excellent example of resource approaches in the writing of Chinese immigrant college students.
3. Some more recent work conceptualizing the nature and benefits of culturally relevant pedagogy has focused on how teachers approach issues of language in their classrooms (Delpit & Dowdy, 2002; Irvine, 2003).
4. We realize that the term "Asian" encompasses many culturally and linguistically distinct communities, and specifies ethnicity in our review.
5. We realize that there are considerable variations and similarities in the cultural practices of individuals in any community (Gutiérrez & Rogoff, 2003).

## REFERENCES

Alim, H. S. (2004). *You know my Steez: An ethnographic and sociolinguistic study of a Black American Speech community.* Durham, NC: Duke University Press.

Au, K. (1980). Participation structures in a reading lesson with Hawaiian children: Analysis of a culturally appropriate instructional event. *Anthropology and Education Quarterly, 11*(2), 91–115.

Ball, A. (1995). Text design patterns in the writing of Urban African American students: Teaching to the cultural strengths of students in multicultural settings. *Urban Education, 30,* 253–289.

Ball, A. F. (2009). Toward a theory of generative change in culturally and linguistically complex classrooms. *American Educational Research Journal, 46*(1), 45–72.

Ball, A. F., & Lardner, T. (2005). *African American literacies unleashed: Vernacular English and the composition classroom.* Carbondale: Southern Illinois University Press.

Cai, G. (1999). Texts in context: Understanding Chinese students' English compositions. In C. Cooper & L. Odell (Eds.), *Evaluating writing* (pp. 279–297). Urbana, IL: National Council of Teachers of English.

Cazden, C., & Leggett, E. (1976). *Culturally responsive education: A discussion of LAU Remedies II.* Washington, DC: U.S. Department of Health, Education, and Welfare, National Institute of Education.

Cochran-Smith, M. (1995). Color blindness and basket making are not the answers: Confronting dilemmas of race, culture and language diversity in teacher education. *American Educational Research Journal, 32*(3), 493–522.

Collins, J., & Blot, R. (2003). *Literacy and literacies: Texts, power, and identity.* Cambridge, UK: Cambridge University Press.

Darling-Hammond, L., & McLaughlin, M. (1999). Investing in teaching as a learning profession. In L. Darling-Hammond & G. Sykes (Eds.), *Teaching as the learning profession: Handbook of policy and practice* (pp. 377–411). San Francisco: Jossey-Bass.

Delpit, L., & Dowdy, J. K. (Eds.). (2002). *The skin that we speak: Thoughts on language and culture in the classroom.* New York: New Press.

Donelson, K. L., & Nilsen, A. P. (2005). *Literature for today's young adults* (7th ed.). Boston: Pearson/Allyn & Bacon.

Dworn, J. (2006). The family stories project: Using funds of knowledge for writing. *Reading Teacher, 59*(6), 510–520.

Fisher, M. (2005). From the coffee house to the school house: The promise and potential of spoken word poetry in school contexts. *English Education, 37*(2), 115–131.

Fogel, H., & Ehri, L. (2006). Teaching African American English forms to Standard American English-speaking teachers: Effects on acquisition, attitudes, and responses to student use. *Journal of Teacher Education, 57*(5), 464–480.

Freire, P. (1970). *Pedagogy of the oppressed.* New York: Continuum.

García, E. (1993). Language, culture, and education. *Review of Research in Education, 19,* 51–98.

Gutiérrez, K. (2008). Developing a sociocritical literacy in the third space. *Reading Research Quarterly, 43*(2), 148–164.

Gutiérrez, K., Baquedano-Lopez, P., Tejada, C., & Riveria, A. (1999, April). *Hybridity as a tool for understanding literacy learning: Building on a syncretic approach.* Paper presented at the American Educational Research Association, Montreal, Quebec, Canada.

Gutiérrez, K., & Rogoff, B. (2003). Cultural ways of learning. *Educational Researcher, 35*(5), 19–25.

Heath, S. B. (1983). *Ways with words.* New York: Cambridge University Press.

Irvine, J. J. (1990). *Black students and school failure: Policies, practices, and prescriptions.* New York: Praeger.

Irvine, J. J. (2003). *Educating teachers for diversity: Seeing with a cultural eye.* New York: Teachers College Press.

Jensen, A. (1969). How much can we boost IQ and scholastic achievement? *Harvard Educational Review, 39,* 1–123.

Jocson, K. (2004). "Taking it to the mic": Pedagogy of June Jordan's Poetry for the People in partnership with an urban high school. *English Education, 37*(2), 44–60.

Kirkland, D. (2008). The rose that grew from concrete: Postmodern blackness and new English education. *English Journal, 97*(5), 69–75.

Klein, H. (2004). *A population history of the United States.* Cambridge, UK: Cambridge University Press.

Labov, W. (1972). The logic of nonstandard English. In *Language in the inner city* (pp. 201–240). Philadelphia: University of Pennsylvania Press.

Ladson-Billings, G. (1994). *The dreamkeepers: Successful teachers of African American children.* San Francisco: Jossey-Bass.

Ladson-Billings, G. (1995). Toward a theory of culturally relevant pedagogy. *American Educational Research Journal, 32*(3), 465–491.

Lee, C. D. (1995). A culturally based cognitive apprenticeship: Teaching African American high school students skills in literary interpretation. *Reading Research Quarterly, 30*(4), 608–630.

Mahiri, J. (2001). Pop culture pedagogy and the end(s) of school. *Journal of Adolescent and Adult Literacy, 44*(4), 382–385.

McCarty, T., & Zepeda, O. (1995). Indigenous language education and literacy: Introduction to the theme issue. *Bilingual Research Journal, 19*(1), 1–4.

Moje, E. B., Ciechanowski, K. M., Kramer, K., Ellis, L., Carrillo, R., & Collazo, T. (2004). Working toward third space in content area literacy: An examination of everyday funds of knowledge and discourse. *Reading Research Quarterly, 39*(1), 38–70.

Moll, L. (1992). Literacy research in community and classrooms: A sociocultural approach. In R. Beach, J. L. Green, M. L. Kamil, & T. Shanahan (Eds.), *Multidisciplinary perspectives in literacy research* (pp. 211–244). Urbana, IL: National Conference on Research in English/National Council of Teachers of English.

Moll, L., & González, N. (1994). Lessons from research with language minority children. *Journal of Reading Behavior, 26*(4), 23–41.

Moll, L. C. (1990). *Vygotsky and education: Instructional instructions and applications of socio-historical psychology* Cambridge, UK: Cambridge University Press.

Morrell, E., & Duncan-Andrade, J. (2002). Promoting academic literacy with urban youth through engaging in hip-hop culture. *English Journal, 91*(6), 88–92.

Paris, D. (2008). *"Our culture": Difference, division, and unity in multiethnic youth space.* Doctoral dissertation, Stanford University, Stanford, CA.

Redd, T. E., & Webb, K. S. (2005). *A teacher's introduction to African American English: What a writing teacher should know.* Urbana, IL: National Council of Teachers of English.

Richardson, E. (2003). *African American literacies.* New York: Routledge.

Smelser, N., Wilson, W. J., & Mitchell, F. (Eds.). (2001). *American becoming: Racial trends and their consequences.* Washington, DC: National Academies Press.

Smitherman, G. (1977). *Talkin and testifyin.* Detroit, MI: Wayne State University Press.

Thompson, G. L. (2004). *Through ebony eyes: What teachers need to know but are afraid to ask about African American students.* San Francisco: Wiley.

Townsend, J. S., & Fu, D. (2001). Paw's story: A Laotian refugee's lonely entry into American literacy. *Journal of Adolescent and Adult Literacy, 45*(2), 104–114.

Vyas, S. (2004). Exploring bicultural identities of Asian high school students through the analytic window of a literature club. *Journal of Adolescent and Adult Literacy, 48*(2), 12–23.

White-Kaulaity, M. (2007). Reflections of Native American reading: A seed, a tool, and a weapon. *Journal of Adolescent and Adult Literacy, 50*(7), 560–569.

Williams, C. H. (2006). "You gotta reach 'em": An African American teacher's multiple literacies approach. *Theory Into Practice, 45*(4), 346–351.

# CHAPTER 20

# Protecting Our Investment

*Induction and Mentoring of Novice Teachers
in Diversity-Rich Schools*

NANCY FREY *and* DOUGLAS FISHER

Professions and trades have long used a model of in-depth supervised work experience following formal training to help the novice to refine his or her professional practice. In medicine, newly graduated doctors enter a phase of residency, where they specialize in a subfield, under the supervision of experienced physicians. Tradespeople such as electricians and plumbers complete an apprenticeship, while working for a master craftsperson. While the probationary member completes preliminary training, the professional community itself uses this time to determine whether the resident or apprentice is suitable for active membership.

Likewise, the teaching profession employs a similar process for novice teachers, called "induction," with successful completion leading to more advanced licensure. This period traditionally lasts 1 or 2 years, and an experienced and expert member is assigned to mentor the candidate. But what happens during the induction years can have a significant effect on the likelihood of the novice's success or failure. Given the need for effective teachers of students in diversity-rich schools, articulated elsewhere in this handbook, it is critical that we protect our investment in these educators. Therefore, in this chapter we discuss the following:

- Historical roots of induction in teaching
- Knowledge bases that inform induction
- Research on teacher retention
- Effects of induction programs
- Implications for induction programs

## HISTORICAL ROOTS OF INDUCTION IN TEACHING

Induction programs designed to support novice teachers have existed in one form or another in American education for nearly as long as there has been a teaching profession. Many of these programs drew from apprenticeship models in other trades, pairing an inexperienced trainee with a master of the craft. This form of on-the-job training has existed for centuries and is still in use in education, medicine, law, and other professions that require a period of internship. However, as educational communities grew in size, both demographically and geographically, through organization into larger school districts, more formal supports for new teachers were created. For example, surveys of county offices of education in California in 1942 and 1946 found that professional development provided new teachers with

> printed statements of the basic philosophy of the county educational program, gave a list of teaching aids available in the county, told the teachers about the county library and other sources of professional materials, discussed with each teacher the county course or study guide, evaluated carefully the past professional and personal records of new teachers, and acquainted them with the county record system. (Johnson, 1947, p. 157)

This approach is more aptly described as "orientation," with its emphasis on procedural processes and cataloging of materials and resources. These efforts lacked any mention of reflective practice or mentoring relationships. In this model, new teachers were expected to solve problems at the local level, usually by seeking out a more experienced colleague who would provide information or direction.

### Establishing Professionalism in Teaching

As education programs were transformed from the normal schools of the past to university degree programs, with accompanying state licensure, the field reorganized as a profession. Education was seen as possessing a body of research-based knowledge, propelled in large part by findings in reading and psychology. The move from trade to profession in turn led to the formation of professional organizations for teachers and administrators.

Many of these professional organizations involved themselves in new teacher orientation, providing a clearinghouse for members to share their ideas and approaches for orienting new teachers. In the 1950s, professional organizations began to call for more formal induction programs in response to the growing complexity of teaching and a burgeoning field of research on effective practices. Cable (1959) noted a "more friendly spirit of help" (p. 103) within education circles and called for formal induction programs that would ensure positive first experiences and build *esprit de corps*.

By the 1960s, professional organizations such as the Association for Supervision and Curriculum Development (ASCD) and the National Association for Secondary School Principals (NASSP) were formalizing teacher induction practices and making these efforts a part of the duties of school administrators. On the one hand, the ASCD model for supervision of new teachers focused mostly on increasing job satisfaction and emphasizing human relations (Burnham, 1976). On the other hand, the NASSP (Hunt, 1967) proposed a three-stage model that took place during the first 1–2 years of employment:

Stage 1: Familiarization with the community, school, and teaching assignment

Stage 2: Pedagogical and organizational matters (lesson planning, classroom management, motivation, grading)

Stage 3: Professional growth (observing experienced teachers, reflective discussion, differentiating instruction, self-evaluation)

Importantly, the NASSP model included the assignment of a mentor teacher (called a "cooperating" teacher), who was released from some teaching duties to guide the novice teacher but did not have any evaluative responsibilities. Aspects of this model endure in many induction programs today. Common features of induction programs include a progression from knowledge of the classroom community to organizational/logistical competence, to self-sustaining reflective practice, as well as the involvement of an experienced peer who does not play an evaluative role.

In the 1980s, many districts began to expand their orientation programs beyond dispensing information to include more formalized mentoring relationships through the assignment of an experienced teacher to shepherd the novice through the first year of teaching. This was influenced in part by the rise of the business model as a method for school reform (Gehrke, 1988; Levine, 1986). Borko (1986) described mentoring of new teachers by a "colleague teacher" who was formally selected and trained, and who received compensation. Not incidentally, the creation of a mentoring position, with its additional pay, was in alignment with a business model of school reform that required more career paths for teachers (Rosenholtz, 1986).

Attention in the last decade has shifted to making induction more meaningful for teachers working in urban and diversity-rich schools. Major societal issues, such as poverty, crime, and unemployment, have detrimental effects on the learning of students in urban schools and challenge their teachers, especially those who have not had similar experiences themselves or exposure to them during their preparation program (Lovette, 1996). A growing number of teacher-educators became concerned with the cultural and economic divide between teachers and the students they teach in urban schools, noting that the majority of teachers are female, white, and come from middle-class suburban or rural settings (Zeichner et al., 1998). Induction and mentoring approaches have begun to expand the scope of work beyond classroom management and planning to include development of culturally responsive instructional and curricular approaches (e.g., Bergeron, 2008; Seidl, 2007).

Taken together, several elements in the decades from the 1940s to the 1980s led to the eventual development of formal induction programs. The growth of school districts made it necessary to set aside time to dispense information to new employees. The explosion of educational research after World War II meant that the corpus of knowledge was growing at a rate that made it necessary to find ways to keep teachers current. In addition, the introduction of reforms based on successful business models led to the creation of mentoring and clinical educator positions that would serve the dual purposes of supporting new teachers and offering a career ladder. However, as schoolchildren became more diverse, teacher demographics remained mostly unchanged. In the coming decade, a body of knowledge about effective professional development, coaching, an understanding of the unique needs of both new teachers and students in diversity-rich schools would spur the development of induction programs.

## KNOWLEDGE BASES THAT INFORM INDUCTION

### Emergence of a Science of Teacher Development

Although educators and administrators recognized that some sort of support was useful for new teachers, most relied on locally developed processes that were a hodgepodge of traditional practices. The work of Joyce and Showers (2002), although not directly related to induction programs per se, elevated the profession's understanding of the relationship among coaching, professional development, and student achievement. Working in collaboration with schools, Joyce and Showers documented the effect sizes, as measured by gains in standardized test scores of students, of professional development experiences that moved away from stand-alone workshop experiences. They described a model that included the following:

- Professional development organized around curriculum, instruction, and the learning climate
- Peer coaching in classrooms for application
- Evaluation of professional development based on student outcomes
- Inquiry-based planning for next steps

In addition, with the recognition that professional development for teachers impacts student achievement, mounting research evidence suggested the existence of both qualitative and quantitative differences across the career of a teacher. Preservice programs were designed to produce skilled novices, but students needed expert teachers.

## Moving from Novice to Expert

Another set of studies explored the meaning and nature of expertise, and the contrast between novices and experts informed induction programming (for an extended discussion on this topic, see Chi, Glaser, & Farr, 1988). Berliner (1994) synthesized research on expertise and applied it to teaching. He described five stages of development:

> *Stage 1: Novice level*—"The deliberate learner." Minimal skills driven by context-free rules ("praise when a student gives the right answer") as seen in student teachers and some first-year teachers.
>
> *Stage 2: Advanced beginner level*—"The insightful learner." Draws upon past experience to inform decisions but does not accept full personal agency for outcomes, as seen in second-year teachers.
>
> *Stage 3: Competent level*—"The arational learner." Sets goals, makes plans, and accepts responsibility but is not yet fluid or fluent. Third- and fourth-year teachers may reach this level, and some teachers never move beyond this stage of expertise.
>
> *Stage 4: Proficient level*—"The intuitive learner." Some teachers reach the stage of being able to teach analytically and intuitively, drawing on both past experience and a deep knowledge base.
>
> *Stage 5: Expert level*—"The arational learner." Teaches fluently and seemingly effortlessly but may have more difficulty in putting instructional decisions into words. Solutions to problems are creative and innovative.

The notion of stages of expertise is useful in understanding the developmental needs of new teachers. Berliner suggests that a major difference between novices and proficient and expert teachers is that they lack pattern recognition—everything that occurs appears unrelated to anything else that has occurred, and they are simply unable to make sense of what is happening beyond the most superficial level. Therefore, a child's misbehavior is understood only by the outward behavior, and is not contextualized by what may have occurred a minute, an hour, a day, or a year before.

Sternberg and Horvath (1995) argued that merely listing the differences between novices and experts is not enough, because it provides a restrictive view of teaching that is then distilled into a list of behaviors. At the same time, they also expressed concern for expert models that focus only on dispositions. The proposed a model that they termed "prototypical," and suggested that more could be learned from noting the similarities among experts, as opposed to a contrastive view of novices and experts. They described their prototypical expert teacher as

> insightful in solving problems ... [and] able to identify information that is promising with respect to a problem solution and is able to combine that information effectively. The prototypical expert is able to reformulate his or her rep-

resentation of the problem at hand through a process of noticing, mapping. And applying analogies . . [and] arrive at solutions that are both novel and appropriate. (p. 14)

Lajoie (2003) reviewed the research on expertise models and described the importance of learner awareness in attaining higher levels of competence. "The transition from student to expert professional can be accelerated when a trajectory for change is plotted and made visible to learners" (p. 21). This echoes the work on the role of metacognition in transfer learning by Bransford and Schwartz (1999), who noted that "people who actively monitor their current levels of understanding are more likely to take active steps to improve their learning" (p. 84).

In summary, research on the novice–expert dichotomy has informed induction supports and programs  Understanding the developmental stages of teacher learning is as useful when working with adults as it is with students. It is not enough to know the behaviors and dispositions of experts; it is also necessary to build the metacognitive awareness of new teachers, so that they can understand their present level of performance and make a plan for advancement. Finally, a path or trajectory of development from novice to expert is also helpful, so that new teachers can act upon their own learning to become more skilled.

## RESEARCH ON TEACHER RETENTION

The need for effective induction experiences for new teachers can be found in one statistic—33.5% of teachers leave the profession in the first 3 years of their career (National Center for Educational Statistics, 2004). The National Commission on Teaching and America's Future (2005) reported than more than 1 million teachers enter or exit school each year, representing one-third of all teachers. Not all of these teachers leave the profession entirely; some simply move to different schools. Although this "revolving door" causes problems in all schools, namely, in program cohesiveness and professional development offerings, it has its largest effect on urban schools (p. 11). Most troublesome, teachers leave urban high-poverty schools at a rate higher than the national average (Cochran-Smith, 2006; Ingersoll, 2002). Thankfully, some teachers stay in teaching, and at the same school for several years.

### Why Teachers Stay

Guarino, Santibañez, and Daley (2006) reviewed empirical studies on teacher retention and reported that the most compelling reason for remaining in the profession was "the perception that among all available alternative activities, teaching remains the most attractive in terms of compensation, working conditions, and intrinsic rewards" (p. 184). They further reported on the demographics of teachers who were more likely to remain in teaching. White males were more likely to remain than white females. In their study of 300,000 Texas teachers, Kirby, Berends, and Naftel (1999) noted that Hispanic males and females had the lowest early attrition rates. In addition, salary had a positive association to retention and a corresponding negative one to attrition (Podgursky, Monroe, & Watson, 2004). In addition, Stinebrickner (2001) found that compensation played an especially strong role in a teacher's decision to remain in the profession during the first 9 years. But for some teachers compensation is not enough. As we have noted, large numbers of teachers leave the profession each year.

## Why Teachers Leave

There is a range of personal and professional reasons why teachers leave the profession. Kersaint, Lewis, Potter, and Meisels (2007) surveyed and interviewed more than 2,800 teachers who left teaching in two very large Florida school districts. They did not differentiate their findings based on years of experience, and participants who left ranged from 1 year to 20+ years of teaching. However, their findings are instructive to administrators and teacher educators. The two most frequently cited reasons for leaving were the wish to spend more time with family and lack of administrative support. The latter reason, much of which was related to disciplining disruptive students, was more important to males and to high school teachers who left than to females and to elementary teachers.

Johnson and Birkeland (2003) conducted a 5-year longitudinal study of 50 first-year teachers. Of the original 50, 11 left teaching during the period of the study. Most reported that they left because they were overwhelmed by their teaching loads and were further discouraged by unsupportive administrators and uncooperative colleagues. Pay played a secondary role but was mentioned as a further irritant in an already intrinsically unrewarding setting.

The problem of teacher attrition is even more acute in urban schools. Weld (1998) found that 50% of novice teachers in diversity-rich schools left the school or the profession in their first years of teaching, compared with 40% in other schools. Ingersoll (2002) found that the annual turnover rate at poor, urban schools was much higher (16%) than that at low-poverty schools (9%). These high rates of turnover and movement between schools leave high-poverty schools with more unqualified and less experienced teachers than other schools within the same district (Lankford, Loeb, & Wyckoff, 2002). Some who have left have attributed this to accountability and testing pressures (Crocco & Costigan, 2007), a perception of violence (Smith & Smith, 2006), and the disproportionately high concentration of student need in high-poverty, urban schools (Ondrich, Pas, & Yinger, 2008).

In summary, teachers do not really leave their positions because of compensation, and some stay because of their pay. Teachers do leave because they are not sure how to do their job, and they do not feel supported by colleagues and administrators. Novice teachers in urban schools are especially vulnerable to the school climate, and their movement often leaves the schools with less experienced staff.

In other words, a significant part of teacher turnover is related to the culture of schools. In part, induction programs are designed to change the culture of isolation that new teachers feel and to provide them with tangible support to do their jobs.

## EFFECTS OF INDUCTION PROGRAMS

Ingersoll and Smith's (2004) analysis of the Schooling and Staffing Survey, compiled by the National Center for Educational Statistics (2004), is instructive in understanding the effects of induction programs. They reported that in the 1999–2000 academic year, 8 of 10 new teachers were enrolled in an induction program. This number reflects all schools—urban, suburban, and rural. A report by the Council of Great City Schools (2000) revealed that only 67.5% of their member districts had induction programs for new teachers in the same school year.

The supports available in induction programs vary widely. Ingersoll and Smith (2004) found that "the strongest factors [for retention] were having a mentor from the same field, having common planning time with other teachers in the same subject, having regularly scheduled collaboration with other teachers, and being part of an external network of teachers" (p. 35). These findings were supported in the analysis of empirical studies by Guarino and colleagues (2006). Stoko, Ingram, and Beaty-O'Ferrall (2007) analyzed promising practices for retaining teachers in urban schools, and stated that "for novices, this collaboration provides them with essential support; for experienced teachers, it prevents the common end-of-the-year burnout" (p. 46).

### Criticisms of Induction Program Approaches

Researchers and educators have argued that although induction programs are useful, they do not go far enough in supporting the needs of novice teachers. For example, Schlechty and Whitford (1989) argued that induction programs are less effective than they could be because the novice teacher is expected to do everything an experienced teacher does. They recommended that positions be created to allow new teachers to observe and to meet with more expert teachers. In addition, Schlechty and Whitford noted that most induction programs lacked the resources needed, such as collaborative planning time, to be successful. Finally, they pointed out that many programs were not "integrated into the school structure ... [so] that the programs come to be viewed as one more burden to be borne in an already burdened environment" (p. 444).

The stage-based model of teacher development has been criticized for the narrowness of its scope. Dall'Alba and Sandberg (2006) reviewed professional development models in several professions, including education, and described this as "a traditional notion of professional skill as a set of attributes, such as knowledge, skills, and attitudes ... identified and described in a decontextualized manner, separate from the practice to which they refer—an approach that reflects a container view of practice" (p. 385).

Induction programs have also been criticized both for what they teach and fail to teach. In particular, many induction programs emphasize socializing new members to the profession ("This is the way we do it") at the expense of real content (Fideler & Haselkorn, 1999). When content is taught, it tends to gravitate to classroom management strategies, which, while welcome, do not provide the "silver bullet" for which novices hope. This is likely because classroom management techniques are only part of the solution: Engaged students are ultimately far less disruptive than students who are "managed" (Marzano, Marzano, & Pickering, 2003).

## IMPLICATIONS FOR INDUCTION PROGRAMS

In 2000, the National Research Council published a synthesis of research on teacher learning from the behavioral and social sciences in the book entitled *How People Learn*. While much of the report centered on student learning, the Committee on Developments in the Science of Learning made specific recommendations on how teachers could be supported in their transition from novice to expert. We use their four-part structure—learner-centered, knowledge-centered, assessment-centered, and community-centered environments—to describe our recommendations for supporting new teachers in diversity-rich schools.

### Learner-Centered Environments

We are defining the "learner" as the novice teacher who can benefit from experiences tailored to meet his or her needs. The literature is clear that reduced workload and opportunities for observation and partnering with peers have a positive impact (Johnson & Birkeland, 2003; Schlechty & Whitford, 1989). Gilbert (2005) surveyed hundreds of new teachers in six Georgia districts and asked them what they needed most. Not surprisingly, four of the top five responses involved opportunities to observe and to work with other teachers. District and school administrators can make these opportunities come to fruition. For example, California's Beginning Teacher Support and Assessment (BTSA) program is a state-sponsored, 2-year induction program administered locally by districts and consortiums. A required part of the program is that novice teachers be released from teaching duties to observe other teachers. In addition, the school is provided the funding to hire substitute teachers while novices are observing their peers.

Although a reduced teaching load is rarely possible due to the fiscal impact on the school, the administrator can choose to place the novice teacher in the best environment possible. Too often, we have witnessed placement of new teachers (who are the least capable due to inexperience) in the most difficult classrooms in the school. These classes are often cobbled together at the last moment to accommodate unanticipated enrollment (Stoko et al., 2007). Even worse, we have seen principals ask other teachers to nominate students for the new class. What results is not surprising—the students perceived as the most problematic due to academic or behavioral concerns become members of the novice teacher's class. In addition, they receive the leftover materials and furniture, often castoffs from other teachers in the grade level or department. Is it any wonder that so many fail? Responsible administrators must recognize this as intolerable and take the lead in making sure that novice teachers receive the best possible class rosters that are constructed with care, and that they have adequate supplies and materials. Expert teachers can manage with less, if they must; novice teachers do not have the resiliency to "make do."

## Knowledge-Centered Environments

Critics of induction programs have called for improvement in the content of what is offered (Alliance for Excellent Education, 2004; Feiman-Nemser & Parker, 1990; National Research Council, 2000). Although many novice teachers and induction program personnel identify classroom management strategies as an important topic, research evidence suggests that engagement and motivation are more effective than knowing a trick to get students to line up for lunch. The work of Guthrie and Wigfield and (2000) on engagement and motivation in reading is instructive for new teachers. In particular, they note that the following conditions are necessary to achieve a meaningful level of learner engagement:

- Setting learner and knowledge goals.
- Promoting real-world interactions.
- Providing autonomous support.
- Offering interesting texts for instruction.
- Instruction on the use of reading comprehension strategies.
- Fostering collaboration among students.
- Giving praise and rewards.
- Showing students their progress through evaluation.
- Caring about students.

Content knowledge can be built effectively through collaboration with university personnel. Because novice teachers are recent graduates of university programs, they are already oriented to course experiences. In addition, local university personnel often have an existing relationship with districts, schools, and the new teachers. Innovative programs offered in partnership with a university program provide continued opportunities for teachers to gain content-area and pedagogical knowledge (Frey, 2001, 2002; Kelley, 2004; Quartz & the TEP Research Group, 2003). For example, the Riverside, Inyo, Mono, San Bernardino County Beginning Teacher Support and Assessment (RIMS-BTSA) program, a partnership between the University of California–Riverside, California State University–Riverside, and the County Office of Education in Riverside and San Bernardino counties, serves over 1,400 novice teachers each year.

Partnerships can be locally driven as well. For example, San Diego State University and San Diego Unified School District collaborated on an induction course focused on the instructional needs of English language learners. All new teachers now complete this course as part of their induction program. The course is designed to build on the teachers' experience in their preservice program and to provide them with additional information and instructional routines while they are in the classroom. The course focuses on interactions that teachers can facilitate in their classrooms to ensure that students use academic language while they learn content (Fisher, Rothenberg, & Frey, 2008).

### Assessment-Centered Environments

Feedback through mentoring is an essential part of teacher development. Yost's (2006) study of 17 new teachers revealed that those who participated in induction programs with mentoring had the most positive experiences. A study of 217 first- and second-year teachers identified principal leadership and school climate as the leading factors in their reasons for returning (Wynn, Carboni, & Patall, 2007). Gilbert's (2005) survey found that new teachers were eager to be observed by their mentors and to receive feedback. Novice teachers find it most helpful when they are paired with mentors who teach the same subject and have schedules that allow them to work and plan together (Johnson & Birkeland, 2003). Induction programs should prioritize mentoring relationships that are geographically (ideally, in the same building) convenient and harmonious in terms of content. These partnerships can then blossom as teachers are able to observe one another and even plan together.

Observation can be challenging for the mentor, especially because most induction programs expressly avoid any evaluative relationship. However, this does not preclude coaching practices as a useful source of feedback for the novice. Gottesman (2000) describes an effective nonevaluative coaching system that we have adapted for use with novice teachers:

- *Previsit*: Mentor and novice meet before the visit to plan the observation and determine the focus and objectives for the visit.
- *Visit*: The mentor collects information requested by the novice teacher.
- *Review of notes*: The mentor reviews the information collected and creates a plan for discussion.
- *Postvisit*: The mentor and novice teacher meet, with the observed teacher first reviewing the observation notes. They then discuss what was observed, with the mentor fostering reflective conversation on the part of the novice teacher.
- *Planning the next visit*: The novice teacher and mentor plan the next observation in the mentor's classroom.

The reciprocal relationship between mentor and novice teacher that emerges during observations in each other's classroom has the potential to cultivate a mutually beneficial partnership. In addition, these observations allow the novice teacher to become more comfortable with having others in his or her classroom. And over time, this will change the culture of schools.

## Community-Centered Environments

Promising results are emerging from the Center X Urban Teaching Program at the University of California, Los Angeles (Quartz & the TEP Research Group, 2003). This program, in existence now for more than a decade, combines a teacher preparation credential, master's degree program, and community-based experiences that follow new teachers through their induction years. Center X stresses a critical theory approach that asks teachers to question and challenge assumptions about power, gender, and class. A study of 233 graduates of the program 5 years later found that they remained in education at rates that exceeded the national average (70 vs. 61%). The research reported thus far suggests three themes about why teachers stayed:

- Learning to build on the strengths of urban communities.
- Becoming a change agent.
- Joining a profession (Quartz & the TEP Research Group, 2003, pp. 105–107).

The Center X focus on social justice in urban schools mirrors a critical literacy stance that is essential for teachers in urban schools to adopt as they advocate on behalf of their learners. In particular, critical literacy invites learners to

- Understand that no text is neutral.
- Consider the author's purpose.
- Challenge representations of power, gender, and class.
- Question whose story is not told.
- Take action (Tasmania Department of Education, 2006).

Existing induction programs can incorporate critical literacy by sponsoring book clubs that challenge readers to reconsider the ways in which communities, including the ones in which they teach, are represented (Kooy, 2006). For example, novice teachers can examine picture books and books written for adult audiences to discuss the perspectives of characters and communities not commonly represented in literature. This can lead to powerful conversations about how teachers can and should represent the voices of outsiders in their own classrooms, and whether the community is fairly portrayed in the materials and discourse of their learning environments. Figure 20.1 contains a list of books that might be useful in a critical literacy approach to induction.

| Questioning the commonplace | Gender roles | *Little Women* (Alcott, 2004)<br>*Sisterhood of the Traveling Pants* (Brashares, 2001)<br>*Oliver Button is A Sissy* (DePaola, 1979)<br>*The Paper-bag Princess* (Munsch, 1988)<br>*Prince Cinders* (Cole, 1997)<br>*The First Part Last* (Johnson, 2004) |
| | Power and class | *Something Beautiful* (Wyeth, 2002)<br>*A Day's Work* (Bunting, 1997)<br>*The Hundred Dresses* (Estes, 2004)<br>*When My Name Was Keoko* (Park, 2002) |
| Questioning the author | Understanding the author's motives and perspectives | *The Tequila Worm* (Canales, 2005)<br>*House on Mango Street* (Cisneros, 1991)<br>*The Pact* (Davis, 2006)<br>*Heaven* (Johnson, 2000)<br>*The Name Jar* (Choi, 2003) |
| Seeking alternative perspectives | Listening to the voices of those not represented | *We Were There, Too!* (Hoose, 2001)<br>*A Long Way Gone* (Beah, 2007)<br>*The Spirit Catches You and You Fall Down* (Fadiman, 1998)<br>*Send in the Idiots* (Nazeer, 2006) |
| Taking action for social justice | In the world | *Three Cups of Tea* (Mortenson, 2007)<br>*Mountains Beyond Mountains* (Kidder, 2004) |
| | In the classroom and community | *I Am a Pencil* (Swope, 2004)<br>*True Notebooks* (Salzman, 2003)<br>*Transparent* (Beam, 2008)<br>*Among Schoolchildren* (Kidder, 1989)<br>*Letters to a Young Teacher* (Kozol, 2007) |

**FIGURE 20.1.** Critical literacy books for teachers.

By offering this list, we do not mean to limit the range of what is read and discussed to match the demographics of the school community. The point of a critical literacy stance is that it broadens the vision of the learner. Lisa Delpit said, "I have described what I want for my child as an academic house built on a strong foundation of self-knowledge but one with many windows and doors that look out on the rest of the world" (2006, p. 229). We want the same for our teachers in diversity-rich schools. After all, they are the ones who will open those doors and windows to a generation of children.

## IMPLICATIONS FOR FUTURE RESEARCH

Induction programs have gained popularity in the last decade, and a majority of new teachers now participate in some sort of induction experience during the first years of their careers. However, many questions remain unanswered when it comes to induction experiences for novice teachers in diversity-rich urban schools:

- What experiences are necessary for novice teachers to become culturally responsive teachers?
- What do mentors need to know and do to support these novice teachers?
- How can choice be incorporated into induction programs?
- What are the characteristics of effective induction programs for urban teachers?
- In what ways can administrators ensure that novice teachers receive the best possible start, without compromising the fiscal and operational health of the organization?
- How can supports be developed for novice teachers in crisis?

## Concluding Remarks

Induction has moved from orientations centered on procedures and materials, often conducted in one or two face-to-face meetings, to multidimensional experiences designed to occur over 1–2 years. In many states and districts, the induction process is a requirement for licensure. These programs commonly include workshops or course work and a mentoring relationship with an experienced teacher. Induction is seen as a positive step in ensuring that novice teachers remain in the profession beyond the first 5 years of their careers.

Induction is problematic, however, in that it is rarely differentiated for teachers in diversity-rich schools. Although reflective practice is stressed, content is usually not tailored to meet the unique needs of teachers working in communities challenged by economic and social hardships. In addition, induction programs may not stress the ways in which novice teachers can amplify the experiences of their students as they foster learning. The evidence points to several characteristics of effective induction programs: mentors who are knowledgeable in the grade level or content and are available; common planning time to collaborate with peers; reduced workload; and ample opportunities to observe peers. Induction programs that look to the school community first—the place where expertise about diversity-rich schools resides—will successfully mentor the new generation of teachers our students deserve.

## References

Alliance for Excellent Education. (2004). *Tapping the potential: Retaining and developing high-quality new teachers.* Washington, DC: Author.

Bergeron, B. S. (2008). Enacting a culturally responsive curriculum in a novice teacher's classroom: Encountering disequilibrium. *Urban Education, 43*(1), 4–28.

Berliner, D. C. (1994). Expertise: the wonder of exemplary performances. In J. N. Mangieri & C. C. Block (Eds.), *Creating powerful thinking in teachers and students: Diverse perspectives* (pp. 161–186). Ft. Worth, TX: Holt, Rinehart & Winston.

Borko, H. (1986). Clinical teacher education: The induction years. In J. V. Hoffman & S. A. Edwards (Eds.), *Reality and reform in clinical teacher education* (pp. 45–63). New York: Random House.

Bransford, J. D., & Schwartz, D. L. (1999). Rethinking transfer: A simple proposal with multiple implications. *Review of Research in Education, 24,* 66–100.

Burnham, R. M. (1976). Instructional supervision: Past, present, and future perspectives. *Theory Into Practice, 15*(4), 301–305.

Cable, P. E. (1959). The need for orienting new teachers. *Peabody Journal of Education, 37*(2), 102–105.

Chi, M. T. H., Glaser, R., & Farr, M. J. (1988). *The nature of expertise.* Hillsdale, NJ: Erlbaum.

Cochran-Smith, M. (2006). *Stayers, leavers, lovers, and dreamers: Why people teach and why they stay.* New York: Bank Street College of Education.

Council of the Great City Schools. (2000). *The urban teacher challenge: Teacher demand and supply in the great city schools.* Belmont, MA: Recruiting New Teachers/Urban Teacher Collaborative.

Crocco, M. S., & Costigan, A. T. (2007). The narrowing of curriculum and pedagogy in the age of accountability: Urban educators speak out. *Urban Education, 42,* 512–535.

Dall'Alba, G., & Sandberg, J. (2006). Unveiling professional development: A critical review of stage models. *Review of Educational Research, 76,* 383–412.

Delpit, L. (2006). Lessons from teachers. *Journal of Teacher Education, 57*(3), 220–231.

Feiman-Nemser, S., & Parker, M. B. (1990). Making subject matter part of the conversation in learning to teach. *Journal of Teacher Education, 41*(3), 32–43.

Fideler, E., & Haselkorn, D. (1999). *Learning the ropes: Urban teacher induction programs and practices in the United States.* Belmont, MA: Recruiting New Teachers.

Fisher, D., Rothenberg, C., & Frey, N. (2008). *Developing academic discourse: Strategies for teaching English learners the language.* Alexandria, VA: Association for Supervision and Curriculum Development.

Frey, N. (2001). We grow our own. *California English, 6*(4), 12–13.

Frey, N. (2002). Literacy achievement in an urban middle-level professional development school: A learning community at work. *Reading Improvement, 39*(1), 3–13.

Gehrke, N. J. (1988). On preserving the essence of mentoring as one form of teacher leadership. *Journal of Teacher Education, 39*(1), 43–45.

Gilbert, L. (2005). What helps beginning teachers? *Educational Leadership, 62*(8), 36–39.

Gottesman, B. (2000). *Peer coaching for educators* (2nd ed.). Lanham, MD: Scarecrow.

Guarino, C. M., Santibañez, L., & Daley, G. A. (2006). Teacher recruitment and retention: A review of the recent empirical evidence. *Review of Educational Research, 76,* 173–208.

Guthrie, J. T., & Wigfield, A. (2000). Engagement and motivation in reading. In M. L. Kamil, P. B. Mosenthal, P. D. Pearson, & R. Barr (Eds.), *Handbook of reading research* (Vol. III, pp. 403–424). Mahwah, NJ: Erlbaum.

Hunt, D. (1967). Teacher induction: A key to excellence. *NASSP Bulletin, 52*(328), 68–78.

Ingersoll, R. M. (2002). The teacher shortage: A case of wrong diagnosis and wrong prescription. *NASSP Bulletin, 86*(631), 16–31.

Ingersoll, R. M., & Smith, T. M. (2004). Do teacher induction and mentoring matter? *NASSP Bulletin, 88*(638), 28–40.

Johnson, L. W. (1947). County in-service programs in California. *Educational Research Bulletin, 26*(6), 156–160, 168.

Johnson, S. M., & Birkeland, S. E. (2003). Pursuing a "sense of success": New teachers explain their career decisions. *American Educational Research Journal, 40,* 581–617.

Joyce, B., & Showers, B. (2002). *Student achievement through staff development* (3rd ed.). Alexandria, VA: Association for Supervision and Curriculum Development.

Kelley, L. M. (2004). Why induction matters. *Journal of Teacher Education, 55*(5), 438–448.

Kersaint, G., Lewis, J., Potter, R., & Meisels, G. (2007). Why teachers leave: Factors that influence retention and resignation. *Teaching and Teacher Education, 23,* 775–794.

Kirby, S., Berends, M., & Naftel, S. (1999). Supply and demand of minority teachers in Texas: Problems and prospects. *Educational Evaluation and Policy Analysis, 21,* 47–66.

Kooy, M. (2006). The telling stories of novice teachers: Constructing teacher knowledge in book clubs. *Teaching and Teacher Education, 22,* 661–674.

Lajoie, S. P. (2003). Transitions and trajectories for studies of expertise. *Educational Researcher, 32*(8), 21–25.

Lankford, H., Loeb, S., & Wyckoff, J. (2002). Teacher sorting and the plight of urban schools. *Educational Evaluation and Policy Analysis, 24,* 37–62.

Levine, M. (1986). Excellence in education: Lessons from America's best-run companies and schools. *Peabody Journal of Education, 63*(2), 150–186.

Lovette, O. K. (1996). From the trenches: First year teacher comments and perspectives. *College Student Journal, 30,* 302–306.

Marzano, R. J., Marzano, J. S., & Pickering, D. J. (2003). *Classroom management that works: Research-based strategies that work.* Alexandria, VA: Association for Supervision and Curriculum Development.

National Center for Educational Statistics. (2004). *Teacher attrition and mobility.* U.S. Department of Education.

National Commission on Teaching and America's Future. (2005). *No dream denied: A pledge to America's children.* Washington, DC: Author.

National Research Council. (2000). Teacher learning. In J. D. Bransford, A. L. Brown, & R. R. Cocking (Eds.), *How people learn: Brain, mind, experience, and school* (pp. 190–205). Washington, DC: National Academy Press.

Ondrich, J., Pas, E., & Yinger, J. (2008). The determinants of teacher attrition in upstate New York. *Public Finance Review, 36*(1), 112–144.

Podgursky, M., Monroe, R., & Watson, D. (2004). The academic quality of public school teachers: An analysis of entry and exit behavior. *Economics of Education Review, 23,* 507–518.

Quartz, K. H., & the TEP Research Group. (2003). "Too angry to leave": Supporting new teachers' commitment to transform urban schools. *Journal of Teacher Education, 54*(2), 99–111.

Rosenholtz, S. J. (1986). Career ladders and merit pay: Capricious fads or fundamental reforms? *Elementary School Journal, 86,* 512–529.

Schlechty, P. C., & Whitford, B. L. (1989). Systemic perspectives on beginning teacher programs. *Elementary School Journal, 89,* 440–449.

Seidl, B. (2007). Working with communities to explore and personalize culturally relevant pedagogies. *Journal of Teacher Education, 58,* 168–183.

Smith, D. L., & Smith, B. J. (2006). Perceptions of violence: The views of teachers who left. *High School Journal, 89*(3), 34–42.

Sternberg, R. J., & Horvath, J. A. (1995). A prototype view of expert teaching. *Educational Researcher, 24*(6), 9–17.

Stinebrickner, T. R. (2001). Compensation policies and teacher decisions. *International Economic Review, 42,* 751–779.

Stoko, E. M., Ingram, R., & Beaty-O'Ferrall, M. E. (2007). Promising strategies for attracting and retaining successful urban teachers. *Urban Education, 42,* 30–51.

Tasmania Department of Education. (2006). *English learning area: Critical literacy.* Retrieved December 30, 2007, from *www.fp.education.tas.gov.au/english/critlit.htm.*

Weld, J. (1998). Attracting and retaining high-quality professionals in science education. *Phi Delta Kappan, 79,* 536–539.

Wynn, S. R., Carboni, L. W., & Patall, E. A. (2007). Beginning teachers' perceptions of mentoring, climate, and leadership: Promoting retention through a learning communities perspective. *Leadership and Policies in Schools, 6*(3), 209–229.

Yost, D. S. (2006). Reflection and self-efficacy: Enhancing the retention of qualified teachers from a teacher education perspective. *Teacher Education Quarterly, 33*(4), 59–76.

Zeichner, K., Grant, C., Gay, G., Gillette, M., Valli, L., & Villegas, A. M. (1998). A research-informed vision of good practice in multicultural teacher education: Design principles. *Theory Into Practice, 37,* 163–211.

# CHAPTER 21

# Professional Development

## *Continuing to Understand How to Teach Children from Diverse Backgrounds*

### MARGARITA CALDERÓN

P rofessional development, or staff development, particularly as it relates to teachers with English language learners (ELLs), is exiguous. After extensive reviews of the literature, the National Literacy Panel for Language-Minority Children and Youth found only five studies on professional development that dealt with teachers working with ELLs. From these studies, only two used student outcomes, along with classroom observation protocols and interviews with teachers, to measure the effectiveness of the professional development models. The others relied mainly on teacher self-reporting (August & Shanahan, 2006). The lack of scientific research on professional development has had mixed influence on teacher practice and questionable impact on outcomes for students in general, but for ELLs in particular. This chapter, besides a review, presents a comprehensive program of professional development that has shown a positive impact on the language, literacy, and domain knowledge development of ELLs. In this chapter we discuss:

- The role of professional development in some cases shaping academic achievement and how in others it perpetuates the achievement gap between white Anglo students and ELLs.
- Research on professional development for teachers with ELLs and illustrative cases of ongoing empirical studies.
- Implications for professional development designs for different cohorts of teachers that interact with ELLs in a school, and ways of monitoring teacher quality and measuring the teacher's impact on students.

## The Role of Professional Development
## and Academic Achievement for ELLs

The nation's secondary schools have become increasingly concerned with the need to reduce dropout rates and improve all students' academic achievement. Closing the academic achievement gap between minority students and white students is also a requirement of the No Child Left Behind Act of 2001 (NCLB). Notwithstanding, NCLB has brought more attention to language-minority students. Schools must demonstrate that they are achieving adequate yearly progress (AYP) with ELLs to avoid sanctions. Unfortunately, the investment in quality professional development to build teacher capacity has not been adequate, and some school districts have scurried to find short-term solutions or to purchase materials that reduce English instruction to the lowest levels of language and literacy proficiency.

After decades of politics on bilingual instruction and myths about teaching ELLs, the nation is confronted with an achievement gap between white Anglo students and Latino students that will not close. This gap widens as students get older. Adolescent Latino and other minority students have high dropout rates. Eighty-nine percent of Hispanic middle and high school students read below grade level (National Center for Education Statistics, 2005). From a recent analysis of data collected by the Office of Civil Rights (2006), National Center for Education Statistics (2005), and the National Clearinghouse for English Language Learners, Tienda (2007) found the shockingly shameful fact that *80–91% of ELLs in middle and high school were born in the United States—that is, they are second- or third-generation immigrants—and have been in United States schools since kindergarten.* Do these figures imply that 80–91% of the achievement gap has been created by the way we prepare our teachers to work with ELLs? Are the long-term ELLs in middle and high schools the result of the professional development practices in school districts across the country? According to the Panel on Adolescent ELL Literacy, these high populations of long-term ELLs are in most states and in most schools (Short & Fitzsimmons, 2007).

Literacy development is a particular problem for the ELLs who enter the educational system in middle and high school. These students have to master in fewer years complex content, along with the English language; different sets of reading comprehension skills to match the U.S. assessments; and the structures of U.S. schools. They must thereby perform double the work of native speakers to keep up, and at the same time be accountable for AYP (Short & Fitzsimmons, 2007). Unfortunately, they are entering middle and high schools in which literacy instruction is not provided in the content areas. They are usually placed in classes with secondary teachers who are not trained to teach basic literacy and language skills to adolescents (Rueda & García, 2001).

About 9–20% of older ELL newcomers or refugees who have been in the United States less than 2 years are Students with Interrupted Formal Education (SIFE), which New York State defines as

Students with Interrupted Formal Education who come from a home in which a language other than English is spoken or are immigrant students and enter a US school after grade 2: have had at least two years less schooling than their peers; function at least two years below expected grade level in reading and mathematics; and may be pre-literate in their first language. (New York City Department of Education, 2007).

Current studies conducted in various states (Calderón, 2007b) suggest that the definition of SIFE include many of the long-term ELLs who have been in U.S. schools since kindergarten or early elementary grades, because they have also had interrupted formal education in U.S. schools due to unsystematic instruction and ineffective instructional programs. The following are some of the reasons we have collected from the long-term ELLs we interviewed:

- They attended kindergarten in English and afterward were placed in a bilingual program in first and second grade, then were transitioned into English in the third grade.
- They attended preschool in English, kindergarten in Spanish, then all subsequent years in English.
- They received literacy instruction in their primary language from kindergarten to third grade, but only 30 minutes of oral English each year. They were transitioned into mainstream English in the fourth grade and fell behind all other students in that class;
- They received instruction in both languages until the fifth grade, but only in language arts, and could not keep up with math, science, and social studies in English.
- Their parents signed waivers so they would be placed in English-only programs.
- They have attended U.S. schools since kindergarten but have language and literacy gaps due to shifts between reading approaches (e.g., mostly phonics or no phonics, or only the teacher read to them because they couldn't read; or they were told to read silently without explicit instruction in reading).
- They attended school in one location for a few months, then moved to another location for a few months, with some weeks in between these changes in which they did not attend school.

As we shared the students' views with teachers, their replies echoed their beliefs about their students and their professional preparation:

- From a fourth-grade teacher: "It takes 5–7 years to learn English and I feel my students still have 3 years to catch up."
- From a second-grade teacher: "I don't have to teach reading in English, only in their primary language. Reading skills transfer automatically."
- From a seventh-grade teacher: "ELL middle and high school students who

are struggling readers only need phonics to keep up with their content courses."

The studies reviewed by the National Literacy Panel for Language-Minority Children and Youth did not find evidence that it has to take 5–7 years to become proficient in English. There was only evidence that it took 3 to 4 years, when schools provided systematic quality instruction. Nevertheless, there seems to be a pervasive belief that it takes 5–7 years to learn English. When schools espouse this thinking, the tendency is to set low expectations for students at each grade level. Students at such schools go unchallenged from year to year and sometimes ignored, because, as one teacher stated, "They haven't been in the program 7 years and it's OK if they are not yet proficient in English." When the seventh year is up, the students are blamed for not achieving at grade level. They carry the label of ELL or limited English proficient (LEP) onto secondary schools. This might be one of the reasons for the eighth-grade slump and why so many ELLs drop out of school.

K–12 interventions, according to Gándara (2006), almost always focus on reforming entire schools that enroll large numbers of poor and ethnic/minority students rather than on raising the performance of particular groups of students. She states that data from the Early Childhood Longitudinal Survey illustrate the achievement gap in reading and math at the beginning of kindergarten that exists between Latino and white children. This gap persists into high school. Strengthening the instructional skills of every teacher might begin to address this critical issue. Long-term, preliterate, and low-literate adolescents need teachers who can combine language, reading, and writing skills with subject matter instruction to address what they missed in their K–5 education. This combination calls for all teacher preparation institutions and professional development programs to be proactive in learning new ways of integrating skills and knowledge to accelerate student academic learning. According to the Carnegie Panel on Adolescent ELL Literacy, without reading comprehension, students cannot learn math, science, social studies, and literature.

## QUALITY TEACHING MAKES A DIFFERENCE

Highly qualified teachers can have an impact on student achievement (August & Shanahan, 2006; Timperley & Alton-Lee, 2008) regardless of students' educational and language background. Teacher quality is the most critical factor in improving student performance (Darling-Hammond, 2000). NCLB requires schools to recruit and retain "highly qualified teachers in core subject areas" and to show annual progress for all students. Yet most teachers graduating from teacher education programs are not highly qualified to teach math, science, social studies, and language arts to ELLs. Even though teachers may hold certification specific to ELL instruction, the recent study by EdSource (2007) found that for California teachers who obtain a Crosscultural Language and Academic Development (CLAD) or Bilingual Crosscultural Language and Academic Development (BCLAD) certificate and are trained in English language development (ELD), teacher credentials do not correlate with student higher scores.

Even most staff development programs in vogue today have failed to produce the level of quality demanded by the ELL challenge in K–12 schools. Research on how professional development programs integrate language, literacy, and subject matter for better results has been lacking. For too long, language specialists have ignored the reading and content domains. Reading specialists have isolated themselves from second language practices and upper-grade subject matter reading. High school math, science, and social studies teachers are basically concerned with "covering their subject area," and believe that language and reading do not play a pivotal role in student comprehension and learning of the content they are trying to teach. For the most part, the researchers and content-area university professors in each of these fields have methodically reflected these beliefs. Until teacher preparation programs treat these domains as a triumvirate, it will be very difficult to find teachers with the skills to address language, literacy, and content.

In examining links between professional development and student performance, the National Literacy Panel recommends that other factors should be considered, including school and district policies that influence learning (e.g., class size, allocation of teachers to classrooms, and required curricular materials). For example, there are trends in schools that require specific schedules for teaching literacy components. Most of these programs were developed for mainstream students, and teachers are not allowed to modify them to fit the necessary adaptations to teach ELLs. Larger-scale studies employing more complex designs to examine the relationship between professional development for teachers and the progress of their language-minority students have not been conducted (August et al., 2007).

August and Calderón (2006) found that the attributes of professional development deemed important for all teachers, as described by the American Educational Research Association (2005), were affirmed as important in the five professional development studies conducted in second-language learning contexts. The effective professional development consisted of ongoing meetings between teachers and those providing the professional development, opportunities for classroom practice coupled with mentoring and coaching, and teacher learning communities. The teacher education was always focused on specific strategies for improving instruction for language-minority students, the theory that informs strategies, and applications of the strategies in classrooms, such as improving how teachers read aloud to young children (Hoffman, Roser, & Farest, 1988); combining direct and constructivist methods (Saunders & Goldenberg, 1996); teaching oral language, reading, and writing in different instructional contexts (Calderón & Marsh, 1988); improving early reading interventions (Haager & Windmueller, 2001); and introducing a literacy curriculum for students with learning disabilities (Ruiz, Rueda,

Figueroa, & Boothroyd, 1995). Furthermore, Calderón and Marsh (1988) high-lighted the importance of staff development that builds on theory, effective teacher craft, and close collaboration between researchers and teachers given the paucity of experimental research on literacy instruction for this group of students.

In addition, the studies suggest that to develop a coherent program of instruction for language-minority students, it is important to include all staff involved in their education (i.e., bilingual and English language specialists; learning disabilities specialists, if called for; and classroom teachers) in the same professional development efforts (Haager & Windmueller, 2001; Ruiz et al., 1995). Although this may be important for all students, it is especially important for language-minority students, who tend to be served by multiple school personnel. The studies suggest that "regardless of the specific research questions posed, it is best to think of professional development as including three outcomes: change in teachers' classroom practices, change in their beliefs and attitudes, and change in students' learning outcomes" (Guskey, 1986, cited in Ruiz et al., 1995, p. 622). However, they also suggest that change is not unidirectional. For example, although some researchers found that changing teachers' perceptions may be the first step in this process (Richardson, 1991, cited in Haager & Windmueller, 2001, pp. 247–248), changing instructional practices in ways that produce positive student outcomes can change teacher beliefs more readily (Calderón & Marsh, 1988).

In essence what this handful of studies suggests is that professional developers working with teachers of ELLs need to do the following:

- Integrate language development, reading comprehension skills, and domain knowledge in their designs.
- Build the content of the professional development on research-based instructional approaches, including the appropriate use and reliance on students' home language.
- Present the theories and research behind each instructional strategy, model each strategy, have teachers practice each at the training sessions, and integrate each strategy into their lessons.
- Work in close collaboration with teachers and researchers given the paucity of experimental research on literacy instruction for ELLs.

## AN ILLUSTRATIVE CASE OF TEACHER DEVELOPMENT PROGRAMS

Although NCLB requires that secondary school teachers be highly qualified in teaching core academic subjects, it does not emphasize the need for them to be able to teach reading, vocabulary, or writing, nor does it require that teachers have any training in working with adolescent ELLs (Short & Fitzsimmons, 2007). Nevertheless, one attempt in which all the teachers in each school, the literacy and content coaches and supervisors, and site administrators have a role and responsibility for ELLs is being studied in 43 middle and high schools in New York City.

Two professional development programs were designed for schools with a wide range of student populations: SIFE, special education ELLs, long-term ELLs, low-level readers, and average- and high-achieving students who share these classrooms. These two programs, called Expediting Comprehension for English Language Learners (ExC-ELL; Calderón, 2007a) and Reading Instructional Goals for Older Readers (RIGOR; Calderón, 2007b), can be used side by side in the same school. These longitudinal studies are generating new insights into teacher preparation and impact on student achievement.

## Designs for Mainstream Science, Social Studies, Math, and Language Arts Teachers

The purpose of the ExC-ELL professional development longitudinal studies is to provide middle and high school teachers with empirically tested instructional strategies for language and literacy that cut across all subject areas. ExC-ELL is not a curriculum due to the surfeit of materials used throughout the country by middle and high school teachers. Instead it is a guide that builds new instructional repertoires for teachers. It builds teacher capacity.

There are three basic components of ExC-ELL:

1. A 10-component lesson template with an ever-expanding set of explicit instructional strategies designed to enhance, not replace, core instruction.
2. A professional development program to model the instructional strategies and routines that help ELLs master academic language, reading comprehension, and writing skills for subject-matter learning.
3. An ExC-ELL Observation Protocol that focuses on quality of instruction and student performance, while serving as a template and a tool used by
   - Teachers to design/develop their lessons.
   - Teachers for self-reflection.
   - Teachers to observe and document student performance.
   - Principals and supervisors to observe and coach teachers.
   - Coaches to give concrete feedback to teachers.
   - Researchers to collect data on teacher and student growth and quality of implementation.

A key feature of the implementation and sustainability of the model has been the participation of middle and high school teachers of math, science, social studies, and language arts, along with their literacy coaches, content coaches, and school- and district-level administrators. These schools have relatively recent newcomers, long-term ELLs, non-ELLs reading below grade level, as well as average- and high-achieving students in the participating classrooms. Table 21.1 outlines the key features of the ExC-ELL professional development program developed for these teachers.

**TABLE 21.1. Key Features of the ExC-ELL Professional Development Model**

- A comprehensive set of explicit instructional strategies and routines that have been empirically tested for their effectiveness with ELLs in K–12 classrooms (August & Shanahan, 2006; August et al., 2008; Calderón, 2007a).
- An integrated set of strategies: word knowledge, fluency and reading comprehension, discussion/discourse, grammar, spelling, and writing skills.
- An instructional repertoire linked to teachers' texts and daily lessons and students' learning goals/standards through a 10-component lesson template.
- Designed grouping of teachers—science, math, social studies, language arts, special education, reading specialists, and English as a second language (ESL) teachers—attend the 5-day session but work together by subject area during lesson application activities.
- Five-day institutes are offered in English and in Spanish to further enhance and promote primary language.
- Teachers taught to use the ExC-ELL Observation Protocol and its technology to conduct two self-assessments before they are observed by researchers and coaches. This helps them practice and better understand the purpose of the protocol.
- Literacy or content coaches participate in the professional development program, with additional sessions on how to coach teachers of ELLs.
- Principals and/or assistant principals who participate in the sessions on the ExC-ELL Observation Protocol and how to use its technology.
- Coaches and administrators shadow the researchers/trainers three to five times to practice using the ExC-ELL Observation Protocol, giving feedback to teachers, and getting feedback themselves.
- A requirement that schools institute Teacher Learning Communities (TLCs) as support structures for teachers to share, reflect, and ensure continuous instructional improvement.
- Teacher opportunities to present the successful strategies they are implementing in their classrooms at workshops for other schools and at conferences.
- Teacher opportunities to coauthor articles, chapters, and manuals as they engage in the professional development.

Students in the experimental groups are consistently outperforming control cohorts (Calderón, 2007a, 2007c). Moreover, the schools made AYP targets and improved dramatically in their annual measurable achievement objectives (AMAOs). The experimental schools in New York received an "A" on their report card based on Mayor Bloomberg's criteria for assigning grades: all-student improvement, attendance, and overall services to students.

## Designs for Intensive Interventions by ESL, Reading Specialist, Bilingual, and Special Education Teachers

New York City middle and high schools, just like most other schools in the country, face the daunting task of educating more and more preliterate and low-literate students at the secondary levels. These students are not only LEP but they also read at a K, first-grade, or second-grade level. They fall into the category of SIFE.

To address the specific needs of SIFE, a new professional development program was created, using many of the ExC-ELL strategies but adding the foundation of reading skills (e.g., phonemic awareness, phonics, fluency, grammar) and the basic and academic language that older students need to use on a daily basis in their subject-matter classrooms. This program is RIGOR, whose purpose is to provide more intensive instruction by ESL, reading specialist, special education, or intensive intervention teachers. It complements ExC-ELL. The professional development and assessment assistance to schools includes the following:

1. Onsite preassessment for accurate student placement
2. Initial teacher training plus follow-up coaching and observation
3. Coach and administrator training with the RIGOR Observation Protocol
4. Onsite postassessment to determine student gains
5. Data reports and recommendations for next steps

Schools are implementing RIGOR through various configurations: during language arts, ESL, and bilingual classes; before- or afterschool programs; and Saturday academies or pull-out or push-in sessions. The response to intervention strategy in special education schools is being implemented as a Tier 1 program for special education ELL (SE-ELL) students during ESL or bilingual language arts, and as Tiers 2 and 3 for students who need an extra intervention. Regardless of the implementation variation, what has accounted for the most student progress has been the fidelity and quality of program implementation. Support from the central district administration has been another major positive factor, as well as site administrators' support. Assistant principals placed in charge of implementing the program took on their role very seriously. They attended the professional development program, along with the teachers, and some of them actually taught the program.

The school district gave additional funds to teachers or assistant principal/ SIFE program coordinators who wanted to conduct classroom research on the implementation of RIGOR and other SIFE programs. This enabled teachers to conduct site-based research on SIFE and learn more about what works and how at their schools. It built a stronger capacity at the school and a mindset of confidence in addressing the tough issues that go along with building success for this most challenging cohort of students. Table 21.2 outlines the key features of the RIGOR curriculum materials and professional development that was developed for middle and high school teachers with ELLs or other students reading at K–3rd-grade levels.

## SUSTAINING MEANINGFUL INSTRUCTION AND TEACHER DEVELOPMENT

Most districts are putting in place formative assessments to predict and support student achievement for NCLB. But the instruments are blunt and often not well aligned. Even if they were, middle and high schools have limited capacity to use these data for differentiated, targeted instruction, especially in the skills areas of language and reading for ELLs. Schools need an approach in which teachers are

**TABLE 21.2. Key Features of the RIGOR Professional Development Model**

RIGOR is a professional development, and a language and literacy development curriculum for ESL, bilingual, and special education and reading specialists working with SIFE. Its purpose is to prepare teachers to do the following:

- Develop phonemic awareness and phonics skills from the beginning, so that preliterate or low-literate students can successfully break the code in English or in Spanish.
- Provide intensive vocabulary instruction and practice, thereby enabling students to increase quickly their repertoire of everyday words; complex and information-processing words; and content-specific words, phrases, functions, and syntax.
- Model and guide practice to monitor reading and comprehension strategies that support content-area reading comprehension.
- Model fluent reading and think-alouds for students to practice with peers, and independent audio- and technology-assisted reading experiences.
- Support grade-appropriate content-area science and social studies concepts and language.
- Model shared to independent writing activities that reinforce students' phonics, vocabulary, and content learning.
- Build students' academic oral language skills through classroom discussions, and small-group and partner activities. The 5-day institutes are offered in English and in Spanish.
- Include literacy coaches or content coaches in the professional development program, with additional sessions on how to coach teachers of ELLs.
- Include principals and/or assistant principals in the sessions on the ExC-ELL Observation Protocol and how to use its technology.
- Include coaches and administrators who shadow the researchers/trainers three to five times to practice using the ExC-ELL Observation Protocol, giving feedback to teachers, and getting feedback themselves.
- Incorporate TLCs as a support structure for teachers to share, reflect, and ensure continuous instructional improvement.
- Allow teachers to present at an annual conference on SIFE Solutions, at workshops for other schools, and at national conferences on the successful strategies they are implementing in their classrooms.
- Support selected teachers to conduct action research in their own classrooms, sponsored by the New York City Department of Education Office of English Language Learners.

given professional development and school administrators who lead in directions that encourage the kinds of differentiated instruction that all students need.

K–3 instruments have become powerful, but in grades 3–12 such instruments are still in an early state of development and adoption. The challenge is that at preadolescent and adolescent ages, the basic skills of reading begin to transition to the complex cognitive processes of understanding, communicating, and interpreting. Issues of motivation and interest become increasingly important as children become older. ELLs may be struggling in each of these areas—learning the basics of decoding in English, while dealing with subject matter that requires advanced skills of comprehension and self-expression, and doing so in an environment where they are often discouraged rather than motivated about language. Unless schools and teachers have tools to come to terms with these issues, it will be hard for them to make progress with this population (Calderón, 2007a).

The ongoing substudy on the ExC-ELL Observation Protocol (EOP®) is testing the use of technology as a quick and easy way of determining teacher instructional delivery and how it correlates to student progress. It was designed to provide a more comprehensive look at teacher workflow and how to maximize the amount of data they can gather about students, then to maximize the simplicity and clarity with which findings can provide feedback to teachers, while minimizing the impact on teacher time.

Teacher self-assessment and reflection is the point of departure and the ultimate goal. Teachers begin the school year by conducting two self-assessments with the EOP before anyone observes or coaches them. This gives them familiarity and confidence with the instrument and process. A Logitech digital pen (which teachers call "the Magic Pen"; see Figure 21.1) enables use of the familiar interface of paper and pen but captures quantitative responses, qualitative notes, and details of classroom organization—all time-stamped, then made available through almost immediate feedback.

For research purposes, the EOP provides a better understanding of the effects of the professional development intervention and how these effects vary according to factors such as (1) the quality of implementation and teacher support, (2) prior student performance, and (3) instructional methodologies. The EOP is also used by literacy coaches, content curriculum specialists, principals, and central district administrators who want to know more about how to observe and coach teachers of ELLs. Administrators and coaches were particularly interested in knowing how to observe and give feedback to teachers as they delivered their lessons, integrating reading, writing, and vocabulary development, along with their content.

The software generates six reports: Observation Summary Report, Observation Detail Report, Teacher Profile Summary Report, Component Implementation Summary Report, Vocabulary Usage Report, and Student Application Summary

**FIGURE 21.1.** Tools for capturing teacher impact on student learning.

Report. The EOP keeps the teacher's and each student's data. For example, the reading fluency data can be stored for individual students to keep running records on file. These records can then be downloaded from the digital pen into a computer. Each part of the protocol coincides with the lesson template (vocabulary, discourse, reading comprehension, cooperative learning activities, classroom management).

## IMPLICATIONS FOR STAFF DEVELOPMENT DESIGNS AND FOLLOW-UP TO ENSURE TRANSFER INTO THE CLASSROOM AND POSITIVE STUDENT OUTCOMES

In essence, what have we learned from reviews of the literature on professional development for teachers of ELLs and from ongoing studies? We can reiterate that features of outcome-linked professional learning pose a challenge to researchers and educators in charge of professional development, as Timperley and Alton-Lee cite in their 2008 review. We also concur that systematic responses are needed at all levels. What is important to bring to the forefront is that we must now add a focus to improve the academic achievement of the millions of students placed at risk by our own schools—long-term adolescent ELLs, SIFE, and all others struggling with language and literacy.

Professional development programs need to invest more time and resources into classroom implementation and follow-up systems that ensure transfer from the training site into the teacher's repertoire, and that monitor the impact on individual students. Professional development designers and/or buyers of professional development programs can analyze and predict the type of student outcomes by including tools to track that trajectory.

Figure 21.2 shows two trajectories that trace the routes schools may take with the outcomes they anticipate. After offering the same quality of workshops/institutes, schools can either invest in continuous support of their teachers or move on to another effort. Without systematic support, stagnation of teachers' skills, and unwillingness to adapt to new student populations become evident by the end of the year. But in schools where teachers are offered tools to self-assess and to gauge how each teaching event is or is not reaching all their students, their motivation and instructional growth are sustained. Teachers learn how to be responsive to all students, and as their learning trajectories rise, so do their students' achievement trajectories.

District and site administration personnel must share in the responsibility of monitoring teacher–student progress based on the type of professional development program they offer. What happens in the professional development training stays in the training, if no attention is paid immediately to classroom implementation and student progress. Figure 21.3 offers one example for tracing a component all the way through to the student outcome. Figure 21.4 offers a more micro-level

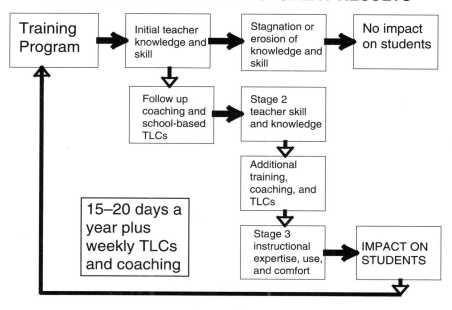

**FIGURE 21.2.** Trajectories of transfer.

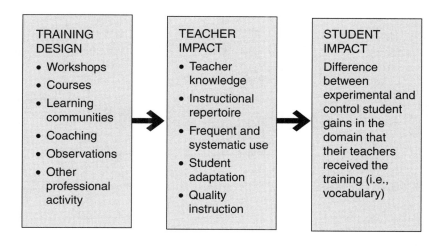

**FIGURE 21.3.** Tracing the relationship between training, teacher outcomes, and student outcomes.

**Example: Vocabulary**

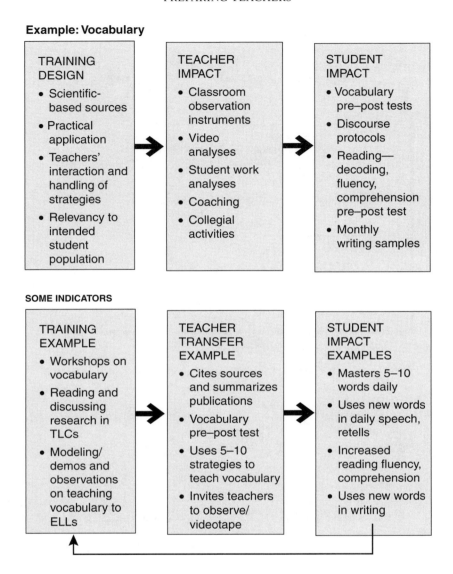

FIGURE 21.4. Measuring components of language and literacy development.

view of a training component, such as vocabulary, which can be traced by different measures and some indicators to monitor continuous learning by both teachers and students.

As school or district managers of professional development track this transfer, teachers are given the power and responsibility to track their learning and application in the classroom. Both systems come together during benchmark assessment periods in which all these data are triangulated through discussions on student progress.

## IMPLICATIONS FOR FUTURE RESEARCH

Teachers play a pivotal role in monitoring the teacher and student trajectory when they are given tools such as the EOP and take ownership of their impact on students. Although this tool is still in its infancy and still undergoing refinement, more such tools need to be developed. The triangulation of data with school, district, and state assessments is still cumbersome at best. Schools do not have the time or resources to conduct such analyses or to apply complex growth models. Future research on professional development needs to include practical systems for measuring the nature of teacher and student joint learning.

Because only five studies on scientifically based professional development for teachers of ELLs were found by the National Literacy Panel, extensive research is needed. Funding has been almost nonexistent for comprehensive studies on teacher development. Until more attention is given to the persons who trigger student outcomes, we cannot continue to expect better outcomes.

## CONCLUDING REMARKS

We have learned the following from both mainstream studies and recent studies on language-minority students' issues:

1. Good teaching makes a difference.
2. Purposeful professional development improves student learning.
3. Adolescent ELLs and low-level readers rise to the challenge of learning language, literacy, and subject matter when teachers are prepared to integrate language, literacy, and domain knowledge.
4. SIFE and long-term ELLs need teachers and specialists in ESL, reading, special education, and bilingual education who can teach phonics, decoding, vocabulary, and reading comprehension, along with academic language and concepts.
5. SIFE and ELLs also need mainstream teachers who can build on language, reading, and writing skills in math, science, social studies, and language arts.
6. The field needs much more longitudinal, scientifically based research on teacher development.

Teachers want to continue to understand how to teach children of all ages from diverse backgrounds. They are always looking for ways to improve, but they rarely encounter school and district support systems such as those described in these case studies. Outcome-based professional development needs to be comprehensive, to include measures to assess the quality of the professional development being offered and the transfer into the teaching repertoire, and to assess the ongoing impact on ELLs. Outcome-based professional development needs to be intensive. It requires a specified time commitment by teachers working with other teachers, principals and assistant principals, coaches, and central administrators; investment of time and resources in assisting teachers; and policies by states, school districts, and the federal government that support all these efforts.

## REFERENCES

American Educational Research Association. (2005, Summer). Teaching teachers: Professional development to improve student achievement. *Research Points, 3,* 1–24.

August, D., Beck, I. L., Calderón, M., Francis, D. J., Lesaux, N. K., & Shanahan, T. (2008). Instruction and professional development. In D. August & T. Shanahan (Eds.), *Developing reading and writing in second-language learners: Lessons from the Report of the National Literacy Panel on Language-Minority Children and Youth* (pp. 131–150). Mahwah, NJ: Erlbaum.

August, D., & Calderón, M. (2006). Teacher beliefs and professional development. In D. August & T. Shanahan (Eds.), *Developing literacy in second-language learners: Report of the National Literacy Panel on Language-Minority Children and Youth* (pp. 555–564). Mahwah, NJ: Erlbaum.

August, D., & Shanahan, T. (Eds.). (2006). *Developing reading and writing in second-language learners: Lessons from the Report of the National Literacy Panel on Language-Minority Children and Youth.* New York: Routledge.

Calderón, M. (2007a). *Expediting comprehension for English language learners (ExC-ELL).* Report to the Carnegie Corporation of New York.

Calderón, M. (2007b). *Reading Instructional Goals for Older Readers (RIGOR): Reading series.* Pelham, NY: Benchmark Education.

Calderón, M. (2007c). *Results from the Reading Instructional Goals for Older Readers (RIGOR) intervention in 17 schools: Report to the New York City Department of Education Office of English Language Learners.* New York: New York City Department of Education Office of English Language Learners.

Calderón, M., & Marsh, D. (1988, Winter). Applying research on effective bilingual instruction in a multi-district inservice teacher training program. *National Association for Bilingual Education Journal, 12,* 133–152.

Darling-Hammond, L. (2000, January 1). Teacher quality and student achievement: A review of state policy evidence. *Education Policy Analysis Archives, 8*(1). Retrieved February 15, 2008, from *http://epaa.asu.edu/epaa/v8n1*

EdSource. (2007, September). *Similar English learner students, different results: Why do some schools do better?* Mountain View, CA: Author.

Gándara, P. (2006). Strengthening the pipeline. *ETS Policy Notes: Latino Achievement in the Sciences, Technology, Engineering and Mathematics, 14*(2), 3–6.

Gitomer, D. H. (2007). *Teacher quality in a changing policy landscape: Improvements in the teacher pool.* Princeton, NJ: Educational Testing Service.

Haager, D., & Windmueller, M. P. (2001). Early reading approach for English language learners at-risk for learning disabilities: Student and teacher outcomes in an urban school. *Learning Disability Quarterly, 24,* 235–249.

Hoffman, J. V., Roser, N. L., & Farest, C. (1988). Literature-sharing strategies in classrooms serving students from economically disadvantaged and language different home environments. *Yearbook of the National Reading Conference, 37,* 331–337.

National Center for Education Statistics. (2005). *The condition of education 2005.* Washington, DC: U.S. Department of Education.

New York City Department of Education Office of English Language Learners. (2007, Summer). *New York City's English language learners: Demographics and performance.* New York: Author.

Office of Civil Rights. (2006). *Civil right data collection.* Available at *oerdata.ed.gov/ocer2006rv30/wdsdata.html.*

Rueda, R., & García, G. (2001). *How do I teach reading to ELLs?: Ninth in a series: Teaching every child to read.* Ann Arbor, MI: Center for the Improvement of Early Reading Achievement.

Ruiz, N. T., Rueda, R., Figueroa, R. A., & Boothroyd, M. (1995). Bilingual special education teachers' shifting paradigms: Complex responses to educational reform. *Journal of Learning Disabilities, 28,* 622–635.

Saunders, W. M., & Goldenberg, C. (1996). Four primary teachers work to define constructivism and teacher-directed learning: Implications for teacher assessment. *Elementary School Journal, 97,* 139–161.

Short, D. J., & Fitzsimmons, S. (2007). *Double the work: Challenges and solutions to acquiring language and academic literacy for adolescent English language learners—a report to Carnegie Corporation of New York.* Washington, DC: Alliance for Excellent Education.

Tienda, M. (2007). Hispanic demographics and implications for schools [Keynote speech]. Washington, DC: Office of English Language Acquisition Summit.

Timperley, H., & Alton-Lee, A. (2008). Reframing teacher professional learning: An alternative policy approach to strengthening valued outcomes for diverse learners. In G. Kelly, A. Luke, & J. Green (Eds.), *Review of research in education* (328–369). Thousand Oaks, CA: Sage.

# Afterword

## From "Just a Teacher"
## to Justice in Teaching—
## Working in the Service of Education,
## the New Civil Right

ERIC J. COOPER

W riting an Afterword based on the excellence between the covers of this handbook is a daunting task. The challenge is to take the extensive research and rich programmatic threads among the pages, to use them and sustain their implementation. It is our hope to erect a bridge across theory, practice, and implementation—leading to what Malcolm Gladwell has called the "tipping point"—for the benefit of all of America's schoolchildren and youth, in particular, those students challenged by poverty, whom we have called "school dependent." Because of family challenges such as poverty, these students are solely dependent on the schools for successful learning and achievement. They must rely on the hearts, minds, and hands of educators to avoid blaming the victim, by recognizing that both the individual and the institutions called schools are responsible for improving the life trajectories of America's young, that they are not mutually exclusive, but two sides of the same coin, if you will.

The words in this volume speak of renewed belief, hope, determination, and confidence. As Walt Whitman has written: "One word can pour such a flood through the soul" (Cooper, in press). So must the reader of this volume come to embrace the words offered by the writers, and by extending them to the context of one's work and mission, frame in those words and actions the foundation of the American democracy—an educated and informed citizenry.

It has been written elsewhere that teachers are uniquely positioned to become the advocates and activists that students in urban, suburban, and rural communities need. Teachers and principals are for the most part trusted by students and parents. Armed with the knowledge and the strategies, broad and specific as they are, that accelerate learning in the classroom, teachers create connections between the school and home that erect partnerships between businesses, universities, policymakers, and politicians, and lead to sustained education reform, while improving and repairing shattered lives. And though education may not be guaranteed by the U.S. Constitution, it is often mentioned as a civil right, and as Jean Anyon (2005) writes in *Radical Possibilities: Public Policy, Urban Education, and a New Social Movement*, "can be located ideologically in the long and powerful tradition of [the American] civil rights [movement]" (p. 178).

For a long period of time during the 20th century, many influential African American leaders embraced the ideas of W. E. B. Du Bois, who called for educating the upper 10% of black Americans. By so doing he felt that these students would lead and bring others along with them. Sadly this has not happened. Students in urban school communities are dropping out at unprecedented rates—ranging from 40 to 70% in many cities and localities. Among African and Hispanic Americans, upwards of 30% of men who do not graduate from high school are in prison. Approximately 70% of black American children are born to unwed mothers. The data are frightening, especially when we consider that America will soon be projected by the Census Bureau to be a majority–minority country by 2042. How will we be able to remain competitive if we do not learn to educate all Americans in a manner that enables them to enter an institution of higher education if they so choose?

Education in America—the kind that is equitable, fulfilling, and meaningful—is in short supply for reasons that are legion, with well-documented results; the real ravages of the system are largely ignored. Despite this, the imperative remains: America's schoolchildren—all of them—deserve powerful classrooms, swirling with powerful ideas, orchestrated by powerful and empowered teachers, and supported by dynamic home–school partnerships, as well as community stakeholders.

The work in this handbook involves developing strategic interventions and policies; improving classroom instruction and schooling through professional development, based on a solid foundation of cognitive, sociocultural, and linguistic research and theories; as well as working to engage communities in conversations that enable parents, teachers, political leaders, stakeholders, and business and university leaders to reach a common ground, so that the future of America is built on hope, not despair.

Given the urgent need for education reform, it is popular today to declare that education policy should be "data driven." In writing this Afterword, I hold that policy should be driven by values and by vision informed by data. For example, the policy that America "doesn't give up on people" is not data driven; it is a statement of values. Policy should begin with values that are formed into a vision of how the world should be. Data should inform the development of policy that guides action, and plans to carry out the policy. Data must inform the "how" of our plans; values must shape the substance of our vision and our mission to make that vision real. Beliefs unite values and information.

It is quite obvious that every writer in this volume believes that virtually no child—which includes no black, brown, Asian, or Native American child—is so compromised by his or her family or community circumstances that he or she cannot be successful in school. I say "virtually" because some children have conditions that impair their ability to fulfill this goal, but they are fewer than the number of children institutionally classified in this way. Here, I am writing about the vast majority of our children.

As readers pour through and labor with the writings, research, and program applications, they struggle to blend the influence of the left brain with that of the right—understanding through neuroscience that the left sees the trees and the right, the forest. This is the challenge of reading, internalizing, and applying a volume such as the one that readers may have skimmed, perused, or are in the process of completing. They work through the millions of data sets the brain takes in over the course of a minute, while understanding that only 2% of the millions of concepts are processed consciously. As George Miller taught us years ago, the challenge of the brain is not storage but retrieval. So it will be for the readers, as it has been for me, in reading this Handbook.

How do we begin to group the information in ways that lead to real-world applications, while answering the challenge that educators face? The task is broad and the challenge of taking each suggestion from each chapter to scale is daunting. Yet, as educators, we are approximately 3.5 million strong—the same number as those who have honored America by joining the armed services. In essence, we represent an army of Americans, capable, if we join through coherent application, of truly changing the world. This will mean, however, that we learn, practice, and extend the research on the pages herein. This will mean that we recognize that teachers are, for many students, the last great hope. This means that we understand that the single most important in-school factor in terms of student achievement is the teacher. So, given our numbers and the moral high ground on which we work, why are successes not far more widespread?

A key to the answer to this question is the will to do the right thing. The often-cited statement of Ronald Edmonds offers one perspective on this fundamental question. In the book *Young, Gifted and Black* (Perry, Steele, & Hilliard, 2003), the late and sorely missed Asa Hilliard III, a professor at George State University and longtime friend of the National Urban Alliance for Effective Education (NUA), quoted Ronald Edmonds: "We can, whenever and wherever we wish, teach successfully all children whose education is of interest to us. Whether we do or do not do it depends in the final analysis on how we feel about the fact that we have not done so thus far." Edmonds often stressed that (in my words) the existence of one's success is proof that one can achieve success in all similar circumstances. He was asserting that the nation, states, school districts, schools, and educators—those at home and in the community—lack the will to bring the achievement distribution of black, brown, and impoverished children in line with the achievement distribution of white middle- and upper-class students.

Many years after the *Brown* decision, we must all recognize that not only are there no separate but equal tables, ultimately, there are no separate tables at all. The education of all children is "of interest" to all of us in the general sense that all in the American economy, policy, and society have a stake—an interest—in all children who grow into contributing members of these elements of America. To be indifferent to this is shortsighted, wasteful, and wrong in a society—one that is still shedding the burdens of pernicious practices and suffering the strains of private prejudices (from all directions) and is the keeper of the American dream held up by Dr. Martin Luther King, Jr., in his speech at the Lincoln Memorial on August 28, 1963. We need to hold on to his dream, both in our dreams and in our waking hours. The need to close the gap between the actual achievement and the potential of the learner is great, national, and urgent. It is also personal and practical. This is what I internalized in reading all the pages of this volume.

The shift of demographics in America to so-called minority–majority, as with school enrollments in which nonwhite students are the majority, should not give false comfort that power or success will follow. In our world, many growing economies and political systems are nonwhite, but they control their own infrastructures. We need look no further than the emerging Asian economies, such as India and China, much of Latin America, or the Middle East. And although the proportion of U.S. African American population is not rising above the 12–13% range held for some time, it is noted in one chapter that 1 out of 4 American children under the age of 6 is Hispanic.

The realities of family circumstances in America—more families with two wage earners; high proportions of Hispanic and African American children living with one parent, relative, or caregiver; and an acknowledgment that many African American and Hispanic American children are "school dependent" for their learning of both basic and advanced subject matter, skills, and behaviors that are advantageous in the world, do not shield families and communities from challenges to do more and to do better by their children. The world economy is changing rapidly, and those behind or beneath the curve of those changes will just lose more ground, unless we act on the genius that is America—our ability to absorb all citizens on "common ground" and toward the "common good."

To this end, educators and leaders must believe in the potential of their students—all their students—to achieve at levels that advance them to the next school grade, that tackle postsecondary education or a job that requires postsecondary literacy and critical thinking. This belief should apply whether a student desires to be an auto mechanic or a technology engineer. Educators must believe in their ability to engage and to educate their students, and in their ability to gain the professional knowledge and skills to do so. This is the purpose of this handbook. It is written to convey a knowledge base that can lift the achievement of all students. It is crafted so that the knowledge translates to a variety of classroom, school, and community circumstances.

Armed with this knowledge applied coherently across schools and throughout districts, communities must believe in the ability and willingness of their educators to engage and to educate all the students. The hope I write about here is a bridge between belief and action. We are sustained not by taking cover when times are hard or challenges are great, but by taking courage from both historical figures in our struggles and the innocent yet strong hopes of our children. Hope, however, is not a strategy that sustains; hope begets strategy. Determination is the express of belief and hope in action, and confidence must be rooted in educator competence and high expectations for all students.

This, then, is our challenge. All who read this book, all who share knowledge with their colleagues must come to embrace a comprehensive, cohesive, and coordinated effort that engages the many parts of a school, a school system, and the surrounding social–political–economic system: moving, as described by one writer, from novice to expert; embracing a voice of advocacy through expert positions that enable rather than disable the learner; implementing instructional, administrative, and organizational arrangements that best guide and nurture student and teacher alike; and finally seeking the "uncommon common ground" where one group or individual is not pitted against another. As the African proverb puts it so well: "If you want to go quickly, go alone, but if you want to go further, go together."

This, then, is our challenge. The research base is clear and focused. The landscape has been cleared sufficiently to recognize that teaching is that center of the combination of policies, programs, practices, and beliefs that lifts and accelerates student achievement. Educators are the professionals who craft and deliver that teaching. Their professional skills and professional behavior, their beliefs that undergird and guide that behavior, are targeted and fine-tuned by professional development activities, before and during their service. Because most of the teachers in classrooms over the coming 15–20 years are already teaching, in-service professional development delivered by universities, agencies, and membership groups has a great mission and is the binding agent for most reforms.

Yes, it is a truism that learning occurs one person at a time, for learning is within each of us. And school change takes place one classroom at a time, for our schools are organized so that the primary "unit of production" is the classroom. And teaching only improves one teacher at a time, for no public policy, outrage, or outcry can force teachers to do what they will not do, certainly not for as long as it will take for their student to overcome external deficiencies, to gather external supports, and to build internal strengths. Thus, progress must occur one teacher, one classroom, one student at a time. Yet there is nothing in this formulation or in nature that denies that this can take place simultaneously with many places and people. This combination of efforts is demanding, but it is doable and long overdue. The formulations in this handbook provide the markers and beacons that enable coherent and sustained education reform. *Si se puede*!

## REFERENCES

Anyon, J. (2005). *Radical possibilities: Public policy, urban education, and a new social movement*. New York: Routledge.

Cooper, E. J. (in press). Realities and responsibilities in the education village. In L. C. Tillman (Ed.), *The Sage handbook of African American education*. Thousand Oaks, CA: Sage.

Perry, T., Steele, C., & Hilliard, A. G. III. (2003). *Young, gifted, and black: Promoting high achievement among African-American students*. Boston: Beacon Press.

# Author Index

Abbott, R. D., 280
Abello, B., 368
Aber, J. L., 106
Abu-Rabia, S., 282
Adams, M., 295, 300, 308, 309, 315
Adams, M. J., 367
Adger, C., 138
Afflerbach, P., 266
Ageyev, V., 106
Al Otaiba, S., 2
Albers, P., 165
Alexander, P. A., 162, 181, 185
Alexandra, D., 57
Alim, H. S., 146, 387
Allen, J., 86
Allensworth, E., 353
Allington, R. L., 5, 240, 241, 257, 263, 265, 354
Almy, M. C., 82
Althusser, L., 60
Alton-Lee, A., 416, 424
Alvarez, H., 220, 224
Alvermann, D. E., 67, 164, 166, 167, 168
Amanti, C., 14, 56, 87, 89, 146, 164, 226, 356
Anders, P. L., 324

Anderson, A., 79, 88
Anderson, J. R., 288
Anderson, K., 324
Anderson, R. C., 347
Angelillo, C., 217
Anglin, J. M., 287
Antunez, B., 41, 44, 45
Anyon, J., 432
Apple, M. W., 14, 19, 28
Applebee, A., 223
Arauz, R. M., 217
Ardoin, S. P., 257
Arnold, J., 148
Aro, M., 294, 300
Aronson, J., 202
Arzubiaga, A., 345, 346
Asante, K., 175
Ash, G. E., 324, 346
Askov, E., 168
Asselin, M., 321
Ataya, R., 184
Au, K. H., 158, 209, 259, 342, 346, 351, 352, 353, 384
Auerbach, E. R., 77, 79

August, D., 32, 33, 45, 239, 248, 280, 281, 286, 293, 294, 313, 321, 325, 326, 327, 342, 346, 413, 416, 417, 420
Aukerman, M., 140
Azuara, P., 57

**B**

Baghban, M., 81
Bailey, A. L., 141
Bailey, G., 223
Baillie, S., 300
Baker, E. L., 234
Bakhtin, M. M., 104, 139
Ball, A. F., 146, 147, 223, 224, 383, 390, 391
Ballenger, C., 224
Banks, J. A., 14, 20
Baquedano-López, P., 60, 220, 224, 386
Barab, S., 71
Baratz, J. C., 145
Barker, R. G., 260
Barksdale-Ladd, M., 259
Barnett, W. S., 79
Barrueco, S., 34
Barton, D., 86, 163
Bauer, E. B., 246, 248
Baugh, J., 150, 223
Baughman, J. C., 348, 349
Baumann, J., 324, 330
Bayley, R., 64
Beach, R. W., 341
Beals, D. E., 79
Bean, T. W., 325
Bearne, E., 165
Beatty, A., 239
Beaty-O'Ferrall, M. E., 403
Beaver, J., 244
Beck, A., 159, 162
Beck, I. L., 323, 324, 326, 327, 328
Beck, J., 370, 371
Becker, W. C., 321
Beeler, T., 295
Beeman, M. M., 325
Behrman, E. H., 161
Bell, M., 71
Benson-Griffo, V., 356
Bereiter, C., 100, 144
Berends, M., 402
Bergeron, B. S., 399
Berkowitz, S. J., 341
Berla, N., 86
Berliner, D. C., 342, 400
Bernhardt, E., 239

Berninger, V. W., 280
Bernstein, B., 55
Bialystok, E., 14, 24, 26, 296
Biancarosa, G., 185, 321, 354
Biddle, B., 100
Biemiller, A., 321
Bilal, D., 179
Birkeland, S. E., 402, 404, 406
Birman, B. F., 39
Bishop-Josef, S. J., 106
Bixler, B., 168
Blachowicz, C. L. Z., 321, 324, 328, 330
Black, M. S., 21
Black, S., 255
Blackburn, M. V., 66, 160
Bleha, T., 177
Block, C. C., 3, 5
Bloodgood, J. W., 300
Blot, R. K., 16, 98, 381
Bober, M., 175
Boethel, M., 86
Boling, E. C., 158, 167
Bond, M. A., 324
Booth, W., 223
Boothroyd, M., 418
Borko, H., 168, 398
Borzekowski, D., 175
Bos, C. S., 324
Bourdieu, P., 17, 21, 78, 79, 120
Bowey, J., 301
Bowles, R., 301
Boykin, A. W., 207, 208
Bradley, B. A., 370
Bradley, R. H., 100
Bransford, J. D., 13, 178, 181, 185, 401
Broaddus, K., 239, 246, 248, 347, 357
Brock, C. H., 137, 139, 342
Broderick, V., 300
Bromley, K., 77
Brooks, W., 84
Brooks-Gunn, J., 97, 100
Brophy, J. E., 255, 257, 258
Brown, A. L., 13, 178, 341
Brown, B., 71
Brown, C., 306
Brown, C. L., 142
Brown, D. L., 225
Bruce, B., 168
Bruner, J. S., 22, 340
Bryant, P., 17
Bryk, A. S., 352, 353
Buck, C., 145
Budwig, N., 60
Buendía, E., 123

Burbules, N., 167
Burchinal, M. R., 207
Buriel, R., 118, 119, 129
Burnham, R. M., 398
Burns, M. S., 280
Burns, S., 44
Butler, F. A., 246
Butler, Y. G., 142
Byrne, B., 297

C

Cable, P. E., 397
Cain, C., 139
Calderón, M., 326, 415, 417, 418, 419, 420, 422
Calif, S., 280, 283
Callahan, R. M., 116, 117, 118, 121, 122, 129, 130
Callister, T., 167
Cambourne, B., 261, 264, 265
Cammack, D. W., 177, 351
Campbell, D. T., 279
Campos, J., 279
Canady, R. L., 255, 256
Cantrell, S. C., 5, 262, 265
Capps, R., 34
Carboni, L. W., 406
Cardenas-Hagan, E., 281, 282
Cardoso-Martins, C., 300
Cardoza, D., 118, 119, 129
Carlisle, J. F., 324, 325
Carlo, M. S., 126, 279, 281, 286, 321, 325, 327, 342
Carlson, C., 281
Carrington, V., 164, 165
Carter, B., 295
Casanova, U., 39
Cascio, J., 68
Casey, H., 254, 263, 266
Castek, J., 178, 183, 186, 187, 188, 189
Castiglioni-Spalten, M., 297
Caughy, M. O., 225
Cazden, C., 56, 148, 208, 265, 266, 384
Celano, D., 80, 258, 357
Chall, J. S., 366
Chamot, A. U., 126, 140
Chan, M., 284
Chapman, J., 304, 307
Chard, D. J., 367
Chavez, V., 67
Chavous, T., 197, 200, 202
Chen, S., 284
Cheng, C., 284
Cheung, H., 284

Chi, M. T. H., 400
Chong, K., 284
Christensen, L., 159, 161
Christenson, S. L., 208
Christian, D., 119, 138
Christie, J. F., 260
Chungmai, L., 105
Church, R. L., 143
Cisero, C. A., 280
Civil, M., 226
Clark, K., 3, 4, 248, 256
Clark, M. M., 78
Clark, R., 79
Clarke, D. K., 116, 117, 118, 129
Clewell, B. C., 47
Cobb, C. E., 224
Cochran-Smith, M., 79, 146, 384, 385, 388
Cocking, R. R., 13, 178
Cohen, C. C. D., 47
Coiro, J. L., 175, 177, 178, 182, 183, 184, 186, 188, 189, 351
Coiro, M. J., 81
Coker, D., 321
Cole, M., 17, 18, 19, 20, 22, 23, 24, 25, 26, 28, 98, 99, 104, 109, 162, 163, 217, 218, 220, 265
Coleman, J. S., 100
Collier, V. P., 103, 118, 119
Collin, R., 14, 19, 28
Collins, J., 16, 98, 381
Collins, M. F., 327
Comber, B., 159, 160, 161, 164
Comeau, L., 280
Compton-Lilly, C., 78, 79, 80, 84
Conant, F. R., 224
Connolly, K. J., 260
Connor, C., 311
Connor, J., 357
Constantino, R., 357
Cooper, E. J., 431
Cooper, M., 185
Cooter, R. B., Jr., 264, 254
Cope, B., 166
Copland, M. A., 352, 353
Cormier, P., 280
Correa, A., 325
Correa-Chávez, M., 217
Corson, D., 137, 141
Corwyn, R. F., 100
Costigan, A. T., 402
Coulter, C., 123
Cowie, R., 368
Coyne, M. D., 321
Crawford, J., 39
Crawford, L. W., 138

Cress, C., 304
Crocco, M. S., 402
Crosland, K., 123
Cross, D. R., 341
Cuban, L., 168
Culler, J., 223
Cullinan, B. E., 346, 347
Cummins, J., 13, 18, 20, 119, 140, 142, 277, 278, 279, 326, 358
Cunningham, A. E., 2, 322
Cunningham, J. W., 340
Cunningham, P. M., 145
Cunningham, T. H., 285


**D**


da Fontoura, H. A., 282
Daley, G. A., 401
Dall'Alba, G., 403
Dalton, B., 189, 330
Dalton, S. S., 100
Darling-Hammond, L., 385, 416
Davidson, R. G., 79
Davies, J., 164
Davis, L. H., 325
Day, J. P., 5, 263
De Abreu, M., 300
Deacon, S. H., 279, 283
DeBruin-Parecki, A., 87
Decker, D. M., 208
Deffes, R., 321
Deffner, N., 302
de Jong, E., 130
DeJong, P. F., 78
Delgado-Gaitan, C., 79
Delpit, L., 18, 20, 79, 143, 146, 153, 224, 342, 393, 408
DeNicolo, C. P., 245, 246, 248
Deno, S. L., 330
Desberg, P., 302
DeTemple, J. M., 79, 323
De Vos, G., 102
Dewey, J., 137
Diamond, J. M., 16, 17, 18, 28
Dickinson, D. K., 2, 322, 323
Dill, E., 207
Dillon, D. R., 326
Diment, K., 330
DiPardo, A., 357
Disney, L., 324
Dobler, E., 178, 182, 186
Dole, J. A., 340, 341, 350
Dona, D. P., 208

Donaldson, M. C., 16
Donelson, K. L., 388
Donnelly, K., 304
Dorian, N., 63
Dorner, L., 226
Douglas-Cowie, E., 368
Doumbia, F., 123
Dowdy, J. K., 393
Dowhower, S. L., 368, 370, 371
Dressler, C., 280, 282, 285, 327, 328
Dressman, M., 357
DuBois, W. E. B., 150, 152
Dudley-Marling, C., 358
Duff, P., 127, 130
Duffy, G. G., 261, 340
Duffy-Hester, A., 308
Duke, N. K., 84, 85, 259, 321, 357
Dummett, L., 146
Dunbar, S. B., 234
Duncan, G., 97, 100
Duncan, L., 300
Duncan-Andrade, J., 223, 387
Dunsmore, K., 28
Durán, B. J., 121, 131
Durán, P., 87
Durgunoglu, A. Y., 280, 282, 285, 327
Durkin, D., 78, 82, 83, 339, 340
Dworin, J., 13, 326
Dworn, J., 386
Dyson, A. H., 146, 160, 164


**E**


Eccles, J. S., 225
Echols, C., 200, 201
Eder, D., 264
Edwards, D. C., 324
Edwards, P. A., 77, 87, 88, 90, 137
Ehri, L. C., 293, 294, 295, 296, 297, 299, 300, 301, 302, 304, 305, 306, 307, 308, 323, 324, 386
Elkonin, D. B., 297, 298, 325
Emig, J. M., 87
Emmer, E. T., 257
Engelmann, S., 100
Engestrom, R., 68
Engeström, Y., 68, 218, 219, 220
Englemann, S., 144
Englert, C. S., 342
Enz, B., 260
Erekson, J., 368
Erskine, J., 294
Escamilla, K., 279
Espinosa, L., 47

Estabrook, L., 175
Estrada, P., 100
Evertson, C. M., 254, 255, 257
Ezzaki, A., 284

F

Fairbanks, M., 323, 324
Farella, M., 279
Farest, C., 417
Farivar, S., 208
Farr, M. J., 146, 224, 400
Fawson, P. C., 256
Fawson, P. F., 260
Feiman-Nemser, S., 405
Ferreiro, E., 78
Fideler, E., 404
Fielding, L. G., 347
Fielding-Barnsley, R., 297
Figueroa, R. A., 418
Fillmore, L., 138
Fingeret, L., 352
Fink, R., 206
Fischer, R., 260
Fisher, C. W., 256
Fisher, D., 78, 146, 342, 396, 406
Fisher, F., 295
Fisher, M. T., 217, 387
Fisher, P. J. L., 328
Fishman, B., 311
Fishman, J., 65
Fishman, J. A., 65
Fitzsimmons, S., 114, 118, 414, 418
Fix, M., 34
Flavell, J. H., 225
Fleisher, L. S., 367
Fletcher, J., 321
Flinspach, S., 323
Flood, J., 78, 137, 144, 146, 342
Florio-Ruane, S., 28
Fobil, J., 175
Foehr, U. G., 175
Fogel, H., 386
Foley, D. E., 99
Folse, K. S., 326
Foorman, B., 295
Ford, D. Y., 200, 201
Fordham, S., 145
Foster, M., 146
Fountas, I. C., 264
Fowler, A., 293
Fox, E., 162
Fox, S., 186

Franklin, S. H., 87
Freedman, S. W., 146
Freeman, D., 209, 326
Freeman, Y., 209, 326
Freire, P., 17, 66, 159, 389
Frey, N., 396, 405, 406
Friedman, T. L., 174, 177
Fry, R., 45
Frye, B. J., 347
Fu, D., 122
Fuchs, D., 2, 205

G

Gadd, N., 148
Gadsden, V. L., 79
Gal, S., 63
Galda, L., 346
Gallego, M. A., 23
Gallimore, R., 23, 25, 79, 101, 118, 208, 209
Gandara, P., 38, 416
García, E. E., 33, 34, 38, 49, 381, 383, 386
García, G. E., 131, 234, 238, 239, 245, 246, 247, 248, 250, 285, 321, 324, 327, 328, 342, 414
García, O., 124
García-Vázquez, E., 118, 119, 120
Garnier, H., 118
Garrett, P., 60
Gaskins, I. W., 304
Gavelek, J. R., 28
Gebhard, M., 142
Gee, J. P., 17, 18, 19, 24, 68, 73, 79, 146, 163, 177, 265
Gehrke, N. J., 398
Genesee, F., 119, 280
Genishi, C., 261
George, M. A., 340
Gersten, R., 326, 355
Gettinger, M., 256
Geva, E., 280, 282, 293
Gholamain, M., 282
Gibson, M. A., 102
Gilbert, L., 404
Gilliam, W., 106
Gilmore, P., 56, 72
Gindis, B., 106
Ginsburg, A. L., 39
Giorgis, C., 347
Giroux, H., 159, 162
Gitlin, A., 123, 130, 131
Glaser, R., 400
Glatthorn, A., 56
Glod, M., 242

Goatley, V. J., 86, 342
Godina, H., 124
Goffman, E., 68
Goldenberg, C., 118, 209, 248, 321, 326, 343, 346, 417
Goldstein, T., 129, 130
González, N., 14, 23, 56, 60, 62, 66, 72, 73, 87, 89, 146, 164, 226, 227, 356, 382, 383
González, R., 38, 116, 117, 122
Good, R. H., 240
Good, T., 258
Goodman, K., 145, 240, 241
Goodman, Y., 80
Goody, J., 17, 18
Goswami, U., 304
Gottardo, A., 280, 284
Gottesman, B., 406
Gough, P. B., 259, 280
Gradmaison, E., 280
Graff, H. J., 114
Graham, C. R., 285
Graham, S., 200, 201
Grant, L., 265
Graves, M. F., 321, 324, 327, 328
Graziano, M., 175
Greaney, V., 346, 349
Greenberg, J. B., 23, 84, 226
Greenfield, P., 217
Gregory, E., 59
Gress, M., 324
Griffin, P., 44, 220, 280
Griffith, L. W., 371
Griffith, P., 259
Grisham, D. L., 330
Guarino, C. M., 401, 403
Guerrero, M. D., 142
Gunderson, L., 116, 117, 118, 129
Guthrie, D., 118
Guthrie, J. T., 179, 206, 207, 213, 344, 345, 346, 349, 405
Gutiérrez, K. D., 19, 66, 218, 219, 220, 221, 224, 247, 386, 393
Gutkin, T. B., 203
Guttentag, R., 305


H

Haager, D., 417, 418
Hacker, D. J., 356
Haertal, G. D., 255
Hagood, M. C., 67, 166
Haith, M., 305
Hakuta, K., 142, 239

Hall, V. C., 198
Halliday, M., 164
Halverson, E., 217
Hamilton, A. M., 368
Hamilton, M., 86, 163
Hamilton, M. A., 66
Hamilton, S. F., 66
Hamilton-Pennell, C., 348
Hamre, B. K., 206
Hancin-Bhatt, B. J., 280, 285, 327
Hanks, P., 368
hAnluain, D. O., 176
Hansen, J., 340, 341
Harklau, L., 122, 125
Harkness, S., 79
Harman, D., 19
Harman, R., 142
Harmon, J. M., 324
Harpalani, V., 24, 218
Harper, B., 200
Harper, C., 130
Harris, J. J., 200, 201
Harris, P., 262
Harris, T. L., 368
Harris, V., 145
Harris, W. C., 176
Harrison, G. L., 280
Harste, J., 165
Hart, B., 79, 97, 100, 258, 294, 306, 321
Hartman, D. K., 180, 183
Haselkorn, D., 404
Hatano, G., 28
Hatch, E., 306
Haveman, R., 100
Haycock, K., 3, 249
Haynes, J. B., 330
Heath, L., 208
Heath, S. B., 13, 22, 55, 78, 79, 80, 83, 98, 99, 137, 144, 146, 163, 217, 342, 380, 381, 383
Hedrick, W. B., 324
Hefflin, B., 259
Hemmeter, J., 81
Henderson, A. T., 86
Henry, L. A., 178, 179, 182, 184, 185, 186, 188, 189, 351
Hernandez, D., 34, 35
Heron, A. H., 164
Hertzman, C., 100
Hess, R., 100
Heubach, K., 371
Hicks, D., 342
Hiebert, E. H., 264, 265, 328
Hilliard, A. G., 143, 433
Hillocks, G., 223

Hindin, A., 87
Hirata, S. Y., 352
Hitlin, P., 175
Hodges, R. E., 368
Hoffman, J., 83
Hoffman, J. L., 241
Hoffman, J. V., 367, 369, 371, 417
Hogan, M., 168
Hohn, W., 299
Holland, D. C., 99, 104, 139, 140, 148, 150
Hollie, S., 147
Holmes, K., 209
Holmes, S., 209
Holt, K., 200
Holt, T., 143
Hoover-Dempsey, K. V., 78
Hopkins, G., 325
Hornberger, N., 65, 326
Horvath, J. A., 400
Howard, J., 224
Howe, A., 198
Hsieh-Yee, I., 179
Hubbard, L., 25
Hubbard, R., 341
Huberman, M., 357
Hudicourt-Barnes, J., 224
Hudley, C., 201
Huey, E. B., 78
Hughes, J., 198, 206, 207
Hull, G., 66, 146, 164, 177
Hulme, C., 304
Hunt, D., 398
Hurley, E., 208
Hwang, Y. S., 200, 201
Hymes, D., 56, 138, 163

I

Iddings, A. C. D., 142
Ingersoll, R. M., 401, 402, 403
Ingram, R., 403
Inklaar, R., 176
Irby, M., 217
Irvine, J. J., 146, 384, 393
Ivey, G., 239, 246, 248, 347, 357

J

Jacob, E., 126
James, C., 285, 327, 328
Jamieson-Noel, D., 321
Janks, H., 160, 161, 164

Jenkins, J., 310
Jenkins, J. R., 367
Jensen, A., 380
Jensen, J., 144
Jetton, T. L., 181, 185
Jewitt, C., 165
Jiménez, R. T., 131, 285, 324, 326, 327, 342, 344, 357
Jocson, K., 217, 387
John, V., 56
Johnson, B., 177
Johnson, K. R., 145
Johnson, S. M., 402, 404, 406
John-Steiner, V., 71
Johnston, P., 105
Johnston, P. H., 5, 263, 266
Jones, G., 223
Jones, L., 257
Jones, S., 160, 161
Jones, S. M., 106
Jones, V., 257
Jorm, A. F., 296
Joyce, B., 399
Juel, C., 259, 309, 310, 321
Justice, L., 301

K

Kalantzis, M., 166
Kamil, M. L., 280, 282, 285, 327, 328
Kaminski, R. A., 240
Kamler, B., 159, 160, 161
Kaomea, J., 342
Karier, C. J., 238
Kastler, L., 83
Katch, L., 311
Katz, L. A., 324
Katz, M. L., 66
Kaufman, M., 277, 279
Kaufman, S., 79
Kendall, J., 279
Kendrick, M., 165
Kenner, C., 165
Kerosuo, H., 68
Kersaint, G., 402
Kessler, B., 301
Kim, D., 330
Kinzer, C. K., 176, 177, 178, 351
Kirby, J., 279
Kirby, P. C., 256
Kirby, S., 402
Kirkland, D., 387
Klauda, S. L., 206

Klein, H., 389
Klein, K., 285, 327, 328
Knobel, M., 68, 69, 161, 164, 175, 177, 351
Knoblauch, D., 200
Koda, K., 342
Kohansal, R., 356
Kohlberg, L., 105
Kohler, K. M., 256
Kolich, E. M., 324
Kolinsky, R., 17
Kooy, M., 407
Koyama, J. P., 122
Kozol, J., 101, 105
Kozulin, A., 98, 104, 106
Krashen, S., 357
Krauss, M., 63
Kress, G., 164, 165, 177
Krol, L., 280
Krol-Sinclair, B., 85, 87, 88
Kruse, S., 353
Kucan, L., 327, 328
Kuhn, M. R., 366, 367, 368, 369, 370, 371, 372
Kuiper, E., 177
Kulick, D., 63
Kulik, C. C., 265
Kulik, J. A., 265
Kunda, Z., 225
Kupersmidt, J. B., 100
Kupper, L., 126
Kwok, O., 198, 206, 207


L

Labbo, L. D., 330
LaBerge, D., 280, 286, 305, 367
Labov, W., 22, 55, 144, 145, 380
Lacey, P., 21
Lachicotte, W., 139
Lacroix, D., 280
Ladson-Billings, G., 14, 146, 358, 384
Lajoie, S. P., 401
Lambert, W. E., 279
Lancaster, L., 163, 165
Lance, K. C., 348, 349
Landry, S. H., 84
Langman, J., 217
Lankford, H., 402
Lankshear, C., 68, 69, 161, 164, 175, 177, 351
Lapp, D., 78, 90, 137, 144, 146, 342
Lareau, A., 78, 79
Lave, C. A., 22
Lave, J., 98, 104, 107, 137, 217, 261
Lawless, K. A., 167, 168

Lawrence, S. M., 146
Lazar, A. M., 146
Leander, K. M., 165, 175
Lederman, N., 198
Lee, C. D., 13, 14, 23, 24, 25, 138, 146, 150, 160,
    208, 218, 222, 223, 224, 225, 382, 383, 393
Lee, C., 60
Lee, T., 62
Lehr, F., 295
Lemke, J. L., 166, 167, 168, 177
Lemos-Britton, Z., 280
Lenhart, A., 175
Lesaux, N., 342, 343
Leseman, P. M., 78
Leu, D. D., 188
Leu, D. J., 175, 180, 181, 182, 183, 184, 187, 188,
    259
Leu, D. J., Jr., 176, 177, 188, 351
Levin, I., 300, 301
Levine, M., 398
Levinson, B. A., 99
Levy, B. A., 368
Lewandowski, L., 330
Lewis, J., 402
Li, G., 79
Liang, L. A., 340
Liberman, I., 295
Lieberman, A., 357
Lightfoot, S. L., 90
Lindamood, C., 297, 298
Lindamood, P., 297, 298
Lindholm-Leary, K., 119
Linek, W. L., 372
Linn, R. L., 234
Lipson, M. Y., 340
Little, J. W., 357
Liu, Y., 284
Livingstone, S., 175
Llosa, L., 142
Loeb, S., 402
Logan, G. D., 370
Long, J. F., 200, 201, 212
Long, S., 60
Lonsdale, M., 347, 349
López, I. C., 118
López, M., 34, 47
Louis, K. S., 353
Love, M. S., 330
Lovette, O. K., 398
Ludlow, A., 177
Luke, A., 114
Luke, C., 167, 168
Lundberg, I., 295
Luria, A. R., 16, 104

Lyman, P., 181, 185
Lysynchuck, L., 368

**M**

MacArthur, C. A., 330
Macedo, D., 66, 159
Maclean, R., 296
Madden, M., 175
Mahiri, J., 387
Majumder, S., 296
Makoni, S., 222
Mandara, J., 225
Marks, H. M., 353
Marsh, D., 417, 418
Marsh, G., 302
Marsh, J., 164
Marston, D., 330
Martens, B. K., 257
Martin, M., 296
Martinez, M., 371
Martinez-Roldan, C. M., 326
Maruyama, G. M., 347
Marvin, C. A., 78
Marzano, J. S., 404
Marzano, R. J., 255, 404
Mason, B., 352
Mason, D. A., 352
Mason, J. M., 209, 346
Mason, P. A., 259
Matteucci, N., 176
Matthee, B., 263
Matthews, R., 296
Matute-Bianchi, M. E., 103
May, S., 62
McAllister, G., 146
McCarthey, S. J., 86
McCarty, T., 62, 65, 138, 383
McClure, K. A., 87
McCutchen, D., 293
McGuckin, R. H., 176
McKay, R., 165
McKeown, M. G., 323, 324, 327, 328
McKinney, J. D., 260
McKoon, G., 239
McLaren, P., 159, 162
McLaughlin, B., 325
McLaughlin, M. W., 217, 385
McMillon, G. M. T., 88, 143, 146
McRae, A., 206, 207
McTavish, M., 86
McVee, M. B., 28
Meece, J. L., 200

Meek, B., 62
Mehan, H., 25
Meisels, G., 402
Meister, C., 187
Melzi, G., 85
Mendez, M., 352
Mendoza-Denton, N., 60
Mercado, C. I., 14, 226
Mercer, J., 238
Merchant, G., 164
Merkel, S., 198
Mertz, E., 65
Messick, S., 234
Metsala, J. L., 262
Meza, M., 226
Michaels, S., 146
Mickelson, R. A., 200
Miller, J., 368
Miller, L., 357
Miller, O., 208
Miller, P. H., 225
Miller, S., 106
Miller-Jones, D., 146
Milner, H. R., 255
Minden-Cupp, C., 310
Mistretta, J., 262
Mitchell, F., 114, 389
Moats, L., 293, 294, 309
Modiano, N., 279
Mohan, L., 352
Mohr, K. A. J., 259
Moje, E. B., 227, 326
Moll, L. C., 13, 14, 23, 24, 56, 66, 84, 87, 89, 146,
    164, 226, 227, 326, 342, 356, 382, 383, 385, 386
Monker, J., 323
Monoi, S., 200
Monroe, R., 402
Montali, J., 330
Montero, K., 369, 370
Monzó, L., 345
Mooney, K., 352
Moore, D. W., 227
Moore, G., 264
Moore, K., 78, 81, 146, 342
Moorman, M., 259
Morais, J., 17
Moran, R. F., 38
Morgan, P. L., 205
Morrell, E., 223, 387
Morris, D., 305
Morrison, F., 311
Morrison, S. B., 260
Morrow, L. M., 254, 257, 260, 261, 262, 265, 345,
    370, 372

Moses, R. P., 224
Mostafapour, E., 280
Mostow, J., 370, 371
Mraz, M., 369
Mufwene, S., 223
Murphy, P. K., 200
Murray, B., 297
Murray, C. B., 225


**N**

Naftel, S., 402
Nagy, W. E., 280, 285, 321, 324, 327, 328
Nalin, K. B., 339
Nasir, N., 218, 221
Nation, I. S. P., 321, 326
Nation, P., 326
Naumann, W. C., 203
Navarro, R. A., 39
Neal, H., 294
Neff, D., 87, 146, 164, 356
Nelsen, G., 352
Neuman, S. B., 80, 258, 260, 261, 323, 357
Newmann, F. M., 353, 354
Nickerson, K., 225
Nies, A., 340
Nieto, S., 14, 18, 19, 20, 21, 23
Nilsen, A. P., 388
Nixon, A. S., 220
Nowak, R., 240, 241
Nunes, S., 296, 299, 308
Nunes, T., 17
Nurcombe, B., 21, 22
Nussbaum, E. M., 128, 130


**O**

Oakes, J., 122
Obrochta, C., 324
Ochoa, S. H., 47
Ochsner, M., 261
Ogbu, J. U., 103, 145, 202, 203, 213
Ogle, D. M., 325, 328, 341
Ogonowski, M., 224
Olsen, L., 101
Olson, D. R., 16, 17
Olson, M. R., 183
Olson, R., 293
Omar, M. H., 246
Ondrejka, C., 68
Ondrich, J., 402
Ordonez, C. L., 325
Orellana, M., 226

Orfield, G., 105
Ortiz, S. O., 47
Orwig, R., 352
Osborn, J., 295
Osborne, J. W., 202, 203, 204
Ost, J., 34
Oxford, R. L., 260


**P**

Paciga, K. A., 241
Padak, N. D., 372
Padilla, A. M., 116, 117, 122
Paffendorf, J., 68
Page, S. E., 176, 186, 188
Pahl, K., 164, 165, 266
Palincsar, A. S., 341, 342
Pany, D., 367
Paradise, R., 217
Paratore, J. R., 77, 79, 85, 87
Paris, D., 379, 389
Paris, S. G., 340, 341, 356
Parker, M. B., 405
Parks, L. A., 139
Pas, E., 402
Passel, J., 34
Patall, E. A., 406
Patrick, S., 126
Pearson, P. D., 3, 4, 7, 131, 212, 234, 238, 239, 247, 248, 250, 256, 263, 264, 324, 340, 341, 342, 351, 354, 355, 356, 358
Peisner-Feinberg, E., 207
Pence, K., 301
Pennycook, A., 72, 114
Perez, B., 138
Perfetti, C. A., 280, 284, 321
Perney, J., 305
Perry, T., 143, 153, 224, 433
Peske, H. G. K., 3
Peters, P., 161
Peterson, B., 347
Peterson, D. S., 3, 212, 263, 351
Peyton, J., 310
Philips, S. U., 55
Phillips, B. N., 208
Phillips, D. A., 100, 106
Piaget, J., 105
Pianta, R. C., 206, 207
Pickering, D. J., 404
Pikulski, J. J., 367
Pinnell, G. S., 264, 352
Pleasants, H. M., 87
Podgursky, M., 402
Pollard-Durodola, S. D., 281

Pomplun, M., 246
Portes, A., 102, 114, 115, 117, 119, 121, 122, 123
Portes, P. R., 98, 99, 100, 102, 103, 104, 105, 106, 107, 108, 109
Potter, G., 78
Potter, R., 402
Povich, E., 145
Powell, S., 209
Powers, K. M., 210
Pressley, M., 3, 4, 5, 257, 258, 261, 262, 324, 330, 341, 350, 352, 353, 356
Proctor, C. P., 189, 286, 330, 342, 343
Pungello, E. P., 100
Purcell-Gates, V., 78, 79, 80, 84, 85, 86, 90, 146
Purkey, S. C., 352, 353
Purves, A., 223
Putnam, R. T., 168

**Q**

Quartz, K. H., 405, 407
Quirk, T. J., 339
Quiroga, T., 280

**R**

Rack, J., 304, 305
Rainie, L., 175
Ramey, C., 98, 100
Ramey, S., 98, 100
Ramirez, J. D., 44
Randolph, S. M., 225
Rankin, J., 3, 4, 261, 262
Raphael, L. M., 352
Raphael, T. E., 158, 340, 341, 342, 352
Rasinski, T. V., 367, 368, 369, 371, 372
Read, C., 300, 368
Readence, J. E., 227
Reardon-Anderson, J., 34
Redd, T. E., 386
Reese, L. J., 118, 119, 208, 209
Reeves, J., 123, 131
Reinking, D., 179, 186, 187, 188
Resnick, G., 260
Retting, M. D., 255
Reutzel, D. R., 254, 256, 257, 260, 264
Reyes, I., 56, 57, 72
Reynolds, J., 226
Rezaei, A., 321
Rhodes, R. L., 47
Richardson, E., 143, 150, 386
Rickford, J., 146, 153, 223
Rideout, V., 175

Riedel, B. W., 240, 241
Risko, V., 77
Risley, T. R., 79, 97, 100, 258, 294, 306, 321
Riveria, A., 386
Rivlin, L., 261
Robb, L., 265, 266
Robbins, C., 323
Roberts, D. F., 175, 176
Roberts, T., 294, 300, 301, 306
Roberts, T. A., 81
Robinson, C., 176
Rodney, M. J., 348
Rodriguez, K., 300
Rodriguez, M. C., 263, 351
Roehler, L. R., 261, 340
Roessingh, H., 120, 125, 130
Rogers, D., 330
Rogoff, B., 13, 19, 20, 23, 66, 217, 218, 393
Rollow, S. G., 352
Romero-Little, M. E., 62
Roos, P., 36, 49
Roper-Schneider, D., 309, 310
Rosebery, A. S., 218, 224
Rosedale, P., 68
Rosenholtz, S. J., 398
Rosenshine, B., 187, 340
Rosenthal, J., 304, 306, 307, 324
Roser, N., 81, 83, 371, 417
Rosier, P., 279
Roskos, K., 260, 261
Ross, G., 340
Rothenberg, C., 406
Rothenberg, J., 265
Rottenberg, L., 126
Rowan, B., 352, 353
Rowsell, J., 164, 165, 266
Royer, J. M., 279, 280
Rubinstein-Áavila, E., 56, 66, 67, 72, 73, 165
Ruddell, M. R., 324
Ruddell, R. B., 262
Rueda, R. S., 248, 326, 345, 346, 414, 417
Ruiz, N. T., 417, 418
Ruíz, R., 14, 26
Rumbaut, R. G., 102, 114, 115, 117, 119, 121, 122, 123
Russo, R. P., 126
Ryan, S., 261
Ryan, T., 330

**S**

Sáez, R., 13, 326
Sailors, M., 263
Salas, S., 103, 105, 107, 109

Saltmarsh, J., 305
Samuels, S. J., 206, 241, 280, 286, 305, 367, 370
Samway, K. D., 323
Sandberg, J., 403
Sanders, E., 310
Sanders, M. G., 199
Sandler, H. M., 78
Sandoval, S. R., 203
San Francisco, A. R., 281
Santibañez, L., 401
Saunders, W. M., 119, 343, 417
Saville-Troike, M., 285
Scarborough, H., 293
Scarcella, R. C., 137, 141
Schatschneider, C., 311
Schatz, S., 71
Schecter, S., 64
Schekler, R., 71
Schiefele, U., 225
Schieffelin, B., 56, 79
Schiff, R., 280, 283
Schilling-Estes, N., 138, 139, 153
Schlechty, P. C., 403, 404
Schleppegrell, M. J., 137, 140
Schmandt-Besserat, D., 16
Schmidt, P. R., 146
Scholes, R., 223
Schreiber, P. A., 368
Schultz, K., 66, 146, 164, 177
Schumm, J. S., 259
Schunk, D. H., 201
Schwanenflugel, P. J., 323, 368, 370, 372
Schwartz, A., 165
Schwartz, R. M., 341
Schwebel, E. A., 370
Scott, D. M., 101
Scott, J., 300
Scott, J. A., 321, 323, 324, 330
Scribner, S., 17, 18, 19, 20, 22, 99, 104, 109, 162, 163, 217
Sedlak, M., 143
Seger, W., 142
Seidl, B., 399
Sellers, R., 197
Selman, R., 105
Sénéchal, M., 323
Serpell, R., 28
Seymour, P., 294, 295, 300
Shah, P. P., 325
Shanahan, T., 32, 45, 256, 257, 280, 293, 294, 313, 321, 325, 326, 327, 342, 369, 413, 416, 420
Shankweiler, D., 295
Share, D. L., 296, 300, 301, 305, 306, 307
Sharp, C., 83
Sharp, D. W., 22

Shearer, B. A., 324
Shepherd, J., 305
Shipman, V., 100
Shmidman, A., 303
Shonkoff, J. P., 100
Shor, I., 161
Short, D. J., 114, 118, 414, 418
Showers, B., 399
Shreyar, S., 142
Siegel, L. S., 100, 280, 282, 293, 294, 342
Simmons, D. C., 321
Simon, M., 175
Simon, S., 259
Simons, H. D., 145
Singley, M. K., 288
Skinner, D., 139
Skobel, B. J., 328
Slater, W. H., 321
Smalls, C., 197, 213
Smart, E. J., 68
Smelser, N., 389
Smith, B., 353
Smith, B. J., 402
Smith, C., 357
Smith, D. L., 402
Smith, E. G., 348, 349
Smith, E. W., 81
Smith, J., 100
Smith, J. A., 256
Smith, K. E., 84
Smith, M., 223
Smith, M. L., 123
Smith, M. S., 352, 353
Smith, M. W., 322
Smith, P. K., 260
Smith, T. M., 403
Smitherman, G., 138, 144, 223, 380
Smolin, L. I., 167, 168
Snow, C. E., 2, 13, 79, 185, 237, 238, 280, 281, 282, 286, 321, 322, 323, 325, 327, 342, 354
Snow, D., 44
Snowling, M., 304
Soep, E., 67
Solano-Flores, G., 240
Sonnenschein, S., 90
Sparks, R., 306
Spear-Ellinwood, K., 57, 69, 70, 71, 72, 73
Spears, A., 223
Spencer, M. B., 24, 218, 225
Spharim, G., 325
Spratt, J. E., 284
Squire, J., 144
Stahl, K., 308
Stahl, S. A., 295, 297, 308, 321, 323, 324, 328, 367, 368, 370, 371

Stanley, J. C., 279
Stanovich, K. E., 2, 322, 347, 348, 366, 367, 369, 372
Steele, C. M., 202, 225, 433
Steiner, L. M., 88
Sternberg, R. J., 400
Stevens, K. C., 323
Stevens, R., 246
Stewart, J. P., 80
Stewart, M. T., 241, 242
Stewner-Manzanares, G., 126
Stief, T., 81
Stinebrickner, T. R., 402
Stodolsky, S. S., 260
Stokes, S., 79, 88
Stoko, E. M., 403, 405
Strahan, D., 353
Strecker, S., 371
Street, B. V., 66, 146, 163, 177, 218, 263, 265, 266
Strickland, D. S., 255
Stringfield, S., 256
Sturtevant, E., 372
Suárez-Orozco, C., 109
Suárez-Orozco, M. M., 102, 109
Sudweeks, R., 260
Suizzo, M. A., 208
Super, C., 79
Swap, S. M., 224
Swartz, D., 120


T

Taaffe McLearn, K., 106
Taboada, A., 179, 207, 212
Tabors, P. O., 2
Tatum, B. D., 146
Taylor, A. Z., 201
Taylor, B. M., 3, 4, 5, 212, 248, 256, 263, 264, 341, 347, 351, 352
Taylor, D., 77, 79, 80, 84, 86, 90
Teague, B. L., 131
Teale, W. H., 79, 80, 83, 84, 85, 86, 241, 242, 249
Teberosky, A., 78
Teddlie, C., 256
Tejada, C., 224, 386
Téllez, K., 14
Tenent, A., 356
Terman, L. M., 320
Tharp, R. G., 23, 25, 100, 101, 106, 209
Thomas, E., 323
Thomas, W. P., 103
Thompson, G. L., 386
Tienda, M., 114, 414
Tierney, R. J., 340

Timpeley, H., 416, 424
Tomlinson, C., 263
Torrey J. W., 144
Townsend, J. S., 122, 387
Trabasso, T., 223
Tracey D. H., 262
Treiman, R., 300, 301
Trisman, D. A., 339
Trumbell, E., 240
Truxaw, M. P., 183
Tse, L. 129
Tucker, G. R., 279
Tudge, J. R. H., 208
Tunmer, W., 304, 307
Turkle S., 69
Turner, J. D., 77
Turner, T., 259
Tyler, K. M., 208
Tyner, K., 17, 18


U

Uhry, J., 297, 305
Underwood, P., 311
Unsworth, L., 350


V

Vadasy, P., 310
Vadeboncoeur, J. A., 106
Vaden. N. A., 100
Valdés G., 79, 124, 130, 226
Valencia, R. R., 13, 21
Valsiner, J., 104
van Ark, B., 176
van den Broek, P., 223
Varian, H. R., 181, 185
Vázquez, L. A., 118, 119, 120
Venezky, R. L., 294
Villanueva, I., 25
Voelkl K. E., 196
Volk, D., 60
Volman, M., 177
Voss, M. M., 80
Vukelich, C., 260
Vyas, S., 387, 388
Vygotsky, L. S., 6, 139, 331


W

Wade-Woolley, L., 279, 280
Wagner, D. A., 284

Wainer, A., 185
Walberg, H. J., 255
Walker, S., 21
Walpole, S., 3, 248, 256
Wang, M., 284, 286
Wang, M. C., 255
Ward, W., 118
Wardhaugh, R., 138
Ware, D., 324
Warren, B., 218, 224
Washington, V., 146
Wasik, B. A., 324
Wasik, B. H., 87
Watson, D., 402
Watt, D., 120, 130
Watt, I. P., 18
Watts, S. M., 321
Watts-Taffe, S., 328
Waxman, H. C., 14
Webb, K. S., 386
Webb, N. M., 208
Webber, S., 177
Weber, C. M., 340
Weffer, R. E., 121, 131
Weinberg, S. F., 339
Weinstein, C., 261
Weisner, R., 79
Weizman, Z. O., 322
Welborn, L., 348
Weld, J., 402
Wells, G., 265
Wells, J., 328
Wendon, L., 302, 303
Wenger, E., 98, 104, 107
Wertsch, J. V., 104, 106, 137
West, M., 326
Wharton-McDonald, R., 262, 356
Wheeler, E., 126
White, D., 81
White, R., 197
White, T. G., 321
White-Kaulaity, M., 387, 388
Whitford, B. L., 403, 404
Wichmann, A., 368
Wiese, A., 33, 49
Wigfield, A., 225, 405
Wiggins, A., 301
Wightman, J., 304
Wilce, L., 300, 302, 305
Wilder, P., 357
Williams, C. H., 386
Williams, E. J., 244
Williams, K. B., 67
Williams, K. T., 241
Willows, D., 296, 299, 308

Wilson, P. T., 347
Wilson, W. J., 389
Windmueller, M. P., 417, 418
Winograd, P. W., 341
Wisenbaker, J., 368
Witt, D., 142
Witt, E., 175, 209
Wixson, K. K., 340
Wolf, M., 14, 16, 24, 28
Wolfe, B., 100
Wolfe, L. A., 257
Wolfe, P., 128, 130
Wolfersberger, M., 260
Wolfram, W., 138, 139, 150, 153
Wong, H. K., 254
Wong, R. T., 254
Wong-Fillmore, L., 63
Wonnacott, C. A., 341
Woo, D. G., 262
Wood, D., 340
Wood, K. D., 324
Wortham, S., 64
Worthy, J., 81, 259, 357
Wright, D., 78
Wright, W. E., 247
Wyckoff, J., 402
Wyman, L., 56, 63, 72
Wynn, S. R., 406


Y

Yaden, D., 79
Yamauchi, L. A., 100
Yan, B., 280
Yarnall, M. M., 261
Yeung, W. J., 100
Yinger, J., 402
Yinger, R. J., 257
Yokoi, L., 3, 261
Young, J. P., 227


Z

Zawilinski, L., 178, 180, 182
Zeichner, K., 398
Zentella, A. C., 35, 65
Zepeda, O., 62, 383
Zhou, M., 102
Zigler, E., 106
Zill, N., 81, 260
Zimmerman, B. J., 201
Zolkower, B., 142
Zwick, T., 176

# Subject Index

Page numbers followed by *f* indicate figure, *n* indicate note, and *t* indicate table.

Ability grouping of students, 264–265
Academic achievement
    adolescent English language learners and, 129–130
    home language environments and, 100–101
    independent reading time and, 347–348
    prior schooling of immigrant students and, 116–118
    professional development and, 414–416, 424–426, 425*f*, 426*f*
    second-language development and, 278
    valuing of, 199–202
    *See also* Achievement gap in reading and math
Academic English
    African American vernacular English and, 137–153
    classroom practices and, 146–148
    cross-language transfer and, 286
    future research regarding, 148–152
    literacy learning and, 141–142
    overview, 140–141, 152
    research regarding, 138–140, 139*t*
Academic learning time (ALT), 256–257
Academic programs, 121–125

Access to print, 258–260. *See also* Text availability
Accountability
    comprehension instruction and, 344
    informal learning environments and, 221–222
    No Child Left Behind Act of 2001 (NCLB) and, 45–48, 46*t*
Achievement gap in reading and math
    classroom practices and, 106–108
    cognitive development and, 105–106
    comprehension instruction and, 358
    cultural historical theory and, 97–109
    misidentification with schooling and, 202–206, 204*f*
    No Child Left Behind Act of 2001 (NCLB) and, 184–186, 250
    online reading comprehension and, 184–186, 259
    overview, 1–2, 102–103
    professional development and, 414
    text availability and, 259
    *See also* Academic achievement
Achievement testing. *See* Testing

Achievement Via Individual Determination
    (AVID) program, 25
Acquisition of language
    adolescent English language learners and,
        118–120
    linguistic diversity and, 79
    poverty and, 101
Activity-theoretical perspective, 218
Adaptation, literacy as, 19–20
Adequate yearly progress (AYP)
    literacy assessments for Title I and, 243
    No Child Left Behind Act of 2001 (NCLB) and,
        45, 47, 236
    online reading comprehension and, 185
    overview, 52n, 243
    poverty and, 101
Adolescence
    literacy development and, 66–68
    online reading comprehension and, 175–176
    See also Adolescent English language learners
Adolescent English language learners
    academic English and, 141–142
    academic programs and, 121–125
    assessment and, 422
    classroom practices and, 129–131
    instructional activities, 125–129
    overview, 114–131
    professional development and, 418–421, 420t,
        422f, 427
    programs and, 121–125
    research regarding, 115–121
    See also Adolescence; English language
        learners
Advanced beginner level of teacher expertise,
    400–401
African American students
    classroom practices and, 207–212
    Cultural Modeling Project and, 222–225
    disidentification with schooling and, 204–206,
        204f
    engagement and motivation and, 196–199,
        207–213
    valuing of achievement and, 199–202
African American vernacular English
    classroom practices and, 146–148
    Cultural Modeling Project and, 222–225
    literacy learning and, 137–153, 145–146
    overview, 142–145, 152
    research regarding, 138–140, 139t, 148–152,
        382–383, 386–387, 389–390
    terminology, 153n
Alphabet knowledge, 300–303, 302f
Alternative pedagogies, 66–68
Analogizing, 304

Annual measurable achievement objectives
    (AMAOs), 236
Annual objectives, 46t
Asian American and Asian students, 387, 393n
Aspira of New York, Inc. v. Board of Education
    (1975), 36
Assessments
    classroom practices and, 247–249
    differentiated instruction and, 263
    with English language learners, 245–247
    Expediting Comprehension for English
        Language Learners (ExC-ELL) and,
        422–424, 423f
    formal literacy assessment, 237–240
    literacy assessments for Title I, 242–245
    No Child Left Behind Act of 2001 (NCLB) and,
        46t, 47–48, 233–251
    online reading comprehension and, 181–182,
        189, 190
    professional development and, 421–422
    research regarding, 237–247, 249–250
    teacher development and, 406–407
    See also Testing
Assimilation, 102–103. See also Segmented
    assimilation
Association for Supervision and Curriculum
    Development (ASCD), 398
Authentic assessments, 248–249
Automaticity
    overview, 367–368
    text selection and, 370–371
    See also Fluency
Availability of texts. See Text availability


B

Background knowledge
    comprehension instruction and, 350
    engagement and motivation and, 211
    vocabulary instruction and, 323–324, 329
Basic interpersonal communication skills (BICS),
    278
Bay Area School Reform Collaborative (BASRC),
    352
Beating the Odds project, 256
Beginning Teacher Evaluation Study (BTES), 256
Beginning Teacher Support and Assessment
    (BTSA) program, 404
Biases, in the development of formal assessments,
    238–239
Bicultural identity, 387
Bilingual Crosscultural Language and Academic
    Development (BCLAD) certification, 417

Bilingual Education Act, 1968–1988, 33, 38–39
Bilingual education programs
    cross-language transfer of literacy skills and, 277–288
    No Child Left Behind Act of 2001 (NCLB) and, 236–237
Bilingual learners. *See* English language learners
Black English. *See* African American vernacular English
*Black English Case* (1979), 143–144
Black students. *See* African American students
Blending, phonemic awareness and, 295–296
Book availability. *See* Text availability
*Bradley v. Miliken* (1977), 143–144

C

*Castaneda v. Pickard* (1981), 36–37
Center for Mathematics Education of Latino Students (CEMELA), 224
Center X Urban Teaching Program, 407
Centers in classrooms, small-group instruction and, 264–265
Choice, student, 344–345
Civil Rights Act of 1964
    Bilingual Education Act, 1968–1988 and, 38–39
    rights of English language learners and, 36, 37
Classroom environment
    classroom management and, 260–261, 267
    cultural development and, 107–108
    exemplary literacy practices and, 5, 262
    vocabulary instruction and, 322–323, 325–326
Classroom management
    classroom environment, 260–261
    engagement and motivation and, 255–260
    exemplary literacy practices and, 5
    fluency and, 372–373
    overview, 254, 254–268
    research regarding, 255, 267
    teacher–student relationships and, 265–266
    vocabulary instruction and, 328
    *See also* Classroom practice
Classroom practice
    achievement gap and, 106–108
    adolescent English language learners and, 125–129, 129–131
    African American vernacular English and, 146–148
    assessment and, 247–249
    comprehension instruction and, 350–358
    cross-language transfer and, 286–287

engagement and motivation and, 207–212
fluency and, 372–373
induction and mentoring of new teachers and, 404–408, 408*f*
learning to read in English and, 313–315
multiple literacies and, 167–169
No Child Left Behind Act of 2001 (NCLB) and, 247–249
online reading comprehension and, 182–183, 186–188
policy and, 33, 48–49
vocabulary instruction and, 328, 328–330
    *See also* Classroom management; Instruction
Coaching system, teacher development and, 406–407
Cognitive abilities, deficiency ideology of diversity and, 21–22
Cognitive Academic Language Learning Approach (CALLA), 140
Cognitive academic language proficiency (CALP), 278
Cognitive development, literate achievement and, 105–106
Collaborative approaches
    African American students and, 207–208
    comprehension instruction and, 345, 354
    exemplary literacy practices and, 5
    family literacy and, 89–90
    small-group instruction and, 264–265
Commission on No Child Left Behind, 2007, 48
Community cultural resources, 14
Compensatory approach to instruction, 22
Competence, 204*f*
Competent level of teacher expertise, 400–401
Complex learning, 225
Comprehension
    assessment and, 237–238
    diverse learners and, 341–349
    instruction and, 338–341, 342–344, 350–358
    overview, 337–358
Consequential validity of assessments, 234
Constructivist perspective, 340
Content area integration
    adolescent English language learners and, 127–129, 130–131
    exemplary literacy practices and, 5
    professional development and, 418–421, 420*t*, 422*f*
"Cooperating" teachers, 398. *See also* Mentoring of novice teachers
Cooperative learning, 126. *See also* Collaborative approaches
Corrective Reading program, 243–244
Critical evaluation, 180, 186–187

Critical literacy
  classroom practices and, 168–169
  overview, 159–161
Critical pedagogy, 161–164
Crosscultural Language and Academic
    Development (CLAD) certification, 417
Cross-cultural research, 217–218
Cross-language transfer
  classroom practices and, 286–287
  within components of reading, 280–286
  developmental interdependence hypothesis
      and, 278
  overview, 278–280
  research regarding, 279–280, 287–288
Cultural deprivation ideology. See Deficit
    ideology of diversity
Cultural development, 107–108
Cultural factors
  achievement gap and, 1–2
  family literacy and, 78–79, 89
  learning and, 217–218
  overview, 13–15
Cultural historical theory
  group-based inequality and, 103–106
  informal learning environments and, 216–228
  learning and, 217–219
  overview, 98
Cultural Modeling Project, 222–225
Culturally relevant pedagogy, 384
Culturally responsive teaching, 208–209
Culture, literacy as the processes and products
    of, 19–20
Curricular learning paradigm, 167–168
Curriculum
  comprehension instruction and, 353–354,
      356–358
  differentiated instruction and, 263
  fluency and, 372–373
  informal learning environments and, 221–222
  new literacy studies (NLS) and, 164
  sociocultural theory and, 160


D

Decoding
  decodable books, 309–310
  fluency and, 367
  phonics instruction and, 293
Deficit ideology of diversity
  African American vernacular English and,
      144–145, 152
  diversity-in-literacy matrix and, 25f
  overview, 21–22

Demographic trends
  education in America and, 432
  English language learners and, 34–35
  policy and, 33
  shifts in, 434
Deprivation-deficit ideology, 22. See also Deficit
    ideology of diversity
Development
  disidentification with schooling and, 205–206
  informal learning environments and, 219–221
  poverty and, 97–109
  research and theory regarding, 98–103
  valuing of achievement and, 201
  vocabulary instruction and, 320–322, 329–330
  word reading skills and, 305–306
Developmental interdependence hypothesis, 277,
    278
Developmental Reading Assessment (DRA and
    DRA2)
  English language learners and, 246
  overview, 244
  research regarding, 244
Dialect
  language variation and, 138, 139t
  terminology, 153n
DIBELS. see Dynamic Indicators of Basic Early
    Literacy Skills (DIBELS)
Difference theory, African American vernacular
    English and, 145, 152
Differentiated instruction
  research regarding, 263
  systematic phonics instruction and, 311
  See also Instructional quality
Digital divide, 184–186. See also Achievement
    gap in reading and math; Online reading
    comprehension
Disadvantage ideology. See Deficit ideology of
    diversity
Discourse patterns
  academic English and, 141
  adolescent literacy development and, 66–68,
      128
  African American vernacular English and,
      146
  diversity-in-literacy matrix and, 25–26, 25f
  endangered language settings and, 62–65
  home language environments and, 87–88
  immigrant context, 57–60
  implications of, 72–73
  language socialization, 60–62
  overview, 18–19, 55–57
  virtual worlds and, 68–71
Discrimination, rights of English language
    learners and, 36

Disidentification with academics, 202–206, 204*f*

Distributed leadership, overview, 352–353

Diversity as difference ideology
diversity-in-literacy matrix and, 25–26, 25*f*
overview, 22–23

Diversity as strength ideology
diversity-in-literacy matrix and, 25–26, 25*f*
overview, 23–24

Diversity overview, 20–21

Diversity-in-literacy matrix
overview, 15, 24–26, 25*f*
resource orientation and, 27

Downward assimilation, achievement gap and, 102–103

Dropouts, 120. *See also* School completion

Dynamic Indicators of Basic Early Literacy Skills (DIBELS)
English language learners and, 246
overview, 240
research regarding, 240–242, 244, 249

**E**

Early Childhood Longitudinal Study, Birth Cohort (ECLS-B), 34–35

Early Reading First program
English language learners and, 33
overview, 41–45, 42*t*–43*t*

"Education debt" concept, 358

Education of teachers. *See* Teacher education

Educational policy
demographic trends and, 34–35
federal legislation, 38–48, 40*t*–41*t*, 42*t*–43*t*, 46*t*
future policy and, 48
implications for the classroom, 48–49
online reading comprehension and, 176–177, 184–186
overview, 32–33, 49–51, 50*t*–51*t*
poverty and, 100–101
recommendations regarding, 432–433
rights of English language learners and, 35–38
*See also* No Child Left Behind Act of 2001 (NCLB)

Effective teaching
classroom management and, 261–265
research and theory regarding, 3–6
*See also* Instructional quality

Elementary and Secondary Education Act
Bilingual Education Act, 1968–1988 and, 38–39
overview, 33

Elementary and Secondary Education Act
reauthorizations of 1994 and 2001, 39–41, 40*t*–41*t*. *See also* No Child Left Behind Act of 2001 (NCLB)

Elkonin boxes, 325

Embedded letter mnemonics, 302–303, 302*f*

Enculturation, literacy as the processes and products of, 19–20

End of grade (EOG) exams, 101

Endangerment of language, 62–65

Engagement of students
African American and European American students, 196–199
classroom practices and, 207–212, 255–260, 267
comprehension instruction and, 344–347
disidentification with schooling and, 202–206, 204*f*
exemplary literacy practices and, 5
multiple literacies and, 158–169
overview, 195–213, 204*f*
research regarding, 159–167, 212–213
valuing of achievement and, 199–202
vocabulary instruction and, 329

English as a second language (ESL) programs
No Child Left Behind Act of 2001 (NCLB) and, 236–237
overview, 236

English for speakers of other languages (ESOL), 107

English language arts (ELA), 356–357

English language learners
academic English and, 140, 141–142
academic programs and, 121–125
adolescents, 114–131
assessment and, 239–240, 245–247
classroom practices and, 129–131
comprehension instruction and, 342–344, 355
demographic trends regarding, 34–35
fluency and, 366–374
learning to read in English and, 292–315
No Child Left Behind Act of 2001 (NCLB) and, 45–48, 46*t*, 236–237
professional development and, 413–428
Reading First and Early Reading First programs and, 43*t*, 44–45
rights of, 33, 35–38, 50*t*–51*t*
vocabulary instruction and, 321, 325–330
word reading skills and, 306–307
*See also* Adolescent English language learners

English learners. *See* English language learners

English writing system, 294–295

Environment, classroom. *See* Classroom environment

Environmental press, 260
Equal Education Opportunity Act of 1974
    (EEOA), 36–37
Equal education rights, 33
Ethnicity
    academic achievement and, 101
    achievement gap and, 1–2, 102–103
    culture and, 218
Ethnographic research
    family literacy and, 79–80
    new literacy studies (NLS) and, 162–163
    overview, 55–57
    sociocultural theory and, 160
European American students
    classroom practices and, 207–212
    disidentification with schooling and, 203,
        204–206, 204f
    engagement and motivation and, 196–199,
        207–212, 212–213
Evolution of literacy, 16–18
Exemplary teaching
    classroom management and, 261–265
    research and theory regarding, 3–6
    See also Instructional quality
Expectations of students
    comprehension instruction and, 352
    small-group instruction and, 264–265
Expediting Comprehension for English Language
    Learners (ExC-ELL), 418–421, 420t,
    422–423, 423f
Expert level of teacher expertise, 400–401
Expertise of teachers, 399–401
Explicit literacy instruction
    comprehension instruction and, 350–351
    exemplary literacy practices and, 5
    See also Instruction

F

Failure Free Reading program, 243–244
Fairness of assessments, 234
Family, 78–79. See also Parent–school connection
Family literacy
    academic achievement and, 100–101
    comprehension instruction and, 345–346
    contexts for, 79–80
    engagement and motivation and, 208–209
    funds of knowledge and, 226–227
    future research regarding, 90
    implications for the classroom, 89–90
    importance of, 78–79
    overview, 77–78, 90–91
    parent–school connection and, 86–89

research findings regarding, 89
texts in the home and, 80–86, 85f
See also Home language environment
Federal courts
    African American vernacular English and,
        143–144
    rights of English language learners and, 35–38
Federal legislation, 38–48, 40t–41t, 42t–43t, 46t.
    See also individual legislative acts; Policy,
        educational
Feedback, 406–407
Fiction writing, exemplary literacy practices and,
    5
Fifth Dimension, diversity-in-literacy matrix and,
    25
Fluency
    classroom practices and, 372–373
    overview, 366–374
    research regarding, 368–371, 373–374
Formal literacy assessment, 237–240. See also
    Assessments
Formative assessments, 248–249
Full alphabetic phase, 305–306
Funds of knowledge
    home language environments and, 87
    overview, 87, 226, 382
    research utilizing, 385–386
Funds of Knowledge Project, 222, 226–227

G

Gatekeeper, literacy as
    diversity-in-literacy matrix and, 25f
    overview, 16–17
Gender
    comprehension instruction and, 346–347
    development of formal assessments and, 238
    engagement and motivation and, 212
Goal setting, 344–345, 352
Golden age of research, 382–385
Government Accountability Office (GAO), 47–
    48
GRA+DE. See Group Reading Assessment and
    Diagnostic Evaluation (GRA+DE)
Grammatical components of language, 141
Grapheme–phoneme (GP) mapping
    phonics instruction and, 293
    word reading skills and, 306
Graphemes, 294
Group Reading Assessment and Diagnostic
    Evaluation (GRA+DE)
    overview, 241
    research regarding, 241

Group-based inequality (GBI)
  achievement gap and, 102–103
  classroom practices and, 106–108
  cultural historical theory and, 103–106
  institutionalization of, 101
  overview, 97–98
  underachievement and, 102–103
Grouping of students, 264–265
Guided instruction, small-group instruction and, 264–265
Guided introspective writing, teacher education and, 391
Guided writing, exemplary literacy practices and, 5

**H**

Head Start programs, 107
High school dropouts. *See* Dropouts
High-stakes testing
  overview, 235–236
  poverty and, 101
  *See also* Testing
Historical perspectives, language variation and, 139–140
History of literacy, 16–18, 380–385
Holistic development, 222–225
Home language environment
  academic achievement and, 100–101
  African American vernacular English and, 146
  comprehension instruction and, 345–346
  demographic trends regarding, 34–35
  engagement and motivation and, 208–209
  funds of knowledge and, 226–227
  parent–school connection and, 86–89
  research regarding, 79–80
  texts in the home, 80–86, 85*f*
  *See also* Family literacy
Home–school connection
  exemplary literacy practices and, 5
  funds of knowledge and, 226–227
  home language environments and, 86–89
  research findings regarding, 89
Homework, 209–210
Horizontal knowledge, 218–219

**I**

Identification with academics, 202–206, 204*f*
Ideologies regarding diversity
  interrelation of with literacy theory, 24–26, 25*f*
  overview, 15, 20–24

Immigrants
  achievement gap and, 102–103
  adolescent English language learners and, 144
  funds of knowledge and, 226
  *See also* English language learners
Inclusion, 123–124
Independent reading time
  comprehension instruction and, 347–349
  fluency and, 374
Independent writing, 5
Induction of novice teachers
  effects of induction programs, 403–404
  future research regarding, 408–409
  historical roots of, 397–399
  knowledge bases that inform, 399–401
  overview, 396–409
  recommendations regarding, 404–408, 408*f*
Informal learning environments
  in formal school settings, 221–227
  future research regarding, 227
  literacy learning and, 219–221
  overview, 216–228, 227
Instance theory of automaticity, 370–371
Instruction
  comprehension and, 338–341, 342–344, 350–358
  exemplary literacy practices and, 5
  fluency and, 372–373
  letter-name knowledge and, 301–303, 302*f*
  phonemic awareness and, 297–300, 298*f*
  professional development and, 421–424, 423*f*
  vocabulary instruction and, 320–331
  word reading skills and, 306, 308–312
  *See also* Classroom practice
Instructional quality
  assessment and, 248–249, 250
  classroom management and, 261–265, 267
  cross-language transfer and, 286–287
  issues related to, 2–3
  learning to read in English and, 293–294, 313–315
  research and theory regarding, 3–6
  *See also* Effective teaching; Exemplary teaching
Interactive learning paradigm, 168
Interdependence hypothesis, 119
Interest levels of children, 346–347
Internet
  achievement gap and, 184–186
  additional skills and strategies for, 177–184
  classroom practices and, 186–188
  comprehension instruction and, 348
  independent reading time and, 348
  No Child Left Behind Act of 2001 (NCLB) and, 184–186

Internet (cont.)
    research regarding, 188–189
    See also Online reading comprehension
Internet reciprocal teaching, 187
Interpersonal processes, group-based inequality
        and, 104
Intertexts
    overview, 178–179
    synthesizing information and, 180
    See also Online reading comprehension
Interventions
    achievement gap and, 106–108
    adolescent English language learners and,
        121–125, 125–129
    classroom practices and, 106–108
    poverty and, 99
Ireland, online reading comprehension and,
        176
IRF model, teacher–student relationships and,
        265
iSkills Assessment, 189


J

Japan, online reading comprehension and, 177
Journal writing, exemplary literacy practices
        and, 5


K

Kamehameha Early Education Program (KEEP),
        209


L

Language endangerment, 62–65
Language Experience Approach, 247
Language policy, 14
Language proficiency
    adolescent English language learners and,
        118–120, 120–121
    demographic trends regarding, 34–35
    developmental interdependence hypothesis
        and, 278
    No Child Left Behind Act of 2001 (NCLB) and,
        236–237
    vocabulary instruction and, 321
Language socialization
    discourse patterns and, 56, 60–62
    language endangerment and, 64–65

Language variation, 139t
    overview, 138
    terminology, 153n
    See also Dialect
Language-as-problem orientation, 14
Language-as-resource orientation, 14–15
Language-as-right orientation, 14
Language-minority students, 292–315. See also
        English language learners
Latino population
    achievement gap and, 414
    Cultural Modeling Project and, 224
    demographic trends regarding, 34–35
    Funds of Knowledge Project and, 226–227
    rights of English language learners and, 36
    terminology, 51n–52n
Lau v. Nichols (1974)
    Bilingual Education Act, 1968–1988 and, 38
    legacy of, 38
    overview, 35–36
Learning, informal learning environments and,
        216–228
Learning to read in English
    classroom practices and, 313–315
    future research regarding, 312–313
    overview, 292–315
Lesbian, gay, bisexual, transgender, and
        questioning (LGBTQ) youth, 160
Letter-name knowledge, 300–303, 302f
Lexical components of language, 141
Library use
    comprehension instruction and, 347–349
    overview, 80–81
    research regarding, 347–349
Lifespan model, classroom practices and,
        106–108
Limited English proficient (LEP)
    No Child Left Behind Act of 2001 (NCLB) and,
        236–237
    overview, 236
    See English language learners
Lindamood Phoneme Sequencing (LIPS)
        program, 297–299, 298f
Linguistic Affirmation Program (LAP), 147
Linguistic diversity
    academic achievement and, 101
    family literacy and, 78–79, 89
    negative responses to, 13–14
    as a resource, 14
Literacy development
    academic English and, 141–142
    African American vernacular English and,
        145–146

classroom practices and, 106–108
learning to read in English and, 292–315
literate achievement and, 105–106
poverty and, 97–109
research and theory regarding, 98–103
Literacy learning
in formal school settings, 221–227
future research regarding, 227
informal learning environments and, 219–221
Literary reasoning
Cultural Modeling Project and, 223
overview, 223
Longitudinal study
immigrant context, 57–60
new literacy studies (NLS) and, 163
phonological knowledge, 281

**M**

Management of the classroom. *See* Classroom management
Marginalization
adolescent English language learners and, 123–124
tracking and, 122
*Martin Luther King Elementary School Children v. Ann Arbor School District Board* (1979), 143–144
"Matthew effect" of reading
fluency and, 369
overview, 347
Meaning construction, 178–179
Memory
instance theory of automaticity and, 370–371
word reading skills and, 305–306
Mentoring of novice teachers
overview, 396–409
recommendations regarding, 404–408, 408f
research regarding, 397–399, 408–409
Metacognitive instructional conversations, 223–224
Mexico, online reading comprehension and, 177
Migrant Program, informal learning environments and, 221
Mnemonic devices, 301–303, 302f
Monolingualism, language endangerment and, 62–65
Morphology, 324–325, 327
Motivation
classroom practices and, 207–212, 255–260, 267
comprehension instruction and, 344–347

deficiency ideology of diversity and, 21–22
disidentification with schooling and, 202–206, 204f
overview, 195–213, 204f
research regarding, 212–213
valuing of achievement and, 199–202
Multicultural literature, 258–259. *See also* Text availability
Multiliteracies, 165–167
Multimodality
classroom practices and, 168–169
overview, 164–165
Multiple literacies
classroom practices and, 167–169
engagement of students and, 158–169
overview, 19
research regarding, 159–167

**N**

National Assessment of Educational Progress (NAEP)
literacy assessments for Title I and, 245
No Child Left Behind Act of 2001 (NCLB) and, 249
National Association for Secondary School Principals (NASSP), 398
National Clearinghouse for English Language Acquisition and Language Instruction Educational Programs (NCELA), 39
National Commission on Teaching and America's Future, 401
National Literacy Panel on Language—Minority Children and Youth
policy and, 32
Students with Interrupted Formal Education (SIFE) and, 416
National Longitudinal Survey of Labor Market Experience of Youth (NLSY), 81
National Reading Panel
cross-language transfer and, 280
fluency and, 369–370
overview, 44
phonemic awareness and, 299
time management and, 257
vocabulary instruction and, 321–322
word reading skills and, 308–309
New literacies
additional skills and strategies for, 177–184
online reading comprehension, 173–190, 174t
overview, 177–178

New literacy studies (NLS)
  classroom practices and, 168–169
  overview, 162–164
New London Group, 167
No Child Left Behind Act of 2001 (NCLB)
  achievement gap and, 184–186
  assessment and, 233–251
  Bilingual Education Act, 1968–1988 and, 38
  classroom practices and, 247–249
  English language learners and, 33, 245–247
  future policy and, 48
  overview, 2, 39–41, 40t–41t, 41–48, 42t–43t,
    46t
  poverty and, 99
  professional development and, 414, 421–422
  research regarding, 249–250
  sociocultural–historical perspective and,
    20
  teacher quality and, 2–3, 416–417
Nonfiction writing, exemplary literacy
    practices and, 5
Norm-referenced assessments, 233. See also
    Assessments
Novice level of teacher expertise, 400–401


O

Observational assessments of teachers, 406–
    407
Office of English Language Acquisition,
    Language Enhancement, and Academic
    Achievement for Limited English Proficient
    Students (OELA), 39
Online reading comprehension
  achievement gap and, 259
  additional skills and strategies for, 177–184
  classroom practices and, 186–188
  compared to offline reading comprehension,
    181–184
  overview, 173–190, 174t
  research regarding, 188–189
  See also Internet
Opportunities to read, 347–349
Oral language, sociocultural–historical
    perspective and, 15–16
Oral proficiency, word reading skills and,
    306–307
Oral reading, fluency and, 373
Organizational skills, 5
Orthographic knowledge
  cross-language transfer of, 277–288
  research regarding, 282–285

Otero v. Mesa County School District No. 51 (1975),
    36
Outcome-based professional development,
    427–428. See also Professional development
Out-of-school spaces, 66–68
Overcompensation, group-based inequality and,
    106–108


P

Parallel block scheduling (PBS), 256–257
Parenting, academic achievement and, 100–
    101
Parents
  comprehension instruction and, 345–346
  home language environments and, 86–89
  parent–school connection and, 5, 86–89,
    226–227
Parent–school connection
  exemplary literacy practices and, 5
  funds of knowledge and, 226–227
  home language environments and, 86–89
  research findings regarding, 89
Peabody Picture Vocabulary Test (PPVT), 285
Pedagogies, alternative
  adolescent literacy development and, 66–68
  multiliteracies and, 166, 167
Peer-scaffolding, 183. See also Scaffolding
Permeable curriculum, 164
Phonemes, English writing system and, 294
Phonemic awareness
  classroom practices and, 314
  overview, 295–300, 298f
  phonics instruction and, 292–293
Phonics instruction
  to beginning readers from diverse
    backgrounds, 292–315
  classroom practices and, 313–315
  comprehension instruction and, 342
  overview, 292–293
  word reading skills and, 308–312
Phonological components of language, 141
Phonological knowledge
  cross-language transfer of, 277–288
  research regarding, 280–282
Phonological recoding, 293, 304
Policy, educational. See Educational policy
Poverty
  classroom practices and, 106–108
  critical literacy and, 160–161
  cultural historical theory and, 103–106
  development and literacy and, 97–109

language proficiency and, 35
literate achievement and, 105–106
research and theory regarding, 98–103,
    160–161
*See also* Socioeconomic status
Power
    African American vernacular English and,
        150–151
    discourse and, 18–19
    language variation and, 138–139, 139*t*
    literacy as, 17
Practice/tool, literacy as
    diversity-in-literacy matrix and, 25*f*
    overview, 19–20
Prealphabetic phase, 305
Prediction, 304
Prejudice, 105–106
Print, access to, 258–260. *See also* Text
    availability
Print-based reading strategies, 307
Prior knowledge
    comprehension instruction and, 350
    engagement and motivation and, 211
    vocabulary instruction and, 323–324, 329
Privilege, language variation and, 139*t*
Problem–resource continuum, 26
Professional development
    academic achievement and, 414–416
    comprehension and, 352, 353
    example of, 418–421, 420*t*, 422*f*
    future research regarding, 427
    importance of, 27
    instruction and, 421–424, 423*f*
    overview, 413–428
    poverty and, 101
    recommendations regarding, 424–426, 425*f*,
        426*f*
    teacher quality and, 416–418
    vocabulary instruction and, 330
Proficiency, language. *See* Language proficiency
Proficiency in reading
    fluency and, 374
    word reading skills and, 306–307
Proficient level of teacher expertise, 400–401
Program for International Student Assessment
    (PISA), 189
Progress, literacy as
    diversity-in-literacy matrix and, 25*f*
    overview, 17–18
Progress in International Reading Study (PIRLS),
    189
Prosody, 368. *See also* Fluency
Proximal zone of development, 108

Q

Quality of teaching. *See* Teacher quality
Quitting school. *See* Dropouts

R

Race, 218
RAND Reading Study Group
    assessment and, 250
    reading comprehension assessments and,
        237–238
Reader response writing, 5
Reading First program
    assessment and, 234–235
    diversity-in-literacy matrix and, 25
    English language learners and, 33
    overview, 41–45, 42*t*–43*t*, 235
    research regarding, 240–242
    sociocultural–historical perspective and,
        19–20
Reading in English, learning to, 292–315
Reading Instructional Goals for Older Readers
    (RIGOR) program, 418–421, 420*t*, 422*f*
Reading materials. *See* Text availability
Reading proficiency
    fluency and, 374
    word reading skills and, 306–307
Rehearsals, 370–371
Relationships between teachers and students
    engagement and motivation and, 208
    overview, 265–266
Reliability of assessments, 233–234
Repeated readings, 370–371
Resource orientation
    diversity-in-literacy matrix and, 25–26, 25*f*
    overview, 14–15, 26–27
Resource pedagogy
    future research regarding, 389–393, 391*f*
    history of, 382–385
    implications of, 388–389
    in the new century, 385–388
    overview, 379–393
Retention of teachers, 401–403
Rights of English language learners
    federal legislation regarding, 38–48, 40*t*–41*t*,
        42*t*–43*t*, 46*t*
    overview, 50*t*–51*t*
    policy and, 33
Risk factors
    achievement gap and, 1–2
    No Child Left Behind Act of 2001 (NCLB) and, 2

Rosenberg Self-View Inventory, 203
Routines, classroom
    fluency and, 372–373
    time management and, 257
    *See also* Classroom management
Rules, classroom, 257. *See also* Classroom
    management


S

SAIL (Students Achieving Independent Learning)
    strategy, 341
Scaffolding
    comprehension instruction and, 340
    Cultural Modeling Project and, 222
    fluency and, 367–368, 371, 372–373
    instance theory of automaticity and, 371
    online reading comprehension and, 183
    sociocultural theory and, 6
    time management and, 256
    vocabulary instruction and, 323, 325, 329
School completion, 120
School cultures, group-based inequality and, 107
"School dependence," 431
School–home connection. *See* Parent–school
    connection
Schooling and Staffing Survey, 403
Schools
    informal learning environments and, 221–227
    literacy development and, 66–68
    *See also* Parent–school connection
Search engine use, 179–180. *See also* Online
    reading comprehension
Second Life virtual world, discourse patterns
    and, 68–71
Second-language development, 278
Segmentation
    instruction and, 299
    phonemic awareness and, 295–296
Segmented assimilation
    overview, 114–115
    prior schooling of immigrant students and,
        116–118
    tracking and, 122
    *See also* Assimilation
Selection of texts. *See* Text selection
Self-esteem, disidentification with schooling and,
    203–204
Semantic knowledge, 277–288
Semantic manipulation, 329
Shared writing, 5
Sight word knowledge, 307

Signifying, 393*n*
Silent reading, 374
Small-group instruction
    effectiveness of, 264–265
    exemplary literacy practices and, 5
    time management and, 256
Social change, curriculum and, 160
Social collaboration in reading, 345. *See also*
    Collaborative approaches
Socialization
    classroom practices and, 106–108
    literate achievement and, 105–106
Sociocritical literacy, 220–221
Sociocultural theory
    new literacy studies (NLS) and, 163–164
    overview, 5–6, 160
    teacher–student relationships and, 266
Sociocultural–historical perspective on literacy
    diversity-in-literacy matrix and, 25*f*
    overview, 15–20
    resource orientation and, 26
Socioeconomic status
    academic English and, 142
    achievement gap and, 1–2, 184–186
    deficiency ideology of diversity and, 22
    family literacy and, 89
    learning to read in English and, 292–315
    letter-name knowledge and, 301
    No Child Left Behind Act of 2001 (NCLB) and,
        2, 184–186
    online reading comprehension and, 182,
        184–186
    text availability and, 81, 83–84, 259
    time management in the classroom and, 257
    vocabulary instruction and, 321, 322–325
    *See also* Poverty
Sociohistorical perspective, 143
Special education services
    group-based inequality and, 107
    rights of English language learners and, 36–37
Spell Read P.A.T. program, 243–244
Spelling knowledge
    English writing system and, 294–295
    word reading skills and, 305–306
Staff development. *See* Professional development
Stage-based model of teacher development,
    403–404
Standardized testing. *See* Testing
Standards, state. *See* State standards
Standards-based assessments
    overview, 233
    research regarding, 249–250
    *See also* Assessments

Standards-Based Change Process (SBCP), 352
State standards
    informal learning environments and, 221–222
    No Child Left Behind Act of 2001 (NCLB) and, 46t
    online reading comprehension and, 184
Statistical trends
    education in America and, 432
    English language learners and, 34–35
    policy and, 33
    shifts in, 434
Stereotypes
    classroom practices and, 211
    engagement and motivation and, 211
Strengths
    assessment of English language learners and, 239–240
    diversity as, 14
    diversity as strength ideology and, 23–24
Struggling readers, 369, 373
Students, 344–345. See also African American students; Engagement of students; English language learners; European American students; Latino population; Motivation
Students with Interrupted Formal Education (SIFE)
    overview, 414–415
    professional development and, 414–416, 418–421, 420t, 422f, 427
    See also English language learners
Subtractive schooling, 101
Supreme Court decisions, 35–38
Systematic phonics instruction, 308–312. See also Phonics instruction
Systemic functional linguistics (SFL), 140–141


T

Teacher education
    African American vernacular English and, 146
    future research regarding, 408–409
    historical roots of, 397–399
    importance of, 27
    induction and mentoring of new teachers and, 396–409
    recommendations regarding, 390–392, 392f, 404–408, 408f
    teacher quality and, 416–418

Teacher knowledge
    future research regarding, 389–393, 391f
    gaining, 388–389
    history of research and, 380–385
    overview, 379–393
    resource pedagogy and, 379–393
Teacher quality
    achievement and, 416–418
    comprehension instruction and, 344–347
    issues related to, 2–3
    overview, 379–393
    research and theory regarding, 3–6
    teacher retention and, 401–403
    See also Effective teaching; Exemplary teaching
Teacher retention, research regarding, 401–403
Teacher scaffolding, 183. See also Scaffolding
Teachers
    African American vernacular English and, 145–146
    home language environments and, 86–89
    parent–school connection and, 86–89
Teacher–student relationships
    engagement and motivation and, 208
    overview, 265–266
Teaching English to Speakers of Other Languages (TESOL), 326–327
Technology
    achievement gap and, 259
    comprehension instruction and, 348
    Expediting Comprehension for English Language Learners (ExC-ELL) and, 422–424, 423f
    independent reading time and, 348
    multiliteracies and, 166
    overview, 168–169
    professional development and, 422–424, 423f
    vocabulary instruction and, 330
    See also Online reading comprehension; Virtual worlds
Testing
    adolescent English language learners and, 119
    comprehension and, 351
    No Child Left Behind Act of 2001 (NCLB) and, 47–48, 235–236
    poverty and, 101
    rights of English language learners and, 36
    See also Assessments; High-stakes testing
Text availability
    classroom management and, 258–260
    comprehension instruction and, 345
    home language environments and, 80–86, 85f
    resource pedagogy and, 390